FIFTH EDITION

*E*INTERNATIONAL*S* *E*CONOMIC*S*

A Policy Approach

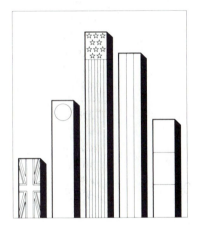

Mordechai E. Kreinin
Michigan State University

Harcourt Brace Jovanovich, Publishers
and its subsidiary, Academic Press

San Diego   New York   Chicago   Austin
London   Sydney   Tokyo   Toronto

To my daughters

Tamara

Elana

Miriam

Preface

*A*lthough Americans have gained a better understanding of our domestic economy since World War II, our knowledge of international economics has remained limited. In recent years, however, international economic matters so frequently occupied the financial headlines that our attention has been forced beyond domestic concerns to those of the world market.

The Previous Editions

Through its five editions, this book has provided a simplified yet comprehensive analysis of international economic relations, with the fundamental objective of extracting maximum policy insight from a minimum number of theoretical constructs. Written for students with only one or two previous courses in the principles of economics, it is designed primarily as a basic text for a one- or two-term undergraduate sequence in international economics. Although the volume contains analytical tools, the material is arranged so that the theoretical sections may be omitted and the main text used also in policy-oriented noneconomics courses. Finally, the book is useful as supplementary reading for students of international relations and business administration, as well as for economics students in money and banking courses.

The method of presentation has remained unchanged through all editions. Each subject is expounded verbally before any use is made of analytical tools beyond simple supply and demand curves. Whenever technical terms and tools are needed, they are carefully explained. Although the focus is on policy, the necessary theoretical underpinnings are fully presented.

As in previous editions, Parts One and Two are devoted to international finance and trade respectively. The order in which Parts One and Two can be studied is fully interchangeable. The sole exception is the short section in Chapter 11 entitled

v

"The Limits to Sustained Exchange Rates," which requires at least minimal familiarity with exchange rates. Instructors using Part Two before Part One can either omit this section or have students read the first section of Chapter 3 as a prerequisite.

The original arrangement that enabled uninitiated readers to skip over the technical sections without loss of continuity has been retained. Each technical section is set off by a short horizontal line at ᴄ.ιe beginning and end. Each paragraph within the section begins with an open square (□) and the complete section ends with a closed square (■).

The appendixes are intended for students interested in more complex theoretical and policy formulations. Additional readings are suggested in footnotes, while sources of relevant statistics are cited for various topics under discussion. A *short bibliography* at the end of the text lists (1) books of readings, (2) a selection of single-topic survey articles that have extensive bibliographies, and (3) sources of international, regional, and national statistics.

Updated Coverage

Some major events have occurred on the international economic scene since publication of the Fourth Edition in 1983, and they have all been included in this edition. Examples are:

- the rise in the exchange value of the dollar from 1980 to 1985, and its decline as of March 1985
- the oil glut and the attendant decline in the price of oil
- the emergence of LCDs' (Less Developed Countries) external debt as a major issue confronting the global economy
- increased protection on both sides of the Atlantic, and proposals for a new round of trade negotiations

All of these and other recent events are discussed in the Fifth Edition. *All statistics, theoretical formulations, and other ongoing events have been brought up to date.*

New Topics

New topics added to the book include (but are not limited to):

- expanded discussion of the unique features of international economics (in Chapter 1)
- sector-specific factors (in Chapter 12 and also in Appendix VII)
- international trade under monopolistic competition (Chapter 12)
- export subsidies (Chapter 14)
- the political economy of protectionism (in Chapter 15)
- trade policy under oligopoly (in Appendix X)

And new to this edition are *end-of-chapter review questions,* to assist students in identifying and retaining the key points of the chapter.

Acknowledgments

My deep gratitude is due the many professors who took the trouble to write words of encouragement, suggestions, and constructive criticism of previous editions. Special thanks for their many helpful comments go to:

W. Max Corden, *Australian National University*
Gerald M. Meier, *Stanford University*
Robert E. Baldwin, *University of Wisconsin*
Franklyn D. Holzman, *Tufts University*
Philip S. Thomas, *Kalamazoo College*
Lawrence H. Officer, *Michigan State University*
Elias Dinopoulos, *Michigan State University*
Steven Matusz, *Michigan State University*
Henry Thompson, *University of Tennessee, Knoxville*
Richard L. Lucier, *Denison University*
Sohrab Behdad, *Denison University*
Gerald V. Egerer, *Sonoma State University*
William J. Baumol, *Princeton University and New York University*
Robert W. Gillespie, *University of Illinois*
Norman N. Mintz, *Columbia University*

Mordechai E. Kreinin

Contents

5 National Income Determination in an Open Economy / 75

6 Balance-of-Payments Adjustment Policies Under Fixed Exchange Rates / 101

7 Exchange-Rate Adjustment / 132

8 The Monetary Approach to the Balance of Payments / 161

13 *Protection of Domestic Industries: The Tariff / 284*

14 *Non-Tariff Barriers (NTBs) to Trade / 324*

15 *U.S. Commerical Policy / 349*

16 *International and Regional Trade Organi-zations among Developed Countries / 360*

17 *Selected Trade Problems of Developing Countries / 381*

1/
World Trade and the American Economy

Definition

*I*nternational economics deals with the flow of commodities, services, and capital across national boundaries. Trade in commodities refers to imports and exports of merchandise. Service transactions involve such activities as shipping, travel, insurance, or tourist services performed by companies of one country for residents of another. And finally capital flows refers to setting up plants in foreign countries or to acquisition of bonds, stocks, and bank accounts in one country by residents of another country.

What Is Unique About International Economics?

In a very real sense international transactions constitute an extension of domestic transactions. In both cases, trade offers the benefits of *specialization*. Exchanges of goods and services among individuals enable them to specialize in what they do best. Domestic exchange enables regions of the country to specialize in the same manner. Thus, the exchange of Idaho potatoes, Florida oranges, and Washington-produced aircraft enhances efficiency of production and improves living standards for each of these states as it specializes in what it does best. Internationally, the U.S. import of Japanese cars and Brazilian coffee and the U.S. export of grains, aircraft, and sophisticated computers enables the three participating countries to specialize in what they do best; thereby producing more than they could without trade and increasing the living standards of all.

The reasons for and the benefits from international transactions are no different from the reasons for and the benefits from internal transac-

1

tions: to reap the fruits of increased output from a given amount of resources attendant upon greater specialization.

Why then is it necessary to distinguish between domestic and international economic relations? Why study international economics as a separate field? Because the existence of national boundaries has profound implications for the *conduct* of trade. The following are a few of the differences between domestic and foreign trade that emanate from this fact.

Exchange Rates   Transactions within a country are financed by the country's own currency, usually through the writing of checks. But a universal currency does not exist. Instead, each country issues its own currency. The price of one currency in terms of another is called an *exchange rate*. Many exchange rates vary from day to day in response to supply and demand conditions in the foreign exchange markets. International transactions require payments or receipts in foreign currencies, and these must be converted to domestic currency through the exchange rates, which themselves are subject to change. This process introduces risks and complications that do not exist in domestic trade. Exchange rate variations can have profound effects on the domestic economy.

Commercial Policies   A national government can introduce a variety of restrictions on international transactions that cannot be imposed on domestic transactions. Examples are:

(a) A tariff, which is a tax on an imported commodity.
(b) An import quota, which places a maximum limitation on the *amount* of the commodity that may enter the country (for example, one million tons of steel).
(c) A "voluntary" export restraint (VER), where the governments of an importing country and an exporting country (say, the U.S. and Japan) negotiate a quantitative limitation on the export of a certain commodity. The Japanese government limited automobile shipments to the United States during the years 1981–1986 under such an agreement.
(d) An export subsidy, where a country subsidizes its exports in order to make them more competitive abroad.
(e) Exchange control, where a country, such as India, restricts the ability of its citizens to convert their money (rupees) to foreign currencies, such as the U.S. dollar.

Such measures may have profound effects on the economy. Yet they apply only to international and not to domestic transactions.

Different Domestic Policies   Each country has its own central bank and finance ministry, and hence its own monetary and fiscal policies. In turn these determine its rate of inflation, economic growth, and unemployment. Such policies are common to all regions within the country; but they vary from one country to another. Consequently, whereas the rate of inflation is reasonably the same throughout regions of France, it differs between France and Germany. And that affects the two countries' competitive position in each other's market, as well as in third markets. Indeed, many changes in international trade and financial transactions can be traced to differences in the domestic policies pursued by different governments.

Statistical Data   We know more about the composition, size, and direction of international trade than about the same features of domestic transactions. No one is sure of which commodities in what quantities are traded between New York and California. There are no "border regulators" along state lines to compile such information. But when a shipment of merchandise leaves or enters the country, the exporter or importer must fill out an export or import declaration describing the shipment, its weight, its value, its destination or source, and other characteristics. From these trade declarations, which are required by all countries, detailed statistics can be compiled on international trade that are not available for domestic trade.

Relative Immobility of Productive Factors   Factors of production are much more mobile domestically than they are internationally. No one can prevent workers from moving between Virginia and Texas. But immigration restrictions, language barriers, and different social customs constitute formidable barriers to people's mobility between countries. While capital can move between countries much more easily than labor, it is more mobile domestically than internationally.

Marketing Considerations   Differences in demand patterns, sales techniques, market requirements and the like make international transactions more difficult than domestic ones. The Japanese sleep on futon beds and have little use for American sheets and pillowcases. American exports of electrical appliances to Europe must be adjusted for use by European electric current. Automobiles exported to the U.K. require steering wheels on the right side of the vehicle, as the British drive on the left side of the road. And automobiles exported to the U.S. must be fitted with the U.S.-mandated pollution control equipment.

In sum, exporters need to make special adjustments in their product design in an attempt to penetrate a foreign market.

Summary   The preceding six areas of significant difference between domestic and foreign transaction refer to the conduct of, rather than the reasons for, and benefits from, trade. They highlight important and unique features that require a special field of international economics.

International Transactions—An Empirical Glimpse

International economics is the oldest branch of economics, dating back to David Hume (1752), Adam Smith (1778), and David Ricardo (1817). Interest in this field has expanded in recent years, partly as a result of the vast growth of international transactions.

A case in point is the phenomenal and uninterrupted expansion of international merchandise trade. The value of world exports grew from $108 billion in 1958 to $1.9 trillion in 1985. The greatest increase was in the trade of manufactured products (from $64 billion in 1960 to $1.1 trillion in 1984), followed by minerals and agricultural products. Particularly remarkable was the expansion of trade among the score of industrialized nations who are members of the Organization for Economic Cooperation and Development (OECD)—Western Europe, North America, Japan and Australia (see Appendix I). Intra-OECD trade accounts for nearly one half of total world trade. Table 1-1 shows the network of total exports by major areas in 1985. The 5th column shows that most of the exports of manufactured products originate in the industrial countries, although the manufacturing exports of certain developing countries have grown rapidly in recent years. All the figures in this paragraph are expressed in current dollars. Thus the increases in trade value over time are made up of price increases as well as expansions in the real volume of trade. The real volume of world trade grew at an annual rate of 9 percent between 1964 and 1973, of 4.5 percent between 1973 and 1979, and of 2 percent between 1979 and 1984.

Figure 1-1 depicts the expansion of the physical volume (value, net of price increases) of world trade in 1980–85. It is seen that exports of minerals declined while that of manufactures and agricultural products expanded during these years.

Commodity trade is not the only component of international transactions that has expanded rapidly. The combined export of services by

Table 1-1
Network of World Trade, 1985, in $ billions

Exports From	Destination				Export of Manufactures to World, 1984
	Industrial Countries	Developing Countries	Eastern Bloc	Total World	
Industrial Countries	898	288	57	1,243	885
Developing Countries	296	120	38	454	151
Eastern Bloc	61	27	105	193	104
Total World	1,255	435	200	1,910*	1,149

SOURCE: GATT, *IMF Survey*, May 19, 1986.

*Includes Australia, New Zealand, and South Africa, which are excluded from the individual areas.

Figure 1-1
Volume Indices of World Exports, 1980–85 (1980 = 100)

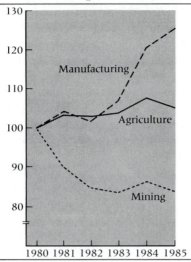

SOURCE: GATT release No. 1382, March 21; 1986, p. 7.

the industrial countries more than doubled in eight years, rising from $259 billion in 1977 to $532 billion[1] in 1984. And, finally, there has been a massive increase in private capital flows. In 1984 the United States experienced a net inflow of over $100 billion, while nine other major industrial countries experienced a combined capital outflow of over $40 billion.

Foreign Trade in the U.S. Economy

Aggregate Measures   As the analysis of international economic relations unfolds in subsequent chapters, the United States will be seen as a pivotal member in the world trading and financial community. Two features of its economy make this country ideally suited for such a central role: It is simultaneously a giant among nations and a *relatively* "closed economy." The first feature refers to the fact that the U.S. gross national product (GNP)[2] makes up 40 percent of the combined total of all industrial countries and is the leading importing and exporting nation. As a consequence, whatever occurs in the U.S. may have profound implications for the rest of the world. For example, a recession in the United States lowers our demand for imported materials and other goods, which may cause problems for exporting countries for which we are such an important market. Thus, American economic

---

[1] About 40 percent is shipping and other transport, and one quarter is travel and tourism.

[2] Total value of final goods and services produced during a one-year period. In 1984 U.S. GNP stood at $3,663 billion, and that of the world at over 12 trillion. Thus, the U.S. accounts for a quarter of worldwide GNP.

policies that affect our trade position are important not only to us but to our trading partners.

On the other hand, the term "closed economy" refers to the fact that the United States is comparatively independent of foreign trade. Quantitatively, exports (or imports) occupy a relatively small proportion of its total economic activity, although that proportion has increased in recent years. Because of its size and the diversity of its resources, the American economy can satisfy consumer wants and national needs with minimum reliance on foreign trade. This is in contrast to other industrial economies in which foreign trade plays a significant, if not a dominant, role. Thus, merchandise exports constitute 6 percent of GNP in the U.S. (up from about 4 percent in the 1960s), 15 percent of GNP in Japan, between a quarter and a third of GNP in the large European countries, and around one half of GNP in the small European countries. The United States is more immune than other countries to disturbances originating abroad.

In 1985, U.S. gross national product amounted to $3,988 billion. Exports of goods and services were $370 billion or 9 percent of GNP. Imports of goods and services stood at 11 percent of GNP (Table 1-2).

Disaggregation   Yet this should not be construed to mean that the American economy is completely independent of foreign trade in either a quantitative or qualitative sense. The quantitative importance of foreign trade cannot be judged solely on broad aggregative measures, because its impact is not spread evenly over all sectors of the economy. A substantial portion of GNP is made up of such items as construction activities and various services—many of which never enter international trade and are therefore termed *nontraded goods*—and is not directly affected by changes in trade policies. Most of the direct effects of such changes are concentrated in the commodity-producing sectors. Exports appear to be most important in the agricultural sector, while imports are most significant among mineral commodities.

Table 1-2
Gross National Product of the United States, ($Billions)

	1981		1985	
Personal Consumption Expenditures	1,843		2,582	
Gross Private Domestic Investments	472		669	
Government Purchases of Goods and Services	597		815	
Net Exports of Goods and Services	26		− 78	
Exports:		367		370
Imports:		341		448
Total GNP	2,938		3,988	

SOURCE: *Federal Reserve Bulletin*, various issues, p. A51.

But even these figures are too aggregative. Foreign trade among industrial nations is extremely specialized, and the manufacturing sector in particular contains variations that are not reflected in the sectoral average. In assessing the role of foreign trade in individual industries, it is customary to examine the ratio of exports to output and the ratio of imports to apparent consumption, where apparent consumption is measured as output plus imports minus exports. There are numerous industries in which one or the other of these ratios is very high, at times upward of 15 to 20 percent. Such industries are often termed, respectively, *export- and import-competing industries*. In the United States, steel and motor vehicles are examples of import-competing industries with imports amounting to a quarter of U.S. consumption in recent years; whereas aircraft, chemicals, and office equipment are examples of export industries. Thus, there are industries in which foreign trade plays an important role.

Table 1-3(a) shows U.S. foreign trade by sectors and Table 1-3(b) shows U.S. foreign trade with major trading partners. In 1984, merchandise exports and imports amounted to $210 billion and $338 billion respectively. The United States is a net exporter of farm products, chemicals, machinery, and aircraft; and a net importer of fuels, iron and steel, motor vehicles, and certain consumer goods. Its main trading partner is Canada, followed by Japan.

Similar tabulations can be constructed for each trading nation. Consider Japan. Devoid of natural resources, Japan imports most of the raw materials and other primary products it requires. In 1984 it imported $101 billion of such products and exported only $5 billion. On the other hand, Japan imported only $32 billion of manufactured goods and exported $164 billion. Within the manufacturing sector, Japan had sizable trade surpluses (exports greater than imports) in: iron and steel, motor vehicles, certain types machinery, and household appliances. Canada, being well endowed with land and natural resources, had a sizable surplus in primary products but a deficit in manufactured goods. Finally, all the European countries have a combined deficit in primary products and a surplus in manufactured goods. But much of their trade is among themselves.

Qualitative Considerations   Nor can the United States be considered independent of foreign trade in the qualitative sense. To say that imports of goods and services amount to 11 percent of the gross national product is to understate their importance in several respects. American imports contain important primary commodities that cannot be produced domestically but are crucial for numerous productive processes. Their absence would considerably curtail domestic production, lower consumer satisfaction, and interfere with our ability to meet national goals. Over 70 percent of U.S. agricultural imports are "complementary commodities"—commodities such as tropical products that cannot easily be grown in the United States. Likewise, the absence of imported fuel could have severe effects on the nation's output and/or environment. In the future, the same may apply

Table 1-3
(a) U.S. Merchandise Trade by Sectors, ($ Billions)

Sector	Exports		Imports	
	1981	1984	1981	1984
Food	42	35	21	24
Raw Materials	10	10	6	8
Ores and other minerals	4	4	4	3
Fuels	10	9	84	63
Nonferrous metals	3	2	7	8
Primary Products (total)	69	61	123	107
Iron and steel	3	1	12	12
Chemicals	25	24	11	16
Semi-manufactures	7	6	12	16
Specialized machinery	28	19	12	17
Office and telecommunications equipment	14	23	11	25
Road motor vehicles	16	17	29	48
Aircraft and aircraft engines	⎫	13	⎫	5
Power generating machinery	⎬	10	⎬ 19	9
Other machinery and transportation equipment	⎭ 43	15	⎭	16
Household appliances	3	3	10	16
Textiles and clothing	5	3	11	19
Other consumer goods	7	6	15	25
Total Manufactures	152	141	143	225
Total Trade	226*	210*	271	338

(b) U.S. Merchandise Trade with Major Trading Areas ($ Billions)

Trading Partner	Primary Products				Manufactures			
	U.S. Exports		U.S. Imports		U.S. Exports		U.S. Imports	
	1981	1984	1981	1984	1981	1984	1981	1984
Canada	6	6	17	21	30	35	26	42
Japan	12	12	1	1	9	11	39	59
Western Europe	21	16	15	17	39	37	38	55
Developing Countries	22	21	85	63	62	47	35	62

SOURCE: GATT, *International Trade*, 1984/85, Appendix tables.
*Includes "special category" exports not broken down by sector.

to other basic materials. Although most manufactured imports compete directly with domestically produced substitutes, foreign trade increases economic welfare (Chapter 11), widens consumer choice through diversification of available products, and expands producers' horizons in marketing their products and investing their capital. Opening the economy to the fresh winds of foreign competition also adds to its viability by curbing domestic monopoly power and spurring technological progress. And foreign imports can also be used to curtail inflationary pressures at home. Countries often relax import restrictions to cope with domestic inflation by increasing supply. Moreover, the external payments position of the country influences aggregate output and income, both directly and indirectly, through its effects on government fiscal and monetary policies. Finally, American imports constitute an important source of dollar earnings for many underdeveloped countries whose stability is vital to the United States. Similar considerations can be articulated with respect to exports. Thus, it would be misleading to suggest that the elimination or diminution of foreign trade would work no hardship on the American economy.

Summary   These are important qualifications, but they do not change the position of the United States *relative* to that of other countries. Comparatively speaking, this country is indeed a giant among nations and is also a closed economy. Whatever happens in the American economy has more important repercussions abroad than foreign developments have on the United States. And this dual characteristic qualifies this country to play a pivotal role in the world economy.

Organization of This Book

This book is concerned with the functioning of the international economy. It analyzes general principles and avoids listing factual details except to document and apply these principles.

In line with the traditional approach, the book is in two parts. Part 1 (Chapters 2 through 10) is devoted to international financial relations. It explains the present currency arrangements, dwells at length on the policies of individual countries within the framework established by the community of nations, and concludes with a discussion of reform plans for the international financial system. The analysis is accompanied by examples of financial episodes of the 1970s and 1980s.

However, remember that a smoothly functioning international financial system is not an end in itself. Rather, it is designed to lubricate the wheels of international trade and investments, to ensure that these activities—conducted by a multitude of profit-seeking individuals and private corporations—can be carried on unobstructed in the interest of the trader and the investor as well as the community at large.

Part 2 outlines the principles that govern world trade and investment and discusses the factors that determine the direction of that trade. It then analyzes the effect of various policies that obstruct the free flow of trade and deals extensively with regional and international organizations that are designed to promote the orderly functioning of the trading system and to increase the welfare of their member states. A list of the major international organizations dealing with trade and financial matters is offered in Appendix I.

A short section in Chapter 16 offers some observations about the system of state trading practiced in the socialist states, while Chapter 17 is devoted to the special trade problems of the underdeveloped world and to the demands that these problems place on the industrial countries. Factor movements are analyzed in Chapter 18. The book concludes with a short bibliography and a list of the most widely used sources of statistics about individual countries and the world economy.

Review Questions

1. What features distinguish international from domestic transactions?

2. What can you say about the growth of world trade in both nominal and real terms?

3. Evaluate the statement, "The U.S. is a closed economy, hence foreign trade is of no consequence to it."

4. Distinguish between: (a) export industries, (b) import-competing industries, (c) nontraded goods. Give examples of each.

5. Using the figures in Tables 1-2 and 1-3, what can you say about the changes in U.S. trade (and its composition) between 1981 and 1984? Make a similar comparison between 1970 and 1986, using the resources in your library.

Part ONE

International Financial Relations

The Alleged Mystique of International Finance

International financial matters have often captured the news headlines in recent years: Fluctuating exchange rates, the sharp escalation in the value of the U.S. dollar relative to other currencies during 1980–85, and its decline during 1985–86; the European Monetary System (EMS); adjustments in the European exchange rates, such as the devaluation of the Italian lira in mid-1985; devaluations of the Mexican peso in 1982 and in 1985; devaluation of the Brazilian cruzeiro in 1983, and of the Greek drachma and the Portuguese escudos in 1985; and a 1982 Presidential Commission exploring the merits and drawbacks of the gold standard; are but a few examples. Neither the meaning nor the implication of these matters is understood clearly by even well-informed citizens. The baffled reader of news reports regards them all as part of the "mystique" of international finance understood only by highly specialized experts, and so he usually skips over to the next story. Yet there is nothing mysterious or bewildering about these occurrences. They all reflect the periodic adjustments of the international financial system and have at their root the fact that each country must, over the long run, live within its means.

Each nation has its own currency, issued by its central bank, and used to finance transactions within the country. Among the Western countries, the five major currencies are: the U.S. dollar ($), the British pound sterling (£), the Japanese yen (¥), the German mark (D.M.) and the French franc (F.F.). The U.S. dollar is the most important among them. It is widely used in international transactions, and it serves as the unit by which the prices of truly international goods and services (such as oil and ocean freight rates) are priced. International trade statistics of all countries, compiled by the United Nations, are also reported in dollars.

The price of one currency in terms of another is called an *exchange rate*. For example in a recent period $1 was worth £0.7; $1 = 2.2 D.M.; $1 = 6.8 F.F.; and $1 = ¥ 160. Exchange rates can fluctuate in response to market supply and demand conditions, just like any other price. The dollar, pound, and yen are examples of such fluctuating currencies. Alternatively the government can fix the exchange value of its currency by buying and selling foreign currencies out of stock (reserves) at a fixed price. This is known as a fixed exchange rate. Whatever the system, the exchange rate is used to convert prices quoted in one currency into another. For example, a British coat which costs £100 is worth $200 at an exchange rate of £1 = $2, and a German automobile costing 10,000 D.M. is worth $5,000 at an exchange rate of 2 D.M. = $1. Each country measures its exports and imports in its own currency. Conversion of the exports of all countries into their dollar equivalents via the exchange rates has made possible the compilation of Table 1-1.

A country must balance its international financial accounts in much the same way as a family deals with its finances. In the short run, any deficit in a family budget can be financed by depletion of previously accumulated assets (spending from savings) or by accumulation of liabilities (buying on credit or obtaining a loan). But this process cannot go on forever. Sooner or later the family must adjust its behavior: either lower its expenditures or raise its income. The inability to go on financing deficits forever acts as a constraint on the economic behavior of the family. An analogous rule applies to a country in its relations with the rest of the world. In the short run, an external deficit can be *financed* by drawing down previously accumulated assets or by accumulating debts to other countries. In time, however, an *adjustment process* must set in to eliminate the deficit.

But a country is not a family, and the analogy cannot be carried to the point of equating the adjustment processes. Family decisions concerning income and outgo are made by a single decision-making unit with reasonably full information and control over its position at any given time. The action involved is both direct and prompt. No elaborate mechanism is required to balance the accounts. By contrast, millions of individual decision makers affect a country's international accounts. They include importers and exporters who in turn must be responsive to the demands of consumers and producers, all individuals engaged in overseas travel, and all companies involved in the transfer of investment and other capital across national boundaries. Consequently, balancing the accounts becomes an objective of national policy, which differs considerably from family decisions.

In a free-market economy the government has no direct control over individual decisions. Most policies subject to government jurisdiction are aggregative in nature, in the sense that they are aimed at the overall performance of the economy. They work through indirect effect on individuals and organizations who are the actual decision makers. While the individual family balances its accounts by direct action, all the government can do is to press one or more policy buttons. It thereby sets in motion a sequence of internal (*endogenous* in economists' parlance) processes as the various economic agents, individuals as well as institutions, react to the external (*exogenous*) policy push. The hope is that the series of interactions will lead the economy toward the prescribed goal.

What in the individual's case is a direct action with immediate and certain effects becomes a lengthy process with uncertain results in the case of government policy. Consequently, the study of economic policy is rather complex; it calls for a full understanding of what happens in the economy between the time a certain policy is adopted and the time when its impact is felt. The mechanisms involved in this process may be cumbersome, they may have conflicting effects, and they may be slow in working their way through the economy.

Not only that, unlike a family, a nation has no automatically generated information about its position at any given time on which to base policy decisions. Therefore, each government must establish an elaborate reporting mechanism to compile the necessary statistics and to perform the analysis needed to guide the policymakers. Moreover, if the policies of trading nations are not to conflict with one another, those nations must act in concert to set up a framework within which their policies are to be formulated. Such a framework is known as an international monetary or financial system.

In a sense, a nation operating within the system of state trading as it is practiced in Eastern Europe is more like a family than is a free-market country. That system requires no elaborate national and international mechanisms. International transactions are handled by a state trading authority, which can balance the external accounts at whatever level suits the national economic plan. The government can determine the degree of autarky under which it chooses to operate. However, a system so divorced from the workings of the market mechanism can result in an inefficient allocation of resources. Equally important, by denying it the right to deal in foreign markets, such a system deprives the consuming and producing public of personal freedom.

Thus the periodic adjustments in the system are the price that the Western countries pay for the freedom of persons to trade and speculate coupled with the freedom of the nation-states to pursue their national objectives. The function of the monetary system is to provide a well-lubricated mechanism by means of which a multitude of traders and investors can each pursue his own goal and yet result in one harmonious whole. On the national level, each country compiles detailed statistics on international transactions on which to base policy decisions, and such decisions are subject to the constraints imposed by the international system. The nature of the statistical compilations involved, the policy options (along with the costs and benefits of each option) open to a country under various conditions, and consideration of the international currency system are the subjects of Part 1 of this book.

Review Questions

1. What is the meaning of: "exchange rate?" Give examples.

2. Suppose that the price of a German automobile is 60,000 D.M. How much would it cost the American consumer at each of the following exchange rates: (a) $1 = 2 D.M. (b) $1 = 3 D.M. (c) $1 = 4 D.M.

   Assume next that the price of an American-made aircraft is $10 million. How much would that aircraft cost the German buyer at each of the above exchange rates?

   Does the exchange rate affect the price of foreign goods sold at home and of home goods sold abroad? If so how?

2 / Statement of International Transactions

A statement of all the transactions between one country and the rest of the world, usually reported annually, is known as that country's *international transactions statement*, alternatively referred to in common parlance as the country's *balance of payments*. The transactions included are merchandise trade, exchange of services (sometimes referred to as *invisible* items, because unlike commodities they cannot be seen), and transfers of capital in both directions. In order to facilitate the understanding of the various items appearing in the statement, it is useful to divide them into two groups: those giving rise to dollar *inpayments* (*plus* or *credit* items) and those resulting in dollar *outpayments* (*negative* or *debit* items). This dichotomy should be kept in mind throughout the exposition.

Main Items in the Statement of International Transactions

In the explanation that follows we shall make use of the U.S. International Transactions Statement for 1985, adapted from the U.S. Department of Commerce publication. A highly condensed version of the official statement appears in Table 2-1, where all entries are divided into current account and capital account transactions.

The Current Account

Merchandise trade constitutes the largest item in U.S. international transactions; exports of goods are an inpayments or plus item, whereas imports of goods are an outpayments or negative item. The two are shown on lines 1 and 2 in Table 2-1; the difference between them is the *balance on merchandise trade* or simply the balance of trade (line 3). In 1985 the U.S. had a trade deficit of $124 billion—a record high. This balance is reported by

Table 2-1
U.S. International Transactions 1985 and 1981 ($ billion)

Current Account Transactions	1985		1981	
1. Merchandise exports	+214		+236	
2. Merchandise imports	−338		−264	
3. Balance on Merchandise Trade (line 1 plus 2)		−124		− 28
4. Service transactions (net) [Exports 146] [Imports 125]	+ 21		+ 41	
5. Balance on goods and services (line 3 plus 4)		−103		+ 13
6. Private remittances and government grants (unilateral transfers)	− 15		− 6	
7. Balance on current account (line 5 plus 6)		−118		+ 7
Capital Account Transactions				
8. U.S. assets abroad other than official reserves, net [increase/capital outflow (−)[1]]	− 34		−101	
9. Foreign assets in the U.S. other than official reserves, net [increase/capital inflow (+)[2]]	+125		+ 69	
10. Statistical discrepancy[3]	+ 33		+ 25	
11. Capital account balance (lines 8−10)		+124		− 7
12. Official Reserve Transactions Balance (line 7 plus 11)		+ 6		0
13. U.S. official reserves, net [increase/outflow (−)]	− 4		− 5	
14. Foreign official reserves, net [increase/inflow (+)]	− 2		+ 5	

SOURCE: *Survey of Current Business,* March 1986, p. 36.

[1]An increase in U.S. assets abroad means capital outflow from the U.S. and has a negative sign. A decrease means capital inflow and has a positive sign.

[2]An increase in foreign assets in the U.S. means capital inflow into the U.S. and has a positive sign. A decrease has a negative sign.

[3]What is the nature of the statistical discrepancy and how does it arise? In compiling the statistics, the U.S. Department of Commerce uses two sources of information for each transaction: the transaction itself and the means of payments for it. For example, information of a given U.S. export transaction can be obtained from the exporter who shipped the merchandise and from the bank through which the payment was made. All goods and services as well as capital transfers are treated in the same manner. Theoretically, the value of all transactions should add up exactly to the value of all payments. But in fact they do not. The difference is called a statistical discrepancy.

the Department of Commerce on a monthly and quarterly basis and is given wide attention by the national media.

Line 4 shows the export minus the import of service transactions. On the export (inpayments) side these consist of U.S. receipts for transportation, insurance, and other services rendered by Americans to foreigners; foreign tourists visiting the United States and spending money here; and *receipts of income on U.S. investment abroad.* This last item is the biggest in the service category. It includes repatriated earnings on U.S. direct investments abroad (35 billion in 1985), as well as dividends and interest received by American owners (including the U.S. government) of foreign stocks, bonds, and bank accounts ($55 billion in 1985). It bears emphasizing that these are *returns* on foreign investments accumulated over previous years. The annual U.S. *investments* themselves are shown in the capital account, (line 8). Imports of services (outpayments) include U.S. payments for insurance transport and other services purchased from foreigners, American tourists visiting foreign lands and spending money there, and foreign receipts of earnings on their investments in the United States. This last item (totalling $66 billion in 1985) includes foreign receipts of interest and dividends earned on bank accounts, bonds, and stocks that foreign private institutions and governments own in the United States. In 1985 the export of services exceeded imports by $21 billion, yielding a surplus on service transactions in that amount (line 4).

Exports minus imports of goods and services constitute the *balance on goods and services*. Shown on line 5 of Table 2-1, this balance amounted to a deficit of $103 billion in 1985 and is a main link between the international transactions statement and the national income accounts. It is conceptually related to the "net exports of goods and services" in the expenditure side of the GNP (see Table 1-2 in Chapter 1), where GNP is the sum of consumption (C), investments (I), government spending (G), and net exports (X_n). However, there are two statistical differences between them: The GNP definition of "net exports" excludes both special military sales under grant from exports and U.S. government interest payments from imports. Consequently the two figures do not match.

Throughout the 1950s and 1960s, the United States had sizable surpluses (excess of exports over imports) on merchandise trade. But in 1971–81 deficits occurred in all years except for 1973 and 1975. The annual deficits grew to the $25–34 billion range beginning in 1977 (see Table 2-2), partly because of the rise in price of imported oil in the 1970s. However, the trade deficit shrank between 1978 and 1980, only to rise sharply again in 1983–86.

Table 2-2
U.S. International Transactions in Selected Years ($ Billions)

	1960	1971	1977	1980	1983	1984
Export of goods and services	29	66	184	345	332	362
Import of goods and services	− 24	− 67	− 194	− 334	− 365	458
Balance on merchandise trade	5	− 2	− 31	− 25	− 61	− 114
Balance on goods and services	5	2	− 9	11	− 33	− 96
Balance on current account	3	− 1	− 14	4	− 36	− 107
Increase (−) in U.S. official reserve assets	2	2	0	− 9	− 1	− 3
Increase (+) in foreign official assets	1	27	35	15	5	3

SOURCE: *Survey of Current Business*, various issues.

Despite the large trade deficits in the 1970s, the balance on goods and services showed a surplus in all years except 1977 and 1978. Sizable earnings on U.S. investments abroad represented the main positive item in the service transactions responsible for offsetting the trade deficits.

Unilateral transfers are a major outpayments item in the U.S. They include the government foreign aid program as well as private remittances and are shown in line 6 of Table 2-1. Adding this item to the balance on goods and services, we obtain the "balance on current account" (line 7), which was $118 billion in 1985.

All transactions considered thus far are current account items and do not include foreign investments or any other form of capital transfers. The resulting balances are therefore strictly partial. But they are reported regularly, as memoranda items, at the bottom of the official statement for several reasons: The balance on goods and services is a useful link to the national income accounts; all three partial balances are comparable to similar balances reported by other countries and therefore make possible intercountry comparisons; and the public and the press have become accustomed to monthly and quarterly reports of the trade balance, a balance that receives wide attention in the media. Additionally, the balance on trade and, to some extent, the balance on goods and services are measures of the macroeconomic effect of international transactions. Although international trade is a small component of the American economy, large swings in the trade balance can have significant effects on the aggregate level of economic activity. And large swings have occurred in recent years: from a surplus of $9 billion in 1975, to a deficit of $34 billion in 1978; and from a deficit of $36 billion in 1982 to a deficit of $118 billion in 1985. Such swings can have important effects on the economy.

The Capital Account

We next turn to the capital account of the statement. Line 8 in Table 2-1 shows the net change over the year in U.S. assets (other than official *reserve* assets) held abroad. This change is a result of U.S. capital outpayments (minus items) of the following varieties: (a) direct private investments abroad by American corporations, such as the establishment of foreign subsidiaries; (b) purchases of foreign securities (stocks and bonds, for example) and deposits in foreign banks by Americans; and (c) U.S. government loans to foreign countries, less repayment of loans by foreigners. In all cases, repatriated U.S. capital is netted out. All these net outflows increase U.S. asset holdings abroad. Therefore an increase (decrease) in U.S. assets abroad means capital outflow (inflow) and has a negative (positive) sign. In 1985 U.S. assets abroad increased by $34 billion.

Line 9 in Table 2-1 shows the net change over the year in foreign assets (other than official reserves) in the United States. Such capital inpayments (positive items) include (a) direct investments in the U.S. by foreign corporations and (b) purchases of American securities (that is, stocks and bonds) and deposits in U.S. banks by foreigners. An increase (decrease) in foreign assets in the U.S. means a capital inflow (outflow) and has a positive (negative) sign. In 1985 foreign assets in the U.S. increased by $125 billion.

While all items reporting the transfer of capital are included in the capital account component of the balance of payments, the income on foreign investments—whether interest, dividends or repatriated profits—is part of the goods and services section. These earnings, of course, are a result of investments made in previous years.

U.S. corporations generally prefer *direct* investments, such as the establishment of foreign subsidiaries, which give the American investors a significant degree of control over the overseas operations. In contrast, until the early 1970s, most foreign investments in the United States have been of the *portfolio* variety, such as stock or bond ownership, not involving a controlling interest in American enterprises. This preference on the part of foreign corporations was changing in the 1970s and 1980s, as an increasing number of them have established branch plants in the United States.

Finally, a large statistical discrepancy, amounting to $33 billion in dollar inflow, appeared in 1985. Its nature is explained in footnote 3 in Table 2-1 and it need not detain us here.

Inspection of lines 7 and 11 reveals a dramatic change in the U.S. external position, from a small current account surplus in 1981 to a sizable deficit in 1985; and from a small capital account deficit in 1981 to a large surplus in 1985. The table does not reveal whether the capital or current accounts was the driving force behind these changes (this must await discussion in subsequent chapters). It only shows that in each of the two years the current and capital accounts nearly balanced each other out.

All the entries covered thus far constitute a response to general economic or political factors. Trade in goods and services is mainly a result of competitive position or of relative prices in different countries, the relative purchasing power of their populations, and the geographical distribution of natural resources around the globe. It is also affected by such intangible factors as taste and marketing ability. Foreign investments reflect relative profit opportunities at home and abroad that in turn can be traced to a number of economic (and political) factors. Short-term capital may be attracted to the financial centers that pay the highest interest rate, although not all flows can be so explained.

Autonomous and Accommodating Items

All items considered so far are known as *autonomous* transactions. They owe their existence (and size) to general economic conditions and are not caused by the state of the balance of payments itself. Because they are motivated independently of one another by a multitude of traders and investors, they may not automatically produce a balance. When these items do not add up to zero, the balance of payments is considered out of balance or out of equilibrium. It is in *deficit* when their sum is negative and in *surplus* when it is positive. This difference between the inpayments and outpayments must somehow be settled; the means for settling it—gold, official foreign currency reserves, and official debt—are known as the *balancing* or *accommodating* items (the term "official" refers mainly to the central bank). These entries are brought into being by the very existence of imbalance in the autonomous transactions. In Table 2-1 they are shown on lines 13 and 14. Their total must equal the imbalance of items 7 and 11 combined but bear the opposite sign, thus making the entire statement add up to zero.

Changes in Official Reserves

More specifically, the accommodating or financing items include changes in official liabilities to foreign official authorities, or exchange of official assets that are acceptable means of payments to all countries. These assets, known as "official reserves," include widely used foreign currencies (mainly dollars for countries outside the U.S.), gold, reserve position in the International Monetary Fund (IMF) (explained in Chapter 4), and Special Drawing Rights (SDRs)—assets that the IMF created and distributed to its member countries and that the official monetary institutions of these countries accept from one another in settling debts. Most of the annual change in official reserves is composed of variations in *foreign* currency holdings of central banks.

How do central banks come to play the balancing role in the balance of payments that consists mainly of private sector transactions? The answer is that central banks buy and sell *foreign* currencies in exchange for their *own* currency in order to influence the exchange rate. Such activity is referred to as official intervention in the foreign exchange market.

Under a regime of fixed exchange rates, which was prevalent before 1973, each central bank buys and sells foreign currencies in exchange for its own currency at a *fixed price* (exchange rate). Private traders either sell their accumulated foreign currencies to the central banks (in which case the central bank's official reserves rise) or they buy foreign currencies from the central bank (in which case its official reserves decline). That is how variations in official reserves played a residual role of balancing the external accounts.

Today the exchange rates of several major currencies (including the dollar) are allowed to fluctuate. Yet central banks continue to intervene on their respective foreign exchange markets. They buy and sell their own currencies in exchange for foreign currencies for a variety of reasons, but mainly to influence the exchange rate. The Federal Reserve Bank of New York (FRB) conducts such activities on behalf of the U.S. government, buying and selling marks, pounds, yen, or francs in exchange for dollars. Each foreign central bank carries on similar transactions in its own financial center. Because of the importance of the dollar in international finance, most (but not all) of these transactions in foreign markets are conducted in dollars. Thus the Bank of England buys and sells pounds for dollars on the London market to influence the pound exchange rate, and the German

Central Bank trades marks for dollars in Frankfurt to influence the mark exchange rate. Because they intervene mainly in dollars, the outcome of their activity may be an increase or a decrease in their dollar asset holdings, which is correspondingly either an increase or a decrease in U.S. liabilities (IOUs).

These activities result in a net change, over the year, in the U.S. official reserve holdings (line 13 in Table 2-1) and in foreign official holdings of U.S. dollars. The latter are official liabilities of the U.S. (line 14).

Line 13 in Table 2-1 shows a $4 billion increase in U.S. official reserve assets. A negative sign indicates an increase in U.S. government assets held abroad.[1] By the same token foreign central banks decreased their dollar reserve holdings in the United States (line 14) by $2 billion.[2] The sum of these two items is shown in line 12. In 1985 U.S. international transactions were in surplus to the tune of $6 billion. The surplus was financed in two ways: U.S. official reserves rose by $4 billion, while foreign central banks drew down their reserves by $2 billion. To summarize, reserve assets and official debt instruments constitute the means of financing imbalances. As do the totals on all balance sheets, the balance sheets for all international transactions, including those of the central banks, totals zero. This is so for all items in Table 2-1; both inflow (+) and outflow (−) items added up to $518 billion in 1985.

Changes in official reserves, which are noted in line 12 of Table 2-1, are the only overall measures of the surplus or deficit in the balance of payments. Known as the "official reserve transactions balance," it arises because the central banks choose to intervene on their respective market and buy or sell foreign currencies.

In the absence of such intervention, any difference between private inpayments and outpayments would be fully reflected in variations of the value of the currency (its exchange rate), and the official reserve transactions balance would be zero. For a country with a freely fluctuating exchange rate (to be described in the next chapter), an external deficit would be reflected in a decline in the value of its currency relative to other currencies. Conversely, an external surplus is reflected in an increase of the value of the currency. With official intervention, part of the exchange variations are blunted by central bank sale and purchase of foreign currencies. Considerable intervention by the United States took place in the Fall of 1985, as reflected in Table 2−1.

Because most of the imbalance on autonomous transactions results in variations of the exchange rate rather than in a change in reserves, the latter magnitude tends to be small and it is not fully indicative of the imbalance.

---

[1] A net increase in U.S. official reserve assets is shown with a negative sign, indicating an outflow of capital; an increase in U.S. liabilities to foreign official agencies is shown with a positive sign, indicating an inflow of capital so as to agree with the method used to indicate flows of other capital transactions.

[2] A positive sign indicates an increase of foreign official holdings in the U.S. or inflow of such capital into the U.S.

Summary

To recapitulate, the size of the country's external imbalance depends on which items in the statement are considered autonomous and which are considered balancing (or accommodating). Although the conceptual distinction between the two categories is clear-cut, in practice it is difficult to determine how to classify certain transactions. For example, not all transactions in official reserves can be considered "balancing" because some such transactions are not strictly passive consequences of all other transactions. Foreign governments can build up official reserve deposits in the United States on their own initiative rather than as an outcome of a U.S. deficit (as implied by the term balancing or accommodating transactions).

Another source of uncertainty arises from the present fluctuating exchange rate system. When a country experiences an external deficit, at least part of it is reflected in a decline in the value of its currency relative to other currencies. Conversely, a surplus is partly reflected in an increase in the value of the currency. In consequence, even if it were possible to compute them perfectly, the imbalances shown in the country's statement of international transactions would not accurately reflect the country's external position. Part of the deficit or surplus is absorbed in variations in the currency's values (that is, exchange rate) rather than being represented in the statistical statement.

Under a *freely* fluctuating exchange rate (one without government intervention), the entire imbalance would be reflected in exchange rate variations. The exchange rate, which is the price of foreign currencies, would settle at a level that clears the market—namely, the *level that equates autonomous inpayments and outpayments*. There would be no change in official reserves, and hence no external deficit or surplus. It is government intervention designed to influence exchange rate movements that yields changes in official reserves.

Uses and Misuses of International Transactions Statistics

In attempting to simplify the exposition, we have glossed over many vexing problems embodied in the international transactions statistics. Readers who need more detailed information may refer to the U.S. statement published in the Department of Commerce monthly *Survey of Current Business*.[3] The annual *Economic Report of the President* contains data and analysis of developments in international finance and trade. Information for other countries may be found in *International Financial Statistics* and the *Balance of*

---

[3] The *Survey of Current Business* also publishes tables showing: (a) U.S. international transactions with individual countries or regions; (b) a commodity breakdown of U.S. merchandise trade; (c) a breakdown of U.S. government transactions; (d) a breakdown of U.S. direct investments abroad and of foreign direct investments in the United States; (e) an account of capital flows other than direct investments; and (f) a detailed account of the change in foreign official assets in the United States.

Payments Yearbook, both published by the International Monetary Fund. International transactions statistics are reported annually, but quarterly data for the United States are also available.

Little or no credence should be given to the occasional news reports that draw conclusions from monthly trade returns, for these data may result from special circumstances. Even quarterly statistics can be unrepresentative and misleading. Normally an imbalance must persist for a year or longer before it can be determined whether it is in some sense a fundamental phenomenon rather than a temporary one likely to reverse itself in due course. A warning against some common misuses of international transactions statistics is in order.

Long-Run Shifts in the Balance on Merchandise Trade

Because of its importance in the total payments position, the balance on merchandise trade merits special attention. Commodity trade is the largest single category in the balance of payments. Yet, in line with the previous section, the trade balance should not in and of itself be a cause for alarm or jubilation, nor should it serve as the sole guide to policy making. In what follows, we attempt to place the balance on commodity trade in its proper perspective, particularly as it relates to the balance on capital account.

For more than twenty years following World War II, the United States mounted huge surpluses on its balance of trade, amounting to several billion dollars in practically every year. At the same time, the capital account showed substantial outflows of investment funds, often exceeding the surplus on merchandise trade.

This relationship between the two subaccounts is not accidental; it is characteristic of a capital-exporting nation. Although the causal relation is rather complex, we can say that a capital-exporting country must generate large trade surpluses in order to offset the deficit on capital account. In part, these surpluses are a direct result of the capital export, because overseas investment projects use American materials and equipment and thereby foster exports. But mainly there is an indirect process, internal to the economic system, through which capital export generates trade surpluses. By the same reasoning, one would expect a capital-importing country, as Australia and Canada have been in the recent past, to have a deficit on merchandise trade. Here we may say either that the deficit is financed by the import of capital or that the import of capital generates the trade deficit. Whatever the line of causation, these tend to be companion phenomena that offset each other so as to yield an overall balance.

What does that relation imply for the U.S. trade position, past, present, and future? It should come as no surprise that, during the era of large inflows of investment capital into this country, the United States experienced continuous deficits on merchandise trade. As the importation of capital subsided and gradually declined below the annual outflow of repatriated earnings as well as debt servicing and repayment to Europe, the trade deficit diminished and slowly gave way to surpluses. For it is only through trade surpluses that foreign debts can be paid and earnings can be remitted abroad. Those surpluses grew to huge proportions as the United States became the world's major exporter of capital. Certainly this situation prevailed in the period 1944–1970. In recent years this country approached the stage of the "mature economy"—namely, a stage in which repatriated earnings exceed the net outflow of investments capital. And to accommodate large net inflows of such earnings, the trade balance must transform into a deficit position. In 1983–85 the United States sustained sizable trade and current account deficits, and these were offset by substantial capital inflows.

It should now be realized that a trade deficit is not inherently bad, and that a surplus is not inherently good. Just to drive home the point that a trade surplus is not necessarily a favorable phenomenon, think of the country giving up more goods than it receives in return and ask yourself: "What is so favorable about that?" The term "favorable balance" as applied to a surplus is a leftover from the mercantilist period when one overriding objective of nations was to accumulate gold. Because countries that do not possess gold mines can acquire the yellow metal only through surpluses on merchandise trade, having such a surplus came to be regarded as favorable. But it is easy to realize that by giving away goods we lose the pleasure or satisfaction of consuming them, while little gain accrues to the citizenry from having stocks of gold buried in Fort Knox. However, all this should not be construed to mean the reverse—that a trade surplus is necessarily unhealthy. Each circumstance must be assessed on its own merit.

Placing Balance-of-Payments Considerations in Proper Perspective

A country as wealthy, diversified, and productive as the United States should not subject its foreign policies to the requirements of the balance of payments. Two examples will serve to illustrate the point. Decisions concerning foreign aid to underdeveloped countries and its distribution among donor nations should not be based on balance-of-payments considerations. Rather, they ought to relate to overall national priorities and to what the country can afford to spend. And it is per capita and total national income, not the balance of payments, that best indicate our ability (or any country's ability) to engage in foreign assistance. Likewise, only the income criterion can properly be used in any attempt to arrive at an equitable distribution of the aid burden. The fact that Ghana may have a balance-of-payments surplus and Great Britain a deficit does not mean that Ghana should initiate a foreign aid program to the United Kingdom. Assuming that we are able and willing to pursue a certain national objective, the balance-of-payments position should not stand in the way.

Another example concerns the U.S. commitments abroad, such as the maintenance of troops in Europe and direct involvement in foreign conflicts. Any such commitments must be made in terms of the ranking of national objectives. This is not to suggest that cost considerations play no role in decisions of war and peace. They must certainly be weighed alongside any noneconomic costs and against whatever potential benefits can be expected from a given policy. The major economic burden resulting from war or foreign commitments is in the form of annual domestic budgetary expenditures. The pressure on the balance of payments resulting from any conflict is subsidiary in nature and can be removed by economic adjustment mechanisms discussed in subsequent chapters.

Limitations of Balance-of-Payments Information

Like any statistics collected from a great variety of reporting sources, the international transactions data are far from perfect. Without going into the methods of gathering the figures, we might mention that the merchandise component is allegedly the most reliable, since traders are required to make detailed reports on both volume and value when goods cross national boundaries. Probably the least dependable are accounts of private capital flows.

But even if it were thoroughly accurate, the international transactions statement does not contain all the useful information about a country's international position. The merchandise account, for example, which is by far the largest item, appears in an aggregative form followed by a list of selected items in the supplementary tables. If an investigator wished to discover the commodity composition of this trade in its entirety he or she would have to turn elsewhere. One source of such data for all countries is the United Nations *Commodity Trade Statistics,* in which a standard classification of commodities (known as SITC[4]) is employed. More importantly, the international transactions statement only shows *changes* in a country's positions, not the positions themselves. All items in the statement refer to *flows* of goods, services, and capital over the one-year period covered. Total American holdings of overseas investments at a point of time, which are the product of flows over many previous years, are not given. Nor are the sales of foreign subsidiaries reported. Since these activities have important bearing on the strength of the dollar, information about them is collected and published separately by the U.S. Department of Commerce. At the end of 1984 U.S. direct private investments abroad totaled $233 billion, while foreign direct investments in the United States amounted to $160 billion. Similar information is available for other assets.[5]

Next, it should be recognized that individual items in the international transactions statement are interrelated. Consider for example the U.S. foreign economic assistance program (a unilateral transfer). Most of the foreign-aid money is spent in the United States, partly because the grants

[4]This is formally called the Standard International Trade Classification.
[5]*Economic Report of the President,* 1986, p. 371.

contain a stipulation that ties them to purchases of American products (known as "tied aid"). Thus, any curtailment of aid would reduce United States exports by nearly an equal amount; the improvement in the balance on current account would be minimal.

Finally, although the balance of payments is a global statement, it is often subdivided into the country's relations with separate continents. But the common belief that there is somehow a need to balance the external accounts vis-à-vis individual countries or groups of countries is erroneous. Such concern would be valid only if currencies were subject to government control and were not freely convertible to each other. Under the conditions of currency convertibility prevailing among the industrialized countries today, the United States can use its surplus with one country to pay for a deficit with another. It is only the overall external position that matters. And even that need not be in balance all the time. Just as a family can run into short-run deficits and cover them out of previous savings or by borrowing, so can a country finance temporary deficits out of reserves or by incurring foreign debts. It is only if the deficits persist over a period of years that they provide a cause for concern.

A Nation Versus a State

Why, it may be asked, is a country the smallest unit to have an international transactions statement? Every region, state, and other subdivision conducts transactions with the world outside it: Why does one never hear of a balance-of-payments deficit of the state of West Virginia or the Rocky Mountains region? A superficial difference is that there exist no comprehensive data on the economic transactions of a state with the world outside. Only countries, with political boundaries through which goods and services must pass, collect such information.

More important is the way the problem manifests itself in the context of a state. Let us suppose that because of a technological change or a shift in consumer taste, there occurred a sharp decline in demand for the products of West Virginia. That state's exports would drop sharply, and in all probability it would develop an external deficit. Yet there would be no press reports to that effect. Instead, public discussion would emphasize the fact that workers in the export industries were thrown out of work and that production and income declined all around. If the situation persisted and nothing were done to rectify it, the state would become a depressed area, and eventually people would start migrating to other parts of the country where jobs were more plentiful—that is, to states producing the type of products for which national and world demand were booming. Such migration is much more difficult, if not impossible, between countries. In other words, whereas an independent country is said to have an external deficit or surplus, a state with a similar trade position is said to be depressed or flourishing.

But the difference does not stop here. A country has its own currency and a national government that can pursue fiscal, monetary, and commercial policies aimed at curing the external imbalance. If nothing else works, it may impose import controls or exchange restrictions. By contrast, a state government can take few measures to alleviate a depression within its borders; its ability to act is much more limited. A state cannot pursue independent fiscal and monetary policies. It does not issue its own currency or control the supply of money; neither can it impose restrictions on "foreign" trade and payments. In a more general way, regions of the same country are subject to uniform economic policies affecting income and prices and, therefore, the balance of payments. Such uniformity does not exist between countries that pursue independent policies. Finally, a country can change the exchange rate of its currency; in the present system of fluctuating exchange rates such changes occur every day. In contrast, the ratio, say, of the New York to the California dollar is immutably fixed at one to one.

On the other hand, the national government of which the state is a part can take steps to help the state by direct government assistance, by a variety of transfer payments, or by encouraging private capital to move in. In general, given the proper business environment, capital is more mobile between states than between countries. Certainly, in the short run, the existence of an integrated capital market within a nation makes it easier to finance imbalances within itself than between nations. And if such financing is not adequate, the adjustment can take the form of outflow of labor from the deficit (depressed) region. The result of this comparison between a country and a political subdivision such as a state is that in the context of a state an external deficit is manifested differently; it is more likely to be offset by movement of the factors of production such as labor and capital, and it cannot be handled by policy measures, which are the prerogative of the central government.

Review Questions

1. You are given the following figures for U.S. international transactions in 1983 (in $ billions):

Merchandise imports	−$300
Merchandise exports	+$200
Investments *income* (net)	+$ 30
Other Service Transactions (net)	+$ 20
Foreign Private Assets in the U.S. (net increase)	+$100
U.S. Assets abroad (net increase)	−$ 50
Change in U.S. or foreign official reserve holdings	0

a. *Calculate* the

  • balance of trade
  • balance of goods and services; and balance on current account
  • official reserve transactions balance.

b. Explain the relation between the current and the capital accounts.
c. Can you suggest what possible exchange standard (fixed? floating?) the U.S. dollar is on? Explain fully.

 d. How do the above figures relate to the expenditures side of the U.S. income and product (GNP) accounts?

2. Based on Tables 2-1 and 2-2 explain the changes in the U.S. external position between 1980 and 1984, and between 1981 and 1984.

3. Why doesn't the state of California publish annual balance of payments statistics? In what way is it different from a country?

3/
Market-Determined Exchange Rates

*U*nlike the situation in the period immediately following World War II, the currencies of most industrialized countries are today freely convertible to one another, some at a fixed ratio and others at a ratio subject to daily fluctuations. This ratio—the number of units of one currency that are exchangeable for a unit of another—is known as the *exchange rate*.[1] Thus, on a certain date, the British pound sterling (£) was worth $2.00 in American currency, and the West German mark (D.M.) was valued at 50 cents, which in turn means that £1 = 4 D.M. The fact that every exchange rate has a corresponding inverse is frequently a source of confusion. The dollar-mark rate can be expressed by saying that 1 mark = 50 cents or, equivalently, that $1 = 2 marks. An *increase* in the value of the mark to 60 cents is equivalent to a *decrease* in the value of the dollar to 1.7 marks. Consequently, a statement that the exchange rate has gone up (or down) requires further clarification, because its meaning depends on how the exchange rate is defined. To avoid confusion, one can use such phraseology as "the exchange value of the dollar went up" (or "down") in terms of other currencies.

Exchange rates by themselves tell us nothing about the relative strength of the currencies involved or the economies behind them. The fact that the pound sterling is set at $2 and the West German mark at 50 cents is not to be construed as an indication that the first currency is four times as strong as the second. It may simply reflect the difference between the denominations into which the two countries have chosen to divide their respective currencies. When first decreed, the external value of each currency presumably reflected the country's economic conditions in general, and the purchasing power of the currency (that is, the internal costs and prices) relative to that of other currencies in particular. This relative position changes

---

[1] Exchange rates are published monthly in the *Federal Reserve Bulletin*.

over time, and such changes may either weaken or strengthen the currency vis-à-vis other currencies. A currency is considered externally weak if the government is having difficulty maintaining the predetermined exchange rate under a fixed-rate system, or if the currency declines in value on the foreign exchange market under a fluctuating exchange-rate system.

Since 1973 important currencies have been fluctuating in response to supply and demand conditions. These market fluctuations are explained in this chapter.

Demand and Supply of Foreign Currencies

When the exchange value of a currency is permitted by the government to fluctuate freely on the foreign exchange markets, with its value determined daily by supply-and-demand conditions, it is known as a *freely fluctuating* or a *floating* exchange rate. In such a situation, market forces determine each exchange rate at the level that clears the market. A floating currency is said to *appreciate* when its exchange value increases and to *depreciate* when its exchange value decreases.

To illustrate how the exchange rate of a floating currency is determined, Figure 3-1 shows the German foreign exchange market, where marks

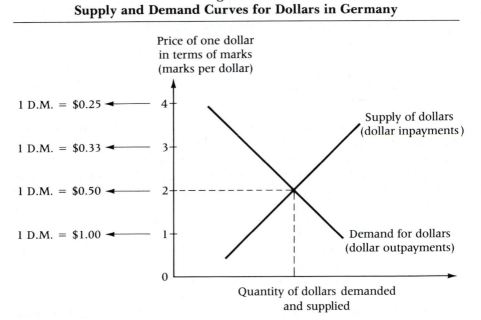

Figure 3-1
Supply and Demand Curves for Dollars in Germany

NOTE: The vertical axis shows the number of marks per dollar along with the corresponding inverse: the equivalent number of dollars per mark in each case.

are traded for dollars, which for simplicity are taken to represent all foreign currencies as far as Germany is concerned. The two intersecting curves show the demand for and supply of dollars at various mark prices. They exhibit "normal" slopes: as the mark price of the dollar declines, more dollars are demanded and fewer are supplied. The equilibrium exchange rate for this particular pair of curves is 2 marks = $1; it would vary with shifts in either demand or supply. The quantity axis indicates the number of dollars changing hands. This is similar to the price determination mechanism in the market for any commodity.

But the analysis begs the more fundamental question of what gives rise to such supply and demand, because foreign currencies are not commodities. A commodity is demanded by consumers for its own sake, to enhance consumer satisfaction, and is supplied by producers through the use of productive factors. By contrast, people do not normally require foreign currencies for their own sake, and foreign currencies are not manufactured in the same manner as are commodities. Rather, the demand for dollars in our illustration reflects German desire to purchase foreign goods, to travel abroad and buy other foreign services, or to transfer capital abroad for investment and other purposes. Together these items constitute the *outpayments* side of the German international transactions statement. On the other hand, the supply of foreign currencies is derived from commodity and service exports and from the inflow of foreign capital. These entries make up the *inpayments* side of the German international transactions statement. Thus, the demand curve in Figure 3-1 is tantamount to a German dollar outpayments curve, and the supply curve, to a German dollar inpayments curve.[2] Since the exchange rate is determined by the intersection of the two curves, it ensures equality between inpayments and outpayments. A shift in one or both curves will also change the exchange rate to a new level, which again clears the market. In other words, a freely fluctuating rate will ensure equilibrium in the balance of payments.

□ This discussion invites an important question: If the demand and supply for foreign currencies is not the same phenomenon as the demand and supply for a product, but is instead "derived" from a desire to trade on foreign markets, how can we be sure that the curves have the usual slopes of demand and supply, as shown in Figure 3-1? Consider the two curves in turn.

□ *Demand for Dollars* Suppose for the sake of simplicity that all international transactions consist of commodity trade. Then the German *demand* for dollars represents indirectly German demand for American goods. If the price of $1 rises from 2 to 4 marks (moving upward along the price axis), then an American product costing $1 would double in price to the German consumer (from 2 to 4 marks), shrinking Germany's volume of

---

[2]Given the German demand for dollars, one can derive the German supply of marks. This relationship is shown at the end of Appendix II-A.

imports and with it the number of dollars required to finance imports. In a more general way, consider the price of a $10,000 American automobile to the German consumer at four alternative exchange rates:

Exchange Rate	Cost in Marks of a $10,000 American Automobile
$1 = 1 D.M.	10,000 D.M.
$1 = 2 D.M.	20,000 D.M.
$1 = 3 D.M.	30,000 D.M.
$1 = 4 D.M.	40,000 D.M.

As the mark price of the dollar rises (moving upward along the vertical axis), the price of American goods to German buyers (the price expressed in marks) rises. As a result, Germans would purchase fewer American goods and demand fewer dollars to buy them. An upward movement along the vertical axis is associated with a leftward movement along the horizontal axis, giving the "demand for dollars" curve a negative slope. In other words, a rise in the mark price of a dollar is associated with a decline in dollar outpayments, and conversely a reduction in the mark price of a dollar is associated with a rise in dollar outpayments. This explains the negative slope of the "demand for dollars" curve.

☐ *Supply of Dollars*   By the same token, the *supply* of dollars is derived from German merchandise exports to the United States. An increase in the price of $1 from 2 to 4 marks means that American consumers of German imports would find that for $1 they can now get 4 marks' worth of German goods instead of 2 marks' worth. In a more general way consider the price of a 1,200 D.M. German camera to American consumers at four alternative exchange rates:

Exchange Rate	Cost in Dollars of a 1,200 D.M. German Camera
$1 = 1 D.M.	$1,200
$1 = 2 D.M.	$ 600
$1 = 3 D.M.	$ 400
$1 = 4 D.M.	$ 300

As the mark price of the dollar rises (moving up along the vertical axis of Figure 3-1), the price of German goods to American buyers (the price expressed in dollars) declines. As a result, Americans would purchase more German goods, and (subject to a certain elasticity assumption to be explored in Chapter 7) would spend more American dollars to buy them, raising German dollar inpayments. An upward movement along the vertical axis is associated with a rightward movement along the horizontal axis explaining the positive slope of the "supply of dollars" or inpayments curve.   ■

At any one time, the supply-and-demand forces emanating from international transactions exert their influence on the foreign exchange market to determine the exchange rate. Thus, a currency is fundamentally "strong" and its value may be pushed upward, when the country's autonomous inpayments (exports of goods and services plus inflow of capital) exceed outpayments (imports plus outflow of capital)—that is, when it has a surplus in the balance of payments. It is "weak" when this situation is reversed and the country's balance of payments is in deficit. In turn, the country's inpayments and outpayments are determined by a host of domestic and foreign factors, including prices (its competitive position, for example), income, and interest rates. Anything that affects these factors at home and abroad influences the position of the supply and demand curves and therefore affects the exchange rate. The exchange rate is deeply rooted in the country's economic conditions; in no way can it be divorced from its own and other countries' general economic policies. The entire constellation of economic circumstances exerts its influence on the exchange rates through its effect on internationally traded items.

Shifts in the Demand and Supply Curves

Although a systematic treatment of the factors that affect the exchange rate must wait until Chapters 6 and 7, a short *intuitive* discussion is appropriate here. Three main factors determine a country's inpayments and outpayments and therefore its demand and supply of foreign currencies: its real income relative to foreign incomes, its rate of inflation relative to inflation abroad, and its rate of interest relative to rates abroad.[3] The higher the country's real income, or the growth rate of its real GNP, *the more its residents can afford to spend on imports*, the greater the volume of imports of goods and services, and the greater the demand for foreign currencies. Thus the exchange value of the home currency declines (depreciates) with the rise in income relative to the rest of the world. As the country's rate of inflation rises, its products in domestic and foreign markets become less competitive, it will import more from foreign lands, and it will export less to them. This raises demand for, and lowers supply of, foreign currencies. The home currency depreciates with the rise in its rate of inflation relative to the rest of the world. The higher the country's rate of interest, the more foreign funds will be attracted to it; the demand for the home currency will be greater, and consequently the supply of the foreign currency will be greater. The exchange value of the home currency increases (appreciates) with a rise in its interest rate relative to the rest of the world. In addition to income (Y), prices (P), and the rate of interest (i), a variety of psychological factors—originating in political disturbances and even rumors, economic expectations, and the like—affect the exchange rate. Unfavorable expectations about

---

[3] The relationships stated here are commonplace in international economics. But a new school of thought, known as "the Monetary Approach," postulates a different set of relationships. These are explored in Chapter 8.

the country's economic conditions and the strength of its currency may lead to depreciation as people sell the currency, while the reverse is true in the case of favorable expectations. The above factors will be considered one at a time, in each case assuming that "other factors are held constant."

Real Income   Suppose that the U.S. real GNP grew at a faster rate than that of other countries such as Germany, as it did in 1976–77. The high growth rate of U.S. real income would enable Americans to increase their purchases of foreign goods and services. German exports to the United States would rise, increasing the supply of dollars in Germany, or German dollar inpayments.

This is shown in Figure 3-2 as an increase in the supply curve of dollars: At each price a greater quantity of dollars is supplied to Germany through German exports to the United States; the supply curve (dollar inpayments) shifts to the right (to the dashed S'). The new intersection with the demand curve would be at, say $1 = 1.9 D.M.: The dollar declined in value (depreciated) from 2.0 to 1.9 marks, and correspondingly the mark appreciated from 50 cents to 53 cents. Indeed, the high U.S. growth rate was a major reason for the decline in the exchange value of the dollar in 1977.

Conversely, a sluggish U.S. economy and a high German growth rate would increase German demand for American goods and services (through such things as German tourists visiting the U.S.). The dollar *outpayments* line in Figure 3-2 would shift to the right, establishing a new equilibrium.

Figure 3-2
Effect of U.S. Income Growth on the $–D.M. Exchange Rate

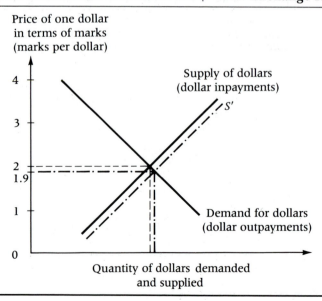

Quantity of dollars demanded
and supplied

The dollar would rise in value, say from 2 D.M. to 2.1 D.M., and correspondingly the mark would depreciate from 50 cents to 47.6 cents. The deep U.S. recession of 1981–82 helped curb imports into the United States and contributed somewhat to the strength of the dollar on the foreign exchange markets.

Relative Price Change   Assume next that the U.S. inflation rate far exceeded that of Germany and other major trading nations. This means that American goods and services would become more expensive relative to their German counterparts on both the U.S. and foreign markets. The American competitive position would deteriorate, and Germany would *sell more* on the U.S. market and *buy less* American goods and services.

In that case Germany would export more to the U.S.—increasing its supply of dollars; and it would import less from the U.S.—reducing its demand for dollars. The dollar inpayments curve in Germany would rise or shift rightward to S'. At each and every exchange rate more dollars would be supplied. Concurrently the dollar outpayments curve in Germany would decline, or shift leftward to D': At each exchange rate fewer dollars would be demanded to finance purchases in the United States.

These shifts are illustrated in Figure 3-3; both cause a reduction in the exchange value of the dollar. The dollar depreciates from 2 D.M. to 1.625 D.M., and correspondingly, the mark appreciates from 1 D.M. = 50 cents to 1 D.M. = 61.53 cents. Differential inflation rates between countries have been a prime cause of currency fluctuations.

Figure 3-3
Effect of U.S. Inflation on the $–D.M. Exchange Rate

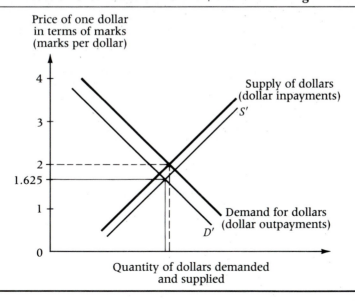

Because money growth is a main determinant of inflation, a sharp *expansion in a country's money supply,* which tends to stimulate inflation, would *cause its currency to depreciate.* Conversely, monetary contraction would cause the currency to appreciate. Additionally, depreciation could be caused by other factors that increase production costs (and hence the price level) such as labor and energy costs, governmental regulations, and the like. For example, in the mid-1970s, high inflation, labor unrest, and other economic dislocations reduced the competitive position of Italy and the United Kingdom, causing depreciation of their currencies.

On the other hand, not only was the 1976–77 U.S. growth rate faster than that of Germany, but the German inflation rate was lower than its American counterpart. This raised German sales in the United States (as German goods became more competitive), and increased Germany's supply of dollars (shifting the supply curve to the right). At the same time German purchases from the United States declined, reducing German demand for dollars (shifting the demand curve to the left). On both the income and price counts, the mark appreciated against the dollar.

A country with an inflation rate well above the world's average would see its currency depreciate continuously. This phenomenon is of paramount importance to the high inflation countries of South America whose currencies depreciate on a monthly basis.

In the very long run, the relative price behavior of any two countries is the most powerful determinant of the exchange rate between their currencies. Put differently, *the exchange rate reflects the relative rate of change in their respective domestic price levels, or the purchasing power of their currencies.* This proposition is known as the *purchasing power parity (PPP) doctrine.*

Its simplest version states that if $1 buys the same quantity of goods and services in the U.S. as 2 D.M. buy in Germany, then the *long-run* equilibrium exchange rate would be $1 = 2 D.M. But because the exchange rate is affected by influences other than relative price levels, the actual exchange rate can depart from purchasing power parity for extended periods. For example, over several years during the 1981–85 period, the dollar exchange rate was above 3 D.M. (driven mainly by high U.S. interest rates). Yet the purchasing power of $1 in the U.S. was equivalent to that of about 2 D.M. in Germany. In other words the dollar was overvalued relative to PPP. But in 1985–86 the dollar depreciated, reaching 2.3 D.M. in June 1986. In the long run, relative price changes have a powerful influence on the exchange rate.

Relative Interest Rates   Suppose that U.S. interest rose sharply relative to interest rates prevailing abroad. Then individuals, corporations, and other economic institutions would transfer funds to the United States to be placed in high-interest-yielding securities and other financial instruments. Americans as well as foreigners would convert currencies into dollars to take advantage of high stateside interest rates. The demand for dollars would rise, and with it, its value on the foreign currency markets.

Figure 3-4
Effect of a Rise in U.S. Interest Rates on the $–D.M. Exchange Rate

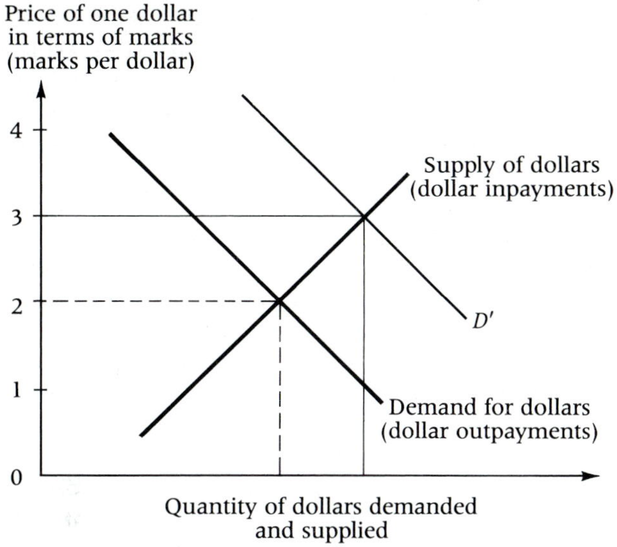

This is seen in Figure 3-4, which describes the German foreign currency market. Demand for dollar increases to D': At each exchange rate, more dollars are demanded to take advantage of high U.S. interest rates. The dollar appreciates from 2 D.M. to 3 D.M.; correspondingly, the mark depreciates from 50 cents to 33.3 cents.

Fluctuations in the exchange value of the dollar in 1980–86 were dominated by variations in interest rates. U.S. real interest rates, high relative to those prevailing abroad, attracted foreign funds to these shores and propelled the exchange value of the dollar to a 15-year high. Between 1980 and February 1985 the dollar rose from 1.7 to 3.4 D.M. (although there were some temporary up and down fluctuations). Dollar appreciation occurred in terms of other currencies as well. In 1985–86 the dollar drifted downward with the decline in U.S. interest rates, dropping to 2.3 D.M. by June 1986.

Countries sometimes adjust their interest rates in order to affect the exchange value of their currencies. Thus, in the 1980s the central banks of Canada and the U.K. often kept their interest high to shore up their depreciating currencies.

Expectations Often market participants anticipate any or all of the preceding changes based on information available to them, and act before the change actually occurs. For example, a sudden spurt in the growth of the money supply leads people to expect an acceleration of the inflation rate. Anticipating that a depreciation of the currency will follow, they sell ("unload") their holdings of the currency, and as a result its value declines, even before the acceleration of inflation is evident.

Similar action may be triggered by a sharp increase in the government budgetary deficit or by a substantial rise in wage rates throughout the country (and the attendant rise in production costs). These factors raise real incomes as well as the rate of inflation; on both counts, the currency would be expected to depreciate. Market agents acting on such information may sell the currency in question; it would depreciate in a manner of self-justifying expectations.

Finally, the very rise (or decline) in the value of a currency may trigger expectations of further change in the same direction. Speculators would then buy (sell) the currency, in the hope of realizing profits; and by that action they push the value of the currency upward (down). Such a "speculative bubble" is said to be partly responsible for the dollar's appreciation in 1984.

Other Factors   Besides the price and income factors, the trade position of a country is affected by such imponderables as international shifts in taste and the quality and design of the country's products and accompanying services. Practically any economic change—such as the lengthening of workers' coffee breaks or an increase in the price of fuels—would affect the exchange rate through its impact on costs, prices, interest rates, and incomes, which in turn influence inpayments and outpayments.

For example, in the late 1970s, the United Kingdom became self-sufficient in oil, as the North Sea fields came into full production. This reduced British outpayments for imported oil, and the pound advanced from $1.60 in 1976, to $2.33 in 1980. With the subsequent dollar climb in 1980–85, the pound depreciated against the dollar reaching an all-time low of $1.1 in the Winter of 1985 before climbing during the remainder of that year. But the sharp drop in oil prices in 1986 prevented the pound from appreciating beyond $1.5.

A new discovery or a technological breakthrough in a certain country increases the profitability of investments there. Direct foreign investments may be attracted to that country, increasing the demand for its currency and causing its exchange rate to appreciate.

Political and psychological influences can also affect the exchange rate. For example, in 1977 fears that Quebec would secede from Canada caused many Canadians to transfer their funds to the United States. To do so they had to convert Canadian dollars to American dollars, causing a depreciation of the Canadian dollar. Likewise, the 1982 war in the Falkland islands (between Britain and Argentina) caused a depreciation of the pound sterling. In 1981, the election of the Socialist government in France caused currency jitters as many Frenchmen transferred their capital abroad. The franc slumped on the foreign currency markets.

Summary All events in the economy, and all government policies, influence real income (*Y*), prices (*P*), and the rate of interest (*i*). These include changes in wage rates and productivity which affect labor production costs (and the price level); changes in energy costs; fiscal and monetary policies; and a multitude of other factors. Through their impact on *Y*, *P*, and *i*, they influence the exchange rate. Schematically, these relationships can be shown as follows:

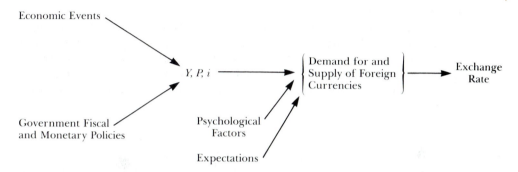

The exchange rate is deeply embedded in the economy.

It bears emphasizing that in all cases what counts are the changes inside the country relative to changes in the rest of the world. If prices and income rise commensurately on both sides of the border, the outpayments and inpayments may be similarly affected, with no change in the exchange rate. By definition an exchange rate involves at least two countries.

In all cases the effect of income, price, interest rate, and other changes on the exchange rate can be analyzed in terms of Figure 3-1, by shifting the demand and/or the supply curve and examining the results. In each case, it is important to know which curve to shift and in what direction.

Several factors affecting the exchange rate may change simultaneously. If one of them does not dominate, and if the changes influence the exchange rate in offsetting directions, it is not possible to draw a clear-cut conclusion about the expected direction of change. A decline in real income (causing appreciation) accompanied by a rise in the rate of inflation (causing depreciation) is one such example; political fears accompanied by a sharp boost in the interest rate is another.

One important conclusion of this discussion is that *depreciation is not necessarily bad, nor is appreciation necessarily good.* It all depends on the factor(s) causing the exchange rate to fluctuate. If the currency depreciates because real income rose sharply, as the dollar did in 1977, it is viewed as a favorable development. But if the depreciation is caused by a high rate of inflation, it is viewed unfavorably.

A second important conclusion is that a *freely* fluctuating exchange rate would settle at a point that clears the market; that is, *with inpayments and outpayments equated.* Both are defined to include transactions in goods and services as well as capital transfers. This takes us back to the discussion of the balance of payments in the last chapter. Had there been absolutely no government intervention in the foreign exchange market (that is, a free float), there would be no change in official reserve holdings and no deficit or surplus in the balance of payments. Exchange-rate fluctuations would preserve a balance in the external account, and there would be no change in official reserves (the measure of a surplus or deficit). External imbalances exist because central banks do intervene in the foreign currency markets to influence the exchange rate in a direction they consider desirable. That is how changes in international reserves occur. A regime in which the central bank intervenes in the foreign exchange market is called a *managed* float. Most currencies of the industrial countries are under a managed rather than a free float. Under a free float the balance of payments is kept in equilibrium by exchange fluctuations. But that does not mean that each category of the international transactions is in balance. In 1984 and 1985 the United States sustained annual trade deficits well in excess of $100 billion. And these were balanced by private capital inflows of similar amounts. A country concerned about its trade balance, because of the implications of exports and imports for domestic output and employment, would find such a situation unsatisfactory.

The Foreign Exchange Market

In the preceding discussion references were made to the foreign exchange market. It is therefore useful to provide a short institutional description of this market.

Market Organization

International transactions call for the use of the foreign exchange market. Although the market is highly competitive and provides traders with full information at all times, it is not to be equated with the stock exchange in terms of its organization. There is no "Big Board" on which instant price quotations (that is, exchange rates) are posted for all currencies. The foreign exchange market consists of the foreign exchange departments of the large New York banks as well as a number of specialized traders. They keep in instant communication with each other by telephone, continuously exchanging price and quantity information. It is therefore useful to think of this market as a network of telephone lines and cables. In addition, each of the large New York banks maintains correspondent banks in all major cities throughout the world, and it is through this relationship that the network of foreign exchange transactions is conducted.

This communication ensures that the foreign exchange markets will be *orderly:* that the value of one currency in terms of another will be the same in all major financial centers. If the franc is worth 20 cents in Paris and 21 cents in London, any financier can purchase francs in Paris, sell them immediately in London, and realize a 1-cent profit on each franc. In doing so he demands francs in Paris, thereby exerting an upward pressure on their price, and supplies them in London, with a resulting downward pressure. The process goes on as long as there are profits to be realized—that is, until the price differential disappears. The transactions described here are called *arbitrage,* for they involve no risk. Profit is realized simply by taking advantage of the geographical price differential. But the arbitrager performs the useful function of ensuring that each currency has the same value on all financial markets.

An equally important feature of this arrangement is the existence of "orderly cross rates." By this we mean that if at a given instant the franc is worth 20 cents and the pound sterling is valued at $2.40, then the pound is worth 12 francs. We prove this by showing that no deviation from this price is sustainable. Suppose that a freak situation developed on the Swiss foreign exchange market, and the pound dropped to 10 francs in value (but with the ratios of 1 franc = 20 cents and £1 = $2.40 maintained in Paris and London, respectively). Then it would pay a financier with 10 francs to convert them into 1 British pound on the Swiss market, exchange the pound for $2.40 in London, and for that sum purchase 12 francs in Paris. Disregarding transaction costs, he makes 2 francs in profit by taking advantage of existing price differentials between geographical locations. In the process he demands pounds and supplies francs on the Swiss market, thereby pushing up the pound–franc ratio. This process, known as *triangular arbitrage,* goes on as long as there is a profit to be made—that is, until the pound is pushed up to 12 francs and the profit opportunities cease to exist.

If, on the other hand, the pound were equal to 15 francs on the Swiss market, it would pay our financier to do the reverse. He would convert a pound into 15 francs, use them to buy $3.00 in Paris, and exchange this for £1.25 in London, thereby realizing a profit of one-fourth of a British pound. In the process he supplies pounds and demands francs, thereby pushing down the franc value of the pound on the Swiss market. The process will continue as long as it provides an opportunity for profit, or until the value of the pound declines to 12 francs. Simple arithmetic will convince the reader that no further profits could then be realized.

The Forward Exchange Market

Institutionally, however, the story does not end here. Partly because of the large distances involved, international transactions are not usually consummated in a short time. Months elapse between the time that a London importer of automobiles places an order in Detroit and the time that the goods are delivered. Because of this and other factors, the conduct of foreign trade necessitates the use of special payment instruments not normally employed to finance domestic transactions.[4] But more important for our purposes, it often calls for making future payments. The British importer deals in cars and assumes the normal risks involved in the automobile trade. However, inasmuch as there is a lapse of several months between the time the order is placed and the time he must make payment, additional uncertainty may arise from exchange fluctuations in the intervening period.

When the order for cars is placed, the importer undertakes to pay a certain dollar sum upon delivery. But in the meantime the dollar value of the pound sterling may change, affecting the sterling cost of the merchandise on which his calculations are based. For example, if the exchange value of the pound sterling drops from $3 to $2, then the sterling cost of a $3000 car rises from £1000 to £1500. The importer would wish to insure against this contingency. Such insurance, known as *hedging*, is available to him in the *forward exchange market*. This market allows him to determine, at the time he orders the merchandise, what the sterling price of dollars will be

[4] Here is an example of the financing of foreign trade. Assume that exporter A in New York exports $2000 (£1000) worth of merchandise to importer B in London. The exporter loads the merchandise on ship and obtains the shipping documents from the ship's officer. He draws a draft for $2000 on B, attaches the shipping documents, and sells these papers to his bank in New York. Exporter A gets paid immediately by his bank. The New York bank airmails the entire documents package to its London correspondent, who in turn notifies importer B of their arrival. B signs ("accepts") the draft to indicate that he accepts the obligation of payment when it falls due, and in return he receives from the bank the shipping documents that will enable him to get control of the merchandise when the freighter finally arrives. Once the draft is signed, it becomes an "acceptance." The London bank credits the account of its New York counterpart and sells ("discounts") the acceptance on the local money market. The investor who purchases the acceptance thus actually finances the transaction while the goods are in transit. Upon its maturity he will present it to B for payment. Availability of funds to finance acceptance is a prerequisite for a city to become an international trade center.

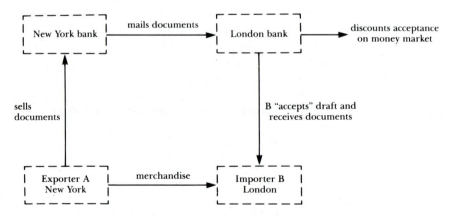

For further discussion see "Recent Developments in the Bankers Acceptance Market," *Federal Reserve Bulletin*, January 1986. For a general discussion of international financial markets and of international payment instruments see F. Weston and B. Sorge, *International Managerial Finance*, Homewood, Illinois: Richard D. Irwin.

when payment falls due. And he can therefore fully account for this price in his original calculations.

In particular, the trader would approach his bank and purchase x number of dollars for delivery, say, six months hence. The price of dollars in terms of sterling is agreed upon immediately, but the transaction on both sides—the exchange (or delivery) of dollars for sterling—does not take place until six months later. The price involved here is known as the *forward exchange rate,* as distinguished from the *spot exchange rate,* which applies to transactions consummated the following day. In a well-developed financial center there are always markets for forward dealings—and therefore market-determined forward exchange rates—for thirty and ninety days hence, as well as for other periods.[5] It bears repeating that, were it not for the risk of exchange variations, the spot and forward exchange rates would be the same, as they are between California and New York dollars. In other words, with complete certainty, there would be no forward exchange market.

Under orderly market conditions, the forward and spot exchange rates are related to one another in a way that reflects the interest-rate differential in the two financial markets. As an example, let us further pursue the case of the British importer, purchasing from his bank six-month-forward dollars. The selling bank is not a speculative institution; it would normally wish to make sure not only that it is in possession of the dollars on delivery date but also that it does not lose money on the transaction from exchange fluctuations. The bank can *cover* itself by immediately purchasing spot dollars and then holding them in New York for six months, when they are scheduled for delivery to the importer in exchange for pounds. In doing so, the British bank earns the New York interest rate instead of the London rate on these funds for the period under consideration. If the interest rate in New York is lower than that in London, the importer would have to pay the differential; forward dollars would sell at a premium compared to spot dollars, the premium being equivalent to the interest differential. On the other hand, should the New York interest rate exceed the London rate, it is actually advantageous for the bank to keep the funds there, and under competitive pressure the gain would be passed on to the importer. Forward dollars would sell at a discount compared to spot dollars, the discount equaling the interest differential between London and New York. In other words, the importer's demand for forward dollars makes it possible for the bank to enjoy a higher interest return, and these extra earnings are passed on to the importer. Without this demand the bank

---

[5] These are the most common delivery dates for which daily quotations are readily available. But bankers and dealers supply quotations for other periods (up to four years) on special request.

There exists also a *futures* market in foreign currencies. It provides standardized contracts in predetermined amounts and with standardized delivery dates. In contrast, the forward market offers contracts in any amount, and the contract can be written for the exact date that the foreign currency is needed or is to be disposed of. See N. Fieleke, "The Rise of Foreign Currency Futures Market," *New England Economic Review,* March 1985.

would not shift the funds to New York for fear of exchange losses in case of revaluation of the pound sterling in terms of the dollar.

A numerical example will help clarify the point. Suppose the British importer requires $2000 in six months and that the spot exchange rate is £1 = $2. If the six-month interest rate is 4 percent in New York and 5 percent in London, then the British bank selling 2000 forward dollars to the importer will charge him £1000 (the spot rate) plus the 1 percent loss it incurs by having to keep the funds in New York at 4 percent instead of in London at 5 percent. His total charge would be £1000 + £10 (1 percent of £1000) or £1010. The six-month forward exchange rate is £1 = (2000/1010 =) $1.98: The forward pound is at a 1 percent discount relative to the ($2) spot pound, and correspondingly, the forward dollar is at a premium relative to the spot dollar. Conversely, if the six-month interest rate is 4 percent in New York and only 3 percent in London, then the British bank selling 2000 forward dollars to the importer would charge him £1000 *less* the 1 percent profit it makes by keeping the funds in New York at 4 percent instead of in London at 3 percent. Competitive pressure would force the bank to pass this differential on to the customer. His total charge for 2000 forward dollars would be £1000 minus £10, or £990. The six-month forward exchange rate is: £1 = (2000/990 =) $2.02: The forward pound is at a 1 percent premium relative to the ($2) spot pound, and correspondingly the forward dollar is at a discount relative to the spot dollar.

As long as orderly conditions prevail, information is complete, and fluid funds are abundantly available, the ratio of the forward exchange rate to the spot exchange rate would reflect the interest differential. Any divergence between them opens up an opportunity for riskless profit, and arbitragers would operate until the relation is restored. In this case the arbitrage equalizes prices over time, instead of between geographical centers at a given point of time, but the principle is the same.[6]

---

[6]An alternative way of looking at this relationship will clarify the principle of "equalization through time." Each currency's future value is equal to its present value plus the interest that can be earned on assets denominated in that currency over the period under consideration. (Conversely, to convert a future monetary value into its present equivalent, we *discount* it by the interest rate.) Thus, if the annual interest rate in London is labeled i_L, then the value of the pound sterling one year in the future (denoted $£_f$) is its present value ($£_p$) plus the added interest:

$$£_f = £_p (1 + i_L)$$

The same relation applies to the dollar with respect to the interest rate prevailing in New York:

$$\$_f = \$_p (1 + i_{NY})$$

Dividing the second equation by the first, we obtain the relation

$$\frac{\$_f}{£_f} = \frac{\$_p}{£_p} \times \frac{1 + i_{NY}}{1 + i_L}$$

The two currency ratios shown are the future and spot dollar-to-sterling exchange rates, respectively, and they can be denoted r_f and r_p. Thus:

$$r_f = r_p \frac{1 + i_{NY}}{1 + i_L}$$

In reality the expected relationship often does not exist. This is due partly to market imperfections (such as imperfect knowledge of the type that accounts for differences in interest rates on savings accounts paid by two banks in the same town). Also, because of such risks as the possible imposition of exchange control by foreign governments, domestic and foreign assets are not perfect substitutes. Another important reason is the desire of people to diversify their asset holdings in order to minimize risk. We might think of every financier as having a portfolio of various financial assets, consisting of stocks, bonds, commercial papers, and the like. If he is a "risk averter" (likes to avoid risk), then he will choose to diversify his portfolio as much as possible to minimize risk of default (which is to say, he will not put all his eggs in one basket). Purchasing foreign assets, as we shall see later on, is one way of accomplishing this. Thus, people can move in and out of foreign assets (so as to reduce risk) and thereby cause international capital flows even when no interest differentials exist.

Speculation

In contrast to the arbitrager, the speculator does not take covered positions (as did the bank in our example). Instead, he sells forward dollars, hoping to deliver cheaper dollars at the future date should the value of the dollar decline in the intervening period. Specifically, a speculator is said to take a *short position* when he sells foreign currency forward without at the same time owning an equivalent amount of this currency (that is, he sells what he does not have), in the expectation of buying it at a lower spot rate when the contract matures. He is said to take a *long position* when he purchases foreign currency forward without incurring an obligation to make a spot payment at the time of delivery (he buys what he does not need), in the expectation that a spot sale of the foreign currency at that time will produce a profit. Because a speculator does not take a covered position, the relationship between interest rates is of no concern to him. What is most important to the speculator is the relation between the forward exchange rates prevailing on the market and his personal expectation about the spot rate at some future date.[7] Indeed, speculative funds may create interest differentials that can then be covered by arbitrage funds if they are available in sufficient quantity and if market conditions are not so unsettled (such as under expectations of an immediate exchange-rate adjustment) that they are completely dominated by speculative activity.

Speculators demand and supply currencies in anticipation of changes in their price. If a currency is weak and the government's ability to defend it is suspect, speculators can exert additional pressure by selling the currency en masse in exchange for other currencies. Short-run capital, sometimes referred to as "hot money,"[8] would then leave the country for other

[7]Since expectations are uncertain, the government can affect speculative activity by floating rumors and otherwise influencing expectations.

[8]Strictly speaking, the term "hot money" is capital flowing against the dictate of interest rate differentials. But the financial press often uses the term to refer to any type of speculative flow.

financial centers that were thought to have strong and therefore desirable currencies. These currencies would be purchased by the speculators. This is the type of pressure that has often created grave disturbances on the international financial markets. For example, in July 1985, pressure on the Italian lira forced an 8 percent devaluation of that currency relative to other European currencies. Speculative activities have been carried out not only by professional speculators but also by the large international corporations, who adjust their transactions to accommodate anticipated changes in the exchange rates, and by the corner shopkeeper in Europe, who converts his surplus cash to the currencies considered strong.

Thus, speculators, as distinguished from traders and investors, purchase foreign currencies and hold them for their own sake. Their demand is derived not from a demand for goods and services but from a desire to profit from changes in the price of the currency itself, and is therefore an exception to the statement made in the first section of this chapter that people do not usually demand foreign currencies for their own sake.

Review Questions

1. Assume that on a certain date the following exchange rates prevail:

   £1 = $1.33; $1 = 2.5 D.M.; $1 = 7.5 F.F.; $1 = ¥187.5

   a. What is the inverse of each of the above exchange rates?
   b. Calculate the bilateral exchange rates between each two of the *non-dollar* currencies, and their inverses.
   c. Suppose that: $1 = 2 D.M. and $1 = 6 F.F. Can 1 D.M. equal 4 F.F.? Why or why not? Can it equal 2 F.F.?

2. In March 1986 the exchange value of the French franc was: $1 = 6.8 F.F.

   a. Show that exchange rate on a diagram similar to that of Figure 3-1.
   b. Using your diagram explain how the dollar—franc exchange rate would be affected by each of the following events:

   • A sharp rise in French interest rates.
   • The appearance of double-digit inflation in France.
   • A prolonged general strike in France.
   • An expected downfall of the French socialist government in the next elections.
   • A 20% increase in the French money supply.
   • A sharp rise in U.S. real income.
   In each case assume that "all other things are constant."

   c. How do you explain the slope of the demand and supply curves in your diagram?

3. What accounts for the large appreciation of the dollar during 1980–85, and its depreciation in 1985–86? Did the exchange value of the dollar during 1984 conform to the *purchasing power parity doctrine?* (Explain) Suppose the dollar rose from $1 = 2 D.M. to $1 = 4 D.M. What is the

effect on the price of U.S. goods sold in Germany, and the price of German goods sold in the U.S.

4. Explain the following terms:
   a. Arbitrage
   b. Triangular arbitrage
   c. Speculation
   d. Spot exchange rate
   e. Forward exchange rate
   f. Future market
   g. Short position
   h. Long position

5. How do interest rates enter into the determination of the forward exchange rate? Explain fully with an illustration.

6. How would each of the following developments affect the exchange value of the (floating) Canadian dollar:
   a. Hydro-Quebec raises $100 million (U.S.) on the New York money market by selling bonds.
   b. Foreign Corporations increase direct investments in Canada by 10 percent.
   c. Because of a booming Soviet harvest, Canada's wheat exports decline.
   d. By order of the Canadian government, Canadian natural gas exports to the U.S. are cut by 5 percent.

4
The International Currency System

For nearly thirty years following World War II, world currencies were maintained at a fixed ratio to one another (a system of fixed or pegged exchange rates). But this system broke down in March 1973 and was replaced by a mixture of fluctuating and fixed exchange rates. Alternative exchange-rate regimes will be explained in the following sections, leading up to the contemporary system that has prevailed since 1973.

Fixed Exchange Rates

In direct contrast to freely floating exchange rates is the fixed exchange-rate system. As the name implies, fixed exchange rates are not permitted to fluctuate freely on the market or to respond to daily changes in demand and supply. Instead, the government fixes the exchange value of the currency. This is illustrated in Figure 4-1. Germany fixes its exchange rate at $1 = 2 D.M. or equivalently at 1 D.M. = $0.50; it imposes upper and lower limits to the exchange rate. Exchange variations, triggered by shifts in the demand and/or supply curves, are permitted only within these limits. The German central bank maintains the limits by buying and selling dollars on the Frankfurt foreign currency market. For the purpose of clarity the limits shown in Figure 4-1 are drawn wide, far wider than in any fixed-rate system used in practice.

If the dollar drops to its lower limit of 1.80 D.M. (which means that the mark rises to 55.5 cents), the central bank *buys* as many dollars, in exchange for marks, as are necessary to "defend" that limit. Conversely, if the dollar rises to 2.20 D.M. (which means that the mark declines to 45.5 cents), the central bank *sells* as many dollars, for marks, as are necessary to defend the limit. Recall that a country's money supply is measured by the

Figure 4-1
A Fixed Exchange-Rate System

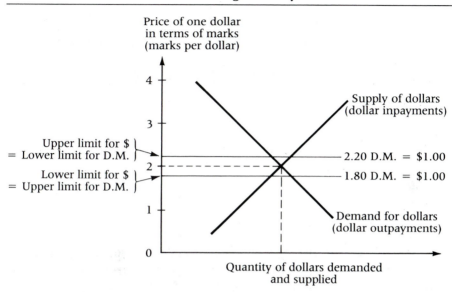

Price of one dollar
in terms of marks
(marks per dollar)

domestic currency (marks in the case of Germany) held outside its central bank. A country's international reserves are in the form of *foreign* currencies held by its central bank; therefore, dollars are reserves for Germany, but not for the United States. Hence, when the German central bank buys dollars and sells marks, its dollar reserves rise and the domestic German money supply, measured in marks, expands. Conversely when the central bank sells dollars and buys marks, its dollar reserves decline, and the German money supply contracts.

Figure 4-2 illustrates the first case in which the supply of dollars rises to S'. Under a freely floating exchange rate, the equilibrium would shift to *e*. But at the government limit set at 1.80 D.M. = \$1, an excess supply of dollars in the amount $\overline{ab}$ emerges. The German central bank buys an amount $\overline{ab}$ of dollars in exchange for marks, and adds them to its central foreign currency reserves in order to maintain the limit. *Its dollar reserves rise and the domestic German money supply expands.* In fact all the bank has to do is stand ready to buy an unlimited amount of dollars for marks at that price. Note that an excess supply of dollars can also be created by a reduction in demand (leftward shift in the demand curve), such that the resulting equilibrium exchange rate moves below the lower limit.

Figure 4-3 illustrates the second case in which the demand for dollars is raised to D'. Under a freely floating exchange rate, the equilibrium rate would shift to *e*. But at the government set limit of 2.20 D.M. = \$1, an excess demand for dollars in the amount $\overline{cd}$ is created. The German central

Figure 4-2
Excess Supply of Dollars (or Excess Demand for Marks)

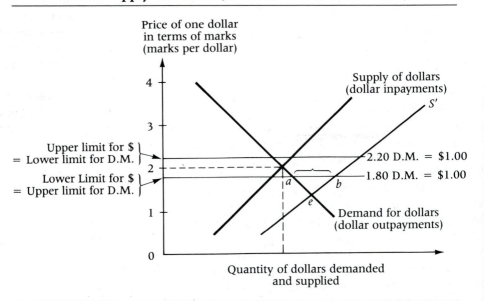

Figure 4-3
Excess Demand for Dollars (or Excess Supply of Marks)

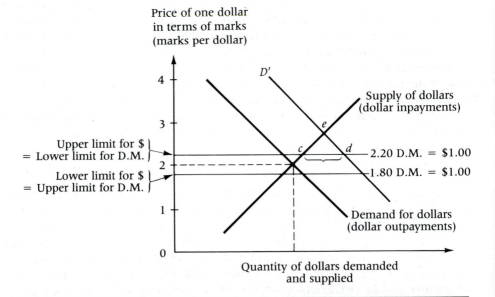

bank sells $\overline{cd}$ dollars (in exchange for marks) out of its central foreign currency reserves to maintain the limit. *Its dollar reserves are depleted, and the domestic German money supply (in marks) contracts.* In fact, all the bank has to do is stand ready to sell an unlimited amount of dollars at that price. Note that an excess demand for dollars can also be created by a decline in supply (leftward shift in the supply curve), such that the resulting equilibrium exchange rate moves above the upper limit.

Under a fixed exchange rate, the exchange rate is set at a predetermined level. Consequently, it cannot be expected to clear the market—a function performed by the price system only if the price is allowed to vary continuously. Hence variations in official foreign currency reserves must fill the gap in cases of excess supply or excess demand for foreign currencies. Variations in official reserves are then a proper measure of a surplus or deficit in international transactions (Chapter 2).

The official exchange rate remains at the same level until such time as the government decides to change it, and with it, the limits of official intervention. Such changes normally occur in discrete amounts and at infrequent intervals, as distinguished from the very small daily variations under a fluctuating exchange-rate system. A government-decreed decrease in the value of a fixed-rate currency, such as from 1 D.M. = $0.50 to 1 D.M. = $0.30, is known as *devaluation* of the mark; and an increase, such as from 1 D.M. = $0.50 to 1. D.M. = $0.70, as *revaluation*. The mechanics of exchange stabilization under two systems of fixed exchange rates, the gold standard and the dollar standard, is described in the following sections.

Exchange Stabilization Under the Gold Standard

Although the gold standard is a relic of the past, public interest in the glittering metal has not fully subsided, and even official interest is revived on occasion. For example, in 1981 President Reagan appointed a Gold Commission to look into the alleged merits of the system. But the only suggestion included in the 1982 Report of the Commission is that the U.S. government start minting gold coins.

Domestically the gold standard required each country to limit its money supply to some given multiple of the gold reserves held by its central bank. Thus the domestic currency issued was "covered" by (fractional) gold reserves. Each central bank was committed to buy and sell gold at a fixed price (redeem the currency in gold); that is, the currency was convertible into gold at a fixed price. The fact that monetary expansion is constrained by the supply of gold is viewed by proponents of the system as its desirable feature. It would avoid the oversupply of fiat money and thereby control inflation. Our interest lies in the external feature—the maintenance of a fixed exchange rate under the gold standard. For the sake of generality, the mechanism is illustrated by reference to the pound–dollar exchange rate rather than to the dollar–mark rate.

During the days of the gold standard, before World War I, the external value of all currencies was maintained by fixing their prices in terms of gold. Each government or central bank stood ready to buy and sell unlimited quantities of gold at a fixed price in terms of its currency. Since the price was set at a predetermined level, it could not be expected to "clear the market." In other words, at the given price there were periods during which the supply of gold exceeded the demand; the difference was then purchased by the central bank and retained in its vaults as reserves for future contingencies. Conversely, there were periods when demand exceeded supply, and the shortage in private supply was met out of the reserves of the central authorities; the country was then losing gold reserves. Indeed, it is to meet such unforeseen contingencies that central bankers insist on accumulating and maintaining reserves in a form (such as gold) acceptable to all countries. Were it not for the fixed price of gold, there would be no need for gold reserves, since unlimited fluctuations in the price of gold would equate supply and demand on a daily basis.

Under the gold standard, the price of each currency in terms of gold was known as its *par value,* and each currency could fluctuate by a very small amount around that par, the degree of fluctuation being determined by the cost of shipping gold. Assume, for example, that the United States fixed the price of gold at $2 for each one-tenth of an ounce, that the United Kingdom fixed its price at £1 for each one-tenth of an ounce, and that the cost of shipping gold across the Atlantic was 2 cents for each one-tenth of an ounce. Each government would then stand ready to buy and sell gold in unlimited quantities at the fixed price. In that case, the exchange rate between the dollar and the pound sterling could vary only between $1.98 and $2.02; that is,

$$£1 = \begin{cases} \$2.02 \text{ (known as the "gold import point" for the United Kingdom)} \\ \$1.98 \text{ (known as the "gold export point" for the United Kingdom)} \end{cases}$$

We demonstrate this by showing that it was impossible for the pound value to be outside this range. Suppose that on some foreign exchange market a situation developed where the pound equaled only $1.50. Then it would pay an American to convert $1.50 into £1 on that market, purchase one-tenth of an ounce of gold from the Bank of England (Great Britain's central bank), ship it to the United States, and sell it to the U.S. Treasury for the fixed price of $2. He would make a profit of 48 cents (50 cents minus the 2 cents cost of shipping gold). In doing so he would demand pounds and supply dollars, thereby pushing up the value of the pound. The process would go on as long as it was profitable or until the value of the pound was pushed to $1.98, when the cost of shipping gold would be equal to the gold price differential between the two markets. Indeed, the price of the pound could hardly go below $1.98 without triggering this process of shipping gold from London to New York.

Conversely, the upper limit of the pound's value would be maintained at $2.02 by a reverse procedure involving gold shipment from New York to London. To demonstrate this, assume that a freak market developed somewhere, in which £1 equaled $3. Then it would pay an Englishman to convert £1 into $3, purchase .15 ounce of gold from the U.S. Treasury, ship it to the United Kingdom, and sell it to the Bank of England for £1.5. He would make a profit and in the process he would have supplied pounds and demanded dollars, thereby depreciating the value of the pound in terms of dollars. The process would go on until £1 was equal to $2.02, when profit opportunities would cease to exist (because the cost of shipping the gold is 2 cents).

In either case, the shipments would be executed by *private arbitragers*, who would stand to make riskless profit, and not by an official institution such as the government or the central bank. Unlike a speculator, an arbitrager assumes no risk. He makes his profit by taking advantage of price differentials existing between geographical locations or points of time. The lower limit of the pound ($1.98) is known as the gold export point for the United Kingdom, while the upper limit ($2.02) is the United Kingdom gold import point, indicating the prices at which gold is exported or imported as a result of the fixed price. The difference between them is the *spread;* in our example it is 2 cents on either side of par, for a total of 4 cents. The same mechanism would work for all other currencies so defined in terms of gold, with the spread setting the limits to exchange fluctuations.

When the central bank buys gold in exchange for its own currency, the domestic money supply expands. When it sells gold for its own currency, the money supply contracts.

Since gold was a common denominator in terms of which all currencies were fixed, it also served to maintain fixed-exchange ratios among the currencies themselves. For example, if one ounce of fine gold was worth £22, $44, 88 D.M., 264 F.F., and ¥ 8800, then the exchange rates would be fixed at: £1 = $2 = 4 D.M. = 12 F.F. = ¥ 400. (And $1 = £0.5 = 2 D.M. = 6 F.F. = ¥ 200; while 1 D.M. = 3 F.F., and so on.) Only small fluctuations could occur around the exchange rates, with the spreads determined by the cost of shipping gold between the financial centers involved.

An alternative system for maintaining fixed exchange rates, based on the U.S. dollar, was in operation between 1944 and 1973. It was known as the *Bretton Woods System.*

Exchange Stabilization Under Bretton Woods

After World War II, gold no longer reigned supreme; it shared the spotlight with the dollar. True, gold still played a reference role, and portions of currency reserves were maintained in gold. But the stabilization operations of central banks were no longer conducted by buying and selling gold, and it was not usually shipped across the ocean.[1] The U.S. dollar had become the more meaningful standard in terms of which all other currencies were

---

[1] Much of the gold belonging to foreign monetary authorities is kept "earmarked" for them at the Federal Reserve Bank of New York.

fixed and the major asset, along with gold, in which most countries maintained their international reserves.

Foreign central banks were not committed to redeem their currencies in gold. Only the United States maintained (until August 1971) a commitment to exchange dollars for gold, at $35 an ounce, when the dollars were presented for redemption by foreign central monetary authorities. This system, under which other countries settled their debts in dollars, which could then be exchanged for gold, was known as the *gold exchange standard*. It grew out of an international conference in Bretton Woods, New Hampshire, immediately after World War II (in 1944), which established the International Monetary Fund (IMF) as the central instrument to develop and oversee the ground rules of an international financial system.

Each central bank maintained the value of its currency in terms of the dollar by standing ready to buy and sell unlimited quantities of dollars on its money market at fixed buying and selling rates.[2] The pound sterling, for example, was valued at $2.40, but the Bank of England permitted a range of fluctuations between $2.38 and $2.42—approximately 1 percent on either side of par:

$$£1 = \$2.40 \left\{ \begin{array}{l} \$2.42 \quad \text{(the dollar buying point)} \\ \\ \$2.38 \quad \text{(the dollar selling point)} \end{array} \right\} \text{spread}$$

Whenever the pound became weak under selling pressure (as a result of a British balance of payments deficit) and its price dropped to $2.38, the Bank of England sold as many dollars as necessary, in exchange for sterling, to maintain the lower limit. The limit was so maintained because no private trader would sell his sterling for less than the $2.38 he could get from the central bank. Conversely, whenever the pound became strong under buying pressure (a British balance of payments surplus) and its value reached $2.42, the Bank of England purchased dollars in exchange for sterling to maintain the upper limit. No private trader would purchase sterling for more than $2.42 if he could get it for that price from the central bank. Since the Bank of England bought pounds (for dollars) when the pound was weak and sold pounds when the pound was strong, its stabilization operations were profitable.

The two support limits, the floor and the ceiling, were known as the *dollar selling and the dollar buying points,* respectively. The difference between them, the *spread,* was no longer determined by the cost of shipping gold but by the central bank's decision concerning the support limits. Under the original regulations of the IMF, support prices could not be more than 1

---

[2] A noted exception was the Sterling Area, which consisted mainly of British Commonwealth countries (except Canada). It became a semiformal organization after the devaluation of the pound sterling in 1930 and a formal one when exchange control was practiced by Great Britain during and after World War II. The countries of the Sterling Area pegged their currencies to the pound sterling and maintained much of their reserves in pounds. In turn, they relied on the Bank of England to maintain the fixed rate between the pound sterling and the dollar. A similar arrangement was maintained by France with respect to its former colonies in Africa.

percent on either side of the currency's par value, for a total spread of 2 percent. At the end of 1971 the permissible spread was widened to 2¼ percent on either side of par, for a total spread of 4½ percent between each currency and the dollar.

When a central bank buys dollars in exchange for its own currency, its dollar reserves rise and the domestic money supply expands. When it sells dollars for its currency, its dollar reserves decline and the money supply (domestic currency outside the central bank) contracts.

If each currency is allowed to vary 2 percent with respect to the dollar, the total permissible variation between any two nondollar currencies becomes 4 percent. To see this, assume two arbitrarily selected exchange rates, designed to make the calculations easy: £1 = $4 and 1 mark = $1. Permit each nondollar currency to fluctuate 1 percent on either side of its dollar value, to obtain the following ranges of fluctuations vis-à-vis the dollar.

$$£1 = $4 \begin{cases} $4.04 \\ $3.96 \end{cases} \quad \text{and} \quad 1 \text{ mark} = $1 \begin{cases} $1.01 \\ $0.99 \end{cases}$$

Then the range of fluctuations between the pound sterling and the mark becomes

Strongest Position of Mark	to	*Strongest Position of Sterling*
$\dfrac{$3.96}{$1.01} = 3.92 \text{ marks}$		$\dfrac{$4.04}{$0.99} = 4.08 \text{ marks}$

In other words, the sterling fluctuates in terms of marks from £1 = 3.92 marks to £1 = 4.08 marks, a spread of 0.16 mark:

$$£1 = 4 \text{ marks} \begin{cases} 4.08 \text{ marks} \\ 3.92 \text{ marks} \end{cases} \text{Spread} = 0.16 \text{ mark}$$

Thus the percent sterling–mark fluctuations were 0.16/4 = 4 percent. The *dollar*, by reason of its role as the common denominator, was *the only currency for which the spread was 2 rather than 4 percent.*

It was through such stabilization measures in the marketplace that all exchange rates were kept fixed (except for the very narrow range of fluctuations), with the dollar serving as the *intervention currency* as well as a common denominator and a standard of value. For example, if $1 equaled 2 marks, 6 francs, and 200 yen, then the mark must have equaled 3 francs or 100 yen, while the franc was worth 33⅓ yen. Much of world trade was (and still is) financed or denominated in dollars. The United States, in turn, was in a unique position; it did not as a rule intervene in the foreign exchange market but only stood ready to buy and sell gold (from and to foreign central banks) at a fixed price. When the United States was in deficit, it was the surplus countries that were obligated to buy the excess dollars so that their currencies would not appreciate above the upper limit. Conversely, during an American surplus, it was the deficit foreign countries that sold dollars to keep their currencies from depreciating. And, in order to accomplish this, all countries had to maintain central reserves in the form of dollars. Thus, the dollar came to play a role similar to that occupied by gold in an earlier period. All currencies were tied to the dollar, which itself was tied to gold.

Market Forces Under Fixed Exchange Rates

So far the discussion has concentrated on the mechanical aspects of exchange stabilization. The reader may reasonably ask two interrelated questions: Can the government choose any exchange rate it wishes? What determines the exchange value of a currency within the limits set by a central bank's intervention?

Under a fixed-rate system a government cannot pick an exchange rate or a par value for its currency "out of a hat," for such a value may be artificial and cannot be defended. Only "realistic" exchange rates are sustainable over the long run. To be "realistic," an exchange rate must reflect supply and demand conditions on the foreign exchange markets and the whole constellation of economic circumstances that affect the country's international transactions, outlined in Chapter 3. Thus the exchange rate must be rooted in the economic conditions of the country relative to conditions prevailing elsewhere. In particular, it must reflect relative prices, interest rates, and income levels as well as other factors that affect dealings in foreign exchange. Any change in the underlying conditions would make the exchange rate either weak or strong and would affect the government's ability to defend it. Like any other price, the exchange rate cannot be divorced from supply and demand conditions. Government intervention to maintain a fixed price can succeed only if in the long run the exchange rate reflects these basic influences.

Within the intervention limits the exchange rate is governed by supply and demand for goods and services, and international capital movements. If the exchange rate hits the lower support limit of the home currency, the government can support it only as long as its international reserves and possible lines of credit last (hence the need for reserves). Once those are exhausted, it may have to devalue the currency to a level that better reflects the country's competitive standing. The upper limit can be supported as long as the government wishes to accumulate reserves. However, such accumulation of reserves is inflationary at home. For the government pays for the dollars it buys in domestic currency, thereby increasing the money supply (a multiple increase under a fractional reserve banking system). Often it is the inflationary pressures that induce a surplus country to stop accumulating reserves. If it wishes to stop the accumulation the country may have to revalue its currency (increase its value in terms of other currencies) or take some other steps.

Only an exchange rate that balances the country's external accounts over the long run, under acceptable domestic conditions, can be supported by the government. Such a rate is known as the *equilibrium exchange rate.* Seasonal or even cyclical fluctuations in the balance of payments, and therefore in the exchange rate, can be ironed out by the government through accumulation or decumulation of reserves and by granting or receiving international loans. This is not so if the imbalance persists over several years and appears to be fundamental in nature. That can easily mean that the exchange rate is not in equilibrium and needs to be adjusted along with the support limits.

The Role of the Dollar in the Bretton Woods System

From 1944 to 1973 the dollar served as the intervention currency and international standard of value. How did this situation, involving such a pivotal role for the dollar, come about? Mainly it evolved out of a constellation of circumstances prevailing after World War II, and in some measure, it was established by design. The "design component" of the system was the creation of the International Monetary Fund, which today has a membership of 149 nations.[3] Following the international financial chaos of the 1920s and 1930s, the Western nations yearned for order and cooperation—order that would make possible a smoothly functioning trading system. A return to the pre-WWI gold standard, with all the rules governing the financial behavior of governments, was thought to be neither possible nor desirable. However, the original IMF charter provided for fixed exchange rates and outlawed exchange control except when a currency was subject to massive speculative attack. The exchange system prevailing during 1944–1973 was often referred to as the *adjustable peg* system, for under it currencies were pegged to each other but each exchange rate was allowed to adjust by discrete amounts whenever it moved out of its long-run equilibrium position. The main functions of the IMF were to lay down ground rules for the conduct of international finance; to serve as an instrument of consultation, advice, and cooperation between countries; and to provide short- and medium-term financial assistance to countries in external deficit. In recent years added functions of the IMF have been to create and distribute international reserves (in the form of SDRs), and to oversee foreign currency intervention by central banks attempting to influence their floating exchange rates.

Turning now to the evolutionary process through which the dollar emerged into a new central role, we will recall that immediately after World War II there were intense "dollar shortages." Most European countries were engaged in intensive efforts to reconstruct their war-ravaged economies, for which they needed large amounts of materials and equipment. The only source for such materials at the time was the United States, so the dollar

---

[3] Also established at that time was the International Bank for Reconstruction and Development (now called the World Bank) to extend reconstruction and development loans to needy nations. Over the years the Bank developed into the main agency for extending development loans out of subscription capital, as well as money raised on the international capital markets. It also has a "soft-loan" subsidiary known as the International Development Association.

was in great demand to finance the necessary purchases. Consequently, most countries saw absolutely no reason to hold gold. Instead, whenever they managed to run an external surplus, they were extremely happy to accumulate dollar balances. The dollar was a much better asset than gold. It was the asset most sought after, and therefore enjoyed full confidence. Like gold, it gave holders access to the vast American market where all the necessities of life were abundantly available, but as a reserve asset *dollars earned interest*[4] *while gold reserves did not.*

Many private international transactions not involving the United States— transactions in goods, services, and capital—began to be financed in dollars. Indeed, a major market known as the *Eurodollar market* developed in Europe in the 1960s, under which European banks and European branches of American banks accepted deposits and financed transactions in American dollars. The Eurodollar market consists mainly of short-term funds with maturities of less than half a year. There is a counterpart long-term market for "Eurobonds"—bonds offered in Europe but denominated in dollars.

☐ Eurodollars come into being when an American or a foreign owner of a dollar deposit with a bank in the United States transfers these funds and places them on deposit with a foreign bank or a foreign branch of an American bank. Normally such transfers are prompted by higher interest rates on short-term deposits prevailing abroad, and foreign banks accept the deposits because they can in turn lend them at still higher rates. Often these funds belong to corporations which intend to use them in short order to finance international trade or investments; they are kept in dollars (rather than converted to local currencies) because of the general acceptability of the U.S. dollar in settling international transactions. The phenomenal growth of the Eurodollar market was in part a result of various U.S. credit restrictions, inducing corporations to move funds to Europe.

☐ Once Eurodollars come into being in the form of an interest-bearing dollar deposit having a stated maturity in a foreign bank, they may be lent out and redeposited in a succession of banks before being ultimately used to finance a business transaction. Eurodollar deposits thereby multiply just as the domestic money supply does under a fractional reserve banking system.[5] The multiplier effect depends on the magnitude of leakage at each stage (similar to reserve requirements on the domestic banking scene). Generally speaking, the deposits and redeposits are of large sums of money at rather narrow interest rate margins. The interest rate is related to rates prevailing in New York.

☐ Finally, the term Eurodollars is somewhat deceptive. It is true that most of the market consists of dollars held in Europe. But European banks also

---

[4] Because foreign holders of dollars placed them in U.S. treasury bills, U.S. bank accounts, and similar instruments.

[5] For a system of T accounts detailing this process of expansion, see R. L. Reierson, *The Eurodollar Market,* New York: Bankers Trust Co., 1964.

accept deposits denominated in nondollar currencies other than their own, and Japanese banks hold deposits in currencies other than the yen (mainly, but not exclusively, dollars).[6] Total *Eurocurrency* deposits are estimated at a trillion dollars. ∎

Along with the emergence of the dollar as the *reserve, transaction,*[7] and *intervention* currency, New York has become the major capital market of the world. Funds in large sums can be obtained on the New York market for a great variety of purposes; by reason of its size, fluidity, and flexibility, traders and investors from all over the world are drawn to it to supply their capital requirements. The vast array of financial assets available on the New York capital market makes it possible to accommodate diverse tastes for varying degrees of risk and return on investments. Concomitantly, the New York foreign exchange market has emerged as the major one in the world. Unlike similar markets on the other side of the Atlantic, it has always been reasonably free of government regulation and has afforded its users an opportunity to deal in practically all currencies in both spot and forward transactions.

In effect, this pivotal role of the dollar under the Bretton Woods system made the United States the world's central banker and thus sometimes referred to as the "center country." American balance-of-payments deficits supplied dollar assets, and therefore international reserves (liquidity), to the surplus countries that cared to hold them. In much the same way as in family finances, a country's deficit can be financed by owing the money. The United States accumulated dollar liabilities to foreign countries, the counterpart being that these surplus countries accumulated dollar assets. As long as the dollar was generally acceptable as a means of settling international imbalances, central bankers went on holding dollars as a reserve asset along with gold.

Central bankers accumulate international reserves for a variety of reasons. In some cases, such as in the United States until 1968, national law requires that gold or foreign currency be held as a cover for domestic currency issue. In other cases it is a matter of prestige or a belief that large international reserves (especially gold) inspire confidence. But *under a system of fixed exchange rates* the most rational reason for a country to hold reserves

------

[6]Banks in the Eurocurrency markets carry on arbitrage operations between the (dominant) dollar and nondollar markets. Thus if Euromark loans are in excess demand relative to Euromark deposits, the Eurocurrency banks would convert dollars obtained from Eurodollar deposits into marks and lend the marks thus obtained. To cover the exchange risk, the banks would purchase a forward contract in dollars. Each nondollar Eurocurrency interest rate is determined by the dollar rate and the forward premium on the nondollar currency. Arbitrage is so extensive that interest parity is maintained. Thus, a sizable inflow of capital into, say, Euromarks will not induce a large drop in its interest rate because the Euromarks will be exchanged for other currencies.

[7]The dollar is also a major *vehicle currency*. Because minor currencies are not widely traded on the main foreign currency markets, it is more convenient to convert (say) Turkish liras into dollars and then into Greek drachmas than to convert liras into drachmas directly. Also many international transactions are invoiced in vehicle currencies.

is so that it can tide itself over a period of external deficits. This is analogous to a family holding reserves against a "rainy day." It should be emphasized, however, that reserves only buy time; they postpone but do not obviate the need for balance-of-payments adjustment. Under a freely fluctuating exchange rate no reserves are needed. The exchange rate settles at a point that clears the market—namely, where autonomous inpayments and outpayments are equated.

Under the Bretton Woods system, reserves were held in gold and foreign currencies, mainly in dollars. For the world as a whole, dollar reserves held an advantage over gold because the mining of new gold is wasteful of resources engaged in the mining and transport activities. For the United States, the main advantage of a currency system based on the dollar was the ability to mount huge cumulative balance-of-payments deficits and pay for them with IOUs (U.S. liabilities) that the world accepted as reserves. Against this benefit there were several disadvantages: First, there was interest cost, for foreign nationals and official institutions held their dollar balances in interest-bearing, money-market instruments and demand deposits in the United States. Not only that, but large-scale transfers of such funds in and out of the center country may cause disturbances in its money markets. But the main drawback of the system was in depriving the U.S. government of the ability to change the exchange value of the dollar. For when all foreign currencies were pegged to the dollar, the value of the dollar in terms of these currencies was determined (as a residual) by the *foreign* monetary authorities. And even the width of the *spread* of fluctuations of the dollar in terms of other currencies was only half that of any two other currencies. *It was this inability to change the value of the dollar that became increasingly irksome to U.S. policymakers* and led to growing American dissatisfaction with the system and finally to its demise. As will become clear in subsequent chapters, the inability to change the exchange rate imposes a severe constraint on the pursuit of economic policy objectives.

For the countries that maintain dollar reserves, the main advantage (compared to gold reserves) lies in the ability to earn interest on reserves. The risk is that the United States may lower the value of the dollar in terms of gold. In that case, if they were holding gold, they would be protected. Foreign countries would go on accumulating dollar reserves only as long as they were confident that the value of the dollar would not decline.

Over a long period after the war, confidence in the dollar was abundantly in evidence, and for good reasons. The dollar was widely used in international transactions and had general acceptability.[8] It was free of government controls. It was and still is backed by the strongest economy in the world. Also, the United States was a net creditor on the long-term investments account, as American holdings of direct and portfolio foreign investments exceeded foreign long-term investment holdings in the United States. And for the first twenty years of the Bretton Woods system, the rate of

---

[8] Only an asset or currency that is widely used in the private sector can serve as an "intervention currency" for stabilizing the exchange rate.

inflation in the United States—which measures the purchasing power of the dollar—fell short of the rate prevailing in other countries. Finally, the United States had a wide and diversified internal capital market, which offered foreign central banks a variety of liquid, low-risk financial instruments (such as U.S. Treasury bills) in which to invest their dollar reserves. The huge U.S. (domestic) public debt provides a wide array of instruments in which foreign central banks can place their dollar holdings.

Throughout the 1950s and 1960s the main source of international reserves was dollars supplied by U.S. balance-of-payments deficits. But as the 1960s wore on, confidence in the dollar gradually eroded. Continual U.S. deficits resulted in a gradual decline of the U.S. gold stock and in massive increases in foreign official holdings of dollars. Western Europe and Japan were *becoming satiated with dollar assets and increasingly unhappy about having to finance the American balance-of-payments deficits* under the Bretton Woods system, indirectly enabling American corporations to accumulate large foreign investments. Thus, Europe and Japan had their own reasons to push for a change in the system.

Although the need for such a change was widely recognized on both sides of the Atlantic, the change was not brought about by an orderly deliberative process. Instead the demise of the Bretton Woods system came about only after three years of upheaval on the international currency markets. In March 1973 a new system went into operation.

The Contemporary International Currency System

Since March 19, 1973, the international currency system has been a mixture of fixed and floating exchange rates.

Fluctuating Currencies   Of the major currencies the U.S. dollar, the pound sterling, the Japanese yen, and the Canadian dollar, are allowed to float on the market, with their exchange rates determined by demand-and-supply conditions. Often the monetary authorities of each country intervene in the foreign exchange market in order to smooth out fluctuations, to maintain orderly conditions, or to prevent their currency's exchange rate from moving upward or downward to a degree that they consider "excessive" or undesirable.

When an excess of inpayments over outpayments pushes up the exchange value of the currency by an amount the authorities consider excessive, the central bank sells its country's currency in exchange for foreign currencies to moderate the rise. Conversely, when, say, an outflow of capital pushes the exchange value of the currency downward, the central bank may moderate the decline by selling foreign currencies in exchange for the country's currency. Such intervention can, at times, be massive.[9] Such floats

---

[9] Reports on exchange movements and on governments' intervention on the foreign exchange markets are published in the *Federal Reserve Bank of New York Monthly Review.*

are known as *managed* or "dirty" floats, as distinguished from *free* or "clean" floats, which occur when no official intervention takes place.[10] But even under heavily managed floats there is no official commitment to maintain fixed limits to the fluctuations.

This point suggests that the contrast between fixed and floating exchange rates should be viewed as a continuum rather than as a two-way dichotomy. At one extreme, an exchange rate can be freely floating, while at the other extreme it can be immutably fixed. The freely floating rate can be subject to intervention by the central bank. And as the degree of intervention or management rises, we move gradually toward a fixed-rate regime. Conversely a "spread" can be added to the fixed exchange rate, within which the exchange rate may fluctuate. As the width of the spread increases, we move gradually toward a floating rate. When that width reaches infinity and government intervention is absent, the regime becomes one of a free float.

Two differences between free and managed floats should be noted. While under a free float the exchange rate would settle at a value that yields equilibrium in the balance of payments (that is, equalizing inpayments and outpayments), there is no such presumption in the case of managed floats. For central bank intervention may lead the exchange rate away from its equilibrium value rather than toward it. Second, no reserves are accumulated or needed when the exchange rate floats freely, for the exchange rate will always clear the foreign exchange market. By contrast, a country whose floating currency is continuously managed accumulates reserves when the central bank moderates an increase in the value of the currency and needs reserves to moderate a decline in its value.

Under a free float, an external deficit (surplus) is reflected in depreciation (appreciation) of the currency; under a fixed exchange rate, an external imbalance causes a change in international reserves, and the accumulation or depletion of reserves constitutes a measure of the surplus or deficit respectively (see Chapter 2); under a managed float system an external imbalance results in a combination of variations in the exchange rate and a change in international reserves. Because under a managed float part of the imbalance is absorbed in exchange variations, the interventional transactions statement provides no clear indication of the country's external position. A major question facing the community of trading nations is the extent to which official intervention in the foreign exchange markets should be subject to certain rules and limitations, enforced by the surveillance of the IMF.

Figure 4-4 (top panel) shows the fluctuations of three individually floating currencies vis-à-vis the dollar in 1985–86.

The European Monetary System   Seven European currencies—the West German mark, French franc, Italian lira, Belgian-Luxembourg franc, Danish kroner, Netherlands guilder, and Irish pound—are pegged to each other.

---

[10]See, for example, P. Wannacott, "U.S. Intervention in the Exchange Market for D.M.," Princeton, *Studies In International Finance*, Dec., 1982.

Figure 4-4
Spot Exchange Rates, 1985–86

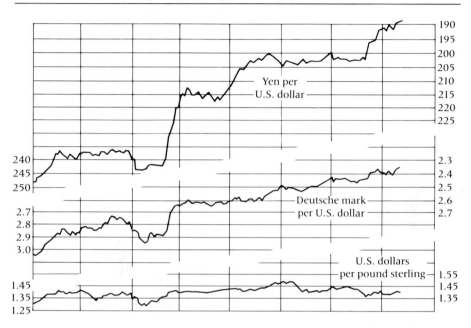

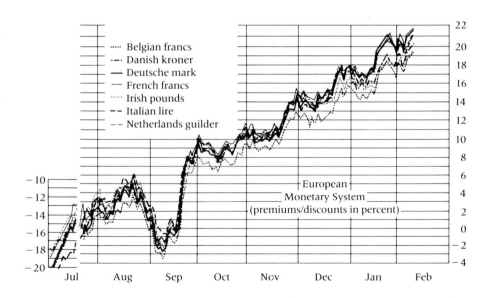

SOURCE: *IMF Survey,* July 29, 1985 and March 31, 1986.

Known as the European Monetary System (EMS), they float *jointly* against the dollar, with a maximum spread of 2¼ percent between the dollar rates of the strongest and weakest participants. Because the resulting movement of the jointly floating currencies produces a "snake-like" pattern, the arrangement is sometimes referred to as the "snake." Figure 4-4 (bottom panel) illustrates the joint movement in 1985–86.

Introduced on March 19, 1979, the EMS links the currencies of members of the European Community (Appendix I), except for the U.K. and Greece, into a reasonably fixed exchange-rate system. It succeeded the "joint float" of five European currencies. Under EMS rules no member currency can move by more than ± 2.25 percent against any other currency; the Italian lira is an exception that is allowed a ± 6 percent band of fluctuations. The limits to fluctuations are maintained by central banks' intervention on their respective foreign exchange markets. Each country conducts its intervention in other members' currencies or in dollars.

However, there is a "warning system" indicating that a country, whether in a "strong" or a "weak" position, should take some action to forestall hitting the intervention limits. These warnings signals take the form of "divergence indicators" from the European Unit of Account (ECU).

The ECU is a weighted average of EC currencies in which the weights are derived from each country's share in intra-European trade and in EC output. (The German mark has about one third of the total weights.) These weights are revised periodically. The divergence indicator is calculated against the ECU at 75 percent of the allowed maximum spread for each currency. When the limit of the divergence indicator is reached, the country is under presumption to act so as to move the exchange value of its currency back toward the "center." Such action may take the form of changes in domestic fiscal and monetary policy or an adjustment of the currency's central rate. Thus, there exists no irrevocable commitment to the central rates. In this sense the EMS **constitutes an adjustable peg system for the countries** that are included in it. In fact, nine realignments of exchange rates within the EMS occurred during its first seven years.[11] Despite these changes, there is evidence that exchange rate variability of the EMS currencies has diminished since the EMS was introduced. In contrast the exchange rate variability of the major currencies not tied to the EMS—the pound sterling, the U.S. dollar, and the Japanese yen—appears to have increased. This is one reason the London *Financial Times* and other influential circles in the U.K. called (in August 1985) for Britain to join the EMS.[12]

To facilitate intervention in EMS member currencies, short-term (up to 45 days) credits are exchanged between the central banks. In addition,

---

[11]The ninth adjustment occurred on April 6, 1986, when the French franc was devalued by 3 percent and the mark and the guilder were revalued by 3 percent. This realignment meant that the franc was devalued by 6 percent relative to other EMS currencies. Previous adjustments occurred on September 24, 1979; November 30, 1979; March 23, 1981; October 5, 1981; February 22, 1982; June 14, 1982; March 21, 1983; and July 22, 1985.

[12]See G. Dennis and J. Nellis, "The EMS and U.K. Membership," *Lloyds Bank Review*, October 1984.

medium-term financial assistance is available through the European Monetary Cooperation Fund, to which each EMS member contributed 20 percent of its gold and dollar reserves in exchange for ECU accounts. The ECU is not a circulating currency; it is only a theoretical unit of account for the EMS, although it is also used as an accounting unit for a variety of private transactions.

Fixed Exchange Rates   About 55 of the world currencies, particularly those of many developing countries (LDCs), are pegged by government action to one of the major currencies—mainly the dollar, but also the French franc or the pound sterling. Additionally, 35 currencies are pegged to a weighted basket of major currencies, such as Special Drawing Rights (SDRs) of the IMF (a weighted average of the five major currencies) or to a specially designated basket. Finally, very few countries pursue a policy of frequent minidevaluations relative to a major currency (mainly the dollar) to accommodate the differential rate of inflation at home and abroad. Dealing in many LDC currencies is subject to government restrictions.

Summary

Clearly the prevailing system is a "hybrid" of four exchange-rate regimes: *single floats, joint floats, currencies pegged to a major currency, and currencies pegged to a basket of major currencies.* Individual countries sometimes switch from one regime to another, as when New Zealand replaced a pegged exchange-rate regime with a free float (in 1985); when Zaire adopted a floating currency (1983); or when Mexico introduced (1982) a two-tier exchange-rate system: a "preferential" rate for crucial imports, and a market rate for all other transactions. In general, since 1973 there has been a movement away from pegged regimes; and within the peggers, from a single currency toward composite or basket pegs. Although two-thirds of all currencies are "pegged," most of world trade is conducted among coun-

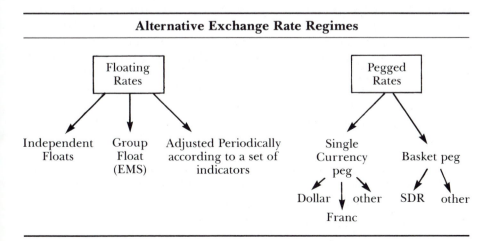

Alternative Exchange Rate Regimes

tries whose exchange rates float against each other. The international currency system is summarized in the scheme on page 65.

Under the present currency arrangements, the European and Japanese currencies are no longer pegged to the dollar. That makes the dollar *a fluctuating currency,* somewhat free of the constraints imposed by the Bretton Woods system. Yet even without the official pegging, the dollar continues to play an important role. It remains the major currency for financing international transactions by the private sector of all countries, and the Eurodollar market is both vast and active. It retains its *reference role* for exchange rates, since countries measure their fluctuations vis-à-vis the dollar and often use dollars to *intervene* on the market to affect these fluctuations (managed floats). Because of its continuous role as the main intervention currency in the managed float system, the dollar is still not completely free of the Bretton Woods constraints. Through their currency intervention, other countries influence the exchange value of the dollar. Finally, many international statistics, such as those relating to commodity trade and published by the United Nations, are still measured in dollars. Such data now embody the fluctuations in the value of the dollar in terms of other currencies. On the other hand, the IMF now uses SDRs, and the EC employs the ECU in their statistical tabulations.

Indices of Effective Exchange Rates

Because the major world currencies are floating independently or in a group (EMS), it is impossible to determine by direct inspection what happens to a country's exchange rate. For example, suppose that in a simplified world there were only three currencies: the U.S. dollar, the Canadian dollar, and the mark. Assume that the U.S. dollar *depreciated 10 percent* relative to the mark, and *appreciated 12 percent* relative to the Canadian dollar. Then the change in the value of the dollar is some *weighted average* of the changes in the two *bilateral* exchange rates. Since in effect the dollar may change in varying degrees against any number of individually floating currencies, a weighted average of all the bilateral changes is required to determine the change in the exchange value of the dollar. Such an average is called the dollar's *effective exchange rate.* It is calculated for all major currencies. In calculating the index, a weight representing the comparative importance to the home economy of each foreign country is applied to the value, relative to a chosen base period, of the bilateral exchange rate between the foreign currency in question and the home currency.

Several possible weights can be used in calculating the average, and correspondingly, each currency can have several effective exchange rates. The weights employed depend on the purpose for which the index is developed. Thus an import-weighted index—where each partner country's share in the home country's imports is used as a weight—measures the effect of exchange-rate changes on the cost of imports into the home country. Likewise, an export-weighted index—where each partner country's share in the home country's exports is used as a weight—measures the average changes in the cost of the home currency exports to foreigners. A third alternative is to weight each partner country by the sum of the home country's export to and import from it (namely, total bilateral trade flows), while a fourth possibility is a global trade-weighted index, where each partner country's weight is equal to its share in worldwide trade. Finally, the IMF developed weights that are designed to assess the effect of exchange rate changes on the country's trade balance. These weights incorporate both the price changes of exports and imports, and the responsiveness of trade flows to these changes, occasioned by a 1 percent movement in each bilateral exchange rate.

Both the bilateral and effective exchange rates mentioned so far are known as *nominal* rates because they do not account for differential inflation in the home and the foreign country or countries. For that reason they do not adequately measure the change in the country's competitive position relative to its competitors. Suppose that the dollar depreciated from 3 D.M. to 2 D.M., but over the same period the U.S. domestic inflation was one-third higher than German inflation, then the U.S. competitive position relative to Germany has not changed.

To measure the changes in a country's competitive position we employ *real* exchange rates. The bilateral real exchange rate is the nominal rate adjusted for the differential inflation between the two countries. The effective real exchange rate is the effective nominal rate adjusted for the differential between the country's inflation rate and a weighted average of foreign inflation rates.

Figure 4-5 shows the real and effective exchange rates of the five main industrial countries, where the weights are those of the IMF. Despite short-run fluctuations, the real and nominal value of dollar rose by more than 60 percent between 1980 and 1985, before declining by 27 percent in the year following February 1985. There was a divergence between the real and nominal effective rates for other countries, although in Germany, France, and Italy both rates declined during 1980–85. The mark, franc and yen then appreciated during 1985–86.

The International Monetary Fund

Occupying a pivotal role in the international currency system is the IMF. In addition to its consultative functions, it coordinates and advises on central banks' intervention on their respective foreign currency markets. These surveillance activities will be discussed further in Chapter 10. Furthermore, the IMF provides short-run credit and supplementary reserves through its regular and Special Drawing Rights (SDR) accounts.

Regular International Monetary Fund Procedures

There are 149 member countries in the IMF, of which the Group of Ten major industrial countries are the most important in terms of the volume of their international payments and their voting power within the organi-

Figure 4-5
Five Industrial Countries: Nominal and Real Effective Exchange Rates

(Index 1978 = 100)

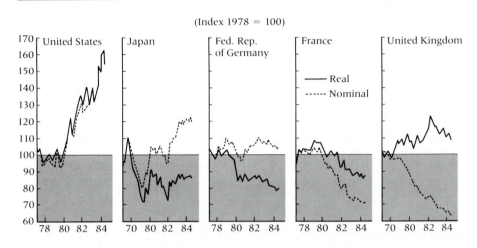

The above charts show indexes of nominal and real effective exchange rates for 5 industrial countries, calculated from the base year of 1978. The *nominal* effective exchange rate index for each country's currency is calculated using the Fund's Multilateral Exchange Rate Model; it is a measure of each currency's trade-weighted average appreciation or depreciation vis-à-vis the currencies of 13 other industrial countries. The *real* effective exchange rate index is the nominal effective exchange rate adjusted for inflation differentials, which are measured by cyclically adjusted unit labor costs. The real effective exchange rate index is an attempt to measure overall cost and price competitiveness; an increase in the index indicates a loss of competitiveness, and a decrease in the index indicates an improvement in competitiveness.

SOURCE: *IMF Survey*, July 29, 1985.

zation. Each member country is assigned a quota, of which it must contribute to the IMF 25 percent in gold or convertible foreign currencies and 75 percent in its own currency. The quota is based on a rather complicated formula[13] that need not be elaborated on here. In turn the quota determines the voting power of each member country as well as the amount of loans it is eligible to receive. The initial resources of the IMF consisted of 25 percent in gold and 75 percent in holdings of a variety of currencies.

Loans granted by the Fund to member countries require approval by the Board of Directors. The loans are given to a country in a specific foreign currency in exchange for an equivalent amount of the borrowing country's own currency. If, for example, France desires supplementary resources, it applies for a loan in the currency it needs, say German marks. If the loan is approved, the Fund provides the marks in return for an equivalent amount of French francs. Thus the Fund does not really make loans in the conventional sense of the word; it sells currencies. The French *purchase* German marks with French francs, and that is the official term used by the Fund

---

[13]A country's national income, international reserves, imports, the variability of its exports, and the ratio of exports to national income are all part of the formula.

for all borrowing activities. When the French repay the loan (in 3–5 years), they *repurchase* their own currency from the Fund for such currencies as are acceptable to the Fund at the time.

There are limits to how much a country can "borrow" from the Fund, and these are expressed in terms of how much of a given currency the Fund is permitted to accumulate. If the French continue to borrow from the Fund, that means they continue to purchase foreign currencies with French francs, which in turn implies that the Fund is accumulating francs. The IMF may do this only to the point at which its franc holdings reach 200 percent of the French quota. Since its initial holdings of francs were 75 percent of the French quota, the total advance that can be made to France in foreign currencies is limited to 125 percent of the French quota. The same rules apply to all countries.

Cumulative purchases of a given currency (in this example, the mark) from the IMF would deplete the Fund's holdings of that currency. When these holdings fall below 75 percent of that country's quota, its currency becomes *acceptable to the Fund for repayment (repurchase) purposes*. It also makes that country eligible for larger future drawings on other currencies because it increases the shortfall of the Fund's holdings from the 200 percent of the quota limit.

If the Fund runs out of currency altogether—something that has not happened thus far—that currency can be declared "scarce," permitting other countries to discriminate against it.

Returning to the borrowing country of our example, France, we see that not all "loans" from the Fund are automatic. Indeed, the larger the cumulative drawings, the greater the Fund's holdings of francs, and the more difficult it becomes for the French to obtain additional loans. Specifically, the 125 percent of quota in total potential drawings is divided into 5 tranches (slices) of 25 percent each. The first one is known as the reserve tranche (used to be called the "gold tranche"). The subsequent four slices are known as the credit tranches. Advances within the reserve tranche are automatic, as is the right to draw on any credit balance that the country may have built up by having its own currency drawn upon.

Any drawings beyond that are subject to the discretionary decision of the Fund, and the Fund may extract pledges from the borrowing country in return for the loan.[14] These pledges usually concern policies to be undertaken by the country to put its international payments situation in order. Known as the *conditionality* criteria, these conditions consist of a set of measures designed to ensure a reduction in the country's external deficit. They are usually formulated in terms of limits on the growth of the domestic money supply or on the size of the budget deficit, perhaps coupled with currency devaluation. As such they may prove embarrassing or unacceptable to the country concerned. And countries at times avoid drawing on the IMF so as not to subject themselves to the conditions that the IMF would

---

[14]The Fund's interest charges, which are levied on any drawings beyond the reserve tranche, also increase with the rise in cumulative drawings. In addition to interest, there is a service charge on each transaction and standby commitment.

impose. Developing countries often must prove compliance with IMF rules before they can obtain loans from private sources. In 1982 Argentina and Mexico cut domestic budgetary spending to qualify for IMF loans. On the other hand, Peru rejected a visit by an IMF team in October 1985, and decided to bypass the IMF in negotiating with private banks.

The automatic-drawing component constitutes the country's "reserve position in the Fund." At any given moment, this equals 25 percent of its quota minus its previous drawing plus previous drawings made by other countries on the Fund's holdings of its currency. In other words, a country's reserve position in the IMF is the shortfall in the Fund's holdings of the currency from 100 percent of the country's quota.[15] Even the automatic drawings carry an obligation to repurchase, usually within three to five years.

Since the reserve tranche is equal to the original gold or foreign currency contribution of the member nation, these drawings do not constitute a net increase in reserves. Thus the net effect on global reserves of any increase in the Fund's quotas is zero. This applies to the several general increases in the Fund quotas, the latest one taking place in 1984 when the total quotas were raised to about $90 billion (90 billion SDRs). But in line with the general downgrading of the role of gold at the Fund, members no longer contribute gold. They may instead contribute "freely usable currencies"—a term that applies to the currencies widely used in international transactions.

Special Drawing Rights Procedures

An increase in international liquidity could be accomplished only by making advances within one or more of the credit tranches automatic, which would require revision of the IMF charter. In a sense this is the essence of its Special Drawing Rights (SDRs). The IMF created and distributed to its members 9.3 billion SDRs in 1970–72 and another 12 billion SDRs in 1979–81, the allocation being proportional to their regular IMF quota. Thus the United States[16] received nearly 25 percent of the total, and the industrial countries combined received nearly two-thirds of the total allocation.

All SDR operations are administered by a special drawing account at the IMF. Each unit of SDR was originally defined in terms of gold or dollars. But in mid-1974 the IMF adopted another valuation system for the SDRs, one better suited for an era of fluctuating exchange rates: The SDR value was calculated daily as the weighted average value of a "basket" of 16 impor-

---

[15] Suppose the country's quota is $200,000, its reserve tranche would then be $50,000. If its drawings on the Fund amounted to $40,000 while other countries purchased $30,000 of its currency from the Fund, its reserve position would be $40,000 ($50,000 − $40,000 + $30,000). The Fund's holding of its currency would be $160,000 (the original contribution of $150,000 plus a net addition of $10,000), or $40,000 short of 100 percent of its quota.

[16] Since the agreement required approval by countries having a total of 85 percent of the quota, it gave veto power to the EC along with the United States.

tant currencies. Since 1981 the SDR has been valued as a weighted average of the *five* most important currencies. As of January 1, 1986, the weights (in percentages) are: U.S. dollar—42; Deutsche mark—19; Japanese yen—15; French franc—12; British pound sterling—12. They are subject to change every five years. The dollar value of SDRs fluctuates on a daily basis. Early in 1986 one SDR was worth about $1.10. Appendix II explains the daily SDR valuation method. Interest charges on SDR transactions are a weighted average of charges on three-month market instruments in the five major countries. Transactions in SDRs and other vital economic statistics of IMF members are reported in the IMF's *International Financial Statistics* and in the *IMF Survey*.

For explanation, let us return to the French and German example and assume that each of the two countries receives an allocation of $100 in SDRs. The allocation is executed by making credit entries for each country on the ledger of the special drawing account, but no country need make a contribution to the Fund. The attractiveness of the SDRs as a reserve asset derives from the obligation of all members to accept them. Thus, if France, the deficit country in our example, finds itself in need of convertible foreign currencies, it can acquire German marks (or any other currency) in exchange for SDRs. The purchase is made directly from Germany (following its designation as the lender by the IMF) and does not affect any of the IMF holdings of the currencies involved. The transaction will deplete France's holdings of SDRs while increasing those of Germany. The French are not required to meet any fixed repayment or "repurchase" schedule, however, as under normal IMF quota operations. Should any other country subsequently require French francs in exchange for SDRs, the French SDR holdings would increase correspondingly. Conversely, should Germany acquire any other currency in exchange for SDRs, its SDR holdings would decline.

We now turn to the surplus country (Germany in the present example), whose currency is presumably in great demand. Each participating country is obligated to provide its currency in exchange for SDRs freely, until its total SDR holdings are equal to three times the amount of its allocation. In our example, if Germany (with an initial allocation of $100) uses none of its SDRs, then its acceptance obligation is $200. If it uses the original allocation, its acceptance obligation becomes $300. The plan contains incentives for a country to exceed this limit, but this is not a requirement.

Because of their universal acceptability in settling imbalances between countries, SDRs are part of owned international reserves. But because they are held only by central banks, they cannot be used for intervention purposes, that is, to peg the value of currencies. Only if commercial banks and other nonofficial institutions were allowed to deal in SDRs, as they now deal in dollars, would it be possible to use SDRs as an intervention asset. On the other hand, SDRs are used as a standard of value of 14 currencies for which it is important to value the exchange rate in terms of a basket of major currencies. Additionally, private transactions, such as bonds floated on the European markets, may be valued in SDRs.

A country generally deals in SDRs for one of three principal reasons: (1) To obtain foreign currencies. To meet its balance-of-payments needs, one country may transfer SDRs to another member country designated by the IMF to receive them in exchange for its currency. The countries designated (by the Fund) to receive the SDRs are usually in a strong external position. (2) To redeem a balance of its own currency held by another member country. (3) *To pay charges and to "repurchase" its own currency* from the General Account of the IMF. All IMF accounts are denominated in SDRs. Between 1970 and 1985 total transfers between countries amounted to SDR 100 billion.

Special Facilities

In addition to the regular and SDR accounts, the IMF operates special facilities through which credit is extended to member countries. An example is the compensatory finance facility designed to help countries that specialize in the export of primary commodities to deal with large fluctuations in their export earnings. Also there exist "enlarged access" and "extended fund" facilities which provide assistance to members with unusually large and protracted deficits who also need help above and beyond their credit tranches. And a special facility to provide balance of payments assistance to low-income developing countries came into being in 1986. Because of these special facilities, a country's potential drawing on the Fund is 500–600 percent of its quota. The pursuit of specified domestic policies designed to improve the country's balance of payments is an IMF condition of any drawing on the advanced credit tranches or the enlarged facilities. These are known as the "*conditionality*" provisions. Finally, the IMF charges interest on debtor countries and pays interest to creditor countries.[17]

International Reserves

A country's demand for international reserves depends on several factors, first among which is the degree to which its currency is allowed to fluctuate. A country on a fixed exchange rate requires more reserves than one on a managed float, which in turn requires more reserves than a country on a free float regime. Also, the need for reserves is positively related to the size of the country's outpayments; and to the size as well as variability of the external imbalances that the reserves must finance. That need is inversely related to the country's willingness to engage in adjustment policies (to be described later) required to restore external balance. The combined demand of all countries indicates the amount of reserves needed by the international community.

On the supply side, each country's **official reserves consist of four**

---

[17] For a concise summary of the IMF and its various activities see: *IMF Survey,* Supplement on the Fund, September 1985.

components: gold, SDRs, reserve position in the IMF, and convertible foreign currencies (mainly dollars, but with the mark increasing in importance). Members of the EMS have additional reserves in their central pool to help stabilize intra-EMS exchange rates. On March 31, 1986, combined official reserves of all countries totaled 422 billion SDRs, most of which were in foreign currencies. The industrial countries owned 250 billion in reserves; and developing countries 150 billion SDRs.

In addition less formal forms of reserves exist. An example is the "swap"[18] network between the major central banks. Under it, central banks undertake to loan one another their own currencies, up to a certain limit (now 17 billion SDRs), for the purpose of intervention in the foreign exchange markets.

This concludes the discussion of the international currency system. Chapters 6 and 7 are devoted to balance of payments policies. Because the international currency system is at present a hybrid of floating and fixed exchange rates, it is necessary to explain the policies under both regimes. In the case of fixed exchange rates the policy problem is how to restore balance of payments equilibrium in times of a deficit or a surplus and how these policies affect the domestic economy. In the case of a floating exchange rate, the question is two-fold: How the exchange rate is determined (Chapter 3) and how changes in the market exchange rate affect the external accounts and the domestic economy. Following the analysis in Chapter 5 of national income determination in an open economy, we shall turn to the balance of payments adjustment mechanism under alternative exchange rate regimes.

Review Questions

1. Using the diagram from Question 1 of Chapter 3, explain how the French central bank may maintain a fixed dollar–franc exchange rate. What happens to the French money supply in each type of intervention?

2. a. What types of exchange rate regimes exist in the contemporary international currency system?
   b. How is an external deficit reflected in each one of these regimes?
   c. Does the U.S. dollar play a special role in the system? If so, what?

3. What is the difference between:
   a. Bilateral and effective exchange rates.
   b. Nominal and real exchange rates.

4. How does the IMF make, and receive payments of, "loans" under the:
   a. Regular account procedure?
   b. SDR procedure?

5. How is the value of SDRs determined?

---

[18] Known as the General Agreement to Borrow.

6. What are the forms of international reserves?

7. Explain the terms:
   a. Free float
   b. Managed float
   c. European Monetary System
   d. Reserve currency
   e. Vehicle currency
   f. Intervention currency
   g. Transactions currency
   h. Reserve position in the IMF

8. The following are hypothetical U.S. International transactions (in billions of dollars) for a certain year.

a. Merchandise exports	300
b. Merchandise imports	500
c. Service transactions (imports and exports): NET	+100
d. Private capital flows: NET	+90
e. Official liabilities to foreign monetary authorities	+10

   Would you deduce from the above statistics that the dollar is a *freely floating* currency? Why or why not?

9. On April 15, 1985, the *New York Times* quoted a certain report released by a Senate working group.
   a. The senators were concerned that the *effective nominal and real* exchange values of the dollar were 50 percent above those of 1980.
   b. The senators recommended seeking something between "the excessive exchange rigidities of Bretton Woods and the excessive gyrations we are seeing now."
   c. The Senators recommended greater intervention in the foreign currency markets (in coordination with other countries).

   Explain the above statements!

5/
National Income Determination in an Open Economy

*T*he discussion of the statement of international transactions (Chapter 2) indicated that the balance on goods and services provides the link between the country's external transactions and its national income accounts. This chapter shows how the foreign trade sector is embedded in the national economy by incorporating the external sector into the Keynesian analysis of income determination. For the sake of simplicity we deal with an economy in which there is a private sector but no government. Also, in order to focus attention on income changes, prices and interest rates are assumed to be constant, a situation that results when there is significant unemployment in the economy. We begin by considering the case of a closed economy (one in which there is no foreign trade), and introduce foreign trade at a later stage.

Output Determination in a Closed Economy

During any one-year period the economy produces a given value of goods and services known as the gross national product (GNP). (Since under our simplified assumptions of fixed prices and no government this is roughly equal to real national income, it will be denoted by Y.) Output can be in the form of investment goods (I) or consumption goods (C): $Y = C + I$. Over any given period, the value of goods produced must equal the income generated in their production. This is easy to see in a Robinson Crusoe economy. If Robinson Crusoe catches 10 fish each day, then 10 fish is both his output (production) and his income. In a complex society this relation is less visible, but it remains valid nonetheless. The value of any good produced in the economy equals all incomes—in the form of wages and salaries paid for labor, rent paid for resources, interest paid on capital, and *profit*—

generated in its production. What is true of one product is equally true of all goods and services put together: output produced equals income earned by all productive factors in the economy.

The income earned in the productive process can be spent on consumption (C) or not. The part that is not spent is called savings (S). Thus, by definition, $Y = C + S$. Combining the two equations we obtain the famous accounting identity:

$$Y = C + I = C + S. \text{ Hence, } I = S. \tag{1}$$

This relationship holds for any period; at the close of the period, realized savings must always equal realized investment. However, it does not necessarily reflect what people intended or wished to do at the beginning of the period, for there is no guarantee that savers and investors—two distinct groups of people—would have identical plans. At the end of each period, therefore, many individuals may find that their initial plans have been frustrated. That is, realized savings and investment are not generally equal to planned savings and investment. The relationship between plans and realization is explained next.

☐ The circular flow diagram of Figure 5-1 portrays a simple economy in which firms produce goods and services, employing members of households in the productive process. If the firms produce $100 worth of goods and services, then this is the income earned by the households. If the households spend it all on consumption and save nothing, the $100 returns to the firms in the form of purchases, and the circle is complete. No saving and no investment take place, and the economy cannot grow in productive capacity or future output. All its capacity is employed in producing for current consumption.

☐ But suppose that, at the beginning of the period, firms planned some investments while households intended to save some of their income. If the two plans were identical (intended $S = I = \$20$), then both plans could be realized, as shown in Figure 5-2. This would always be the case in a Robinson Crusoe economy, where the same person decides how much to save and how much to invest. Suppose this individual has been catching 10 fish a day

Figure 5-1
Circular Flow

$100 *(Y)*

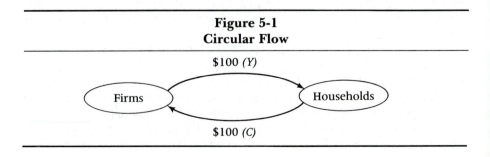

$100 *(C)*

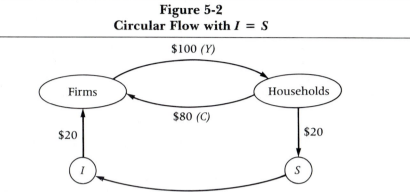

Figure 5-2
Circular Flow with $I = S$

and now decides to cut his daily consumption to 8 fish. He can transform his savings (2 fish not consumed) into a productive investment by using the resources freed from producing for consumption (time freed from fishing) to produce for investment (constructing a fishing net). The net will enable him to save even more time from fishing, which can then be invested in other productive activities. This is how savings are transformed into investments, making possible greater production (economic growth) in subsequent periods.

☐ But when millions of individuals are involved in making these decisions, the two sets of plans (the aggregate plans of all persons saving and all persons investing) are unlikely to match. Let us assume that at the beginning of the period firms plan to produce $120 worth of goods and services, generating an equal amount of income. Households plan to save $30 and spend $90 on consumer goods, while business firms intend to invest $20 out of their total planned output of $120. In other words, firms set their production schedules to manufacture $100 worth of consumer goods and $20 worth of investment goods, while consumers plan to consume $90 worth and save $30. Planned output of $120 exceeds planned spending by consumers ($90) and investors ($20) of $110; and, correspondingly, intended savings ($30) exceeds intended investments ($20). In both cases the excess is $10. These intentions are depicted in Figure 5-3. The outcome of this set of plans must be that some business people in the economy are stuck with "unplanned" inventories ($10), because they would find customers for only $110 worth of the goods that they had intended to market. Since the national-income accounts include inventory changes as part of investments, the realized savings–investments identity is preserved at $30. But the investments part includes $10 in unwanted inventories (along with $20 in desired or intended investments). The natural reaction of business people would be to cut down orders from the factories, thereby reducing production, employment, and income. $Y = \$120$ is not a sustainable equilibrium output. The economy will contract.

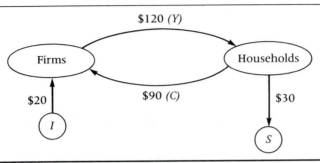

Figure 5-3
Circular Flow with *I* < *S*

$120 (*Y*)

Firms   Households

$20 $90 (*C*) $30

I   *S*

☐ Conversely, assume that firms plan to produce $80 worth of goods and services, generating an equal amount of income. Households plan to save $10 out of an income of $80 and spend $70, while firms intend to invest $20. Here planned spending ($70 by consumers and $20 by firms) exceeds planned output ($80) by $10, and intended investments exceed intended savings by $10. This is shown schematically in Figure 5-4. The excess of aggregate spending over output necessarily results in a depletion of inventories through which realized savings and investments would be equalized (at $10). But this would lead business people to raise orders from the factories, with the attendant increase in output and employment. The difference between what is planned and what is realized causes adjustments in the economy. *Y* = 80 is not a sustained equilibrium output. The economy will expand.

☐ Clearly, only the case portrayed in Figure 5-2—with income or output at $100—is an example of equilibrium, inducing no change in the level of output (*Y*). Intended expenditures on *C* ($80) and *I* ($20) equal planned output ($100), which is equivalent to saying that intended *S* equals intended *I*. By contrast, in Figure 5-3, planned output exceeds the sum of intended

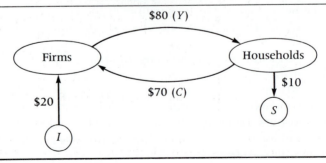

Figure 5-4
Circular Flow with *I* > *S*

$80 (*Y*)

Firms   Households

$20 $70 (*C*) $10

I   *S*

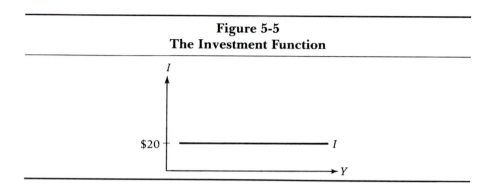

Figure 5-5
The Investment Function

C and I, or planned S exceeds planned I. And in Figure 5-4, the opposite is true: Planned expenditures on C and I exceed planned output, or intended S falls short of intended I. Although *realized* savings and investments are always equal, it is the relationship between *planned* savings and *planned* investments that determines the course of the economy. And this relationship is analogous to the relationship between Y and C + I.

☐ Because of its analytical importance, we proceed with a diagrammatic representation of the relation between the "intended" magnitudes. We have postulated that income produced is made up of consumption and investment. As a first approximation, investments are assumed to be independent of current income. Thus, although changes in I definitely bring about changes in Y, the reverse is not true; changes in Y are assumed not to induce changes in I. This is shown in Figure 5-5 by a straight horizontal investment function. Relating I (vertical axis) to Y (horizontal axis), it postulates that regardless of the level of income, intended investments are always the same ($20).

☐ Consumption, by contrast, is functionally dependent upon income. Any change in income (ΔY) is bound to change consumption (ΔC) in the same direction, though by a smaller magnitude.[1] This proposition, demonstrated time and again in empirical studies,[2] is shown graphically in the upper panel of Figure 5-6, where consumption is plotted against income. The line labeled "consumption function" shows that as Y rises so does C, but by a lesser amount. For simplicity it is drawn here as a straight line (linear relation). The consumption function shows how much is consumed (vertical axis) out of various levels of income (horizontal axis). From this it follows that savings (income not consumed) is also determined by income. The relation between them, known as the savings function, is depicted in the lower panel of the figure. It shows the amount saved (vertical axis) out of various levels of income (horizontal axis). This function is derived from the consumption function in the upper part as follows: An imaginary reference line is drawn

[1] The Greek letter Δ, read "delta," denotes change.
[2] In fact, consumption has a component that is independent of income in addition to the one that is dependent on income. This is expressed by the relationship: $C = C_0 + cY$.

Figure 5-6
Income Determination in a Closed Economy

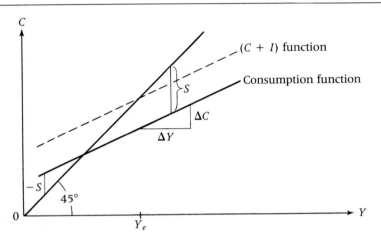

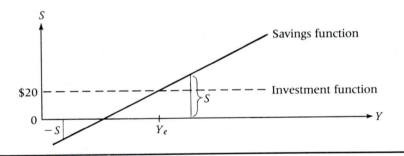

to bisect the 90° angle between the axes. Known as the 45° line, it has the geometrical property of being at equal distances from the two axes. In other words, it is the locus of points for which $C = Y$ and therefore $S = 0$. Thus, for any level of income, the vertical distance between the consumption function and the 45° line indicates savings. It is by transposing these distances to the lower part of the chart that the savings function is formed. Note that $S = 0$ at the level of Y at which the consumption function intersects the 45° line.

☐ Two terms must be defined for each relation: The *average propensity to consume* (APC) is the ratio of total consumption to total income (C/Y), and the *marginal propensity to consume* (MPC) is the ratio of change in consumption to the change in income ($\Delta C/\Delta Y$). Analogously, the *average propensity to save* (APS) is S/Y, and the *marginal propensity to save* (MPS) is $\Delta S/\Delta Y$. For straight-line consumption and savings functions, the MPC and MPS are the constant slopes of the functions. Also, since any additional income (ΔY) must be added either to consumption (ΔC) or to savings (ΔS), the sum of the marginal propensities equals 1: MPC + MPS = 1.

☐ We next add investment to Figure 5-6. This can be done in the upper panel by superimposing a fixed investment on the consumption function. The $(C + I)$ function (broken line) becomes a line parallel to the C function and the fixed vertical distance between them equals investment. Alternatively, it can be done by superimposing Figure 5-5 onto the lower panel of Figure 5-6 (broken line). The two methods yield identical results. The level of income at which $S = I$ is also the one at which $(C + I)$ intersects the 45° line—that is, intended C plus intended investment equals planned output. As the discussion of the circular flow diagrams indicated, this is the equilibrium level of income, Y_e. At points to the right of Y_e, intended savings exceeds intended investments, and forces will come into action to lower income, while the converse is true of points to the left of Y_e. These are equivalent to the situations depicted in Figure 5-3 and 5-4, respectively. Level Y_e corresponds to income in the circular flow chart of Figure 5-2, in which equilibrium prevails.

The Domestic Multiplier

☐ Suppose now that the annual level of investment is doubled from $20 to $40 as shown in Figure 5-7. Then the equilibrium level of income will rise from Y_1 to Y_2 (for the sake of simplicity we omit the upper panel of Figure 5-6, although the analysis is analogous). The increase in income raises savings to the new level of investments, so that $\Delta I = \Delta S$. Clearly, given the increase in investment (ΔI), the increase in income (ΔY) depends on the slope slope of the savings function, or the marginal propensity to save. In fact, the geometrical definition of a slope shows that $\Delta S/\Delta Y = \Delta I/\Delta Y = $ MPS, or that

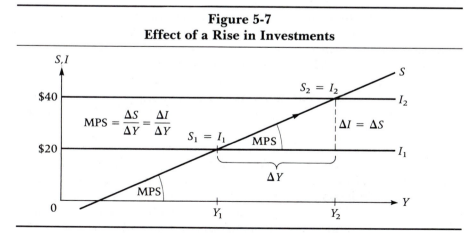

Figure 5-7
Effect of a Rise in Investments

$$\Delta Y = \Delta I \frac{1}{\text{MPS}} = \Delta I \frac{1}{1 - \text{MPC}}$$

Because the MPS is a fraction (say 0.2), the increase in income is several times (five times in this example) the rise in investments. The ratio between the change in income and the change in investments ($\Delta Y / \Delta I$) is known as the *domestic multiplier* and is labeled k. It is equal to 1/MPS or 1/(1 − MPC). It can also be derived directly from equation (1):

$$k = \frac{\Delta Y}{\Delta I} = \frac{\Delta Y}{\Delta Y - \Delta C} = \frac{1}{1 - \Delta C / \Delta Y} = \frac{1}{1 - \text{MPC}} = \frac{1}{\text{MPS}} = \frac{1}{\text{leakage}} \qquad (2)$$

☐ To gain further insight into the economic behavior underlying this relation, we can reformulate our earlier discussion. Suppose, starting from equilibrium income Y_1, that annual investment rises by $20. The immediate impact would be to raise by $20 the incomes of the newly hired workers and sellers of materials used in the new projects. In other words, $20 would be *injected* into the income stream in the first period. But the recipients of the added income will raise their level of consumption by spending part of these receipts. They would increase their consumption by MPC × ΔY (and raise their savings by MPS × ΔY), which in our numerical example (where MPS = 0.2 and MPC = 0.8) equals 0.8 × $20 = $16. The balance of $4 (= MPS × ΔY) *leaks* out of the income stream into savings. Next, the recipients of the $16 in the second round of spending would consume 0.8 of that, or 0.8 × $16 = $12.8. Consequently, the increase spreads through the economy in successive rounds of new spending, which can be represented by a declining series. This succession, which carries the economy from the initial equilibrium to the new one, takes a long period of time to complete. The relation obtained in equation (2) only shows the change in income between the initial and the final points of equilibrium, after successive rounds of the multiplier process have been completed. The total change in income resulting from the change in investment is ΔI times the multiplier change in (k). ■

Introduction of Foreign Trade

In introducing foreign trade, two items must be added to the previous analysis: (1) Exports of *Goods and Services*, labeled X. Because exports must come out of domestic production, they involve the sale of goods manufactured by domestic factors of production. *Exports constitute injections into the income stream,* much the same as investments. (2) Imports of *Goods and Services*, labeled M, give rise to outflow of dollars. Consequently *imports constitute a leakage out of the domestic income stream,* much the same as domestic savings. Any income generated in the productive process can now be spent on domestic goods and services (C) or leaked out of the income stream in one of two forms: domestic savings, or spending on *foreign* goods and services.

The National Income Accounts

It was stated in Chapter 2 that net exports of goods and services (namely, exports minus imports) constitute the link between the national income and the international transactions accounts. Net exports is one of the four expenditure components of GNP: $C + I + G + (X - M)$. For the sake of simplicity, we deal with an economy in which there is only a private sector and no government, so that: GNP $= C + I + (X - M)$. If imports were netted out of consumption and investment, so that C and I refer only to domestically produced consumption and investment goods, they must also be subtracted from $(X - M)$, and the expenditures side of the accounts becomes: GNP $= C + I + X$. Over any given time period, output produced (GNP) equals income (Y) generated in the production process; and that income can be spent on domestic consumption, on imported goods and services, or it can be saved: GNP $= Y = C + S + M$. Consequently

$$C + I + X = C + S + M; \quad \text{or} \quad I + X = S + M \tag{3}$$

An alternative formulation of this identity is:

$$S = I + (X - M) \tag{4}$$

If we think of the external surplus $(X - M)$ as representing accumulation of foreign assets and label it net foreign investments (NFI), then equation (4) is the savings–investment identity, with I extended to include NFI.

These are national income identities, and in a *realized* sense they are true at all times. But an identity does not necessarily reflect what people *planned* to do at the beginning of the period because the four distinct groups of people (investors, exporters, savers, and importers) do not coordinate their plans. When equation (3) holds in a "planned" sense, the economy is at an *equilibrium* level of output. The relationship between plans and their realization is examined next. We start by relating a country's import and export of goods and services to its national income, namely by developing its import and export schedules.

Total Injection and Leakage Functions

☐ **The Import Function** With prices and interest rates assumed to be constant, imports—like savings, vary positively with income: The higher the income, the more goods and services people are able and willing to import. An example of this relationship is shown in the first two columns of Table 5-1. As income rises, so do imports. This relationship is represented graphically in the import-income space (Figure 5-8). The figures were deliberately selected so as to generate a straight line. Points A, B, C, D in Figure 5-8 correspond to the rows in Table 5-1. To each level of output or income measured on the horizontal axis, there corresponds a unique level of imports measured on the vertical axis. Moving up *along* the import function shows that imports increase as income rises.

Figure 5-8
A Hypothetical Import Function Based on Table 5-1

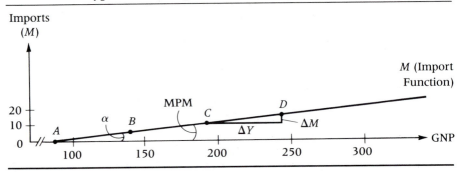

☐ Two concepts are associated with the import function: (1) The *average propensity to import* (APM) is the portion of income spent on imports: APM = *M/Y*. It is computed in column 3 of Table 5-1 and is shown to increase with income for a straight-line import function. (2) The *marginal propensity to import* (MPM) is the portion of an increase (decrease) in income translated into an increase (decrease) in imports: MPM = $\Delta M/\Delta Y$, where Δ (delta) denotes change. Computed in columns 4, 5, 6 of Table 5-1, it is constant (at 0.1) for a straight-line import function.[3] The diagrammatic expression for the MPM is obtained by selecting the change in income between two points, such as *C* and *D*, and relating it to the corresponding change in imports. For a straight-line import function, the ratio $\Delta M/\Delta Y$ *is constant* through the function; *it is equal to the slope of the import function* in Figure 5-8.

☐ In an open economy, income (*Y*) can be spent on consumption of domestic goods (*C*), on imports (*M*), or it can be saved (*S*). Consequently,

$$APC + APS + APM = 1$$

Since any addition to (or deletion from) income can also be channeled in the same three ways,

$$MPC + MPS + MPM = 1$$

☐ While moving along the import schedule shows how a change in income affects imports, there exist other influences on imports. These are represented by a shift in the entire import function. For example, suppose for some reason the price of domestic products becomes *less competitive* with

---

[3]Another frequently used concept is the income elasticity of demand for imports, η_Y. It differs from the MPM in that it represents a ratio of *percentages:*

$$\eta_Y = \frac{\text{percentage change in imports}}{\text{percentage change in income}} = \frac{\Delta M/M}{\Delta Y/Y} = \frac{\Delta M/\Delta Y}{M/Y} = \frac{MPM}{APM}$$

For the U.S. this elasticity is estimated at 1.7.

Table 5-1
A Hypothetical Import Schedule ($ billions)

	GNP (Y) (1)	Imports (M) (2)	AMP (M/Y) (3)	ΔY (4)	ΔM (5)	MPM ($\Delta M/\Delta Y$) (6)
(A)	90	0	0			
(B)	140	5	0.03	50	5	0.1
(C)	190	10	0.05	50	5	0.1
(D)	240	15	0.06	50	5	0.1

imports (that is, it rises relative to foreign prices). Then at each level of income more will be imported than before, and the entire import function will shift upward. On the other hand, if consumer taste shifts away from imports and towards domestic products, then at each level of income less will be imported than before, and the entire import function will shift downward.

☐ **The Export Function**   U.S. exports are rest-of-the-world imports. With constant prices, their size depends on income in the rest of the world (that is, the importing countries); *it does not depend on U.S. income.* The export function plotted in the U.S. export–income space is shown as a straight line (Figure 5-9): Regardless of income, exports are the same, assumed here to be 15. It is important to recognize that the statement "exports are invariant with respect to income" means that income does not affect exports. But the reverse is *not true:* As in the case of investments, a change in exports does affect income and in the same direction.

☐ **The Total "Injection" and Total "Leakage" Functions**   Since exports must come out of domestic production, they constitute an injection into the income stream, along with investments. Imports, on the other hand, constitute a leakage out of the income stream, along with savings. It is now

Figure 5-9
A Hypothetical Export Function

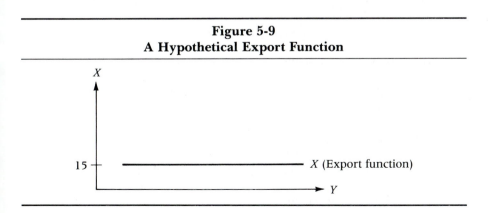

Figure 5-10
Derivation of Total Injection and Total Leakage Functions

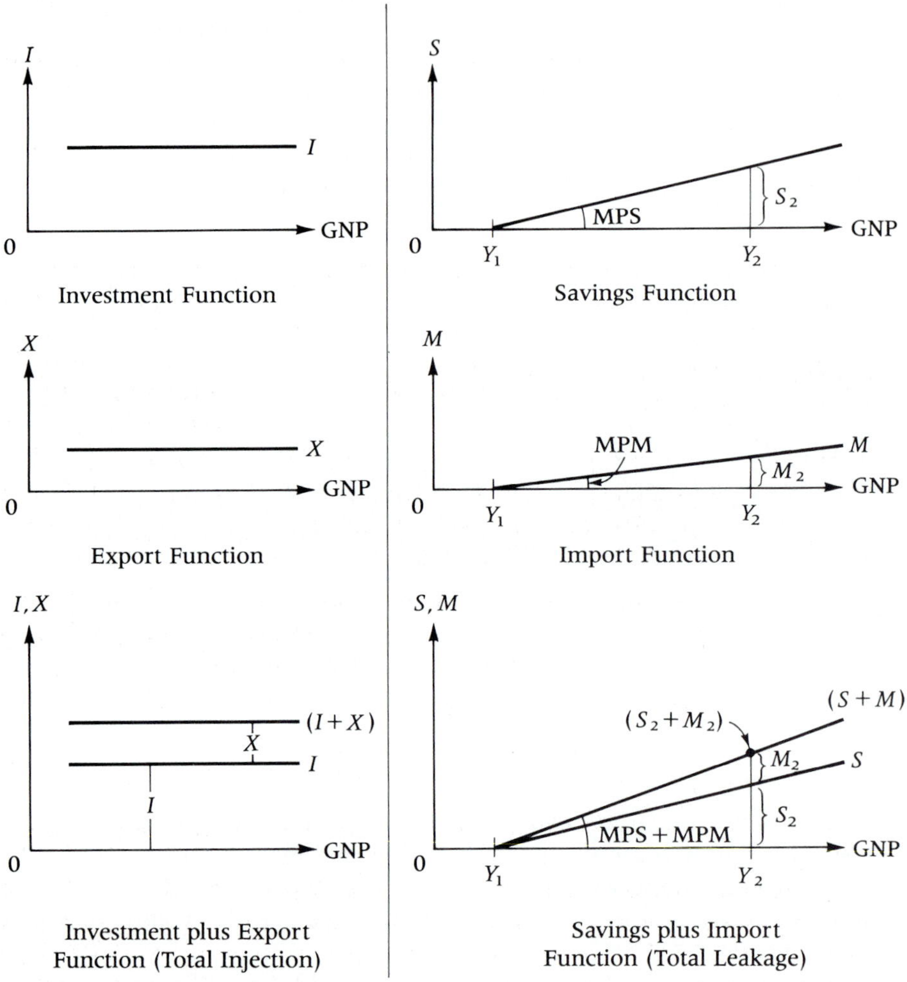

Investment Function

Savings Function

Export Function

Import Function

Investment plus Export
Function (Total Injection)

Savings plus Import
Function (Total Leakage)

NOTE: This analysis is restricted to the private sector. Addition of government would add government expenditures (G) to the injection side and taxes (T) to the leakage side.

possible to combine the two injection functions (investments and exports) on the one hand and the two leakage functions (savings and imports) on the other. This is done in Figure 5-10. The top two left-hand panels show the investment and export functions separately. Then, in the bottom panel, exports are superimposed upon investment to obtain the ($I + X$) or total injection function. It shows the size of investments plus exports at each level of GNP. The straight horizontal line reflects the notion that ($I + X$) is invariant to the country's own GNP: Regardless of the GNP, the ($I + X$) is the same. $(I + X)$ is not influenced by GNP, but the reverse is not the case: GNP is profoundly affected by $(I + X)$.

☐ A similar procedure is followed in the three right-hand panels with respect to the total leakage, or $(S + M)$, function. The two top panels present the savings and imports schedules separately. At each level of income, the functions show, respectively, the amount saved and the amount spent on imports. Two features are introduced for the sake of simplicity (but without loss of generality): The schedules are drawn as straight lines; and the level of GNP (or income) at which savings are zero is the same as that at which imports are zero: $0Y_1$.

☐ In the bottom panel, the import function is superimposed upon the savings function to obtain the total leakage or the $(S + M)$ function. This is done as follows: First, reproduce the savings function. Then at each level of income, add *vertically* the amount of imports (from the middle panel) *above* the amount of savings. Because the functions are linear, only two points are needed to construct the entire line. At income or output $0Y_1$, both savings and imports are zero, so that their sum is zero. At income or output $0Y_2$, savings is segment S_2 and imports is segment M_2. Their sum is $(S_2 + M_2)$, with M_2 superimposed vertically upon S_2. Connecting the two points yields the $(S + M)$ function.

☐ At each level of GNP or income, measured on the horizontal axis, the $(S + M)$ function shows the amount of savings plus imports, measured on the vertical axis. The slopes of the savings and import functions are respectively the MPS and MPM. Consequently, *the slope of the (S + M) function equals the MPS + MPM.*

Output Determination in an Open Economy

☐ *Equilibrium output or income is the level at which aggregate supply (GNP) equals aggregate demand, which now consists of C, I, and X. Alternatively, it is the level of output at which the planned injection into the income stream (I + X) equals the intended leakage out of the income stream (S + M).* The two propositions are equivalent.

☐ We demonstrate the preceding propositions by using hypothetical figures for the economy, and show that from any other position the economy will be propelled toward the level of GNP at which the preceding conditions are fulfilled. Table 5-2 contains hypothetical consumption, savings, imports, investments, and exports schedules for an economy. Here C refers strictly to consumption of *domestically* produced goods, and imports are shown separately under M. The *differences between* the five rows show that as income changes by 50, C changes by 30, S by 15, and M by 5. Therefore, MPC = $\Delta C/\Delta Y$ = 0.6; MPS = $\Delta S/\Delta Y$ = 0.3; MPM = $\Delta M/\Delta Y$ = 0.1. The three marginal propensities add up to 1.

Table 5-2
Hypothetical Y, C, S, M, I, and X for an Economy (billions of dollars per year)

| Possible Levels of GNP or Y | Planned | | | | | Aggregate Demand ($C + I + X$) | Change in Inventories | Change in Output | Relation between Planned S, M, I, X |
	C	S	M	I	X				
(1)	(2)	(3)	(4)	(5)	(6)	(7)	(8)	(9)	(10)
A 90	90	0	0	25	15	130	Depleted	Increase	$(I + X) > (S + M)$ by 40
B 140	120	15	5	25	15	160	Depleted	Increase	$(I + X) > (S + M)$ by 20
C 190	150	30	10	25	15	190	Constant	Equilibrium	$(I + X) = (S + M)$
D 240	180	45	15	25	15	220	Accumulated	Decrease	$(I + X) < (S + M)$ by 20
E 290	210	60	20	25	15	250	Accumulated	Decrease	$(I + X) < (S + M)$ by 40

☐ **Row B**   Firms produce $140 in goods and services during the year and generate an equal amount of income for households. Of that income households spend $120 on consumption of domestically produced goods (*C*), $5 on imported goods (*M*), and they save (*S*) $15. The last two items are withdrawn out of the domestic income stream. Firms, in turn, invest (*I*) $25 and export (*X*) $15. These items constitute injections into the domestic income stream. This information can be summarized in the form of a circular flow diagram (Figure 5-11).

☐ In total, firms produce $140 in goods and services; that amount is the aggregate supply or GNP (top flow). They sell $120 to consumers (bottom flow), $25 to investors, and $15 to exporters for a total of $160. That amount represents aggregate demand. The left side of Scheme A (next page) summarizes this information and shows a $20 excess of aggregate demand over aggregate supply. With prices assumed constant, this excess must be supplied out of inventories. As inventories are depleted, firms step up orders from the factories, and output, income, and employment rise.

☐ How is the relation between aggregate supply and demand reflected in the relation between savings plus imports (leakages) on the one hand and investments plus exports (injections) on the other? Plans for each of the four categories are made independently of each other by different groups of people. Therefore the plans need not be equal. At the beginning of the year, households plan to save $15 and to spend $5 on imported goods— that is, to "leak" $20 out of the income stream. Firms, in turn, plan to invest $25 and export $15 for a total injection of $40. The excess of planned (*I* + *X*) over planned (*S* + *M*) is $20 (last column of Table 5-2)—precisely

---

Figure 5-11
Circular Flow Diagram Describing Row B of Table 5-2

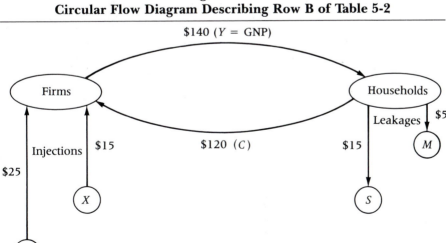

Scheme A   Analysis of Row B in Table 5-2

Aggregate Supply and Demand Approach		Planned $(I + X)$ and $(S + M)$ Approach		
Aggregate Supply (GNP)	$140	$(S + M)$	$(I + X)$	
			Planned	
Aggregate Demand	$160	Savings $15	Investments	$25
$C = \$120$		Imports $ 5	Exports	$15
$I = \$ 25$		$(S + M)$ $20 <	$(I + X)$	$40
$X = \$ 15$			*Realized*	
			Planned $(I + X)$	$40
			Unplanned I	−$20
			(Δ in Inventories)	
Excess of Aggregate Demand over Aggregate Supply	$20	$20 =	Total	$20

the amount by which aggregate demand exceeds aggregate supply. The difference is supplied out of inventories. Since depletion of inventories is counted as negative investment, there is equality between *realized* $(I + X)$ and *realized* $(S + M)$. This is summarized in the right side of Scheme B. It is the depletion of inventories that brings the unequal plans for $(S + M)$ and $(I + X)$ into equality in a realized sense. And this "valve" or regulatory mechanism is what causes firms to step up production, income, and employment.

☐ Clearly the results obtained from the aggregate supply-and-demand approach and from the planned $(S + M)$ and $(I + X)$ approach are identical. Row B, with GNP = $140 is not sustainable, for it leads to unplanned depletion of inventories. It does *not* represent equilibrium output or income. Rather, output and employment expand, say to the level indicated in Row C.

☐ **Row D**   As an opposite case, consider the position of the economy described in row D of Table 5-2. Firms produce $240 of goods and services and generate an equal amount of income for households. Out of that income households spend $180 on consumption of domestically produced goods (C), $15 on imported goods and services (M), and save (S) $45. The last two items constitute leakages out of the domestic income stream. Firms, in turn, invest (I) $25 and export (X) $15, for a total injection of $40 into the income stream. This information is summarized as a circular flow diagram in Figure 5-12.

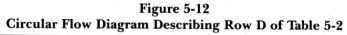

Figure 5-12
Circular Flow Diagram Describing Row D of Table 5-2

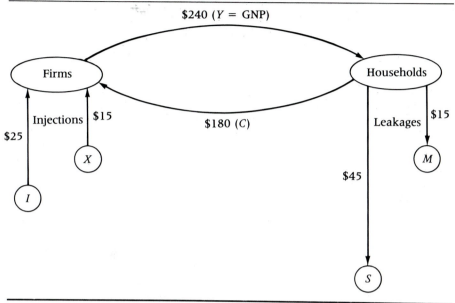

Scheme B   Analysis of Row D in Table 5-2

Aggregate Supply and Demand Approach		Planned $(I + X)$ and $(S + M)$ Approach		
		$(S + M)$	$(I + X)$	
Aggregate Supply (GNP)	$240		*Planned*	
Aggregate Demand	$220	Savings $45	Investments	$25
$C = \$180$		Imports $15	Exports	$15
$I = \$\ 25$		$(S + M)$ $60 >$	$(I + X)$	$40
$X = \$\ 15$				
			Realized	
			Planned $(I + X)$	$40
			Unplanned I	$20
Excess of Aggregate Supply over Aggregate Demand	$20	$60 =$	(Δ in Inventories) Total	$60

☐ Aggregate supply (or GNP) is $240, while aggregate demand is $220, which consists of $180 in consumption, $25 in investments, and $15 in exports. The $20 excess of aggregate supply over aggregate demand represents unsold output, which is added to inventories. This is not a sustainable situation. Firms will not go on producing output which cannot be sold. Instead, they are led to curtail output, lay off workers, and reduce employment (column 9 of Table 5-2).

☐ How is this outcome represented in the $(I + X)$ and $(S + M)$ analysis? At the beginning of the year, households plan to save $45 and to spend $15 on imports. Firms, in turn, plan to invest $25 and to export $15. The excess of planned $(S + M)$ over planned $(I + X)$ is $20—precisely the amount by which aggregate supply exceeds aggregate demand. That difference is made up by unintended accumulation of inventories. Since an addition to inventories is counted as investment, $(I + X)$ equals $(S + M)$ in a *realized* sense. The two approaches are summarized in Scheme B.

☐ While planned $(S + M)$ may diverge from planned $(I + X)$, in a realized sense they are always equal. It is the unintended accumulation of inventories that brings about equality between realized $(S + M)$ and $(I + X)$. But such an accumulation constitutes an inducement for firms to curtail orders from the factories; the factories then reduce output and lay off workers. GNP of $240 is not sustainable. It is not equilibrium output. Consequently, GNP declines.

☐ **Row C: Equilibrium**   Firms produce $190 of goods and services over the year. This aggregate supply equals the income received by households. Out of that income, households spend $150 on purchases of domestically produced goods and services (C), $10 on imports (M), and they save (S) $30. The last two items constitute leakages out of the income stream. In turn firms invest $25 and export $15. This is displayed in the circular flow diagram of Figure 5-13.

☐ Aggregate supply (or GNP) is $190, and aggregate demand is also $190, consisting of $150 in consumption, $25 in investments, and $15 in exports. Precisely the entire output is sold to consumers, investors, and foreigners. There is no depletion or accumulation of inventories, and hence no inducement to change the level of output. Given the C, S, M, I, and X schedules, a GNP of $190 is sustainable—it is equilibrium output. An identical result follows from the second approach. Planned $(I + X)$ equals planned $(S + M)$ at $40. No change in inventories is required to bring the planned magnitudes into equality in a realized sense. There exists no inducement to change the level of output, and hence of employment. This equilibrium position is summarized in Scheme C.

☐ Equilibrium output is the level at which aggregate supply (GNP) equals aggregate demand $(C + I + X)$, or alternatively the level at which intended

Figure 5-13
Circular Flow Diagram Depicting Row C of Table 5-2

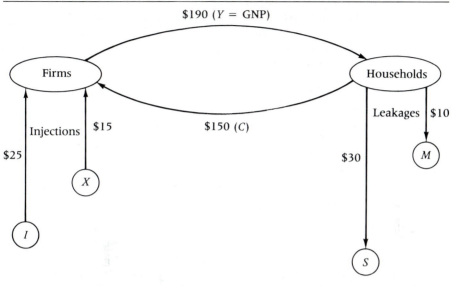

Scheme C   Analysis of Row C in Table 5-2

Aggregate Supply and Demand Approach	Planned $(I + X)$ and $(S + M)$ Approach			
	$(S + M)$		$(I + X)$	
Aggregate Supply (GNP) $190			*Planned*	
Aggregate Demand $190	Savings $30		Investments $25	
$C = \$150$	Imports $10		Exports $15	
$I = \$\ 25$	$(S + M)$ $40		$(I + X)$ $40	
$X = \$\ 15$				
			Realized	
		$40	= Planned $(I + X)$ $40	
Excess of Aggregate Supply over Aggregate Demand 0		(No change in inventories)		

$(I + X)$ equals intended $(S + M)$. The following section offers a diagrammatic presentation of the second approach.

Diagrammatic Presentation of Equilibrium GNP

☐ In portraying equilibrium output diagrammatically, it is necessary to
combine the two bottom panels—the total injection and total leakage functions—of Figure 5-10. This is done in Figure 5-14. Equilibrium output or
income (Y_E) occurs at the intersection of $(S + M)$ and $(I + X)$. At all output
levels higher than (to the right of) Y_E, $(S + M) > (I + X)$, leading to
unintended accumulation of inventories; the economy contracts. At income
levels lower than (to the left of) Y_E, $(I + X) > (S + M)$, leading to unintended depletion of inventories; the economy expands. Given the four
schedules, only Y_E represents equilibrium output or income, a level which
is sustainable.

☐ There is nothing desirable or undesirable about Y_E. It is merely the level
of output that is sustainable. If full employment output exceeds the equilibrium output, the difference between them is a GNP gap of the inadequate
aggregate demand variety and represents unused capacity and unemployment. It is often referred to as "underemployment equilibrium." Conversely, if $Y_E > Y_{FE}$, the difference between them is a GNP gap of the
excessive aggregate demand variety and represents an increase in the average price level.

☐ The equilibrium depicted in Figure 5-14 is characteristic of *a capital-
exporting country;* we saw in Chapter 2 that such a country typically has an

Figure 5-14
Equilibrium Output (Y_E) Occurs Where $(S + M) = (I + X)$

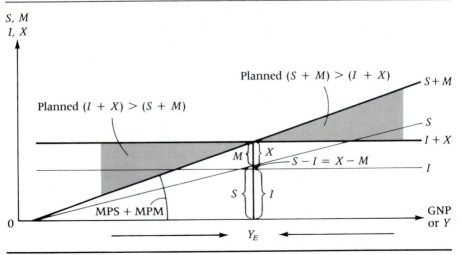

export surplus. It now appears that the export surplus is embedded in the domestic economy; it equals the excess of savings over investments: $S - I = X - M$. Conversely, in a capital-importing country, imports exceed exports by the excess of domestic investments over savings. We might say that the foreign country's savings are channeled into investment projects in the capital-importing country by means of an excess of imports over exports (Figure 5-15). Finally, if $S = I$, then $X = M$, and trade in goods and services is in balance.

☐ During most of the postwar years the United States was a capital exporting country. It had an external current account surplus, and correspondingly, its domestic savings exceeded domestic investment—the condition portrayed in Figure 5-14. Then in the decade 1971–80 national savings equalled domestic investments, and at the same time, the current account balance stood at zero. Finally, in the years 1983–86, with the emergence of sizable trade and current account deficits, the United States became a capital importing country, and domestic investment exceeded domestic savings[1]— the condition portrayed in Figure 5-15. By contrast Japan's large trade surpluses in the 1980s reflect the fact that it is a high-saving economy: Its domestic savings exceed domestic investment, as shown in Figure 5-14. While the Japanese save 17 percent of disposable income, the U.S. saving rate is about 5 percent.

☐ Consider China as another example. For many years its external current account was in balance (or even in surplus) so that its domestic savings and

---

[1] In 1984 private and business savings amounted to 7.4 percent of GNP while government dissaved 3.4 percent for a total domestic savings of 4.1 percent. Domestic investment was 6.6 percent of GNP. Concurrently, the current account deficit stood at 2.8 percent of GNP.

Figure 5-15
A Capital-Importing Country: $I > S$ and $M > X$; $(I - S) = (M - X)$

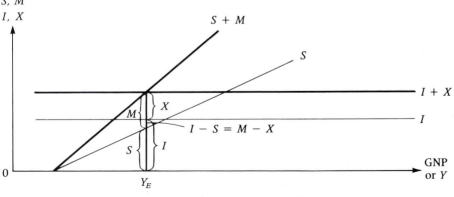

investment were roughly equal. It was developing "by its own bootstraps." But as of the mid-1980s, China began to accelerate its development efforts, relying partly on foreign investments. It moved toward the situation portrayed in Figure 5-15: domestic investment in excess of domestic saving and a corresponding current account deficit.

The Foreign Trade Multiplier

The Multiplier Process

☐ For any given S, I, M, and X schedules, a unique equilibrium out (Y_E) is established. But any of the four functions can shift in its entirety, changing that equilibrium. For analytical purposes, and based on much empirical evidence, the savings and imports functions, and therefore the ($S + M$) function, are considered relatively stable. By contrast, the investments and/ or export schedules are more volatile, subject to frequent gyrations. If either of them shifts, then the ($I + X$) function shifts in the same direction and by the same amount.

☐ A change in exports is subject to the same multiplier process as a change in investments. Starting from a position of underemployment equilibrium, assume that exports rise in response to an increase in foreign demand. In order to increase exports on a permanent basis (that is, an upward shift in the export function), firms must hire factors of production to expand their output. During the first period in which the expansion (ΔX) occurs, income in the economy rises by the amount of the expansion. In the second period, ΔX continues. But in addition, income recipients of the first period spend *part* of that income on additional consumption of domestically produced goods (ΔC), returning that part into the income stream. However, only a portion of the added income is so spent, with the size of the portion determined by the MPC. The remainder is "leaked" out of the income stream. In an "open" economy (without government), the leakage occurs in two forms: Part is "leaked" into savings, its size determined by the MPS, while part is "leaked" into imports, its size determined by the MPM. In an open economy, MPC + MPS + MPM = 1; the three components add up to the incremental income. Note that consumption is now interpreted as consumption of domestically produced goods. Only the part spent on such goods contributes to income of domestic factors of production, which in turn produce a subsequent round of spending. Imports, like savings, constitute a "leakage" out of the spending stream.

☐ In the third period, the original ΔX continues, but income recipients from the "second-round spenders" spend part of their newly earned income on consumption. This amount is returned into the income stream, the size of the portion determined by the MPC. The remainder is "leaked out" in the form of savings and imports, depending respectively on the MPS and MPM. The process continues through successive and ever-decreasing rounds of spending, with two leakages occurring at each round, until the economy gradually achieves a new equilibrium level of output or income.

☐ Once the process is completed, the rise in income is a multiple of the original increase in exports. And the ratio between them ($\Delta Y/\Delta X$) is the multiplier. But because there is an additional leakage (into imports) at each round of spending, the size of the multiplier is smaller than in the case of a "closed" economy. It is called the *foreign trade multiplier.*

☐ A permanent rise in investments also produces a succession of spending rounds with leakages (into savings and imports) at each round of spending. The foreign trade multiplier determines the effect of ΔI on equilibrium output or on the level of economic activity.

☐ This analysis applies equally to a *decrease* in either investments or exports. It would generate a multiple *contraction* in equilibrium output, depending on the size of the foreign trade multiplier.

The Multiplier Formula

☐ To derive the formula for the foreign trade multiplier, we reproduce in Figure 5-16 the $(S + M)$ and $(I + X)$ functions of Figure 5-14. The initial investments and exports are presented as $(I + X)_1$ generating equilibrium output $0Y_1$. Either investments or exports increase so that the $(I + X)$ function rises to level $(I + X)_2$, yielding a new, higher, equilibrium output $0Y_2$. And at that new GNP higher levels of savings and imports are generated to equal the new $(I + X)_2$. Only the initial and final equilibria, and not the spending–income process in between, are shown on the diagram.

Figure 5-16
Effect on GNP of an Increase in $(I + X)$

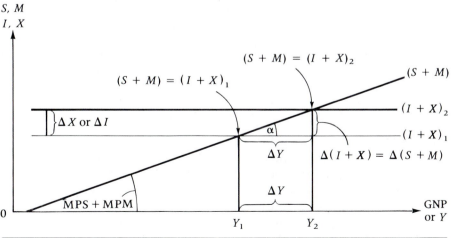

Because at each of the two income levels $(I + X) = (S + M)$, it follows that the changes in the two magnitudes are equal: $\Delta(I + X) = \Delta(S + M)$. This is indicated on the diagram.

☐ Geometrically, the ratio $\Delta(S + M)/\Delta Y$ equals the slope of the $(S + M)$ function, which in turn is the (MPS + MPM). The multiplier is $\Delta Y/\Delta(I + X)$ or the inverse of that ratio. Consequently, the foreign trade multiplier, k, is:

$$k = \Delta Y/\Delta I \quad \text{or} \quad \Delta Y/\Delta X = \frac{1}{\text{MPS} + \text{MPM}} = \frac{1}{\text{leakage}} = \frac{1}{1 - \text{MPC}}$$

Conceptually, the formula for the multiplier is expanded to incorporate the newly added leakage into imports:

$$k = \frac{1}{\text{MPS} + \text{MPM}} \tag{5}$$

☐ To illustrate the use of the formula, assume that the marginal propensities contained in Table 5-2 prevail in the economy; that is, MPC = 0.6 and MPS = 0.3, so that MPM = 0.1, with all three adding up to 1. Then the foreign trade multiplier is:

$$k = \frac{1}{0.3 + 0.1} \quad \text{or} \quad \frac{1}{1 - 0.6} = \frac{1}{0.4} = 2.5$$

A rise (decline) in investments *or* in exports of $10 will increase (lower) output by $(10 \times 2.5 =)$ $25. In turn, consumption, savings, and imports will rise (decline) by:

$$\Delta C = \Delta Y \times \text{MPC} = 25 \times 0.6 = \$15$$
$$\Delta S = \Delta Y \times \text{MPS} = 25 \times 0.3 = \$ \ 7.5$$
$$\Delta M = \Delta Y \times \text{MPM} = 25 \times 0.1 = \underline{\$ \ 2.5}$$
$$\text{and } \Delta C + \Delta S + \Delta M = \$25 = \Delta Y$$
$$\Delta S + \Delta M = \$10 = \Delta I \text{ or } \Delta X \quad \blacksquare$$

Some Conclusions

Exports is a channel of expenditures, much the same as investments or consumption. A rise in exports can come about because of a variety of reasons: The country's prices may become more competitive; foreign taste may shift in favor of the country's products; or foreign countries may lower barriers to their imports, such as their import tariffs. If exports increase, then the nation's output rises by a multiple of that increase, and with it income and employment expand. In other words, one way to move the economy from an underemployment equilibrium toward full employment is to increase exports. Conversely, a contraction in exports—for whatever reason—produces a multiple reduction in GNP and an associated cut in employment.

Imports are a function of income; therefore, as U.S. income rises so do imports of goods and services. A protracted and strong economic expansion will cause imports to increase, and could bring the U.S. external balance (exports minus imports) into deficit, as it did in 1983–86. Conversely, when the U.S. economy plunges into a recession, imports decline on a wide front. Consequently, it should come as no surprise that the U.S. trade balance improves, as it did in the first quarter of 1982. Incidentally, U.S. petroleum imports along with other raw materials used in manufacturing industries are some of the imports that decline during a recession.

However, U.S. imports are other countries' exports. A decline in U.S. imports, occasioned by a recession, necessarily means that the exports of raw materials and manufactured goods of, say, Latin America and Canada, contract. Since these countries depend heavily on the U.S. as a market for their output, the reduction of their exports may be severe. Such a reduction would have a multiple effect on their GNP—reducing output, income, and employment. Thus, a recession in the U.S. can indirectly cause a recession in countries that depend heavily on the U.S. market. Conversely, economic expansion in the U.S. raises American imports, which in turn means that exports of other countries increase, producing a multiple expansion of their output and income. Indeed it was the robust U.S. recovery in 1983–85 that helped generate trade surpluses in many LDCs. There is obviously a link between the economies of various nations.

Thus far we have assumed that the U.S. import function—namely, the relationship between imports and income—is stable. Although this is generally the case, there are exceptions. Many U.S. imports have close domestically produced substitutes. Automobiles are a case in point. Suppose that concern over gasoline supplies causes the buying public to switch from domestic automobiles to small, energy-efficient foreign cars. Imports rise, but not because income has increased. Rather, at every level of income, more is imported and fewer domestic goods are consumed. The entire import function shifts upward, and the consumption function correspondingly shifts downward. The result is a multiple reduction in U.S. GNP and a consequential decrease in income and employment.

Conversely, a change in consumer taste from imported goods to domestic substitutes will increase GNP and, therefore, income and employment.

Finally, it should be noted that the country's external transactions—both imports and exports—are intertwined with the level of domestic economic activity. They are both affected by that level (imports), and in turn they affect GNP through the multiplier process (exports).

Review Questions

1. Assume that the Canadian dollar is pegged to the U.S. dollar. A Canadian news report in 1986 expressed concern over a possible future slow-

down in U.S. economic activity and its impact in the Canadian economy.

a. By what mechanism would such a slowdown affect Canada and how? In your answer incorporate graphs and formulas as necessary.

b. Suppose U.S. imports from Canada decline by 100. Assume that Canada's MPS $= \frac{1}{8}$ and its MPM $= \frac{1}{8}$. By how much precisely would Canada's *income* (GNP), *imports, consumption,* and *savings* be affected (and in which direction)? Show your work, and explain.

c. What would happen to Canada's balance of trade?

2. In a 1985 article, the *Wall Street Journal* suggested that the European recovery rather than being internally generated, was largely induced by the U.S. recovery (the U.S. was the "locomotive").

a. Using graphs and/or formulas as needed, explain how U.S. recovery can stimulate European recovery.

b. What would happen in case of a U.S. economic slowdown?

3. Prove the formula for the foreign trade multiplier.

4. Suppose that in recent years Germany had large trade surpluses and France sustained substantial deficits.

What does that imply for the relationship between domestic savings and investment in each of the two countries? Explain with the help of diagrams.

5. In 1985 the U.S. had a large current account deficit, and Japan—a sizable surplus. Various commentators suggested that some or all of the following steps must take place before these imbalances can be eliminated:

- A rise in the U.S. private savings rate.
- A substantial cut in the $200 billion deficit in the U.S. Federal budget.
- A rise in Japan's private domestic investments.
- A decline in Japan's private saving rate.
- A rise in Japan's government deficit.

Explain how each of the above steps may affect the external imbalances.

6

Balance-of-Payments Adjustment Policies Under Fixed Exchange Rates

Short-Run Imbalances

*W*hat policy options are open to a country with a *fixed exchange rate* that is subject to a deficit in its balance of payments? If the deficit is strictly seasonal or short-run in nature and likely to reverse itself in due course, little action need be taken. As long as there is full confidence in the ability of the government to maintain the exchange rate, private short-term capital can be relied upon to bridge the gap. Suppose that the British pound became weak in the fall, because of a seasonal balance-of-payments deficit, and dropped toward the lower support limit of $2.38.

$$£1 = \$2.40 \begin{cases} \$2.42 \\ \\ \$2.38 \end{cases}$$

Individual financiers would be certain that there was only one way the pound could go: up. After all, it was only temporarily depressed and the lower support limit could not possibly be penetrated. They would act accordingly. Foreigners owning money to Britons could accelerate debt payments to take advantage of the "unusually low" pound price, while Britons having debts denominated in foreign currencies would postpone payments whenever possible, until dollars became somewhat cheaper in terms of pounds.

In general, financiers would be induced to buy and hold pounds, expecting a profit when the "normal" price was restored. They would be certain that they could not lose by such action. Thus, a downward movement in the value of the pound generates inflow of short-term funds, which itself tends to arrest and reverse that movement. Since the expectations of people differ, one might expect the inward flow of these funds to accelerate as the pound moves gradually downward, until at some point the decline in the value of the pound is arrested.

A precisely reverse phenomenon occurs when the pound is seasonally strong and reaches toward the upper support limit. Since everyone knows that it cannot rise in value above $2.42, there is a potential gain and no risk from selling pounds for other currencies, thereby generating an outflow of funds.

These are *stabilizing* short-run capital movements. Caused by public expectations with respect to exchange-rate variations, they offset temporary deficits in the balance of payments and narrow the range of exchange fluctuations to something less than the official spread.

Variations in interest rates also bring about stabilizing capital movements. An external deficit is an excess of autonomous outpayments over inpayments. But this net excess implies that, on balance, Britons are withdrawing sterling deposits from their bank accounts to convert them into foreign currencies in order to make overseas payments. Temporarily, at least, there is a decline in the British domestic money supply and a stiffening of short-run interest rates. As interest rates rise, foreign capital is attracted to Great Britain to take advantage of higher earning opportunities. Conversely, an external surplus means an excess of inpayments over outpayments and a rise in the money supply. Interest rates are nudged downward, and short-term capital tends to leave the country.

On both counts, therefore, private short-term funds bridge temporary imbalances and stabilize the exchange rate. But it is worth repeating that all this is contingent upon confidence in the long-run value of the currency. If the government's ability to maintain the exchange rate is suspect when the pound hovers around its lower support limit, precisely the opposite movement can occur. Fearing devaluation, say to £1 = $2, the possible small gain of two or three cents from an appreciation within the official spread no longer looms important. The same may be said about small interest gains. Instead, the feared loss from a sizable devaluation may drive people away from the pound to strong currencies, as they were driven away from the French franc in the spring of 1982, and from the Mexican peso in the 1980s. Conversely, if revaluation is expected when the currency is at its upper support limit, short-term funds tend to flow inward instead of outward. These capital movements are *destabilizing* in nature and usually occur when confidence in the currency is shattered. Whether speculation is stabilizing or destabilizing depends on people's expectations with respect to future movements of the currency, which in turn depend on their confidence in the economy.

Returning to the stable case, the inflow of private capital can be reinforced by official action. The government may raise interest rates or manipulate the forward exchange market to attract short-term funds from abroad, or it can fall back on its accumulated reserves. If necessary, recourse might be sought in borrowing from other countries or from international organizations such as the International Monetary Fund. However, should the deficit last for several years and prove fundamental in nature, a deliberate course of action would have to be pursued. Even so, the more international reserves the country has, the less the pressure is on it to act. But as in the case of a family, reserves can only buy time; if they dwindle, an adjustment mechanism must be set in process to eliminate the deficit.

The first option open to the country is the classical prescription of inducing domestic contraction by monetary and fiscal means. Indeed, some contraction in the level of economic activity (in employment, production, and income) will occur automatically in the deficit country, because external trade and domestic economic activity are intricately interrelated. Specifically, the contractionary effect will operate through both the expenditures and monetary mechanisms, leading to a curtailment in imports and perhaps an expansion of exports, thereby reducing the deficit. Since the purpose of government adjustment policy is to reinforce these tendencies, a detailed explanation of the processes involved will help clarify the mechanism through which government domestic policies affect the balance of payments.

"Automatic" Processes

Direct Effect on Private Expenditures

Income Changes   Consider the case in which a deficit appears in a country's balance of payments, and assume that the deficit is brought about by a reduction in exports as foreign buyers shift to alternative sources of supply. The immediate consequence on the home front is a decline in production, employment, and income in the export industries. But that decline tends to spread throughout the economy in a multiple fashion. Workers and officials in the export industries, who suffer the original impact, have less money to spend on consumption of goods and services produced by other industries. To be sure, they are unlikely to reduce consumption by the full amount of the decline in their purchasing power, since it is just for such a circumstance that they have accumulated savings. But some reduction would undoubtedly occur. In turn, as income and employment decline in the "second round" of industries, their wage-earners spend less elsewhere. And so the process spreads throughout the economy in a wavelike fashion, with its force declining as it becomes further removed from the primary impact areas. At every stage at which the decline occurs, income recipients lower their consumption by something less than the cut in purchasing power, simply because it is human nature to cushion the impact of income reduction on the standard of living by drawing on one's savings. The extent of the total effect is positively related to two factors: the size of the original income reduction in the export industries and the proportion of any income reduction that is translated into reduced spending by the citizens (the *marginal propensity to consume*) at each "round." This multiplier process obviously takes time to work its way through the economy.

When the deficit is caused by an increase in imports (rather than a reduction in exports) the process is somewhat analogous. There is a direct effect on income and employment in the domestic import-competing industries only to the extent that the new imports displace the consumption of domestically produced goods (imports that are not financed out of a reduction in the rate of consumer saving). Production of such commodities declines, and the attendant reduction in income and employment spreads throughout the economy in the manner just described.

It is an integral part of economic analysis that imports vary positively and closely with variations in income. In other words, income is an important determinant of imports (though not the only one). Thus the decline in income induces a reduction in imports. It also brings about a cut in the consumption of domestically produced goods, thereby leaving more of them available for exports and exercising greater pressure on producers to market abroad. The upshot of this income–expenditures mechanism is that part of the original decline in exports is offset by an induced reduction in imports and an increase in exports. These automatic tendencies narrow the balance-of-payments deficit by, say, as much as one-fourth (to 75 percent of its original size). They certainly are unlikely to close it altogether. Also, it takes time before their full impact is felt.

Precisely the reverse process takes place in the surplus country, which experiences an increase in world demand for its exports. The primary impact occurs in the export industries, where employment and income expand to satisfy the increasing world demand. Income recipients save part of their additional earnings but spend a large share of them, which leads to an expansion of output and income in the industries producing the goods that they purchase. In turn, part of the incremental income is translated into purchases elsewhere, channeling purchasing power into a "third round" of industries. And so the process spreads in a declining sequence throughout the economy, where at each round, part of the added income is withdrawn from the spending stream. It is useful to liken this sequence to the effect of a stone dropped into a pond of water; the initial splash in the area of impact is followed by a series of waves, which spread in concentric circles throughout the pond in ever-declining intensity. This is how the expansion of income spreads throughout the economy. The total effect on income is likely to be much greater than the primary impact; the ratio between total effect and primary impact is known as the *multiplier*. Its magnitude varies inversely with the proportion of the added income withdrawn (or leaked) from the income stream at each stage.

If the surplus is brought about by a reduction in imports, then the primary impact area consists of the industries producing domestic substitutes (to the extent that domestically produced goods, rather than savings, take the place of imports). From there, successive rounds of consumer spending carry the expansion into other sectors of the economy. If the surplus is brought about by the investment of foreign capital in new plants and equipment, the expansionary effect is virtually the same as when exports rise.

The income increase produced through the expenditure mechanism raises imports; it also brings about an increase in the consumption of domestically produced goods, thereby leaving fewer goods available for export and reducing the pressure on producers to export. On both counts— the induced rise in imports and the decline in exports—the initial surplus would be reduced, again exhibiting an automatic tendency toward partial adjustment of the balance of payments.

To sum up, a disequilibrium in the balance of payments contains the seeds of its own partial reversal. A newly developed surplus increases income by a multiple of that surplus, and the rise in income brings about an increase in imports (and a cut in exports) that partly offsets the original surplus. Conversely, a newly developed deficit results in a multiple income reduction, which in turn lowers imports (and expands exports) and offsets part of the deficit.

☐ In the years since World War II, economists have developed a body of analysis based on the ideas of John Maynard Keynes that provides a more rigorous formulation of the relationships outlined above. This is useful for two reasons: It sharpens our understanding of the processes involved, and it makes possible, at a subsequent stage, the measurement of the magnitude of each effect. In what follows we employ the tools of income determination and the foreign trade multiplier, developed in Chapter 5, to the problem at hand.

☐ **Implications of the Multiplier Formula**   Let us assume that the economy we are considering has an MPS of 0.3 and an MPM of 0.1. Its foreign trade multiplier will be (see Chapter 5):

$$k = \frac{1}{0.3 + 0.1} = 2.5$$

This means that any exogenous change[1] in spending, be it investment or exports, will change the income of the community in the same direction, by 2.5 times the original change. In turn, the variation in income induces

[1] By an *exogenous change* we mean a change that is not itself a result of a change in the country's own income. It includes a shift in the entire consumption function (as opposed to movement along the function) and the changes in investments or government expenditures. Government spending (usually labeled G) is excluded from the discussion in the text but could be incorporated without undue difficulty.

a change in imports of $\Delta M = \Delta Y \times$ MPM. Thus, any rise or fall in domestic expenditures must produce changes in the balance of payments. In other words, the country's internal and external positions are interrelated by the income (and other) mechanism, and at no time can they be regarded as separate.

☐ There is a difference between the effect on the balance of payments of an exogenous change in domestic spending such as investment or government expenditures on the one hand, and the effect of a change in exports, on the other. A $100 rise in domestic expenditures will raise income by 100*k* = $250 once the multiplier process has worked itself out. This will increase imports by $250 × MPM = $25, causing a balance-of-payments deficit of like magnitude. This is an important reminder that any domestic expenditures program, governmental or private, not only raises income but also results in an external payments deficit. Thus, the large U.S. trade deficits in 1983–85 were due in part (but only in part) to the rapid recovery of the American economy relative to that of its trading partners.

☐ By contrast, if the exogenous increase in expenditures is in the export sector (foreigners demanding more of the country's products), then the immediate result is a balance-of-payments surplus of $100. The rise in domestic income of $250 follows as before, but the $25 induced increase in imports will not cause a $25 deficit. Instead it partly offsets the original surplus, lowering it to $75. Since our main interest is the second case, we shall pursue it step by step.

☐ A $100 increase in exports (*X*), everything else remaining the same, produces immediately a surplus of $100 in the balance of payments. Next there is a gradual effect on domestic income through the multiplier mechanism: $\Delta Y = \Delta X \times k$. With an MPM of 0.1 and an MPS of 0.3 as before, this becomes: $100 × 2.5 = 250$. (It takes a long time to approach the new equilibrium.) Given the rise in income (which may be further magnified by the acceleration principle), there will be an induced increase in imports of:[2] $\Delta M = \Delta Y \times$ MPM $= \$250 \times 0.1 = \$25$. The original balance-of-payments surplus, $\Delta X = \$100$, is now partially offset by $\Delta M = \$25$, the difference being $\Delta X - \Delta M = \$75$. In other words, the increase in imports induced through the domestic expenditures–income mechanism will reduce the balance-of-payments surplus from $100 to $75. This is a movement in the "right" direction but it is not sufficient to restore balance-of-payments equilibrium.

---

[2]Other induced effects of the increase in income will be on savings (*S*) and domestic consumption (*C*): $\Delta S = \Delta Y \times$ MPS $= \$250 \times 0.3 = \$75$. And since MPC + MPS + MPM = 1, $\Delta C = \Delta Y \times$ MPC $= \$250 \times 0.6 = \$150$. Thus, the increase in imports, savings, and consumption adds up to the rise in income of $250.

☐ The above equations can be combined to describe fully the effects of income on imports:

$$\Delta M = \Delta Y \times \text{MPM} = \Delta X \times k \times \text{MPM} = \Delta X \times \frac{1}{\text{MPS} + \text{MPM}} \times \text{MPM} \qquad (1)$$

In our example this becomes: $\Delta M = \$100 \times \dfrac{1}{0.3 + 0.1} \times 0.1 = \$25.$

The induced effects of a $100 increase in exports with MPM = 0.1, but with alternative values of the MPS, are tabulated below, and all are calculated in the same way as the figure of $25 we have just obtained.[3] (The reader can experiment with other numerical examples by selecting alternative marginal propensities.)

ΔX	MPM	MPS	k	ΔY	ΔM	ΔS	ΔC
$100	0.1	0.4	2.0	$ 200	$ 20	$80	$100
$100	0.1	0.3	2.5	$ 250	$ 25	$75	$150
$100	0.1	0.1	5.0	$ 500	$ 50	$50	$400
$100	0.1	0.0	10.0	$1,000	$100	$ 0	$900

As we lower the MPS, the induced increase in imports (ΔM) rises. But only at zero MPS does it completely offset the $100 original increase in exogenous exports. This is a general result, for when MPS = 0,

$$\Delta M = \Delta Y \times \text{MPM} = \Delta X \times \frac{1}{0 + \text{MPM}} \times \text{MPM} = \Delta X \qquad (2)$$

That is, ΔM = ΔX. In other words, if MPS is zero, the induced change in imports equals the original change in exports. In all other cases the induced movement will stop short of restoring balance.

☐ If the first change is a $100 *reduction* of exports, where a *deficit* of $100 is created, then income would *decline* by: $100 × 2.5 = $250 and imports by $25. Again there is an automatic income mechanism that pulls the balance of payments toward equilibrium. But the induced change in imports is less than the original change in exports, leaving some imbalance in the external accounts.[4] Apart from the extreme case of zero MPS the income

---

[3] MPC = 1 − MPS − MPM.

[4] The cause of the deficit can also be a $100 exogenous increase in imports (an upward movement of the entire import function). To the extent that these imports substitute for the consumption of domestically produced goods, there will be a primary reduction in domestic expenditures. This reduction will be short of the rise in imports to the extent that they are financed out of savings rather than substituted for domestic consumption. In terms of the example in the text, the primary impact could be, say, $80 instead of $100. It would cause a decline in income of $80 × 2.5 = $200 and an induced reduction in imports of MPM × $200 = $20. This would partly offset the original increase in imports.

mechanism induced by changes in expenditures constitutes only a partial correction to the imbalance. Additional, though probably still insufficient, automatic help may come from other areas to be explored next.   ∎

Price Changes   In today's industrial economies, variations in the level of economic activity are usually accompanied by price movements. Thus, in the deficit country, the reduction in the level of income and employment has the side effect of curtailing the rate of price increases. When jobs are scarcer, unions tend to be more restrained in their wage demands, thereby holding production costs down; and as sales decline, producers are more likely to "hold the line on prices." It is true that since World War II, industrial wages and prices have become rather rigid or sticky in a downward direction, considerably weakening the effectiveness of the price-adjustment mechanism under fixed exchange rates. But since our main concern is with the country's position *relative* to other countries, even a decline in the rate of price increases helps make the country more competitive, assuming that no such reduction occurs in other countries. This decline encourages exports and discourages imports, thereby contributing to automatic adjustment. The strength of this effect depends on the degree to which trade flows respond to variations in relative prices (namely, price elasticities).

Precisely the reverse happens in a surplus country, where the expansion of income and output is likely to be accompanied by an acceleration of domestic price increases. And this has the salutary effect of reducing the original surplus. In sum, these price changes reinforce the income mechanism by partially offsetting the payment imbalances caused by autonomous factors.

The Monetary Mechanism

The level of economic activity will be affected, in the directions described in the previous section, not only through the expenditure mechanism but through a set of monetary factors. Money affects the level of real production and employment through its availability and cost (the rate of interest) to producers and consumers alike. Indeed, the direct real impact of an external deficit or surplus on the economy, discussed in the previous section, is generally confined to cases where the imbalance originates in the current account sector or when direct foreign investments—in the physical sense of plants and equipment—are involved. By contrast, regardless of its source, whether it is the current account or the capital account, an external imbalance affects the economy indirectly through the monetary route in a manner that tends to reduce or even remove the imbalance.

A surplus or deficit in the balance of payments, whatever its source, means that autonomous outpayments do not equal inpayments. Inpayments are received in foreign currencies either in return for exports or in the form of capital inflow. Their local recipients exchange them for domestic currency, which in turn is deposited in local banks, mainly in checking accounts, thereby creating new demand deposits. In a modern economy these deposits (that is, checking accounts) constitute the bulk of the money supply. And in a banking system that operates on the fractional reserves principle, new deposits serve as a basis for a multiple expansion of the money supply. Thus, unless *offset* (or "sterilized") by deliberate action of the central bank, a net inflow of foreign exchange (currencies) results in a multiple expansion of the domestic money supply. The reverse process takes place as a result of outpayments. The buyer of foreign goods and services or the exporter of capital acquires the foreign currency necessary to make payment in exchange for his domestic currency. And the latter is usually drawn out of his demand deposit, thereby causing a multiple contraction in the money supply.

In case of a surplus, inpayments exceed outpayments resulting in a new inflow of funds, and in increase in money supply. For example, suppose Germany has an external surplus of 100 million marks. German bank deposits rise by the same amount. If the required reserve ratio of the banks is 20 percent (or one fifth), excess reserves of 80 million D.M. are created. The money multiplier, being the inverse of the required reserve ratio, is 5. Thus the banks are able to expand money supply by $(80 \times 5 =)$ 400 million D.M. The converse happens in a deficit country: outpayments exceed inpayments, and the net outflow of funds reduces bank deposits and causes a multiple contraction of money supply.

Consider the case of a deficit country whose money supply shrinks. Much spending in the economy, and therefore output employment and income, depends on the availability of bank loans. As money becomes "tight," or less readily available, it is reasonable to expect certain marginal business-investment projects and consumer purchase plans to go unrealized. Also because the rate of interest is determined by the demand and supply of credit, the effect of monetary stringency is to raise interest rates on the money markets, thereby adding to the cost of investment, home construction, and other economic activities that depend on borrowed funds. The resulting curtailment of such activity reduces employment and income in the community, and any such reduction spreads through the economy through the multiplier mechanism. Finally, the tighter money supply curtails the rate of price increases. Both the *income* and *price* changes have the effect of reducing imports and encouraging exports, thereby partly offsetting the balance-of-payments deficit.

In the case of the surplus country, money supply expands. This eases the supply of bank credit and lowers interest rates—both factors contributing to increased income and employment and to a higher rate of price increases. In turn, these increases curtail the original surplus.[5]

---

[5] Note however that this effect may be mitigated by international capital flows. When capital is free to move internationally, it is attracted to deficit countries (where interest rises) and it leaves surplus countries (where interest declines). And these capital movements moderate considerably the changes in interest rates.

□ **The Specie-Flow Mechanism**   In the preceding paragraphs, the equilibrating effect of changes in the money supply was said to operate through the domestic income and price channels. Classical economic doctrine—the body of economic doctrine in vogue before the appearance in 1936 of John Maynard Keynes' *General Theory of Employment, Interest, and Money*—placed primary emphasis on the money supply–price approach. Indeed, this was an integral part of the way the classical economists viewed the aggregate level of economic activity.

□ One convenient way of looking at the economy is through the so-called equation of exchange:

$$MV = PO$$

M is the quantity of money in circulation, consisting of bank notes, coins, and demand deposits, and *V* is the income velocity of circulation, the number of times per year the average dollar changes hands to finance transactions in *final* goods and services (excluding goods in intermediate stages of production). Therefore, *MV* equals the aggregate annual monetary expenditures designed to finance all transactions in final goods and services.

□ *P* is the aggregate price level (index), and *O* is the real volume of final goods and services produced during the year. Thus, *PO* is the money value of goods and services produced during the year, or the gross national product (GNP).

□ This equation is in fact a truism. It is true by definition, for it states that the number of dollars spent on purchases of all goods and services equals their money value (GNP). The classical economists, however, proceeded a step further and made two important assumptions (that may or may not be true): First, that the velocity of circulation (*V*) is constant, for it depends on the payment habits of the community, which rarely change. And second, that the volume of final output is fixed in the short run at the full-employment level.[6] With *V* and *O* constant, any changes in *M* must produce proportional variations in *P*.

□ All this is immediately applicable to the balance-of-payments adjustment mechanism. Under the gold standard, a deficit country lost gold. And since the domestic money supply was based on fractional reserve requirements held in gold, the country experienced a multiple contraction in its money supply and a consequent reduction in prices. This improved the country's competitive standing by encouraging exports and discouraging imports, and thereby partly redressed the deficit. Precisely the reverse happened in a surplus country, where the expansion of the money supply raised prices,

---

[6]Strictly speaking, the full-employment condition is not an assumption but a result of other postulates in the classical model: Complete price and wage flexibility, and savings as well as investment, are considered a function of the rate of interest.

thereby impairing the country's competitive position and reducing the surplus. Under the *rules of the game* of the gold standard, central banks were supposed to *reinforce* these automatic tendencies by contracting money supply (by selling government bonds) in case of a deficit and by expanding money supply (by purchasing government bonds) in case of a surplus. This process came to be called the *specie-flow mechanism*. In short, the classical specie-flow mechanism focused on variations in relative prices (variations in the price ratio between two countries), which under a system of fixed exchange rates must be brought about through domestic price changes.

☐ These ideas were first challenged after World War I in connection with the transfer of reparations. Germany at the time needed to generate an export surplus to be able to effect the payment of huge reparations imposed by the victorious powers. In the ensuing debate on how this could be accomplished, Keynes took a classical position: the money-supply–price-change mechanism would bring about the necessary adjustment. On the other hand, the Swedish economist Bertil Ohlin took what fifteen years later would become a Keynesian position. He emphasized the transfer of purchasing power (income) from Germany to the United Kingdom as the main regulatory device but, lacking the post-Keynesian analytical tools, his exposition was not fully convincing.

☐ In a totally different context, a number of empirical studies convinced economists that as often as not the adjustment mechanism worked too fast and too smoothly to be satisfactorily explained by the money supply–price forces. In short, when the "Keynesian revolution" came in 1936, economists were receptive and ready to apply the new ideas to the international trade field. These adaptations came after World War II.

☐ In particular, some of the classical assumptions were questioned. It was asked: Can it be assumed that gold gains and losses produce multiple changes in the money supply? The central bank can easily *neutralize* their effect by what are called *offsetting policies*. Instead of reinforcing any loss (gain) of gold by contractionary (expansionary) monetary policy, as was required under the *rules of the game* of the gold standard, the central banks could and often did precisely the reverse. In such cases, gains and losses of gold reserves would not produce the expected changes in the money supply.

☐ Another classical assumption that came under scrutiny was the constancy of V. Keynes held that money is used either for transactions or for speculative purposes. In the transactions sphere, velocity does indeed depend on the payment habits of the community and is therefore roughly constant. But speculative funds are kept idle by those who expect to benefit from an increase in the value of money in terms of other financial assets (that is, by those who expect the prices of these assets to decline). The amount so held depends on the cost of idle funds in terms of forgone earning opportunities elsewhere. This cost can be measured by the rate of interest; the higher the interest rate, the more costly it is to maintain idle speculative balances. The velocity of these balances is zero, for they do not circulate. Total velocity is a weighted average of the zero and constant velocities in the two sectors, and thus it changes as funds are switched between speculative and transactional balances. Since the rate of interest determines the division of balances between the two sectors, it also affects the velocity of circulation. Thus, changes in the money supply (M) may affect the interest rate and produce offsetting variations in V. Indeed, when M rises (declines) there is a tendency for the interest rate to decline (rise), thereby increasing (decreasing) speculative balances and lowering (raising) V. Variations in V have an inherent tendency to offset variations in M, so that spending (MV) and, therefore, PO need not be affected at all.

☐ Keynes challenged the idea that physical output is constant at the full-employment level, by questioning the constructs of the classical model that lead to this result.[7] Instead, he advanced the proposition that in industrial economies wages and prices are rigid in a downward direction. Thus, even if MV did vary, the impact might be on physical output (O) rather than on prices (P).

☐ Finally, it was said, even if prices do move in the desired direction, this is not a guarantee of success. A decline in the relative prices of the deficit country means that it will sell more goods abroad. But since each unit of the commodity sold now brings a lower price, there is no assurance that total inpayments (price times quantity) will rise. That depends on whether the increase in the quantity sold is proportionally larger than the decline in price—whether the increase is large enough to offset the fact that now every unit sells for less. This would be the case only if the demand for the country's exports is responsive to price change.[8]

☐ We sum up the challenge to the specie-flow mechanism is terms of the equation of exchange $MV = PO$ as follows: (a) M may not vary in the expected direction; (b) even if it did, its variations may be partly offset by changes in V; (c) changes in MV may affect O as well as P; and (d) even if

---

[7] In particular, he made savings a function of income rather than of the rate of interest, introduced rigidity into money wages in a downward direction, and added a "liquidity trap" that set a lower limit to the rate of interest.

[8] Economists measure the degree of response in terms of *price elasticity* (η_p), which is defined as the ratio

$$\eta_p = \frac{\text{percentage change in the quantity purchased}}{\text{percentage change in price}} = \frac{\Delta Q/Q}{\Delta P/P} = \frac{\Delta Q}{\Delta P} \times \frac{P}{Q}$$

It is negative because price and quantity move in opposite directions. However, it is common practice to ignore the negative sign and discuss elasticity in terms of its absolute value. Thus, the necessary condition of response described in the text is such that $\eta_p > 1$, and is known as *relatively elastic demand*. Chapter 7 offers a more extensive discussion of this concept.

P varied as predicted, the expected change in the trade flows may not materialize.

☐ Not only did these criticisms run deep, but economists had an alternative explanation of the adjustment mechanism. It was rooted in the Keynesian ideas that became widely accepted after World War II. Instead of the money supply–price approach, the focus was shifted to the expenditures–income approach, utilizing the marginal propensities and the multiplier as analytical tools. The role of the money supply in affecting domestic income and prices, and therefore imports, was downgraded.

☐ Today economists are no longer so sure. One school of thought maintains that velocity is a more stable and predictable relationship than the multiplier and that the money supply affects economic activity more than expenditures. Indeed, there is a debate going on among economists concerning the relative effectiveness of aggregate expenditures and the money supply in influencing the course of the economy. Consequently, it is necessary to take a balanced view of the adjustment mechanism, and to incorporate both the money and expenditure approaches as they affect income as well as prices. ∎

Summary of the "Automatic" Balance-of-Payments Adjustment

The automatic adjustment mechanism under fixed exchange rates is a function of aggregate expenditures and the money supply, both operating in the *same direction* and both affecting the economy through the income and price mechanisms. The four linkages involved may be diagrammed as:

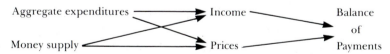

A deficit in the balance of payments automatically brings about a slowdown in the country's economic activity and a slowdown of the rate of price increases through both monetary and nonmonetary (sometimes referred to as "real") factors, while a surplus increases economic activity and accelerates the rate of price increases.

The economic slowdown resulting from a deficit contains the seeds of a mechanism that reverses the deficit in part, for it is primarily the income of the community that determines imports. A reduction in national income means that consumption of goods and services is curtailed, including the consumption of imported goods. Likewise, there is a decline in the importation of materials used in the production process. The proportion of change in national income translated into a change in imports is known as the *marginal propensity to import* (MPM). The higher the MPM, the larger the effect on imports of a given reduction in national income. Furthermore, the reduction in the level of aggregate demand in the country means that a larger portion of its productive capacity is freed to produce for export markets. The lower the level of demand is at home, the greater the pressure will be on producers to market their products overseas, for when home demand is high producers have little incentive to seek overseas markets.

Complementing the increased availability of productive resources, and continuously interacting with it, is the improved competitive position of the country on both its own and world markets. For it is the relative behavior of prices at home and abroad that determines a country's competitive standing, and the deficit country normally experiences a slowdown in the rate of price inflation. The extent to which the improved competitive position lowers imports and raises exports depends on the degree of community response to price change (or what economists call *price elasticity*). The greater the response is, the greater will be the improvement in the balance of payments that can be expected from a given reduction in relative prices. In sum, the income–price mechanism set in motion by the deficit tends to reduce the deficit.

Accompanying the expenditure mechanism is the money supply mechanism. Unless the monetary authorities act to offset or "sterilize" it, the money supply of the deficit country is reduced. That causes a decline in the rate of inflation as well as a reduction in the level of income or at least in its rate of growth. On both counts, imports decline and exports rise, thereby reversing the external deficit at least in part.

By the same token, it has been shown that surplus countries experience expansion in income and money supply and deterioration in competitive standing caused by the acceleration of price increases. Both lead to higher imports and lower exports. Thus, a surplus as well as a deficit contains in it the seeds of its own reversal. Furthermore, if the surplus and deficit countries are important trading partners, the changes occurring in them reinforce each other. Figure 6-1 presents a schematic illustration of the processes just described. In sum, *under a fixed exchange-rate regime, income and price influence the balance of payments in the same (corrective) direction.*

Government Policy

The automatic income and price mechanisms interact and reinforce each other in the direction of restoring balance. Since they may be insufficient in magnitude and slow to take effect, however, they need to be further reinforced by government policy. But in a free, private-enterprise economy, the government does not have direct control over international transactions. It can influence them only indirectly. Because income and prices (and perhaps the rate of interest) are the crucial determinants of inpayments

Figure 6-1
Automatic Processes that Reverse External Imbalance

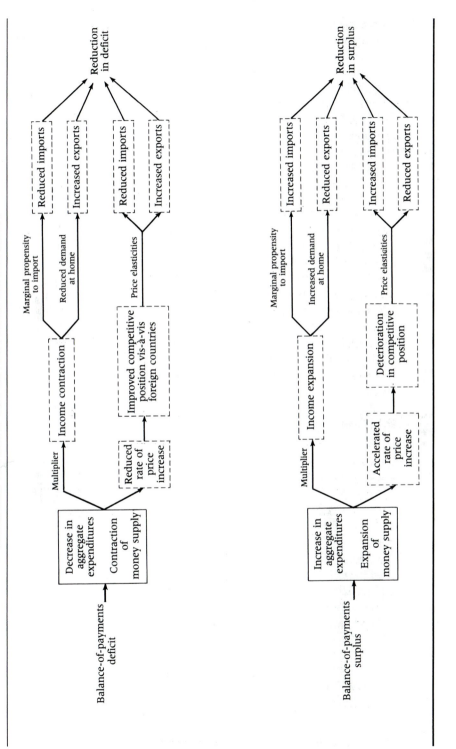

and outpayments, the government must use measures that affect income and prices and, through them, influence the balance of payments. Thus, two links must be crossed: Government policy → Income, prices → Balance of payments.

Domestic Measures and the Balance on Goods and Services

Two sets of policy instruments are available to the government to affect the level of economic activity (that is, income and prices) and through it the balance of payments. They are monetary policies, influencing the economy through control of the supply of money, and fiscal policies, influencing the economy through changes in government revenues and expenditures. Consider first the case of a deficit in the balance of payments. On the monetary side, the central bank can raise the rate of interest, thereby making borrowing more costly;[9] it can increase reserve requirements of the commercial banks, making less money available for loans; and it can sell government bonds to the public and the banks (known as open-market operations), thereby withdrawing money from the economy. These measures restrict public access to funds for spending purposes and render such funds more expensive. As spending for goods and services declines, so do production and income. And the decline spreads through the economy in a magnified fashion through the multiplier process. At the same time contractionary monetary policy reduces the rate of inflation and changes in both price and income serve to reduce the deficit on goods and services.

On the fiscal side, the treasury can raise taxes or lower government expenditures, or both, thereby withdrawing purchasing power from the public and bringing about a direct slowdown in economic activity, which spreads through the economy through the multiplier process. The decline in income is accompanied by a slowdown in the rate of price increases, and both factors work toward elimination of the deficit in the manner described in the previous sections.

This analysis explains the *conditionality* policy of the IMF. When countries experiencing external deficits wish to draw on the resources of the IMF, the Fund often insists on the adoption of contractionary monetary and/or fiscal policies (as well as other measures) by the borrowing country. This is done to insure restoration of balance-of-payments equilibrium, so that the loan can be repaid. The requirement, known as "conditionality," ... "reflects the principle that balance-of-payments financing and adjustment must go hand in hand." (IMF *Survey*, September 1985, p. 1).

Precisely the opposite policies are called for in the case of a surplus. Expansion of the money supply and an increase in the budgetary deficit inflate the economy, with both the income and price effects leading to the

---

[9] In an open economy with international capital movements, the monetary authorities may not have full control over the rate of interest.

removal of the surplus. Indeed, in 1986, the Japanese government undertook to stimulate the domestic economy in an effort to reduce its external surpluses. But Germany refused to do likewise for fear of kindling inflation.

Effect on Direct Investment Capital

There is a possibility that the equilibrating mechanism brought about by government policy may be partly offset by international movement of direct investments. Often such capital responds to relative profit opportunities at home and abroad, being attracted to high-profit locations.

The expected level of profit on investments is related positively to the level of income and employment. When a surplus country experiences automatic expansion reinforced by government policy, the effect on the balance of trade is to reduce the surplus. But the expansion also attracts foreign investments, an inpayment item that increases the surplus. The converse is true of the deficit country, where domestic contraction reduces the deficit but may also encourage outflow of long-term capital (or discourage inflow), thereby aggravating the deficit. Although the strength of these influences is not known, they offset part of the equilibrating effect of domestic policies.

Effect on Other Capital Movements

Apart from direct investment people also invest in *foreign* bonds, stock, commercial paper, bank accounts, and the like. Such funds are referred to as *portfolio capital*. A large share of it, especially the short-run variety, is sensitive to interest differentials between financial centers. If interest rates in London exceed those in New York by more than the discount on forward pounds (that is, if a covered interest differential exists), then it pays to transfer funds to London. Consequently, the British government can deal with a temporary balance-of-payments deficit by raising the rate of interest and attracting short-term capital.[10] How helpful this might be, even in the short run, depends on the sensitivity of capital movements to interest differentials. In the case of the United States, the high interest rates in the early 1980s attracted massive amounts of capital to these shores. But various empirical studies on the question have yielded mixed results, to the extent that economists have been led to reformulate their thinking on the subject. It used to be thought that barring undue disturbances in the foreign exchange markets (such as expected devaluation), the existence of a *fixed* interest differential would result in a *continuous flow* of funds until the differential was eliminated. The "portfolio approach" developed in recent years leads to a different conclusion.

---

[10] This can be costly to the British government because it means higher interest payments on the internal public debt (that is, on government bonds). To avoid this cost and still achieve the same result, the government can manipulate the forward exchange market.

This approach views each financier as holding a portfolio of financial assets, the composition of which is designed to maximize his return subject to minimum risk. A major determinant of this composition (besides the level of national income) and therefore of its distribution between domestic and foreign assets, is the constellation of interest rates prevailing on domestic and foreign money markets. This portfolio grows each year as additional assets are acquired, but these increments are very small in comparison to the total assets already in the portfolio; their distribution between foreign and domestic assets is governed by the same considerations as that of the entire portfolio and is therefore in the same proportion. For example, a New York financier may have a portfolio worth $1000, divided equally between domestic and foreign assets, with an annual increment of $100 also equally divided between the two types of assets.

If the foreign central bank (for example, the Bank of England) raises the rate of interest, two things happen. First and foremost, the financier readjusts his portfolio to account for the fact that foreign assets now have a higher yield (assuming no increase in risk). He may now decide to hold $400 in domestic and $600 in foreign assets. This is the major impact, but it is a one-time rather than a continuous effect. Second, the small annual flow into new assets will also be adjusted to account for the new level of foreign interest and divided on a 40:60 percent basis. This is a continuous effect, but it is rather small. All it does is increase the annual flow into British securities by $10. Summarized, these changes are:

	Before Foreign-interest Increase		After Foreign-interest Increase	
	Domestic Assets	Foreign Assets	Domestic Assets	Foreign Assets
Portfolio	$500	$500	$400	$600
Annual increments	50	50	40	60

Generalizing from the behavior of this financier, we see that a rise in the interest rate has a substantial one-time effect in attracting foreign capital and only a minor continuous effect in the same direction. Empirical studies indicate that most of the portfolio adjustment occurs within one year of the change in the interest rate (or national income) that brought it about, and that the annual flow effect is less than one-tenth of the one-time portfolio adjustment. Therefore, a country that wishes to continuously attract large amounts of foreign capital will have to keep raising its rate of interest to ever higher levels. A one-time increase can produce only a one-time sizable infusion of foreign capital.

But suppose a country wanted to attain just that type of infusion—for example, because its deficit was expected to be reversed within one year. How could that be accomplished with the policy tools under discussion? In other words, what are the effects of monetary and fiscal policies on the rate of interest?

Monetary contraction (assuming no fiscal change) *raises* the interest rate both because of direct action of the central bank—as it raises the discount rate and as it sells government bonds on the market, thereby depressing their price (which means higher interest)—and because of the reduction in the money *supply*. On the other hand, fiscal contraction (assuming no monetary change) brings about a reduction in aggregate expenditures (both private and public) and therefore a reduction in the *demand* for credit. Assuming that nothing is done on the monetary side to offset it, this *lowers* the price of credit—that is, the rate of interest.[11] For the country in deficit, therefore, monetary contraction helps restore balance in two ways: Exports of goods and services rise relative to imports, and there is an influx of foreign capital in response to an increase in the rate of interest. Only the first salutary effect, not the second, is present in the case of fiscal policy.

An equally important difference between them is that monetary policy does not require legislative approval, whereas under our institutional arrangement fiscal measures are less flexible; on the tax side, especially, they require a long time for enactment. Consequently, many economists recommend the use of monetary policy for dealing with external imbalances while reserving fiscal measures for internal stabilization objectives.[12] Indeed,

[11] This distinction can easily be understood by those readers familiar with the Hicks–Hansen *IS* and *LM* functions, which determine equilibrium combinations of interest rate (r) and national income (Y). Starting from equilibrium (Y_1, r_1), *monetary contraction* is shown by shifting the *LM* function to *LM'*, leaving the *IS* curve unchanged. The effect is to lower income to Y_2, but raise the interest rate to r_2. Next we show *fiscal contraction* by shifting the *IS* function downward to *IS'*, leaving the *LM* curve unchanged. In this case both income and interest rate are reduced, to Y_3 and r_3.

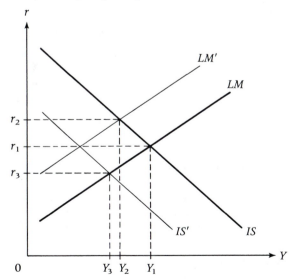

[12] Since fiscal and monetary policies are often handled by two separate government agencies (the treasury and the Federal Reserve, respectively, in the case of the United States), each agency should be assigned a policy objective most amenable to the policy instrument under its control. The allocation of such objectives is known as the "assignment problem."

Table 6-1
Policies for Dealing with External Imbalance

Economic Processes at Work	Deficit Country	Surplus Country
1. Fiscal measures	Contraction	Expansion
2. Monetary measures	Contraction	Expansion
3. Implications for production, income, and employment	Contraction	Expansion
a. Effect of 3 on trade in goods and services	Imports down, exports up	Imports up, exports down
b. Implication of 3 for direct foreign investments	Outflow	Inflow
4. Implication for rate of domestic price increase	Slowdown	Acceleration
a. Effect of 4 on the country's competitive position	More competitive	Less competitive
b. Effect of 4 on the current account balance	Imports down, exports up	Imports up, exports down
5. Implication of 2 for interest rates	Up	Down
a. Effect of 5 on short-term capital flows	Inflow	Outflow

empirical investigations show that changes in the rate of interest are the measure most commonly used by industrialized countries for dealing with external imbalances.

Table 6-1 summarizes the economic processes described above. It is clear from lines 3a and 4b that fiscal and monetary measures bring forth an income–price mechanism that works in the direction of restoring balance to the goods-and-services account. This process is partly offset by the effect of the same mechanism on direct foreign investments, indicated by item 3b. Monetary policy has a further equilibrating effect on the balance of payments through the rate of interest and its impact on short-term capital movement, as seen in line 5a.

Foreign Repercussions

The analysis can be pursued further. Whenever nations are tied to each other by fixed exchange rates (such as the EMS), any action taken in one country affects economic conditions in the others, especially in the countries that trade heavily with that country. And these effects reverberate back to the original country, with the changes in employment, income, and trade coming full circle (though in diminished strength).

Consider a country (country A) that for reasons of its own pursues contractionary fiscal and monetary policies. The reduction in its income lowers imports, implying reduced exports of its trading partners, countries

B and C. This in turn lowers income and employment in the export industries of countries B and C, and the reduction spreads in them through the multiplier mechanism. This has the further effect of lowering their imports from A, which accentuates the reduction in its national income. Precisely the reverse process holds if country A pursues domestic expansionary measures. These effects clearly indicate that a system of fixed exchange rates links together the economic fates of countries that have close trade relations. Both depression and inflation spread from one country to the next, and no one is isolated from outside disturbances.

What are the implications of this circular mechanism? In the first place, it gives additional responsibility to the leading industrial nation, if it wishes to concern itself with the fate of others. After World War II it used to be said that when the United States sneezed, Europe caught pneumonia; in other words, Europe was so dependent on the American market for the export of goods and services that each deep recession on this side of the Atlantic brought about severe economic contraction on the other. Although this is no longer true, there are still vast areas of the world, notably Canada and Latin America, dependent on American prosperity for the maintenance of a high level of exports and therefore national income. Of course, these relations hold among units of any closely knit trading system, such as members of the European Common Market.

In 1974–75 most industrial economies experienced a severe economic slump. Triggered partly by external shocks, such as the quadrupling of oil prices by the OPEC cartel, and partly by government anti-inflationary policies in 1973–74, it was the most prolonged recession since the war. No single country could extricate itself by expansionary policies, because of the balance-of-payments constraint: A higher growth rate than the OECD (Organization for Economic Cooperation and Development) average would induce an unacceptable balance-of-trade deficit (superimposed upon deficits occasioned by higher prices for imported oil). The only way out was coordinated growth-oriented policies by all countries. Particular responsibility rested upon the three "locomotive economies" of the West: the United States, Germany, and Japan. Because of their size, an accelerated growth of these three economies would stimulate imports from other industrial countries (as well as from the less developed countries, LDCs), thereby stimulating their growth as well. That was the announced strategy of the OECD in 1976–77. But the plan ran into problems in 1977–78 because the growth rates of Germany and Japan were less than half that of the United States, producing trade surpluses in the first two countries and deficits in the United States. And European economies remained at a low ebb.

In 1983–86, the U.S. economy staged a robust recovery from the 1981–82 recession. That, along with an overvalued dollar, led to massive trade deficits in the United States. But the increased exports of other countries (the counterpart of our imports) helped alleviate the recessionary conditions prevailing there.

The second implication is that, to properly calculate the multiplier effect of any policy, one must allow for foreign repercussions as they complete the circuit and affect the country in which the policy originated. It will be recalled that the foreign trade multiplier was developed by using an example of a country experiencing an autonomous expansion of exports. If it is in a *large and important* country, that increase necessarily implies a significant and autonomous rise in imports of its trading partners. The resulting decline in the income of trading partners lowers their induced imports from the home country, curtailing its exports and reducing the size of the calculated foreign trade multiplier. The foreign repercussions can be shown schematically for a two-country world, where country A experiences an autonomous increase in its exports to country B:

Country A	Country B
+ X	+ M
+ Y	− Y
+ M	− M
− X	+ X
− Y	+ Y
− M	+ M
+ X	− X
+ Y	− Y
·	·
·	·

These foreign repercussions diminish in strength as we move down the columns. Nevertheless, they dampen the effect of the original autonomous increase in exports of country A. The multiplier formula given earlier ignores these repercussions and to that extent is applicable only to small countries. For a large country, the multiplier is smaller, since a term representing the foreign repercussions is added to the denominator. Its derivation is given in Appendix III.

A third implication of the interdependence under fixed exchange rates is that no country is completely free to pursue independent domestic policies: All countries are subject to outside discipline exercised through the balance of payments. When a country gets out of line, a crisis can easily result. Thus, when the French labor unions demand and get higher wages, as they did in the spring of 1968, a general weakening of the franc is signaled. Since an increase in wage rates increases production costs, French products become less competitive and at the same time French incomes are raised, thereby encouraging imports and discouraging exports. If all its trading partners faced the same wage demands, these factors might roughly cancel each other. But when it happens only in France, the franc is weakened and may become subject to further pressures exerted by alarmed speculators. In 1982 French and Italian domestic expansionary policies weakened the franc and the lira within the EMS and led to their devaluation in June of that year. Similar crises may follow from such actions as the British trade unions demanding and obtaining a doubling of their tea break, British workers engaging in a "go-slow" work policy or wildcat strikes on a large scale, the Dutch government embarking on a policy of huge new expenditures to reclaim the North Sea, or the West German central bank doubling the country's money supply.[13]

What is common to all these measures is that they disturb the price and income relationships between countries, and through them, affect the balances of payments and the stability of currencies. Under a system of fixed exchange rates, the world is linked by exchange rates, but governments desire—or are forced—to pursue policies that are independent of other countries while at the same time they wish to preserve the freedom of private citizens to trade and speculate. These three features of the system are not always compatible and they need not lead to one harmonious whole. It is impossible to be completely linked yet completely independent at the same time, all the time. To put it differently, a combination of fixed exchange rates, currency convertibility, and imperfect harmonization of national economic policies that affect incomes, prices, and interest rates cannot work well. When these features clash, a crisis results. It spreads from the country that triggered it to other countries, because all nations are linked by fixed exchange rates. "International financial crises" are the periodic adjustments of the system to these conflicting forces. It was this kind of clash that produced the recurrent crises during 1967–73 and finally led to the demise of the Bretton Woods system of pegged exchange rates in March of 1973.

In fact, the issue of interdependence can be carried further. In recent decades a truly international capital market has developed. One important feature of this integrated market is the one trillion of so-called Eurodollars. These come into existence when dollars are deposited by their owners in foreign banks. Being a fully convertible and universally acceptable asset, such dollars know no national boundaries; they are moved from one country to another in search of higher interest return, which in turn reflects the needs of commerce.

If a country wishes to pursue domestic contractionary policies by raising the rate of interest, the higher rates may simply attract funds into the domestic money market, thereby providing new liquidity and negating the intent of the policy, at least in part. The opposite may occur when a central bank lowers the interest rate to promote expansion but all that happens is that funds are withdrawn from the country in favor of higher rates else-

---

[13] Even the normal process of economic growth disturbs the balance of payments because it raises income and therefore imports. Of course, other countries also grow and import more from any country in question, but growth rates differ among nations and so does their effect on trade. Even if growth rates of all countries were equal, the resulting effect on trade would be unbalancing because the marginal propensity to import differs among nations. For example, empirical studies suggest that if Japanese income grew at the same rate as that of the rest of the world, the world's demand for Japanese exports would grow three times as fast as Japanese demand for imports. The reverse is true for the United Kingdom.

where, thereby contracting domestic liquidity. This demonstrates the limitations that an integrated capital market imposes on the conduct of an independent national monetary policy. In order to gain more independence, some European countries have found it necessary to impose certain controls on the movement of short-term capital.

There is another side to this story. The existence of Eurodollars has provided some countries with a new monetary tool for the pursuit of domestic stabilization policies. For example, if West Germany wishes to bring about contraction in its money supply, its central bank sells on the market not only government bonds but also dollars in exchange for marks. Such sales are normally accompanied by an agreement to repurchase these dollars from their holders (usually commercial banks) at a future date, so as to eliminate the risk from possible exchange fluctuations.

A degree of interdependence exists even under fluctuating exchange rates. In various periods during the 1980s, the United States pursued a policy of fiscal expansion and monetary tightness. As a result, U.S. interest rates, and especially the real rates (nominal interest minus the expected rate of inflation) rose, attracting massive amounts of foreign capital to the United States (and raising the exchange value of the dollar). That forced other industrial countries to raise their interest rates in order to forestall some of the capital outflow, thus hampering their ability to reflate their economies. International conferences at that time were replete with foreign criticism of high U.S. interest rates. When U.S. interest rates declined foreign rates followed the same downward trend. Conversely, in 1986 the European and Japanese central banks reduced their interest rates in order to enable the Federal Reserve to lower U.S. rates without fear of large-scale withdrawal of capital. This episode represented an attempt to coordinate a reduction in interest rates among the main industrial countries.

It should not be concluded from all this that an integrated capital market is a bad phenomenon. In fact, it is far superior to a system beset by an assortment of controls over international capital movements. What the foregoing examples show is that a high degree of interdependence calls for regular policy coordination among central bankers. "We are all in this together," one might say, and the economic navigators of nations, especially of small open economies, must take account of outside restrictions in formulating their policies. Indeed, in 1986 the U.S. administration was formulating proposals for worldwide coordination of economic policies.

With this short but important digression completed, let us return to the vantage point of the individual country.

The Balance of Payments in the Context of General Policy Objectives

Since every economic measure taken by the government affects both the balance of payments and domestic conditions, the economist needs to concern himself with the total situation. If a country suffering from a balance-of-payments deficit happens to be subject to domestic inflationary pressures at the same time, it is in a relatively fortunate situation, because the domestic remedies required to cure the domestic inflation are also those needed to cope with the external deficit. In both cases contractionary fiscal and monetary policies are called for, and the situation is known as "consistent." Such was the situation confronting the United States late in the 1960s.

Similarly, when a country experiences simultaneously a domestic recession and a balance-of-payments surplus (as Germany and Japan did in 1977), it is in a consistent situation, because both predicaments call for expansionary policies. On the monetary side, the central bank should lower the rate of interest, lower the reserve requirements to which commercial banks are subject, and purchase government bonds on the open market. On the fiscal side, the government should curtail taxes or raise expenditures (or both), pumping purchasing power into the economy. The resulting increases in income and prices have the effect of increasing imports and lowering exports, thereby eliminating the balance-of-payments surplus. Thus, the same set of policies can be used to deal with both internal and external problems.

But a country can also find itself in an "inconsistent" combination of circumstances. It may have a balance-of-payments deficit and domestic unemployment at the same time, or a balance-of-payments surplus along with domestic inflation. In the first case the deficit calls for contractionary policies but the unemployment necessitates expansionary measures. In the second case the surplus requires internal expansion but the inflation necessitates domestic contraction. Table 6-2 should help clarify the four combinations.

While the first two situations can be handled by proper domestic policies, the second two are problematical. Thus, the United States in the early 1960s was plagued by a combination of unemployment and deficit. On the other hand, in the early 1970s West Germany and Japan confronted a combination of an external surplus and an inflationary boom.

Under the "rules of the game" of the gold standard, the guide to government policy was the balance-of-payments position of the country.

Table 6-2
Combinations of Economic Conditions and Policy Requirements

Internal Conditions	Domestic Policies Called For	Balance of Payments	Domestic Policies Called For	Nature of Situation
Unemployment	Expansion	Surplus	Expansion	Consistent
Inflation	Contraction	Deficit	Contraction	Consistent
Unemployment	Expansion	Deficit	Contraction	Inconsistent
Inflation	Contraction	Surplus	Expansion	Inconsistent

Policymakers were expected to subjugate internal stabilization needs to the requirements of balance-of-payments adjustment. But with the depression of the 1930s and the advent of Keynesian economics, governments began to assume increasingly greater responsibility for domestic employment and prices. This brought the conflict in inconsistent situations into sharper focus, and it is said to have been partly responsible for the breakdown in the international financial system in the 1930s. In particular, with respect to the United States, it is often claimed that it is unreasonable to expect a $4 trillion economy to be subservient to the needs of the relatively small external sector.

It is this conflict of policy goals that was foremost in the minds of the 1944 Bretton Woods conferees, who established the International Monetary Fund and hammered out the rules by which the world's financial system was thereafter governed for almost thirty years. Their objective, not quite successfully met, was to strike a compromise between the two goals, leaving countries scope for independent domestic action while at the same time helping to finance external imbalances out of reserves and loans. On the whole, however, it is the adjustment mechanism that has suffered in the process.

Readers familiar with domestic economic problems will recognize that this inconsistency is superimposed upon another troublesome conflict: that between inflation and unemployment. Contractionary measures designed to combat inflation often create unemployment, as they did in 1982, while expansionary measures designed to cure a recession can easily bring about or accelerate inflation. By adding the international dimension, a further source of possible inconsistency between policy objectives emerges. A broad discussion of such conflicts is beyond the scope of this volume.[14] We merely wish to emphasize that at no time should the balance-of-payments objective be viewed in isolation. There is no such thing as a single, isolated policy goal. At any given time, the government has several targets relating to the domestic and external performance of the economy. These goals may include full employment, high growth rate, price stability, external balance, and the like. The government also has an arsenal of policy instruments, including monetary, fiscal, exchange rate, and other policies.

Application of each instrument would have different effects on each of the policy goals. The rational policymaker would view the situation in its totality and select a proper mix of instruments to deal with his set of targets. The greater the number of policy objectives (or targets) and the larger the potential conflict between them, the larger the number of instruments that must be employed to meet these objectives. If a government avoids using any one of the instruments at its disposal for political or other reasons, or if it does not have the capacity to use domestic instruments in the required

---

[14] For simplicity, "internal balance" is assumed to represent whatever compromise is considered "best" between the goals of full employment and price stability.

combinations, it may have to choose among conflicting objectives or strike a compromise between them.

Having said this, let us return to the inconsistent positions described in Table 6-2. Assume that a country is faced with unemployment and a deficit at the same time. A temporary remedy can be found in a proper combination of domestic measures. Remember that monetary contraction has a dual effect on the balance of payments: It not only improves the current account balance, but attracts short-term capital from abroad by raising the interest rate. Suppose the government combines a policy of monetary contraction and fiscal expansion. Depending on the relative size of the doses applied, the fiscal measure can more than offset its monetary counterpart in its effect on the domestic economy. We thereby obtain a net expansionary effect, desirable for internal purposes but which increases the current account deficit. On the other hand, the increase in the rate of interest embodied in the monetary contraction attracts funds from abroad, more than offsetting the adverse impact on the current account position. This combination of measures is particularly attractive if the country has a current account surplus less than its capital outflow, yielding (under full employment) a total external deficit—a situation typical of the United States in the early 1960s. A precisely reverse combination of measures can be pursued in the case of inflation coupled with surplus, especially when the surplus is a result of a current account deficit smaller than the capital inflow. For example, in the first half of 1974, large inflows of short-term funds into the United Kingdom—attracted by high interest rates—offset the large current account deficit and helped prop the external value of the (floating) pound sterling.

But with the policy combinations described above, the authorities can deal only with temporary conditions of deficit and unemployment. If the inconsistent situation was brought about by deeply rooted causes such domestic measures are unlikely to constitute a sufficient remedy, because they do not contain a mechanism to realign the country's prices (under full employment) with those of the rest of the world. More drastic action is needed. One step in the arsenal of the policymaker is exchange-rate adjustment, which will be addressed in the next chapter.

Some Unanswered Questions

Apart from the difficulty of resolving conflicts between objectives, most of what has been said so far has revolved around one main topic: the *direction* in which the economy moves as a result of the application of various policies. But the direction of change is not a sufficient guide for policy making. Two other interrelated pieces of information are essential. First, we must know how strong a force is exerted on the economy by each policy measure. This in turn determines how far in the direction of the target the economy moves in response to the policy measure—or, put differently, how great an application of each instrument is required to reach the target. Second, we need to know how long it takes for the full impact of the various instruments to be felt throughout the economy and what sort of time path the economy follows in its movement toward the target position. The second point, classified by economists as "economic dynamics," enables public officials and concerned citizens to know roughly what to expect at various intervals after the policy button has been pressed.

The Degree of Impact

Consider the internal measures designed to eliminate a balance-of-payments deficit. On the fiscal side the initial instrument at the disposal of the authorities is a reduction in government expenditures or an increase in taxes, or both. Such action lowers the income and the rate of inflation, which in turn lower imports and raise exports. In each of these phases the question is: By how much?

All that the government can control is the initial fiscal action. That step is *exogenous* to the economy in the sense that it is "arbitrarily" determined at a political level outside the economy. Once the action is taken the government has no further control over the final outcome, unless it wishes to take some other deliberate steps, such as a mid-course correction. The initial action sets in motion a sequence of interrelated economic processes, each depending on other economic magnitudes and therefore considered *endogenous* or internal to the economy.

In the case of a reduction in government expenditures, the following sequence of questions can be articulated:

1. By how much does gross national product decline for a given cut in government expenditures? The answer depends on the size of the multiplier (which is measurable), and on possible reduction in interest rates, which has the opposite effect of stimulating the economy and offsetting part of the contraction.
2. What proportion of the total reduction in gross national product is translated into lower imports and higher exports? Again, these have measurable magnitudes, especially the marginal propensity to import. *A priori* reasoning would suggest that the less dependent the economy is on foreign trade, the smaller is the effect on imports of a given change in gross national product. Put differently, the more closed the economy is, the larger is the income adjustment required to achieve a given reduction in imports.
3. Will there be an "unfavorable" side effect to the economic contraction as long-term capital is encouraged to seek more profitable investment opportunities abroad? If so, how significant is it?
4. To what extent does the reduction in the level of economic activity force producers to curtail the rate of price increases?
5. To what extent do lower prices stimulate exports and discourage imports? This depends on various price elasticities.

6. Will the reduction in interest rates result in significant outflow of short-term capital?

Similar questions can be asked with respect to an increase in taxes or, if the country wishes to eliminate a balance-of-payments surplus, with respect to an increase in government spending and a reduction in taxes.

When it comes to monetary policy, the main instrument in the hands of the central bank is control over the money supply. In the case of an external deficit, the money supply would be contracted and interest rates would be raised. Once administered, the policy must operate through processes internal to the economy and must push the economy toward the preassigned target. Whether it will actually get there depends on the answers to the following questions:

1. To what extent does a contraction in the money supply lower the level of economic activity and slow the rate of inflation? U.S. experience in 1981–82 demonstrated that a combination of fiscal expansion and monetary tightness had a powerful effect both in reducing the rate of inflation and in causing a deep recession. The subsequent reversal of monetary policy produced a robust recovery in 1983–86.
2. By how much do a given economic contraction and price reduction discourage imports and encourage exports?
3. To what extent does an outflow of long-term investment capital occur as an unfavorable side effect to the economic contraction?
4. How sensitive is short-term capital to interest differentials between financial centers, and therefore how strongly is it attracted to the deficit country when its interest rates rise?

Answering the questions is no mean task. At any given moment a multitude of forces is operating on the economy, and it is necessary to isolate the effect of the policy under investigation. In order to find out the effect of a policy, we need to compare situations with and without the policy, all other things assumed to remain unchanged. It is the validity of this *ceteris paribus* assumption that laypeople often question when they read the writings of economists. How can it be valid if the economy is always in a state of change? The answer is that all other changes take place in the presence or in the absence of the policy under investigation. And making the assumption "other things being equal" is equivalent to comparing the situation with and without the policy. In the physical sciences this is accomplished by controlled laboratory experiments. Since this is not possible in economics, we must use theoretical abstractions and statistical techniques to achieve the same objective.

This is the role of model building in the social sciences. It is often necessary to build a simplified model of the whole economy in order to draw inferences concerning the size of the parameters being estimated. Model construction means the mathematical formulation of the relationships between various economic variables in a manner that lends itself to statistical estimation. The branch of economics concerned with such studies is econometrics. Thanks in no small measure to improved estimation techniques, policymakers today have at least a rough idea of the magnitudes of the variables involved. The following are some examples drawn from an econometric study pertaining to the 1970s decade of floating exchange rates.[15] For U.S. trade:

> A one percent increase in real GNP increases import volume by 1.7 percent. This income elasticity of import demand has risen from one decade to the next, indicating an *increased openness of the American economy.*
>
> A one percent decline in the import price index relative to the domestic whole-sale price index increases imports by 1.2 percent. Most of that effect takes place two quarters following the change.
>
> A one percent increase in the rest of the world's GNP raises U.S. exports by 1.3 percent.
>
> A one percent decline in the competitors' prices reduces U.S. exports by 0.9 percent.

Similar information is available for other industrial countries. Although these are merely orders of magnitude, they help determine the optimal dose of each measure that needs to be administered.

Time Lags

The second crucial question concerns the timing of policy and the time path followed by the economy as it moves toward the target position. It certainly makes a great deal of difference whether a policy instrument attains its objective in one year or five years, if for no other reason than because many things can happen in the longer time span to change the course of the economy. Thus, the longer the lag is, the greater is the need for further application of policies to maintain the economy on the proper course during the intervening period.

There are two time lags common to practically all policies that are external to the economy: the lag between the need for action as reflected in the economic conditions and the recognition of that need by the policymaker, and the lag between the recognition and the point when economic action is initiated. Economists and statisticians can help reduce the recognition lag by speeding up the collection and evaluation of data about the state of the economy and the dissemination of the analytical conclusions and their policy implications. The second lag results from administrative delays and at times from the need for legislative action, as in the case of tax-rate changes.

---

[15] D. Warner and M. Kreinin "Determinants of International Trade Flows," *Review of Economics and Statistics,* February 1983.

Next in sequence come the endogenous lags—those that depend on the working process of the economic system itself. Two questions are relevant here: How long does it take for a certain fiscal or monetary action to work its way through the economy before its full impact is realized in terms of changes in gross national product and the price level? And how long is it before the effect of income and price changes on the balance of payments is manifested in whole or in part? These questions call for dynamic studies, based on quarterly data, that specify the time path followed by the economy as it adjusts gradually to the shock of new policy.

Review Questions

1. a. Suppose that the Belgian government increased its annual domestic spending by 10 billion Belgian francs. Assuming that the MPS $= \frac{1}{4}$ and the MPM $= \frac{1}{4}$, compute the effect of that act on: GNP; C, S, M, and the balance of trade (compute the changes in the above magnitudes).
   b. What would be the effects on the above variables had Belgium experienced a trade surplus of 10 billion Belgian francs? Assume that Belgium trades only with members of the EMS.
   c. Trace the effects of each of the above developments on the other members of the EMS combined.

2. Summarize the automatic mechanisms (expenditures and money) of the balance of payments (B. of P.) adjustment under a fixed exchange rate.

3. Prove that when the MPS $= 0$ the expenditure mechanism insures full adjustment in the B. of P.

4. a. In 1983 Mexico faced a combination of external deficit and internal unemployment (under a fixed exchange rate regime). Does this represent a consistent or an inconsistent situation? Why? Can it be handled by domestic policies? Why or why not?
   b. What about a combination of external surplus and inflation?

5. How does: (a) fiscal policy; (b) monetary policy affect domestic interest rates? How do interest rates affect capital flows under the Keynesian and portfolio approaches?

7/Exchange-Rate Adjustment

*D*uring the reign of the Bretton Woods system, there were many revisions in the par value of currencies. And since 1973 there have been frequent changes in the exchange rates of currencies that are on fixed rate regimes. For example, Portugal devalued its currency in 1983; Thailand in 1984; Greece in 1985; and the French franc was devalued in 1986 relative to other EMS currencies.

Under a fixed exchange-rate regime, the term "devaluation" refers to a decrease in the value of a currency in terms of other currencies, while "revaluation" describes an increase in that value. Any consideration of a change in the exchange rate is usually shrouded in secrecy and denied publicly, in order to prevent unbearable speculative pressure against the currency. Public suspicion of an impending devaluation inevitably invites speculative activity, as holders of the currency try to avoid losses or realize gains by shifting to other currencies.

In order to understand what can be accomplished by changing the exchange rate, we must inquire into its economic effects. It is instructive to discuss four separate effects, assuming in each case that all other things are held *constant.* In fact various influences continuously interact with one another. Let us assume that the United Kingdom (in a fixed exchange-rate regime), *facing a persistent balance-of-payments deficit and sizable unemployment,* devalues the pound from $3 to $2, or equivalently, raises the price of the dollar from one-third to one-half pound sterling. (Under a managed float the corresponding event is for the government to permit the currency to depreciate from the old to the new level; under a free float, market forces would bring about the decline.) What will be the effects of such an action?

Relative Price Effect

The immediate impact of the devaluation is to lower the prices of goods and services produced in the United Kingdom relative to prices in other countries, making British products more competitive both at home and on foreign markets. In other words, British imports become more expensive in terms of pounds, making the home-produced substitutes relatively cheaper, while British exports become cheaper in terms of the foreign currencies in which they are sold. Thus, a $6000 American automobile will cost the British customer £3000 instead of £2000 as a result of the devaluation, while the price to the American consumer of a £10 English shirt declines from $30 to $20 as the pound is devalued from $3 to $2. Likewise, an American tourist to the United Kingdom must now spend only $400 instead of $600 on a £200 package tour. Conversely, the cost to a British traveler of a $900 trip to the United States rises from £300 to £450 as a result of the devaluation. Indeed, when the exchange value of the dollar rose during 1981–85, foreign vacations became cheaper for Americans whereas U.S. vacations became more expensive for Europeans and Japanese. The reverse happened in 1985–86 with the decline in the exchange value of the dollar. Finally, a potential American investor in the United Kingdom finds his dollar cost of a given pound expenditure reduced by one-third, while the converse is true for an English investor who contemplates buying American securities. The same change applies to all traded goods and services as well as to capital flows: Relative U.K.–U.S. prices decline, even when domestic prices remain unchanged in both countries.

Becoming more competitive by lowering relative prices is not an end in itself, however. It is a means toward eliminating the external deficit, which is usually measured in terms of dollars, dollars being the internationally accepted medium for settling imbalances. In other words, the aim of British policy is to *reduce* the dollar value of *imports* (total dollar outpayments) and *raise* the dollar value of *exports* (total dollar inpayments). It is to that end that prices are reduced. The effect of the relative price change on the value of trade flows depends on the degree of quantity response to price change. But since the results in the case of inpayments and outpayments are not symmetrical, each flow will be considered separately.

Before proceeding with the analysis, we need to define more precisely the meaning of "degree of response to price change," a term we used loosely in a previous chapter. Consider the demand curve shown in Figure 7-1(a). It shows the quantities (on the horizontal axis) that would be purchased at alternative prices (on the vertical axis). It slopes downward and to the right (that is, it has a negative slope) in accord with the inverse relation between prices and quantities: The lower the price, the greater the quantity purchased. In the present case, as price declines from P_1 to P_2, quantity increases from Q_1 to Q_2. This inverse relation between price and quantity is assumed to hold for most products. But the dollar value of purchases may or may not increase. Since value is price times quantity ($V = P \times Q$), and since

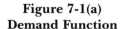

Figure 7-1(a)
Demand Function

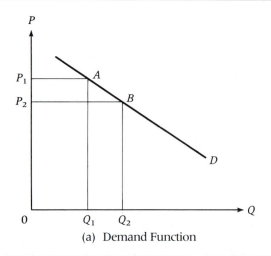

(a) Demand Function

price has fallen while quantity has risen, we cannot say, in general, whether their product ($P \times Q$) has risen or fallen. This product is represented by the rectangular area under the relevant point on the demand curve, since that area is $0P \times 0Q$, or price times quantity. In our case this area has changed from $0P_1AQ_1$ to $0P_2BQ_2$. Since the area ($P \times Q$) corresponds to dollar payments by the importer or, equivalently, to dollar receipts of the exporter, we are concerned with the manner in which it changes as a result of the price changes.

The effect of a given price change on $V = P \times Q$ depends on how large the quantity response is. Clearly, the flatter the demand curve is, the greater the quantity response that it represents. The standard measure of the degree of response is called the *price elasticity of demand* (η_p):

$$\begin{matrix} \text{elasticity} \\ \text{coefficient} \end{matrix} = \eta_p = \frac{\begin{matrix}\text{Percentage Change} \\ \text{in Quantity Purchased}\end{matrix}}{\text{Percentage Change in Price}} = \frac{\Delta Q/Q}{\Delta P/P} = \frac{\Delta Q \times P}{\Delta P \times Q}$$

where Q and P are used as bases to convert the absolute changes ΔQ and ΔP into percentage terms. Since price and quantity normally move in opposite directions, the elasticity will usually have a negative value. However, it is common to ignore the negative sign and measure elasticity of demand in terms of its absolute value.

Consider the value $\eta_p = 1$. By definition, this means that any given percentage change in price will exactly equal the resulting percentage change in quantity purchased. In other words, the increase in quantity is exactly sufficient to offset the reduction in the amount for which each unit now

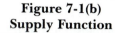

Figure 7-1(b)
Supply Function

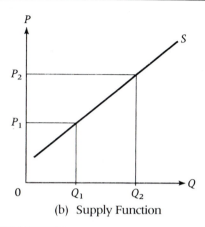

(b) Supply Function

sells. This leaves dollar value $P \times Q$ (the area under the demand curve) unchanged. When the demand elasticity is greater than 1, the percentage increase in the quantity purchased is larger than the percentage decrease in price, so that a decline in price yields an increase in the dollar value of purchases. Precisely the opposite is true when the elasticity is smaller than 1. In that case a price reduction produces a less-than-proportionate increase in the quantity purchased, so that the dollar value (the area under the curve) declines. We call the first case *demand of unitary elasticity,* the second case *relatively elastic demand,* and the third case *relatively inelastic demand.*

The value of the elasticity changes as one moves along a straight-line demand curve. In particular, for a demand curve that stretches from the price axis to the quantity axis, the midpoint represents unitary elasticity ($\eta_p = 1$); points above it represent the relatively elastic segment of the curve, and points below it, the relatively inelastic segment. A demand curve along which $\eta_p = 1$ at all points is a rectangular hyperbola, under which the area is the same at all points. Demand is said to be infinitely elastic ($\eta_p = \infty$) when the demand curve is horizontal, because in that case the percentage change in price is zero. On the other hand, a vertical demand curve, where quantity is unchanged, portrays zero elasticity.

We are also interested in the response of suppliers to price change. The supply curve slopes upward and to the right (positive slope), indicating a direct relation between price and quantity: As price rises so does the quantity supplied, and vice versa (Figure 7-1(b)). The elasticity of supply is therefore positive; it is defined in the same manner as the demand elasticity, except that Q refers to the quantity supplied:

$$\eta_s = \frac{\Delta Q / Q}{\Delta P / P}$$

Figure 7-2
Demand and Supply

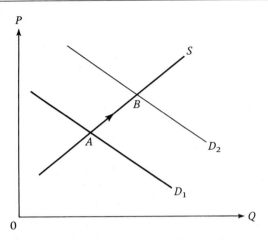

Loosely speaking, the flatter the supply curve is, the higher is the elasticity that it implies. A horizontal supply curve indicates infinite elasticity of supply, while a vertical curve shows zero elasticity.

The intersection of the supply and demand curves (or schedules, as they are also called), determines the price prevailing in the market and the quantity exchanging hands. A shift in one of the curves, say a rise of the demand curve, means that at every price more of the product is demanded (for example, because of higher income). It is not to be confused with a movement along that curve. The shift from D_1 to D_2 (Figure 7-2) causes a movement along the supply curve from A to B and establishes a higher price as well as a greater quantity.

We are now in a position to analyze the effects of sterling devaluation upon the dollar inpayments and outpayments of the United Kingdom. Note, however, that in this discussion the supply schedules refer to each country's supply of exports to its trading partner and the demand schedules refer to each country's demand for imports from its trading partner.

Effect on Dollar Outpayments

Sterling devaluation has made British imports (an American automobile in our earlier example) more expensive in terms of pounds, with *dollar* prices remaining the *same*. Since English consumers deal in pounds, the volume[1] of imports inevitably declines, and dollar outpayments (volume of imports times the constant dollar price) must also decline. The amount by which

---

[1] The words *volume* and *quantity* are used interchangeably to refer to the physical amount of goods measured by units or aggregated by the use of index numbers. *Value*, on the other hand, is volume times price.

dollar outpayments are reduced is determined only by the decline in the volume of imports, since dollar prices are unchanged. In turn, the extent of this decline depends on how responsive British consumers are to the increase in the pound price of imports, or the price elasticity of demand for imports. The more responsive they are, the greater the reduction is. One factor that invariably affects the degree of responsiveness is the availability of acceptable substitutes produced at home. The more readily available they are, the more likely it is that consumers will switch to homemade goods and thereby reduce outpayments. Thus, other things being equal, the import demand elasticity of a large country with a diversified economy is likely to be greater than that of a small country, because the large country tends to produce adequate substitutes for most of its imports.

Similar reductions in outpayments occur as British tourists are discouraged from going abroad by the fact that they must pay more pounds for the dollars they need, and as British companies contemplating overseas investments are held back by the increase in the pound cost of such ventures. In short, *dollar outpayments* in all forms *necessarily decline,* the extent of the reduction being determined by the degree of responsiveness to price change.

The simple analytical tools of supply and demand can be used to demonstrate the point. The two panels of Figure 7-3 are the usual price–quantity diagrams. They differ from each other in only one respect: Prices are expressed in dollars on the upper panel, but in pounds on the lower panel. The quantity axes are identical in all respects. We begin by observing the curves that represent the predevaluation situation. American supply to the United Kingdom ($S_{U.S.}$) is assumed, for the sake of simplicity, to be infinitely elastic, or horizontal. (A small country normally faces an infinitely elastic supply curve.) Its predevaluation level is \$3 or £1. British demand for imports from the United States ($D_{U.K.}$) assumes the normal shape. The predevaluation volume of British imports from the United States is Q_1 and is shown in both panels.

Devaluation of the pound does not affect American supply in terms of dollars or British demand in terms of pounds. This is not so for the U.S. supply expressed in terms of pounds, however, or for the British demand expressed in terms of dollars. The fact that the pound is now at \$2 means that the \$3 supply price translates into £1.5 instead of £1, indicated by the postdevaluation $S'_{U.S.}$ shown in the lower panel. It results in reduced volume of imports—from Q_1 to Q_2. Since the dollar price remains unchanged, the reduced quantity *necessarily* translates into a reduction in *dollar* outpayments. The size of this reduction depends only on the change in quantity, which in turn is a function of the British demand elasticity; the more elastic the demand the larger the decline in dollar outpayments.[2]

---

[2] Note that total outpayments expressed in sterling may increase (but by proportionally less than the devaluation) or decrease, depending on the elasticity of $D_{U.K.}$. But the main interest attaches to *dollar* outpayments.

Figure 7-3
Effect of Devaluation of the Pound on U.K. Dollar Outpayments

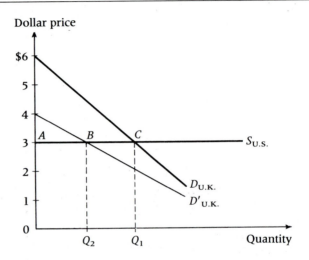

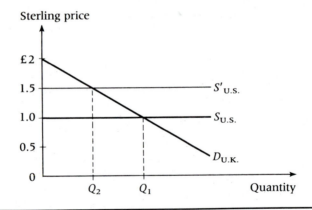

Only in the extreme case of zero elasticity of British demand (when $D_{U.K.}$ is a straight vertical line) will the quantity imported, and therefore outpayments, remain unchanged. In that case sterling prices rise in exact proportion to the devaluation and dollar prices remain unchanged. In other words, there is no competitive gain for British products.

Precisely the same result can be demonstrated on the upper panel of Figure 7-3. Although $S_{U.S.}$ remains at $3, $D_{U.K.}$ must change when expressed in terms of dollars. The British demand curve shows the quantities that consumers are willing to buy at various hypothetical sterling prices. These remain unchanged. But each such sterling price now translates into one-third fewer dollars than before the devaluation. Consequently, the British demand curve on the dollar price scale (upper panel) must be lowered from

$D_{\text{U.K.}}$ to $D'_{\text{U.K.}}$, yielding import volume Q_2. Dollar outpayments—the volume of imports times their dollar price—is the area under the equilibrium point. It declines from $0ACQ_1$ to $0ABQ_2$. The only case in which no such reduction occurs is when the demand curve is of zero elasticity (it is vertical) and does not shift. In general, the larger the elasticity of demand, the greater will be the decline in outpayments.

Effect on Dollar Inpayments

When it comes to the inpayments side, the picture is less clear-cut. British exports become more competitive because their *dollar* prices to foreign customers are down one-third. This decline is certain to induce American consumers to purchase more English goods. But the interest of the British government is not in selling more goods in the United States per se; it lies in earning more dollars. And, as a result of the devaluation, each unit of British exports sells for fewer dollars than before. The total inflow of dollars into the United Kingdom is made up of the volume of British exports *times* the unit dollar price the exports fetch abroad. Since that price has declined by one-third, the quantity sold would have to increase by *more* than a third in order for dollar inpayments to rise. More generally, inpayments rise only if the increase in the volume of sales is more than proportional to the decline in price—more than sufficient to compensate for the fact that each unit now sells for less.

In turn, that condition depends on the degree of foreign response to the decline in prices of British goods. If foreign customers are responsive enough to offset the decline in price (if the foreign demand for British goods is *relatively elastic*), then dollar inpayments rise. The same principle holds with respect to foreign tourists visiting the United Kingdom and foreign users of all British services. It also applies to foreign corporations wishing to invest in the United Kingdom. They all find it possible to purchase each pound necessary for their transactions for fewer dollars. But whether or not they spend more dollars in the United Kingdom depends on their response to the decline in price. Only if they increase the purchases of British services more than proportionately to the decline in their dollar price will the flow of inpayments increase. (This is the qualification hinted at in the first section of Chapter 3 in connection with the slope of the German inpayments line.)

As before, this conclusion can be clarified by simple demand-and-supply analysis, except that in this case the United Kingdom is the supplier, with an infinitely elastic supply curve ($S_{\text{U.K.}}$), and the United States is the demanding country. The curves labeled $S_{\text{U.K.}}$ and $D_{\text{U.S.}}$ in Figure 7-4 show the predevaluation situation in terms of dollar prices on the upper panel and sterling prices on the lower panel. $S_{\text{U.K.}}$ and $D_{\text{U.S.}}$ appear in both panels at the predevaluation exchange rate of £1 = \$3. The quantity traded is Q_1.

Dollar inpayments, which are our main concern, are shown on the upper panel as the area under the equilibrium point, $0ABQ_1$. They equal

Figure 7-4
Effect of Devaluation of the Pound on U.K. Dollar Inpayments

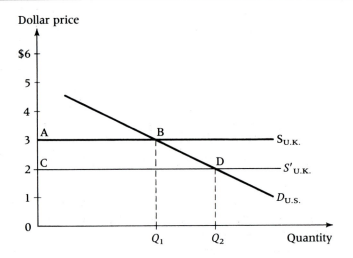

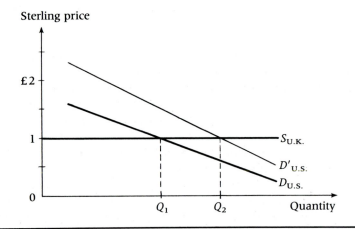

price times quantity ($\overline{0A} \times \overline{0Q_1}$), here $\overline{0A} = \$3$. Devaluation does not affect the American demand relationship $D_{U.S.}$ when it is expressed in terms of dollar prices. But $S_{U.K.}$, which remains unchanged with respect to sterling prices (lower panel), is affected when expressed in terms of dollar prices (upper panel). Specifically, the £1 supply price was equivalent to \$3 before devaluation, but it is equal to \$2 after devaluation. Correspondingly, $S_{U.K.}$ is shifted downward to $S'_{U.K.}$; that is, the devaluation has made British goods cheaper for American consumers. The new equilibrium point is D. The quantity traded rises to Q_2. Total dollar inpayments are now equal to the area $0CDQ_2$. They are larger than the predevaluation inpayments ($0ABQ_1$) if the U.S. demand elasticity is greater than 1 over the relevant range, smaller if the elasticity is smaller than 1.[3] In general, the more elastic the American demand for British imports, the greater will be the increase in dollar inpayments into the United Kingdom following devaluation.

Outpayments and Inpayments Combined

To recapitulate, while U.K. dollar outpayments are certain to decline, the impact of the devaluation on dollar inpayments to the United Kingdom is uncertain. Here not only the size of the increase but its very occurrence depends on the responsiveness of American consumers to the reduction in the dollar prices of British goods. The reason for the difference is as follows. Because of the increase in sterling prices of British imports, the volume of these imports declines. Since their dollar prices remain unchanged, their total dollar value (outpayments) is also certain to decline, the size of the reduction depending on the response of British consumers. On the inpayments side, the increase in the quantity of British exports results from a *decline* in their *dollar* prices. Their total dollar value rises only if the percentage increase in quantity is larger than the percentage decline in price. Whether or not that happens depends on the response of American consumers to the reduction in price.

Of course the British government is interested in the net effect of devaluation on its foreign exchange position. Its target is an *increase* in *inpayments minus outpayments* (or a decrease in outpayments minus inpayments), both being expressed in terms of dollars. While ideally outpayments should decline and inpayments should rise, the two components of the equation can compensate for each other. Even if the inpayments actually decline, the reduction may be more than offset by a larger cut in outpayments, thereby improving the balance of payments.

Economists have worked out complicated formulas for the conditions that must prevail if devaluation, in its immediate impact, is to reduce the excess of outpayments over inpayments. Known as the *stability condition,* or alternatively as the Marshall–Lerner condition (after the scholars who developed it), this condition can be seen intuitively by referring to Figures 7–3 and 7–4. Assume that the elasticity of $D_{\text{U.K.}}$ is zero and that of $D_{\text{U.S.}}$ is 1. Then dollar outpayments and inpayments remain unchanged when the pound is devalued. Thus, the critical values of the demand elasticities that would leave the British trade balance unaffected (when supply elastic-

---

[3]On the bottom panel in Figure 7-4, where the prices are expressed in terms of pounds, British supply ($S_{\text{U.K.}}$) remains unchanged. But the American demand curve is shifted upward as a result of the devaluation, reflecting the fact that a given number of dollars now buys more pounds. The quantity traded rises to Q_2, and so total sterling inpayments necessarily rise. But whether or not this rise translates into an increase in *dollar* inpayments depends on whether it is proportionately larger than the devaluation.

ities are infinite) are such that they sum up to one: $\Sigma D_E = 1$. From that point, we can raise the $D_{\text{U.K.}}$ elasticity above zero and obtain a decline in outpayments, and/or an increase in the $D_{\text{U.S.}}$ elasticity above 1 and obtain an increase in inpayments. In fact, the two elasticities can compensate for each other. Therefore, in the case where the two supply elasticities are infinite,[4] the condition for success is that the sum of the *demand elasticities* of the two countries must exceed unity. When supply elasticities are less than infinite, the formula becomes more complex. Also, in realistic situations, the sum of the elasticities must exceed the bare minimum so as to allow for reversal factors (discussed in the next sections). It bears emphasizing that this entire discussion relates to the size of the elasticities necessary to move the balance of payments in the *desired direction,* and not to the degree of impact that a given devaluation would have or to the time lag between devaluation and its effects.

There is abundant empirical evidence to suggest that in the case of industrial countries these conditions are indeed met. The response to price change is large enough to ensure that the relative price change has the salutary effect of both raising inpayments and lowering outpayments. Devaluation or depreciation of the currency is likely to decrease the country's external deficit. Whether the shift in the balance-of-payments position is sufficiently large to eliminate the deficit altogether depends on the size of the devaluation itself and on factors to be considered next. (Under a freely fluctuating exchange rate, the depreciation will continue until the deficit is eliminated.)

☐ The analysis of the relative price effect of devaluation can be expanded in several directions:

1. Figures 7-3 and 7-4 relate price to the quantity of a traded commodity. The upper panels can be translated into a relationship between the exchange rate and total foreign currencies demanded and supplied (as in the first section of Chapter 3) by transforming (or "mapping") the area under the equilibrium point (price times quantity) onto the horizontal axis. The horizontal axis then shows quantity of foreign exchange (dollars). Figure 7-3 would then illustrate the outpayments, or demand for dollars, while Figure 7-4 would show the inpayments, or supply of dollars. The resulting diagram depicts the foreign exchange market; it is discussed in Appendix IV.
2. The analysis of Figures 7-3 and 7-4 can be extended to the more general case in which the supply curves are less than infinitely elastic.
3. A similar analysis can be employed to show the effect of devaluation on

---

[4] Another assumption embodied in the analysis is that the devaluation occurs from an initial position of balanced trade ($X = M$).

the commodity terms of trade of the devaluing country (that is, the price of exports divided by the price of imports).[5]   ■

Domestic Income Effect

On the domestic front, the result just obtained implies an expansion of output, and therefore of employment and income, in the industries producing export goods and import substitutes. This expansion is brought about by an increase in demand from foreign and domestic sources, respectively, with the initial impact on output amounting to the rise in exports plus the decline in imports[6] $(\Delta X - \Delta M)$. This expansion spreads throughout the economy through the multiplier mechanism, generating a multiple increase in gross national product. As before, the multiplier is 1/(MPS + MPM), so that the increase in income is

$$\Delta Y = (\Delta X - \Delta M) \times \frac{1}{\text{MPS} + \text{MPM}}$$

As income rises so do imports, reversing *part* of the relative price effect on the balance of payments. The size of this *reversal factor* depends on the ΔY and the MPM. (It may be partly offset by the attraction of foreign investments.) *In the case of exchange rate adjustment, the relative price and income changes influence the balance of payments in opposite directions.*

Yet the domestic expansion of income and output is desirable in an economy suffering from unemployment, as the U.K. is assumed to be in our example. This explains why devaluation is a potent instrument for dealing with a combination of an external deficit and domestic unemployment: it lowers the deficit and increases output and employment.

Domestic Price Effect

Once full employment resources is approached, a likely companion to the increased level of economic activity is a rise in domestic prices. It affects the balance of payments adversely, constituting a second reversal factor. But unlike the income expansion it is also undesirable on domestic grounds. In fact, an increase in the domestic price level can be anticipated independently of the income expansion, dissipating part of the competitive edge gained by the devaluation. The very fact of a 33⅓ percent devaluation raises sterling prices of all imported commodities by 50 percent. And, since many imports enter as raw materials into the productive process, while others

---

[5] Readers interested in these extensions (numbers 2 and 3) may wish to consult pp. 412–21 of the third edition or obtain the material from the author upon request.

[6] Or rather the portion of the decline in imports that translates into expanded output of domestic substitute products.

(like food) enter into the cost of living, which partly determines wage rates, a wage-price inflationary spiral might be triggered as producers attempt to pass on the increase in production costs to consumers in the form of higher prices.[7] The extent of inflation depends on the degree of "openness" of the devaluating country—that is, on how dependent it is on foreign imports whose prices must rise—and on the success of the government in controlling the inflationary trends by contractionary policies. Intransigent labor unions that insist on tight escalator clauses (tying wage rates to the cost of living) and other benefits can negate many of the benefits of devaluation.

Both income expansion and increases in the domestic price level have the effect of encouraging imports and discouraging exports, thereby reversing part of the relative price effect *on the balance of payments*. Therefore the elasticity conditions necessary for the success of devaluation are actually more exacting than those outlined previously, because the buyers' response to price change must be high enough to allow for the offsetting influences of domestic income and prices.

For this reason it is incumbent upon government to contain the increase in prices as much as possible. Spiraling inflation can wipe out the entire competitive gain and lead to successive but useless devaluations. There is even a danger of the development of an inflationary psychology that feeds upon itself. People begin to expect prices to rise every year, and they purchase commodities as a hedge against inflation. By that very act, they push prices up and add to the inflationary flame. In time, money may even lose its usefulness as a store of value, which harms not only the balance of payments but also the domestic growth rate, as people are induced to curtail their rate of saving. The experience of some Latin American countries is a case in point.

This explains why the 1986 devaluation of the franc within the EMS was accompanied by a cut in French government spending, tight monetary policy, and abolition of control over currency movements. Similarly, the 1985 (15 percent) devaluation of the drachma was accompanied by contractionary policies in Greece. The two devaluations of the dollar in 1971 and 1973 brought about a sharp improvement in the U.S. balance of payments by 1973. At the same time they contributed to the domestic expansion of 1972–73. Conversely, the rise in the value of the dollar in 1981–85 produced a sizable trade deficit, but helped curb inflation in the U.S.

---

[7]Some economists, known as "global monetarists" (see Chapter 8) carry this point much further. They maintain that with open worldwide markets, the price of every commodity—be it a homogeneous good like wheat or a differentiated product like automobiles—must be the same in all countries. Under such an assumption, the dollar price of British exports cannot be affected by the pound devaluation. Pound prices of these goods must rise in full proportion to the devaluation to ensure this result. In these conditions the analysis of U.K. dollar outpayments remains intact, for it rests solely on the rise in domestic U.K. pound prices. But what about U.K. dollar inpayments, whose rise in the foregoing analysis depended on a decline in their dollar price? Adherents to the "global monetarist" view suggest that an inpayments increase is still possible: The rise in the domestic pound prices of exports, in proportion to the devaluation, would increase the profitability of exports and induce exporters to draw resources from other industries and expand their overseas shipments.

As a final illustration, during 1982, the value of the Mexican peso dropped from 4¢ to 1¢ in several steps. By August of that year, the change in relative prices had exerted a devastating effect on U.S. towns bordering on Mexico: Mexicans stopped shopping there altogether, while Americans in large numbers began shopping south of the border, where dollar prices dropped to a fraction of the predevaluation level. But domestic inflation in Mexico jumped to triple digit levels through the mechanism described in this section. When another devaluation of the peso was announced in 1985, it was to be accompanied by a sharp reduction in government expenditures and a tighter monetary policy, to prevent an inflationary spiral.

It is not possible, nor is it desirable, for a devaluating country to eliminate all income expansion. An increase in output and employment is, after all, one objective of a devaluation. In an inconsistent situation involving both an external deficit and a domestic recession, such as the United Kingdom faced in our hypothetical example, the devaluation should be large enough to allow for some offset to the relative price effect emanating from the real income sources. Only when full employment is approached and when the main impact of further expansion will fall on the price level is the policymaker obligated to slam on the brakes.[8] Considering the possible conflict between output expansion and price stability, the policymaker is required to walk the tightrope among several objectives: achieving the necessary improvement in the external trade position, maintaining a desirable expansion in employment and output, and containing the domestic price increases. He must also remember that all these influences take time to work their way through the economy.

Redistribution of Domestic Resources

While domestic price and income effects operate against the relative price effect in improving the balance of payments, devaluation also brings about domestic redistribution of resources favorable to its success. It will be recalled that exporters gain a considerable competitive edge abroad, while at the same time the prices of imports increase in terms of the domestic currency. Consequently, British producers can afford to raise the sterling price of both export and import substitutes to some extent and still remain competitive. In other words, the tendency toward domestic price increases as a result of devaluation is not evenly spread. What occurs is a differential increase because prices rise more in the foreign-trade industries (export and import substitutes) than in the purely domestic sectors (construction, services, and so on). Thus, there appears an *important change in relative prices within the economy:* The price ratio of traded to nontraded goods increases. This attracts resources to industries that produce internationally traded goods, which in most cases makes the economy more efficient and at the

---

[8]This is an oversimplification. In actual fact, there are large gray areas here, calling for different doses of contractionary measures.

same time promotes the type of production that improves the balance of payments. Many economists consider this to be a very important effect in the analysis of devaluation.

Revaluation (or appreciation) of the currency has the reverse effect of shifting resources away from the export- and import-competing industries to the nontraded sectors of the economy. This helps to explain the lopsided nature of the U.S. recovery in 1983–85. Although generally robust, it was concentrated mainly in the nontraded industries, such as construction and services. Certain traded goods industries failed to participate because the 60 percent appreciation of the dollar during 1981–85 made them noncompetitive with foreign products both at home and abroad.

In the previous four sections, four effects of devaluation were traced one by one and their possible interactions were analyzed. Because of the importance of product market elasticities in the analysis, these effects are lumped into what is known as the *elasticity approach* to devaluation. Specifically, the analysis showed that devaluation is likely to help a country's external position and at the same time promote an expansion of income and employment. Although this was not explicitly stated, domestic expansion is often considered a prerequisite for improvement in the balance of payments, because the increased production of export goods and import substitutes requires the employment of new resources. Clearly the ready availability of labor and machinery to be put to productive use is of crucial importance to the success of devaluation.

Another View of Devaluation—The Absorption Approach

In order to highlight the relationship between the external and internal effects of devaluation, we turn to an alternative way of analyzing devaluation—the *absorption approach*. Focusing on the relation between the balance of payments and domestic conditions, this approach complements and sheds additional light on what has been said thus far.

For simplification, consider an economy that produces, consumes, and trades only commodities. The imbalance of trade is then identical to the imbalance of payments. The following equality between two pairs of magnitudes must hold for all periods: The difference between the value of goods *produced* in the economy (Y) and that of goods *absorbed*[9] domestically by all users (A) must equal the difference between exports (X) and imports (M). In other words,

$$A - Y = M - X \text{ or } Y - A = X - M$$

If absorption exceeds production, the difference between them must be made up of excess imports over exports; and when production is higher

---

[9] Absorption means the total of private and public consumption and capital accumulation.

than domestic absorption, the difference must be expressed in excess exports over imports.[10] This is the fundamental identity of the absorption approach.

☐ The identity can be derived from the national income accounts. National income consists of four types of expenditure: consumption, investments, government expenditures, and net exports:

$$Y = C + I + G + (X - M) \tag{1}$$

If we omit the import component of C, I, and G, and confine these terms to spending on domestically produced goods, we must also delete M. We obtain:

$$Y = C_d + I_d + G_d + X \tag{2}$$

where d denotes "domestic." Equation (2) states that national product or income consists of what is produced and absorbed domestically ($C_d + I_d + G_d$) plus what is exported (X). The goods and services produced and absorbed domestically are called domestic absorption (A_d). That is, $A_d = C_d + I_d + G_d$. Therefore,

$$Y = A_d + X \tag{3}$$

☐ On the other hand, total absorption (A) consists of what is produced (and absorbed) domestically (A_d) plus imports (M). In our notation,

$$A = A_d + M \tag{4}$$

and therefore $A_d = A - M$. We may combine this with equation (3) to obtain

$$Y = A_d + X = A - M + X = A + X - M \tag{5}$$

Hence, $Y - A = X - M$, or $A - Y = M - X$ ■

Starting from a deficit position where imports (M) exceed exports (X), absorption (A) must exceed production (Y) by the same amount. This is essentially a case of *a country living beyond its means* (absorbing more than it produces), or a country investing in excess of domestic savings. When the currency is devalued, the price and income effects come into force and work their way through the economy. If the relative price effect on the balance of payments is more powerful than the interacting income effect, the final outcome is a reduction in the trade deficit ($M - X$). But that

[10] Think in terms of a one-good economy—one that produces cars, for example. If production is 1000 cars each year and domestic absorption into all uses (including inventories, whether desired or not) is 800, then exports must exceed imports by 200. Exports of 300 and imports of 100 would thus yield an appropriate balance. Alternatively, assume that production is 1500 and imports are 500. Then the total number of cars available for disposition is 2000. If 1700 cars absorbed by domestic users, then 300 are left over for exports. Hence, again:

$$1700 - 1500 = 500 - 300$$
$$(A) \quad (Y) \quad (M) \quad (X)$$

Given three of the four magnitudes, the fourth can be found by using the identity.

necessarily implies an equivalent reduction in $A - Y$: Either absorption (A) is reduced or domestic production (Y) is increased or a combination of the two occurs.

When devaluation occurs under conditions of unemployment, the main impact is on Y: Production of exportables and import substitutes rises, and the effect spreads throughout the economy by means of the multiplier mechanism. Resources that were previously unemployed are put to work to produce the goods whose sale was made possible by the improved competitive position.[11] It is for this reason that persistent balance-of-payments deficits combined with unemployed resources in the domestic economy constitute an "ideal" situation to be met by devaluation.

Under full employment, there are no free resources to be put into production to increase Y. Devaluation, which necessarily exerts pressure on scarce resources, is likely to dissipate in domestic inflation. Prices rather than real output would rise. To be sure, there is reason to expect more efficient allocation of resources to follow the devaluation, so that more goods can be produced with existing resources. This is particularly pronounced when the devaluation replaces an assortment of exchange and import controls. In underdeveloped areas it is often the case that countries with overvalued currencies resort to complicated systems of control, inevitably leading to gross misallocation of resources and widespread inefficiencies. When devaluation finally comes, economic efficiency can be expected to improve. But this is not the situation in industrial countries, where the effect of improved allocation is not likely to be great.

Thus, under full employment, the crucial question revolves around the economy's ability to reduce domestic absorption. Only a reduction in absorption can release otherwise occupied resources in order for the production of export goods and import substitutes to take advantage of the devaluation. There are reasons to expect some reduction in absorption to follow from the devaluation itself. One of them is the resource redistribution effect discussed in the previous section. Even under conditions of full employment, some resources would be drawn to the export- and import-competing industries from the nontraded sectors of the economy. Other reasons to expect a reduction in absorption follow from the alleged reaction of the public to a general increase in domestic prices following devaluation. They involve fine points of economic theory and need not detain us here.[12] In the final analysis, success depends on the ability of the government to

---

[11] As a result of the increase in production and income, absorption will also rise, but by less than the rise in income, because part of the increase will leak away into savings. The higher the MPS, the larger will be the difference between ΔY and ΔA, and the more successful will be the devaluation.

[12] Here is an example of such an effect. A general rise in the price level lowers the real value of people's savings inasmuch as these are invested in fixed money-value assets such as bonds and savings accounts. To the extent that people's behavior is governed by a desire to attain some level of real saving, they would try to save more to make up for the loss by building up their monetary balances. They can do that by lowering consumption out of any given income, which in turn means that absorption is reduced.

bring about a reduction in absorption through appropriate domestic measures.

Chapter 8 will present an alternative view of devaluation, known as "The Monetary Approach."

Summary of Devaluation Analysis

Need for Policy Mixes

By now it should be clear why a change in the exchange rate is recommended for countries in inconsistent situations. Since *devaluation improves the balance of payments and also expands output and employment,* it is well suited for dealing with a combination of domestic unemployment and external deficits. The fact that under the Bretton Woods system the dollar could not be devalued (when the United States experienced deficits and unemployment) made U.S. policymakers increasingly discontent with that system and was one of the factors responsible for its demise.

Exchange revaluation has the opposite effects (requiring the reader to reverse the thought processes employed above): The deterioration in a country's competitive position lowers inpayments or increases outpayments or both. At the same time, output and employment decline in the export- and import-competing industries, and from there the contraction spreads throughout the economy. Consequently, an upward adjustment of the exchange rate is well suited for a country experiencing persistent surpluses in the balance of payments and inflationary booms (overemployment) at the same time. *Revaluation removes the surpluses and dampens the inflation.*

Attainment of the desired results on the external and internal fronts requires that exchange-rate adjustment be accompanied by appropriate domestic measures. In practice, all cases require a mix of policies rather than one measure. The final aim of policy is to satisfy the combined external and internal objectives, including balance-of-payments equilibrium, price stability, full employment, desirable growth rate, and whatever other goals the community agrees upon. Starting from a given situation, any one policy instrument designed to attain one objective is likely to overshoot or undershoot the mark in terms of the other objectives. Such is the nature of the beast. Other instruments must then be brought into play to bring about the necessary adjustments in these areas and put the economy on an even course. It is a rare (perhaps even nonexistent) case when one instrument can properly deal with more than one target. Normally, it is necessary to employ as many instruments as there are targets to attain the final objectives. The appropriate combination of instruments often necessitates a delicate balancing of the policy doses administered; the nature of the mix depends on the objectives as well as on the circumstances. Appendix V contains a geometric exposition of the policy mixes required to attain internal and external balance.

Effectiveness of Policy

So far, the proper policy mix has been dealt with only in terms of the situation confronting the country and its policy target. But the optimal mix depends not only on the situation but on the relative effectiveness of the policy itself—and that varies from country to country.

Consider, for example, the effectiveness of expenditure policies in dealing with a balance-of-payments deficit. A reduction of $1 million in GNP lowers imports and stimulates exports by a fraction of that amount. The size of this fraction depends on the marginal propensity to import and other variables relating to the degree of openness of the economy, or the degree to which it depends on foreign trade. In an oversimplified fashion, it might be stated that the more open the economy is, the greater will be the effectiveness of expenditure policy in dealing with external imbalances, since a given change in GNP would have a greater effect on the balance of trade than in a closed economy. Conversely, in a closed economy (such as the United States) with a low marginal propensity to import, a given change in GNP would produce a much smaller change in the trade balance. In other words, it would take a huge reduction in the gross national product to bring about any noticeable improvement in the trade balance.

On the other hand, for a closed economy the cost of engaging in a switching policy, such as devaluation, is likely to be less than for an open economy. "Switching policy" is a catch-all phrase for measures that rely primarily on changes in relative prices (the ratio of import prices to domestic prices) to improve the balance of payments. Switching policies are distinguished from income and expenditure policies, which focus on the income mechanism. An exchange-rate adjustment that affects the ratio of domestic to import prices and causes purchasers to switch to the cheaper goods is a prime example: Devaluation induces a switch from imports to domestic substitutes, whereas revaluation does the reverse.

In a small open economy, the cost of switching can be high. Under the elasticity conditions that normally obtain in the industrial countries, the commodity terms of trade deteriorate as a result of devaluation.[13] When a large share of production and consumption is accounted for by foreign trade, a profound effect on domestic economy activity results. Foreign imports play an important role in production as well as in the cost of living, and a rise in their prices can cause many dislocations in the economy and reduce real income. The reallocation of resources (as between industries) following devaluation may also be on a large scale. On the other hand, in a relatively closed economy all these effects are smaller in size and more minor in consequence; it is *relatively* less costly and less disruptive to adjust by switching than by means of an income policy. In addition, a large country may need a smaller switching dose to rectify a given imbalance than a small country

---

[13] *Commodity terms of trade* are defined as the ratio of the export price index to the import price index. Their deterioration means that the country can obtain less imports for a given quantity of exports, or, equivalently, it must give up more goods by way of export to obtain a given quantity of imports.

would. Thus, the effectiveness of switching policies, or their cost, varies among countries.

In sum, it is not only the situation confronting a country that determines the optimal policy mix. It is also the relative cost or effectiveness of the various policies, which varies from one country to another, depending on how closed or open the economy is or on the magnitude of foreign trade relative to the gross national product. Both the targets and the relative effectiveness of various policies must be considered before the optimal mix can be determined.

Foreign Retaliation

This discussion cannot end without a reminder that devaluation, like domestic policies, has foreign repercussions. When a country devalues its currency, it experiences an increase in output, employment, and income, because exports expand and imports contract. But, by implication, its trading partners suffer a reduction in exports and an increase in imports, with an attendant decline in output and employment. The larger and more important the devaluating country is, the greater are the effects elsewhere. If the country devalues in order to get itself out of a domestic recession, then it merely inflicts a recession on other nations. Such a "beggar thy neighbor" policy was fairly common during the worldwide depression of the 1930s. Trading partners can easily retaliate by devaluating their own currencies competitively as they did in the 1930s. This danger is enhanced in a period of managed floats. In a system of heavily managed floats, a country can maintain an artificially undervalued currency, givings its export- and import-competing industries a competitive advantage. This is sometimes referred to as "exchange-rate protection."[14] And it clearly underscores the need for international harmonization of economic policies. In a multicountry world, it is no longer possible for a country to attain internal and external balance by use of its own policy instruments. Other countries can easily frustrate the balance.[15]

Fluctuating Exchange Rates

Thus far, the balance-of-payments adjustment mechanism has been discussed within the context of fixed exchange rates or highly managed floats.

---

[14] See M. Corden, "Protection, the Exchange Rate, and Macroeconomic Policy," *Finance & Development,* June 1985.

[15] Another feature of policy mixes in a multicountry world is known as the "redundancy problem." Since the balance of payments of all countries in the world combined necessarily adds up to zero (shows neither deficit nor surplus), external balance can be achieved if all countries *but one* achieve it. Thus, if each of N countries has two policy objectives—internal and external balance—except for one country, which is concerned with only one of these, the total number of objectives, and therefore the total number of policy instruments required, is $2N - 1$. There is, in a sense, a spare policy instrument in the system, giving one country some freedom for maneuverability. In the 1950s this freedom belonged to the United States, which did not have to be concerned with its balance-of-payments problem, because foreign countries were content to pile up dollar assets.

In what follows, we consider some implications this analysis holds for the case of freely fluctuating exchange rates discussed in Chapter 3.

What Governs Exchange Variations

What factors determine the exchange rate when it is free to respond to market forces? In the short run, the exchange rate is a price that equalizes the demand and the supply of *stocks* of financial assets.[16] The price of a currency represents a balance between the desire to hold stocks of assets denominated in that currency and the quantity of such assets in existence. And of all the assets, particular importance is attached to money. Thus, relative rates of money growth between two countries is a prime determinant of the exchange rate between the two respective currencies in the short run.

But in the longer run, the exchange rate is the "price" that equalizes inpayment and outpayment *flows* in the balance-of-payments statement.[17] Economic events and policies influence the exchange rate through their effect on these flows, as illustrated in Chapter 3. While it is impossible to provide an exhaustive list of all factors that may come into play, it is still useful to sort them out under broad headings and emphasize the lines of causation to be observed.

First, there are foreign developments beyond the control of the country in question that bear directly on its balance of payments. An international shift in demand that increases demand for the country's traditional exports would raise the volume and price of these exports and cause its currency to appreciate. Conversely, a shift in demand away from its traditional exports, or an economic slump in its major markets, would harm its export performance and depress the exchange value of its currency. A similar outcome would result from a sharp rise in the price of its imports, other things being equal. Oil prices quadrupling in 1973 engineered by the OPEC cartel, and their doubling again in 1979, brought about wide fluctuations in the value of practically all important currencies. Countries possessing no energy sources of their own, and therefore depending largely on imported petroleum, witnessed the value of their currencies decline relative to that of countries less dependent on imported petroleum. Conversely, the sharp decline in international oil prices in the 1980s resulted in depreciation of the currencies of several oil-producing countries. It was one of the factors responsible for the decline in the exchange value of the British pound and of the Mexican peso.

Under a second broad heading, we classify all policies of the country's own government that bear directly on the balance of payments. Thus, the imposition of import restrictions or limitations on capital outflow raises the value of the currency. The converse of this was illustrated when, following the removal of government controls on the outflow of investment capital

---

[16] Hence, this view is known as the *asset markets approach* to exchange-rate determination.

[17] One way of reconciling the *stock* and *flow* formulations of exchange-rate determination lies in viewing flow information as being capitalized into stock variables.

from the United States in January, 1974, the dollar slumped on the foreign exchange markets. Likewise, the imposition of a tax by Switzerland on bank deposits of foreign residents (negative interest) in 1978 curtailed the inflow of funds into that country and abated the appreciation of the franc.

Third, domestic economic events and government policies are likely to *depreciate* the exchange rate *if* they:

1. Interfere directly with the capacity to produce and export.
2. Raise GNP in the country relative to that of the outside world, thereby stimulating imports more than exports.
3. Raise domestic prices relative to prices in other countries, thereby impeding the country's ability to compete on both the foreign and domestic markets.
4. Reduce the country's interest rate relative to those in the outside world, thus stimulating the outflow and discouraging the inflow of short-term capital.

In each case, opposite policies or economic events would *appreciate* the country's currency.

An interesting case of currency appreciation is worth a special note. Consider a country like the U.K. where the traditional exports originate in the manufacturing sector. The discovery and development of North Sea oil in the 1970s has freed the U.K. of dependence on imported petroleum. As a result, the exchange value of the pound sterling rose precipitously. This had the salutary effect of dampening the rate of inflation. But, on the negative side, the competitive position of the manufacturing sector (both at home and abroad) deteriorated sharply. The long-term effect may be to erode the country's industrial base to a point from which it would be difficult to recover. A similar phenomenon was caused in Holland by the development of natural gas,[18] and such an effect is common in countries with a newly developed natural resource base.

While the foregoing factors are fundamental in nature and likely to govern exchange variations in the long run, short-run fluctuations may also result from speculative capital movements that can be triggered by *expectations* and rumors. Expectations may be based on underlying economic trends, or they may result from sheer confidence factors in the political or sociological arena.

The Role of Fluctuating Rates

Empirical studies suggest that, at least in the industrial countries, elasticities in international trade are generally large enough to meet the conditions for a stable foreign exchange market outlined earlier in this chapter. It is the relatively elastic demand for traded goods that ensures the "normal"

---

[18] Hence, it is sometimes referred to as the "Dutch disease." Another source of pressure on the manufacturing sector arises from its reduced ability to compete with the natural resource sector for productive factors when natural resources command exceptionally high prices on world markets. For a survey of this literature see Max Corden, "Booming Sector and Dutch Disease Economics: Survey and Consolidation," *Oxford Economic Papers,* 1984, 359–80.

slopes of the demand and supply curves for foreign exchange shown in Figure 3-1. Under stable conditions, the foreign exchange market determines the exchange rate at a level that clears the market for foreign currencies. Automatic exchange fluctuations can be relied upon to ensure equilibrium in the balance of payments: A deficit would cause currency depreciation and a surplus, appreciation. These adjustments contain the equilibrating mechanism that restores equilibrium to the balance of payments. The marketplace, rather than the judgment of government officials, determines the extent of exchange-rate adjustment necessary to restore external equilibrium. (Note however that overall balance-of-payments equilibrium does not mean that each subcategory of the international transactions statement is in balance.)

A freely fluctuating exchange rate frees the government of direct responsibility for balance-of-payments adjustment; it can rely on the market to provide the necessary equilibrating mechanism. The government in turn can concentrate on domestic policy goals, and thus the conflict between policy objectives in "inconsistent" situations is removed. Also, *there is no need to accumulate and hold international reserves, for these are only required to maintain a fixed exchange rate.* By contrast, in the case of a *managed* float, the exchange rate may sometimes be nudged away from its equilibrium level, yielding deficits or surpluses in the balance of payments; for that reason, reserves are required to manage the float. As long as floats are managed the balance of payments remains a policy objective that cannot be disregarded. Inasmuch as the dollar continues to be the main intervention currency in the present-day system of managed floats, the exchange value of the dollar is partly determined by the activities of foreign central banks.

Exchange fluctuations also affect the domestic economy—affecting money, income, prices, and resource allocation between the production of traded and nontraded goods—in a manner similar to that of a government-sponsored exchange-rate adjustment. Thus, depreciation of the currency raises domestic income and prices and shifts resources from production of nontraded goods to the export- and import-competing industries, while appreciation does the reverse. The difference between the two systems is that under fluctuating rates the adjustments occur in small daily intervals rather than in one sizable discrete step (although many small changes in the same direction can add up to a substantial change over a relatively short period) and in response to market forces rather than to a governmental decree.

Because the exchange rate responds to market forces, a fluctuating rate regime is capable of insulating a country from disturbances *originating abroad*, at least in part. In the section "Foreign Repercussions" in Chapter 6, it was seen that the fixed exchange rate serves as a link between countries. Such a link is absent under freely fluctuating rates. If country A experiences a depression and lowers its imports from its trading partner, country B, then under a fixed rate the depression would spread to B (via the decline in its exports and the multiplier mechanism), whereas under a fluctuating exchange rate, B's currency would merely depreciate. Likewise, under a fixed-rate system, an inflation in country A would spread to B, but under a fluctuating rate regime it would merely cause B's currency to appreciate. On the other hand, under a free float, *internal* economic fluctuations tend to be "bottled up" in the country in which they occur.

However, the insulation of the economy from the effects of outside fluctuations is not complete, because exchange variations produce domestic disturbances via variations in the terms of trade and shifts of resources between industries. Still, some measure of insulation is attained. Indeed this is one reason why Canada, fearing economic fluctuations imported from its giant neighbor south of the border, opted for a fluctuating exchange rate during 1951–64, and again in recent years.

The discussion of the foreign trade multiplier is not fully applicable to the fluctuating exchange-rate regime. An autonomous rise in a country's exports or an autonomous decline in its imports will not necessarily expand its income, and certainly not by the amount indicated in the multiplier analysis. Rather, an increase in exports or a decrease in imports will appreciate the exchange value of the country's currency until equilibrium is restored in the balance of payments. Depreciation will occur in the cases of an autonomous decline in exports or increase in imports.

When domestic policies are not coordinated among countries, each jealously guarding its right for independent economic action, fluctuating exchange rates are more appropriate than fixed rates. However, even with fluctuating rates there is a need for some measure of consultation and coordination. At the very least, it is important to avoid competitive depreciation of currencies when the float is "dirty." The record of the industrial countries in meeting this requirement during the floating rates period has been satisfactory.

Some Unanswered Questions

Much economic research has been devoted to determining what combinations of policy instruments are most appropriate for moving the economy toward certain targets, and much has been learned about the processes involved. But the gaps in our knowledge are still wide. They are reflected in comments that frequently emanate from high quarters to the effect that "fine tuning of the economy" is all but impossible, given our present state of knowledge. As in the case of the last chapter, we conclude with a discussion of some unanswered questions.

The Degree of Impact

In the case of persistent balance-of-payments deficits, perhaps coupled with unemployment and excess productive capacity, the economist must determine whether the currency is overvalued and whether the overevaluation is amenable to cure by a downward adjustment in the exchange rate. If so, he must estimate the degree of devaluation required. The same principle applies to revaluation in the case of persistent surpluses. But to arrive at a precise figure is all but impossible. Theoretically, an equilibrium exchange rate between two currencies must in some sense reflect the purchasing power of these currencies in their respective countries; that is, it must reflect their relative price levels. The method that relies on price comparison between the two countries to determine the equilibrium exchange rate is known as the *purchasing-power parity* (PPP) doctrine.

Developed originally in the 1920s, the doctrine has *absolute* and *relative* variants. Under the first version, a comparison of the average price levels between two countries is carried out at a given point in time, and the exchange rate between the two respective currencies at that time is said to reflect that relative price level. If the two countries use the same assortment of goods, that representative basket can be priced in both currencies. If it costs £1,000 in the U.K. and $2,000 in the U.S., then the exchange rate is £1 = $2. The problem is that the representative basket of goods is not the same in both countries (different consumption habits and the like), and different commodity baskets produce different results. To avoid this difficulty, the relative version was developed. It relates the exchange rate to *changes* over time in the purchasing powers of the two currencies as measured against a prior base period, when the actual exchange rate was supposedly in equilibrium. If, for example, prices in the United States doubled while prices in the United Kingdom tripled, then the sterling would have to be devalued by one-third relative to its dollar exchange rate in the base period.[19]

Yet, either variant of the purchasing-power parity doctrine leaves many questions unanswered. Where does one find an ideal equilibrium period to serve as a base (in case of the relative version)? Which of the many price or production-cost indexes should be used for the comparison?[20] How can we account for changes in the living and buying habits of the two populations being compared? How do we incorporate the effect of changes in income and employment that might have occurred in the intervening period? How can we allow for the effect of capital flows that are not even reflected in the

---

[19] For a comprehensive treatment see L. H. Officer, *Purchasing Power Parity: Theory, Evidence, Relevance*, Greenwich, Conn.; IAI Press, 1982.

[20] Most widely used in this connection is the wholesale price index, because the consumer price index includes services and other items that never enter international trade. It is interesting to note that the prices of such services (haircuts and dry cleaning, for example) are higher in the United States than in the less developed countries, such as Mexico. One reason for this may be that the prices of internationally traded goods, such as manufactured products, tend toward some degree of equality between countries because of trade flows. Since labor productivity is several times higher in the United States (because of more mechanized production, among other things), American wage rates in the foreign-trade industries are much higher than their Mexican counterparts. Within each economy, mobility of labor exerts a strong pressure toward equalization of wage rates (for equal skills) in all industries. This means that wage rates in the U.S. service industries are much higher than those in Mexico. But since there is no such international productivity difference in these industries, American prices end up being several times higher than those in Mexico. And such price differences can exist in service industries because they are not traded internationally.

price levels? All these factors affect the balance of payments and therefore the exchange rate. They make it impossible to apply a simple rule of thumb in constructing an estimate. They do not render the price comparison operationally irrelevant, however. It must be regarded as a general guide, to be coupled with other considerations, and used with discretion.

While the PPP has been shown to hold when a very long period of adjustment (such as 30 years) is allowed for, prolonged departures[21] from it have been rather common in the floating rates period. For example, the dollar exchange rate clearly departed from PPP value during 1981–85.

In countries where inflation is rampant, price level changes tend to dominate all other factors affecting the exchange rate, and the doctrine emerges as a powerful guide to exchange-rate determination. Thus, in 1982–85 annual inflation in Israel was in the triple-digit range. And the Israeli shekel depreciated continuously against the dollar in a manner that reflected roughly the differential inflation rates between the two countries. The same rule applies to certain Latin American countries.

But where inflation differentials are small, other factors in the exchange-rate equation become important. And the inability to pinpoint the equilibrium exchange rate is one reason why many economists have been moved to advocate exchange-rate flexibility where market forces determine the exchange rate.

Another way to approach the problem is to turn it around and ask what the impact of a given devaluation would be on the balance of payments and on the gross national product. This too is a rather complex question, because devaluation has several effects that all interact with one another and because the relative price and income effects exert opposite influences on the balance of payments. However, economists have been able to devise mathematical formulas that incorporate the main influences. In such formulas the price effects are measured in terms of price elasticities, while the income effects are shown through various marginal propensities. Estimating the size of these responses is a statistical task to which much effort has been devoted. For countries where such estimates exist, the effect of alternative devaluations of different sizes on the external trade accounts can be roughly approximated. (Even here, however, we know next to nothing about the effect of devaluation on capital flows.)

Thus, the problem of magnitude can be approached from both sides, giving the policymaker an idea of the degree of adjustment necessary in

---

[21] Vast and prolonged departures of exchange rates from PPP values often invalidate international comparisons of living standards. The most common indicator of the standard of living is per capita GNP, or GNP divided by the population. This is calculated by each country in its own currency, and then converted into dollars via the prevailing exchange rate. Therefore the international comparison depends on the exchange rate. The sharp rise in the exchange value of the dollar in the first half of the 1980s raised U.S. per-capita GNP relative to that of other countries. Yet there has been no commensurate increase in the relative U.S. living standards. For that reason it may be advisable to use some measure of relative prices (PPP) rather than the exchange rate to convert per-capita GNP from one currency to another.

the exchange rate. What he actually does often depends on political as much as economic considerations. Such questions as how much the currency can be devalued without eliciting retaliation by the country's trading partners or without undue loss of prestige at home and abroad are usually foremost in the minds of any government officials contemplating exchange-rate adjustment.

Time Path

The time path of the economy once its currency has been devalued or depreciated is equally important. For example, as the dollar declined from the lofty level it attained in 1985, how long would it take before the U.S. trade balance improved?

In the case of a fixed exchange rate, such knowledge helps the policymakers determine the need, magnitude, and timing of supplementary measures. Immediately following the dollar devaluation of 1971, for example, the U.S. balance of payments deteriorated because the dollar cost of previously contracted U.S. imports went up while the dollar value of American exports remained unchanged. Only when the volume of imports declined in response to higher import prices and the volume of exports rose in response to lower prices in terms of foreign currencies did the balance of payments improve. And that did not happen until 1973 when the dollar devaluations in December 1971 and February 1973 converted the U.S. external deficit into a surplus. Similarly, in the year beginning March 1985 the dollar depreciated by over 25 percent forcing a rise in the dollar price of Japanese goods.[22] At the same time it has made U.S. goods more competitive abroad. Yet the immediate effect was an *increase* in the U.S. trade deficit. An improvement can be expected only after a time lag. This phenomenon is commonly described as a "J-curve."[23]

The time lag involved in exchange-rate adjustment is important in a system of fluctuating exchange rates, for in that case it determines the efficiency of the system. If the lag is long and trade flows respond slowly to exchange-rate adjustments, then exchange variations cannot be relied upon to produce equilibrating trade flows with dispatch. Rather, in the short run, equilibrating capital movements will have to be relied upon to bridge

---

[22] The mark and the yen rose by about 35 percent, but the Canadian dollar declined by 8 percent against the dollar over that year. Some scholars maintain that the yen would have to rise further to ¥150 = $1 or higher, to attain balance in Japan's external accounts.

[23] The term "J-curve" refers to the shape of the adjustment path frequently followed by the trade balance of countries in response to an exchange-rate devaluation. The initial impact of a depreciation is often negative because import prices rise more rapidly in local currency than export prices and there has not been time for the volume of trade to adjust. After a lag, however, the trade balance improves with a reduction in the rate of growth of imports, a rise in the rate of growth of exports, and a reduction in the gap between the price indices of imports and exports. As a result of these factors, there is an initial decline in the trade balance, but this adverse movement will be checked and reversed, leading the trade balance to follow the rising portion of the "J." See M. Kreinin, S. Martin, and E. Sheehey, "Differential Response of U.S. Import Prices and Quantities to Exchange Rate Adjustments," Michigan State University Discussion Paper No. 8406, December 1984.

the balance-of-payments deficit until the necessary adjustment in trade flows come about. However, for a variety of reasons, short-term capital may be destabilizing: It may move in the direction opposite to what is desirable. For example, if a currency depreciates as a result of a balance-of-payments deficit, financiers may expect further depreciation and sell the currency rather than buy it. In other words, capital movement may not be a reliable temporary mechanism to bridge a balance-of-payments gap. In that case the efficiency of the system of floating exchange rates must depend on a relatively quick response of trade flows to exchange variations.

The following are selected results pertaining to the period of floating exchange rates:

A one percent depreciation of the U.S. dollar increases the export volume by 1.5 percent.

Most of the effect of exchange-rate changes on the volume of imports occurs in the three subsequent quarters.

Expected movements in the dollar exchange rate influence the current volume of both U.S. exports and imports.

Similar estimates are available for other countries.[24] But at best they yield rough orders of magnitude.

Review Questions

1. a. Between 1981 and 1985 the exchange value of the dollar increased by 50 percent. Explain the effects of this advance on the U.S. trade position and the domestic economy. Make use of charts and formulas as needed.
   b. In the year following February 1985 the dollar declined by 25 percent. Explain the effect of this depreciation on the U.S. trade position and the domestic economy. Would you expect these effects to take place in 1985–86 or in subsequent years? Why?

2. In 1983 the Mexican government, faced with external deficits and domestic unemployment, devalued the peso by 50 percent. Explain the effects of this devaluation, using:
   a. Elasticities approach (four effects)
   b. Absorption approach
   c. Internal and external balance approach. (Demonstrate why other policies must accompany devaluation to reach a certain combination of targets).

   Repeat the analysis for the 1986 (6 percent) devaluation of the French franc within the EMS.

3. Why does the IMF often require both currency devaluation and domestic contractionary measures, of countries seeking to draw on its resources?

---

[24] Warner and Kreinin, "Determinants of International Trade Flows," *Op. cit.*

4. Explain the *absorption approach* to devaluation. What does it say about the effectiveness of devaluation at a time of full employment?

Does the existence of a large current account deficit mean that the country is "living beyond its means"? Why?

In 1986 the U.S. was urging Japan to increase domestic consumption and investment, in an effort to reduce its external trade surplus. How would such a domestic policy affect Japan's trade position?

5. What is meant by the statement: Under a fixed exchange rate, changes in income and prices influence the B. of P. in the same direction, but in the case of exchange rate adjustment they influence the B. of P. in opposite directions?

6. The 1985–86 depreciation of the dollar may in time:
   a. Increase $(X - M)$, and GNP.
   b. Shift resources from the nontraded to the traded sectors.
   c. Precipitate domestic inflation.

   Explain.

7. Explain the following terms:
   (a) "J" curve, (b) Relative PPP, (c) Absolute PPP.

8. On June 25, 1986 the *Wall Street Journal* carried the following story:

   > Japan's economic output fell 0.5% in the first quarter (of 1986), the first GNP decline in 11 years. The drop was attributed to a sharply stronger yen, which caused Japanese exports to fall 4.9% during the quarter.

   Explain the above statement showing the relation between the rise of the yen and the decline in Japan's exports; and between the change in exports and the drop in GNP. Use diagrams and formulae as needed.

9. In July 1986 China devalued its currency, the yuan, "in a bid to revive exports, tourism and foreign investments." Explain how the 13 percent devaluation would have these effects.

10. In mid-1986 U.S. auto sales jumped, "while sales of Japanese cars slowed as the stronger yen pushed prices higher in the U.S." Explain.

8

The Monetary Approach to the Balance of Payments

Chapters 6 and 7 reviewed several mechanisms through which equilibrium in the balance of payments is maintained and restored. Although the theories involved are largely reconcilable and are certainly not mutually exclusive, they differ from one another in the economic processes each emphasizes. It has become the conventional wisdom to label them *approaches;* they are commonly referred to as the "elasticities approach," the "income-multiplier approach," the "absorption approach," and the policy approach that stresses "internal and external balance." The policy discussion in this book (except for this chapter) is based on the "traditional" approaches.

In the 1970s there emerged a new approach that highlights the role of money in the adjustment process. Labeled the *monetary approach* to the balance of payments, it is offered as an alternative to the traditional theories. Developed partly in the tradition of domestic "monetarism,"[1] its predictions and policy implications are different from those obtained from the other approaches.

Monetarists do not use the term "balance of payments" in its conventional sense, which is the statement of international transactions. Rather, they take it to mean one of the balances or, better yet, imbalances. In particular, they deal only with the accommodating or financing (as distinguished from autonomous) transactions, as defined in the discussion that appeared in Chapter 2. The most useful concept for the monetarists' formulation in the case of fixed exchange rates would be an accommodating item that shows the effect of a balance-of-payments deficit or surplus on

---

[1] Both the domestic and external varieties find their intellectual homeground at the University of Chicago. For extensive discussion of the monetary approach see M. Kreinin and L. Officer, *The Monetary Approach to the Balance of Payments: A Survey,* Princeton Studies in International Finance No. 43, 1978, and K. Clements, "The Monetary Approach to Exchange Rate Determination: A Geometric Analysis," *Weltwirtschaftliches Archive,* 1981, no. 1.

the domestic monetary base (the latter consisting of commercial-bank reserves and currency in the hands of the nonbank public), which in turn determines money supply. The nearest approximation to this balance is the "official reserve transactions balance."

Clearly, the monetary approach to the balance of payments does not attempt to explain the behavior of individual balance-of-payments components, such as trade and service flows, long-term capital, or private short-term capital. These are all lumped together into one "above the line" category. Nor is the approach concerned with any of the "partial balances." Consequently, it has been described as analyzing the problem "from the bottom up," in contrast to other approaches, which pay attention to the composition of the balance or imbalance.

The Underlying Cause of External Imbalances (Under Fixed Exchange Rates)

As defined above, the balance of payments is viewed by the monetarists as *essentially a monetary phenomenon.* Payments imbalances are rooted in the relationship between the demand for and the supply of money. The monetary approach rests on the basic premise that over the long run—usually taken to mean a period longer than a year, but shorter than a decade—there exists a stable demand function for money as a *stock.*[2] The quantity of nominal money balances demanded is a positive function of nominal income.

Demand and Supply of Money

It will be recalled that the equation of exchange is $MV = PO$. The terms can be rearranged to obtain $M = 1/V(PO)$. Labeling $1/V = k$ and substituting y for O, we obtain an equation that represents the demand for money: $M^d = kPy$,[3] where

M^d = desired nominal money balances
k = desired ratio of nominal money balances to nominal national income
y = real output
P = domestic price level
$\left.\right\}$ Therefore, $yP = GNP$

---

[2] A *stock* variable is distinguished from a *flow* variable in that it indicates a magnitude at a point in time. By contrast a flow shows movement of the variable per unit of time (such as a year). Thus the quantity of water in a filled tub is a stock. Inflows and outflows of water are flows that change the stock. The amount of capital in the economy is a stock, whereas annual investments are flows that add to that stock. The outstanding public debt is a stock, whereas the annual budget deficits are flows that add to that stock. Money supply at a point in time is a stock, whereas annual changes in money supply are flows that add to or subtract from the stock.

[3] In a more complete statement, it is also a function of the rate of interest, viewed as the opportunity cost of holding money.

The demand for nominal money balance is a stable positive function of the price level and of real income. For example, if the GNP ($= Py$) is $4 trillion and $k = \frac{1}{5}$ (velocity $= 5$), then the desired stock of money is $800 billion.

Money supply (M^s), for which demand is a stable function, is a constant multiple (m) of the monetary base. In turn, that base has two components: domestic credit created by the monetary authorities (D), and an international component (R). The latter component can be increased or decreased by any inflow or outflow, respectively, of money from foreign countries when the balance of payments as defined previously is in a surplus or a deficit, respectively. In notational form, $M^s = m[D + R]$, where M^s is total money supply, D is the domestic credit component, R is the international reserve component, and m is the money multiplier, which for simplicity is viewed here as a constant.

These two equations constitute the centerpiece of the monetary approach:

> (1) Demand for money: $M^d = kPy$
>
> (2) Supply of money: $M^s = m[D + R]$

Demand for money can be satisfied either from domestic or international sources. Thus, if the demand for money rises—say, because of an increase in real income—while domestic supply remains unchanged, the excess demand would be satisfied by an increase in the international component—that is, by drawing foreign-source funds into the country. And that generates a balance-of-payments surplus. Conversely, a rise in domestic money supply (D), with demand for money (M^d) remaining unchanged, would produce a deficit. In general, any change in the domestic component of the money supply is ultimately offset by an equal and opposite change in the international reserve component through the balance of payments.

External Surplus

A surplus or deficit in the *balance of payments reflects stock disequilibrium between demand for and supply of money.* A surplus on the basis of "official reserve transactions" occurs when demand for monetary balances exceeds the money stock. If the excess demand for money is not satisfied from domestic sources, such as by an increase in domestic money supply, funds will be attracted from abroad to satisfy it. And such an inflow can be generated through a surplus on commodity trade or on the service account, direct investments by foreign companies, or an attraction of private long-term or short-term portfolio funds. The precise composition is immaterial; the important thing is that the excess demand for money stock will generate a balance-of-payments surplus. But *assuming no intervention by the monetary authorities to "offset" or "sterilize"* the resulting inflow of funds, such a surplus is necessarily *temporary and self-correcting.* It will continue only until the money stock rises to the level necessary to satisfy the demand for money balances—that is, until the excess demand for money is eliminated.

The reason for the "self-correction" feature is that the stable demand function for money relates to money as a stock rather than a flow. When the desired stock is reached, the inflow of foreign funds—which is the counterpart and the cause of the external surplus—ceases, and so does the balance-of-payments surplus. If starting from an equilibrium money stock of $800 billion and GNP of $4 trillion, GNP sustains a once-and-for-all growth to $4.2 trillion, then the demand for money holdings would grow to $840 billion. In the absence of any growth in the domestic money stock, the extra $40 billion will be drawn from abroad in the form of balance-of-payments surplus (ΔR). The surplus will last until money balances are bought up to the newly desired level of $840 billion. A circumstance under which a surplus can be more than temporary is official sterilization of the incoming funds that would prevent the money stock from rising to the desired level.

Alternatively, in a "flow" formulation, continuous surpluses can occur under conditions of a *continuous* increase in demand for money over and above the rise in the domestic component of the money supply. And that can be brought about by a continuous rate of increase in income in excess of the rate of growth in domestic credit creation, causing continuous excess demand for money—that is, disequilibrium in the money market. This was advanced as an explanation of the continuous surpluses of Germany in the 1960s and 1970s—namely, a growth rate of real income that exceeded the rate of growth in real money balances.

External Deficit

Conversely, a balance-of-payments deficit reflects excess supply of money as a stock. When the stock of money exceeds the demand for money balances, people try to get rid of the excess supply. They do that by increasing purchases of foreign goods and services, by investing abroad, or by transferring short- or long-term portfolio funds abroad to acquire foreign assets.[4] Thus, the deficit on official reserve transactions is viewed as a spillover of the excess supply of money; its composition is immaterial. The *deficit is temporary and self-correcting.* Assuming that the monetary authorities do not replace the outflowing funds by creating new domestic credit (in other words, that they do not pursue a sterilization or offsetting policy), the deficit will last only until the excess supply is dissipated abroad and will stop when stock equilibrium in the money market is restored—namely, when the total money stock declines to the level of desired money balances. Starting again from an initial equilibrium money stock of $800 billion and GNP of $4 trillion, suppose that the Federal Reserve increases money supply to $820 billion

---

[4] Some critics of the monetary approach maintain that people get rid of excess money balances first by purchasing *domestic* financial assets as well as goods and services and only then buying foreign goods, services, and assets.

without any increase in the demand for money. This would produce external deficits ($-\Delta R$), lasting until the excess of $20 billion is dissipated abroad. When the money supply declines to $800 billion, the deficits would disappear. Continuous deficit is possible if a "neutralization" policy is followed by the monetary authorities.

Alternatively, in a "flow" formulation, continuous deficits can occur if the conditions causing the excess of supply of money persist. In turn, this may be caused by a growth rate in the domestic component of the money supply in excess of the growth rate in income.

The self-correcting apparatus outlined above takes time. Except for suggesting that the period required might be between a year and a decade, the monetary approach describes neither the dynamic process that the economy must undergo to reach the new equilibrium nor the elapsed time necessary to reach it. It is concerned strictly with the *final, long-run equilibrium* position.

Role of Money

Clearly, money plays a central role in the approach. It is viewed as an *active* agent, not merely as fulfilling a passive role in transactions. In other words, people's crucial decisions concern the adequacy of their money balances. Their demand for such balances relative to supply determines the level of their expenditures on goods and services. Indeed, aggregate spending is a function of real balances. The converse view of treating purchase and investment decisions as central, and viewing money as a passive agent used to finance these transactions, is rejected by the monetarists. The self-correcting feature of the analysis derives from the focus on money as a stock. What the public demands is a stock of money balances.

As under the "traditional" approaches, a rise in the country's money supply produces an external deficit, and a decline in money supply causes an external surplus. But in the monetary approach these imbalances are arrived at by a different mechanism and they are viewed as temporary, lasting only until (stock) equilibrium in the money market is restored. Since external imbalances are viewed as self-correcting, balance-of-payments adjustment policies are considered *unnecessary*. They are considered *ineffective*, except in the short run. The only possible long-run remedy to a deficit is a reduction in the rate of money creation.

It is often suggested that the monetary approach is the intellectual grandchild of the "specie-flow" mechanism developed by David Hume in the last century and described in Chapter 6. Indeed, monetary flows are central to both theories, and both regard external imbalances as self-correcting. But in the specie-flow mechanism, monetary flows rectify external disequilibria through their effect on relative commodity prices. By contrast, the monetary approach views a stable demand for money as the core of the mechanism, and relative commodity prices play no role in the adjustment process. Price elasticities are therefore considered irrelevant. Many monetarists believe that perfect international arbitrage ensures that the one price would prevail internationally on all commodity and capital markets. So no changes in relative commodity prices are even possible, let alone necessary, for international adjustment.

Monetary Policy

Domestically, the monetary approach implies that under fixed exchange rates a country's central bank has no control over its money supply. The pursuit of any domestic objective (such as price stability) by altering the domestic component of the money supply will be frustrated by equal and offsetting changes in the international component through reserve flows. In the absence of offsetting policies (or in view of government inability to pursue them), all the government can do is control the *composition* of the money supply, not its aggregate. *A change in* D *will produce an equivalent and opposite change in* R. *And the direction of causation is from* D *to* R, not the other way around. Changes in the demand for money (M^d) and in the domestic component of the monetary base (D) are the active ingredients that disturb money market equilibrium. *Changes in R maintain and restore that equilibrium under fixed exchange rates.* Such changes (ΔR) constitute balance-of-payments deficits or surpluses.

To a monetarist, there is no essential distinction between a central bank's intervention in the foreign-exchange market, which involves the direct exchange of domestic for foreign currency, and its open-market operations, which directly exchange bonds for local currency. The reason is that (in the case of expansionary open-market operations, for example) any excess supply of domestic currency will be exchanged by the public for foreign currency. For the central bank, buying bonds or buying foreign exchange has the same effect. An analogous argument applies to contractionary open-market operations.

Global Monetarism

To recapitulate, the monetary approach to the balance of payments is concerned strictly with long-run equilibrium and rests on two central assumptions: (a) The demand for money is a stable function of very few variables; and (b) countries do not pursue sterilization or offsetting policies, either because they cannot sterilize over a long period or because they do not wish to do so. Although not central to the approach itself, many of its adherents also believe that (c) wage-price flexibility fixes output at the full employment level, at least in the long run, so that the Keynesian income adjustment mechanism is irrelevant; and (d) perfect substitution in consumption (that is, infinite cross elasticity of substitution) across countries in both the product and the capital markets ensures a single price for each commodity and a single rate of interest. In other words, the *world consists of a single integrated market* for all traded goods and for capital; the "law of one price" obtains throughout the globe. Consequently, changes in relative prices are not possible and the elasticities approach is rejected. Adherents to assumptions (c) and (d), in addition to (a) and (b), are often called "global monetarists." Thus, global monetarism is a subset of the general monetary approach.[5]

Policy Implications

Devaluation

It is only through possible effects on the demand for and supply of money balances that devaluation can have an impact on the balance of payments. And any such effect must come about through the increase in domestic prices caused by a downward adjustment in the exchange rate.

Through its direct effect, devaluation of a country's currency raises domestic currency prices of importables and exportables; and because of interproduct substitution, the prices of nontraded goods will also rise, although to a lesser degree. The general price rise increases the demand for nominal money balances, which is a stable function of money income. If that (stock) demand is not satisfied from domestic sources, an inflow of money from abroad would occur, producing a balance-of-payments surplus and therefore a gain in international reserves. Devaluation reduces real domestic money balances and forces residents to restore them through the international credit or commodity markets. However, the resulting balance-of-payments surplus will continue only until the stock monetary equilibrium is restored. In other words, the effect of devaluation will be strictly *transitory*. In the long run, devaluation has no effect on real economic variables; it merely raises the price level.

By the same reasoning, revaluation (currency appreciation) would produce a transitory balance-of-payments deficit if it lowered domestic prices,

---

[5] If global monetarism is a subset of the general monetary theory, then there also exists a subset of global monetarism itself. Under it exchange fluctuations not only fail to equilibrate the balance of payments, they also may be the prime cause of worldwide inflation. The argument runs roughly as follows: The law of one price guarantees that, given sufficient time for adjustment (and abstracting from transport costs), all internationally traded goods will command the same price everywhere; this applies to homogeneous and differentiated products alike. Thus, a currency devaluation cannot, over time, change a country's prices relative to those of its competitors; either its prices would rise or foreign prices would decline until prices were fully equalized internationally. Here, Mundell and Laffer introduce a second supposition—namely that the price response to exchange-rate adjustment is not symmetrical. Export prices (denominated in local currency) rise in the devaluing country, but import prices fail to decline in the revaluing one. This asymmetry is often referred to as the "ratchet effect." As a consequence, the equalization of international prices is accomplished strictly through price increases in the devaluing country. Since, in a regime of fluctuating exchange rates, some currencies depreciate and others appreciate over one time period, while the reverse tends to occur during some subsequent period, and because domestic price changes (such as increases) occur only in the depreciating countries and not in the appreciating ones, the net effect is a worldwide increase in the prices of traded goods. This is very much a minority view.

thereby reducing the demand for monetary balances and producing (stock) excess supply of money.

In sum, exchange-rate changes are incapable of bringing about a *lasting* change in the balance-of-payments position. Furthermore, since all external disequilibria are self-correcting, exchange-rate changes are viewed as unnecessary. Still devaluation hastens the process of restoring balance-of-payments equilibrium by absorbing excess money balances.

But the transitory effect of devaluation does not depend on changes in relative prices and on product-market elasticities. For the monetarists, devaluation operates through a totally different mechanism—the stock demand for and supply of money. This effect is supplemented by an increase in the domestic currency prices of traded goods (exports and import substitutes) relative to those of nontraded goods. As a result, resources shift from nontraded to traded-goods industries, while demand shifts in the opposite direction. These changes in the production and consumption mixes help increase exports and reduce imports.

Tariffs, Quotas, and Exchange Control

Monetarists analyze the effect of import restrictions on the balance of payments similarly to the way they analyze devaluation. A tariff increases domestic prices of imports, and through substitution, prices of domestically produced goods. This raises the demand for money. If that demand is not satisfied out of domestic sources, it will produce a transitory balance-of-payments surplus until monetary (stock) equilibrium is restored. Import quotas and exchange control have a similar temporary effect.

Economic Growth

When the economy is growing in real terms, there is a continuous growth in the demand for real and therefore nominal money balances. The portion of this growth not supplied from domestic sources is reflected in a balance-of-payments surplus. Translated into a multicountry context, the monetarists maintain that the growth rate of a country's reserves is faster than the world's average if its real growth rate is faster than the world average.

This conclusion, of a positive relation between the rate of income growth and the balance of payments, *all other things being held constant,* is diametrically opposed to the prediction of the Keynesian analysis, where imports are a function of income. However, the latter prediction applies only to the "goods and services" component of the balance of payments, while the monetarist prediction applies to the "official reserve transactions" balance. The two can be reconciled via the capital account, if economic growth attracts foreign capital in excess of the deficit on goods and services. For example, if economic growth generates a $100 rise in imports, but also stimulates a capital inflow of $150, the balance on goods and services may move into deficit, while the official reserve settlement balance would show a surplus.

Change in the Rate of Interest

An increase in the domestic rate of interest raises the opportunity cost of holding money, producing a decrease in the demand for money. The resulting excess supply of money would be dissipated abroad in the form of an external deficit, lasting until stock equilibrium in the money market is restored. Conversely, a decline in the domestic interest rate lowers the opportunity cost of holding money, which produces an excess demand for money. In turn, that creates a balance-of-payments surplus, which lasts until the stock imbalance is eliminated.

As in the case of a change in real income, this prediction of the monetarist approach is diametrically opposed to that of the traditional theories. According to the latter, a rise in domestic interest rates (relative to interest rates abroad) produces an external surplus, while a decline in domestic interest rates results in a deficit.

Fluctuating Exchange Rates

Freely floating exchange rates maintain continuous equilibrium in the balance of payments. Since reserve changes (ΔR) are held at zero, the monetary authorities maintain control over the money stock. For example, suppose the central bank increases the money supply, so that an excess supply of money is created. The resulting outflow of money depreciates the currency (in contrast to the fixed rate case where a deficit is created, and a change in R offsets the change in D). This raises the price level, thereby increasing the demand for money. M^d rises to the new level of M^s, and a new equilibrium is established in the money market with a higher money stock. Thus, floating exchange rates restore the effectiveness of domestic monetary policy.

With universally floating rates, domestic prices adjust continuously to give the existing stock of money the real value the public desires. The nature of the adjustment process is different under the fixed and fluctuating rates systems. Under fixed exchange rates, quantities of money adjust *gradually* through reserve flows to bring *equality between actual and desired money stock*. Under floating rates, changes in the valuation of the money stock occur instantaneously through domestic price changes (caused by exchange-rate adjustments), bringing full stock adjustment.

How is the exchange rate determined in a regime of freely floating rates? *It is determined by the relationship between the price levels of the two countries, which in turn depends, in each country, on the relation between the desired and actual stock of national money.* Put differently, the price of a currency is viewed as a relationship between a desire to hold *stocks* of assets denominated in that currency and the quantity of such assets in existence. Because the most stable demand function for a financial asset is that for money, the exchange rate is assessed through a comparison of the supply and demand for money in different countries. Since the demand for money depends on real income, on the price level, and on the interest rate, all these variables—along with expectations—enter into the monetarists' model of exchange-rate determination. The direction of their effects is as specified in the section on fixed exchange rates: factors that were shown to cause a deficit result in currency depreciation, and those shown to cause a surplus result in currency appreciation.

Other things being equal, the exchange rate appreciates or depreciates as the country decreases or increases its money supply (in relation to its money demand); raises or lowers its real income, relative to the rest of the world.[6]

Floating rates are not necessary for the maintenance of balance-of-payments equilibrium in the long run. Since imbalances are self-correcting even under fixed exchange rates, a preference for a fixed-rate system is indicated; why not enjoy the greater efficiency obtainable from a single worldwide currency area?

The monetary approach has serious implications for international policy coordination of *managed floating*. The traditional approaches call for surveillance and coordination of central bank direct intervention in the foreign exchange market. Under the monetary approach, this is not sufficient. A government can cause its currency to depreciate by buying domestic bonds as well as by buying foreign currencies. What is crucial is the relation between the demand and supply of money, not whether money is created by domestic or foreign assets. So policy coordination requires rules governing the compatibility of monetary policy, not just of intervention in foreign exchange markets. This implies greater restrictions on national economic sovereignty.

Finally, according to the monetary approach, the most effective way of arresting, and perhaps reversing, the depreciation of a currency is to have a preannounced permanent reduction in the rate of growth of the domestic money stock. The announcement itself would have an immediate impact on the exchange rate through the price-expectations channel. However, for this effect to be sustained beyond the initial impact period, the *actual* rate of growth in money supply must conform to the newly announced target. Only then would the public regard the target as an indicator of the future rate of money expansion.

---

[6] Recall that: $M^d = kPY$. In equilibrium money supply (M^s) equals money demand (M^d), so we can write: $M^s = kPy$. Transposing we obtain: $P = M^s \cdot \frac{1}{ky}$. Similarly for the foreign country: $P^* = M^{s^*} \cdot \frac{1}{k^*y^*}$. According to the PPP doctrine, the exchange rate (E) reflects the ratio between the price levels of the two countries. Hence $E = \dfrac{P}{P^*} = \dfrac{M^s}{M^{s^*}} \cdot \dfrac{k^*y^*}{ky}$.

General Evaluation

Thus far, insufficient work has been done on reconciling (as opposed to comparing) the monetary with the traditional approaches. One possible conception of the various theories is as follows. The absorption approach highlights the fact that a balance-of-payments deficit (at least on current account) represents the fact that a country is living beyond its means. If imports exceed exports of goods and services, then absorption exceeds income (or output), and by the same amount. To remove the deficit, the country must reduce absorption or increase output until the two are equal. This proposition is pertinent to all theories. The monetary and traditional (elasticities or income) approaches differ in the mechanism by which this is accomplished. Thus, the absorption approach can be merged with either the elasticities/income or the monetary theories. But the monetary approach is distinctly different from its traditional counterparts in its analytical framework, predictions, and policy implications.

There is little doubt that highlighting the role of money in the adjustment process is a significant contribution because it counteracts the frequent tendency to ignore money and concentrate exclusively on real variables. But it is possible that the monetarists have gone too far in emphasizing monetary variables to the nearly complete exclusion of everything else and in offering their approach as a full substitute for the traditional approaches. It can also be questioned whether by ignoring the composition of imbalances the monetary approach overlooks matters that are significant to the economy. It matters for the generation of domestic output and employment (and consequently for foreign economic policies) whether the source of the disturbance is in the capital account or in the goods and services account. Also if a deficit on goods and services is continuously financed by private short-term capital, it would cause no imbalance on official reserve transactions; yet the country's foreign indebtedness would rise over time, and that may have serious economic implications.

More fundamentally, the assumptions and predictions of the monetary approach must be tested against its alternatives. The numerous tests performed to date do not provide a clear-cut answer, for the results are rather mixed. Future work would have to concentrate on additional testing, and at the same time theoretical attempts must be made to reconcile the various approaches.

Summary

At this point it is convenient to offer a tabular summary of the various theories of the mechanism of balance-of-payments adjustment:

Table 8-1
Summary of Balance-of-Payments Theories

Theory	Exchange Rate Regime or Policy to Which the Theory Applies	Essence of the Adjustment Mechanism
"Specie-Flow"	Fixed	Money Flows → Relative Prices
Income-Expenditures	Mainly Fixed	Income-Multiplier → Imports
Elasticities	Devaluation	Relative Prices and Other Effects
Absorption	Devaluation	Changes in Income (Output) Relative to Changes in Absorption
Internal-External Balance	Fixed	Income Effect on Current Account Interest Rate Effect on Capital Account
Monetary	Fixed, or Floating	Demand for and Supply of Money Stock

Review Questions

1. How would each of the following developments affect the exchange value of the (floating) Japanese yen? Assume that all other things are constant):

   a. A sharp drop in Japan's interest rate
   b. A decline in Japan's real income
   c. A sharp drop in Japan's money supply
   d. Elimination of all tariffs and quotas on Japan's imports.

   In each case explain *fully* the result and the reasons for it under the *traditional* and the *monetary* approaches. Can the two be reconciled?

2. What would be the effect of each of the above developments on Japan's balance of payments had the yen been on a fixed-rate regime?

3. Distinguish between *stock* and *flow* variables. What does this distinction have to do with the monetary approach to the B. of P.?

4. What are the implications of the monetary approach for the effectiveness of monetary policy under fixed and floating exchange rates?

9/
Exchange Control; Bilateralism; Financial History

Exchange Control

A country with a fixed exchange rate may choose to maintain an overvalued currency. Refusal to devalue in the face of persistent deficits may be based on such reasons as the prestige accorded the exchange rate in the popular mind or the existence of large government debts denominated in foreign currencies. Under such conditions, the government may be forced to impose exchange control, because, if foreign currencies are undervalued in price (priced below the equilibrium level), or, equivalently, if the domestic currency is overvalued, the price mechanism cannot clear the market. Instead, it generates excess demand for the undervalued, or "cheap," foreign currencies.

This situation can be met temporarily by using reserves or by borrowing. But if it persists over a period of years, the country may be forced to seek an alternative to the market mechanism by resorting to direct exchange control. Although comprehensive exchange control is only of historical interest for the industrial countries, it is very common in the developing nations. On the other hand, the European countries were subject to such controls after WWII until late in the 1950s; the persistent deficits were attributed by some experts to structural causes not curable by devaluation. Even in recent years, the capital movements in many industrial nations have been subject to varying degrees of mild government controls, and disguised forms of control are at times exercised even on current transactions. In the 1970s, several European countries imposed restrictions on the inflow of capital, especially when it was considered disruptive of domestic monetary conditions. And in March, 1982 the French government tightened its control on capital transfers from France in an effort to forestall devaluation of the

---

Figure 9-1
French Foreign Exchange Market

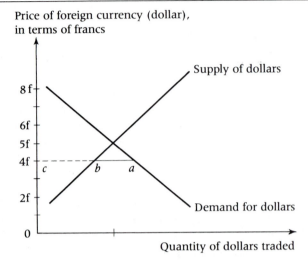

Price of foreign currency (dollar),
in terms of francs

---

franc within the European Monetary System (EMS). The IMF publishes annually *A Report on Exchange Restrictions*, which gives a country-by-country account of existing regulations.

In Figure 9-1, French francs are represented as the home currency and foreign currencies are represented by the U.S. dollar. The vertical axis shows the price of one dollar in terms of francs; the horizontal axis indicates the number of dollars traded. Normal supply and demand curves for dollars are also shown: the equilibrium price or exchange rate being $1 = 5 francs, or 1 franc = 20 cents. This is the price that clears the market. It performs the function of allocating available dollars among competing uses.

Suppose the French government decides to fix the dollar at 4 francs. The dollar will then be *undervalued* compared to its equilibrium price; and the franc, at 25 cents instead of 20 cents, will be correspondingly *overvalued* compared to the equilibrium price. This arbitrary exchange rate cannot be sustained for a long period of time, because it creates excess demand for dollars in the amount $\overline{ab}$. If the government refuses to devalue the franc to 20 cents, it will be forced to impose exchange control. This makes it possible to maintain an exchange rate that departs from its equilibrium value. Instead of the market price performing the allocative function, a government agency must now determine how to allocate the $\overline{bc}$ available dollars among the larger quantity demanded, $\overline{ac}$.

Under a system of comprehensive exchange control, all earners of foreign currencies must surrender their proceeds to the control authority, be it the central bank or a special division set up in the treasury, while users of such currencies must obtain a government license before engaging in international transactions. This may sound strange to Americans, who are accustomed to exchanging their dollars for any other currency at the bank window without ever needing a license. Most Americans could not imagine their government telling them what they may or may not do with their dollars or how many dollars they may exchange at the border on crossing to Canada or Mexico. This reflects the fortunate experience of the inhabitants of the United States. Most other countries have resorted to exchange control at one time or another in their history.

Under an exchange-control system, government officials rather than market forces determine how the available foreign exchange is to be distributed among various goods and services, among sources of supply (supplying countries), among importers and other users, and over time. Such decisions are likely to be arbitrary and at times even capricious. Furthermore, because the supply of imported commodities is restricted, their price on the domestic market rises with the imposition of controls. The importers therefore realize more profit per unit than they would have enjoyed in the absence of exchange restrictions. Thus, the foreign exchange license itself assumes a considerable market value, occasionally inviting corruption and fraud on the part of the officials issuing the licenses. On occasions, governments practicing exchange control have auctioned foreign currency licenses.

☐ An illustration can show the extent of price increase and the consequent monopoly profit. Assume that the Belgian government imposes exchange control and decides to restrict the number of dollars spent on imported automobiles to one-half the free market amount. Because Belgium does not produce cars, the supply-and-demand curves in Figure 9-2 refer to imports. Free market price P_1 is established, Q_1 cars being imported at total dollar expenditures of $0P_1RQ_1$. This is the amount that the control authority decides to cut in half. In other words, importers would be allowed to spend only $0P_1MN$ dollars.

☐ While the consumer demand curve remains unchanged, the importers' demand curve now diverges from it, because it is governed by the amount of foreign exchange allocation. The new importers' demand curve is now characterized by the fact that the area under it (total dollar expenditures, or price times quantity) is fixed at $0P_1MN$. Such demand conditions are represented by a rectangular hyperbola passing through point M. This curve intersects the foreign-supply function at point L. Thus, the quantity imported is reduced to Q_2 and the import price is set at P_2. Total dollar cost is $0P_2LQ_2$ and is equal to the official allocation.

☐ But the demand of domestic consumers has not changed. Quantity Q_2 will command price P_3 on the internal market, $P_3 - P_2$ being the importers'

Figure 9-2
Effect of Exchange Control

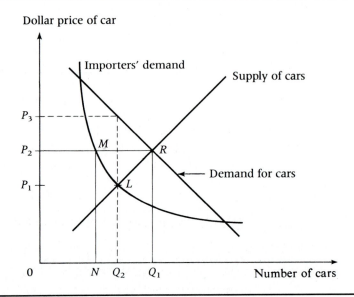

Dollar price of car

Importers' demand

Supply of cars

P_3

M

P_2 R

Demand for cars

P_1 L

0   N Q_2 Q_1 Number of cars

---

monopoly profit per car.[1] Clearly, the less elastic the local demand is for the product, the higher the profit will be.   ■

Exchange control can be used as a device for limiting commodity imports in much the same way that tariffs or quotas limit imports. It makes little difference whether the authorities restrict the number of cars that may enter the country or whether they limit the quantity of foreign exchange allocated for automobile imports. In either case, the domestic automobile industry obtains protection and the balance-of-payments position improves. An exchange-control system is more effective for dealing with the balance of payments, however, because it encompasses all transactions, including services and capital movement, while tariffs and quotas are restricted to commodity trade. Also, the usual focus and intent of exchange control is to maintain external balance, while that of tariffs is to offer protection to domestic industries from foreign competition.

A government may wish at times to place under control only capital transfers, not current transactions. This was the original intent of exchange control when it was introduced in Europe in the 1930s. The IMF charter permits the imposition of exchange control only to combat severe capital

---

[1] This is a potential source of corruption for government officials. The foreign currency license is valuable to the (often wealthy) importer in terms of his profits, and it is issued by government officials with modest incomes. This is a clear invitation for bribes.

outflow, because under certain conditions, direct control may be the only way to combat speculative flight of short-term funds. Such limited exchange control may succeed as a temporary device, but people can generally make capital transfers under the disguise of regular transactions, thereby evading the regulations. Exporters *underbill* the foreign importers and instruct them to deposit the difference in the exporters' foreign bank accounts, while importers *overpay* the foreign exporters, with the difference deposited in the importers' foreign bank accounts. It is also easy to see that, like any other rationing system, exchange control generates a black market. That partial evasion by commodity traders gives rise to an undeclared supply of foreign currencies was just illustrated. On the other side of the market are potential users of foreign exchange, such as travelers, who, because they are denied an allocation by the control authority, are willing to pay a higher price than the official exchange rate. They constitute the demand side of the equation. Thus, in terms of the domestic currency, foreign currencies are traded at a higher price than the official rate.

From an economic standpoint, exchange control and the attendant rationing of foreign exchange often result in misallocation of resources. Market prices no longer indicate priorities concerning what or how much is needed by producers and desired by consumers. Nor is there a guarantee that the arbitrary decisions of government officials will conform to these priorities.

Furthermore, in attempting to promote exports with an overvalued currency, governments often resort to a *multiple exchange-rate* system that further distorts the structure of the economy (in addition to being complicated to administer). If the official value of the pound is £1 = $4, the British government may place the commodities whose export it desires to encourage and whose import it wishes to discourage, at a lower rate of, say, £1 = $3. This amounts to (partial) devaluation of the pound with respect to the specified commodities, because they are traded at a lower exchange value. Exporters obtain one-third more pounds for their foreign-currency proceeds, while importers must pay more pounds for the dollars that they need to buy the merchandise—precisely the same as under devaluation.

Government may adopt a more discriminatory approach and introduce a whole array of exchange rates, with commodities classified according to the degree of encouragement or discouragement attached to their exportation and importation, respectively. By shifting commodities among the various exchange rates, the government has the virtual decision-making power on what is exported and imported. And in an open economy, which is highly dependent on foreign trade, the government can also determine the structure of investments and production by giving hidden subsidies to certain investment goods (through the exchange rate). These decisions do not usually coincide with what is dictated by consideration of comparative advantage (see Chapter 11). Yet by the end of 1984, 25 countries (all LDCs) were on a multiple exchange rate regime, some with as much as four or five exchange rates.

Incidentally, many types of interference with free trade and payments are tantamount to partial and disguised forms of devaluation. For example, assume that a country tries to combat an external deficit by levying import taxes and providing export subsidies, both to the extent of 10 percent. In terms of government revenue, these may roughly balance each other out to effect neutrality. But their real effect is to make imports more expensive and simultaneously to cheapen exports—precisely the effect of a 10 percent devaluation. However, whereas devaluation affects all balance-of-payments items, including service and capital transactions, the trade measures apply only to merchandise.

In general, imports can be discouraged by a whole maze of trade restrictions and exchange controls, whereas exports are encouraged by offering to exchange the foreign-currency proceeds for domestic currency at a more favorable rate, by arranging for cheaper raw materials for the producers of export goods, by offering cheap official credit to finance exports, and by other measures. Indeed, the granting of official export credit at subsidized interest rates has become common among industrial countries. Many developing countries suffer from elaborate systems of control that replace the simple market mechanism and leave a large measure of latitude to government officials in making arbitrary decisions. The result frequently is gross misallocation of resources, which radically distorts the structure of trade, investments, and production, and hampers the development process. Overt devaluation quite often replaces this disguised devaluation when the controls become so cumbersome as to be unmanageable. On occasion, a country is led to scrap its complex system of many exchange rates and substitute a dual exchange-rate regime: a fixed rate for certain specified transactions, and a floating rate for all other transactions.

Since 1982 Mexico had a dual exchange rate for the peso: a floating rate and a fixed "preferential" rate for both crucial imports (such as food and certain capital goods) and interest payments on the external public debt. A similar system had been tried in other Latin American countries. However, apart from the distortions such a system introduces, it is difficult to enforce.

Bilateral Clearing Agreements

If a country is completely devoid of foreign-currency holdings, or nearly so, and still wishes to stimulate private trade, it may impose barter-trade conditions on individual traders. In other words, it may permit an importer to import only if he can team up with a local exporter of some product, who would be paid by the importer in local currency. But this is a rather cumbersome procedure.

To avoid the problems of such barter trade and still stimulate trade, nations uses exchange-clearing agreements. These were introduced on a large scale in Europe immediately following World War II, when countries lacked foreign currencies with which to finance foreign trade.[2] Such agreements are designed to permit trade by a multitude of exporters and importers working independently of one another but without the transfer of foreign exchange. A typical agreement between countries A and B would work as follows: Each country's central bank establishes an account for transactions with the other country, as illustrated in Figure 9-3. A's importers from B pay in their own currency into B's account in A's central bank while exporters to B draw payments from the same account. Likewise, B's importers from A make payments in their own currency into A's account in their central bank, while exporters to A are paid out of the same account. If the bilateral trade position balances over the month, then the two accounts will show zero balances. Trade between the two countries is reduced to its barter essentials, and no currency changes hands to finance it.

But complications arise if trade is out of balance. Suppose country A has a surplus with country B and then A's exporters to B draw more out of B's account (in A's central bank) than A's importers pay into it, leaving the account in deficit. Conversely, A's account in B's central bank shows a surplus, because if B has a deficit with A, its importers pay into their account more than B's exporters draw out of it. B could pay up its deficit by transferring the accumulated surplus to A, but that would involve transfer of foreign exchange, which is what the whole system was set up to avoid. Instead, the two countries agree in advance on a mutual line of credit, known as the *swing* (since it can shift directions), up to a predetermined level. Only if the cumulative deficits exceed the limit is the debtor country obligated to pay up in gold or dollars.

A network of four hundred such agreements covered Western Europe immediately after World War II, as every nation had bilateral agreements with each of the other countries. (These were invariably superimposed upon an exchange-control system.) The economic implications of these agreements derive from the reaction of the participating countries to possible imbalances. In order to avoid paying foreign currencies, deficit country B might halt purchases from its surplus counterpart A and encourage sales there, before the limit of the swing is reached. In fact, much before that point, surplus country A is likely to take action, because, within the limits agreed upon, A is obligated to extend credit to B even if its overall position (with respect to all countries) is weak. Country A cannot use its surplus with B to pay up deficits to other countries C, D, and E. It must grant credit to B, even when A has a deficit with all its trading partners combined. Consequently, A would try to curtail the surplus as soon as it appeared, by encouraging purchases and discouraging sales to B regardless of prices.

The economic implications of this action are adverse on two counts. The volume of trade is reduced to the lowest common denominator. And, since exchange of services is hardly ever covered by the agreement, service

---

[2] Today there are over 100 bilateral clearing agreements, mainly among the LDCs and between socialist states.

Figure 9-3
Bilateral Clearing Agreement

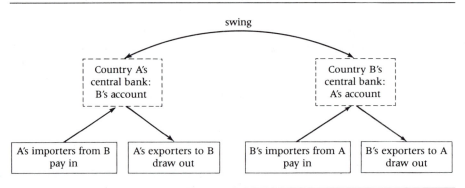

and capital transactions are both reduced to a bare minimum. Equally important, the pattern or direction of trade is no longer governed by comparative advantage, as is the case if each trader sells where it is most expensive and buys where it is cheapest. Instead, trade is channeled into lines dictated by the need for bilateral balancing of the accounts. Relative prices in various sources and destinations are relegated to a secondary role, as buyer and seller alike follow government directives concerning their trading partners.

A network of such agreements is an administrative nightmare to finance ministers. Because a surplus with one country cannot be used to pay up a deficit with another, ministers must worry about bilateral balancing of numerous external accounts rather than about one overall position. This leads to some conceptual distinctions employed to describe currency convertibility.

A currency is considered *fully convertible* if its holders can convert it freely (without a government license) to any other currency, regardless of either the purpose of conversion or the identity of the holder. The two qualifications provide the distinctions for cases of partial convertibility. A currency can be convertible for current transactions but subject to government controls with respect to capital transfers. This is known as *current account convertibility* and was adopted by many European countries in the 1950s as a first step toward full convertibility. A more important distinction (employed on a different plane) relates to the holder of the currency. When a country imposes exchange control, its currency becomes *nonconvertible to its own residents.* But once payment is made to a foreign person or corporation under license by the control authority, the foreigner is free to use it anywhere and convert it to any other currency. In other words, the currency is convertible when held by nonresidents of the country concerned. Such nonresident convertibility disappears if the country enters upon bilateral clearing agreements in addition to exchange control. In our example, the currency of B could not be used by A's citizens (nonresidents of B) to settle deficits with third countries. Since the verdict against bilateralism is more severe than that against exchange control, the attainment of nonresident convertibility was an important step in the European drive toward full convertibility.

It is worth noting that, even under the tightest and most comprehensive control discussed here, actual transactions are still in the hands of private traders. The ultimate degree of government intervention is state trading, in which all international trade is conducted by government corporations or trading authorities. This practice is universally adhered to by the Eastern bloc countries.

The European Payments Union (EPU)

How was convertibility attained in post–World War II Europe? The European economy emerged from the war with its productive capacity destroyed. The network of bilateral clearing agreements is what made possible any trade at all. As an immediate objective, the European countries, organized in the OEEC,[3] wished to attain nonresident convertibility within Europe. This was achieved by the European Payments Union (EPU), which functioned from 1950 to 1958.

Assume that Western Europe consists of three countries, all having exchange-clearing agreements with each other. At the end of the each month of transactions they bring their accounts to the central agent for clearing, with the results shown in Figure 9-4 (arrows show the direction of total

[3]The Organization for European Economic Cooperation was designed to coordinate the reconstruction efforts under the Marshall Plan; it later became the Organization for Economic Cooperation and Development (OECD) with the United States, Canada, Australia, and Japan joining in.

Figure 9-4
Bilateral Accounts

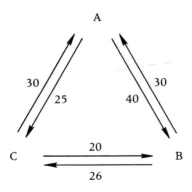

debts).[4] These figures can be netted out on a bilateral basis with the following results:

Country A		Country B		Country C	
Owes B:	10	Owes C:	6	Owes A:	5
Owed by C:	5	Owed by A:	10	Owed by B:	6

In our hypothetical example, country A has a deficit of 5, while B and C show surpluses of 4 and 1, respectively. But these surpluses do not relieve the two countries of worry. In the absence of nonresident convertibility, B cannot use its surplus with A to pay C, nor can C use its surplus with B to pay A. Each country must concern itself with many bilateral positions, not with its overall balance. The EPU eliminated such anxieties by offering its members unlimited clearing facilities. Instead of owing money to each other, they could shift their debts and credit to the EPU, and all accounts would be brought to settlement with the EPU (see Figure 9-5). In the context of our example, the net accounts within Europe of Figure 9-5 are reduced to the following magnitudes:

$$A: \quad -5 \qquad B: \quad +4 \qquad C: \quad +1$$

In other words, because of the opportunity for unlimited clearing, member countries can now concentrate on their overall position within Europe and need not concern themselves with a multitude of bilateral accounts. Lest the reader be misled by the smallness of the differences between this tabulation and the preceding one, it should be pointed out that this is a highly oversimplified example. In actual postwar Europe, each of 18 countries had bilateral agreements with 17 other countries, so that the net position of each member was a result of 17, not 2, bilateral accounts. Therefore, the salutary effect of the clearing mechanism is much larger than the example indicates.

A second provision of the EPU was automatic credit. Each member had a quota interpreted as a reference number rather than as a financial contribution.[5] Initially, creditor countries were obligated to extend credit to the EPU amounting to 50 percent of their surpluses, the balance being received in gold or dollars. Debtor countries received full automatic credit of up to 20 percent of their quotas. Beyond that, a sliding scale was agreed on, with an increasing proportion of the cumulative deficits being paid in gold or dollars. The EPU itself was endowed with a sizable grant from the Marshall Plan to meet deficits.

[4] The "agent" in the case of the EPU was the Bank for International Settlements (BIS) in Basel, Switzerland. It was established in the 1930s to facilitate the transfer of reparations. Today the BIS is used as an instrument of consultation and cooperation among the world's central bankers. See Appendix I.

[5] The quota amounted to 15 percent of the country's trade with the EPU areas in 1949, the year before the EPU was set up.

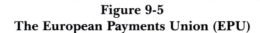

Figure 9-5
The European Payments Union (EPU)

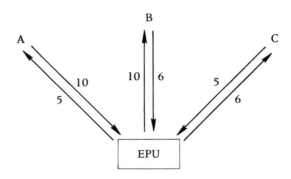

The main shortcoming of the EPU was that it was restricted to Europe. Creditor countries had an incentive to discriminate in favor of purchases inside the EPU while encouraging exports to non-EPU countries in order to avoid granting automatic credits. Likewise, a member country in an over-all balance-of-payments equilibrium—consisting of a surplus with the EPU area and an equal deficit with the dollar area—could not declare nonresident convertibility (vis-à-vis the world as a whole), because it had to extend credit to the EPU. It is for this reason that the payment rules were gradually revised, reducing the automatic credit component. In 1958, member countries felt sufficiently strong to introduce nonresident convertibility.

Having met its original objective, the EPU was dismantled at the end of 1958 and replaced by another instrument of regional cooperation, the European Monetary Agreement (EMA).[6] However, the EPU is more than merely of historical interest. Regional groups of developing countries operate, or attempt to set up, such multilateral clearing arrangements, as do the socialist states of Eastern Europe.

---

[6] Although trade among industrial countries is now financed by transfers of largely convertible currencies, transactions with communist or underdeveloped countries often necessitate barter arrangements. An exchange of Iranian oil for Czechoslovakian power-generating stations is a case in point, and a barter of Yugoslavian railroad cars for New Zealand butter is another. More complicated cases arise when there is nothing in the buyer's country that the seller wants. In a typical instance, an American exporter sold some used tiremaking machinery in Eastern Europe for a very attractive price but in a nonconvertible currency. Because of a surplus in a trade agreement between the buying country and Turkey, the money could be used to buy Turkish lira and, with those funds, Turkish chromium. The chromium, in turn, was sold in a fourth country for hard currency. Such transactions, known as "countertrade," are also used by companies that find themselves holding funds blocked in a country that is under exchange control ("blocked accounts"). As they are not allowed to convert their pesos or rupees into dollars or marks, they often have to purchase local products for sale abroad. Countertrade has increased in recent years, and it now accounts for 1–5 percent of total world trade. See: "Countertrade: Trade Without Cash," *Finance and Development*, December 1983.

Historical Survey

In order to place the current international financial scene in proper perspective, it is useful to survey one century of global financial history. The century is divided into several periods, distinguished on the basis of major financial events.

The Gold Standard (1870–1914)

These are the years described in economics textbooks as the golden age of the gold standard. Most currencies were pegged either to gold or to a currency (mainly sterling) that was itself on the gold standard (in a manner described in Chapter 4). London was the main financial center of the world. Although exchange-rate adjustments were not unheard of, there was a core of major European currencies whose exchange rates were kept completely fixed. This was allegedly accomplished by the central bankers adhering strictly to the "rules of the game" in their domestic monetary policies (fiscal policies of any kind were not commonly in use). They deflated in times of external deficit and inflated in times of surplus thereby reinforcing the automatic effects of imbalances on the domestic money supply. (If a central bank pursues reverse policies, contracting during a surplus and expanding in time of deficit, it offsets the automatic tendencies. Such action is therefore known as "offsetting" or "neutralizing" policy.) The attainment and maintenance of external balance was the paramount concern of policymakers and domestic stabilization needs were secondary in importance. Domestic economic conditions were manipulated to the extent necessary to maintain external equilibrium.

Several factors helped this endeavor. Prices and wages were flexible in a downward as well as an upward direction. Thus, by deflating the economy in times of deficit, both the price and income mechanisms exerted a powerful balancing pressure. Prices in the deficit country could actually decline while those in the surplus country increased. As a consequence, large changes in relative prices in the desired direction could be attained under fixed exchange rates.

Also, wage–price flexibility took some of the sting out of contractionary policies, because a large component of the total effect of such policies was on prices rather than on income and employment. It will be recalled that the equation of exchange, $MV = PO$, is an identity that holds at all times. If total spending on goods and services in the economy declines because of contractionary policies, the impact can be felt either on the price level or on the volume of output (and therefore employment) or on both. To the extent that prices are flexible, variations in them can absorb part of the impact, and the painful effect on output and employment is thereby mitigated. This flexibility must have made central banks during that period more willing than they are now to accept the domestic consequences of the rules of the game.

Furthermore, Europe at that time was reasonably free of direct government controls over trade and payments in the form of import quotas and exchange controls. Even tariffs, although common, did not vary much over the years. Consequently, the price mechanism was permitted to function almost freely in the international arena and to exert its stabilizing influence.

Finally, capital movements were generally stabilizing in nature. They responded swiftly to positive interest differentials, making it easy for a country to bridge short-term balance-of-payments deficits by raising interest rates.

The gold standard was brought to an abrupt end by World War I. The ravages of war and the differential rates of inflation in various countries destroyed the underlying price–cost relationships on which the prewar exchange rates had been based. For lack of a better alternative, many currencies were left to fluctuate freely as the war ended.

Fluctuating Exchange Rates and Currency Stabilization

Under the system that emerged from World War I, major currencies were left to fluctuate in response to demand-and-supply conditions. But the arrangement (1918–23) was viewed as an interlude until conditions stabilized and countries could go back to the gold standard. The *purchasing power parity* theory was originally developed in that context. Starting from an equilibrium pre–World War I exchange rate of £1 = $5, if U.S. prices doubled during the war while the U.K. price index quadrupled, the postwar exchange rate should have been set at £1 = $2.50. Yet, despite the fact that cost and price ratios between countries changed radically during World War I, it was considered a matter of national prestige by every country to restore its prewar parity.

During 1923–28, one country after another returned to the gold standard at the prewar exchange rate. The British pound, for example, was stabilized at $5. This was done by unilateral action on the part of the countries concerned; international cooperation, so vitally necessary in these matters, was totally lacking. For the now-overvalued currencies, this action contained the seeds of further disturbances. It brought a strain on the balance of payments as well as on the domestic economies that had to bear the brunt of the adjustment process.

The "Devaluation Cycle," (1930–39)

Several countries yielded to pressure and went off the gold standard. The pound sterling in particular became a freely fluctuating currency in 1930. Since the fluctuations were at times violent, a special agency was established in 1931 to help smooth them out. Known as the British Exchange Equalization Account (BEEA), it was to operate secretly in the marketplace by buying and selling foreign and domestic financial assets.

Other countries, primarily those of the Sterling Area,[7] followed the British example and pegged their currencies to the fluctuating sterling. It was through this action that the Sterling Area first assumed a formal economic status. In most cases devaluations were taken at that time either to bridge balance-of-payments deficits or to help decrease domestic unemployment by raising exports and lowering imports. Since this was done at the expense of the country's trading partners, it was subject to retaliation by competitive devaluation.

Not all countries devalued. The French led a small group of nations that remained on gold at the previous exchange rates and became known as the "gold bloc." France chose to tackle the resulting balance-of-payments deficits by imposing import quotas. Thus, the first time an import quota was used by a major power, it was for the purpose of dealing with balance-of-payments deficits rather than for protection. Germany, on the other hand, imposed exchange control to avoid devaluation and subsequently used its control system to manipulate international power politics. The pound sterling, the franc, and the dollar became the major convertible currencies.

In 1936 France, the U.K., and the U.S. negotiated an agreement to enable France to devalue without retaliation. The resulting *tripartite declaration*, subsequently adhered to by four additional countries, ushered in a period of informal cooperation in international finance—the only such period between the two world wars. Cooperation was short lived, however, being abruptly interrupted by World War II, during which most combatants imposed exchange control. The British operated a "dollar pool," through which they centralized and controlled the dollar dealings of the entire Sterling Area.

Bretton Woods (July 1944)

At the end of the war, delegates of forty-four nations held a conference in Bretton Woods, New Hampshire, to discuss pressing economic problems. The painful lessons of the 1930s were not lost on the participants, so the aftermath of World War II was characterized by cooperation in international financial matters. Because there had actually been no system functioning since the breakdown of the gold standard, there was a widespread desire to restore fixed exchange rates. But it was also widely recognized that the rules of the game would have to be changed as countries now wished to accord a relatively higher priority to domestic stabilization.

Two plans for an international monetary system were considered at the conference: the British plan authored by Keynes and the American plan of Harry White. Keynes was concerned about the excessive reliance on bilateral payments arrangements after the war and about the deflationary bias imparted to the international economy when the responsibility of adjustment rests primarily with deficit countries. He proposed the creation

---

[7]Members of the British Commonwealth and other countries attached to the sterling.

of an international clearing union with unlimited opportunity for clearing balances, large automatic credit provisions, and the ability to create international reserves (that is, a sort of international EPU). Also, the code of behavior he proposed placed many of the responsibilities of adjustment on the shoulders of the surplus countries.

What emerged from Bretton Woods was a fund (the IMF) rather than a clearing union. It was akin to the White plan presented on behalf of the American delegation. In fact, the conferees agreed to set up two sister institutions: The International Bank for Reconstruction and Development, now called the World Bank,[8] which was to help in European reconstruction and later serve as an instrument for financing economic development, and the IMF, which was to become the central international financial institution. Fixed exchange rates were an integral part of the Bretton Woods system.

European Reconstruction (1945−58)

The years 1945−50 witnessed intense reconstruction efforts in Europe, with the outpouring of American aid first under the Anglo-American loan agreement and then under the Marshall Plan. Intra-European trade, such as it was, was conducted through a network of bilateral clearing agreements. The continent was starved for dollars because the United States was the only source of plant and equipment as well as consumer goods. So intense was the *dollar shortage* that prominent economists suggested that it might become a permanent feature of the financial scene, in defiance of all theoretical expectations.

The European Payments Union was established in 1950 and functioned in Europe until convertibility was restored in 1958. The fact that the European Common Market (see Chapter 16) came into being in 1958 is no coincidence; it makes little sense to set up a common market for the purpose of freeing trade among nations while foreign payments remain subject to government control.

The "Dollar Glut" (1959−70)

As of the late 1950s, the United States was running balance-of-payments deficits that averaged $3 billion per year. Their counterpart was European surpluses which enabled Europe to accumulate dollar reserves. But in the 1960s European countries began to feel saturated with dollar reserves and demanded conversion into gold, the more traditional reserve asset. The U.S. attempted to cope with the deficits through a variety of administrative measures. For example, Congress eliminated the federal gold reserve requirement for all domestic currency except notes, in order to free our gold for foreign transactions. And the Department of Commerce embarked on an export-promotion program.

---

[8] Despite its name, the World Bank is in no sense an international central bank. It makes long-term loans to developing countries out of subscription capital and from funds raised on the world's capital markets.

In an attempt to discourage European companies from raising capital in New York, a tax was imposed on American purchases of European securities. Finally, the main brunt of government policy was to directly restrict American corporate investments in Europe and limit American bank loans to European borrowers. These controls were eliminated in January 1974.

In the circumstances prevailing in the 1960s, it would have been far better to lower the value of the dollar relative to the continental currencies. However, because of the dollar's unique role as the international "standard of value," it could not be devalued. Rather, it was incumbent on the surplus countries to revalue their currencies relative to the dollar. Such a step would have improved the competitive position of the United States; and at the same time it would have been in the best interest of the revaluating countries themselves. West Germany had not only been "suffering" from balance-of-payments surpluses, but was also experiencing a domestic inflationary boom. Exchange revaluation would have raised the standard of living of the West German consumers as their mark wages would have purchased more foreign goods. It also would have helped to bring German inflation under control. Moreover, since there is a limit to how much reserves a country is likely to need, it did no good for West Germany to go on piling up reserves indefinitely. Revaluation is merely one way of reaping and distributing the fruits of increased productivity throughout the economy.

Beyond this, placing the burden of adjustment on the surplus countries (revaluation) is beneficial to the system as a whole. Traditionally that burden has fallen on the deficit countries. But a deficit country can only apply contractionary policies, which may bring about a recession, or it can impose exchange and trade restrictions. Both methods are undesirable. Indeed, the whole international financial system was discredited in the interwar period because its net effect was deflationary. If surplus countries were to assume more of the responsibility for adjustment, confidence in the system would be restored.

Why did West Germany resist revaluation? The answer is that two powerful economic groups were vehemently opposed to revaluation: the big export interests, who wished to maintain their competitive position in foreign markets, and the small farmers, who feared the effects of a reduction in the import prices of foreign farm products.

By 1970 another important currency had emerged with considerable strength, namely the Japanese yen. Japan's GNP has grown at the amazing annual rate of 10 to 13 percent in real terms. At the same time Japan rolled up massive trade surpluses. Along with the mark, the Japanese yen became a major candidate for revaluation early in the 1970s. Throughout the period the United States continued to mount sizable deficits, with Japan and Europe accumulating large dollar reserves. Confidence in the dollar, the cornerstone of the Bretton Woods system, was continuously eroding.

A "two-price system" for gold was introduced in 1968, separating official dealing from private dealings in the yellow metal. It marked the first step in downgrading the role of gold in international finance. Accompanying this decision of the world's major central bankers was a decision to introduce, beginning in 1970, the Special Drawing Rights (SDRs) of the IMF as a new form of reserve assets.

The Smithsonian Agreement

By 1971 the U.S. deficit on official reserve transactions reached $30 billion, and a trade deficit ($2.7 billion) appeared for the first time in this century. In addition, the United States was suffering from unemployment as well as an unacceptably high rate of inflation. To deal with these circumstances President Nixon introduced (in August 1971) stimulative fiscal and monetary measures, and imposed price and wage controls to curb the inflation. The controls lasted, in one form or another, until April, 1974. On the international front, the president announced a series of measures designed to bring about devaluation of the dollar in terms of other major currencies.

Under the newly announced policy, dollar holdings by foreign central banks would no longer be redeemable in gold by the United States. Although the closing of the gold window was merely a *de jure* recognition of a previously existing situation—in which the U.S. gold stock was only a fraction of foreign official holdings of dollars—it had an important symbolic value. From then on, dollar reserves could not be exchanged for other types of reserve assets, such as gold, so that continued pegging to the dollar by foreign central bankers would place the world on a straight dollar standard. At the same time, foreign countries were invited to revalue their currencies against the dollar. To further encourage revaluation of the yen and the continental currencies, the president imposed a 10 percentage point tariff surcharge on imports to the United States, to last until the exchange-rate adjustments took place.

The immediate response of most major countries was to stop pegging their currencies to the dollar and to adopt a regime of "managed float." Most currencies were allowed to appreciate 5 to 8 percent in terms of the dollar, but the United States did not consider this level of currency appreciation adequate.

On December 18, 1971, at the Smithsonian Institution in Washington, the major financial nations announced that they had reached an agreement on the realignment of exchange rates and restabilization of currencies. Under it the price of gold was raised from $35 to $38 per fine ounce, while the major currencies were revalued against the dollar in proportions ranging from 8.5 percent (the pound and franc) to 17 percent (the yen). The weighted value of gold, and more importantly of the SDRs, in terms of all currencies remained unchanged. From that point on, IMF accounts were to be maintained in SDRs.

As a part of the package, the United States removed the import surcharge, but the dollar remained nonconvertible into gold, and the U.S. "gold window" remained closed. Subsequent legislation created the Domestic International Sales Corporations (DISC). Under DISC, companies conducting 95 percent of their business in export trade were allowed to defer one-half of their corporate profit tax obligation. In some cases the deferral became a total exemption because DISC corporations were taxable only when their profits are distributed to shareholders. Thousands of U.S. companies had set up export subsidiaries to qualify as DISC corporations. The DISC device (discontinued in 1984) was intended to offset certain European export subsidies.

The international financial system itself was hardly changed. The dollar was maintained at the intervention currency and the standard of value to which all other currencies were pegged, although these currencies would now be pegged at new exchange rates. However, the range of permissible fluctuations for each currency vis-à-vis the dollar (that is, the "band") was widened from 2 percent to 4½ percent—2¼ percent on either side of the currency's "central rate," namely, the dollar value in which it is defined. This implied a 9 percent range of fluctuations between each two nondollar currencies.

One major exception to the 9 percent range of fluctuations between any two nondollar currencies was the exchange fluctuation among the currencies of the EEC. Striving to attain or at least to display a measure of financial integration, the six members of the Community (France, West Germany, Italy, and the three Benelux countries—Belgium, Luxembourg, and the Netherlands) decided in March, 1972 to limit the range of fluctuations between their currencies to only 4½ percent. This arrangement, known as the "EEC snake," lasted until March 1973.

After several months of post-Smithsonian calm, renewed international financial jitters again affected the United States. The $7 billion U.S. trade deficit in 1972 created widespread suspicion that the Smithsonian Agreement "was not working." This suggested the possibility of further dollar devaluation and triggered a massive flight from the dollar, mainly toward the West German mark. The United States used the situation to achieve a further devaluation of the dollar in February 1973.

March 1973—The Collapse of Bretton Woods

Both the United States and Europe had reasons to be dissatisfied with the Bretton Woods system: The United States because it could not change the exchange value of the dollar, and Europe (as well as Japan) because of waning confidence in the dollar. Yet the demise of the system was brought about by the onslaught of market forces, rather than by a deliberate decision of the world's central bankers. The tranquility following the February 1973 devaluation was short-lived, lasting no more than a few days. Fresh currency jitters erupted, leading to the closing of the foreign exchange markets for a two-week period in March to give central bankers a breathing spell during which a solution could be worked out.

What emerged from these deliberations is a new exchange-rate regime: a system of *generalized managed floats*. This spelled the end of Bretton Woods and resulted in its replacement by the contemporary system described in Chapter 4. Because of frequent disparities in inflation, growth, and interest rates, most major currencies have fluctuated sharply since 1973, with movement in one direction or another lasting from one to five years.

The 1974–75 World Recession and Its Aftermath

In late 1973 and early 1974, the world financial scene came to be dominated by cutbacks in the supply of Arab oil and by a great increase in the price of oil introduced by the oil-producing cartel (OPEC). During 1973, the price of crude oil quadrupled (from $3 to $12 per barrel), with profound effects on the economies of most countries, developing and developed alike. Globally, the price increase implies a transfer of real resources from all oil-importing to all oil-producing countries. But different groups of countries were variably affected by the increase. The developing countries can be divided into three groups: oil-producing desert countries with sparse populations, such as Saudi Arabia and Kuwait; oil-producing "high absorption" developing countries, such as Iran, Indonesia, and Nigeria; and oil-importing countries. The main problem facing the first group was that of excess riches: what to do with the immense fortune amassed, and how to ensure accumulation of enough real and financial earning assets to provide a substitute for the oil revenues once the wells run dry. For the most part the countries of the first group placed their earnings in American and European banks, and contracted with the industrial countries for the establishment of new industries on their soil. For the second group of oil producers, the high prices constituted an unmitigated boon. Practically all their oil revenues were spent on imported capital equipment. Their economic development was speeded up, and the problem of investment outlets for the additional earnings did not arise. It is the third group of developing countries that was subjected to an immense burden. Not only did they lack resources to pay the added cost of oil, but they encountered increased prices of essential oil-based products such as fertilizers, which raised the specter of a cutback in farm output. Certainly there has been a setback to their economic development. To cushion the impact these LDCs borrowed heavily in financial markets. Thus petrodollars were "recycled" from OPEC to oil-importing countries through the major banks[9]. While this alleviated the immediate problem of the oil-importing LDCs, it planted the seeds for the LDCs' debt problem of the 1980s.

In the industrial world, the rise of petroleum prices has had three effects: (1) It contributed to the subsequent double-digit inflation experienced in 1974–75, because energy inputs enter the production of practi-

---

[9]A problem created by the "recycling of petrodollars" in 1974 was that Arab countries preferred to place their funds in short-term deposits, while the (Eurodollar) banks receiving these deposits were faced with demands for long-term loans. Much of this demand came from countries in balance-of-payments difficulties. Prudent banking policy dictates a limitation on such "borrowing short and lending long." Therefore intergovernmental loans were used to supplement the private capital market.

cally all products. (2) It contributed to the longest recession in the postwar period (1974–75), because the sum of $80 billion a year was transferred—in a form similar to a tax—out of the industrial and into the OPEC countries. Combining the two effects, the increase in oil prices contributed to—but was not the sole cause of—the "stagflation" of the mid-1970s. (3) The higher import bill for petroleum caused widespread external deficits[10] with their magnitude varying from country to country according to its dependence on imported energy. A special IMF loan facility was in existence during 1974–77 to help both developed and developing countries finance oil imports.

Oil prices continued to advance gradually through the 1970s, and then doubled again in 1979–80 reaching over $35 per barrel. But the price increase had the expected effects on the energy sector: Oil consumption declined gradually, as consumers began to use less energy and as industrial users switched in part to non-oil forms of energy. At the same time production of oil substitutes, such as coal, expanded dramatically. These factors, plus the worldwide economic slump, combined to produce an oil glut on the world market in the 1980s. Prices slumped, and OPEC annual surpluses were reduced to a fraction of their previous size. Several oil-producing countries, such as Nigeria and Mexico, ran into severe financial difficulties. OPEC was faced with an urgent need to cut production in order to prevent prices from falling further, exacerbating tensions within the cartel.

Returning to the mid-1970s, only the United States among the industrial countries adopted the necessary monetary and fiscal stimulus in 1976 and 1977. In contrast, partly because of concern over inflation and partly because of institutional constraints, the German and Japanese economies remained at a virtual standstill over the two-year period. While the growth rate of the U.S. GNP was at the 5 to 6 percent level, that of Germany and Japan remained at 2 percent or less. The inflation rate in the U.S. was twice that of Germany and Japan. The differential inflation and growth rates go a long way toward explaining the large U.S. trade deficit in 1977 and 1978 and the massive surpluses in Germany and Japan.

Together these factors led to a sharp depreciation of the dollar. Relative to the yen and the mark, the dollar declined by 28.4 and 15.7 percent respectively. Aided by resumed growth in Europe, the depreciation (after a 2–3 quarter lag) helped reverse the U.S. trade performance. A turnaround occurred in 1979 and 1980 when a surge in overseas shipments increased this country's share in the manufacturing exports of all industrial countries from 14.7 to 15.6 percent. The surge in exports occurred across most commodity categories. Only autos, steel, and household appliances failed to participate. This improved U.S. trade position continued into the first half of 1981.

---

[10] As people dipped into their savings to pay for the higher cost of oil, there was a reduction in $(S - I)$, corresponding to a decline in $(X - M)$.

Figure 9-6
U.S. Dollar Trade Weighted Exchange Rate

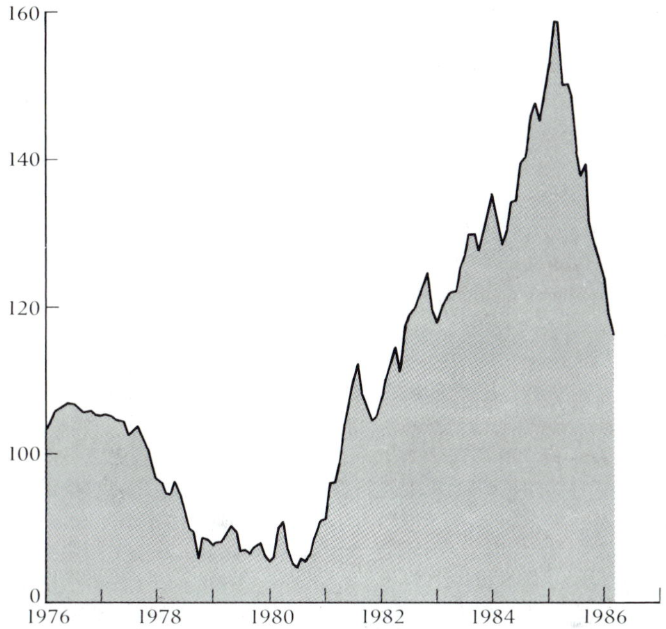

SOURCE: Board of Governors of the Federal Reserve System

The Rise of the Dollar (1980–85), and Its Decline (1985–86)

The situation changed dramatically during the next four years, when the international financial scene came to be dominated by the sharply rising exchange value of the dollar (Figure 9-6). Tight monetary policy combined with a $100 billion budget deficit in 1981–82 propelled U.S. interest rates to unprecedented heights, and plunged the economy into a recession. Subsequent expansion in the money supply turned the economy around, and a robust expansion followed in the years 1983–85.

Despite the economic recovery, U.S. budgetary deficits continued to grow through the 1980s, largely as a result of the Reagan tax cut early in the decade. Reaching $210 billion in 1985 (or over 5 percent of GNP, up from 2 percent in 1971–81), the deficits caused real interest rates (nominal interest minus the expected rate of inflation) to remain high both by U.S. historical standards *and* relative to foreign rates. In contrast, tight fiscal policies in Europe helped keep European interest rates lower than U.S. rates. This attracted large sums of capital from Europe and Japan for investment in U.S. financial instruments, including treasury bonds.[11] For investment purposes, foreigners had to convert their currencies into dollars, thereby raising the demand for dollars. This capital influx was supplemented by a reduction in U.S. capital outflow, as U.S. banks witheld loans to the LDCs. Indeed the massive availability of foreign funds kept U.S. interest rates lower than they would have been in the absence of capital inflow. Finally, the high exchange value of the dollar contributed to record-high trade deficits. The linkages between the budget deficit and the trade deficit are as follows:

Linkages Between the U.S. Budget Deficit and Trade Deficit, 1983–85

U.S. Budget Deficit →	Contributes to High → U.S. Real Interest Rates	Attracts Funds from → Abroad, to be Invested in U.S. Financial Instruments	Raises Demand → for Dollars	Increases Exchange → Value of the Dollar	Makes the U.S. Less → Competitive at Home and Abroad	Increase U.S. Trade Deficit

---

As the demand for dollars on the foreign exchange markets rose so did their value. Between 1980 and February, 1985 the effective exchange rate of the dollar increased by over 60 percent. Its value rose from 1.71 to 3.48 D.M. and from 4 to over 10 F.F. Limited intervention in the foreign currency markets by the central banks failed to stem the tide of the rising dollar. While the dollar receded from its lofty heights during 1985/86 (as U.S. interest rates declined), it remained (by mid-1986) 35 percent above its 1980 value, and was still grossly overvalued relative to PPP.

The overvaluation of the dollar helped keep down inflation in the U.S. But, on the other hand, it discouraged exports and encouraged imports, producing massive trade deficits in 1983–85. The strong dollar explains two-thirds of the deficit, while the other third is attributed to the rapid rise in U.S. real income and the reduction of Latin American imports from the U.S., caused by the external debt of LDCs.[12]

Another way of viewing the deficit is by emphasizing its macroeconomic nature. We have seen in a previous chapter that: $I - S = M - X$. Because U.S. domestic investments exceed private saving minus the government budgetary deficit (negative public saving), imports must exceed exports. A mechanism by which this equality was preserved when U.S. national saving declined (by an increase in the budget deficit) relative to national investment was the appreciation of the dollar.

As the 1985 trade deficit approached $150 billion, it offset much of the stimulative effect of the budget deficit. Indeed, the overvalued dollar

---

[11] In 1984 the attraction of high interest rates may have been supplemented by a "speculative bubble," as market actors expected to profit from further appreciation of the dollar.

[12] See: Stephen Morris, *Deficits and the Dollar: The World Economy at Risk*, Institute for International Economics, 1985; and "The Strong Dollar," Hearings Before the Joint Economic Committee of the Congress, November 29, 1985.

slowed if not halted altogether the recovery in the traded-goods industries, mainly agriculture and certain manufacturing industries. These sectors failed to participate in the general recovery. In 1984 the United States became a debtor nation for the first time since WWI: Foreigners owned more assets in the U.S. (in all forms) than Americans held abroad.[13]

A serious repercussion to the sharp swings in the value of the dollar (from a low in 1980 to a high in 1985) was the reallocation of domestic resources. Resources moved into the traded-goods industries in 1979–80 and out of them in 1982–85. For example, the low dollar signaled an expansion of U.S. agricultural capacity, supplying the export markets. The subsequent high dollar made that capacity obsolete, as U.S. farm products could not compete on world markets. This contributed to serious American farm problems in the mid-1980s.

A strong protectionist sentiment swept the Congress as a result of the overvalued dollar and the mounting trade deficits. But import restrictions in whatever form were never the proper response to what is essentially a macroeconomic phenomenon. They would invite retaliation by our trading partners, raise the cost of goods to the consumer, and perhaps be partly offset by further appreciation of the dollar.

Apart from that, it must be remembered that the trade deficits have their counterpart in capital inflows. Indeed it was the capital account that drove the trade account in the mid-1980s. Both the trade deficit and the capital account surplus reflect the fact that the U.S. economy invests more than it saves. A reduction in the trade surplus through protectionism implies a comparable cut in the inflow of funds. And that means sharply higher interest rates, which in turn may depress the economy. Alternatively, if the Federal Reserve replaces the foreign funds by pumping up the money supply, a step-up in the rate of inflation would occur.

Protectionism attacks the symptom of the problem rather than its root cause. Two thirds of the deficit can be attributed to the overvalued dollar. In turn, the overvaluation of the dollar could be attributed to a U.S. expansionary fiscal policy and tight monetary policy, whereas an opposite combination of policies prevails in other industrial countries. It is by reversing these two sets of policies that the deficits could be reduced.

In Europe, the rising dollar stimulated the export-and import-competing sectors. On the other hand, high U.S. real interest rates forced the European countries to maintain higher rates than they considered desirable in order to avoid undue depreciation of their real exchange rates. And that had a dampening effect on economic activity. This suggests that, contrary to prior expectations, domestic monetary policy did not become independent in the period of floating exchange rates. The widespread recognition that changes in real exchange rates have undesirable side effects meant that monetary policy still faces a balance of payments constraint: it must approx-

---

[13] Note however that the U.S. debt is denominated in dollars and not in foreign currencies as is the LDCs debt.

imate the monetary policy being pursued abroad in order to avoid large exchange rate movements. "In the years of fixed exchange rates, the Europeans and Canadians had to follow U.S. monetary policy to avoid excessive swings in their payments balances; under flexible exchange rates, they have had to follow U.S. monetary policy to avoid excessive swings in their real exchange rates."[14]

But the European economy also suffers from structural rigidities which sharply curtail the mobility of resources (mainly labor) between sectors of the economy. In a period of rapid technological change, such rigidities produce unemployment, especially in the declining industries.[15] European unemployment stood at around 10 percent through the 1980–85 period, generating protectionist sentiments in Europe. Again protectionism was not the answer. The proper response is to attack the root cause of the problem, which in this case was internal structural rigidities.

In general, protectionism is not a proper response to various domestic ills, be they budget deficits or structural rigidities.

Partly in an attempt to stem the protectionist tide in the Congress, the finance ministers of the big five industrial countries agreed on September 22, 1985, to massive coordinated currency intervention to drive down the value of the dollar. This was a departure from the Reagan administration's earlier stance of non-intervention in the currency markets. The President also announced some mild measures to deal with "unfair" trading practices of foreign governments.

In the Fall of 1985 central banks sold about $12 billion to drive down the value of the dollar. Much of the dollar sales was "sterilized" by open market operations (sale or purchase of government bonds) in the five countries' money markets. Under *sterilized* intervention the central bank does not permit the domestic money supply to be influenced by its foreign exchange operations. Thus, if the German central bank sells dollars for marks in order to depress the dollar, it would accompany that sale by a purchase of German government bonds (for marks), so as to avoid a decline in the domestic money supply. The net effect of the two transactions is an open market sale of dollars for German government bonds by the Bundesbank. In contrast, under *unsterilized* intervention no sale or purchase of domestic assets (namely, government bonds) accompanies the foreign exchange transactions, so that the domestic money supply is not insulated from central bank operations in the foreign currency market.

Because the market intervention by the five governments was consistent with direction of market forces, it pierced the "speculative bubble," and accelerated the decline of the dollar that began in March 1985. By mid-1986, the dollar lost nearly 30 percent of its peak (February 1985) value,

---

[14]See R. M. Dunn, *The Many Disappointments of Flexible Exchange Rates*, Princeton Essay in International Finance, No. 154, December 1983.

[15]See Chapter 3 in Bela Balassa, *Change and Challenge in the World Economy*, New York: St. Martin's Press, 1985.

but it remained overvalued relative to PPP. Although the depreciation of the dollar makes U.S. goods more competitive at home and abroad, it can be expected to improve the trade balance only after a time lag.[16]

In the long run the best solution is a reduction in the budgetary deficit in the United States, so as to reduce the excess of domestic investments over domestic savings. Precisely the opposite measure is needed in Japan: domestic demand must be stimulated by government policy, so that future growth need not depend on exports.

The LDC[17] Debt Problem

In 1983–84 the world became painfully aware of the fact that the developing countries owe some $700 billion in external debt, which constitutes nearly 40 percent of their combined GNP. Their annual debt service exceeds one fifth of their combined export earnings. The LDCs were having great difficulty in servicing (paying interest on) the debt, far less making payments on the principal. The burden of this debt is most heavily felt in Latin America.[18] As the problem captured the news headlines, a series of arrangements was made by governments, the IMF, and the large commercial banks to postpone payment on the debt and reschedule it to later years. In 1983 and 1984, $168 billion of external debt was rescheduled. Although the problem was thereby alleviated, it was by no means solved. It may reappear in all its severity at a future date.

What was the origin of the LDC debt problem? Mismanagement of their domestic economies played a central role. Overexpansionary fiscal and monetary policies, overvalued real exchange rates, and price and interest rate rigidities were key elements. From 1979 to 1982, for example, the public sector deficit as a proportion of GDP [gross domestic product] rose from 7 to 15 percent in the main Latin American countries. These deficits were associated with inflationary pressures, weakening balance of payments positions, and heavy external borrowing. Overvalued real exchange rates produced a bias against the production and competitiveness of exportables while simultaneously encouraging imports. Furthermore, fears of impending depreciation, combined with high and variable inflation rates, often produced serious bouts of capital flight. Failure to adjust public sector prices and interest rates put heavy strains on government budget positions and weakened incentives for savings and the efficient allocation of investment.

Adverse developments in the world economy were also an important cause. In part they can be traced back to the oil crises of 1973–74 and 1979–80. While the export earnings of the OPEC countries skyrocketed,

---

[16] Remember also that the depreciation is part of the price mechanism, while the trade balance is affected by differentiated growth rates in real incomes as well as by relative price changes.

[17] Less Developed Countries, otherwise known as the developing countries.

[18] It owes 40 percent of the total LDC debt, and its ratio of debt service to exports is double that for other developing countries.

the oil importing countries—developed and developing alike—ran up sizable deficits. Since OPEC could not use up its surpluses fast enough, the accumulated petrodollars were placed on deposit in the large banks of Europe and the United States. Thus, the industrial countries experienced capital inflows that offset their trade deficits. They were able to manage their balance-of-payments problem until proper adjustments could be made in the trade sector.

Not so the oil importing LDCs. To pay for their oil import (now costing a multiple of the pre–1973 prices) they borrowed vast sums from commercial banks and other sources. Thus the petrodollars were "recycled" from OPEC to oil-importing LDCs through the large international banks.

When the time came to pay up, the LDCs were dealt a multiple blow. The worldwide recession of 1981–82 made it harder for them to export to the industrial countries and to earn the foreign currencies needed to service the debt. Prices of primary commodities, the LDCs main export items, plummeted. The rise in global interest rates increased the cost of servicing the debt.[19] And finally, since this debt was denominated in U.S. dollars, the sharp appreciation of the dollar raised the value of the debt in terms of all other currencies.

As a result, countries such as Brazil, Argentina, and Mexico, encountered immense difficulties in meeting their debt obligations. In Mexico the problem was compounded by slumping oil prices and by the 1985 earthquake. The massive U.S. trade deficits of 1984 and 1985 helped somewhat in the adjustment problem, because they enabled Mexico and Brazil to mount substantial trade surpluses. But for the most part debt payments were rescheduled by their creditors (banks) to later years. The problem may re-emerge on a crisis scale in future years.

The key to the solution of their debt problem is an overhaul of domestic economic policy in the LDCs themselves, including the introduction of fiscal and monetary discipline, realistic exchange rates, and proper economic incentives. Equally important is the need for robust growth in the United States and resumed economic growth in Europe, which would increase imports from the LDCs; and continued reduction of interest rates which alleviates the burden of servicing the debt. Finally, the industrial countries must keep their markets open to the exports from the LDCs, avoiding import restrictions on traditional LDCs' exports such as textiles and footwear. Only by mounting trade surpluses can the LDCs service their external debt.[20]

---

[19] Much of this debt was contracted at "variable" interest rates. Hence the cost of servicing it rises and declines with the movement of world interest rates, which in turn were dominated by rates prevailing in the United States. Thus between 1980 and 1983 the interest rate on the debt rose from 9.7 to 13.1 percent, raising the annual interest payments by over $20 billion. The real interest rate on Latin American debt rose from minus 10 percent in 1973–78 to plus 8 percent in 1979–82.

[20] For an excellent discussion of the causes and possible solutions of the debt problem see the *IMF Survey*, November 25, 1985.

Review Questions

1. a. Explain the effects of exchange control on the economy.
   b. How do you think the monetary approach would differ from the traditional approach in the analysis of exchange control?

2. a. Describe a possible bilateral clearing agreement between Rumania and Bulgaria.
   b. Describe a possible payments union among the countries of Eastern Europe. What would be its main advantages and shortcomings?
   c. What is "countertrade"?

3. Compare and contrast the functioning of the gold standard with that of Bretton Woods. (Draw on Chapter 4 as well.)

4. What was the Smithsonian agreement, and what led to the breakdown of Bretton Woods?

5. Discuss two problems of the contemporary world financial scene.

6. In 1984, Mexico and Brazil (two principal debtor nations) experienced a resurgence in exports.

   a. How is this related to the U.S. recovery?
   b. Would a strong recovery in all OECD countries help to alleviate the debt problem? If so, how?
   c. How would the 1986 decline in world interest rates affect the LDC debt position?

7. In what sense was the U.S. trade deficit of the mid-1980s a macroeconomic phenomenon? How was it related to the fiscal and monetary policy mix in the U.S. and abroad?

   In mid-1986 both houses of Congress wished to counter the trade deficits by increased protectionism. Was that the proper response? Can you think of a more appropriate response within the constitutional responsibility of the Congress?

8. Did the system of floating exchange rates lead to national independence in the pursuit of monetary policy?

9. Distinguish between "sterilized" and "unsterilized" intervention in the foreign currency market.

10. Stimulating the European and Japanese economies (in the mid-1980s) would help alleviate the U.S. trade deficits and the LDC's debt problems. Why?

10/ Reforming the International Monetary System

*E*conomists have developed far-reaching reform plans for the international currency system. The *Wall Street Journal* once noted that any economist can compose such a plan in forty-five minutes and "the trouble is that most of them have done so." Although many exchange rates are now floating, discussions continue about reforming the system, and possibly even "relinking" the major currencies to one another. Indeed, widespread dissatisfaction with what is viewed as excessive exchange fluctuations has given added momentum to these discussions in 1986. Four main lines of approach have been selected for review: a full-fledged gold standard, a dollar exchange standard, an international reserve-creating institution or central bank, and freely fluctuating exchange rates. The selection is not exhaustive, but it serves to delineate the range of possibilities and to illustrate some possible combinations. The first three proposals involve a return to fixed exchange rates and therefore require a mechanism for reserve creation. The chapter concludes with a discussion of problems encountered by the present system of managed floats.

The Gold Standard

For many generations now, gold—known to chemists and physicists as element 79—has aroused more passion and emotion than any other natural element, such as copper or lead. Witness the comment of William Jennings Bryan in the last century, during the debate over bimetallism, decrying the crucifixion of mankind on a "cross of gold." More recently, humorist Art Buchwald suggested that gold be replaced by moon rocks as a monetary asset. In an opposite vein, General de Gaulle proclaimed in 1968: "A monetary system based on the foundation of gold, which is alone in having a character of immutability, impartiality, and universality, should therefore be applied." Against such a background, it is no wonder that even today there exists a body of opinion that considers gold more a blessing than a nuisance and favors return to the pure gold standard.

Indeed, this has long been one of the proposals for basic reform in the system. Under it, foreign currencies would be withdrawn from service as a reserve asset and be replaced entirely by gold. A sizable increase in the official price of gold in terms of all currencies is proposed to provide the massive infusion of reserves required for this system. This would immediately increase the monetary value of existing gold stocks in the coffers of central banks, thereby adding considerably to reserves. More important, a higher price would induce increased mining and attract privately held gold, to an extent sufficient for the maintenance of the gold standard. Some proponents of the return to a pure gold standard (which also implies fixed exchange rates) argue that such a system would exercise discipline on the domestic policies of nations, inducing them to avoid inflationary measures that lead to balance-of-payments deficits.

The contrary view is that such a system would be wasteful of resources devoted to gold production; that the benefits from gold revaluation would be unevenly distributed, benefiting mainly the countries that hold their reserves in the form of gold rather than those that very much need additional reserves; that sizable revaluations under this system would have to come at periodic intervals, resulting each time in excess liquidity to be "dissipated" gradually as trade expands; and that the reaction of hoarders and speculators to price increases is far from certain, because it depends on their expectations concerning possible further increases in gold prices.

In this view it is desirable to move in precisely the opposite direction and *demonetize gold*—namely, remove it from its position as an international reserve. Although this step may reduce aggregate reserves in the short run, it would eventually make the system more rational. Within domestic economies, this process has been going on for generations. Gold used to be a circulating currency; then it was withdrawn into national reserves for use in settling international imbalances. A final step in the process is suggested: Just as the management of our internal monetary affairs is subject to the discretion of human managers, so can the international system be managed, although the latter requires much cooperation since it is not backed by an international government. Gold is too expensive (in terms of the resources required to dig it up) and too unreliable a reserve item to occupy such a pivotal role in the currency system. Indeed, the world has moved away from any semblance of a gold standard.

In March 1968, the central bankers of the ten major industrialized countries met in Washington and took a major step toward demonetizing gold: They separated the private gold market from the official market. With governments no longer dealing in the private gold market,[1] private hoarders

---

[1] Foreign official gold stocks are held in part in the basement of the New York Fed.

could no longer bleed the U.S. Treasury of its cherished gold stock. On August 15, 1971, the United States announced that it would no longer redeem in gold (at a fixed price) dollar assets held by foreign central banks. This closing of the gold window officially made the dollar no longer convertible to gold. Thus, the fact that the official price of gold was raised twice in the ensuing year and a half—to $38 an ounce in December 1971 and to $42.20 an ounce in February 1973—was of little consequence to official behavior. In the words of one U.S. congressman: "What does it matter if we don't sell gold at $35 or we don't sell gold at $42.20 per ounce?" Also, the large increases in the price of gold on the private market in recent years increased the value of official gold holdings;[2] it did not affect the market behavior of central banks. Throughout much of the 1970s and 1980s, the private price of gold fluctuated between $200 and $800 per ounce. In mid-1986 it stood at $345 per ounce.

Except for sales in small quantities, most individual countries are not yet ready to unload their gold stock. However, the IMF auctioned off one-third of its gold holdings (in the late 1970s), with proceeds going to the developing countries. Further sales, with the proceeds mainly benefiting the African countries, were proposed in September 1985. The Fund also downgraded the role of gold in other ways: Gold no longer serves as a common denominator of the par value system, its official price was abolished, and the Fund's transactions in gold with member states ceased. All other reform proposals involve a considerably reduced role for gold as a monetary asset.

A Dollar Exchange Standard

Under certain conditions, the U.S. dollar is in a fairly ideal position to serve as a reserve currency. A major reason for the periodic loss of confidence in the past was the American commitment to convert official foreign dollar holdings into another reserve asset, gold. But suppose the U.S. completely severed the relation between the dollar and gold, and all countries agreed to peg their currencies to the dollar and maintain their reserves in interest-bearing assets on the New York money market. The world would be on a straight dollar standard. Countries wishing to increase (or decrease) their rate of reserve accumulation could devalue (or revalue) their currencies vis-à-vis the dollar. But to avoid competitive devaluation, the IMF would have to establish and administer international rules for exchange-rate adjustment. The United States would play a passive role. With the dollar serving as the anchor currency, it could maintain complete freedom of international transactions and permit other countries to determine their exchange rates vis-à-vis the dollar. The extent of the American external deficit would simply be a by-product of foreign demand for dollar reserves.

---

[2] Whereas the U.S. and 20 other countries still value gold at $42.20 per ounce, many countries now price their gold reserves according to a market-related formula.

Although theoretically workable, it is unlikely that the international community would move to such a system. International confidence in the dollar fluctuates over time, and at the same time, the U.S. is reluctant to relinquish control over the exchange value of the dollar.

An International Reserve-Creating Institution

Why, asks Robert Triffin of Yale University, should *international* reserves be in the form of a national currency—dollar, sterling, or whatever? Why should the creation of reserves for the system have to depend on balance-of-payments deficits of the center country, with the attendant threat of erosion of confidence in that country lurking in the background? Why not adopt the model of domestic monetary systems and establish some form of an international reserve-creating institution to perform tasks similar to those of domestic central banks?

Under Triffin's proposal, all central banks would be required to maintain a portion (say, one-quarter) of their total international reserves (gold and foreign currencies) on deposit with an expanded IMF (XIMF). The XIMF, in turn, would serve as a clearing house for all intercountry financial transfers, in much the same way as the EPU served the European countries. The main function of the expanded Fund would be to create international reserves in an orderly fashion, to coincide in time and place with the needs of central banks as indicated by the value of international commerce and other considerations. As shown in Figure 10-1 (for a three-country system), central bank deposits with the XIMF would be assets and reserves to the member countries and liabilities to the XIMF in much the same way as commercial bank deposits with their respective central banks are assets and reserves to them and liabilities to the central banks. However, in a more meaningful sense, national currencies would be replaced as a reserve instrument by a truly international asset acceptable to all: deposits with the XIMF. The dangers arising from a multiple-reserve-asset structure would then be removed. Excess reserves of central banks would be freely transferred between countries.

Equally important are the proposed new means for the creation of reserves. Reserves can be created by the Fund extending loans to countries in need. In this case, the initiative is taken by the borrowing country, and the loan is made by setting up a deposit on the books of the Fund, against which the country can draw. Such drawings are reserves by virtue of their universal acceptability. To the country receiving the loan, these are *owed* reserves. But once transferred to other nations in the form of a Fund deposit, they become *owned* reserves. Reserves can also be created through periodic allotments (as under the SDR provisions), where the XIMF distributes reserves among its members by crediting their accounts in accordance with some predetermined formula. These immediately become owned reserves acceptable to all, and can be used to settle international imbalances.

Figure 10-1
A Schematic Representation of the Triffin Plan

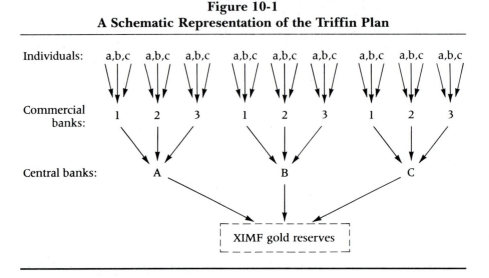

An equally important way of creating owned reserves is through open-market operations. With the consent of a country's government, the Fund can go into that country's financial market and purchase national currencies, government bonds, or other securities, including bonds and obligations of international organizations. Because the Fund pays by check drawn upon itself, the payment, once transmitted through the domestic clearing mechanism, will necessarily end up in the hands of the country's central bank. That bank, in turn, must deposit the payment with the Fund, thereby gaining owned reserves—that is, assets that are a liability of the XIMF. Because the Fund holds the initiative in such operations, it can control the overall amount of reserves being created and abide by whatever agreement is reached on the annual accretion of reserves. Limits can be imposed on the annual addition to reserves as a guard against inflation. The Fund can also determine which countries may obtain the new reserves. Indeed, a variant of the plan centers on this determination.

As long as the only purpose of the arrangement is to create reserves, their distribution can follow the present IMF quota allocation, giving the developed countries most of the newly created reserves. But an important body of professional opinion believes that there is nothing sacrosanct about the present quota distribution and that the creation of reserves should be linked to assistance for economic development (this is often referred to as the *link* proposal). In other words, the savings of real resources derived from the creation of fiat reserves (as against the mining of gold) should be assigned mainly or wholly to developing countries. Such a combination is particularly desirable in view of the mounting need for aid coupled with the increasing reluctance of legislatures in industrial nations to allocate funds for that purpose. In a sense, what is proposed is to remove a component of the aid allocation from the political process in the donor countries.

This can be accomplished by the Fund channeling its investments to the securities and currencies of developing countries, thereby giving them the newly created reserves. Most developing countries tend not to accumulate reserves, and they would spend most of the new acquisition on capital goods in the developed countries. Thus the new reserves would end up in the hands of the industrial nations. But since they would pay for these reserves in real resources, the industrial nations would be providing badly needed developmental assistance. This can also be accomplished under the SDR agreement by the allocation of a special SDR issue of predetermined size to the developing countries. In addition, the Fund can combine reserve creation with developmental assistance by purchasing the securities of international and regional development institutions, such as the World Bank.

All proposals to create new reserves depend on the reserve needs of the international currency system. And these vary inversely with the degree of exchange-rate variability.

Freely Fluctuating (Floating) Exchange Rates

A system of *free* floats would require central bankers to abandon intervention in the foreign exchange markets. It is instructive to compare the system of free floats with a regime of fixed rates by presenting an imaginary debate between a proponent and an opponent of fluctuating rates. Although such a presentation necessarily reflects a consensus of views on each side (which in fact does not exist), and is therefore oversimplified, it at least captures the essence of the controversy.

Proponent   The main advantage of freely fluctuating exchange rates is that the values of all currencies settle at a price that clears the market for foreign currencies; that is, changes in the exchange rate equate demand and supply for foreign exchange. We can then rely on exchange fluctuations to maintain equilibrium in the balance of payments, which thereby removes one of the thorniest problems of economic policy—a problem compounded by the fact that countries are often reluctant to assign high priority to external adjustment when it conflicts with the need for domestic stabilization.

Not only does this system solve the adjustment problem, but it also eliminates the need for reserves. Only when the price is fixed is there a need for reserves. Two great issues facing the international financial community—how to improve the balance-of-payments adjustment mechanism and how to generate adequate reserves—would be solved by one act. Economic policy could then concentrate on the domestic objectives of full employment and price stability.

Fluctuating rates also make monetary policy more effective for domestic stabilization. To see this, assume that a central bank wishes to cope with a depression by lowering interest rates. Under a fixed exchange rate, this is supposed to work by encouraging investments that are sensitive to the cost of credit. With a fluctuating rate, this policy can be expected to operate through an additional channel: The reduction of interest rates induces outflow of short-term capital to other countries where rates are higher. This depreciates the exchange rate and thereby encourages exports and discourages imports. The improvement in the trade balance implies a domestic expansion in employment and output that spreads through the economy through the multiplier mechanism. The reverse sequence takes place when the central bank combats inflation by raising interest rates. Thus, under fluctuating rates, monetary policy affects the domestic economy through the trade balance in addition to investments.[3]

Opponent   Fluctuating exchange rates introduce considerable risk into all international transactions and therefore lower the volume of foreign trade and investments relative to what it would be under fixed rates. Exchange rates are not like any other price, for they involve monetary values, and money is the standard by which everything else is measured. Just as it is essential to have a fixed ratio between the New York dollar and the California dollar, so it is useful to have fixed ratios between national currencies. Otherwise, commodity traders and investors cannot make advance estimates of costs and prices.

All this is particularly true in open economies, which are highly dependent on foreign trade. Constant exchange fluctuations will introduce continuous variations in the domestic price level as well as in the structure of relative domestic prices. That can result in turn in incessant reallocation of resources and perhaps even in loss of confidence in the currency as a store of value. At the very least, such fluctuations can be highly disruptive.

Domestic stabilization of income and employment can be adequately handled by fiscal measures. In fact, under fixed rates the balance of payments constitutes a restraining influence on governments, forcing them to avoid excessive inflation because it leads to balance-of-payments deficits. With fluctuating rates, all that happens in case of inflation is exchange depreciation and the anti-inflationary discipline exercised by the balance of payments is lost.

Proponent   The risk introduced by fluctuating exchange rates, and therefore its effect on the volume of transactions, is vastly exaggerated. In reality the risk depends on the size of the fluctuations: If they are small, it should

---

[3] On the other hand, fiscal policy is less effective under fluctuating rates. In a recession, fiscal expansion *raises* interest rates, attracts foreign capital, and *appreciates* the currency. The adverse effect on the trade balance offsets the stimulative effect of fiscal deficits, as illustrated by the U.S. experience in 1981–1985. Thus, monetary policy is more effective than fiscal policy for domestic stabilization under flexible exchange rates. If international capital movements are not responsive to interest-rate differentials, both monetary and fiscal policies are more effective under flexible exchange rates than under fixed rates. For flexible rates maintain balance-of-payments equilibrium and prevent leakages through imports, thereby increasing the size of the multiplier. Indeed, one objection to floating exchange rates is that they "bottle up" economic fluctuations inside the country rather than permit them to spread to other countries. The last part of Appendix VI-B offers further analysis of the relative effectiveness of fiscal and monetary policy under alternative exchange-rate regimes.

be relatively cheap to ensure against fluctuations in the forward exchange market. Indeed there has been a marked increase in the role of forward currency markets since 1973.

Theoretically, fluctuating rates can be expected to be reasonably stable because exchange markets are highly competitive and the underlying demand-and-supply factors involve a high measure of response to price change. Under such conditions, it takes only a small change in price (that is, in the exchange rate) to bring forth whatever quantity response is made necessary by changing circumstances on either side of the market. For example, if for some reason there is an increase in demand, it takes only a small rise in price to bring forth the needed increase in supply to clear the market. Similarly, a decline in demand would require only a small reduction in price to induce suppliers to withdraw the amounts needed from the markets.

In the market for any commodity, there is a positive correlation between the degree of response to price change (elasticity) and price stability. To see this, compare the effect on prices of a downward shift in the demand schedule under high and low response conditions (Figure 10-2). Starting from equilibrium position at P_1, Q_1, we shift the demand curve from D_1 to D_2. Clearly the price reduction resulting from the same shift in demand (the horizontal distance (a) between D_1 and D_2 is the same in both panels) is much sharper in the low-response (inelastic) case than in the high-response (elastic) case. Precisely the same result may be obtained by shifting the demand curve to the right or by shifting the supply curve in either direction while holding demand unchanged. High elasticities are associated with price stability, low elasticities with sharp price fluctuations.

Since the foreign exchange market is characterized by strong responses to price change on both the demand and supply sides, a fluctuating exchange

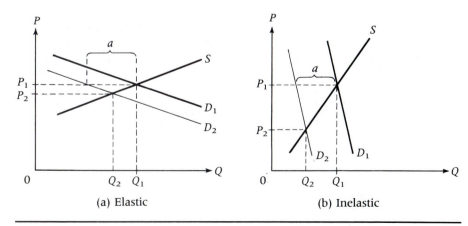

Figure 10-2
Elastic and Inelastic Supply and Demand Schedules

(a) Elastic

(b) Inelastic

rate would be relatively stable. Exchange fluctuations as such need not constitute an impediment to trade and investments. On the other hand, fixed exchange rates often lead to the imposition of exchange and import controls as a means of coping with deficits in the balance of payments and these limit international transactions much more than moderate exchange fluctuations.

Furthermore, the analogy to a ratio between New York and California dollars does not hold, for not only are regions of the same country subject to the same monetary and fiscal policies, but factors of production (such as capital and labor) can move between them without government restrictions and compensate for external deficits. In other words, the adjustment mechanism under fixed exchange rates works far better interregionally than internationally. This strand of the argument leads to a possible compromise between the two positions that will be discussed later.

If small countries with open economies face especially severe problems under fluctuating rates, the way is always open to them to peg their currencies to the currency of a large country with which they trade a great deal. This indeed is what many developing countries do.

Finally, the monetary authorities can be relied upon to exercise their own anti-inflationary discipline in the management of internal economic affairs.

Opponent   The view of quick adjustment is contradicted by the time lag in the response of trade flows to price changes in general and to exchange fluctuations in particular. Estimated price elasticities in international trade are higher in the long run than in the short run. In addition, merchandise trade *may* be characterized by high elasticities for large price changes and low elasticities for small price changes—a phenomenon resulting from the significant transactions costs in international trade. Consequently, it takes a considerable price change to induce traders to switch from domestic to foreign sources and destinations. If this were the case then exchange fluctuations might be more violent than the previous argument indicates. Also, if elasticities are low in the short run, then the immediate response to exchange variations falls on (stabilizing) capital movements. But depending upon expectations, capital movements may be destabilizing in nature.

Other opponents concede that the underlying factors of goods and services transactions make for reasonably stable exchange rates, but they worry about the nature of capital movements that respond to exchange fluctuations. Even small exchange fluctuations can elicit and feed upon speculative activity; as the value of a currency rises in terms of foreign currencies, speculators may expect it to rise further and may therefore *purchase* that currency in large quantities. This would indeed bring about the anticipated increase in its value (as self-fulfilling expectations). The reverse would occur in the case of a decline. Thus, speculation superimposed upon the underlying market factors would aggravate fluctuations and be destabilizing in nature.

The mild variations shown here by the solid line will be converted by the speculators to the sharper fluctuations illustrated by the dashed line.

Proponent It is unreasonable to assume that speculation would be destabilizing over the long run. In fact, to be profitable, speculation requires its practitioners to sell when the currency's price is high (not to purchase on the basis of expectations) and to buy when it is low. On the average, therefore, speculation must be a stabilizing phenomenon that has the effect of narrowing rather than aggravating the range of fluctuations. On the other hand, speculation can be highly destabilizing under a regime of fixed rates. When a currency is weak, the speculator knows with reasonable certainty that if it moves at all it can move in only one direction: It can be devalued. He can hardly lose by selling it and buying a strong currency that can only be revalued. Indeed, in a regime of fixed exchange rates, speculative activity can bring about changes in the exchange rate when it is superimposed on a certain underlying weakness or strength. Because the risk involved is very low, such speculation is often both destabilizing and excessive. Even the IMF recognizes that fact and permits the imposition of exchange control in cases of speculative attack. By contrast, fluctuating rates may dampen speculative activity by introducing more risk into it. **End of Debate**

The Record of 1973–86

What is the evidence of the floating rates period? The amplitude of exchange fluctuations has been high and often unsettling. Exchange variability has been substantial for both nominal and real exchange rates; bilateral and effective exchange rates; and over short- or long-term time horizons. It has been greater under the floating rate system than in the earlier period of adjustable pegs. And it has been greater among currencies floating independently than for those within the EMS. Variability did not decline over time; it was substantially higher during 1979–86 than in the previous five years. Additionally there have been many significant cases of exchange rate "overshooting"[4] superimposed upon changes in fundamental market conditions. Overshooting may have been experienced by Germany in 1975–76, Japan in 1976–78, the U.K. in 1979–80, and the U.S. in the 1980s.

Throughout the floating rates period, official intervention in foreign exchange markets persisted, indicating a growing demand for international

[4]Overshooting, or the excessive movement of exchange rates, results from the overreaction of exchange rates to policy developments. Usually it reflects the fact that financial markets normally adjust much more rapidly to new conditions than do contract prices in labor and product markets. For example, an unanticipated change in a country's monetary policy stance could cause interest rates to overadjust in the short run, which in turn could lead to overshooting of the exchange rate.

reserves. Even U.S. intervention, dormant throughout the first term of the Reagan administration, intensified greatly in 1985. Finally, for extended periods, exchange rates departed considerably from PPP values.

But much of that volatility was a result of unsettled global economic conditions: oil shocks, draughts, stagflations, differential inflation rates between countries, and vastly different growth rates. These events could not have been accommodated by a fixed exchange-rate system. Thus the appropriate question is: were exchange fluctuations of greater magnitude than that warranted by the economic disturbances that triggered them, so as to send improper signals to business and governments? One measure of the intensity of changing economic circumstances is fluctuation in the prices of stocks and bonds. The fact that exchange rates exhibited *less* variation than the prices of other financial assets suggests that exchange fluctuations were not excessive relative to changes in fundamental conditions.

International economic relations have not been disrupted by floating exchange rates, and the system weathered well the economic crises of the 1970s.[5] Whether the value of trade and investments has been reduced by floating rates is still an open question.

Concern over the amplitude of exchange fluctuations can best be met by improved coordination among countries of their fiscal and monetary policies. This implies that countries do not gain independence in domestic monetary policy even under floating rates, for such policy is targeted in part at stabilizing the exchange rate. A return to fixed exchange rates, desired by some observers, may not be practical as long as the underlying economic conditions vary greatly among countries. However, there are a number of possible currency arrangements that lie between the two extremes of fixed and floating rates.

Wider Bands and Crawling Pegs

One proposal is to adopt fixed exchange rates but widen the spread within which exchange rates are permitted to fluctuate (the "wider band" proposal). It would contribute to speeding up balance-of-payments adjustments and at the same time would reduce the need for reserves.

Other ideas bandied about include the so-called crawling peg which would permit a country in disequilibrium to make preannounced small changes in its parity every month until equilibrium is attained. The proposal has the dual advantage over an "adjustable peg" system of permitting parity adjustments before the pressure on the country has reached a boiling point and of removing some of the political stigma attached to large, discrete exchange variations. On the other hand, preannounced exchange adjustments can stimulate speculative activity, and the country would need to manipulate its interest rates to stem destabilizing capital flows. Brazil has functioned under this system in recent years.

---

[5] For further discussion see R. Blackhurst and J. Tumlir, "Trade Relations Under Flexible Exchange Rates," Geneva, GATT Studies No. 8, September 1980; and M. Goldstein, "Whither The Exchange Rate System," *Finance and Development*, June 1984.

An automatic variant of the crawling peg has also been discussed. It would make the parity on any business day a moving average of the exchange rates (or of reserve movements) over a predetermined preceding period. Thus, if the exchange rate bounces along the floor—the lower support limit—for a specified period, the official parity rate along with the entire band would gradually be nudged down. Conversely, it would move upward should the rate move along the ceiling for a time. In other words, the movements of the par value of each currency (along with its support limits) would depend on the relation between the actual exchange rate and the support limits over a certain past period. Schematically, the crawling rate proposal can be illustrated as follows:

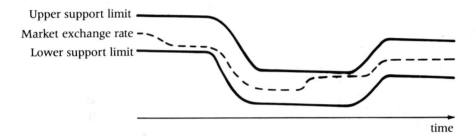

Target Zones

Finally, it has been proposed that the IMF establish "target zones" for the major currencies, and that central banks maintain their respective exchange rates within those zones through market intervention. The "zones," which would be subject to periodic changes, would delineate limits to sustainable exchange rates. In determining the target zones the IMF would use a variety of indicators, such as cost-price comparisons and indicators pertaining to capital flows. But given the uncertainties surrounding the future flow of international transactions, it would be difficult to determine the target zones.[6]

All the proposals mentioned above involve some central bank intervention in the currency markets, and hence would call for increased demand for international reserves. Also any attempt to link the exchange rates of the major currencies would require coordination of domestic economic policies.

Optimum Currency Areas

Another proposal is to establish fixed exchange rates within a group of closely knit countries, and to permit free fluctuations between the blocs of countries, each floating jointly. Such groups of countries are often referred to as "optimum currency areas." While there are no specific rules that define

[6] For discussion see John Williamson, *The Exchange Rate System*, Policy Analyses in International Economics No. 5 (Washington: Institute for International Economics, 1983), and Hans Genberg, "On Choosing the Right Rules for Exchange Rate Management," *The World Economy*, Vol. 7, December 1984.

exactly what groups of countries may qualify for inclusion in any one area, some guidelines can be articulated. It is desirable for the countries composing a currency area to have a high measure of coordination in fiscal and monetary policies, as well as a high level of factor mobility between them. These conditions help lubricate the adjustment mechanism under fixed exchange rates. Recall that when resources are highly mobile, as within a country, the adjustment process entails the movement of resources from the deficit (depressed) region to the surplus (prosperous) region. In addition, the currency area ought to be large enough, with most of its international transactions conducted within its own boundaries, so that fluctuations between its composite exchange rate and the rates of other areas cannot affect its domestic price levels to any great degree.

Behind these criteria for optimum currency areas is the relative ease of the balance-of-payments adjustment process under the two alternative regimes. A region that is reasonably independent of foreign trade would sustain a lower adjustment cost in a system of flexible rates than in a system of fixed rates, where it requires substantial income adjustment to produce a change in the trade balance. The reverse is true for open economies. For them the cost of balance-of-payments adjustment is lower via the income adjustment mechanism. There is some degree of "closedness" of a country or group of countries for which the costs of adjustment under the income and switching mechanisms are equal. That break-even point can be thought of as determining the size of the optimum currency area.

Adoption of a common currency is the most extreme form of financial integration within an optimum currency area. Money performs its functions (as a means of exchange and store of value) best if the same unit covers a wide area. Thus, a worldwide currency is the best from the viewpoint of stimulating saving and economic growth. Barring such a currency, the next best thing would be a currency common to several countries willing and able to meet the conditions for such an arrangement. In what follows we explore further the issues involved in forming a currency union in the context of the European Community (EC).[7]

☐ **Monetary Integration in the EC**   EC planners have long considered monetary integration an essential ingredient of European integration. This is expected to have two components: permanently fixed exchange rates within the EC, preferably without a band of fluctuations, which may vary jointly relative to other currencies; and the complete absence of exchange control within the area.

---

[7]The European Community consists of twelve countries: West Germany, France, the United Kingdom, Italy, the Netherlands, Belgium, Denmark, Ireland, Luxembourg, Greece, Spain, and Portugal. Belgium and Luxembourg have long had a monetary union. The EC is discussed in Chapter 16.

☐ Historically, the move toward a common currency received a sharp stimulus from the adoption of the "Barre Plan" in February 1969, which set up a commission to coordinate the members' economic policies, and in particular to harmonize their monetary policies. A further step was taken in the May 1970 "Werner Report," which went into the specifics of monetary integration. Operationally, the move was reflected in the adoption of narrow exchange-rate margins for EC currencies after the 1971 Smithsonian agreement, the joint currency float agreed upon in March 1973, and currently the EMS. However, the EMS does not coincide with EC membership, because some members, including the United Kingdom, do not participate in it; and exchange-rate adjustments within the EMS occur frequently.

☐ Is a currency union a desirable objective for the EC? Alternatively, what type of countries can be viewed as an "optimum currency area"? At one extreme, the population of a mini-country would choose to strike bargains and accumulate liquid wealth in terms of foreign currency.[8] Such a country clearly should join a monetary union with other countries, as Luxembourg does with Belgium, Lichtenstein with Austria, and Monaco with France. Advancing to larger states, the same reasoning does not necessarily apply to most of the small European countries. Before a country the size of Norway or the Netherlands joins a currency union, it must weigh the costs of balancing its external accounts through domestic policy, as would be required of a member of the union, and of balancing them through exchange-rate adjustment (remembering that as a member of a customs union the country has already given up its right for independent action on trade controls). The higher the country's marginal propensity to import, the lower are the costs of adjustment via domestic fiscal and monetary policy. For in case of a deficit, the higher the MPM, the more a given reduction in GNP will curtail imports and the less the domestic unemployment necessary to eliminate a given deficit. Likewise the higher the MPM, the smaller will be the increase in domestic expenditures necessary to eliminate a given external surplus. As a general rule, this implies that the smaller the country and the more open its economy, the less the cost of adjustment will be via domestic policies. The costs of adjusting to external imbalances through variations in the exchange rate are (a) the domestic price instability generated by exchange fluctuations, which would reduce the value of the currency as a store of value, and (b) domestic economic instability, which would arise as resources shift between the traded and non-traded goods industries in response to exchange fluctuations. Also, in the case of depreciation, there are losses in the terms of trade. These costs of adjustment tend to be larger in the case of small open economies, where foreign trade may occupy as much as one half of GNP, than in large countries. In general, the more

---

[8] The chief disadvantages of floating rates for a small open region are the thinness of the foreign-exchange market and therefore the market's vulnerability to the machinations of individual speculators, the sensitivity of the domestic price level to changes in import prices, and the sheer cumbersomeness of the many foreign-exchange transactions that are necessary when most goods, and perhaps many services, are bought from and sold to other regions.

important that trade is in a country, the greater will be the potential gain from price certainty in international trade and hence from the assurance of fixed exchange rates. Thus, while the small European countries *may* do well to join a currency union, the same need not apply to the large members of the EC, such as Italy, France, Germany, or the United Kingdom. For the large countries, the cost of balancing the external accounts is less via exchange-rate adjustments than it is via domestic measures.

☐ Are there circumstances under which even the large European countries would benefit, on balance, from a currency union? Two alternative sets of conditions can be so visualized: The first is a set of prerequisites which, if met, would minimize or eliminate external imbalances between members of the currency union so as to minimize the need to adjust. Ideally these countries should have identical growth rates in productivity and identical preferences concerning the unemployment–inflation mix that they consider desirable; their position on the Phillips curve (for example, trade union aggressiveness, industrial concentration, and structural unemployment) should be the same. A difference in any one respect can create problems, unless it is offset by a difference in another respect. Members of the EC have exhibited nonoffsetting differences in all three respects.

☐ A second set of conditions that would (by minimizing intra-union imbalances) increase the benefits, relative to costs, of a currency union would be for members of the union to behave as though they were regions of one country. This would include a common monetary policy and a common central bank, a high level of capital and labor mobility between members so that the depressed–flourishing area dichotomy would not be translated into unbalanced trade accounts; and an aggressive large-scale "regional policy" that would transfer resources to the depressed areas of the Community and stimulate economic activity in those areas by direct action of the central authorities of the union. This set of conditions is not fulfilled in the case of the EC, where each country jealously guards its independent monetary policy, where there are cultural and even political obstacles to labor mobility, and where regional policy is still in its infancy. And indeed the EMS does not constitute irrevocably fixed exchange rates.

☐ On the other hand, fixed exchange rates within the EC *could* "force" members to coordinate their domestic policies, and thereby produce a greater convergence of inflation and growth rates. Indeed, some observers maintain that this has already happened on the European continent, and it may account for the lower variability of EMS exchange rates relative to those of the independently floating currencies. This proposition of "putting the cart before the horse," is used by some British observers in arguing for U.K. accession to the EMS. ■

Living with Floating Exchange Rates

The IMF Charter

The original IMF charter displayed a distinct preference for fixed exchange rates. Floating rates were permitted only as a temporary device. When generalized floating was introduced in 1973, it was first viewed as a temporary aberration. A committee of the IMF was set up to consider an overhaul of the system, preferably including a return to fixed exchange rates. But these attempts were abandoned in the currency turmoils that followed the 1973–74 oil crisis. The resiliency of floating rates in weathering out the crisis came to be generally recognized as a big advantage. In 1978 the IMF charter was revised to legitimatize floating rates, to downgrade the function of gold and enhance that of SDRs in the international currency system, and to expand IMF quotas.

Most important of these changes is the provision to legitimatize floating rates. It permits countries to choose between several alternative exchange rate systems: a freely floating exchange rate; a managed float, under which currency intervention by the monetary authorities could be subject to IMF guidelines and surveillance; and a fixed exchange rate, under which the par value may be set in terms of SDRs or any other asset, but not in terms of gold. Return to a full-fledged fixed exchange-rates system would take place if countries holding 85 percent of IMF quotas agreed to do so. The monetary role of gold was downgraded and its official price was abolished. The Fund's transactions in gold with member states ceased, except under special circumstances; the expression "gold tranche" in the Fund's regular account was replaced by "reserve tranche." Use of SDRs between official institutions of member states was expanded in the hope that the SDR would develop into the financial reserve asset of the international monetary system. The 25 percent of members' quotas that used to be paid in gold is now payable in SDRs or in currencies that are widely used in international transactions ("freely usable currencies").

The IMF exercises surveillance over the foreign exchange intervention of member governments. Through bilateral and multilateral consultations, it attempts to ensure that members do not manipulate their exchange rates to gain competitive advantage, and that they intervene only to counter disorderly conditions. The following developments signal the need for IMF consultation with a member about its exchange-rate policies: "(1) persistent sales or persistent purchases of foreign exchange by a member's authorities; (2) an unsustainable level of official borrowing or prolonged official lending for balance-of-payments (BOP) purposes; (3) the introduction, intensification, or prolonged maintenance for BOP purposes of restrictions on trade or capital flows; (4) the pursuit for BOP purposes of monetary or other domestic financial policies that provide an abnormal incentive for capital inflows or outflows; and (5) behavior of the exchange rate that appears to be unrelated to underlying economic and financial conditions."[9]

Although the role of the dollar as the numeraire of the system has been downgraded somewhat, it remains the most widely used transaction and vehicle currency. As a consequence it is still the most important intervention asset in use by countries to manage their floats, and the most widely "pegged currency" among LDCs. Although the SDR can now serve as a unit of account, it cannot be used in market intervention as long as it is held exclusively by official institutions. Even for the purpose of reference value, the dollar is still in wide use. And, finally, the dollar is still the most commonly used reserve currency.

Developed Countries

Currencies of the industrial countries are floating either individually or jointly. Yet, despite some trying times, countries have exhibited a satisfactory degree of cooperation in their exchange-market interventions. But it would be an error to project these conditions into the indefinite future. The possible development of friction between the policy objectives of different countries, and even of competitive exchange depreciation, suggests a need for the adoption of rules to govern market intervention coupled with IMF surveillance.

Following is a taxonomic listing of alternative objectives for official intervention in the foreign exchange market: (1) "Neutral" intervention, designed to smooth out short-run exchange fluctuations without interfering with long-run trends. In practical terms such an objective implies that there would be no net change in the countries' reserve position in either direction over a certain given period such as three months. (2) Intervention to offset or moderate the effect of political and economic "shocks," or nonrecurring events, such as a prolonged general strike, or a drought. (3) Intervention to offset seasonal and cyclical movements in the trade balance. (4) Extensive intervention to maintain exchange rates consistent with long-run basic balance. In its extreme form such a rule would imply unlimited intervention, and it is based on the supposition that the authorities are better judges of the long-run equilibrium exchange rate than is the market. If so, why not opt for a fixed exchange-rate regime? (5) Intervention to adjust the volume or composition of official reserves. (6) Intervention to maintain joint floats or pegged currencies. If such intervention employs only the jointly floating currencies, its effects on the exchange value of third currencies will be neutral. But if it is undertaken in third currencies, the value of the latter can be affected.

This brings into focus a general problem affecting all official intervention. Extensive intervention by many countries in their respective foreign exchange markets, using one of very few intervention currencies (such

---

[9]W. C. Hood, "Surveillance Over Exchange Rates," *Finance and Development*, March 1982, pp. 9–12.

as the dollar) will affect the ability of the latter currency to float freely. Because the dollar is the major intervention currency, its fate is most affected by action of countries other than the issuing country. To some extent this places the U.S. in the same straitjacket as in the period of Bretton Woods. To cope with this problem some rule may have to be adopted to guard the interest of the country issuing an intervention currency. An example of such a rule is that a country may not accumulate the currency of another country beyond a specified limit without the permission of the latter.

Against this spectrum of possible objectives, we might consider the guidelines promulgated by the IMF: Intervention is permitted to *moderate* sharp and disruptive fluctuations in the exchange rate and to offset the effect of temporary factors. Countries should *not* intervene aggressively, that is, in such a way as to *aggravate* exchange fluctuations (depress the currency value when it is falling or enhance it when it is rising). Exceptions to the above "do" and "don't" rules could occur only if a currency is recognized by the IMF to be clearly outside the range of a reasonable estimate of the "medium term norm" exchange rate (that is, a rate that would bring about balance-of-payments equilibrium over a four-year period so as to balance out seasonal and cyclical variations). Such intervention may also be permitted by the Fund in order to adjust the country's reserves (up or down) to what it considers a desirable level. A specific proposal for IMF surveillance of country intervention is described in Appendix VI-A.

Developing Countries (LDCs)

LDCs' Preference for Stable Exchange Rates For the less-developed countries (LDCs), the introduction of generalized floating presented new and unfamiliar conditions. Indeed in international conferences most of them display a strong preference for a return to fixed rates among the industrial countries. Possible reasons for this preference are four-fold: First, the lack of high-quality banking services compounded by the scarcity of expertise makes it difficult for LDCs to deal with and take advantage of fluctuating rates. Foreign currency markets are rudimentary at best, and the forward markets vary from nonexistent to poor. This makes it impossible for traders to obtain forward cover for commercial transactions and thus insure against exchange fluctuations. Even if the LDC currency is pegged to that of its main trading partner (as most of them are), it necessarily fluctuates against the other major currencies, introducing uncertainty into the finance of international trade. Second, pegging to a major currency which is itself fluctuating can have destabilizing effects, such as imported inflation or deflation (see next subsection). Third, the real value of LDC reserves changes with the fluctuations of the major currencies, especially if an LDC's reserves are made up of one dominant currency. Reserve diversification is a possible way out, but may be somewhat costly and complicated to maintain. A fourth reason for preferring fixed rates is an LDC's hope for a "link" between reserve creation and foreign assistance. Since under floating rates few reserves need be created, there is also no prospect for any link arrangement.

But some of these reasons are not as powerful and convincing as they sound. The technical deficiencies can be remedied over time. Experts can be trained; forward exchange markets can be developed privately or the central bank can offer forward cover; and reserves can be diversified and managed so as to avoid losses in their real value. And with respect to the "Link" proposal, considering the political opposition in the industrial countries, it is doubtful whether any meaningful arrangement would have come into being even under fixed exchange rates.

More importantly, the LDCs often overlook the potential benefits to them that flow from freeing the industrial countries from the balance-of-payments constraint. Under the fixed exchange-rate system balances-of-payments deficits often resulted in internal contractionary policies in the industrial countries and led to reduced demand for raw materials from the LDCs. And at other times external deficits led to the imposition of import restrictions, restricting LDCs' exports, as well as to the curtailment of foreign aid and investments. This is less likely to occur under floating rates.

In sum it is not at all clear that LDCs fare better under fixed than under floating exchange rates. Yet a September 1985 Report of the "Group of 24" LDC representatives in the IMF supported the principle of "target zones" among the major currencies, to attain greater exchange stability. Some of the group's other recommendations were: increased IMF surveillance of the industrial countries to insure that the burden of adjustment does not fall disproportionately on the LDCs; new annual allocations of SDRs with a LINK provision; a general increase in IMF quotas, an enlargement of its other loan facilities, and a new facility to finance interest rate increases on external debt; and a reorientation of the IMF conditionality criteria from demand deflation to growth-oriented adjustment.

In any event, the LDCs have little influence on the type of currency arrangement chosen by the industrial countries; they have to accommodate themselves to whatever the major nations decide. The question arises: Given floating rates of the Western currencies, what alternatives are open to the developing countries?

LDCs' Options in a World of Floating Exchange Rates As a first possibility, LDCs can adopt independent floating. But very few of them have opted for that regime, and probably for good reasons. In the first place, most developing countries have a set of distinguishing characteristics: They are highly specialized in the production of very few commodities; they are too small to affect their terms of trade (especially with respect to their imports); they have relatively inelastic import-demand and export supply, particularly in the short run; and they have rudimentary financial markets, making international capital flows relatively nonresponsive to interest differentials. And these features suggest that a floating LDC currency can easily be subject to extreme gyrations. Secondly, the short-run market-clearing exchange rate of a developing country may diverge considerably from the long-run equilibrium rate, defined as the exchange rate that should prevail after the appropriate or desired structural changes in the economy have been instituted. Third, rightly or wrongly, LDCs often use exchange-rate policy—including exchange control and multiple exchange rates—as a major instrument in guiding the course of their economic development. They may not wish to give up this policy tool by letting market forces determine the exchange rate.

A second alternative, favored by most developing countries, is pegging to a single currency—perhaps that of their main trading partner. Not only is this regime simple to implement, but it has the advantage of eliminating the exchange risk from a large share of the country's international transactions. If prices in the partner country are relatively stable, such a regime may also increase confidence in the LDC. Against these advantages there are several drawbacks. The movements in the LDC's exchange rate reflect the external position of its main trading partner rather than balance-of-payments developments in the LDC itself. If the factors affecting the two external positions are unrelated, this will increase the need for reserves on the part of the LDC and the maintenance of reserves can be costly. Equally important, such a regime often interferes with the LDC's domestic objectives and imparts a large measure of instability to its economy. Appreciation of the "partner currency" stimulates imports and discourages exports, thereby harming the LDC's balance-of-payments position, and at the same time dampening its level of economic activity. Thus if the Thai baht is pegged to the dollar, it necessarily fluctuates against the yen and other currencies, Japan being Thailand's second most important trading partner. And during 1980–85, the baht appreciated with the dollar, which caused strains on the Thai economy. In November 1984, the baht had to be devalued against the dollar. Conversely, depreciation of the main currency would be inflationary in the LDC. In 1973, currencies pegged to the pound sterling depreciated with it, and this depreciation exacerbated the inflation and the excess domestic liquidity created by the commodity boom of that period.

A less important problem is intra-LDCs exchange fluctuations. To the extent that various LDCs peg their currencies to different major currencies, they fluctuate vis-à-vis each other, making it difficult to promote intra-regional trade. Francophone and Anglophone Africa are cases in point.

These problems led several LDCs to abandon the single currency peg and switch to a basket of currencies. That basket may be either "tailor made" for the LDC in question, or alternatively it may be the SDR. The choice depends on the objective of pegging and on the geographical distribution of the country's foreign trade. If the country wishes to stabilize its import prices and the sources of its imports are concentrated in very few countries, a "tailor-made" import-weighted basket is appropriate. The country must then select the currencies to be included in the basket and their weights, and develop a formula to compute the daily changes in the exchange rate that would stabilize its currency in terms of the basket. By contrast, if imports are widely distributed, an SDR link may be appropriate. However, the SDR serves only as a numeraire, while the actual intervention is usually done in dollars.

Review Questions

1. a. Compare and contrast a fixed and a floating exchange-rate system. What is the historical evidence concerning their relative advantage?
   b. Compare the relative effectiveness of fiscal and monetary policies under the two systems. (Advanced students may wish to consult the Appendix.)
   c. What possible compromise systems lie between the two extremes?

2. Is the EC an ideal "optimum currency area"? Why or why not?

3. Evaluate the LDCs' position concerning the international currency system.

4. Explain the following: (a) Triffin Plan (b) Link proposal (c) Dollar standard (d) Target zones (e) IMF surveillance.

International Trade Relations

Introduction

A smoothly functioning international financial system is not an end in itself; it merely makes possible an unobstructed trade in goods and services as well as transfers of capital in order that it may serve the interests of the international community. In Part 2, therefore, we turn our attention to the advantages of such unobstructed exchange, and to public policies that affect the flow of trade. This part of international trade theory is known as the pure theory of international trade to distinguish it from the mechanism of the balance-of-payments adjustment, or monetary trade theory. The word "pure" carries no moral connotation. It underscores the fact that the theory deals with trade in its barter essentials and that monetary phenomena do not occupy a central role in it.

Of the various items in the balance-of-payments statement, merchandise trade is the main concern of Part 2. The only exception is the last chapter, which is devoted to direct foreign investments and labor mobility.

Data on International Commodity Trade

☐ In the balance-of-payments statement, all commodities are lumped together into one item. But there are statistical sources that break this item down into its components and show the sources and destinations of each product. Thus, the United Nations and other international organizations classify all commodities according to the Standard International Trade Classification (SITC). The SITC comprises one-, two-, three-, and four-digit classes. Commodity groups in the one-digit class are fewest in number and least detailed; those in the other classes are greater in number and more detailed, up to the four-digit class, which has the most commodities and is the most refined in detail. Items 5 through 8 of the one-digit class, for example, are manufacturers: Item 5 is chemicals, 7 denotes machinery and transport equipment, and 6 and 8 are other manufactures. Each of these items is further subdivided into its components and subcomponents. For example SITC 7 is divided into categories 71, nonelectrical machinery; 72, electrical machinery; and 73, transport equipment. Category 71 is subdivided into 711, nonelectrical power machinery; 712, agricultural machinery; 714, office machines; and so on. And 714 is further subdivided into 714.1, typewriters; 714.2, accounting machines; and so forth.

☐ The most comprehensive quarterly and annual statistics for all countries, using four-digit (and sometimes five-digit) SITC, are published by the United Nations in *Commodity Trade Statistics.* For Europe and North America, a detailed commodity breakdown appears in OECD statistical publications.[1] These reports are based on data collected by member countries from import and export declarations filed by traders. Information on trade flows as well as on domestic economic variables for the industrialized countries is contained in the OECD's publications, *Main Economic Indicators,* and *Economic Outlook.*

☐ For the United States, a very detailed classification of traded commodities is published quarterly in the U.S Census Bureau report of exports and imports. U.S trade may be compared with domestic consumption or production of a given commodity by means of Census Bureau publication, *United States Commodity Imports and Exports as Related to Output.* For other countries, such a comparison may be found in the United Nations publication *The Growth of World Industry.* Finally, the United Nations' *Monthly Bulletin of Statistics* offers trade and other information for various nations. Information on East–West trade is contained in surveys published by the U.N. Economic Commission for Europe.[2] ■

Part 2 begins by considering why nations trade and what determines the types of commodities that are imported and exported—that is, the commodity composition of trade. In the process it sheds additional light on the relation between national economic conditions and trade and exchange relations. The discussion then turns to government policies that obstruct the free flow of goods across national boundaries when protection of domestic industry is the foremost objective. Subsequent chapters discuss regional and

---

[1] "Partner country" statistics contain many sizable discrepancies: a country's export of a given commodity does not always match the importing country's reported import of that commodity. This is true of both volume and value figures. Some of the reasons for the discrepancies are that different countries often categorize the same product differently; there is a time lapse between departure and arrival of goods; traders may under- or over-invoice exports or imports to take advantage of government policies (subsidies, exchange controls); and discrepancies and inaccuracies exist in official calculations.

[2] See also Paul Marer, *Soviet and East European Foreign Trade 1946–1969,* Indiana University Press, 1972.

international organizations designed to promote free trade or to advance the interests of a certain group of countries. Chapter 18 is concerned with international flows of investment capital.

Review Question

- How would you go about comparing the export/output ratio of commercial aircraft between the U.S and France?

11 / *Why Nations Trade*

Nations trade with each other for fundamentally the same reasons that individuals or regions engage in exchange of goods and services: to obtain the benefits of specialization. Since nations, like individuals, are not equally suited to produce all goods, either because they are differently endowed or for other reasons, all would benefit if each specialized in what it could do best and obtained its other needs through exchange. The point is self-evident, for in a free society communities would not engage in trade if it did not benefit them. This chapter focuses on the gains to individual nations from an international exchange of goods, it demonstrates the conditions under which trading countries may benefit from trade, and in the process it develops a method of determining which goods are exported and which are imported by each country.

The Principle of Comparative Advantage

The Gains from Trade

Asked why she engages in foreign trade, any businessperson can promptly offer a superficial, yet correct answer: she purchases a commodity abroad if and when it is cheaper abroad than at home, and she sells a commodity abroad when it fetches a higher price abroad than it does domestically. She buys where it is cheapest and sells where it is dearest in order to maximize her profit. In other words, relative prices at home and abroad determine which goods are exported and which are imported by any given country— the commodity composition of trade.

But what makes some goods cheaper in one country and others cheaper in another? To the businessperson this is of no consequence; she simply converts one currency into another at the prevailing exchange rate and compares prices. But to the economist this is the crux of the matter, for it is only by answering this question that she can determine whether such profit-maximizing behavior on the part of individual traders is beneficial to the country. And, equally important, saying that a commodity is cheaper in one country than in another implies the use of an exchange rate. But the exchange rate itself must in some way be determined by relative costs and prices as well as by other economic conditions in the two trading countries. Thus, by simply falling back on the businessperson's statement, we are, at least in part, explaining relative prices by relative prices. In order to break out of the circular reasoning, it is necessary to investigate what determines the relative cost–price positions of the two countries.

To do this we go to a principle originally enunciated early in the nineteenth century by the English economist David Ricardo: the principle of comparative advantage or, stated inversely, comparative cost. It is most easily explained by a simplified example similar to the one Ricardo used. Assume that the world consists of two countries, say the United States and the United Kingdom, which produce two commodities, wheat and textiles. Suppose further that the only factor of production employed in producing the two goods is labor in a homogeneous form. This means that the value of each product is determined exclusively by its labor content (yielding the so-called labor theory of value). Goods move freely between the two countries but labor is mobile only domestically, not internationally. Transport costs are also assumed not to exist. Technology is presumed to remain constant, unaffected by trade. Although this is a highly simplified case, it yields considerable insight of general application, as we shall see.

Suppose that the production conditions prevailing in the two countries are those of Scheme 1.

Scheme 1	Production Conditions
In	One Person-Day of Labor Produces
United States	60 bushels of wheat *or* 20 yards of textiles
United Kingdom	20 bushels of wheat *or* 10 yards of textiles

Clearly, labor is more productive absolutely in the United States than in the United Kingdom in both the textile and the wheat industries: it produces more of everything in the United States than it does in the United Kingdom. (At a later point it will be shown that the existence of this *absolute* advantage has important implications with respect to the relative wage rates in the two countries.) It should not be inferred from these figures that because the United States is more efficient in the production of both commodities, it would produce both of them when trade opens up or that the United Kingdom would produce none. To suggest this is to deny the mutual advantage to be derived from international trade. The condition postulated here, that one country is absolutely more productive than another in most of their mutual pursuits, is not uncommon. Yet mutually beneficial trade does take place, even between countries as extremely different in productive efficiency as the United States and India.

What is important in the problem at hand is *comparative,* not absolute, advantage. A vertical comparison of the figures in Scheme 1 shows that the degree of American advantage over the United Kingdom is not the same in both industries. The United States has a 3 to 1 advantage in wheat, but only a 2 to 1 advantage in textiles. Comparatively speaking, therefore, the United States has a greater advantage in wheat and a lesser advantage in textiles. The United Kingdom is in the reverse position; it has an absolute disadvantage in both goods, but the extent of disadvantage is greater in wheat and lesser in textiles, because labor can produce only one-third as much wheat as in the United States, but it can produce fully one-half as much textiles. Since we are merely comparing the degree of advantage and disadvantage in producing the two goods, the analysis can be expressed by asserting that the United States has a comparative advantage in wheat while the United Kingdom has a comparative advantage in textiles.

This situation is analogous to that of a doctor who is absolutely more efficient than his nurse in the performance of both medical and paramedical duties. But the degree of his advantage is much larger in the first type of duty than in the second. And just as it pays the doctor to concentrate on the former and hire a nurse to do the latter, so it is to America's advantage to specialize in wheat and purchase British textiles.

But this is running somewhat ahead of our story. The productivity comparison between the two countries is possible only because of the existence of an international common denominator—a given quantity of homogeneous labor. Had this been absent, the vertical comparison in Scheme 1 would have been impossible. Consequently, it is more general and meaningful to focus on the horizontal, *within-country,* comparison, although the conclusion is the same in both cases.

What do we see from that vantage point? Domestically, the United States must give up 3 bushels of wheat to obtain 1 yard of textiles. Obviously, wheat is not convertible into textiles in any mechanical sense; but by forgoing 3 bushels of wheat, enough labor (and other resources if present) is released to be put into textile production to produce 1 yard of textiles. This is what the internal cost ratio of 3 to 1 (or 60 bushels of wheat for 20 yards of textiles) means: The resource cost, sometimes called the "opportunity cost," of 1 yard of textiles in the United States is 3 bushels of wheat. The United States would be unwilling to trade 3 bushels of wheat for anything less than 1 yard of textiles, for it can do better at home. But it would be eager to purchase textiles abroad if a yard could be obtained for less than 3 bushels of wheat, because then the resource cost of textiles embodied in the wheat traded is less than that of forgoing wheat production in order to produce the textiles at home.

What is the situation from the British point of view? Domestically, the resource cost of 2 bushels of wheat is 1 yard of textiles, because by giving up 1 yard of textiles enough labor is released to produce 2 bushels of wheat. If the United Kingdom is able to obtain through trade more than 2 bushels of wheat per yard of textiles, it will trade, for the resource cost of obtaining wheat by trading away textiles is less than that of giving up textile production to produce wheat at home. But the United Kingdom would be unwilling to trade 1 yard for less than 2 bushels, for it can do better at home.[1]

In sum, the appropriate comparison for each country is between the resource cost of the commodity produced at home and the cost when it is acquired from abroad in exchange for the export good. The figures of Scheme 1 can be transformed into the limits to mutually beneficial trade, as given in Scheme 2.

Scheme 2   Limits to Mutually Beneficial Trade

---

1 yard of textiles $\begin{cases} = \text{maximum of 3 bushels of wheat for the United States} \\ \\ = \text{minimum of 2 bushels of wheat for the United Kingdom} \end{cases}$

The United States is willing to purchase 1 yard of textiles for anything less than 3 bushels of wheat, while the United Kingdom is willing to sell 1 yard of textiles for anything more than 2 bushels of wheat. Trade can take place anywhere between these limits. Stated differently, the domestic cost ratios of the two commodities in the two countries constitute the limits to mutually beneficial trade. Within these limits, it is to the advantage of each country to concentrate on the production of the good in which it has a comparative advantage and to obtain the other product through trade.

To see that trade is indeed beneficial to both nations, select any international price ratio within the specified limits, such as 1 yard of textiles = 2½ bushels of wheat. Trading at this ratio enables each country to consume more than is possible without trade. Let us say that the United States, employing its entire labor force, produces 600 bushels of wheat, of which it consumes 400 and exchanges 200 for textiles. The United Kingdom at full production manufactures 200 yards of textiles, of which it consumes 120 and exchanges 80 for wheat. With international trade, the 200 bushels of wheat are exchanged for 80 yards of textiles, permitting the United States to consume 400 bushels and 80 yards and the United Kingdom to consume 200 bushels and 120 yards. Without trade, the United States can transform (in terms of resource conversion) the 200 bushels into only 66⅔ yards of

---

[1] Put differently, the relative cost of producing the two commodities in the two countries can be summarized as follows:

1 unit of textiles cost 3 units of wheat in the U.S. and 2 units of wheat in the U.K. *Textiles are cheaper* (in terms of wheat) *in the U.K.*

1 unit of wheat cost one-third unit of textiles in the U.S. and one-half of textiles in the U.K. *Wheat is cheaper* (in terms of textiles) *in the U.S.*

Each country specializes in the product that it can produce cheaper, and obtains the other commodity through trade.

Table 11-1
Production and Consumption with and without Trade, Where the
International Exchange Ratio Is 1 Yard = 2½ Bushels

	United States	United Kingdom
Production at full capacity	600 bushels of wheat	200 yards of textiles
Consumption with trade	400 bushels of wheat 80 yards of textiles	200 bushels of wheat 120 yards of textiles
Consumption without trade	400 bushels of wheat 66⅔ yards of textiles	160 bushels of wheat 120 yards of textiles

textiles, making available a total of 400 bushels and 66⅔ yards. The United Kingdom, without trade, can transform the 80 yards of textiles into only 160 bushels of wheat, making available 120 yards and 160 bushels. All this is summarized in Table 11-1, showing clearly that both countries benefit from the exchange.

Demand Considerations

Referring back to Scheme 2, it will be observed that the internal cost ratios (namely, supply conditions) provide the limits to mutually beneficial trade. Within these limits, the actual exchange ratio is determined by the relative strength, or intensity, of each country's demand for the other country's product.

Since the demand for the imported good is expressed in terms of units of the country's own export product—the entire exchange being in barter terms—it is known as "reciprocal demand." In other words, production costs determine the limits, while reciprocal demand determines what the actual exchange ratio will be within these limits. Clearly, the further apart the two domestic cost ratios are, the more room there is for mutually advantageous trade, and the larger the benefits are that can be derived from trade by both countries, in the sense that the net increase in available goods over the no-trade position is larger. At the other extreme, when the two domestic cost ratios are identical, there are no advantages to trade. Each country is as well off in isolation (without trade) as with trade, so there is no inducement to engage in trade. In the real world, before trade can commence the difference between the two cost ratios must be large enough to compensate for transport costs and artificial barriers to trade.

Finally, in our simple example, the distribution of the benefits between the two countries depends on where the exchange ratio settles. If it ends up near the British cost ratio of 1 yard of textiles = 2 bushels of wheat, the United States derives most of the gain; if it is close to the American cost ratio of 1 yard of textiles = 3 bushels of wheat, the United Kingdom reaps most of the benefits. The reader may wish to verify this by working a couple of simple numerical examples.

The commodity exchange ratio is often referred to as the "commodity terms of trade," for it shows the price of one product in terms of the other. In a multi-product world, these prices must be expressed in terms of composite indexes, and *the terms of trade* of each country become *the export-price index divided by the import-price index.*

Now the link between the commodity terms of trade and the distribution of the benefits from trade among the trading countries occupies a central role in present-day policy debates involving the developing countries (the subject of a later chapter). However, the exchange ratio is a rather superficial barometer of the division of the gains from trade. If the ratio ends up near the British domestic ratio (say 1 yard = $2\frac{1}{10}$ bushels), this is a result of the high intensity of British desire for wheat compared to the relatively low level of American eagerness for textiles. It is true that this trade ratio is more beneficial to Americans in the sense that it increases their available textiles per unit of wheat given up by more than it increases the wheat available to the United Kingdom per unit of textile given up. *But* the Americans are much less eager for textiles than the British are for wheat. Consequently, in terms of satisfaction, or utility, reflected in the eagerness of demand, the Americans may not gain more than the British. Once the "commodity gain ratio" is translated into "utility ratio," the gain appears rather equally divided.

In reality, demand factors often occupy a more important role than the one ascribed to them here. In the example of Scheme 1, both goods are homogeneous commodities: there is only one universal type of wheat and only one kind of textile. But much of the trade that takes place in the world is in "differentiated products": Each commodity has various gradations of quality, size, flavor, and so on, and even differences in packaging and brand names are important. In such circumstances it is no longer true that identical cost ratios would result in no trade. For example, it is reasonable to assume that automobile production has approximately the same rank of comparative advantage in Italy, France, West Germany, and the United Kingdom. And consequently it would be difficult to explain the intercountry exchange of Fiats, Renaults, Volkswagens, and Austins on the grounds of cost differentials. A large part of the explanation must lie in consumer preferences for the foreign brand, even when the price equals that of its domestic counterpart. Since these cars are of roughly similar quality and size, the benefit from such trade is a psychic gain in the mind of the consumer, derived from having an option to purchase the foreign brand. The fact that there are such psychic benefits is self-evident; otherwise there would be no exchange of cars. But the size of the gain cannot always be measured.

This example can be generalized to most individual products. They are traded even when cost ratios are identical in the countries involved, because consumers may prefer the foreign brands for reasons that have nothing to do with production costs. Since much of world trade is in differentiated products, demand considerations play an important role in determining its composition. They are abstracted from in this exposition only for the sake of simplicity.

Having made this important qualification, we return to the analysis of a world in which all products are homogeneous.

Why Complete Specialization?

A feature of the Ricardian example that may have puzzled the reader is that trade leads each country to specialize completely in the production of the commodity in which it has a comparative advantage. *In isolation,* of course, every country must produce both goods if it wishes to consume both. Production and consumption are necessarily identical. International trade makes it possible for the production mix to be different from the consumption mix, with the differences being made up by trade. But must the United States get completely out of textile production and devote itself exclusively to wheat? Likewise, must the United Kingdom abandon wheat production altogether and specialize in textiles? Certainly this is not true in the real world, where even the most casual observation shows that countries produce some of the same types of goods as those they import.

The answer is that "complete specialization" is unique to this type of example and arises from the assumption that production costs per unit of output remain constant as output expands or contracts. When trade opens up, the United States expands its wheat production and contracts its textile production while the reverse happens in the United Kingdom. If the unit cost rises with output (known as "increasing cost" situations), then the American wheat price rises as production expands and the British wheat price declines as production contracts. Precisely the reverse happens to textile prices. Thus, increasing cost conditions constitute a mechanism that forces prices in the two countries to converge. And once prices of the last ("marginal") unit traded are the same in the two countries, there is no inducement for trade to expand further. Equality of prices is the condition for equilibrium between the two countries after international trade opens up. Prices can easily become equal before complete specialization is reached, resulting in equilibrium with trade, where production is incompletely specialized, as illustrated in Figure 11-1 (prices become equal at the margin: intramarginal units are not equalized in price).

But this mechanism is absent under constant cost. Then production costs remain unchanged as output expands and contracts, and there is no tendency toward price convergence, as is shown in Figure 11-2. Therefore, the process does not stop until complete specialization is reached—until the United Kingdom discontinues wheat production and the United States gets out of textile production. To sum up, production under increasing cost may or may not lead to incomplete specialization, but constant cost conditions necessarily result in complete specialization.[2]

---

[2] The only exception occurs if one of the countries is too small to supply its trading partner with all the partner's needs of the commodity.

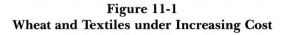

Figure 11-1
Wheat and Textiles under Increasing Cost

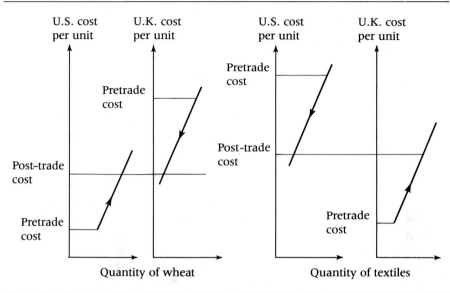

What accounts for the increase in unit production cost as output expands and its decline as output contracts as shown in Figure 11-1? It is what economists call the law of diminishing returns. Suppose it takes land and labor to produce wheat, land being available in fixed quantity while the amount of labor applied to it can be varied. As one increases the number of workers cultivating the fixed acreage of land by successive additions of one worker at a time, the *increment* of wheat output first rises, but then

Figure 11-2
Wheat and Textiles under Constant Cost Conditions

U.S. cost per unit U.K. cost per unit U.K. cost per unit U.S. cost per unit

Quantity of wheat   Quantity of textiles

declines. Stated in technical terms: Diminishing returns set in beyond a certain level of output. Concomitantly, the average amount of wheat per worker also begins to decline. This gradual reduction in the average productivity (output per worker) of the variable factor (labor) is a direct result of the fact that successively large quantities of it are employed with a fixed quantity of the fixed factor (land). Why, then, is that not reflected in our Ricardian example? Simply because only one factor of production (labor) is assumed to exist. It need not be combined with any fixed factor and therefore does not result in diminishing returns. Labor productivity, measured as output per worker, remains constant regardless of the level of output. And under constant cost conditions (portrayed in Figure 11-2), there is no mechanism that leads prices to converge as trade expands; hence the necessary outcome of complete specialization.

Comparative Opportunity Cost

Who Exports What

Having disposed of the puzzle embodied in our example, we are in position to return to the main line of argument. Suppose that labor is not the only factor of production but one of several. Then trade may or may not lead to complete specialization, although at some points in the analysis it helps to assume that it does. Equally important, the common denominator that made it possible to compare productivity between countries is no longer available, for when several productive factors enter into the production process, the productivity of each of them separately is of little consequence. Instead, it is necessary to measure their joint productivity.

For convenience we concentrate on the inverse of productivity, or unit production cost, by aggregating the resources that go into the production of one unit of output. But resources or factors are diverse. The only way to aggregate labor, land, and capital is by adding up their money value. Thus, instead of a Ricardian labor productivity scheme, we end up with a production cost scheme (Scheme 3), where costs in each country are measured in terms of its currency.[3] Although the same two commodities are retained, Scheme 3 differs from Schemes 1 and 2, for it deals with cost of production per unit of output (the inverse of labor productivity). We shall presently see that the principle of comparative advantage (or cost) remains inviolate.

[3] Note that the ratios of Scheme 3 need not be the inverse of those in Scheme 1 because Scheme 3 includes all production costs and is not restricted to labor costs. It would, however, be instructive for the interested reader to work through an example where the production cost ratios are exactly the inverse of the labor productivity ratios postulated in Scheme 1. Scheme 3 would then read

	Wheat	Textiles
United States	$1	$3
United Kingdom	£1	£2

Scheme 3	Production Costs per Unit of Output	
	Wheat per Bushel	Textiles per Yard
United States	$1	$3
United Kingdom	£1	£1

Since we do not know the exchange rate (for there is no exchange rate before trade opens up), there is no way of comparing costs in absolute terms between the two countries. But the intracountry (horizontal) comparison is still possible as before. In the United States, the resource or factor cost of 1 yard of textiles is 3 bushels of wheat. The dollar signs represent composite factor cost—it takes three times as big a resource basket to make 1 yard of textiles as to grow 1 bushel of wheat. It is in this sense that the two goods are interchangeable, but this is the only relevant sense for the economy as a whole.

To restate, the opportunity (or resource) cost of 1 yard of textiles in the United States is 3 bushels of wheat. In the United Kingdom, on the other hand, the resource cost of 1 yard of textiles is 1 bushel of wheat. Comparatively speaking, therefore, textiles are three times as expensive (in terms of wheat) in the United States, as in the United Kingdom. More precisely, the textile/wheat cost ratio in the United States is three times as great as in the United Kingdom. In the same sense, wheat is relatively cheaper in the United States than in the United Kingdom. This establishes the fact that the United States has a comparative advantage in wheat and the United Kingdom, in textiles; they will specialize and trade accordingly.

The Limits to Mutually Beneficial Exchange

Having ascertained the direction of trade should it open up, we next establish the limits to mutually beneficial exchange. Domestically, the United States can obtain 1 yard of textiles for 3 bushels of wheat, for by forgoing 3 bushels of wheat, enough resources are released to produce 1 yard of textiles. It will trade only if it can obtain 1 yard of textiles for less than 3 bushels of wheat. Domestically, the United Kingdom can obtain 1 bushel of wheat per yard of textiles. It would trade only if 1 yard of textiles yielded more than 1 bushel of wheat. As before, the domestic cost ratios set the limits within which the exchange ratio must fall (Scheme 4). If the cost ratios are identical in the two countries, no trade takes place (the limits simply

---

Scheme 4   Limits to Mutually Beneficial Trade

1 yard of textiles { = maximum of 3 bushels of wheat for the United States

= minimum of 1 bushel of wheat for the United Kingdom

Figure 11-3
Region of Mutually Beneficial Trade

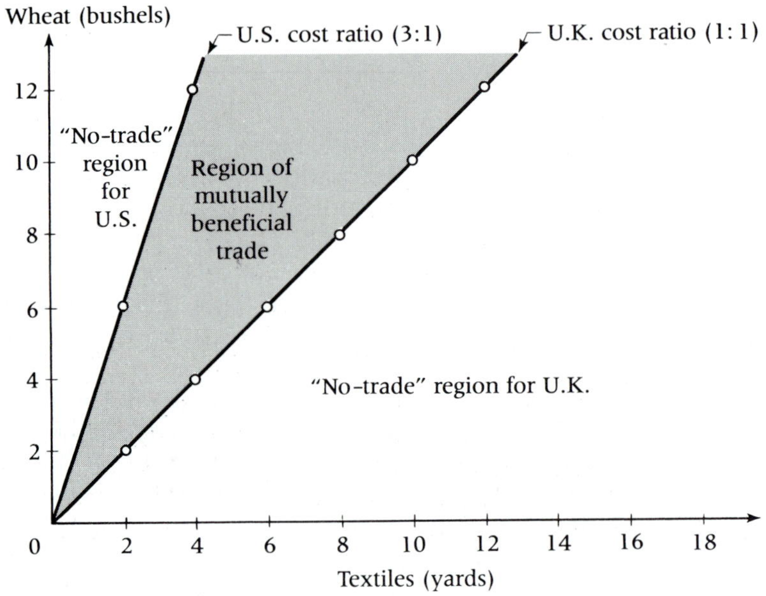

collapse into one point) unless motivated by demand factors as in the case of differentiated products.

Scheme 4 can be transformed into a simple diagrammatic form. In Figure 11-3, yards of textiles are plotted against bushels of wheat. The U.S. cost ratio of 3 bushels of wheat per yard of textile is represented by a straight line from the origin with a slope of 3. A similar line, but showing a 1 to 1 cost ratio, is drawn for the United Kingdom. All exchange ratios falling between the two lines constitute the region of mutually beneficial trade, where for each country the opportunity cost of acquiring the imported good in exchange for exports is less than that of producing it domestically. Outside this region, one or the other of the two countries will not want to trade, for it can do better at home. The "trade region" is bounded by the cost or supply ratios of the two countries. Thus, cost conditions determine the limits to mutually beneficial trade.

Where within these limits trade will take place depends on demand considerations. Because of the barter nature of this presentation, economists constructed a special tool to demonstrate demand in this context. Whereas the "normal" demand curve shows the price of the goods in question on the vertical axis and the quantity demanded on the horizontal axis, Figure 11-3 has total quantities of the two barter goods on the two axes. To cope with this situation, a special tool known as the "reciprocal demand curve" is developed for each country, which shows the respective quantities of the two goods demanded and supplied simultaneously. These curves reflect the intensity of demand on the part of each country for the other country's product. Their intersection determines the precise exchange ratio. If it falls close to the American cost ratio, the United Kingdom reaps most of the benefits from trade; if it falls close to the British cost ratio, the United States reaps most of the benefit. (As articulated on page 229, this commodity-gain ratio does not necessarily correspond to the utility gain ratio.)

☐ **Reciprocal Demand or Offer Curve**   A highly simplistic way to obtain a reciprocal demand curve from an ordinary demand curve is illustrated in Figure 11-4. Part (a) depicts a negatively sloping British demand for American wheat, where the price of wheat is expressed in terms of textiles. Part (b) shows the same demand curve but with respect to different axes. The vertical axis of (b) is identical with the horizontal axis of (a); they both show the quantity of American wheat demanded by Britain. However, the horizontal axis of (b) depicts the *total quantity* of textiles offered by Britain in exchange for the American wheat. It is to be distinguished from the vertical axis of (a), which shows a price ratio: units of textiles offered per unit of wheat. Therefore, the horizontal axis of (b), the quantity of textiles offered by Britain, is derived from (a) by multiplying the price of wheat in terms of textiles by the quantity of wheat; it is equivalent to the area under the ordinary demand curve. Thus, for 1 unit of wheat the British offer 1 × 6 = 6 units of textiles (point *a*); for 2 units of wheat they offer 2 × 5 = 10 units of textiles (point *b*); for 3 units of wheat, 3 × 4 = 12 units of textiles (point *c*); for 4 units of wheat, 4 × 3 = 12 units of textiles (point *d*); for 5 units of wheat, 5 × 2 = 10 units of textiles (point *e*); and for 6 units of wheat, 6 × 1 = 6 units of textiles (point *f*). The resulting curve in (b) is Britain's "reciprocal demand" or "offer" curve.

☐ Unlike the case of an ordinary demand curve, price in Figure 11-4 (b) is not shown explicitly on one of the axes. It can, however, be derived for any point along the reciprocal demand curve by connecting the point with the origin via a straight line, such as line α. The slope of this line shows the quantity of wheat exchanged per unit of textiles. An upward movement along the reciprocal demand curve (from *a* to *b* to *c* and so on) indicates a decline in the price of wheat: fewer units of textiles per unit of wheat or, conversely, more wheat obtainable for a given amount of textiles. This can be verified by comparing price rays α and β. Thus, the reciprocal demand curve shows at once the quantity of American wheat demanded and of textiles supplied by the United Kingdom at various relative prices.

☐ Demand elasticity varies along a straight-line demand curve, with the upper part being relatively elastic and the lower part being relatively inelastic. Translated into the reciprocal demand curve configuration, it is seen that the positively sloped part of the curve (lower segment) is relatively elastic; the negatively sloped part (upper segment) is relatively inelastic, while elasticity equals 1 at the bending point. As the price of wheat (in terms

Figure 11-4
Derivation of Reciprocal Demand Curve

Price of wheat in terms of textiles
(units of textiles per unit of wheat)

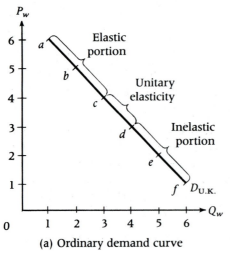

(a) Ordinary demand curve

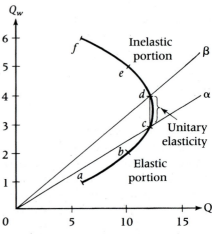

(b) Reciprocal demand curve for
the U.K.

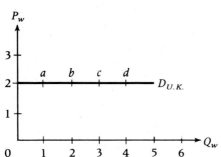

(c) Infinitely elastic demand curve

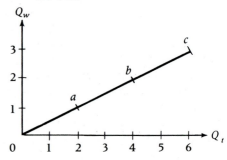

(d) Infinitely elastic reiprocal
demand curve

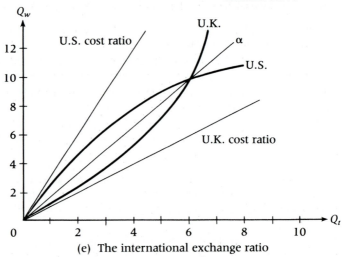

(e) The international exchange ratio

of textiles) declines, the quantity of textiles offered (equivalent to total revenue in the case of an ordinary demand curve) rises along the elastic portion, remains constant in the region of unitary elasticity, and declines along the inelastic segment of the curve.

☐ The extreme case of infinitely elastic demand is shown in (c) of Figure 11-4, where the axes are identical to those of (a). The equivalent reciprocal demand curve, shown in (d), is a straight line through the origin. By inference, the flatter the reciprocal demand curve, the more elastic it is. In what follows we restrict ourselves to the elastic portion of the curve.

☐ Each of the two trading countries has a reciprocal demand curve starting at the origin: The one for the U.K. "faces" the wheat axis, and the one for the U.S. "faces" the textiles axis. Both curves fall within the region of mutually beneficial trade, for no trade can take place outside that region. These curves are drawn in (e). Their intersection yields price ratio α, at which the international exchange of wheat for textiles takes place. ■

The Limits to a Sustainable Exchange Rate[4]

This analysis can be carried further. We know from our example that the United States produces and exports wheat and that the United Kingdom produces and exports textiles. Therefore, the limits to the exchange ratio of Scheme 4 can be translated from commodities into money by assigning to each commodity the price it commands in the country in which it is produced, in terms of the currency of that country. In other words, 1 yard of textiles costs £1, while 1 bushel of wheat costs $1. The limits of Scheme 4 are thereby converted into the respective currency values illustrated by Scheme 5.

Scheme 5   The Limits to the Dollar-Pound Exchange Rate

$$1 \text{ yard of textiles} = £1 = \begin{cases} \$3 \text{ (3 bushels of wheat)} \\ \\ \$1 \text{ (1 bushel of wheat)} \end{cases}$$

Given the production costs of Scheme 3, the values in Scheme 5 must be the limits to the pound-dollar exchange rate. Suppose we arbitrarily select the midpoint of £1 = $2 and apply it to the production cost example on which this is based (Scheme 3). By converting the pounds sterling cost to dollar cost at this exchange rate, we obtain Scheme 6.[5]

---

[4]Note: This section and the next require rudimentary knowledge of exchange-rate determination, offered in the first few pages of Chapter 3.

[5]The example of footnote 2 yields the following limits to the exchange rate:

$$£2 = \begin{cases} \$3 \\ \\ \$2 \end{cases} \quad \text{or} \quad £1 = \begin{cases} \$1.50 \\ \\ \$1 \end{cases}$$

Scheme 6
Production Costs of Scheme 3 in Terms of Dollars where £1 = $2

	Wheat per Bushel	Textiles per Yard
United States	$1	$3
United Kingdom	$2	$2

Clearly, the United States undersells the United Kingdom in wheat, and the United Kingdom undersells the United States in textiles. This is precisely the answer attributed to the businessman at the beginning of this chapter. But now it is clear that comparative advantage lies behind the statement that one buys where it is cheapest and sells where it is dearest after converting foreign prices to domestic currency at the going exchange rate. It is also clear that the limits to the exchange rate are determined by the cost ratios. Any exchange rate outside these limits is not sustainable, because then one country would undersell the other in both goods, thereby forcing an exchange-rate adjustment "into" these limits. To demonstrate this point, select a value of the pound higher than the upper limit, say £1 = $3.50. After conversion of Scheme 3 into one currency, the production costs become those given in Scheme 7.

Scheme 7
Production Costs of Scheme 3 in Terms of Dollars, at £1 = $3.50

	Wheat per Bushel	Textiles per Yard
United States	$1.00	$3.00
United Kingdom	$3.50	$3.50

Here the United States undersells the United Kingdom in both commodities. (However, the degree of underselling is larger in wheat than in textiles, so that the pattern of comparative advantage is preserved.) Not being competitive in any good, the United Kingdom must suffer a fundamental and persistent balance-of-payments deficit, because the pound is overvalued. The $3.50 exchange value of the pound is unsustainable, and the British currency would depreciate.

Conversely, if we select a value for the pound lower than the "floor," say £1 = $0.50, the production cost of Scheme 3 changes to that of Scheme 8. In this case, the United Kingdom undersells the United States in both goods (but the pattern of comparative advantage is preserved), with the United States in fundamental and persistent deficits. The dollar is overvalued in terms of the sterling, and it would depreciate.

Scheme 8
Production Costs of Scheme 3 in Terms of Dollars, at £1 = $0.50

	Wheat per Bushel	Textiles per Yard
United States	$1.00	$3.00
United Kingdom	$0.50	$0.50

Within the limits specified, the precise exchange rate is determined by considerations of reciprocal demand—demand by each country for the other's product—in such a way as to maintain balance-of-payments equilibrium.

Although this two-commodity case vastly oversimplifies what happens in the real world, it reinforces and illuminates what was said in Chapter 3. The exchange rate of a country cannot be arbitrarily determined; it must reflect the cost-price relationship between the country and its major trading partners.

More Than Two Commodities

In reality, each country produces many commodities, but the principle of comparative advantage holds nevertheless. All goods produced by each country must be *ranked internally* in the order of their domestic costs. Each country exports the commodity or commodities in which its advantage is most pronounced or, equivalently, that which ranks lowest on its cost scale. The cutoff point between what is exported and imported depends on reciprocal demand considerations in such a way as to yield a balance-of-payments equilibrium. An example will elucidate the arguments. Suppose the United States and the United Kingdom produce five commodities, A, B, C, D, and E with the production costs as given by Scheme 9 (ranked in order of magnitude within each country).

Scheme 9   Production Costs in Two Countries with Five Goods

	Commodity				
	A	B	C	D	E
United States	$2	$4	$6	$8	$10
United Kingdom	£1	£2	£3	£4	£5

No trade can take place under these cost conditions, for the relative cost ratios between all commodities are the same in the two countries (the case of differentiated products is assumed not to exist). An exchange rate of £1 = $2 would equalize costs of all commodities between the two countries (as the reader can easily verify by converting British costs to dollars at this exchange rate). Consider, however, the ranked production costs in the two countries as given in Scheme 10.

Scheme 10   Production Costs in Two Countries with Five Goods

	Commodity				
	A	B	C	D	E
United States	$1	$4	$9	$15	$20
United Kingdom	£1	£2	£3	£4	£5

Centering attention on the two extremes, A and E, it is immediately apparent that the American comparative advantage is in commodity A, the British in E. The domestic exchange ratios between them set the limits within which the exchange rate must fall (Scheme 11).

Scheme 11   Limits to the Sterling-Dollar Exchange Rate

$$1E = £5 \begin{cases} 20A = \$20 \text{ maximum for United States} \\ \\ 5A = \$5 \text{ minimum for United Kingdom} \end{cases}$$

$$\text{or } £5 = \begin{cases} \$20 \\ \$5 \end{cases} \quad \text{or } £1 = \begin{cases} \$4 \\ \$1 \end{cases}$$

If the exchange rate were outside these limits, one country would undersell the other in all five commodities, leading to a fundamental external imbalance, which in turn would necessitate exchange-rate adjustment. Where within these limits the actual exchange rate lies depends on reciprocal demand. In turn, the exchange rate determines the commodity composition of trade. Having ranked the commodities by degree of comparative advantage, we proceed from the two extremes toward the middle to determine where the equilibrium must settle. Assume, for example, that the exchange rate is £1 = $3. The British cost converted into dollars becomes:

	A	B	C	D	E
U.K. cost (£1 = $3)	$3	$6	$9	$12	$15

The United States exports commodities A and B, while the United Kingdom undersells the United States in D and E and therefore exports them. Commodity C is not traded at all, for its cost is the same in both countries. If this situation balances the accounts, all is well and good. If not, the exchange rate will have to be adjusted. Suppose that the United Kingdom runs a persistent external deficit because its demand for A and B is much more intense than the American demand for D and E. The pound would then depreciate to, say, £1 = $2.50. Under the new exchange rate, British costs become:

	A	B	C	D	E
U.K. cost (£1 = $2.50)	$2.50	$5.00	$7.50	$10.00	$12.50

Commodity C now enters trade, to be exported by the United Kingdom where it is cheaper. Such shifts occur whenever the external accounts are fundamentally out of balance, indicating disequilibrium in the exchange rate. The important thing in considering the position of any country is to rank all commodities by degree of comparative advantage, for it is along such ranking that the shifts occur. Once ranked in that order, the exchange rate determines which commodities are exported and which are imported.

This simple illustration should dispel the popular notion that one country can undersell another in every commodity traded. This is not possible. What is traded and in which direction is determined by the exchange rate. And since underselling in everything means that the balance of payments of the "undersold country" is in fundamental deficit, its currency would depreciate to the point at which it can sell enough goods to balance the accounts. As long as the exchange rate is in long-run equilibrium, the complaints voiced by import-competing industries to the effect that nothing produced at home can withstand foreign competition are baseless. Such competition can affect only the industries that should contract because they rank low in the order of comparative advantage.

More Than Two Countries

If instead of the previous example we have two commodities but many countries, then the countries must be ranked in terms of the cost ratios prevailing in them for the two goods. Suppose goods X and Y have the following cost ratios (cost of X divided by price of Y in respective currencies) in five countries A–E:

	A	B	C	D	E
X/Y cost ratio	1	2	3	4	5

Total world supply and demand determine the worldwide price ratio, somewhere between that in the two "extreme" countries A and E. If that ratio is 3, then country C will not trade, and countries A and B will export X to countries D and E in exchange for good Y. The reader may experiment by changing the world price ratio, thereby affecting the direction of trade; the outcome will still be determined by the established ranking of the X/Y price ratio.

In reality, of course, there are many commodities and many countries, and it is rather difficult to demonstrate the principles involved with simple numerical illustrations. But the principles hold nevertheless.

Before proceeding, a note of caution is in order. Thus far this chapter has been devoted to the gains from international trade. It has been shown that when relative production costs vary between countries there is room for mutually beneficial trade. Nothing has been said about the *causes* of the differences in relative costs, a topic to be taken up in the next chapter. Equally important, we have concentrated on the internal ranking of commodities for the purpose of determining comparative advantage *at a given point of time.* But it cannot be overemphasized that as the ranking of commodities within each country changes over time, so does comparative advantage, and countries must adapt to this continuous change. However, these changes are themselves caused by changes in the factors that determine the ranking of industries in the first place—such as the availability of factors of production and technological advancement—and their implications will be analyzed at the end of Chapter 12.

Examples from U.S. Trade[6]

In recent years, much public attention has been focused on the decline in U.S. exports and the increase in imports of autos and steel. Although the U.S. net trade position (exports minus imports) in all manufactured products improved during the 1970s, the country's position in the two industries under review deteriorated markedly. In part, this is widely attributed to wrong managerial decisions: delays in the introduction of new technology in the case of steel, and the "wrong" product mix in the case of automobiles. However, much of the deterioration can be analyzed in terms of production costs.

It is a common practice to compare U.S. production cost per unit of output (labor compensation divided by productivity) in each of the two industries to those prevailing in a foreign country such as Japan. For example, it has been demonstrated that Japan enjoys a 25 percent cost advantage (over the U.S.) in auto production. But this is not an altogether proper comparison. For example, if Japan had a similar cost advantage in all or most industries, then this simply means that the Japanese yen is undervalued. Another way of viewing the same problem is by understanding that a comparison of labor compensation between countries is inaccurate because it depends on the exchange rate: Japanese wage rates must be converted to dollars via the dollar—yen exchange rate. They would vary with the exchange fluctuations. In sum international comparisons of a single industry must be embedded in the total economy.

In particular, it is necessary to *rank* all industries *within each* country by order of their production cost: from the lowest to the highest cost industries. This is equivalent to ranking them by comparative advantage. A variant of this approach calls for comparing—within each country—the behavior of production cost in motor vehicles and in iron and steel *relative* to their

---

[6]This section is based on: M. E. Kreinin, "Wage Competitiveness in the U.S. Auto and Steel Industries," *Economic Inquiry,* January 1984; and "U.S. Trade in High-Technology Products," *Journal of Policy Modeling,* Winter 1985.

counterpart in the entire manufacturing sector. Such a comparison is made here for labor production costs, which is labor compensations (wages and salaries plus fringe benefits) divided by productivity.

However, labor productivity within each country is available in the form of an index; it shows performance relative to some base period. Consequently, labor cost must also be calculated in the same manner. Should the data reveal that a consistent rise in the labor cost in one of the industries (or both) was far in excess of the national manufacturing average, it can be inferred that the industry moved down in the ranking by comparative advantage.

Table 11-2 shows the 1980 indices of labor compensation, labor productivity, and unit labor cost in the steel industry; and for all manufacturing in five countries. The U.S., along with the U.K. and France, lost comparative advantage in steel as unit labor cost advanced much more than its counterpart in all manufacturing. No such loss occurred in Japan and Germany. The sharp rise of U.S. labor cost in this industry relative to all manufacturing is a result of a long-standing trend, where compensation advanced at a rate far ahead of its counterpart in all manufacturing whereas productivity rose at a much slower rate.

A similar tabulation for the automobile industry (see footnote 6 reference) shows that within the U.S., unit labor cost for motor vehicles edged considerably ahead of that for all manufacturing, primarily due to a faster rise in labor compensation, which more than offset the small differential in productivity. Within Japan unit labor cost in autos moved in tandem with that of all manufacturing.

Table 11-3 shows the unit labor cost (compensation divided by productivity) for each of the two industries *relative* to all manufacturing *within* the U.S., Japan, and Germany at a point in time (1980). U.S. production cost in the iron and steel and the motor vehicle industries exceeds that for

---

Table 11-2
Indices of Unit Labor Cost in Iron and Steel and
All Manufacturing for 1980 (1964 = 100) in Five Countries

Country	HOURLY COMPENSATION		OUTPUT PER HOUR		UNIT LABOR COST	
	Iron and Steel	All Mfg.	Iron and Steel	All Mfg.	Iron and Steel	All Mfg.
United States	382	316	119	141	321	224
Japan	725	807	352	394	206	205
Germany	448	461	227	217	197	212
United Kingdom	827	898	119	167	689	538
France	754	632	221	233	341	271

SOURCE: Complete source information is available in footnote 6 reference.

Table 11-3
Ratios of Unit Labor Cost Within Three Countries, 1980/81

Industry Ratio	U.S.	Japan	Germany
Iron and Steel/ All Manufactures	1.57	0.93	1.02
Motor Vehicles/ All Manufactures	1.42	1.07	1.18
High Technology/ All Manufactures	0.90	0.95	1.08

SOURCE: Complete source information is available in footnote 6 reference.

all manufacturing by 57 and 42 percent respectively. That excess is far smaller, or non-existent, in Japan and Germany. It is these ratios that indicate the loss of U.S. comparative advantage in iron and steel, and an incipient loss in motor vehicles. Note that the inter-country comparison of these *ratios* is not affected by exchange fluctuations.

In contrast to these two industries, the United States does have a comparative advantage in an array of high-technology industries, such as chemicals, computers, medical instruments, and certain specialized machinery. Unit labor cost in this sector is *below* its counterpart in all manufacturing, which cannot be said for our main trading partners. This is shown in the last row of Table 11-3.

It is the industry ranking *within* each country that determines what happened to comparative advantage.

Absolute Advantage and Wage Rates

We now return to the Ricardian example of labor productivity used in the first part of this chapter. While comparative advantage held the center of the discussion, it was also noted that absolute advantage in the Ricardian model cannot be disregarded, for it determines the relative wage level in the two countries. This will be demonstrated presently, with an admittedly over-simplified example. (The model says nothing about what makes American labor more productive in both industries.)

Given the labor-productivity figures of Scheme 1, assume that the wage rate in the United States is $30 per day. Free mobility of labor between industries ensures that wage rates within the country are the same in both industries, for if they were not, labor would move from the low-wage to the high-wage industry until wage rates were equalized. The question is: What must the British wage rate be?

Under the productivity conditions postulated in Scheme 1, the answer can be obtained by determining which wage rate, relative to the one assumed for the United States ($30 a day), would enable the United Kingdom to undersell America in textiles and be undersold in wheat. In other words, the relative wage rate must conform to the entire constellation of comparative advantage developed before, to make possible mutually beneficial trade.

Since an American worker produces 60 bushels of wheat per day, the cost of wheat is (30/60 =) $0.50 per bushel. Similarly, an American worker can produce 20 yards of textiles a day, and at a daily wage of $30 this yields a cost of $1.50 per yard. Because the United Kingdom undersells the United States in textiles, the British price must be $1.50 per yard or less, implying that a British laborer who produces 10 yards a day must earn less than $15 a day. At any higher wage rate the United Kingdom would not remain competitive in textiles. On the other hand, the United States undersells the United Kingdom in wheat, meaning that the British price must be above $0.50 per bushel. Since a British worker produces 20 bushels a day, his minimum wage rate must be $10, for any rate below that level yields a price lower than the American price. Thus if the established pattern of trade is to prevail, the British wage rate must be somewhere between $10 and $15 a day, or between one-half and one-third of the American wage rate. These limits are equal to, and are determined by, the productivity ratios in the two industries.

This result may be used to analyze the frequent complaint of protectionist forces in the United States that they cannot withstand foreign competition because foreign wages are lower than American. Time and again, in hearings before congressional committees, representatives of import-competing industries demand the imposition of a "scientific tariff": a tariff that would equalize wage rates here and abroad. Alternatively stated, their claim is that the tariff level should equal the difference between American wage rates and wage rates prevailing in competing countries. Now we see that this is an untenable position, for if the British wage rate were equal to ours, the United States would undersell the United Kingdom in all commodities. There could be no two-way trade under such conditions. The relative wage rate in two countries is determined by the differences in productive efficiency. And American wages are among the highest in the world because this economy is among the most productive. (We defer to the next chapter the question of *why* it is more productive.) It is true that in our example American textiles cannot compete. But that is because, in the example, the United States does not possess a comparative advantage in that commodity. The same applies to a 1982 complaint of U.S. mushroom growers, that they cannot compete with Chinese mushrooms because of low wage rates in China.

Summary of Policy Implications

To recapitulate, international trade raises the real income of the community by improving the efficiency of resource utilization (the last section of this chapter elaborates on this point). The ranking of industries in the order of their comparative advantage, combined with an equilibrium exchange rate, determines which commodities are to be exported and which are to be imported. The country's resources are most efficiently utilized if they are distributed and employed along this order. Consequently, policies that distort this ranking, such as tariffs and quotas imposed on specific commodities, result in inefficient resource allocation and loss of income to the community.

If the general wage and price level of a country gets out of line compared with other countries, its balance of payments gets out of equilibrium. The solution lies in appropriate fiscal and monetary policies or in exchange-rate adjustment. The situation does not call for tariffs, quotas, exchange control, or other interferences with free trade. These latter measures are usually applied on a selective basis, being most restrictive where politically powerful and vocal interests have to be satisfied. Usually these interests do not include the consumer. As such they distort the aforementioned ranking of industries and result in inefficiencies. The same point applies to various forms of exchange control. By contrast, aggregate domestic policies and exchange-rate adjustments affect all foreign transactions and tend to preserve the ordering of industries by comparative advantage.

As long as the balance of payments is in equilibrium, the demands of import-competing industries for protection—under one guise or another—are often unwarranted. What they are asking for is selective protection or, essentially, tariff protection for themselves. That would distort the industrial ranking and lead to inefficient resource utilization. The claim that they cannot compete may be correct from their own self-centered point of view. But satisfaction of their demand for protection would be injurious to the economy as a whole. The reason they are not competitive is that they rank low in the order of comparative advantage. Allocative efficiency requires that they contract in size and their resources be transferred to the growing industries. Government help in this transfer process—in the form of direct loans, retraining programs, and the like—would contribute to efficiency all around and help alleviate human suffering.

Far from contributing to inflation—as is sometimes alleged by the popular media—international trade is anti-inflationary. Suppose that bad weather conditions cause a poor harvest in the Soviet Union, making it necessary for that country to purchase huge quantities of grain from the United States. The price of grain (as well as of meat and other products derived from grain) will rise in the United States. This always happens to the price of an exported commodity. However, this does not mean that the conduct of trade is inflationary, because it overlooks what happens to the prices of imports. At a simplified level, assume that the United States barters its wheat for Russian crude oil. The United States can obtain the oil it needs either by producing it at home (say, at the Alaskan North slope) or by bartering it for wheat. Given the immensely efficient American agriculture, it is cheaper to obtain oil by bartering it for wheat.[7] The effect on the U.S.

[7]Conversely, the Soviet Union is said to be a low-cost producer of gas and oil and a high-cost producer of grain. By the law of comparative advantage it pays the Russians to import part of the grain they need for domestic consumption in exchange for gas and oil.

price level would be anti-inflationary. If, as is more likely, the Russians pay for the grain in convertible currencies, the dollar would appreciate on the foreign exchange markets. Indeed, this usually happens in years of poor harvests in the Soviet Union. And appreciation of the dollar cheapens foreign imports in the United States. Thus, when imports as well as exports are considered, the effect of foreign trade is to lower rather than to raise the average price level of all goods. Additionally, competitive pressure from foreign producers often constitutes a barrier to price increases by domestic producers. It spurs local producers to introduce the latest technological innovations and greater efficiency. In the case of the auto industry, it is often suggested that foreign competition induced the U.S. producers to introduce small cars in the late 1970s, thereby conforming to consumer preferences.

It is in the interest of a country to engage in balanced, mutually beneficial, and market-directed trade. It is contrary to its interest to pursue policies that distort its comparative advantage by providing protection to inefficient industries. There is no particular advantage in being able to undersell other countries in everything. Giving up commodities in exchange for gold, IOUs, or other paper assets, simply deprives the nation of the satisfactions derived from consumption, especially if international reserves are already adequate. Under such conditions there is little that is favorable about a huge trade surplus.

Dynamic Gains from International Trade

The forgoing analysis of the benefits from international trade followed the traditional line of emphasizing specialization and reallocation of *existing* resources. In fact, these gains can be outweighed by the impact of trade on the country's growth rate and therefore on the volume of *additional* resources made available to, or employed by, the trading country. These are termed "dynamic" benefits, in contrast to the "static" effects of reallocating an unchanged quantity of resources. The reason for the disproportionately little space devoted to these factors is that they are difficult to measure as well as to theorize upon. But their importance should not be underestimated. The short discourse that follows is intended to be indicative rather than exhaustive.

Consider first a fully employed economy. Its income and output are equal and may be considered two sides of the same coin. For what does it imply to state that the price of a desk is $100? First, this is its value as a unit of output. Next, the price reflects the fact that a total of $100 in income was generated and paid to productive factors used in the production of the desk in the following forms: wages and salaries for labor, rental income for the use of natural resources, interest paid on capital, and *profit* return for entrepreneurial ability. This example can be generalized to all goods and services produced in a given year. Their final value, the gross national product, equals the income generated in the production process. In turn, the economy's growth rate is determined by (among other things) the degree to which the population is willing to abstain from current consumption (their propensity to save), so that resources can be released from production of consumer goods and used for investment purposes.

For, if in a fully employed economy all income is spent on consumer goods—meaning that the saving rate is nil—then all resources must be occupied in the production of these goods and no investment is possible. On the other hand, should consumers abstain from consuming part of their income, or save, resources would be freed to produce investment goods, making possible economic growth and the attainment of larger streams of output in future years. It is this saving–investment process that generates growth and development.

It is an integral part of economic theory, demonstrated time and again in empirical studies, that the level of saving in the community, or abstinence from consumption, is positively related to the community's income. The higher the income is, the higher the saving is, too, because it is easier to save out of higher levels of earnings. Thus when the United States gives foreign aid to developing countries, it is in essence doing the saving for them. Since it is difficult to save out of very low incomes prevailing in the underdeveloped world, the process of foreign aid involves diversion of American savings, in the form of productive resources, for investment purposes in the recipient countries.

Since it is safe to assume that the marginal propensity to save (the proportion of added income that goes into added saving) is positive, any positive increment to the community's income necessarily results in added saving. In other words, not all the added income will be spent on consumption. Therefore when income is higher the rate of growth possible is higher.

But this is precisely what international trade was shown to do. Income rises because of more efficient utilization of fully employed resources. This raises savings and makes additional resources available for investment purposes. Furthermore, since the opening up of the economy to foreign trade changes relative prices, the tendency toward higher investments is accentuated if investment goods are imported or are made out of imported materials, for the price of imports goes down relative to that of exports and other goods as a result of trade.

An extreme example of this case is that of developing countries in which capital equipment cannot be produced at all, for technical or other reasons. In such a case, it is not just a matter of forcing resources toward more efficient uses when the country moves to specialize in "simple" products and import capital goods. The resources could not possibly have manufactured the latter goods because they are totally unsuitable for that purpose. In that case the country must worry not only about the saving rate and the release of resources from current consumption, but also about how to convert these resources into investment goods. Because such transformation is not possible at home, it can be accomplished only by exchange of exportables for imported capital equipment. International trade is the only vehicle by means of which the conversion can be carried out, thereby becoming a main instrument of growth. Indeed, when development is inhibited by insufficient imports of capital goods, underutilization of other factors may occur. Trade (and aid) can break this bottleneck.

This point underscores the fact that international trade does not comprise only flows of finished products intended for the final consumer. Rather, much of it consists of exchanges of factors of production in the form of plants and equipment and semiprocessed or raw materials. And since many developing countries do not possess the know-how and ability to produce them at home—even if they were willing to, however inefficiently, devote resources to their production—their importation amounts to much more than specialization in production. It enables the country to reach otherwise unattainable horizons in technology and efficiency. A technological gap of centuries may thus be bridged within a generation.

Thus international trade places the economy on a higher growth path, which tends to feed upon itself as continuously rising incomes make possible ever-rising levels of saving and investments. Because in this model the main obstacle to growth is nonavailability of resources, it may be referred to as "supply-propelled growth" made possible by the introduction of trade to an isolated economy or by removal of artificial barriers to trade.

An equally important stimulus to growth occurs when trade is introduced into a somewhat lagging economy not operating at full capacity. In some underdeveloped countries unemployment can assume a disguised form, as where the indigenous farm population is ostensibly at work but for a variety of reasons the output of each worker is only a fraction of his potential. Similar situations, requiring powerful stimuli on the demand side to "get the economy moving" on a rational path, may occur in any country at certain stages of its economic development. Such stimuli can be provided by international trade.

On the export side, the impact of overseas shipments is not confined to the export sector of the economy. Rather, as these industries expand, they require inputs from other sectors and thereby stimulate investments and technological advancement elsewhere. Thus the benefits of specialization are not limited to the expanding industries but tend to spread to the other areas. By the same token, as the standard of living of those engaged in export production rises, the goods and services they require increase in quantity as well as quality, and perhaps change in composition. In turn, this new demand stimulates growth in the industries producing final goods and services, as well as in those supplying the inputs. Such "export-led growth" is important in many countries.

On the import side, foreign trade makes it possible for a developing economy to obtain capital equipment and other materials necessary for investment. Without trade such goods may be obtainable not at all or only at prohibitive cost. Again, industrial expansion made possible by such imports tends to spread through the economy, generating growth in many sectors.

The broad implications of the foregoing statements become apparent if one looks at total international economic intercourse rather than just the exchange of commodities. Flows of capital in various forms, not the least of which is direct foreign investment, have come to occupy a prominent share of international transactions. Such transfers of capital embody not only plant and equipment, but technology and managerial skills. They make possible a fast diffusion of all the ingredients necessary for economic growth, highly beneficial to the host countries but with some feedback effects on the donor nation itself.

This is not all. There are important benefits to developed and developing countries alike that arise from the fact that foreign trade increases the size of the national market. Exports enable small and moderately sized countries to establish and operate many plants of efficient size, which would be impossible if production were confined to the domestic market. Not only can firms enjoy "internal economies of scale," but the economy as a whole benefits from the salutary impact of competitive pressure on prices, product improvement, and technological advancement. Innovation is often held back when competition is lacking. Furthermore, expansion of an industry ensures the availability of such things as a pool of skilled labor on which individual firms can draw (these benefits are known as economies external to the firm but internal to the industry). And overall industrial expansion usually brings with it the creation and development of the necessary infrastructure, such as transportation and power facilities, on which whole industries can draw (economies external to the industry). In turn, imports assure the existence of competitive pressure on domestic import-competing industries, even those that are internally monopolized. They also dampen inflation in the importing country.

This discussion indicates the immense potential of dynamic benefits that can flow from international trade. They may occur in varying degrees at any stage of a country's growth. That the effect of these benefits is not the same in all countries is due to many causes, not the least of which is the willingness of government to avail itself such "blessings" through free-trade policies.

More On the Static Gains from Trade

☐ Earlier in this chapter we showed that a differential price ratio between two countries gives rise to mutually beneficial trade. The static gains from trade were demonstrated in the case of constant opportunity cost, leading to complete specialization. This section shows the static gains in the context of increasing opportunity cost, where specialization may be incomplete. To do this we utilize more advanced tools: indifference maps and transformation curves. Students not familiar with these analytical tools can skip directly to the next chapter without loss of continuity.

The Consumer Indifference Map

☐ It will be recalled from the theory of consumer demand that the indifference curve represents various combinations of two goods, *X* and *Y,* among which the consumer is indifferent. In Figure 11-5, the consumer presented with a large number of alternative combinations finds himself indifferent to the choice among the following combinations of *X* and *Y.*

Point	Quantity of Y	X	MRS: $\Delta Y/\Delta X$
a	8	1	
			−4
b	4	2	
			−2
c	2	3	
			−1
d	1	4	

☐ These, as well as all the other combinations lying on the curve, yield equal amounts of satisfaction to the consumer. Each of the goods is subject to diminishing marginal utility, meaning that the more of it that there is in the consumer's possession the less intensely he wants additional units. Thus when he has 8 units of *Y* and only 1 of *X* (point *a*), he is willing to give up

Figure 11-5
Consumer Indifference Curve

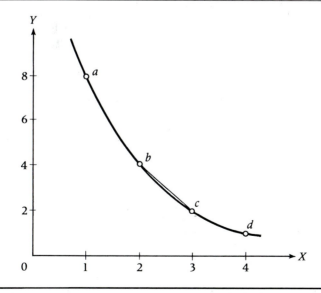

4 of *Y* to get an extra unit of *X*. But once the *Y* in his possession declines to 4 and the *X* rises to 2 (point *b*), he is only willing to part with 2*Y* to get an extra unit of *X*. And beyond that point, an extra unit of *X* is worth to him only one unit of *Y*.

☐ These substitutions that leave the consumer equally well off are summarized in the third column of the table. Using the Greek letter Δ to denote change or increment (negative for decrement), the ratio $\Delta Y / \Delta X$ stands for what economists call the marginal rate of substitution (MRS) of *X* for *Y*. The fact that it is declining is merely a reflection of the law of diminishing marginal utility of each good. And it is this feature that makes the indifference curve convex to the origin. The MRS between any two points along the curve is the slope of the line that connects the two points, such as $\overline{bc}$. And that slope (MRS) declines as we move down from *a* to *d*.

☐ Each consumer has a whole map of such indifference curves (Figure 11-6), with the higher ones (further away from the origin) indicating higher levels of satisfaction. Because utility cannot be measured, all we can say is that combinations represented by indifference curve III are more satisfactory[8] than those depicted by II, but we cannot say by how much. It is an essential feature of the map that the curves composing it do not intersect. For if curve I intersects curve II, then at the point of intersection the two curves yield equal satisfaction, which is clearly inconsistent with the fact that at all preintersection points, curve II represents a higher level of satisfaction than curve I. Ordinarily demand curves can be derived from the indifference map.

The Community Indifference Map

☐ Can indifference curves of many individuals be aggregated to form the locus of points yielding equal satisfaction to the community or country? In other words, can we scale the axes in millions of units and have indifference curve I show all the combinations of the two goods providing a given level of satisfaction to all citizens combined, and so on for curves II and III? Strictly speaking, the answer is No. For one thing, individual ranking of commodity combinations requires the use of majority rule unless the preferences of all are identical. And this need not result in a harmonious or transitive ranking, making it impossible to draw a community indifference curve.[9]

---

[8] It is only with the help of the indifference map of the consumer that we can say that the consumer prefers combination *a* (with more *X* but less *Y*) to combination *b*.

[9] To see what is meant by this possible (though not necessary) outcome, assume that three individuals X, Y, and Z are asked to rank commodity combinations A, B, and C in order of their preferences, and the ranking comes out as follows:

	X	Y	Z
1.	A	B	C
2.	B	C	A
3.	C	A	B

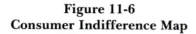

Figure 11-6
Consumer Indifference Map

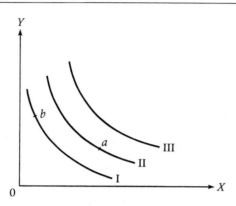

☐ Even if this were not the case, we must remember that the ranking of situations is done by majority rule, with no "protection" offered to the minority. Indeed, if majority rule prevails, no one knows how strongly members of the "losing" minority feel about the outcome. Translated into real-world situations, any change (free trade, technological advance, or what have you) that improves the position of society as a whole (and should therefore place it on a higher community indifference curve) is also likely to change income distribution, so that even if we increase the total amount of goods available to society, it does not necessarily follow that the amount bestowed upon each member of the community would rise. As long as we are unable to compare the intensity of feelings of the gaining majority with that of the losing minority, we must adhere to the rule that the community as a whole is better off (and should be placed on a higher indifference curve) if and only if some of its members are better off, and *none* is worse off, than before the change. This can occur only when the income distribution remains unaffected by the change in total income, or when the losers are compensated to a point at which they are as well off as before.

☐ In sum, the community indifference curve is not a neat concept. It requires some heroic assumptions, such as permitting one dictator to make decisions (and rank combinations) for the entire community. Alternatively we must assume transitivity in ranking, coupled with unchanged income distribution or compensation of losers. Only then can we generalize from an individual to a country and employ the concept of community indifference curves.

Two of three persons (X and Z) prefer A to B, two of three persons (X and Y) prefer B to C, and two of three persons (Y and Z) prefer C to A. This violates the logical rule that if A is preferred to B and B is preferred to C then A ought to be preferred to C. It is known as lack of transitivity in preference ordering.

For pragmatic reasons economists do make these assumptions and use the concept, as we shall do here. Thus, the country will be thought of as having a map of nonintersecting community indifference curves, with the higher ones indicating higher levels of satisfaction.

Transformation Curves

☐ Each country also has a given amount of resources that can be employed to produce two goods X and Y. In Figure 11-7, if all resources are devoted to the production of Y, then 6 million units can be produced. Alternatively, if all resources are employed in producing X, 4 million units of X can be manufactured. In between these two extremes lie all the possible combinations of the two goods that these resources can produce. The locus of these combinations is known as the *transformation function* or curve, because movement along this curve indicates the transformation of one commodity into the other in the sense that resources are transferred from one industry to the other.

☐ If the resources are identically suited for the production of the two goods, they can be shifted back and forth from one industry to another without any loss of efficiency. Certainly this would be the case if there was only one homogeneous factor (such as labor) or if two or more factors were used in a fixed and identical proportion in the production of both goods and were equally suited for the two industries. This is the constant-opportunity-cost case and it is depicted by a straight-line transformation function.

Figure 11-7
Constant Opportunity Cost (in Millions of Units)

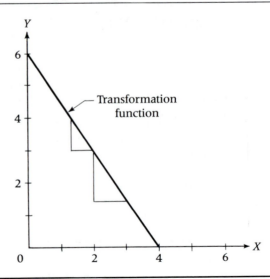

The cost of extra units of *X* in terms of *Y* given up (when the resources are transferred from *Y* to *X*) does not vary along the function and is equal to the constant slope of the curve. This is the Ricardian case, which leads to complete specialization once trade opens up: The country would produce either 6 million *Y* or 4 million *X*, depending on its comparative advantage relative to its trading partner. (See question 7 on page 264.)

☐ More commonly the country's resources are not equally suited for the production of both goods; some are more efficient in *Y* production, others in *X*. In that case the two extreme points of producing only one commodity will exist as before, each point (on one of the two axes) showing how much of a good can be produced if all resources are devoted to its production. But the "transformation" of one good into the other (in the sense of resource transfer) will be different.

☐ Starting, say, from 6 million units of *Y*, the transformation of *Y* for *X* will not be at a fixed ratio yielding a straight line. Instead we encounter a line concave to the origin, depicting increasing opportunity cost (Figure 11-8). At point *a* all the country's resources, presumably including some resources better suited for the production of *X*, are employed in production of *Y*. As we move from *a* to *b* to obtain the first million units of *X*, the resources first transferred from *Y* to *X* are better equipped to manufacture *X* to begin with. Thus, the cost of 1 million *X* is only 0.5 million units of *Y*;

Figure 11-8
Increasing Opportunity Cost (in Millions of Units)

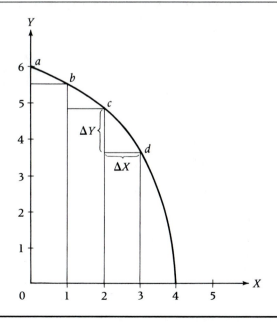

the ratio of 1 to 2 is depicted by the slope of the straight line connecting *a* to *b*. Moving from *b* to *c* we begin to transfer from industry *Y* to *X* some resources that are better suited to produce *Y*. Thus, it costs nearly 0.75 million of *Y* to obtain the second million *X*. By the same token, a move from *c* to *d* shows that the third million units of *X* is obtainable at an opportunity cost of over 1 million units of *Y*. Finally, to obtain the fourth million units of *X* implies transferring all resources to industry *X*, including those that are ideally suited for *Y*. Thus, the cost rises to 3.5 million units of *Y*.

☐ What the concave opportunity-cost curve depicts is a rising ratio of $\Delta Y/\Delta X$. This ratio is known as the marginal rate of transformation (MRT). At any point on the curve, it is equal to the slope of the curve. This is the case of increasing opportunity cost with which we are presently concerned.

Equilibrium in Isolation (Without Trade)

☐ The transformation function shows all the combinations of the two commodities that the country can produce given its resources. Points inside the curve represent unused resources (for example, unemployment), while points outside the curve represent commodity combinations that cannot be reached. Thus, the country will strive to produce somewhere along the curve. But where? That is determined by the pattern of demand, or the community preference scheme for the two goods, as reflected in the community indifference map.

☐ Given its resources, the country attempts to maximize satisfaction—namely, consume on the highest possible community indifference curve. And that indifference curve is one tangent to the transformation function. In Figure 11-9, *P* is the equilibrium point of consumption and production, with $\overline{0Y_1}$ and $\overline{0X_1}$ produced and consumed. Without international trade, domestic production and consumption are equal. The slope of *ML* (the common tangent to the indifference curve and the transformation function) is the commodity price ratio prevailing on the domestic market: $\overline{0M}$ of *Y* is exchangeable for $\overline{0L}$ of *X* (note that in the constant-cost case depicted in Figure 11-7, the domestic price ratio equals the slope of the transformation function and is independent of demand conditions).

International Trade: Similar Tastes

☐ In order to introduce international trade, we must consider two countries. We first assume that the tastes of the two populations, as reflected in the shape of their indifference maps, are identical. On the other hand, their transformation curves are different: Country A is better suited to produce commodity *Y*, and country B is better suited to produce commodity *X*. The heavy curves in Figure 11-10 depict the two countries in isolation. Given its resource endowment, as represented by its transformation curve, each country gets onto the highest possible indifference curve. Equilibrium production and consumption are obtained from the tangency solution at points *E* and

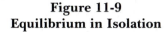

Figure 11-9
Equilibrium in Isolation

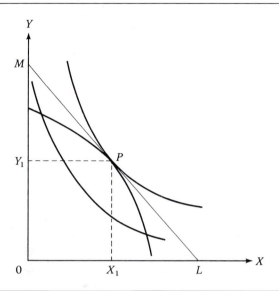

F for countries A and B, respectively. Given equal demand patterns, the supply conditions determine relative market prices.

☐ Relative prices of *Y* and *X* are different in the two countries, as indicated by the different slopes of price lines *MN* for A and *PR* for B. This establishes the fact that there is room for mutually beneficial trade. In particular, commodity *Y* is relatively cheaper in country A, with $\overline{0M}$ of *Y* exchangeable for $\overline{0N}$ of *X*, while commodity *X* is relatively cheaper in country B, where $\overline{0P}$ of *Y* are exchangeable for $\overline{0R}$ of *X*.[10] These relative price ratios establish the fact that country A has a comparative advantage in *Y*, country B in *X*. They would move to specialize accordingly.

☐ Each country would move along its transformation curve toward more specialization in production: country A from point *E* upward, country B from *F* downward. The slopes of the tangents to the two curves (the respective price lines) change as they move; indeed, the two slopes converge. Post-trade equilibrium is reached when the two price lines become parallel, meaning that the price ratios in the two countries are equal. In other words, after trade opens up, it will proceed to the point at which commodity prices are equalized. The two price lines that are tangents to indifference curves II at C_A and C_B meet this requirement. But so do an infinite number of other "pairable" points along the two transformation functions.

[10]Ratios of quantities exchanged are employed to indicate relative prices.

Figure 11-10
Equilibrium with Trade: Different Transformation Curves

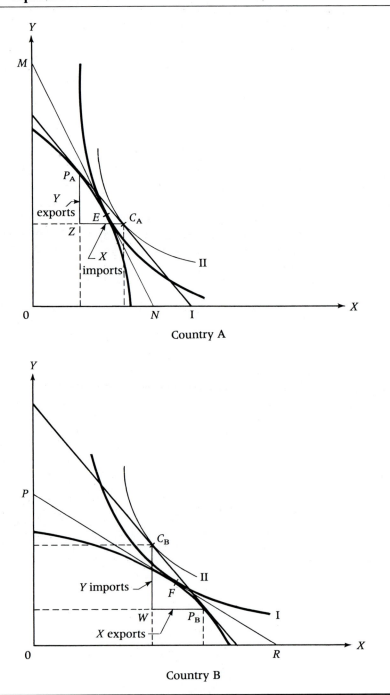

Country A

Country B

☐ To pinpoint the exact equilibrium solution, another condition must be satisfied. In the two-country world depicted here, what one country exports the other must import. The quantity traded by each country is the difference between what is produced and what is consumed domestically. As the production point travels along the transformation curve toward its equilibrium point, the price line tangent to it becomes flatter in country A and steeper in country B. Given the (pre-existing) community indifference map of each country, the price lines become tangent to higher and higher indifference curves as this process proceeds. And it is this tangency position that determines the consumption points.

☐ Suppose that consumption point C_A and C_B in the two countries are such that both equilibrium conditions are met. Thus country A produces at P_A and consumes at C_A, while country B produces at P_B and consumes at C_B, each pair of points is measured with respect to the axes of the country concerned. The difference between production and consumption is made up by trade. Country A produces more Y than it consumes, and the excess $\overline{P_A Z}$ is exported. It consumes more X than it produces, and the difference $\overline{Z C_A}$ is imported. By similar reasoning, country B imports $\overline{C_B W}$ (= $\overline{P_A Z}$) of Y and exports $\overline{W P_B}$ (= $\overline{C_A Z}$) of X. The "trade triangles" of the two countries are thus identical.

☐ It will be observed that both countries land on a higher indifference curve (II) than they were able to attain in isolation (I), thereby demonstrating that both gain from trade.[11] In this case, trade enabled each country to specialize in production according to the "suitability" of its resources and to remain "unspecialized" in consumption. This divergence between production and consumption mixes is not possible without trade. How much the gain is to each country cannot be determined, because there is no way to measure satisfaction. The indifference curves merely tell us the ranking of utility levels in ascending order, as we proceed upward away from the

[11]The benefit from trade for a country (moving from indifference curve 1 to 3 in the chart below) can be decomposed into two parts. This is illustrated here in reference to Country A: The *consumption* gain, obtained when the price to consumers changes from the domestic to the international price ratio while production remains unchanged at E, is shown by a shift from 1 to 2; and the *production* gain, as the country moves to specialize in the production of Y, and output shifts from E to P, is shown by a move from 2 to 3. Because the shift from E to P takes time, the initial benefit is a movement from indifference curve 1 to indifference curve 2. See W. Mayer, "Short-Run and Long-Run Equilibrium for a Small Open Economy," *Journal of Political Economy*, September/October 1974.

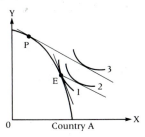

Country A

origin. Readers who are uneasy about using community indifference curves may simply note that trade enables each country to consume outside the region of possible production.

☐ While each country moves to produce more of the commodity in which it has a comparative advantage, specialization in this case is not complete. Commodity prices were equalized before either country got completely out of the production of "the other" product. Thus, the post-trade equilibrium situation finds each country producing some of both products. This is a possible, but not necessary, result of increasing opportunity cost.[12]

Factor Endowments

☐ What accounts for the difference between the transformation curves of the two countries? The answers can be many and varied. It could be that country A has developed a more efficient technique for producing Y, and B employs more efficient means for manufacturing X. Or the two countries may have become equipped by tradition or the skill of their labor forces in the production of their respective products. These as well as other explanations are possible.

☐ But the model that reigned supreme in international trade theory for a long period after World War II discarded these hypotheses and adopted another explanation of the divergent shape of the transformation curves. (This, as well as other models, will be explored in detail in the next chapter.) Each commodity is assumed to be produced in the same manner in both countries; economists say that the production function of each commodity is the same in the two countries. By that they mean that, for each possible pair of factor prices, the two countries would use the two factors in the same proportion in the productive process.[13]

☐ On the other hand, the production functions differ between the two commodities, and they differ in a unique and unequivocal way: At all factor prices one commodity (Y) utilizes more of one factor (say, capital) relative to the other commodity (X), which means that the second good (X) utilizes more of the second factor (labor) relative to the first good (Y). It is in that sense that commodity Y is classified as capital intensive and commodity X as labor intensive, and that relation holds in each of the two countries.

☐ Countries differ from each other in their relative factor endowments— hence the model is known as the "factor proportions theory." Country A is

---

[12] To see that it is not a necessary result, the reader might note that not all points along each transformation are "pairable" with points on the other function in the sense that they have identical slopes.

[13] Another way of stating this is to say that the isoquants of each commodity are identical in the two countries. "Isoquant" describes the various combinations of two productive factors that can produce a given quantity of output. Shaped like an indifference curve, it has quantities of factors on the two axes, the isoquant itself is labeled for the volume of output it represents.

relatively capital-abundant, in the sense that its capital/labor endowment ratio is higher than B's. And that makes country B labor-abundant relative to A. It is now a short step to concluding that country A would have a comparative advantage in producing *Y*, the commodity requiring relatively more capital in the production process. Conversely, country B would have a comparative advantage in producing *X*, the commodity requiring relatively more labor, which that country possesses in relative abundance. (Other assumptions attached to the factor-endowment model will be described in the next chapter.) This model constitutes a very specific explanation of the pattern of trade.

☐ International trade is brought about by the unequal price ratio existing between the two commodities in the two countries when they produce and consume in isolation. In other words, whenever the price lines are not parallel in the pretrade equilibrium position, there is room for mutually beneficial trade. The relative slope of the lines represents relative prices and therefore indicates which country has a comparative advantage in each product. The factor-endowment model is an attempt to explain what gives rise to comparative advantage, and it traces the reason to one specific cause: differences in factor endowments between countries coupled with differences in production functions between commodities.

☐ Clearly, this is one of many possible explanations for the divergent pretrade commodity price ratios. In the first place there are other reasons that may give rise to divergent transformation curves, which the factor-endowment model dismisses. Second, the model's assumption that demand patterns are identical in the two countries need not hold. Thus, differently shaped maps of community indifference curves can result in unequal price ratios even with identical transformation curves.

Differences in Demand

☐ Differences in demand are illustrated in Figure 11-11. The heavy lines represent the pretrade positions; they depict identical transformation functions but different indifference curves. The resulting price lines $\overline{MN}$ and $\overline{PR}$ show that commodity *Y* is relatively cheaper in country A (where consumers prefer *X*), and commodity *X* is relatively cheaper in country B (where consumers prefer *Y*). This establishes the pattern of comparative advantage and the lines of specialization once trade opens up. As before, the posttrade equilibrium position must satisfy the conditions of equal prices in the two countries (parallel price lines) and equal quantities of each commodity imported and exported. The heavier price lines meet these conditions.[14] Given the indifference maps, the two countries will consume at C_A and C_B and produce P_A and P_B. In this case, they move toward less specialization in production and greater specialization in consumption. In other words,

---

[14] The international price line may be thought of as an alternative transformation curve available to the country, along which it might exchange one product for the other.

Figure 11-11
Equilibrium with Trade: Different Indifference Curves

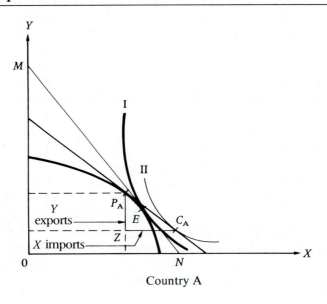

Country A

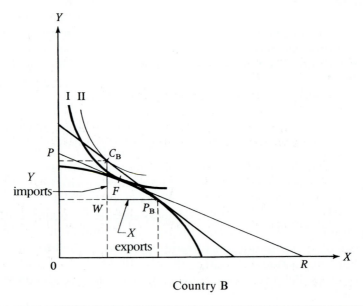

Country B

trade makes it possible to satisfy divergent wants from identical production conditions. Consequently, both countries experience a rise in welfare, as indicated by the fact that they find themselves on higher indifference curves. Country A exports $\overline{P_A Z}$ of Y and imports $\overline{C_A Z}$ of X, while country B exports $\overline{P_B W}$ ($= \overline{C_A Z}$) of X and imports $\overline{C_B W}$ ($= \overline{P_A Z}$) of Y.

The General Case

☐ In the general case, both the transformation curves and the indifference maps may differ. If the resulting pretrade price lines are not parallel, there is room for mutually beneficial trade. The relative prices established before trade determine the pattern of comparative advantage and the direction of trade. Only when the two pretrade price lines are parallel is there no room for trade. This can come about if both the transformation curves and the indifference maps of the two countries are identical. Alternatively, it can happen when the two sets of curves differ in such a way as to precisely offset each other—in other words, if each country prefers to consume the commodity that it can produce best and if that preference exactly compensates for the degree of production advantage so as to produce identical prices. ∎

Review Questions

1. a. In what sense are the cost data of Footnote 3 related to the figures of Scheme 1?
   b. Based on the figures of Footnote 3, determine the:

   • Direction of trade once it develops
   • Limits to mutually beneficial trade
   • Limits to a sustainable exchange rate.

2. Evaluate the following statements:
   a. In international trade, domestic cost ratios determine the limits of mutually beneficial trade, whereas demand considerations show where, within these limits, the actual exchange ratio will lie. In your answer graphically combine the use of domestic cost ratios with reciprocal demand curves.
   b. Comparative advantage is a theoretical concept. It cannot be used to explain any real-world phenomena.
   c. The opening up of trade raises the price of export goods; hence trade is inflationary.
   d. The concepts of regular demand curves and reciprocal demand curves are totally unrelated.

3. Using the figures of Scheme 1, determine the limits to the U.K.—U.S. wage ratio.

4. What can you say about the following relationships:
   a. Absolute advantage and the standard of living
   b. Absolute advantage and the direction of international trade
   c. Comparative advantage and the direction of trade
   d. Comparative advantage and the standard of living

5. Demonstrate the benefits of trade to two trading countries.

6. a. Use the theory of comparative advantage to explain why it pays the:

   • U.S. to export grains and import oil
   • Soviet Union to export oil and import grains

   b. Why does the popular press believe that grain exports are inflationary to the U.S.? What is wrong with this proposition?

7. a. Why must the Ricardian (constant cost) model lead to *complete specialization?*
   b. Demonstrate (with the use of transformation and indifference curves) that trade is beneficial to both trading countries in the case of constant cost.

   Hint: Use (and explain) the following charts and the information contained in them.

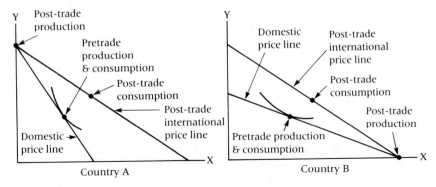

Note that constant cost is represented by straight line pretrade transformation curves. In this case the domestic price ratio is independent of the position of the indifference curves.

8. Suppose that between 1960 and 1980 U.S. steel industry wage rates tripled while general manufacturing wage rates doubled, and that productivity in the steel industry advanced equally with that in all manufacturing. Also suppose that, in Japan during the same period, both wage rates and productivity in the steel industry rose in tandem with that of all manufacturing.

   What happened to U.S. comparative advantage in steel over this period? Explain fully!

9. What can you say about the U.S. comparative advantage in:
   a. motor vehicles and steel
   b. high-technology products

12 / The Commodity Composition of Trade

As long as economists were interested merely in demonstrating the gain from international trade, the analysis presented in the previous chapter was adequate. In a nutshell, it demonstrates the self-evident proposition that whenever the domestic price (or cost) ratio is different in two countries, there is room for mutually beneficial trade, and the greater the difference is in the price ratios, the greater the static gain will be.

But during the present century the attention of international trade theorists turned from the gain from trade to the determinants of the commodity composition of trade. In other words, they attempted to unravel the factors that determine which country exports what commodity. To be sure, this question was not ignored in the last chapter. It was treated as a by-product of the focal issue, the gains from international trade. As such, the answer was given on two levels. In the context of the "opportunity cost" discussion, it was stated that each country exports the commodity that is relatively cheaper in that country, without exploring the reason for this relative cheapness. The Ricardian model with one factor of production (labor) probes a little deeper and hypothesizes that each country exports the commodity that it can produce at lower average labor cost (or higher average labor productivity). In other words, differential labor productivity is said to be the cause of the price differences.

This answer requires no further amplification as long as our concern is with the gains from trade. The very existence of trade under divergent price (or cost) conditions attests to its profitability. But if we wish to focus on the commodity composition of trade, the propositions articulated above may be inaccurate, because in this context they cease to be self-evident and are subject to empirical verification. And even if they are accurate, they are inadequate, because they beg further questions.

With respect to accuracy, the answer centering on labor productivity is more specific and therefore more meaningful than the one postulating differential opportunity cost ratios, even though it is based on a simple assumption. It attributes the price differential to only one factor: differences in average labor productivity. As applied to the real world, this is a testable hypothesis that can be confirmed or rejected by empirical observations. Labor is not the only cost involved in producing a commodity. Although it is the most important single element, its effect can be swamped by other cost components. Moreover, the flow of manufactured products is not determined by cost and supply considerations alone. Manufactures are characterized by what economists call "product differentiation" or lack of homogeneity. What is essentially the same product appears on the market in a great variety of forms that differ from one another in quality, dimensions, packaging, brand name, and so on. The buyer is swayed by many factors other than price. And because industrial goods make up most of world trade, it cannot be concluded *a priori* that costs of production determine the direction of trade flows. The demand side of the equation cannot be ignored.

The Ricardian model, attributing comparative advantage to labor productivity, was tested empirically with reference to U.K. and U.S. exports to third markets (that is, countries other than the United States and the United Kingdom) in both a prewar year and a postwar year. Using a cross section of industries, it was found that American exports to third markets exceeded British exports in industries where U.S. labor productivity (output per worker) was at least two and a half times U.K. labor productivity. Because American wage rates were roughly double the British, this is a successful test of the labor productivity hypothesis.[1]

Even if labor productivity were the determining factor of who exports what, it still begs the question of *what determines labor productivity?* In other words, the theorist wishes to go "behind" productivity to find the answer. A widely studied and rather specific explanation of the commodity composition of trade is the *factor proportions* (or *endowment*) *theory*. First introduced by the Swedish economists E. F. Heckscher and B. Ohlin, the theory was refined after World War II by Paul Samuelson and made into a very elegant, though extremely restrictive, construct. Although its postulates are rather complex, it can be stripped to its bare essentials by ignoring many of the details and drastically simplifying the economics involved. Stated briefly, this theory is a marriage between the resource endowment of the country, on the one hand, and the economic characteristics of the commodities traded, on the other.

The Factor Proportions Theory

Consider a world of two countries, the United States and the United Kingdom, producing two commodities, textiles and machinery, with two factors

---

[1]See G. D. MacDougall, "British and American Exports," *Economic Journal*, Dec. 1951; and R. M. Stern, "British and American Productivity and Comparative Costs," *Oxford Economic Papers*, October 1962.

of production, labor and capital.[2] All production is carried on by purely competitive firms; there are many firms in each industry, none large enough to influence by its own actions the conditions prevailing in the market. Prices of the two products and of the two factors are determined by supply and demand; each firm accepts these prices and adjusts its activities to them. In other words, firms are price takers on both the commodity and factor markets. Also, free internal mobility of labor and capital between industries ensures that the price of each factor is the same in the two industries within each country. On the other hand, factors are not free to move between countries, so that pretrade compensations of each factor can differ internationally.

Each producer of a commodity has a range of production methods available to him, from which he selects one. The basic economic feature that distinguishes various production techniques is the labor/capital ratio. The producer presumably adjusts the factor use ratio to the ratio of factor prices that he confronts in the marketplace. The more expensive labor is relative to capital, the less labor and the more capital he would use. Each commodity is assumed to be produced under identical production conditions in the two countries,[3] in the sense that *if faced with the same factor prices, producers in both countries would use the two factors in the same ratio.* In other words, the processes available in the two countries for the production of a given commodity are the same and, if factor prices were the same, the two countries would select the identical process—or factor use ratio—to produce the product. Economists summarize this by saying that each commodity has identical production functions, or isoquants, in the two countries.

On the other hand, the production processes required differ from one commodity to the other within each country in a definite, unique, and consistent manner: For any given pair of factor prices, the production of machinery utilizes a higher capital/labor ratio than the production of textiles.[4] This is expressed technically by saying that machinery is *capital inten-*

---

[2] This is sometimes referred to as a "2 by 2 by 2" model. See R. Jones, "Two-ness in Trade Theory," Princeton, *Special Papers in International Trade*, No. 12, 1976. Most conclusions generalize to higher dimensional models, such as $3 \times 3 \times 3$. Economists have also studied models with 3 factors and 2 commodities. See for example: R. Jones and S. Eaton, "Factor Intensities and Factor Substitution in General Equilibrium," *Journal of International Economics*, 1983; and H. Thompson, "Complimentarity in a Simple General Equilibrium Production Model," *Canadian Journal of Economics*, August 1985.

[3] An additional assumption is that if a producer increases the use of both factors by a given proportion, his output will rise by that same proportion. This is known in economics as "constant returns to scale." It is to be sharply distinguished from the law of diminishing returns in that it allows both factors to vary, while the concept of diminishing returns operates when one factor is variable and the other remains fixed. Consequently, it is possible for a firm to function under constant returns to scale and at the same time be subject to diminishing returns in a sense that the two possibilities coexist.

[4] Remember that, within each country, factor prices are the same in both industries. This is guaranteed by the free and unobstructed mobility of factors within each country as assumed in the model. Thus, if the price of labor (wage rates) were higher in the machinery than in the textile industry, labor would move from the latter to the former until wage rates were equal in both.

sive relative to textiles or, equivalently, that textiles are *labor intensive* relative to machinery. The extension of this relationship to a world of more than two commodities involves the *ranking* of all goods by their capital/labor ratio. A fundamental assumption of the model is that this ranking (not necessarily the ratios themselves) is the same in the two trading nations. In other words, machinery is the relatively capital-intensive commodity, textiles the relatively labor-intensive product, in both the United States *and* the United Kingdom.[5]

How are countries distinguished from one another? They differ in their *resource endowment:* the United States possesses a higher capital/labor ratio than the United Kingdom. We say it is the relatively *capital-abundant* country, while the United Kingdom is the relatively *labor-abundant* country.[6] Note that it is the endowment *ratio,* rather than the absolute amount of each factor available, that is important. If we assume (as this model does) that demand conditions are similar in the two nations, then relative factor prices are determined by their supply as reflected in the resource endowment. Thus, capital becomes relatively cheaper in the United States and labor relatively cheaper in the United Kingdom. More precisely, the capital/labor *price* ratio is lower in the United States than in the United Kingdom. Combine this result with the earlier postulates concerning manufacture in the two countries and the following conclusions emerge: The United States specializes in the production of machinery, the commodity that uses much of its relatively cheap factor (capital)—it exports machinery and imports textiles; the United Kingdom specializes in textiles, the commodity that uses much of the relatively cheap factor (labor) there—it exports textiles and imports machinery.

This result can be translated into the example of the previous chapter. It was shown there that the United States had a comparative advantage in wheat, the United Kingdom in textiles, with comparative labor cost or productivity determining this outcome. Now we can add that U.S. labor is

---

[5] In the simplest case, where the ratio of factor inputs is fixed, the above statement may be illustrated by the following example:

| | Input Requirement in the Production of: | |
	1 Machine	10 Yards of Textile
U.S.	5 units of capital + 2 man-days of labor	2 units of capital + 4 man-days of labor
U.K.	5 units of capital + 2 man-days of labor	2 units of capital + 4 man-days of labor

The capital to labor ratio is 5:2 in the case of machines and 2:4 in the case of textiles—in both countries.

[6] For example, assume that the U.S. has 100 million workers and $4,000 billion of capital, whereas the U.K. has 30 million workers and $600 billion of capital. This works out to $40,000 of capital per worker in the U.S. and $20,000 of capital per worker in the U.K. It also explains why labor is more efficient in the United States: It has more capital at its disposal than does labor in Great Britain.

relatively more productive in wheat production because wheat is a relatively capital-intensive commodity and American labor has more capital to work with than does British labor, since the United States is the relatively capital-abundant country. On the other hand, the United Kingdom, being the relatively labor-abundant country, acquires *comparative* advantage in textiles, a commodity that requires relatively less capital in its production. This statement has general application. *Each country exports the commodities that are relatively intensive in the factor with which it is relatively well endowed.* In an indirect sense, each country exports the services of its abundant factor and imports the services of its scarce factor—as embodied in the two bundles of traded goods. All phrases in this general rule are couched in relative terms.

Under this model, specialization may be complete or incomplete, although many manipulations and some interesting results derived from the model involve the further assumption of incomplete specialization—in other words, that each country produces some of both commodities (including the imported one). Economists have worked out the conditions that are likely to lead to complete specialization. It turns out that the more diverse (or different) the resource endowment ratios of the two countries are, and the more similar the factor intensity ratios of the two commodities are, the more likely it is that specialization will be complete. The limiting case of the second condition, where the two products use factors in identical ratios, yields the Ricardian case of constant opportunity cost and complete specialization.

For over twenty years economists have been practically wedded to this explanation of the pattern of international trade. The model was refined in many ways and used to examine a host of important questions, such as the effect of economic growth on both the pattern and terms of trade. Even in the face of contrary empirical evidence, to be discussed below, economists were loath to dispense with it as the central theoretical proposition. Appendix VII offers a sketchy graphical explanation of the factor proportions model.

It is interesting to speculate on the attraction that the model holds for economic theorists. In the first place, it is a logically tight structure, where the conclusions follow uniquely and neatly from the assumptions. Second, it is a very simple explanation (perhaps much too simple) that lends itself readily to geometric and mathematical manipulations—a quality that has fascinated modern economists. Also, despite its limitations and the problems discovered in attempts to test it empirically, it is *highly useful in explaining a wide range of observed phenomena.*

Third, the explanation of trade patterns is couched in terms of the most elementary properties of the trading countries. Any other explanatory factor that could conceivably be advanced—labor productivity, production cost, or what have you—begs the question "What determines that factor itself?" By embedding the explanation in the bare essentials of the country's economic structure we minimize the need for such questions. The natural resources of the country are determined by nature and not by any economic factors. Immigration policies and sociological factors affecting birth rates, rather than economic variables, are the main determinants of labor supply, although an important qualification is introduced by the fact that the size of the labor force and its level of participation are at least partly related to economic conditions. The point is probably least valid in the case of capital, where it is certainly legitimate to inquire into the economic causes of past investments that led to today's capital stock. These certainly include the saving behavior of past generations that made resources available for investments, natural resources, entrepreneurial ability of the population, and a degree of destruction through wars and other causes. To the extent that technological developments control investments, we can still ask what (besides human genius) motivates new technology. But all these are causes of past behavior. Today's capital stock can be taken for granted. Consequently, despite these qualifications, the model reduces to the bare essentials of the economic structure, at least when considered as of the period under study.

Last, but not least, because the model employs the country's economic structure to explain trade, the process can be reversed to inquire into the effect of international trade on the economic structure, especially on the remuneration of factors of production and the distribution of income among factors.[7] Since the model implies that each country exports the *services* of its abundant factor (embodied in the bundle of exported goods) and imports the *services* of its scarce factor (embodied in the bundle of imported goods), it follows that the introduction of international trade into an otherwise isolated economy raises the demand for the abundant factor, and therefore its remuneration, while lowering returns to the scarce factor. (The opposite result follows from the imposition of a tariff.) With incomplete specialization, and under the assumption of this model, international trade would lead to the equalization of factor prices between the trading nations.[8]

☐ More specifically, the process of factor price equalization is based on changes in the factor use ratios in the production of the two commodities. In the example used earlier, and under conditions of incomplete specialization, trade causes the United Kingdom to produce more textiles and less machinery, thereby shifting resources from machinery to textiles. But because of the difference in the factor-use ratio in the two industries, resources are released from the machinery industry at a relatively high capital/labor ratio and can be absorbed into the textile industry only at a relatively low capital/labor ratio. Thus the process involves freeing relatively more capital and

---

[7] The distribution of income among factors of production (the total return to labor, to capital, to natural resources, and to entrepreneurial ability) is known as the *functional distribution of income*. It is to be distinguished from the size distribution, designed to assess the degree of income inequality in the population.

[8] These results do not follow the Ricardian model, which immediately leads to complete specialization.

less labor than can be absorbed. In the market scrambling that ensues, the price of capital falls and that of labor rises. This must be the outcome if (as the model assumes) all factors are fully employed before and after trade. Precisely the reverse holds true in the United States, where resources are released from textiles at a relatively low capital/labor ratio and are absorbed into producing machinery at a relatively high capital/labor ratio. This process entails a rise in the price of capital and a fall in the price of labor.

☐ Two consequences of this transformation are among the topics explored by economists since World War II. First, the internal distribution of income in each country has changed, with the relatively abundant factor (capital in the United States and labor in England) gaining and the relatively scarce factor losing from the introduction of trade. These effects occur in both industries as long as specialization is incomplete and both are functioning in the two countries. But in each country the loss to the scarce factor is less than the gain to the abundant factor, so that the community as a whole benefits from the introduction of trade. Conversely, restrictions on trade would benefit the relatively scarce factor. Indeed, Australia, for example, has in the past imposed tariffs in order to affect the internal distribution of income in favor of labor, which is scarce there relative to land. This may also explain why vast segments of the American labor movement favor various forms of protection from imports, labor being scarce relative to capital in the United States. However, there are superior means at the disposal of government to change income distribution, such as taxes and subsidies.

☐ Second, in comparing factor remunerations between countries, we notice that the introduction of trade lowers the price of capital in the United Kingdom and raises it in the United States. Since capital is the relatively scarce factor in the United Kingdom and was more highly priced there than in the United States before the advent of trade, this constitutes a convergence of the two prices. Similar convergence occurs in the price of labor as it rises in England and declines in America. Schematically, these movements can be illustrated as in Figure 12-1. This convergence takes place in both

Figure 12-1
Effect of Trade on Factor Prices

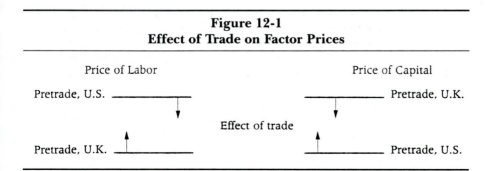

industries as long as specialization is incomplete. And under the strict postulates of the Heckscher–Ohlin model, including the assumption of constant returns to scale,[9] factor prices would be equalized completely.   ■

Empirical Testing

With all these virtues, one may ask whether there is anything wrong with the model. The answer is that empirical tests to date have failed to verify it. An excellent way to test a theory is by examining its ability to predict real-world phenomena (although another method may be to inquire into the realism of its assumptions). For a long time it was impossible to test the factor proportion theory in that fashion, because commodities entering international trade could not be decomposed into their labor and capital components. The production processes in an industrial economy are rather complex. Each final good, such as automobiles, can be decomposed into its labor, capital, and material inputs. And the last item (such as steel and other metals) also must be decomposed in the same procedure, and so on down the line. Only by working backward through the production processes to the crude material stage, which itself is found in natural form, can one sum up the total labor and capital inputs embodied in each final product. Indeed, for most traded commodities, the labor and capital content in the final stage of fabrication is only about half the total.

This procedure presented a monumental obstacle until the impasse was broken in the late 1930s, when mobilization required precise knowledge of the production processes in the economy. If the government decides to increase the production of airplanes by one thousand units, to avoid bottlenecks it must also know what inputs from other industries would be required. In fact, any massive shifts in the commodity composition of production, for demobilization or for any other reason, necessitates such knowledge. Smooth transition of the economy is impossible without it. Nobel laureate Wassily Leontief was the first to develop a method that provided this information for the United States in the form of "input–output tables." These show the inter-industry flows of goods and services as they work their way through the production processes into final form. This work has since been taken over by the U.S. Department of Commerce. Similar studies are available for numerous other countries.

Once input–output statistics became available, it became possible to decompose American exports and imports into their labor and capital components. Leontief did this in the mid-1950s. He discovered that a representative basket of American exports embodied more labor and less capital than one of American imports. Certainly the capital/labor ratio was higher for imports than exports. Since the United States is by far the most capital-abundant country in the world, this result contradicts the factor proportions

---

[9]This implies that the marginal product of each factor depends only on the factor use ratio and is completely independent of the scale of operations.

theory. His finding caused great consternation among theorists and came to be known as the Leontief scarce-factor paradox.

Since that time, similar data from other countries have been subject to the same analysis, but in many cases they failed to verify the theory. It should be pointed out that in the 1950s the United States occupied an extreme position in the spectrum of countries ranked by capital/labor endowment ratio and therefore could be considered the relatively capital-abundant country vis-à-vis the rest of the world. This is not true of other nations. Japan, for example, trades with some countries that are capital abundant (in North America) and others that are labor abundant (in Asia) relative to itself. Consequently, a proper test of the model for Japan requires the breaking up of its trade into two parts according to the nature of the trading partner. In sum, although the tests conducted thus far are not conclusive, such as they are they fail to confirm the accepted doctrine.[10]

These results touched off a heated debate among economists that lasted two decades. Most writers attempted to salvage the factor proportion theory by reconciling it with the empirical findings. Leontief himself pointed to the great effectiveness of American labor, resulting from superior management, better training, and stronger motivation. He concluded that since American labor is three times as effective as its foreign counterpart (even when using the same capital equipment), when labor is measured in efficiency units the United States comes out as the relatively labor-abundant country, and the theory is thus vindicated.

Other economists claimed instead that U.S. import restrictions so heavily protect labor-intensive industries that the observed import basket is artificially biased toward capital-intensive products. Still others maintained that the trouble lies in confining the model to two factors of production and ignoring natural resources. In fact, what the United States imports is natural-resource-intensive products. Because these necessitate much capital in their production, they show up as capital intensive on a capital–labor scale. Finally, some economists emphasized the possibility that strong American demand for capital-intensive goods may have offset the U.S. factor endowment advantage in these goods and raised their relative prices in this country to a point at which they would be imported rather than exported. Other theoretical as well as statistical reconciliations were advanced, and the data were modified and manipulated in various directions.

Although some of the new results were closer to theoretical expectations, it is difficult to overlook the fact that none has yet shown that American exports have a capital-intensity lead over imports. Indeed, in the view

---

[10] A study of the composition of Soviet trade in 1955–68 shows conformity with the factor proportion hypothesis. The study concludes: "When the Soviets trade with relatively developed countries they import capital intensive commodities and export labor intensive goods. When they trade with nations at similar development level, imports and exports embody factors in approximately equal proportions, and when they trade with underdeveloped regions, they export capital intensive and import labor intensive products." Steven Rosefielde, "Factor Proportions and Economic Rationality in Soviet International Trade," 1955–68, *American Economic Review,* September 1974, pp. 674–75.

of some writers, the factor-proportions model should be drastically modified both on the grounds of empirical tests and because it is based on unrealistic assumptions: In a world of free capital movement and integrated capital markets, where the multinational corporation is becoming a dominant force, and in an era in which technical and managerial talent can be transferred between countries and innovations quickly diffused, can one adhere to the classical assumption of factor immobility between countries? Is it correct to assume constant returns to scale? Is it legitimate to postulate that the ranking of industries by capital/labor ratio is the same in all trading nations? Is it legitimate to confine both the analysis and its tests to two factors of production, assumed to be homogeneous in form, when we know that more than two enter the productive process? Is it reasonable to focus almost exclusive attention on supply considerations and assume that demand conditions are largely similar in the trading nations? Both the predictive ability of the theory and the assumptions on which it rests were brought into question. Indeed, relaxation of each of the above assumptions can practically produce a new theory.

Alternative Theories

Although the factor proportion theory cannot explain all international trade, and indeed should not have been expected to do so in the first place, it still has considerable explanatory power. Phenomena such as the stimulus to American investments in Canada provided by the Canadian tariff (which means that Canadians are inconsistent in insisting on a high tariff but complaining about the inflow of American capital) can be explained by reference to the model, as can some of the relationships between economic growth and international trade. But it is unreasonable to expect one simple theory to account fully for such a complex phenomenon as trade in all goods among one hundred nations. In particular this theory cannot adequately explain the vast expansion of trade among the industrial countries whose factor endowment ratios are rather similar. Much of this exchange is *intra-industry* trade; namely, trade in similar products that are differentiated (or distinguished) from each other by some feature(s). It is not surprising, therefore, that during the 1970s and 1980s several alternative explanations appeared in the professional literature.[11] These are reviewed next.

Sector-Specific Factors   This model is a widely used variant of the factor proportion theory. It assumes a two-sector economy, with agriculture (A) using land and labor, and manufacturing (M) employing capital and labor. Labor is perfectly mobile between the two sectors, whereas capital and land are specific to manufacturing and agriculture respectively. In each sector labor is combined with a fixed quantity of the other factor (capital in M or

[11] See for example: R. Baldwin, "Determinants of the Commodity Structure of U.S. Trade," *American Economic Review,* May 1971.

land in A), to produce the product. Hence labor is subject to diminishing returns, and the VMP_L[12] declines in each sector. Labor mobility ensures that the wage rate, which equals the VMP_L, will be equalized across the two sectors. Indeed, this equality condition determines the distribution of labor between the two sectors.[13]

Suppose the country is land abundant so that it has a comparative advantage in A. When free trade is introduced to an otherwise isolated economy, the domestic price of A rises. Labor is drawn from M to A, so that more labor is combined with (specific factor) land, while less labor is combined with capital. The value of the marginal product of land rises and that of capital declines: owners of land gain and capital-owners lose. Hence there is a potential conflict between the owners of factors specific to the expanding and contracting industries (the gainers and losers).[14] The effect of trade on the mobile factor (labor) is discussed in the second part of Appendix VII.

Human Skills In industrial economies, the training and sophistication of the labor force is the most important characteristic distinguishing one country from another. Therefore, countries that are relatively well endowed with professional personnel and highly trained labor will specialize in and export skill-intensive goods. Conversely, relative abundance of unskilled labor promotes the export of commodities embodying mostly untrained labor. A test of this hypothesis requires information on the skill content of products entering international trade and the matching of this information with the relative abundance (or scarcity) of skill in the trading nations.[15]

The skill content of products can be measured as the ratio of professional and technical manpower in the total labor force of the industry or, alternatively, it can be approximated via the average wage rates in the industry, on the assumption that wage rates reflect the degree of training and professionalism. Since interindustry skill differentials are similar the world over, in the sense that the *ranking of industries* by degree of skill used does not vary much between countries, the skill content of each commodity in one country (normally the United States, for which more data are available) is used to represent the skill content of the same commodity in all countries. Of course, the commodity composition of trade, and therefore the "skill

---

[12] The value of the marginal product of labor is the price of the product times the marginal physical product of labor.

[13] See Jones, R. W., "A Three-Factor Model in Theory Trade and History," in J. Bhagwati et al (eds.), *Trade, Balance of Payments, and Growth: Essays in Honor of C. Kindleberger*, Amsterdam, North Holland, 1971.

[14] A possible interpretation of this model is that it corresponds to the short-run version of the Hechchser-Ohlin theory. Because capital is not mobile across sectors in the short run, there is a direct conflict of interest among capitalists in different industries. See Neary, J. P., "Short-run Capital Specificity and the Pure Theory of International Trade," *Economic Journal* 86, (1978).

[15] See D. Keesing, "Labor Skills and Comparative Advantage," *American Economic Review*, May 1966.

mix" embodied in it, varies from country to country. This measure of the skill content of traded goods is matched with the percentage of professional and technical personnel in the labor force of every country, the latter proportion measuring the relative national abundance of trained manpower. The degree of correlation between them indicates whether labor skill is indeed a powerful explanatory variable of the direction of international trade.

An extension of this hypothesis can be used to explain comparative advantage in high-technology products. Because they are produced by knowledge-intensive industries, these products tend to be developed in countries with both a high proportion of research scientists and engineers in the labor force and a willingness to spend a relatively large share of their GNP on research and development.

Economies of Scale   According to another hypothesis, a large home market is conducive to the export of goods produced under conditions of increasing returns to scale—that is, where production costs decline as the scale of operations expands. Conversely, a small home market leads to the export of goods not subject to these conditions. In this case a test would require matching the size of the market with the type of commodities traded, classified by the degree to which their manufacture is subject to economies of scale.

Technological Advance   This hypothesis makes use of the sequence of innovation and imitation as they affect exports. It argues that the industrially sophisticated countries are the early producers of new products; they therefore enjoy easy access to foreign markets at an early stage of manufacture. Later a process of imitation sets in, as other nations start producing and exporting these goods by relying on lower wages or some other factor-cost advantage. An example may be the production of antipollution equipment. Because the United States is the leader in setting up pollution standards, American firms are likely to be the first in developing and producing such equipment. Only later will their manufacture spread to other countries. To test this theory, one would need to inquire whether it is indeed the industrially advanced countries that are responsible for the introduction of new products into international trade.

Product Cycle   Instead of emphasizing the time lag involved in the imitation process (as in the technological-advance hypothesis), the product cycle hypothesis stresses the standardization of products.[16] Early manufacture of a new good involves experimentation with both the features of the product and the manufacturing process. Therefore, in its beginning stages, the good is nonstandardized. As markets grow and the various techniques become

---

[16]R. Vernon, "International Investment and Trade in the Product Cycle," *Quarterly Journal of Economics*, May 1966; and L. Wells, "A Product Cycle for International Trade?," *Journal of Marketing*, July 1968.

common knowledge, both the product and the process become more standardized and perhaps even subject to internationally set standards and specifications. At that time, production can begin in less sophisticated nations. The upshot of this hypothesis is that highly sophisticated economies are expected to export nonstandardized goods, while less sophisticated countries specialize in more standardized goods. A test of the theory must relate the degree of standardization (or, conversely, product differentiation) of the country's exports to the level of its industrial sophistication.

Similarity of Preferences   All the explanations mentioned above, along with the factor-endowment theory, have one thing in common. They maintain that international trade compensates for national deficiencies, whether in capital, labor skill, management, or technological sophistication. The gain from trade derives from the fact that it enables countries to specialize in goods that require the factors that they possess in abundance. It is a gain from reallocating resources among different activities. The result is that countries import and export dissimilar goods—dissimilar in terms of one or more of the characteristics outlined above. Presumably the more divergent the countries' endowments are, the more dissimilar will be the commodities exchanged and the greater will be the gain from trade.

The "preference similarity" hypothesis, applied to trade in manufactured goods, is essentially a different approach.[17] It maintains that a country's exports are merely an extension of production for the home market. Such production caters to the needs of the majority, and it is through producing for that market that the country acquires a comparative advantage in the product and then comes to export it. Since the minority of the population has slightly different demands, these can be met with imports from a country where such tastes are those of the majority. Because the type of goods demanded in a country is thought to be uniquely determined by the level of per capita income, most exchanges of manufactures takes place between countries of similar industrial structures. And because the trading partners export essentially similar goods, each country's exports are similar to its imports. Thus trade extends the variety of manufactured goods available to the consuming public, and the gain from trade stems from the satisfaction of being offered the precise variety or brand of product the consumer desires. This approach was suggested only as an explanation of international trade in manufactured products. In the case of nonindustrial goods that are high in natural resource content, one must rely on the natural resource endowment of the country as an explanatory factor.

Monopolistic Competition   Elements of the previous hypotheses are incorporated in this recently developed theory which attempts to explain the two-way exchange of similar products. It postulates that firms operate under increasing returns to scale: if the firm increases all inputs by a given

[17] S. Linder, *An Essay on Trade and Transformation*, N.Y., Wiley, 1961.

proportion, its output rises by a greater proportion. Put differently, the firm's unit production cost declines as output expands. Because this is not consistent with perfect competition, markets are assumed to be monopolistically competitive; each industry consists of many firms selling differentiated products. Products can be differentiated by such features as size, quality, service after purchase, packaging, and even brand name.

When such an economy is opened to trade, factor endowments determine which major industries the country specializes in, thereby determining inter-industry trade. But because of economies of scale, each country produces only a limited variety of each industrial product, trading them for other varieties imported from abroad. This is the essence of intra-industry trade.

Each country experiences both inter-industry and intra-industry trade. A country is a net exporter in industries in which it has a comparative advantage. But it imports some products (or varieties) within these industries. Likewise, it exports some products in the industries in which it has a comparative disadvantage. The more alike countries are in their factor endowments, the more their trade is intra-industry in nature.[18] Because product differentiation is widespread in the manufacturing sector, countries of similar industrial structure trade heavily with each other and much of their trade is an exchange of similar products. The effect of home-market demand on the varieties that a country specializes in is as postulated in the "similarity of preferences" theory. Indeed, trade liberalization in Europe resulted mainly in the expansion of intra-industry trade. There were no cases of industry collapse with its output replaced by imports; instead, industries in each country moved to specialize in differentiated varieties of products, exchanging their brands for varieties produced abroad.

This analysis adds two elements to the gains from international trade as discussed in Chapter 11. First, consumers gain access to differentiated varieties of products not available at home. Second, because firms operate under increasing returns to scale, production costs and prices decline as output expands to serve export markets. However, there is a trade-off between these two gains: the greater the potential economies of scale (and hence the scope for price reduction) the lesser the scope for new varieties, and the smaller the consumers' gain from increased variety of goods.[19]

Summary International trade theory is now in a state of flux with respect to both formulation and testing. Tests to date have yielded mixed results concerning which of the foregoing hypotheses has the strongest explanatory power. Perhaps some of the explanatory factors can be merged into a

---

[18] If factors endowments are identical between countries, there would be only intra-industry trade, and trade in each industry would be balanced.

[19] E. Helpman, "International Trade in the Presence of Product Differentiation Economies of Scale and Monopolistic Competition," *Journal of International Economics*, August 1981; and P. Krugman, "New Theories of Trade Among Industrial Countries," *American Economic Review*, May 1983.

composite variable and each composite variable would be used to explain a distinct portion of international trade.

In order to see what is meant by a composite variable, consider the factor proportions model based on the capital/labor ratio. Labor is assumed to be a homogeneous factor. Yet we know that it is anything but that. There are different types of labor embodying various degrees of skill and professionalism. In fact, one of the above explanations of the commodity composition of trade that was tested successfully was concerned with human skills—a variable that can be quantified in terms of the education and training needed to acquire them. Education and training are investments in people; they create human capital. And in an economic sense, human capital is no different from physical capital. The two can be combined under the heading "capital" and so used in computing the capital content of commodities for the purpose of estimating capital/labor ratios. The denominator of the capital/labor ratio would then consist only of unskilled labor.[20] Alternatively, capital can be considered an indirect factor of production, to be added to the country's natural endowment of labor and natural resources. In the same vein, one might merge the various technological variables and then match the level of technology required to produce commodities with the degree of technological sophistication of the trading nations.

An Emerging Consensus?

The contemporary view treats separately two components of international trade: (a) *Inter-industry trade* is the exchange between countries of totally different types of commodities, such as textiles and shoes for aircraft and computers; or the exchange of primary materials for finished manufactures. Much of this trade is between nations of vastly different factor endowments, such as the LDCs and the industrial countries, and can be explained by the traditional factor endowment model, or its extension into skills and technology.

(b) *Intra-industry trade* refers to a two-way trade in a similar commodity such as the exchange of automotive products between U.S. and Canada or among some of the European countries. A growing proportion of international trade falls in this category. Much of it is conducted among the industrial countries, whose factor endowments have become increasingly similar.

Two features of the producing firms involved in trade intra-industry are important: (1) They tend to be oligopolies[21] (rather than perfect competitors), mainly with differentiated products; and (2) economies of scale in production and distribution play an important role in their behavior.

---

[20] See P. Kenen, "Nature Capital and Trade," *Jour. of Political Economy*, Oct. 1965.
[21] A few large firms make up each industry.

Under these circumstances, factor endowments determine whether a country will be a net exporter or a net importer within broad commodity classes, but the advantages of long production runs lead each country to produce only a limited range of products within each class. The result is that countries with similar capital–labor ratios and skill levels will still have an incentive to specialize in producing different goods within each industry and to engage in trade—hence the emergence of vast intra-industry trade.

The benefits from such trade are not confined to reallocation of resources. They include the rationalization of industries to take advantage of economies of scale, greater competition among large firms (across national boundaries), and a wider *variety* of products available to consumers. The effects on income distribution and on returns to factors, so prominent in the factor proportions model, may be outweighed by the economies of scale effect. All productive factors may gain from trade.

One reason why the U.S. and Europe find it difficult to adjust to increased imports from the LDCs, even when accompanied by increased exports to them, is that these imports represent inter-industry rather than intra-industry trade. Resources within the importing country must shift from one industry to another rather than within segments of the same industry.

Economic Adjustment to Changing Circumstances

Having outlined the manifold factors that determine comparative advantage, we hasten to add that these influences are never at a standstill. They change over time, both within and between countries. Technological advance, capital accumulation, acquisition of new skills, and invention of new products are commonplace in all dynamic economies. They occur practically every year and in turn change the ranking of industries in terms of comparative advantage. Industries that could easily meet price competition on world markets at one time may suddenly find themselves shrinking in size because of their inability to compete. Under such circumstances it is important that resources in the economy be mobile enough to shift from sluggish to competitive sectors. The economy itself must be in a process of continuing transformation to meet new circumstances. This requirement applies particularly to inter-industry trade.

Consider, for example, the production of desk calculators. Immediately after World War II, this was almost exclusively an American monopoly. But twenty years later—when the technology involved was no longer considered sophisticated—the Burroughs Corporation found it advantageous to move production from Detroit to Scotland where equally qualified but cheaper labor was to be found. Were the Detroit plants shut down? Not at all; they were transformed into the production of more sophisticated electronic computers. While the United States was losing its comparative advantage in calculators, it was gaining a new one in more highly sophisticated equipment.

But at the same time, similar changes were taking place in other countries. Consider the attempts of the developing countries to industrialize. What new industries can they establish? Apart from production based on locally available materials, their comparative advantage lies in industries that are both technologically unsophisticated and labor intensive. Textiles, footwear, and lumber products come immediately to mind as concrete possibilities. More advanced developing countries (where hourly compensation is one-tenth that of the U.S.'s, and the labor is well-trained) have moved to develop steel, auto, and consumer electronic industries. Thus, while India, Pakistan, and Taiwan establish textile mills, it is necessary for some European countries to contract their textile industries and shift to the production of more advanced products, perhaps desk calculators. In terms of their comparative advantage, it pays them to specialize in the latter type of commodities and import the cheaper textiles from abroad.

A reverse change in the structure of comparative advantage may occur if and when developed countries introduce and enforce high antipollution standards. For these standards may raise the production cost of many synthetic materials above that of their natural substitutes, which are produced mainly in the developing countries. These countries would then regain the competitive advantage that they had previously lost to synthetics.

In another example, U.S. domination of the world airplane market is being challenged by the European A300 airbus (which, however, is powered by General Electric engines), produced by a French–German consortium. The same applies to European and Japanese penetration of other high-technology industries.[22]

Perhaps the most dramatic illustration of the dynamic nature of comparative advantage is the recent Japanese concern about textile imports. During the 1970s, in the midst of the American industry's clamor for quota protection from Japanese textile exports, the Japanese mills themselves were becoming increasingly concerned about cheap textile imports from South Korea, Hong Kong, and Taiwan. Likewise, Korea is beginning to export steel to Japan. Japan must gradually shift resources to more sophisticated industries, rather than imposing restrictions on imports from the LDCs.

But here comes the hitch. What on paper is a one-paragraph description of economic transformation is in reality a severe problem of human adjustment. Production equipment must be scrapped and new machinery installed. Workers must be retrained in new skills and sometimes relocated. At times, even entire communities are disbanded, and ghost towns appear where once there were thriving cities. In other words, the shift that benefits the entire nation occurs at the expense of considerable hardship to a minority of dislocated people. This problem is common to any type of economic change, such as the introduction of new technology, not only to change

---

[22] Examples of such industries are robotics, fiber optics and consumer electronics, office automation, computers, microchips, genetic engineering, and specialized oil and gas drilling equipment.

brought about by foreign trade. Public assistance in the adjustment process can help smooth over and speed up the transformation, but hardships remain nonetheless.

Consequently, it is not surprising that the industries directly affected by new import competition strive to protect their interests by demanding tariff or quota protection, with the labor unions joining in. The eventual benefit to all, after the transformation has been completed and workers moved to higher paying jobs, is lost sight of. The vested interest of the minority often prevails; certainly little attention is paid to the consuming public that stands to benefit from cheaper imports. The resulting protection of the textile industry in the United States and Europe has become a major grievance of many developing nations.

Another contemporary illustration is the insistence of the (politically powerful) Japanese farmers on import protection for farm products, which thereby perpetuates their very inefficient agricultural practices. American food exports are not allowed to penetrate that market, much to the chagrin of U.S. policymakers. Within Japan, the policy of protecting agriculture incurs the wrath of the large industrial exporters, who fear American retaliation in curbing imports of Japanese manufactured products.

To all countries, developed and developing alike, inability to transform may spell economic stagnation and continuous difficulties. Difficulties in making the adjustment to new patterns of production as dictated by shifting world demand is one of the problems that has plagued the British economy for the past thirty years. Despite the hardships involved, an economy must maintain the dynamism necessary for continuous change as it adapts to shifts in comparative advantage. The government can help by maintaining a high level of aggregate production and employment so that labor and capital released from declining industries will find alternative employment. It can also provide direct assistance to alleviate the burden of inter-industry transfers.

We close this discussion with a pertinent letter (to the *Wall Street Journal*, July 22, 1969), by W. L. Law, president of a leather company that reacted to Japanese imports by switching to other products.

> Baseball glove leather was the principal product for our firm until Japanese-manufactured ball gloves entered and ultimately captured 70 percent of the United States market. Today we tan no baseball glove leather. Sentiment in the ball glove industry was very strong for protective action but I found that I could not in good faith urge protectionist action. Such action would have been wrong economically, politically, and morally. . . .
>
> Certainly, labor-intensive industries are unable to compete. Give an Italian girl a needle and $20 per week and she will produce lace for one-fourth the cost of the American girl who receives $80 per week. However, give an American miner a giant mechanical shovel and $150 per week and by mining 100 tons he will produce much cheaper coal than the British miner with less efficient tools who receives $50 per week and only produces 20 tons. So we import handmade lace and we export computers.

Review Questions

1. What is meant by "Reactive factor intensity of a commodity" and "Relative factor abundance of a country?" How are these concepts used to explain the commodity composition of trade? Demonstrate that under this analysis "commodity movement and factor movement are substitutes for each other." Was the "Leontief Paradox" a verification of that explanation?

2. Does the factor proportion theory provide a good explanation of "intraindustry trade?" If not, can you outline an alternative explanation for this growing phenomenon.

3. Once the United States acquires a comparative advantage in jet aircraft production it can be sure of a dominant position in the global market forever. Do you agree? Explain.

4. Distinguish between inter- and intra-industry trade. Offer examples of each. Offer possible explanations for inter- and intra-industry trade.

5. Explain and elaborate on the following statement: "Under the factor endowment model, the main gain from trade is found in resource reallocation. Under the monopolistic competition theory, there are other gains as well (what are they?)."

6. Present four alternative explanations of the commodity composition of international trade.

13

Protection of Domestic Industries: The Tariff

*I*n light of the gains from international trade that were articulated in Chapter 11, one would expect free trade to be the prevailing rule and artificial barriers to trade the exception. Yet even casual observation may convince the reader that we live in a protection-ridden world, where government interference with the free flow of goods, services, and capital is anything but an exception. As in other areas of national concern, commercial policies do not represent the reasoned opinions of a single decision maker. They are a product of pressure groups vying for the attention of legislators and policymakers. The result hardly squares with the dictates of economic theory.

Traditionally, the most common instrument of protection, though by no means the only one, has been the tariff, and it has undergone much economic analysis over the years. It is a highly charged political issue, with import-competing industries clamoring for tariff protection, export industries often favoring free trade, and the consumer who pays the cost of protection being neither vocal nor adequately represented.

Some Institutional Considerations

Export Versus Import Duty

The tariff is a tax levied upon a commodity when it crosses a national boundary. The most common tariff is the import duty, although some countries, primarily exporters of agricultural commodities and raw materials, also employ export taxes. Export taxes may be used to produce government revenue, or they may be designed to curtail exports in order to prop up world prices of a primary commodity, as when Ghana discourages the exportation of cocoa or Brazil the exportation of coffee. It is interesting to note that import and export taxes are symmetrical in their effect on a country's resource allocation. A tax on imports raises their prices in the taxing country relative to the prices of other commodities and draws resources from export industries to import-competing industries. A tax on exports discourages overseas shipment of the taxed commodities and lowers their prices in the taxing country relative to other prices. Consequently, resources are pushed out of the export industries into the import-competing industries. Since export taxes are relatively rare, we shall be concerned mainly with import duties.

In the United States, the Constitution prohibits the imposition of a tax on exports. Consequently, whenever the U.S. government wishes to restrict exports so as to keep down domestic prices (as in the case of soybeans in 1972), it resorts to direct quota restrictions or a complete ban on overseas shipments.

Protection Versus Revenue

In times past, tariffs were imposed mainly as a source of government revenue. They are the easiest taxes to administer, because collection can be executed by officers stationed at official points of entry along the border. Many developing nations still rely on tariffs for financing government operations because of this ease of collection. Among industrial countries today, however, tariffs are levied for the protection of domestic industries. The small revenue generated by a protective tariff is a pleasant by-product, not the major objective. A duty is purely for revenue if it does not cause resources to move into industries that produce domestic substitutes for the imported commodities. A tariff levied on a commodity that is not produced at home, such as an import tax on coffee, or on a commodity whose domestic substitutes bear the same taxation, may serve to illustrate such a duty. At the other extreme, a *prohibitive* tariff—one high enough to keep out all imports—yields only protection and no revenue. For the overwhelming majority of taxed commodities, both the protection and the revenue are present. In the U.S. customs duties yield about $12 billion in revenue per year.

Types of Tariff

We distinguish between *ad valorem* duty, specific duty, and compound duty. The *ad valorem* tax is a fixed percentage of the value of the commodity, as when imported cars are taxed at 5 percent of value. A specific duty is a fixed sum of money per physical unit of the commodity, say $100 per imported automobile. A compound duty is a combination of the two, as when a car is taxed at $50 per unit plus 2 percent of value. The United States uses both specific and *ad valorem* duties in roughly equal proportion; European countries rely mainly on *ad valorem* taxes.

What are the advantages and disadvantages of each kind of tax? The *ad valorem* tax is more equitable than the others because it distinguishes among fine gradations of the commodity as they are reflected in its price.

The person importing a Rolls Royce pays more than his counterpart importing a Volkswagen. On the other hand, under a specific duty each person would pay the same amount, resulting in a higher percentage tax on the cheaper import.

In addition, the *ad valorem* tax provides a more constant level of protection to domestic industry in times of inflation than the specific duty does. Since world prices have been rising in recent decades, the level of protection accorded by a fixed sum of money declines as the tax becomes a smaller fraction of value, while the *ad valorem* duty, given as a fixed percentage, is not subject to the same decline.

On the other side of the ledger, a specific duty is easy to apply and administer, while an *ad valorem* tariff requires evaluation of the price of the commodity by the tax official before the tax can be calculated. There are two bases for such valuation: the f.o.b. price and the c.i.f. price. The first stands for "free on board" and indicates the price of the commodity on board ship at the port of embarkation (if ship-loading costs are excluded, we obtain the f.a.s. or "free along side" price). The second designation stands for "cost, insurance, freight" and covers the cost of the commodity up to the port of entry. It includes ocean freight and other intercountry transportation costs, which the f.o.b. price excludes. The United States and Canada use the f.o.b. price for computing the tariff, while most European countries employ the c.i.f. value. Consequently, a given percentage tariff translates into a level of protection about one-tenth lower in the United States than in Europe.

Since there are advantages and disadvantages to both specific and *ad valorem* duties, a sensible compromise may be to use the specific duty for standardized products and the *ad valorem* duty for goods with a wide range of grade variations.

Because tariff-setting in the United States is a congressional prerogative, the American tariff reflects the influence of a great variety of political pressure groups. This is one reason why the tariff classification has traditionally been rather long and complex, compounding the difficulty of administering the tariff. The customs officer must determine the classification within which each imported product falls. Since various categories are subject to different tax rates, this determination is very important to the importer. Indeed, much tariff litigation revolves around the classification of imported commodities, as well as their valuation (in the cases of *ad valorem* duties). The uncertainty that results from the complexity of the list is in itself a hindrance to international trade. To complicate matters further, a given product may be subject to different rates depending on its source of supply. This reflects the fact that an importing country may accord preferential treatment to certain exporting countries in the form of lower rates. In the case of the United States, the statutory tariff, set by Congress in the 1930s, is much higher than the rates charged on imports from most Western countries (known as the most favored nation rates) after a long succession of reciprocal tariff reductions. And in turn the latter duties are higher than those charged on manufacturing imports from many LDCs that are accorded preferential status in the U.S.

A corollary of the two methods of valuation of commodities for tariff purposes is the way the United Nations and other organizations report commodity trade statistics. All products entering trade are classified according to the SITC. But the basic sources from which the data are derived are import and export declarations filed by the traders with the respective governments at the time the commodity enters or leaves the country. The declarations include a detailed description of the products to permit further classification, along with quantity and value information. Import declarations usually require more detailed description than their export counterparts, because they are of direct interest not only to the statistician who compiles data but also to the tax assessor. Export values are reported on the f.o.b. basis by all countries. But when it comes to import statistics, the United States and Canada use f.o.b. values, whereas European countries report c.i.f. values, because the import declarations are so filed for the purpose of computing the tariff. These methods of valuation are used by all data-gathering organizations.

Tariff rates are published by individual countries, in their respective languages, but translations of all tariff schedules into the five major languages are printed in the *International Customs Journal,* published by the International Customs Tariff Bureau in Belgium. Tariff systems of foreign countries are also described in various issues of *Overseas Business Reports* published by the U.S. Department of Commerce. The American tariff is reported in *The Tariff Schedule of the United States, Annotated.* Virtually all European countries, as well as many of the developing nations, adhere to a standardized classification of commodities known as the Brussels Tariff Nomenclature (BTN) in levying their tariffs.

Economic Effects of the Tariff

Who Pays the Tariff?

It is customary to think of the tariff as being paid by the importer when the commodity enters the country and then passed on in whole or in part to the consumer as a price increase. Because this is the administrative procedure, there is a natural tendency to conclude that the tariff is being paid by the citizens of the country imposing it. Often, however, this is not true.

Consider an extreme example of a two-country world: the United States as a coffee importer and Brazil as the exporter. When the United States imposes a tariff on coffee, its domestic price rises, leading Americans to consume less; they either switch to substitute products such as tea or simply cut down on consumption of hot beverages altogether. But this means that the United States imports less coffee, reducing demand on the world coffee markets and leading to a reduction in its world price. As Brazil's export price declines, the coffee exporters are, in effect, forced to absorb part of the duty. The burden or *incidence* of the duty is divided between the Americans and the Brazilians: The U.S. domestic price rises and the Brazilian export price declines, the two changes adding up to the amount of the tariff. Consequently, the Brazilian exporter is forced by the market mechanism to absorb and pay part of the U.S.-imposed tax.

From the point of view of the importing country as a whole (the private sector and government combined), the import is now obtained at a lower cost than before (although private consumers pay more). The terms of trade—export prices divided by import prices—have improved. Conversely, the terms of trade of the exporting country deteriorate as its export prices decline.

The distribution of the burden between the importing and exporting countries is not the same in all cases; it depends on the type of commodity and on the countries involved. Consider first the importing country. If it is a small nation, accounting only for an insignificant share of world import of the product, a reduction in the quantity that its citizens consume is unlikely to influence the world price of the commodity. Thus, while the United States is a customer important enough to affect the world price of coffee and consequently shift part of the duty to foreign exporters, the same cannot be said of Luxembourg. The larger the tariff-imposing country is, the more "monopoly power" it can bring to bear on world markets and the better able it is to "tax the exporter" and thereby affect the terms at which it trades. The term "monopoly power" refers to market power. A small country, like a purely competitive firm, is a price taker. It is too small to affect by its own action the conditions prevailing in the market. A large country exercises monopoly power in the sense that it does not accept market prices as given. Its very actions affect them.

A second question on which the ability to shift part of the tax to exporters turns is the extent to which the increase in the domestic price of coffee would lead Americans to curtail consumption. Availability of adequate substitutes, such as tea, or alternative sources of supply of the same product, domestic or foreign, play an influential role here, as does the general willingness to do without coffee. The more readily available the substitutes are, the easier it is to relinquish consumption of Brazilian coffee and thereby depress the export prices and shift the duty to the exporters.

As for the exporting country, the easier it is to find alternative markets for the product, at home or abroad, or to contract production in the face of a price decline, the smaller will be the proportion of the foreign tax it will have to absorb. Instead of taking a price cut, exporters simply withdraw from the market in question. All these considerations reduce to various elasticities of supply and demand.

In sum, when a sizable country imposes an import duty, part of it is absorbed by the foreign exporter in the form of a lower export price, part by the home consumer in the form of a higher domestic price. A myriad of country and commodity characteristics determines the division of the tax between the two countries.

Graphic Exposition

A visual demonstration of this analysis requires a simple but useful extension of the tools of demand and supply. What follows pertains to a one-commodity, two-country world in which one country is the importer and the other the exporter.

We begin with the importing country B. Figure 13-1 (a) shows supply and demand curves for a single commodity in which country B has a comparative disadvantage compared to country A. P_1 is the equilibrium domestic price, the price that equates domestic supply and demand and thereby clears the market. If the world price is also P_1, country B will not trade in that commodity. But at any price below P_1, country B will import the commodity in question.

Figure 13-1 (b) describes country B's demand for imports: At price P_1 the demand for imports is zero. As the price declines to P_2, two things happen on the domestic market: The quantity demanded rises as we move down the (negatively sloped) demand curve, and the quantity supplied declines as we move down the (positively sloped) supply curve. The divergence, or horizontal distance, between the domestic quantities demanded and supplied at P_2 (distance a) is what the country imports at that price. That distance is plotted in 13-1 (b) to obtain another point of the import-demand curve. Likewise, when price drops to P_3, the quantity demanded increases and the quantity supplied domestically declines further, so that the quantity imported rises to b. Again it is plotted in panel (b). By connecting all points in Figure 13-1(b), we obtain the import-demand schedule.

In sum, the import-demand curve shows the quantities that the country stands ready to import at various prices. In all cases except when one

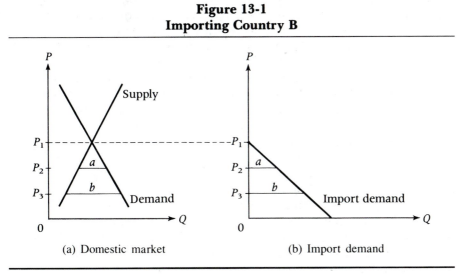

Figure 13-1
Importing Country B

(a) Domestic market   (b) Import demand

of the domestic schedules is of zero elasticity (vertical), import demand is flatter and more elastic than domestic demand. This is so because its slope equals the combined slopes of the domestic demand and supply schedules. Therefore, both the demand and supply schedules affect the shape of the import-demand schedule. (A precise formulation of the relationship is given in Appendix VIII.) At prices above P_1, domestic quantities supplied exceed those demanded, and import demand becomes negative. This simply means that at these higher prices the country becomes an exporter of the commodity—and it is a useful reminder of the fact that whether a commodity is exported or imported depends on its domestic price relative to the international price.

An infinitely elastic (horizontal) import-demand schedule is generated when either the domestic demand or the domestic supply curve is infinitely elastic. The reader can verify this by gradually making one of the domestic curves flatter, until it approaches the infinitely elastic position, and observing the resulting changes in the import-demand curve.

Next we turn to the exporting country in our configuration, country A. Figure 13-2(a) shows domestic demand and supply, with equilibrium price P_1 being established in isolation. At that price, the country will not trade, and therefore zero quantity is shown for export supply in panel (b). When price rises to P_2, the quantity supplied domestically increases as we move up along the (positively sloped) supply curve, while the quantity demanded internally declines as we move up along the negatively sloped demand curve. The divergence, or horizontal distance, between the quantities supplied and demanded domestically at price P_2 is a units of the commodity, the quantity that the country will export at that price. We thus obtain another point on the export-supply curve. By the same token, as

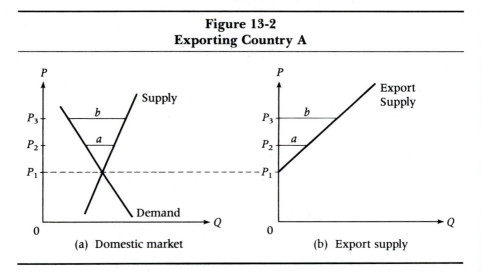

Figure 13-2
Exporting Country A

(a) Domestic market

(b) Export supply

price rises to P_3, the quantity exported increases to b. Connecting all the points in panel (b) yields the export-supply curve.

In sum, the export-supply schedule shows the quantities that the country stands ready to export at various prices. In all cases except when one of the domestic schedules is of zero elasticity (vertical) export supply is flatter and more elastic than domestic supply, for its slope is made up of the combined slopes of the demand and supply functions. Both domestic supply and demand affect the shape of the export-supply schedule. (A rigorous formulation of this relationship is given in Appendix VIII.) An infinitely elastic (horizontal) export-supply schedule is generated when either domestic demand or domestic supply is infinitely elastic. This can be verified by making one of the domestic curves flatter in several successive steps, until it approaches the infinitely elastic position, and observing the resulting changes in the export-supply curve. At prices below P_1 export supply is negative, and the country becomes an importer of the commodity.

We are now prepared to illustrate world trade in one commodity. In Figure 13-3, the fact that country A has a lower domestic equilibrium price than B establishes A as the exporter and B as the importer. Indeed, pretrade price in A is P_1 ($20), while that of B is P_2 ($60). From the exporting country we derive the export-supply curve, and from the importing country the import-demand curve, both plotted in Figure 13-3(b).

Now suppose that trade opens up. Post-trade equilibrium in the absence of transport cost and artificial barriers to trade requires that there be a common price in the two countries and that the quantity exported by one country be equal to the quantity imported by the other. Both conditions are met at price P_3, which is established by the intersection of the export-supply and import-demand curves. Note that the price in the exporting country

Figure 13-3
Equilibrium with Trade

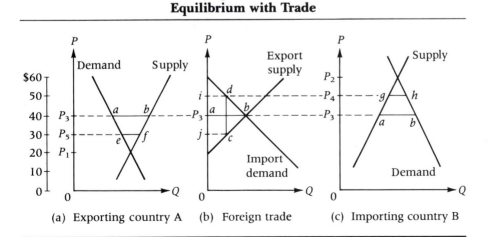

(a) Exporting country A   (b) Foreign trade   (c) Importing country B

rises while that in the importing country declines following the opening of trade. Production expands in the exporting country and contracts in the importing country, but the contraction stops short of complete specialization. The importing country continues to produce some of the product.

This free-trade position is now modified by the introduction of a tariff. For simplicity, we deal with a specific duty of, say, $20 per unit of the product. Since the vertical axis denotes price, the duty can be measured as a $20 segment on that scale. Starting from the intersection of the export-supply and import-demand curves, we proceed left to where the vertical divergence between the curves equals $20. This occurs at $\overline{cd}$.[1] The tariff is a wedge which causes the good's price in the exporting and importing country to differ by the amount of the tariff.

As a result of the tariff, the volume of trade declines to $\overline{ef}$ in the exporting country, which equals $\overline{gh}$ in the importing country and $\overline{id}$ $(= \overline{cj})$ in the center panel. Second, the export price declines to P_5 ($30 per unit) in country A, and the import price rises to P_4 ($50) in country B. The difference between the two is the tax per unit levied by the government of B. Government revenue from the duty equals $\overline{gh}$ units of import times $\overline{cd}$ ($20 per unit). Half of it is paid by the exporters in A and half by the consumers in B. In this example, the incidence of the tariff is divided equally between the two groups—a result of the equal but opposite slopes of the import-demand and export-supply curves. The terms of trade of the importing country have improved, because it now obtains imports from A for $10 per unit less than before. While B's private consumers pay a higher price (P_4) for the commodity than under free trade, the country as a whole (the government and private sectors combined) pays a lower price, P_5. Thus, it is the behavior of A's export price that indicates the changes in B's terms of trade.

To demonstrate unequal distribution of the tax burden between the two countries, observe first the case in which supply and demand in country B are more elastic than those in A, so that the import-demand schedule is more elastic than the export-supply schedule. This is shown in Figure 13-4. The free-trade equilibrium is determined as before, the resulting price being P_3 (in this case, $50 per unit). A $20 specific duty is introduced, and the divergence equaling that amount, $\overline{cd}$, is shown in the foreign trade panel. Here most of the tax burden is borne by the exporting country, whose export price declines to $35 ($P_5$), while the consumers in country B pay $55 ($P_4$) per unit. Geometrically, the difference can be traced to the relative size of the "scissors opening" between supply and demand in the two countries. Since the quantity exported by A must equal the quantity imported by B both before and after the tariff, it simply takes a larger drop in A's price to produce a quantity change comparable to the one produced by a small rise in B's price.

---

[1]Strictly speaking, the imposition of a tariff involves shifts in the demand or supply schedules. For simplicity, all such shifts are omitted here. Only the post-tariff equilibrium points are shown.

Figure 13-4
Unequal Distribution of the Tariff Burden, I

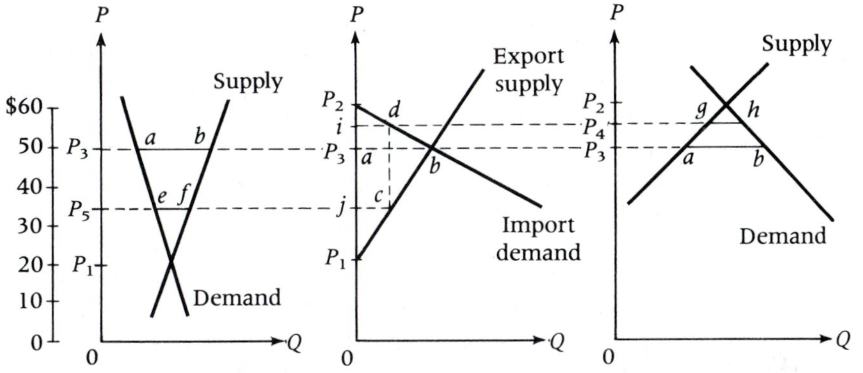

(a) Exporting country A   (b) Foreign trade   (c) Importing country B

But the shape of the curves is merely a representation of economic conditions. Country B does not "tolerate" a large increase in price because its consumers are ready to reduce consumption (elastic demand) or shift to rapidly expanding domestic supply (elastic supply). On the other hand, exporters in A cannot reduce the quantity supplied fast enough (inelastic supply), cannot expand home sales by much (inelastic demand), and (if this were a multicountry world) do not have enough, if any, alternative third-market destinations ready to absorb the product. They are therefore forced to take a sharp price cut. Such would be the result of an import tariff on coffee levied by the United States. Most of it would be absorbed by the Brazilian producers in the form of a price reduction. The extreme case occurs when demand or supply in B is infinitely elastic, producing infinitely elastic import demand. The entire tax burden is then borne by the exporters.

The results are the opposite if the domestic demand and supply conditions in the two countries are such that the export supply is much more elastic than the import demand. This is shown in Figure 13-5. In this case consumers in importing country B are reluctant to reduce the quantity demanded (inelastic demand) while domestic producers are unable to expand the quantity supplied (inelastic supply). On the other hand, exporters in A can easily curtail shipments (elastic supply), expand sales at home (elastic demand), or (if this were a multicountry world) shift to third-market destinations. Consequently, consumers in B must absorb most of the tax in the form of a price increase, while producers in A bear only a small share of the burden. Even so, the terms of trade of country B (consumers and government taken as a whole) improve, albeit by a small amount, since B obtains its imports at lower prices. A more rigorous formulation of the relationship between elasticities and the incidence of the tariff is given in Appendix VIII.

Figure 13-5
Unequal Distribution of the Tariff Burden, *II*

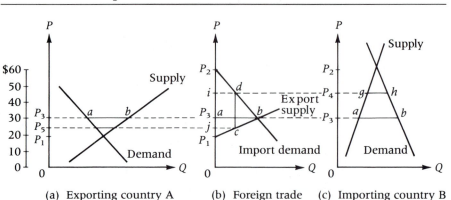

(a) Exporting country A   (b) Foreign trade   (c) Importing country B

Only in the extreme case of infinitely elastic export supply (caused by infinitely elastic supply or demand in country A) is the full burden of the duty borne by B's consumers. And only then do the importing country's terms of trade remain unaffected (they do not improve). This is not a rare and esoteric case, however. It applies to all countries that are not important enough as importers to affect the terms at which they trade. A small importing nation, like a competitive firm, is a price taker. It is faced with an infinitely elastic export-supply curve, and its domestic price must rise by the full amount of any duty it cares to impose. Only the few large countries can improve their terms of trade by levying import duties.

On the other hand, a small country can improve its terms of trade by imposing an export tax, if it is a major supplier of its export commodities. For example, if Ghana is responsible for one-third of world cocoa supply, then an export tax on cocoa would force marginal producers to withhold supplies from world markets, thereby pushing up the world price of cocoa. Ghana's terms of trade, but not necessarily its economic well-being (see next section), would improve as a result.

The foregoing analysis is oversimplified because it deals with only one commodity traded between two countries. This is all that can be handled with the tools of demand and supply. Clearly, the very nature of international trade necessitates one more set of diagrams dealing with another commodity, where B is the exporter and A the importer. Otherwise, the balance of payments of B will be in perpetual deficit, that of A in perpetual surplus. Since, in a manner of speaking, the above demonstration portrays only half the story, it is often referred to as "partial equilibrium analysis." However, the same insights can be gleaned from "full equilibrium analysis," through the use of reciprocal demand or offer curves.

Figure 13-6
International Exchange Ratio Before and After a British Tariff

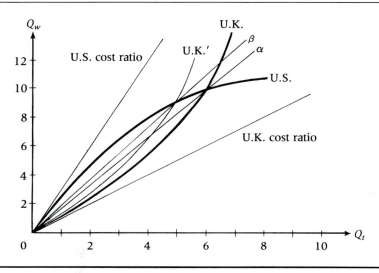

☐ In full-equilibrium terms, the imposition of a tariff by Britain can be shown by shifting the U.K. reciprocal demand curve upward from U.K. to U.K.' as shown in Figure 13-6. For any given quantity of textile exports, Britain will now require the pretariff quantity of wheat imports *plus* the quantity of wheat assessed by the British government in the form of an *ad valorem* tax. As a result of this shift, the British terms of trade (the quantity of wheat imports obtainable for a given amount of textile exports) improve form α to β. The United States can *retaliate* by imposing a tariff of its own, shifting its reciprocal demand curve downward and improving its terms of trade.

☐ It is easily verified that if Britain were facing an infinitely elastic U.S. offer curve (that is, a straight line), the terms of trade would remain unchanged following the tariff. That is the small country case.   ■

Domestic Effects

To recapitulate, a tariff drives a wedge between the price received by exporters and that paid by consumers. In the importing country it causes the appearance of two prices, where before the tariff there was only one. One is the price that the country as a whole (the government and private sectors combined) pays for the product, which equals the foreign country's export price plus transportation costs. This price is generally lower than its pre-tariff equivalent. The other is the price that the consuming public in the importing country must now pay, which is higher than its pretariff equivalent. The discrepancy between the two prices constitutes the import duty, which accrues to the government. Thus, part of that tax is paid by foreign producers and part by domestic consumers. The first component measures the improvement in the importing country's terms of trade, or its equivalent—the deterioration in the exporting country's terms of trade. When it comes to the terms of trade, what one country gains the other loses; the world as a whole is not affected. In our example, Brazil's export/import price ratio declines while that of the United States rises. The second component, the increase in domestic prices, constitutes the protection accorded to domestic producers of import-competing products and is responsible for the changes that occur in the domestic economy of the importing country.

In order to focus attention on the domestic effects in the tariff-imposing country, we assume it to be a small one, facing infinitely elastic export supply. The internal price of imports rises by the full amount of the duty, an increase that has several consequences. In the first place, it forces some consumers to curtail consumption of imports and to switch to domestically produced substitutes. The latter are presumably less desirable; otherwise, they would have been purchased even in the absence of the tariff. Consequently, this change constitutes a welfare loss to the consumer. In other words, the tariff distorts relative market prices by "artificially" raising the prices of imports, thereby inducing the consumer to purchase less desirable domestic products.

Second, production expands in the industries producing substitutes for the tariff-ridden imports. Under conditions of full employment, this is accomplished by drawing resources away from other industries,[2] which presumably rank higher in the order of comparative advantage (otherwise, the resources would have been employed in the tariff-ridden industries even before the tariff). This is a loss in production efficiency for the economy as a whole and is often called "production cost." It is worth emphasizing that the producers of the protected commodity gain from this transformation; the loss occurs in the efficiency of the economy as a whole as these producers are able to attract resources from other sectors. These two losses are partly offset by an increase in government revenue, which under our present assumptions is collected only from domestic sources. Concentrating strictly on what happens within the importing country, we see a net loss in real income coupled with a redistribution of income from the consuming public to the producers of the protected commodities and to the government. Because the tariff raises the price to the consumer and gives protec-

---

[2] For this reason economists would prefer a general tariff of equal rate applicable to all imports over the now common differential tariffs on different goods. An equal across-the-board tariff, coupled with a similar export subsidy is equivalent to currency devaluation (but its effects are restricted to the commodity component of the balance of payments).

tion to the domestic producer, its *domestic effects are comparable to those of a combined tax on the consumers and a subsidy to the producers.*

These changes can be seen in Figure 13-7. The importing country is still assumed to be small enough not to exercise "monopoly power" on world markets, and it faces an infinitely elastic export supply. Figure 13-7 depicts the internal supply and demand conditions for a tariff-ridden commodity— say, cars. In the absence of any international trade, the domestic price is set at P_1. Under free trade and in the absence of transport cost, the domestic price cannot differ from the world price, assumed here to be P_2. Being a small "price taker," the country has no effect on world price. At P_2 domestic consumption is $0b$, production is $0a$, and imports, being the difference between the two, are ab.

A tariff in the amount of P_2P_3 raises the domestic price to P_3 and produces the following effects. Internal consumption of cars declines by $\overline{hb}$ as consumers move along the demand curve from d to f. Thus, the tariff forces consumers to curtail consumption of the taxed commodity and switch to less desirable substitutes (the consumption effect of the tariff). Domestic production of cars rises by $\overline{ag}$ as producers move along the supply curve from c to e (the production effect of the tariff). In a general equilibrium context, $\overline{ag}$ represents the resources that the protected car industry was able to bid away from the other, more efficient, industries. Imports decline by $ag + hb$. Finally, the shaded rectangle, import volume $\overline{ef}$ (= $\overline{gh}$) times tariff per unit P_2P_3, represents government revenue from the tariff.

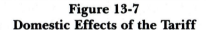

Figure 13-7
Domestic Effects of the Tariff

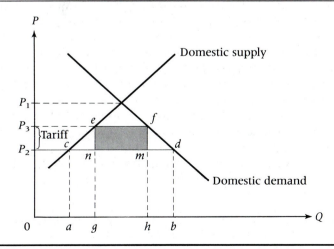

☐ **The Economic Cost of the Tariff—Further Considerations**   The economic cost of the tariff can be examined in greater detail with the tools of welfare economics. These tools will be developed first.

☐ Consider the demand curve D in Figure 13-8. Points on it show the prices that consumers would be willing to pay for various quantities. In conjunction with a supply curve (not shown), a market price is established at $0P_1$. Once determined, all buyers pay this uniform price. But in fact it is the price that only the marginal buyer was willing to pay. Other (intramarginal) purchasers, more eager for the product, would have been willing to pay higher prices, as indicated by points on the demand curve above A. (Less eager buyers, whose preferences lead to points below A on the demand curve, do not purchase the product.) Yet despite this differential eagerness, they all pay the same price. The difference between what consumers would have been willing to pay and the market price that they actually pay is known as *consumers' surplus*. In the diagram it is measured by the area of the triangle P_1AB.[3] If the market price rises to $0P_2$, then the consumers' surplus becomes P_2CB. It *declines* by the shaded area P_1P_2CA. Note that the demand curve need not be extended to intersect the price axis in order to determine the *change* in consumers' surplus.

☐ Next consider the supply curve S in Figure 13-9. Points on it show the quantities sellers are willing to supply at varying prices. In conjunction with a demand curve (not shown), a market price is determined at $0P_1$. Once it is established, all sellers receive this uniform price. But in fact only the marginal seller required this price to effect his sale. More efficient (intramarginal) sellers would have been willing to sell for less, as indicated by points on the supply curve below E. (Less eager sellers, requiring prices above $0P_1$, do not sell). Yet despite this differential eagerness (perhaps reflecting productive efficiency), all sellers obtain the same price. The difference between the price that the sellers would have required to part with the product, and the market price they all actually receive is known as *producers' surplus*. In Figure 13-9, it is measured by triangle P_1GE. If the market price rises to $0P_2$, then the producers' surplus becomes P_2GF. It *increases* by the shaded area P_1P_2FE. Note that the supply curve need not be extended all the way to the price axis to determine the *change* in producers' surplus.

☐ We are now in a position to analyze the welfare effect of the tariff, using Figure 13-7. Tariff P_2P_3 raises the post-trade domestic price from $0P_2$ to $0P_3$. As a result of this increase, the consumers' surplus *declines* by area $P_3P_2 df$, the producers' surplus *rises* by area P_3P_2ce, while government revenue *rises* by the shaded rectangle *efmn*. The net welfare loss from the tariff is therefore equal to the sum of the areas of triangles *cen* and *dfm*. It is

---

[3] The perfect price-discriminating monopolist would charge each consumer what he is willing to pay, instead of one market price for all. He would thereby appropriate the area of the triangle for himself.

| **Figure 13-8** | **Figure 13-9** |
| Consumers' Surplus | Producers' Surplus |

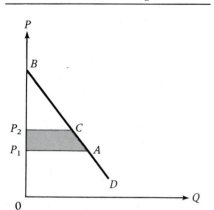

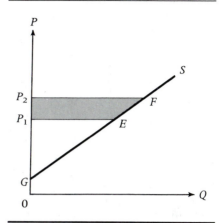

known as the *deadweight loss*. Apart from this net loss, the tariff results in income redistribution away from the consumers and to the government and the producers of the protected commodity.[4] ■

---

[4] In full-equilibrium terms, the consumption and production effects can be shown with the use of indifference curves. The accompanying diagram portrays a country with a comparative advantage in commodity B. Under free trade, production is at P_1, consumption is at C_1, and the level of community welfare is represented by U_1. The international price line is P_1R_1. A prohibitive tariff shifts production and consumption to P_2 and lowers the level of welfare to U_3. This reduction can be viewed as having two components. First, the production mix shifts from P_1 to P_2, but consumers are assumed to continue to face the (more favorable) international price P_2R_2 (parallel to P_1R_1). This represents the production cost, which lowers welfare from U_1 to U_2. Second, the price facing the consumers changes from the international to the domestic (dashed line) price, with the attendant reduction in welfare from U_2 to U_3. This represents the consumer cost of protection.

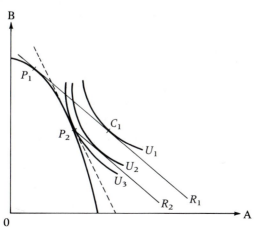

An important consequence of these effects is that the tariff produces a gain to the factors of production that are heavily utilized in the import-competing industries. The textile workers of America, for example, stand to benefit from a high tariff on imported textiles, in much the same way as resources employed in the export industries gain from free trade. Countries have at times levied tariffs with the objective of helping a certain productive factor at the expense of others in the economy. The total loss to the country of such policy far outweighs the gain to the particular resource. Also, taxes and subsidies are better ways to redistribute income in the economy, should such a course be deemed desirable.

Finally, a tariff may have such important indirect consequences as increasing the degree of monopoly in the country, thereby lowering productive efficiency, penalizing consumers, and retarding economic growth. If the country imposing the duty is so small that its internal market can support only one or two firms, foreign competition provides a stimulus to innovation and growth and a necessary check on pricing policies. The tariff reduces or bars such stimuli. Even in a large country, imports may provide the major competitive spirit when the industry is monopolized. This may partly explain the clamor for protection by the U.S. steel industry, where oligopolistic practices prevail. It is also a good reason why such protection is contrary to the public interest. This is particularly true in times of inflation, when removal of import restrictions can help cool the economy and hold back price increases. Indeed, countries often liberalize import restrictions as an anti-inflationary device.

We turn next to the internal repercussions in the exporting country. Nothing happens there if the importing nation is small. But if it is large enough to exercise monopoly power, the price of the export good is depressed, because less of it is now purchased by the country levying the tariff. This leads to a curtailment of production and an increase in consumption of the commodity. Introduction of trade has the opposite effect on the exporting nation; it raises the domestic price of the exported commodity. Thus, it should have surprised nobody that the price of wheat in Canada went up in the mid-1960s when the government concluded an agreement to sell a billion bushels to China, or that the price declined when the agreement expired. It merely reflected the increase and subsequent decline in the demand for Canadian wheat. Likewise, the price of wheat in the United States doubled in 1972 after the large sales to Russia.

In the exporting country, the producers of goods subject to foreign import taxes lose, while the consumers gain. The exporting country as a whole loses, not only because resources are now less efficiently allocated, but because its terms of trade deteriorate. This latter effect reflects the fact that the exporting country pays part of the tax collected by the importing country.

Effect of Real Income

The tariff inevitably causes a reduction in the real income of the world as a whole. The effects on the terms of trade in the importing and exporting countries cancel each other out; all that remains is a reduction in the volume of trade compared to what it would have been under free-trade conditions. This constitutes a reduction in the world's real income, both because the production patterns are distorted and no longer conform to comparative advantage configurations and because consumers are induced to shift from their ideal consumption mix to less desirable substitutes.

This does not mean that every country must lose from the tariff, however. The exporting nation loses because of both the reduction in the volume of trade and the deterioration in the terms of trade. But the importing country is subjected to two conflicting forces: a loss of real income caused by the reduction in the volume of trade and a gain due to improvement in the terms of trade. If the country is large enough to affect the terms at which it trades, the latter effect may be stronger than the first, resulting in a net gain in real income. Economists call the tariff rate that maximizes this net gain the *optimum tariff*.[5] Its size depends on the very factors that determine the "terms of trade effect." (The section on the "Economic Cost of the Tariff" in Appendix VIII offers a graphic exposition of the two-country case.)

Developing countries sometimes attempt to justify their complex and cumbersome systems of protection on the grounds that they provide an optimum tariff. But this is not a defensible position. These countries are much too small relative to total world trade in whatever they import to affect the terms at which they trade—to "force" the exporters to pay part of the tariff. Their optimum import tariff is necessarily zero. In their export trade, however, such countries may be able to exploit monopoly power and pass on a tax to outside interests. But only in the case of primary exports can a single developing country be important enough as a supplier to affect world prices. For example, a tax levied by Ghana on cocoa exports, or by Brazil on coffee exports, may restrict world supply of the commodity and raise its price, so that foreign consumers pay part of the tax. As a major exporter of the product it taxes, a country may in this manner improve its terms of trade.

In the case of developing countries, the taxed export good is usually an agricultural product or a raw material. Such export taxes are sometimes hidden in the activities of marketing boards set up by the government to stabilize prices and thereby stabilize the income received by the growers. Ostensibly designed to iron out excessive price fluctuations, the board can also push export prices above long-run equilibrium levels by withholding supplies or by paying farmers a lower price than it receives abroad, inducing them to produce less. And this action improves the terms of trade of the exporting country.

Some industrial nations are large enough to benefit from an import levy, and there is little doubt that the United States is one of them. Available evidence suggests that the incidence of the American tariff is about equally

[5]Corresponding to the "optimum tariff" on imports, there is an "optimum tax" on capital inflow that could be imposed by a country if it is a big enough borrower to improve the terms of borrowing abroad (interest rates).

divided between the foreign exporters and the domestic consumers. But in many products the height of the American tariff exceeds its "optimum" level in the technical sense of the word. Furthermore, a leading nation like the United States should think twice before using its tariff as a vehicle for taxing other, poorer, nations. It makes little sense to engage in foreign-aid programs and then proceed to nullify part of the aid by imposing import duties. Whatever minor economic gain may accrue could be more than offset by political losses.

Other Effects

Although not purposely designed to deal with balance-of-payments problems, a tariff does have balance-of-payments implications. Because it restricts imports of the products on which it is levied, the duty is generally thought to improve the country's external trade position. This result need not hold if the economy is operating near full employment. Under these circumstances, the shift of consumer demand from imports to domestically produced substitutes requires that labor and machines be shifted from somewhere else in the economy to the import-competing industries. If the factors of production come from the export industries, then exports *may* decline by as much as imports, and there will be no improvement in the trade position. Similarly, if the resources come from other import-competing industries, the net effect on imports will be nil. Furthermore, any bidding away of resources through the price mechanism usually contributes to a general increase in the price level, which in turn impairs the country's competitive standing and may nullify the initial gain of reduced imports. These considerations are less important when the economy is initially at unemployment; then the resources required to produce the import substitutes are abundantly available and need not be attracted from alternative uses.

An immediate implication of the preceding paragraph is that a tariff increases employment if it is imposed during a recession. It is true that unemployed workers and machines are put to work to meet the new demand. It does not follow, however, that the tariff should be used for that purpose; not only can the effect be negated by foreign retaliation (which would cause a reduction in exports), but domestic fiscal and monetary measures are far more effective instruments of domestic stabilization. They can increase employment without the loss in economic efficiency caused by the tariff.

Finally, because a tariff restricts competitive imports, it contributes to whatever monopoly power exists in the domestic economy. This further impairs allocative efficiency, technological progress, and economic growth.

Some Empirical Estimates

With the help of theoretical constructs and statistical tools, we can estimate the various economic effects of the tariff. Most studies of the subject are based on the *reductions* in tariff rates that have taken place multilaterally since World War II. Also, because more information is available for the

Figure 13-10
Schematic Effects of Tariff Reduction

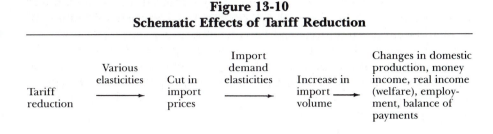

United States than for other countries, our discussion concerns this country, with the latest estimations pertaining to the effects of the "Tokyo Round" of tariff reductions concluded in 1979. The measurements are restricted to the "static" or allocative effect of the tariff.

A possible framework for the analysis of the effect of tariff reductions on the importing country is presented in Figure 13-10. Taking these linkages one at a time, empirical evidence suggests that between one-third and one-half of any reduction in the American tariff accrues to the foreign exporters in the form of increased export prices. The United States is large enough to affect the terms at which it trades. Thus, foreign exporters pay part of its tariff by lowering their export prices. Conversely, when the U.S. tariff is reduced these exporters reap part of the benefit.

It is difficult to determine the effect of these price changes on the volume of imports because it needs to be isolated from other causes affecting imports. Yet the order of magnitude has been assessed. The "Tokyo Round" agreement put into effect during 1980–88, is estimated to raise U.S. exports by $2.7 billion and increase U.S. imports by $2.4 billion. These estimates pertain to the 1974 base period and should be compared with 1974 exports (excluding primary materials) of $64 billion and imports of $58 billion. The estimated employment increase associated with the rise in exports is 190,000 workers, while the rise in imports would lower U.S. employment by 220,000 workers, for a net employment loss of 30,000. The main industries that would benefit from expansion in employment are: machinery, chemicals, metal products, precision instruments, and perhaps aircraft. Contraction would occur in: footwear, leather goods, clothing, and iron and steel. Finally, the welfare effects are relatively small, estimated to yield a net gain of under $.3 billion.[6] These are measured by estimating the size of the two deadweight triangles in Fig. 13–7: $\frac{1}{2} \cdot \Delta$tariff $\cdot \Delta$imports.

Why does the cost of tariff protection appear to be so small? Three reasons come immediately to mind. First, tariff rates in industrial countries

[6] In a separate analysis, the annual welfare cost of the existing U.S. tariff and main quota programs was estimated at $8.5 billion. See D. Tarr and M. Morkre, *Aggregate Costs to the United States of Tariffs and Quotas on Imports*, Washington, D.C., Federal Trade Commission, 1984. For more advanced analysis see A. Dendorff and R. Stern, *The Michigan Model of World Production and Trade*, Cambridge, MA.: MIT Press, 1986; and F. Brown and J. Whalley, "General Equilibrium Evaluation of Tariff—Cutting Proposals," *Economic Journal*, Dec. 1980.

are not extremely high, being concentrated in the 10-to-20 percent range. By comparison, rates upward of 100 percent are common in many developing areas. Second, only a small part of the total production of the large industrial economies is traded internationally, so comparison with total GNP is bound to yield a small ratio. Finally, it should be remembered that in a large country most of the benefits from trade are already realized domestically, because trade is always free within the country. It is the *incremental* benefit that accrues from eliminating the moderate level of protection on external trade that is small. Interestingly enough, although this incremental gain is probably much larger for developing countries, because of the small size of their economies, it is they that insist on having high levels of protection. Indeed, recent empirical studies suggest that developing countries often establish new industries behind a protective wall, which results in "negative value added" when their product is measured at world prices. In other words, the amount of foreign exchange saved by domestic production is less than what it would cost to import the merchandise.

How Protective Is the Tariff?

Public discussions of the tariff issue often involve intercountry comparisons of the level of protection, on which policy decisions frequently are based. But protection cannot be measured or compared simply. What the measure of protection purports to convey is *the amount of potential imports kept out of the country by the tariff.* This is a very difficult figure to derive, and the problems of estimating it are often overlooked or side-stepped in public pronouncements. These problems will now be sorted out.

Ad Valorem and Specific Duty

Whenever specific duties are employed, they must be converted into their *ad valorem* equivalent to facilitate international or intercommodity comparisons. Only when it is expressed as a percent of price is the tariff rate independent of the unit of the commodity on which it is levied, thus making duties on diverse commodities comparable. Normally the conversion is made by dividing the duty by the average price of the transactions undertaken over the preceding year.

Nominal Versus Effective Tariff Rates

Even when expressed as a percent of price, the tariff rate published in the country's tariff schedule (known as the "nominal" rate) does not convey the level of protection accorded to the domestic producers. While nominal tariffs apply to the total value of imports, they protect only the portion of that value produced at home. For example, assume that country A levies a 20 percent import tariff on desks, but imported lumber and other materials that go into the domestic production of desks enter duty-free. Assume further that these imported materials constitute one-half of the final value of the desk, so that the value added in domestic manufacturing is one-half. In other words, if the desk sells for $100, then the manufacturer spends $50 on imported inputs and home production adds another $50 to its value. The 20 percent tax levied on imported desks yields $20 per desk. But this sum protects only that component of the desk's value produced at home, namely half its total value. To that component it accords *effective* protection of 40 percent ($20 as a percentage of $50). If the imported raw materials were taxed at 10 percent, then the effective rate of protection given the desk manufacturer would be 30 percent. It is evident that if the final product entered duty-free, while imported raw materials used in domestic production were taxed, then the domestic producer of the final good would be taxed rather than protected. A tariff on the final product protects domestic import-competing activities; duty on imported materials taxes the users of these materials by raising their cost. Effective protection nets out these two effects.

In essence, the effective protective rate measures the degree of protection given to domestic production activities. It is defined as the percentage increase in *domestic* value added made possible by the tariff structure (that is, tariffs on both the final product *and* on imported inputs) compared to a situation under free trade. The effective protection for a final product increases as the nominal rate imposed on it increases, and as the nominal rate imposed on imported materials used in the production process decreases. It also varies with the proportion of imported inputs that constitute the final value of the product (a proportion that may itself change as the situation changes from free trade to tariff). These relationships can be derived from a mathematical formula.[7] Alternatively, in what follows they are shown in a series of examples.

[7] A simplified formula for the effective protective rate derived from the above definition is:

$$g_j = \frac{t_j - a_{ij}t_i}{1 - a_{ij}}$$

where g_j is the effective protective rate on final product j, t_j is the nominal tariff rate on final product j, t_i is the nominal tariff rate on imported input i, and a_{ij} is the share of i in the total value of j in the absence of tariffs.

The formula is derived as follows. Value added in industry j (per unit of output), without any tariffs, is

$$v_j = p_j(1 - a_{ij})$$

Value added in industry j, with tariffs on both the input and the output, is

$$v'_j = p_j(1 + t_j) - p_j a_{ij}(1 + t_i) = p_j[(1 + t_j) - a_{ij}(1 + t_i)]$$

where p_j and p_i are the prices of the output and input, respectively.

$$g_j = \frac{v'_j - v_j}{v_j} = \frac{p_j[(1 + t_j) - a_{ij}(1 + t_i)] - p_j(1 - a_{ij})}{p_j(1 - a_{ij})}$$

$$= \frac{(1 + t_j) - a_{ij}(1 + t_i) - (1 - a_{ij})}{1 - a_{ij}} = \frac{1 + t_j - a_{ij} - a_{ij}t_i - 1 + a_{ij}}{1 - a_{ij}}$$

$$= \frac{t_j - a_{ij}t_i}{1 - a_{ij}}$$

Consider a leather wallet whose c.i.f. import price in Belgium *under free trade* is $20. The cost of the leather of which the wallet is made is $10 on the world market, so that a wallet made in Belgium out of imported leather would have a domestic value added of $10 at free-trade prices. Translated into Belgian francs at an exchange rate of $1 = 50 francs, we obtain a product (wallet) price of 1000 francs, a world market cost of inputs (leather) of 500 francs, and a free-trade domestic value added of 500 francs.[8]

Case 1   A 20 percent tariff on wallets and on leather will raise the domestic price of a wallet to 1200 francs and that of the leather input to 600 francs. Protection thus enables the Belgian firm to operate at value added of 1200 − 600 = 600 francs, compared with 1000 − 500 = 500 francs, at free-trade prices. The difference of 100 francs, equaling 20 percent of the free-trade value added, is the effective rate of protection. Thus, when the tariff rate on the input equals the tariff rate on the output, the nominal and effective protection on the output are the same. In the present example, they all equal 20 percent.

Case 2   Consider next a case in which the tariff on leather wallets is 40 percent, raising their domestic price to 1400 francs, and the tariff on leather is 20 percent, raising its domestic price to 600 francs. The domestic value added under protection is 1400 − 600 = 800 francs, compared with 500 francs at free-trade prices. The difference of 300 francs constitutes 300/500 = 60 percent effective protection on leather wallets compared with a 40 percent nominal tariff rate. Thus, when the tariff rate on the final output exceeds the rate levied on the input, the effective protection on the output exceeds the nominal rate imposed on it.

Case 3   Next, consider a case in which the tariff on leather wallets is 30 percent, raising their domestic price to 1300 francs, and the tariff on leather is 40 percent, raising its domestic price to 700 francs. The domestic value added under protection is 600 francs, compared with 500 francs at free-trade prices. The difference of 100 francs constitutes a 100/500 = 20 percent effective protection on wallets compared with 30 percent nominal rate. Thus, when the tariff rate on the input exceeds that on the final output, the effective protection accorded the final output falls short of the nominal rate imposed on it.

Case 4   Indeed, the tariff on the input can be so much in excess of the tariff on the output that the effective protection on the output is negative;

---

[8] A problem that arises in obtaining these figures is that the free-trade prices of outputs and inputs, and therefore the value added under free trade, cannot be observed directly in a country under a tariff regime. There are two ways of getting around this problem. The tariff-ridden prices can be deflated by the tariff rates to obtain the implied free-trade prices, or the ratio of the value added to the final product price can be be inferred from that of another country where tariff rates are close to zero.

the product is taxed rather than protected. For example, suppose that the tariff on leather wallets in Belgium is 10 percent, raising the domestic price to 1100 francs, while the duty on leather is 40 percent, raising its domestic price to 700 francs. Value added under protection is then 400 francs, compared with 500 francs under free trade. The result is a *negative* effective protection on wallets of 100 francs or $100/500 = 20$ percent.

In conclusion, the effective protective rate on a product will exceed, be equal to, or fall short of the nominal rate on the product, depending on whether the nominal tariff is higher than, equal to, or lower than the nominal tariffs on material inputs. Negative effective protection results when tariffs raise the cost of inputs by a larger absolute amount than they raise the price of the product.[9]

Case 5   In addition to the tariff rates on the output and input, the effective rate of protection depends also on the share of domestic value added in the product price. This share was assumed to be 0.5 in the above examples. In contrast, assume now that the free-trade c.i.f. import price of a leather wallet in Belgium is $20, but the cost of material input (leather) is $16, so that the value added of $4 constitutes only 20 percent of the price of the wallet. Translated into francs, the price is 1000 francs as before, but the imported inputs are 800 francs and the domestic value added under free trade is only 200 francs. Now reconsider Case 2, above. The 40 percent tariff on wallets raises their domestic price to 1400 francs, while the 20 percent tariff on leather raises its price to 960 francs. The domestic value added under protection becomes $1400 - 960 = 440$ francs, compared with only 200 francs under free trade. This constitutes an effective protective rate on wallets of $240/200 = 120$ percent. This result underscores an important fact. If a country establishes a plant for the final processing of a product, importing most inputs at a semifinal stage of fabrication at zero or very low duties, then even moderate nominal protection on the final product translates into a very high effective protection.

The professional economic literature of the late 1960s and early 1970s is replete with articles refining the concept of effective protection[10] and

[9]In terms of the notation of footnote 7, where g_j is the effective protection on product j,
  If $t_j > t_i$, then $g_j > t_j$.
  If $t_j = t_i$, then $g_j = t_j$.
  If $t_j < t_i$, then $g_j < t_j$.
  If $t_j < a_{ij}t_i$, then $g_j < 0$ (negative protection).

[10]Particular attention has been paid to relaxing the assumptions made in the formula. For example, it was originally assumed that the input coefficient is fixed for each input, as denoted by a_{ij}. But economic theory tells of isoquants that are convex to the origin and along which the firm adjusts its input-use ratio to variations in the relative prices of the inputs. Because tariffs cause such price variations, the fixed a_{ij} should be replaced by a production function in an assumed specified form that allows for price changes. Other assumptions that can be relaxed involve the possibility that some inputs are not traded or that the elasticity of foreign supply of inputs is less than infinite. Finally, a question may be raised about the conformity of this basic concept to general economic theory. Price theory assigns business profits the central role of guiding resource allocation in the economy. By contrast, the theory of effective protection, under which the effective protective rate deter-

measuring its level in many countries—developed and underdeveloped alike. Several important implications follow from this concept, and they will be considered in turn.

First, although the consumer reacts to changes in the final price that reflect the nominal tariff rates, *the producer reacts to changes in the cost of his production processes, and these are affected by the effective rate.* Thus, it is the effective rate of protection that indicates the degree of resource misallocation caused by the tariff structure.

A second corollary to this analysis concerns the tariff structure of most industrial countries. They admit raw materials virtually duty free, semiprocessed goods at moderate duties, and finished manufactures (especially of the labor-intensive variety) at high duty rates. This structure means that the effective protection on finished manufactures is much higher than the nominal rates indicate. Recent calculations suggest that *the effective rates on many finished products are double their nominal counterparts.* Developing countries maintain that the sharp *"escalation"* of effective protection by degree of processing encourages the importation of goods into the developed nations in raw or semiprocessed form and therefore discourages industrialization (in the form of final processing) in the developing world.

A third conclusion, applicable to developed and developing countries alike, is that changes in tariff rates on imported inputs have an inverse effect on the level of protection accorded to final products. The significance of this point becomes apparent when we consider a developing country pursuing an import substitution policy as a road to industrialization. Often in such cases, the country begins by building up a final assembly plant under a high protective tariff and using untaxed imported inputs. As a second stage, the country begins to "deepen" domestic production by manufacturing the inputs at home and according them high protection. And so it proceeds "backward" through the production process adding new "layers" of inputs. What the government often does not realize is the fact that by imposing tariffs on imported inputs, it actually lowers the level of protection accorded the final product. By that very action it may render the final assembly plant unprofitable.

Fourth, this analysis has implications for a country's export position as well. Although export industries must sell at world market prices, they often use imported inputs for which they must pay domestic prices augmented by a tariff. In Case 2 above, if the Belgian producers had to export their wallets at the world market price of $20, or 1000 francs, apiece, but pay a 20 percent tariff on leather, then the tariff would raise the cost of their input from 500 to 600 francs and lower value added from 500 to 400

---

mines the "production effect," assigns this role to value added. But value added contains, in addition to profits, domestic primary (labor, for example) and nonprimary inputs. Thus, profits and value added may not move in the same direction or by the same amounts, and the two criteria may yield conflicting results. This could occur if we were to relax the assumption of fixed input coefficients a_{ij}.

francs. The producers would thus sustain a negative protection—a tax— of 20 percent. To retain the free-trade value added of 500 francs (that is, to compensate the producers for the increased cost of input caused by the tariff) would require that the producers receive an export subsidy of 100 francs, 10 percent of the price of the product. Such subsidies (that is, rebates of the tariff paid on imported materials) are often practiced in developing countries to protect their export position, because in the absence of the subsidy firms may not have any inducement to export.

Finally, rates of effective protection can be used indirectly as a rough guide to determine comparative advantage. The analysis of Chapter 11 revealed that economic efficiency requires the ranking of industries by degree of comparative advantage. A country would then export the commodities ranked high and import those ranked low on its scale of industries. Under free-market competitive conditions, the price mechanism would generate such a ranking, thus bringing about efficient allocation of resources.

But in the developing countries, free-market conditions are rarely in effect. Instead, trade is restricted by a variety of policy instruments, such as high tariffs, import quotas, advance deposits for imports, export subsidies, exchange controls, multiple exchange rates, and so on. Moreover, these restrictions are applied selectively by the government to encourage activities that it perceives to be in the best interest of the country and to discourage others. For example, the government may encourage cheap imports of investment goods (such as machinery) and discourage imports of consumer goods. These restrictions are often coupled with a variety of domestic market distortions, such as artificially high wage rates in certain industries obtained through powerful labor unions. In such cases, not only is the free-market ranking distorted beyond recognition, but producers proceed to use capital-intensive processes relative to the country's factor endowments, because factor remunerations are distorted to such a point that they no longer reflect the factor endowments. (That is, the prices of imported capital equipment are artificially low and the price of labor artifically high.)

Suppose now that, faced with such distorted conditions, the government wishes to embark on a new development plan and decide more rationally which industries or projects it should promote; or, alternatively, an international aid organization must determine what projects to support. How can such new resources be allocated optimally? One possible guide is the effective rate of protection. Because that rate measures the inducement to the protected producer to expand his activity, it also reflects the degree of protection that the industry requires to operate on its present scale. The ranking of industries by the level of effective protection[11] indicates their relative incentive to expand output under the existing structure of protection; it would produce a roughly inverse order to the ranking by comparative advantage. The industries at the low end of the scale in terms of

[11]In one study of the East African tariff, 34 industries were ranked according to their effective protection, with rates ranging all the way from 900 percent to − 46 percent.

effective protection are the ones that should be expanded. (Note that professional opinion is divided on the validity of this use of the effective protection concept.)

A closely related guide to project selection is the domestic resource cost (DRC) of foreign exchange earned by exports or saved by import substitution. Every dollar so earned (or saved) by a developing country costs a certain amount in domestic currency (representing a bundle of domestic resources) expended on processing and other activities. The activities that should be supported are those in which the cost of a dollar earned or saved is least. The ranking of industries from the high to the low domestic currency cost per dollar earned would produce an ordering roughly similar to the ranking from high to low effective protection. In both cases, it is the low-ranking industries that deserve support and encouragement to expand.[12]

This completes the discussion of effective protection. We turn next to other problems encountered in assessing how protective the tariff is.

Aggregation Problems

Suppose we were given the effective rates of protection, expressed in percentage terms, for all commodities and countries. Since all countries do not employ the same tariff classification, it is necessary for comparative purposes to convert all rates into a common classification. Also, because one often wishes to relate tariff rates to trade flows, it is desirable to have this common classification coincide with the SITC, by which all international trade is reported. Indeed, the SITC was revised in 1961 to conform more closely to the Brussels Tariff Nomenclature (BTN). There is now a readily available and easily accessible concordance between the two. It is a common objective of scholars and policymakers alike to aggregate tariff rates from the highly detailed and divergent commodity classifications by which they are reported into, say, the three-digit SITC. Some people may wish further to aggregate them into one average figure for each country, so as to have a ready-made intercountry comparison of the levels of protection.

But the aggregation of tariff rates is a thorny issue; there is no satisfactory way to average out the rates imposed on diverse commodities. The use of simple unweighted averages of tariff rates implicitly assumes that each commodity is of equal importance in the country's import trade. This, of course, is not realistic. An alternative aggregation procedure is to compute weighted averages, but here the problem is what weights to use. Ideally, one should weigh each rate by what imports would have been in the absence

---

[12]A widely used manual on industrial cost-benefit analysis suggests the following method for assessing proposed industrial projects: Evaluate all expected costs and benefits at *world prices*, which (in contrast to the often distorted prices prevailing at home) represent the country's real trading opportunities. The resulting streams of annual costs and benefits should then be discounted at a rate of something like 10 percent in real terms (that is, after allowing for inflation, the rate may be 15 to 20 percent), thereby translating future values into their present worth. Finally, the single cost figure should be subtracted from the benefit figure; if there is a surplus, the project is worth undertaking. (See Little and Mirreless, *Manual of Industrial Project Analysis in Developing Countries*, OECD, Paris, 1969.)

of the tariff. But because this is not known, many investigators employ the country's own tariff-ridden imports as weights. Such a procedure invariably biases the results downward, because the very high tariffs permit fewer imports and therefore receive little weight. At the extreme, a prohibitive tariff excludes all imports and therefore receives no weight and will not be represented at all in the calculation. A better solution is to weigh each tariff by the domestic consumption of the product. But because the two magnitudes are often not available on the same commodity classification basis, a possible compromise is to weigh each tariff by total world (or OECD) trade in the commodity to which the rate applies. Even this procedure incorporates some downward bias because of the similarity in the tariff structures of industrial countries.

It is evident that press reports that use average figures to compare the level of protection of various countries are all subject to errors and biases. To have any value, they should be accompanied by a frequency distribution of the tariff rates as supplementary information or, lacking that, a rough idea of the range within which the country's tariff rates tend to concentrate. Such information is available in the GATT's *Basic Documentation for the Tariff Study* (Geneva, 1971), which presents average pre-Tokyo Round tariff rates and frequency distribution of tariff lines for several countries.

The Response to Price Change

Even in dealing with disaggregative figures, the nominal and effective tariffs do not, in and of themselves, provide a precise indication of the level of protection. In the final analysis, that level refers to the quantity of the imported commodity excluded from the domestic market. And that exclusion operates through the price mechanism; it comes about because the tariff raises the price of imports relative to that of domestic substitutes. But the extent to which the import price rises and the foreign export price falls depends on various elasticities, as was seen earlier in this chapter. More important, the amount of imports excluded by a given percentage increase in import price depends on the response of the public to the price increase (the elasticity of demand for imports). The higher the response, the larger will be the exclusion caused by a given percentage rise in price and the more protective a given tariff will be.

This degree of response depends on a variety of factors, not the least of which is the availability of domestic substitutes. But one important variable determining the import-demand elasticity for any commodity is the share of imports in domestic production and consumption. It can be shown that the larger the share of imports, the smaller will be the elasticity (see Appendix VIII). This relation is important because it permits us to make *a priori* judgments in some cases. Suppose one is comparing the degree of protection afforded by the American tariff with that of a European country, say Italy. Because imports occupy a much smaller share of the U.S. market than of the Italian, the import-demand elasticity is higher in America and so is the degree of protection embodied in a given percentage price rise. Conversely, when we talk of multilateral tariff reduction, a given percentage reduction in the U.S. import price is translated into a larger increase in the volume of imports than in virtually any other country.

Arguments for Protection

Against the background developed thus far, we can briefly evaluate some of the arguments heard in political and economic circles on behalf of the tariff. From the viewpoint of the welfare of the world as a whole, the most popular claim made for tariff protection is the so-called infant-industry argument. It asserts that industries that may benefit from large-scale operations because of the existence of external economies (such as good transport facilities, a well-trained labor force, or the "learning by doing" effect) should be allowed to grow to optimum size under a protective tariff.[13] Once that size is attained, the tariff can be removed, leaving behind a viable and competitive industry. Theoretically, this is a valid argument. Indeed, Japan's development is replete with illustrations of how an industry can be developed and fostered under tariff protection until it reaches an optimum size. In its development policy, Japan made effective use of both tariff protection and imported technology in the form of licensing agreements. Today it is one of the world's largest exporters.

Often there are difficulties with the practical application of this theory. First, the argument can be abused, as it has been at times by declining industries that attempt to protect their position in the market and thereby perpetuate inefficiency. Even the American steel industry advanced the argument once in an effort to convince Congress to impose import quotas on steel. Second, once it has been imposed, a tariff is rather difficult to eliminate, regardless of the industry's competitive standing. And finally, even in cases where the infant-industry position applies, it is more efficient to offer a direct subsidy as a means of helping the industry to expand. While the tariff imposes both production and consumption costs on the economy, a subsidy embodies only production costs, not consumption costs. More generally, a tariff is equivalent to a tax on the consumer *plus* a (disguised) subsidy to the producer. By contrast, a direct subsidy does not contain the tax element, and the subsidy component is provided in an overt fashion. It is then open for all interested parties to inspect and evaluate. And, when the time comes, it is somewhat easier to discontinue.

From the point of view of an individual nation taken as a whole, the only rational argument for the tariff is the improvement in terms of trade (the "optimum tariff"). However, this applies only to the major importers that are large enough to exercise monopoly power and affect the terms at which they trade. In a very real sense, such a tariff must be viewed as a

[13]Recently a group of British economists at Cambridge University recommended import controls for the United Kingdom, in order to assure British industry high-capacity operations.

transfer of resources from the relatively poor nations to the very large and wealthy nations—a transfer that is undesirable on equity and other grounds and is certainly in conflict with the national objectives embodied in a foreign-aid program.

Tariffs may at times be used to increase employment or improve the balance of payments. But both objectives can be met more effectively and more efficiently by fiscal, monetary, or exchange-rate policies. Protection is an expensive way to create jobs. On the other hand, a period of unemployment in the domestic economy is not a good time to reduce tariffs. After all, the main objective of such a reduction is to increase efficiency by transferring resources to industries in which the country has a comparative advantage, and the existence of widespread unemployment would make such a transfer very difficult if not impossible. (Allocative efficiency matters less when resources are not fully employed.) In recent years, the U.S. labor movement has generally favored protectionism for fear of job losses in such import-competing industries as steel, footwear, and textiles. However, foreign retaliation can create equally severe unemployment in the export industries. Labor's argument may be on firmer ground when the U.S. tariff is designed to offset unfair trading practices by foreign countries, such as predatory dumping (see Chapter 14).

In 1977–78 and again in 1981–86, there was a marked increase in the clamor for protection in the United States. In part, this was due to the massive trade deficits, which had adverse effects on employment and output in the traded-goods sectors. Not only that, but the impact was concentrated in a few highly visible industries: footwear and textiles on the one hand, and steel, autos, and certain high-technology items on the other. The first group are labor-intensive industries, with import competition coming mainly from the developing countries. The price differential between imports and domestic substitutes is very large. In the long run, production in these industries would have to contract in the industrial countries, including the U.S., and switch to highly specialized products within the industry. The role of public policy is to make the transition gradual and ease the adjustment through a variety of assistance measures. In the second group, competition comes mainly from Europe and Japan, and the price differential is relatively small. Depreciation of the dollar—coupled with attempts to modernize the industry, hold the line on wages, and reduce costs—ought to make these industries more competitive.

Perusal of testimonies before congressional committees on foreign trade reveals a whole array of arguments for protection, only a few of which can be included here. That the perpetual demand for tariffs to equalize wage rates among nations (known as the "scientific tariff") makes no economic sense was already shown in Chapter 11. It was demonstrated that American wages are higher because productivity is higher than in other countries, and that such a wage differential is necessary to the existence of two-way trade. Empirical studies have shown two things. First, within the United States, the import-competing industries—such as textiles—that complain about low foreign wages are themselves low-wage industries by American standards. The export industries, from aircraft to computers, successfully meet foreign competition on both domestic and foreign grounds, despite the fact that their wages far exceed those paid the textile workers. This is not surprising. It is precisely what one would expect on the basis of productivity differences. Foreign competition would force contraction of the textile industry, and the resources released from it could be devoted to products in which this country possesses a comparative advantage, such as computers. These industries can pay the highest wages and still compete effectively. Second, empirical findings do not support the contention that foreign producers gain access to the American market by paying substandard wages, judged by the standards prevailing in these countries.

Demands to keep out cheap foreign imports—simply because they undersell local produce—go back many years. A famous reply to this argument is contained in a short satire by Fredric Bastiat. Titled "The Petition of the Candlemakers," it is an imaginary petition presented to the French Chamber of Deputies in the early nineteenth century:

> We are subjected to the intolerable competition of a foreign rival whose superior facilities for producing light enable him to flood the French market at so low a price as to take away all our customers the moment he appears, suddenly reducing an important branch of French industry to stagnation. This rival is the sun.
>
> We request a law to shut up all windows, dormers, skylights, openings, holes, chinks, and fissures through which sunlight penetrates. Our industry provides such valuable manufactures that our country cannot, without ingratitude, leave us now to struggle unprotected through so unequal a contest. . . . In short, granting our petition will greatly develop every branch of agriculture. Navigation will equally profit. Thousands of vessels will soon be employed in whaling, and thence will arise a navy capable of upholding the honor of France. . . .
>
> Do you object that the consumer must pay the price of protecting us? You have yourselves already answered the objection. When told that the consumer is interested in free importation of iron, coal, corn, wheat, cloth, etc., you have answered that the producer is interested in their exclusion. You have always acted to *encourage labor,* to *increase the demand for labor.*
>
> Will you say that sunlight is a free gift, and that to repulse free gifts is to repulse riches under pretense of encouraging the means of obtaining them? Take care—you deal a death-blow to your own policy. Remember: hitherto you have always repulsed foreign produce because it was an approach to a free gift; and the closer this approach, the more you have repulsed the good. . . .
>
> When we buy a Portuguese orange at half the price of a French orange, we in effect get it half as a gift. If you protect national labor against the competition of a *half-gift,* what principle justifies allowing the importation of something just because it is *entirely a gift?* . . . The difference in price between an imported article and the corresponding French article is a *free gift* to us. The bigger the difference, the bigger the gift. . . . The question is whether

you wish for France the benefit of free consumption or the supposed advantages of laborious production. Choose, but be consistent.[14]

Industries often claim that their products and the labor skills they utilize are essential to national security, and should therefore be preserved by a tariff. Whether true or not, this is not a subject on which the economist can pass judgment, except to indicate that if it is true the industry should be directly and overtly subsidized out of the defense budget.

Similarly, the argument that a nation needs the tariff in order to have something to bargain down in tariff negotiations is economically unsound, because the country is better off without the tariff, regardless of the level of protection it encounters in the markets of its trading partners. If the argument is modified to suggest that the "bargaining tariff" is used to secure the best of all worlds in which no nation employs a protective tariff, then its validity depends on the effectiveness of the tariff in securing such a situation.

A case for protection is sometimes made from the point of view of a single factor of production: Through its domestic effects, the tariff can be used to redistribute income among factors (in favor of the relatively scarce factors and away from the relatively abundant ones) or income groups. But whether desirable or not, there are other, more efficient, means of redistributing income in society (that is, taxes and subsidies, as mentioned previously).

Finally, many arguments for protection have been advanced in recent years with respect to developing economies. They suggest that the tariff and other means of commercial policy be used to rectify market imperfections existing in the domestic economies of these countries. For example, it has been demonstrated that labor mobility between sectors of the economy is low in many developing countries. This phenomenon is particularly apparent with respect to movement from subsistence agriculture to manufacturing and has its origin in the traditional attachment of the indigenous population to its place of birth and the extended family. But suppose that economic efficiency requires such a move and that the wage differential is not large enough to overcome the inherent obstacles to mobility. The proposed remedy is to impose a protective tariff on manufactured imports. That would enable industrialists to charge higher prices for their products and thus pay higher wages, inducing labor to move to manufacturing. In other words, where the allocative mechanism in the economy is not sufficiently lubricated in the sense that resources do not respond swiftly or in sufficient quantities to market price differentials, there is a need to artificially augment the differential in order to bring about the necessary mobility. The tool suggested for accomplishing this is the protective tariff.

[14]A condensation of Bastiat's petition quoted from Yeager and Tuerck, *Trade Policy and the Price System,* Scranton, Pa., International Textbook Co., 1966. Ironically, in August 1986 candle imports from China were found to injure the U.S. candle industry.

The argument makes sense as far as it goes. It suffers from ignoring the fact that there are far better instruments than tariffs to produce wage differentials and induce mobility. Direct subsidy to labor to help it move, or to the industry itself to help defray the cost of higher wages, comes immediately to mind. The same may be said about the use of tariff policy to eliminate all sorts of domestic distortions,[15] to achieve a desired investment pattern, or to promote rapid growth of certain industries. There is a whole array of instruments at the disposal of the government, and it is usually suboptimal to use international *commercial* policy to influence the *domestic* economy. Distortions should be dealt with by measures that come as close as possible to the source of the trouble; otherwise undesirable side-effects would be created. Hence it is misguided to call upon tariff protection to correct a variety of economic and social ills. But the point is purely academic if the country is so underdeveloped that no policy instruments other than the tariff are available.

In sum, while tariff protection is very common in the present-day world, rational justifications for its use are few and far between. The world as a whole, as well as most individual countries, would be better off if it were dispensed with as an instrument of national policy. The question examined next is whether there has been any progress toward this end.

Approaches to Free Trade

Although it is in the interest of most industrial countries to abolish tariffs, even unilaterally, it is a fact of political and economic life that they are extremely reluctant to do so. There have been instances of unilateral tariff reduction (as in Germany in the mid-1950s and in Japan in 1978), but not many. Either because of prestige attached to diversified industrial production or because of the political pressure of social interest groups, tariff cuts appear to be as painful to the nation as tooth extraction is to the individual.

Any country reducing its level of protection feels that it is giving away something valuable and must obtain something in return from its trading partners. Tariff reduction has come to be regarded as a *concession* to others and is offered only reciprocally. It has also become a subject of tough and prolonged international bargaining, in which each party tries to "extract" as much as possible from its partners and to "surrender" as little as possible in return. Certainly, each delegation returning home from negotiating ses-

---

[15] In developed and devloping countries alike, if factors of production are not mobile between industries, then the introduction of trade into an isolated economy will not produce the expected shift in resource allocation and production mix. The resources that remain "stuck" in the import-competing industries will suffer a reduction in remunerations. But because the consumers will still enjoy the more favorable international prices, society as a whole benefits from the introduction of trade. However, if in addition to factor immobility there is wage rigidity, so that factors refuse to accept a reduction in remunerations, unemployment will result. Under these conditions the economy may be better off without trade than with it. But domestic measures designed to promote factor mobility and wage flexibility are superior to commercial policy for dealing with this situation.

sions attempts to convince local politicians that it obtained more and better tariff concessions than it gave away—clearly an impossible outcome for all parties at one and the same time.

The International Approach

The first approach is associated with the General Agreement on Tariffs and Trade (GATT), an international organization with a membership of 90 countries devoted to the promotion of international trade in general and the reduction of trade barriers in particular. Its members, known as the contracting parties to the GATT, hold periodic negotiating conferences in which tariff "concessions" are exchanged. The reductions agreed upon by any two or more partners are then extended to all member nations. This rule is known as the Unconditional Most Favored Nation Principle (MFN); it guards against discrimination in international trade. The result is successive rounds of tariff reductions, each applying to all sources of supply on a nondiscriminatory basis. The last completed set of tariff reductions, known as the "Tokyo Round," was negotiated during the years 1975–79. It resulted in average tariff cuts of approximately 35 percent of the duties prevailing in the mid-1970s, with the reduction being "staged" over a nine-year period: 1980–88. The negotiating process and the rules under which the GATT operates will be described in Chapter 16.

The approach, although tedious and laborious in the extreme, invariably leads to a worldwide increase in productive efficiency—as the world moves to specialize along lines dictated by comparative advantage—and to more desirable consumption patterns. Although the gains are not equally distributed, and some countries may even lose, there is a gain to the world as a whole. Additionally, small countries may experience important "dynamic" benefits flowing from the increased size of their markets and curtailed monopoly power at home. It can be shown that, starting from a certain nonprohibitive tariff level, each round of tariff reduction is less beneficial than the one before, because it applies to lower protection rates (see "Economic Cost of the Tariff," in Appendix VIII).

The Regional Approach

The regional approach is exemplified by customs unions and free-trade areas. A customs union involves two or more countries that abolish all, or nearly all, trade restrictions among themselves and set up a common and uniform tariff against outsiders. The European Community[16] (EC) or Common Market, is a customs union that originally encompassed West Germany, France, Italy, Belgium, the Netherlands, and Luxembourg. It was enlarged, as of July 1, 1977, to include Great Britain, Denmark, and Ireland. The 1981 accession of Greece and the 1986 accession of Spain and Portugal

---

[16]Originally called the European Economic Community (EEC), the name was changed in the mid-1970s to the European Community (EC). Consequently, we shall retain the name EEC in any references pertaining to years prior to 1976.

increased the Community's size to twelve countries. Trade among members is free of restrictions; nonmembers must pay the common external tariff. An American producer shipping to France is discriminated against in favor of a West German competitor to the extent of the duty.

In a free-trade area, trade among the member countries is also completely liberalized, or nearly so. But there is no common tariff against nonmember countries; each country is free to impose its own duty. The European Free Trade Association (EFTA) is a free-trade area encompassing Sweden, Norway, Switzerland, Finland, Iceland, and Austria. An American exporter to Sweden is discriminated against in favor of a Swiss counterpart by the level of the Swedish duty. The United States concluded an FTA agreement with Israel in 1985, and is contemplating similar negotiations with Canada. Australia and New Zealand are also contemplating a free-trade area. Customs unions and free-trade areas are exempt from GATT's Most Favored Nation rule. The European organizations will be discussed in detail in Chapter 16. It is the approach to trade liberalization that concerns us here. Unlike the international approach, it may or may not lead to an improvement in world allocative efficiency, because it contains an important element of discrimination against nonmember countries.

Indeed, the theory of customs unions, developed since World War II, deals mainly with the effect of regional integration on world allocative efficiency. To be sure, other effects of customs unions—such as the impact on the economic welfare or the balance of payments of a single integrating country—have been treated in some detail, but our main concern is with the first effect. Its theoretical interest lies in demonstrating that not every partial movement toward the optimal world of free trade is necessarily beneficial. Each case must be examined on its merits.

Static Effects   Consider a three-country world in which countries A and B form a customs union to the exclusion of C. In other words, A and B abolish all trade restrictions between themselves, while their imports from C become subject to the common external tariff. The action has two effects. With respect to products in which A and B are competitive, the elimination of tariffs between them causes the replacement of some high-cost production by imports from the partner country. This effect, known as "trade creation," is favorable to world welfare because it rationally reorganizes production within the union. Second, for products in which country C is competitive with one of the integrating countries, A or B begins to import from the other what it earlier imported from C. If C is the most efficient producer, it would be the major supplier as long as its products receive the same tariff treatment as those of its competitor. But the tariff discrimination induces diversion of trade away from C toward a member country. This effect, known as "trade diversion," is unfavorable, because it reorganizes world production less efficiently. Production shifts from the most efficient locations in C to less efficient ones inside the union. Finally, there is a favorable consumption effect, as consumers in each member state benefit

Figure 13-11
Static Effects of a Customs Union

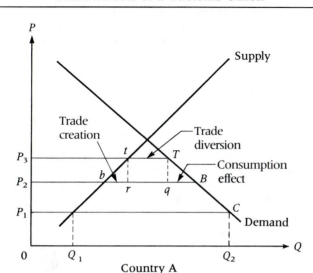

Country A

from price reduction on imports from the partner country when intra-union tariffs are removed. Indeed, a net unfavorable production effect (when trade diversion exceeds creation) may be more than offset by the consumption effect, yielding a net gain in welfare.

These three effects can be illustrated with the help of a partial equilibrium diagram pertaining to one commodity imported into country A. For simplicity, we assume that A is a small country, facing infinitely elastic (horizontal) supply curves from countries B and C (for a more elaborate presentation, see Appendix VIII). Figure 13-11 shows the domestic demand and supply in country A for the imported product; it also shows the horizontal supply curves $\overline{P_1C}$ of country C and $\overline{P_2B}$ of country B. Country C is the least-cost producer.

Under free trade, price $\overline{0P_1}$ will prevail and quantity $\overline{Q_1Q_2}$ will be imported from country C. Next, if A imposes a nondiscriminatory tariff $\overline{P_1P_3}$, the domestic price rises to $0P_3$. Imports decline to $\overline{tT}$, but they come only from the most efficient supplier, country C, because suppliers from B will not be competitive. Finally, when A forms a customs union with B, to the exclusion of C, the tariff $\overline{P_1P_3}$ (assumed for simplicity to remain unchanged) is charged only on imports from C, not on those from B. The domestic price declines to $\overline{0P_2}$ and imports rise to $\overline{bB}$, but they will now come exclusively from B (because supply curves are infinitely elastic).

Our concern is in comparing the last two situations. Imports into A increase from $\overline{tT}$ to $\overline{bB}$. Trade diversion is represented by $\overline{tT}$, the decline in imports from the most efficient producer, country C. On the other hand,

$\overline{br}$, the decrease in domestic output in A and its replacement by imports from B, represents trade creation, while $\overline{qB}$ is the favorable consumption effect representing the increase in domestic consumption.

Although these basic effects need to be modified in various ways to account for such factors as the impact of the customs union on C's trade with D, E, and F in a multicountry world, and for possible balance-of-payments policies in the customs union, they do constitute the major "static" influences. Their relative magnitude determines whether the customs union is, on balance, favorable to worldwide allocative efficiency. The tools of economic and statistical analysis make it possible to measure or at least to approximate these magnitudes. But the estimation is complex. It is not just a matter of looking at the increase in intra-area trade volume: First, because this volume is influenced by many factors other than the formation of the customs union and, second, because even if the "integration effect" were isolated, the observed increase in intra-union trade comprises the trade creation and diversion combined.

The increase in imports into A from B partly reflects a decline in A's own production (trade creation), while in part it is a substitute for imports from C (trade diversion). In order to disentangle the two influences and get at "trade creation," one must subtract from the total increase in imports (adjusted to exclude noncustoms union influences) the decline in imports from nonmember countries (trade diversion) caused by integration. This is a rather complex statistical task, and the reader should not be misled by frequent press reports that identify simple changes in trade values among continental countries with either creation or diversion of trade.

Even without measurement, we can identify some factors that have *a priori* bearing on the relative size of the two effects. The larger the customs union, the smaller is the scope for trade diversion and the better is the chance that the customs union will have a favorable effect. At the extreme lies a "customs union" encompassing the entire world, where only trade creation and no trade diversion can occur, yielding the optimal situation of universal free trade. Second, the more similar the production patterns are within the integrating countries and the larger the differences are in production costs between them, the greater the scope is for trade creation. One proxy for the differences in production costs is the preintegration tariff rates levied by the individual countries to protect their high-cost producers. Considerable variation in preintegration rates on the same product among the countries might be taken as an indication of large differences in production costs. In general, the higher the pre-union tariff rates, the better the chances are for large trade creation as these rates are dismantled. Finally, the lower the common external tariff of the customs union, the less will be the degree of discrimination against outsiders and the smaller will be the scope for trade diversion.

Estimated annual trade creation in manufactures of the original EEC of six countries is $10 billion for 1969–70, and trade diversion is less than $2 billion. The respective figures for the original EFTA are $3 billion and

$1 billion. Enlargement of the EC from six to nine countries is estimated to have resulted in $28 billion and $5 billion of annual trade creation and diversion respectively for 1977–78.[17] (Note however that these estimates are in current dollars; between 1970 and 1978 EC prices doubled.) It may be noted here that the creation of the EEC has not led to large-scale contraction of entire industries in any one country and their replacement by imports from another member. The tendency toward inter-industry specialization has been very limited. Instead, the main trend is toward intra-industry specialization: The same industry in various member countries moves toward specialization in specific types of subproducts (see Chapter 12). This eases adjustment to trade liberalization.

Dynamic Effects   Returning now to the theory of customs unions, there is more to their effect on world welfare than allocative efficiency. At least as important are the dynamic or growth considerations. A customs union expands the size of the market because of both the creation and diversion of trade. This makes possible production on a larger scale and infuses competition into markets from which it might have been absent. Indeed, the United States can be viewed as a large customs union, in which the huge size of the market has made possible the establishment of many competitive units, each with large-scale production. This fact is partly responsible for the tremendous productivity of the American economy.

In the case of a new customs union, the scale effect is likely to be more powerful in the smaller integrating countries, because large countries enjoy these benefits even in the absence of integration. The favorable growth effect also stimulates imports from nonmember countries, partly offsetting static trade diversion. However, nonmember countries may on balance experience a reduction in their exports to the customs union, and this in turn contracts the size of their market and adversely affects their growth rates. The smaller they are to begin with, the more important this factor is likely to be. Again, favorable and adverse influences must be weighed against each other to assess the net impact on worldwide growth. The immense difficulties in doing this arise from the fact that a multitude of factors influence the growth rate, and it is not easy to isolate the effect of integration.

Finally, since the elimination of tariffs in the case of a customs union is not reversible, the expansion of the market is certain to last. This stim-

---

[17] A common measure of trade creation is the change in the ratio of total (external plus intracommunity) imports to consumption in the EEC between two years before and after integration, allowance being made for the effect on that ratio of factors other than integration. This is so because with constant consumption, the rise in imports equals the decline in domestic output. Trade diversion is measured by the change of external imports to consumption over the same period, and with similar allowance for nonintegration effects. See M. E. Kreinin: "Effects of the EEC on Imports of Manufactures," *Economic Journal*, September 1972, and "The Static Effect of EC Enlargement on Trade in Manufactured Products," *Kyklos*, 1981, pp. 60–71. For a study relating to another area of the world, see M. E. Kreinin, "North American Economic Integration," *Law and Contemporary Problems*, Summer 1981, pp. 7–31.

ulates investments, both domestic and foreign, and thereby increases the growth rate. Such "investment creation" can be partly offset by what might be called "investment diversion," when investments are diverted from the most rational location in the world to the integrating region because of the tariff discrimination. Thus, if an American-based company shifts the location of a projected plant from the United States or Canada to the EC in order to circumvent the tariff wall and gain access to a large market, the outcome is unfavorable to worldwide growth. The same may be said of potential foreign-investment projects in nonmember countries (such as a developing country) that never materialize because they depend too much on export to the customs union; and the possibility of such exports comes into question because they would be discriminated against in the customs union.

In sum, the regional approach has a large number of effects that require individual study. The industrial countries have proceeded along both avenues of trade liberalization since World War II. Under the auspices of the GATT, tariffs have been lowered gradually to moderate levels. At the same time, small groups of countries have proceeded to eliminate tariffs altogether, and those in the EC have taken some further measures to form a cohesive group.

Review Questions

1. Distinguish between:
   a. Ad valorem and specific tariff
   b. Nominal and effective protection
   c. Customs union and free-trade area
   d. GATT and the European Community
   e. Discriminatory and non-discriminatory tariff reduction
   f. Trade creation and trade diversion (of a customs union)
   g. An import and export tax

2. a. Explain the concept of "effective rate of protection."
   b. What does the effective rate on final goods depend upon and how?
   c. In what way does the effective rate analysis help to illuminate these policy issues:

      • "Deepening" of production in LDCs
      • Escalation of tariff rates by degree of processing in industrial countries

3. Assume that we have a two-country, tariff-ridden world, and that the countries decide to remove the tariff in two *successive steps* of equal tariff cuts. Using a partial equilibrium diagram, demonstrate that the welfare benefits to the "world as a whole" are greater from the first than from the second tariff reduction. (You may wish to consult Appendix VIII.) What empirical information do you have about the effects of tariff reductions?

4. Explain the concept of the "optimum tariff." How can a tariff improve the welfare of one country and lower that of the world as a whole? (Use diagrams.)

5. "A *customs union* constitutes a partial movement towards free trade and *must* therefore lead to an improvement in world welfare." Do you agree? Explain the statement, using a diagram to show the three effects of a *customs union*. Does the increase in intra-union trade measure trade creation?

6. Suppose the U.S. levied a 20 percent tariff on imported cars. Explain the effects on the:
   a. U.S. terms of trade (Use both partial and general equilibrium analysis.)
   b. Distribution of income within the U.S.
   c. U.S. welfare (or real income).
   Use graphs as needed.

7. Review and evaluate three common arguments for protection.

8. *Evaluate* each of the following statements:
   a. A tariff on textiles is equivalent to a tax on consumers and a subsidy to the textile producers and workers. (Use a diagram.)
   b. A tariff lowers the real income of the country, while at the same time it distributes income from the consumers to the governments and to the import-competing industry. (Use a diagram.)
   c. The best way to reduce the $200 billion U.S. budget deficit is to impose a 50 percent tariff surcharge to collect revenue.
   d. Chinese mushrooms undersell American mushrooms because Chinese labor is cheaper than American labor. We should impose a high tariff on mushrooms until China agrees to raise wage rates to the level prevailing in the U.S.

9. Assess the possible effects of a free trade area between the United States and Canada. Is such a FTA likely to lead to an expansion of inter- or intra-industry trade? How would such a FTA conform to the MFN provision of GATT?

14

Non-Tariff Barriers (NTBs) to Trade

*A*lthough the tariff is a widely used instrument of protection, it is by no means the only one, nor is it the most harmful. Indeed, as tariff rates have been reduced under programs of multilateral trade liberalization, the *nontariff barriers* loom increasingly important. Some of these devices will be considered in this chapter. However, it should be remembered that restrictive as these may be, they are only interferences with an otherwise free-market system. Eastern European bloc trading, in which international trade is conducted by government corporations and is not subject to the decisions of individuals, goes considerably further in the degree of control it implies than any of the methods discussed here.

Import Quotas

Instead of imposing a tax on an imported commodity, as under the tariff, the government may directly restrict the volume of permissible imports to a certain maximum level. The absolute limit is known as the *import quota*. For example, the number of cars imported may be limited to 10,000, or the volume of steel to 100,000 tons. These limits are presumably below what would be imported under free-market conditions, for otherwise there would be no need for the quota. Indeed, if free-market demand for imports falls below the quota, the quota becomes ineffective.

How Common Are Import Quotas?

Although the main purpose of quotas is to protect domestic industries by restricting imports, they have also been employed to cope with balance-of-payments deficits and to raise home employment. Quotas were very common in Western Europe immediately after World War II. Today, international trade in manufactured goods is virtually free of such restrictions in the developed nations. Import quotas are prohibited by the GATT.

Trade in agricultural products is subject to a variety of quantitative restrictions in virtually all the industrial countries, including the United States. They all protect their agricultural sectors because the farmers are politically powerful. In the United States as well as in the European Community, aid to farmers often takes the form of price-support programs— the government sets prices somewhere above the free-market level and purchases the food surpluses that result from that fixed price. If imports were allowed in freely, the government would be supporting the prices (and income) of both foreign and domestic farmers. In order to maintain domestic prices above the international level, the United States imposes import quotas; at the same time, it often employs export subsidies to dispose of the accumulated surpluses overseas. For example, the U.S. sugar import quota is designed to maintain a U.S. sugar price at double the world market level. It will be seen in Chapter 16 that the European Community has devised some new and unique methods of agricultural protection. Tight Japanese import quotas on food products incur the wrath of American farmers and the U.S. government, but their relaxation is furiously resisted by the inefficient Japanese farm industry. On the other hand, the United States and other countries have on occasion liberalized or lifted quota restrictions to combat specific shortages or general inflation. Furthermore, during the food "shortages" of 1973, the United States and the European Community resorted to export bans on certain critical products.

In developing countries quotas are used in all sectors, for a mixture of reasons. Often, these countries attempt to develop new industries to produce substitutes for imported goods and believe that this can be accomplished only under a protective shield of import quotas. Tariffs, even high ones, do not provide the local manufacturer with the same degree of certainty. No one knows the level of supply and demand response to price change nor, therefore, how much of a foreign commodity would be excluded from the domestic market by a given tariff level. Consumers may prefer imported, internationally known brands even at higher prices. And foreign producers may choose to absorb part of the duty in order to avoid losing sales. None of these uncertainties exists in the case of quotas, where the volume of imports is limited by administrative action.

Economic Effects of Quotas

Because it restricts the volume of imports, the import quota raises the domestic price of the imported commodity in much the same way as does the tariff.[1] Consumption declines as consumers switch to less desirable substitutes, while domestic production of substitute products expands under the protection accorded to their producers, with resources drawn from other (presumably

---

[1] The excess of domestic over foreign price can be regarded as the "implicit tariff" equivalent of the nontariff barrier.

more efficient) industries. In contrast to the tariff, however, there is no revenue to the government. In this case it accrues to the importers, who are now able to charge a higher price for each unit of the restricted supply. This is referred to as *monopoly profit,* because a monopolist reaps his profit in the same manner—by curtailing output and thus charging a higher price compared with what he would charge under competition. Only by auctioning off the import licenses can the government recoup this revenue.

But the revenue aspect is not the only important difference between a tariff and a quota. While the tariff interferes with the market mechanism, a quota replaces it altogether with arbitrary government decisions. With tariffs, domestic price cannot differ from world price by more than the duty; and unlimited quantities of a product may be imported by anyone, provided he is eager enough for the good to pay the tax. Thus, starting from a given tariff-ridden situation, with its attendant level of consumption and production costs, any rise in domestic demand can be satisfied from increased imports at the same price. Domestic production does not rise nor does the cost of protection in terms of misallocated resources and reduced desirability of the consumption mix. This is not so in the case of a quota. Here there is no limit to the differential between domestic and world prices. Since an upward quantity adjustment is not possible, any rise in domestic demand will simply raise the domestic price, leaving admissible imports unaltered. Such an increase raises the production and consumption costs of protection by forcing further misallocation of resources and less desirable consumption patterns.

Figure 14-1 describes the domestic situation in the car market of a small car-importing nation that faces infinitely elastic export supply on world markets. In the absence of international trade, domestic price is P_1, while under free trade the price (world price) is P_2 and $\overline{ab}$ ($= \overline{cd}$) units are imported. A tariff t raises the domestic price to P_3, and imports are reduced to $\overline{gh}$ ($= \overline{ef}$). The same effect on the domestic price and the volume of imports would be produced if the government imposed an import quota of $\overline{gh}$. Indeed, if conditions were competitive in all markets, and if the import licenses were auctioned to produce the same government revenue as under the tariff, the initial effects of a tariff and a quota would be identical. This is referred to as the "equivalence" of a tariff and a quota.

But suppose there is an upward shift in domestic demand to D'. Under a tariff t, the domestic price can never exceed world price (P_2) plus the tariff. It therefore remains at P_3, and the volume of imports rises from $\overline{ef}$ to $\overline{ei}$. In other words, the increase in demand is accommodated by an increase in the volume of trade. On the other hand, in the case of an import quota, quantity adjustment is not possible; the volume of imports is fixed at $\overline{ef}$. Consequently, the upward shift in demand will produce a price adjustment. Domestic price rises to P_4, where the quantity imported remains unchanged at $\overline{jk}$ ($= \overline{ef}$). Similarly, if domestic producers become less efficient and the supply curve shifts toward the left, a quota would protect them from increased imports, while a tariff would not. In case of a decrease in domestic demand

Figure 14-1
Domestic Market for Cars in a Small Importing Country

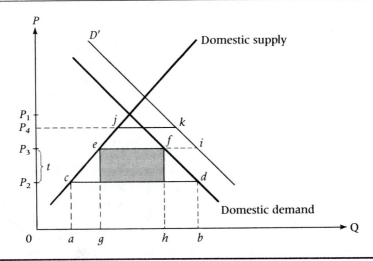

or an increase in domestic supply, the domestic price would decline under a quota, with the quantity imported remaining unchanged; while the volume of imports would decline under a tariff with the price remaining

Figure 14-2
A Tariff and a Quota When Domestic Demand Rises

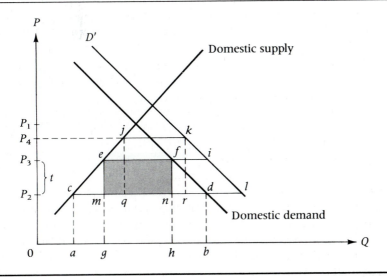

unchanged. The general conclusion is that as long as the quota remains "effective" (the controlled allocation falls short of what would be imported under free-market conditions), the adjustment to any shift in demand or supply occurs in the quantity of imports in the case of a tariff and in the domestic price in the case of a quota.

☐ Before any change in demand or supply, a tariff rate t or import quota gh causes the same deadweight welfare loss. In Figure 14-2 it is shown as triangles cem and nfd. Starting from this position of equivalence, consider four cases:

☐ (a) In a growing economy, the most common occurrence is an increase in demand produced by the rise in income. This is portrayed in Figure 14-2 as a rightward shift to D'. With a tariff t, the price remains at P_3, the quantity imported rises to ei ($= gb$), and the welfare loss becomes triangles cem and dil; it remains roughly unchanged. With import quota gh, the price rises to P_4, where the quantity imported remains unchanged at jk ($= gh$). The welfare loss from a quota is greater, for it consists of the larger triangles, cjq and rkl. The "equivalence" of a tariff and a quota is broken: A quota is more harmful to welfare.

☐ (b) A reduction in domestic supply (caused by a drought, a rise in production costs, or other reasons) would be shown by a leftward shift in the supply schedule (holding demand constant). Following the same procedure as in case (a), the results are similar: A quota is more harmful to welfare than a tariff, as it produces more sizable "deadweight loss" triangles.

☐ (c) A reduction in domestic demand produces the opposite result: A tariff is more harmful to welfare than its originally equivalent quota. Indeed, the downward shift in demand can be so large as to render the import quota ineffective: Free market imports become smaller than the maximum mandated by the quota.

☐ (d) An increase in domestic supply, shifting the entire supply schedule to the right, yields the same outcome as case (c). The reader is invited to pursue cases (b), (c), and (d) diagrammatically.

☐ In all four cases, the "equivalence" of tariff t and quota gh breaks down. But case (a) is the most common of the four. ■

Another possible difference between a tariff and a quota is suggested by the theory of effective protection. When a quota is imposed on an imported raw material, it raises the production costs of the final output of which the material is a part. This is the same effect as that of a tariff on inputs. But whereas import duties on raw materials are sometimes rebated when the final product is exported, no such rebate occurs in the case of quotas.

A third important difference between a tariff and a quota concerns the case where the domestic producer of the import substitute is a monopolist. International trade, even with a tariff, imposes severe limitations on this producer's monopoly power. In particular, he cannot charge more than the world price plus the tariff, for consumers can switch to foreign imports in unlimited quantities. There is always a potential (if not actual) threat to his position. In the case of an import quota, all he needs to do is accommodate a certain fixed amount of imports; beyond that, he is the king of the marketplace. He may certainly charge more than he could with the tariff; he faces less competitive pressure than he would under the tariff; and in general he can cause greater damage to economic efficiency and growth. (Appendix IX demonstrates that a profit-maximizing monopolist would indeed charge more under a quota than under a tariff.) He also is easily assured of any increase in sales resulting from a rise in domestic demand, because the volume of imports is fixed by decree.

Furthermore, for the competitor and monopolist alike, a tariff does not provide protection with certainty. The foreign exporter may choose to absorb all or most of the duty by reducing the export price and leaving the import price virtually unchanged. In that case, the volume of imports would decline very little, much to the dismay of the protection-seeking producer. Such an outcome is not possible in the case of a quota, where the volume of admissible imports is prescribed by the government. More generally, domestic producers, lacking precise knowledge of the supply and demand elasticities for their product, can never be sure how much imports would be excluded from the country by a given level of tariff protection. Certainty does obtain in the case of a quota.

All these differences explain the frequent clamor for import quotas in preference to tariffs by the U.S. textile and shoe industries as well as the oligopolistic steel and auto industries. They also make clear why such demands should be resisted. In terms of its effect on economic efficiency and consumer sovereignty, a quota is much more harmful than a tariff.

In addition, import quotas require a cumbersome administrative apparatus. The administering government agency must decide how to allocate import licenses among importers as well as among sources of supply (exporting countries) and how to distribute the yearly allocation over time. These decisions can be arbitrary and may bear no relation to consumer choice and producer cost. Furthermore, since sales of the restricted commodity yield monopoly profit to the importer, the import license itself assumes considerable value. If there is a free market for such licenses, the license to import a unit of the product would be worth the difference between its domestic and international price. An importer may be willing to bribe government officials to obtain one. Thus, the system contains seeds of corruption.

A final source of inefficiency arises from the fact that the import licenses are usually distributed among the importers who were functioning at the time the control was imposed. The system tends to freeze the situation as it existed at a certain base period. Total sales and profits cease to depend on the efficiency of the importing firms. A tax such as a tariff, while distorting relative prices, still permits competitive-market forces to serve as an allocation mechanism. The importers who are efficient enough to pay the tax get the business. Import quotas displace the market mechanism altogether, and a powerful incentive for business efficiency on the part of importing firms is lost. Despite its high economic costs, it is the LDCs—which can least afford to tolerate inefficiency—that insist on using quotas.

Voluntary Export Restraints (VERs)

Partly because import quotas are not permissible under GATT, countries frequently resort to "voluntary" export restraints (VER). A VER is a bilateral agreement between two governments, under which the exporting country limits its export of a certain product(s) to the importing country. Typically, it is the import-competing industries that pressure their government to negotiate a VER with the exporting country in order to lessen import competition. The exporters are "forced" to accept such quantitative limitations when they are threatened with more restrictive action by the importing country if they fail to agree.[2] The agreement is administered by the government of the exporting country or by the exporters themselves. VERs have become a most important instrument for restricting trade, and its use is spreading.

VERs tend to be less effective than quotas in limiting trade. It is easier to control imports than exports; often the exporting country administering the VERs does not really want the restraint; VERs usually cover only major suppliers, so that supplies from other countries partly substitute for the exports of major suppliers; and sales from restraining countries can be augmented by trans-shipment through nonrestraining countries.[3]

Often VERs are negotiated with one or more major exporting countries. For example, during 1981–86, Japanese auto exports to the U.S. were subject to VER limitations, while European models were exempt. Another illustration is the VER curbing color TV exports to the U.S. from Japan, Taiwan, and South Korea.

Herein lies an important difference between import quotas and VERs. While quotas may be global, VERs are inherently discriminatory as between

---

[2] For an analysis of the nature of such threats and the reaction they elicit see G. Stockhausen, *The Effects of a Quota Threat on the Exporting Country*, Phd. dissertation, University of Michigan, 1985, chapter 1.

[3] Another difference between quotas and VERs may be noted. When they are administered by the exporting country, VERs shift wasteful rent seeking activity from the importing to the exporting country: Firms will spend resources in lobbying activities, to increase their shares of the premium-fetching export licenses. If the exporters, rather than their government, administer the VER, they effectively become a cartel (that distributes export licenses), interested in maximizing joint profit.

sources of supply.[4] This is an implicit violation of the nondiscrimination rule embodied in GATT's MFN principle, and consequently the "new protectionism" increasingly bypasses the GATT mechanism. Exporters not covered by a VER agreement invariably benefit from it, as they can raise both the volume and the price of their exports to the importing market. Thus European auto makers benefited from the U.S.-Japan auto VER; they picked up some of the slack created by the excluded Japanese vehicles.

The VERs restrict supply and therefore raise import prices in the importing country; their welfare effects are similar to those of import quotas. However, because VERs are often administered by the exporting countries, exporters tend to raise their export price and capture much of the "tariff equivalent revenue" (shaded area in Figure 14-1). In contrast, under quota restrictions, that revenue accrues to the importers.[5]

A phenomenon common to both import quotas and VERs, when imposed on differentiated commodities, is known as *product upgrading*. If Japanese auto exporters to the U.S. were restricted to 1.6 million units, without regard to the type of car, they would tend to ship the more elaborate models, loaded with optional equipment, to enhance the profit on each car sold. From the consumer viewpoint a quota or a VER, which raises the absolute dollar price by the same amount regardless of quality or grade, translates into a proportionately larger price hike on low- than on high-cost models. Consequently both supply and demand factors induce a shift towards more expensive Japanese models. Such product upgrading occurs in all cases of quotas and VERs imposed on manufactured goods.[6]

VERs, import quotas, and ICAs are viewed as forms of "managed trade." They have become increasingly widespread as protectionist pressure intensified in many countries. As tariff rates have come down under GATT negotiations (to an average of 5 percent for the U.S.), countries turn increasingly to VERs to protect local industries. It has been estimated that a fifth of U.S. manufacturing imports is covered by such trade barriers, at a cost to American consumers of $50 billion per year. A similar proportion of EC and Japanese imports is affected by non-tariff barriers.

One reason for the intensified protectionism is the desire of politicians to save domestic jobs that would otherwise be destroyed by imports. But apart from the fact that macroeconomic policies are superior instruments to expand employment, protectionism does not usually save many jobs. It

---

[4] See E. Dinopoulos and M. Kreinin: "Import Quotas and VERs," M.S.U. Working Paper, 1986.

[5] W. Takacs, "The Equivalence of Tariffs, Quotas and VERs," *Jour. of Intern. Economics*, 1978, 565–73; and T. Murray, W. Schmidt and I. Walter, "On the Equivalence of Quotas and VERs," *Jour. of Intern. Economics*, 1983, 191–94.

[6] Falvey, Rodney E., "The Composition of Trade Within Import Restricted Product Categories," *Journal of Political Economy*, 1979, pp. 1105–1114; R. Feenstra, "Automobile Prices and Protection: The U.S.–Japan Trade Restraint," *Journal of Policy Modeling*, Spring 1985; C. Rodriguez, "The Quality of Imports and the Differential Welfare Effects of Tariffs, Quota, and Quality Controls as Protective Devices," *Canadian Journal of Economics*, 1979, pp. 439–49; and A. Koo, "Quotas and Product Upgrading," mimeographed, 1985.

often invites retaliation by other nations, hurting employment in the exporting industries, so that the net number of jobs saved is very small at best.

Beyond that, protectionism is an expensive and inefficient way to expand employment. Consider the case of the auto VERs. Robert Crandall estimated that by mid-1984 they caused a $1500 hike in the average price of a Japanese car sold in the U.S., and a $450 climb in the average price of a U.S.-made car. This adds up to an annual cost to the American consumer of $9 billion.

These price increases reduced the number of American and Japanese automobiles sold in the U.S., and also induced some shift toward European models. Taking these factors into account, Robert Feenstra estimates that the auto VERs saved about 10,000 jobs in 1981–82. Suppose the job gains by 1984 were 40,000 (out of total employment of over ¾ million in the industry). Since the quotas cost the consumer $9 billion per year, this works out to a cost of over $200,000 for each job saved. It is a multiple of the annual earnings of the average U.S. auto worker.

Similarly, the annual cost per job saved by protection in the steel industry is set at about $175,000; in textiles—$43,000; and in tuna—$240,000. In Sweden, for every $20,000-a-year job in shipyards, Swedish taxpayers pay a $50,000 annual subsidy. And in Canada, protection of the clothing industry costs consumers $500 million a year to provide $135 million of wages to Canadian workers. Protection in whatever form is an expensive and inefficient way to create jobs.

International Commodity Agreements

International trade in certain primary commodities is governed by International Commodity Agreements (ICAs), allegedly designed to stabilize the world price of the commodity in question or dispose of surpluses. It is usually the producing nations that press for such agreements, claiming that when the response to price change on the part of consumers and producers is low the market mechanism is too sluggish and cumbersome and needs to be modified by some central direction. After all, the performance of the price system as an allocation mechanism is contingent upon reasonably strong and prompt responses to price change. When the response is weak and tardy, violent price fluctuations frequently occur. If a bumper crop raises the supply of the commodity, it takes a huge decline in price to induce consumers to take even part of that increase. Likewise, a shift in consumer demand, for any reason, produces a large price change because producers cannot respond with sufficient speed and vigor to the new situation. Such circumstances may imply large fluctuations in the earnings of growers and in the terms of trade of the countries that produce the primary materials. If a country's economy is largely devoted to the production and exportation of one or two primary products, as economies in many developing countries are, then the entire level of economic activity tends to fluctuate along with these prices.

ICAs involve both the producing and the consuming countries (in contrast to cartels, which are strictly producers' organizations). They take one of three forms.

Export restriction schemes call for control over the quantity marketed internationally by means of national quotas for the production or export of the supplying countries. In some cases, where it is designed to stabilize foreign currency earnings, the agreement can have pervasive effects. A temporary letup in demand would be met by a greater (artificially contrived) reduction in supply, with the hope that the sharp rise in price would compensate for the decline in quantity, leaving total foreign-exchange earnings unchanged. In Figure 14-3 the original situation is described by schedules D and S; equilibrium price and quantity are P_1 and Q_1, respectively. Total foreign exchange revenue, which the agreement seeks to maintain, is the area of $0P_1e_1Q_1$. A decline in demand to D' requires the exporting nations to curtail supply to Q_2, so that the price may be raised to P_2, and foreign exchange earnings would be $0P_2e_2Q_2$ ($= 0P_1e_1Q_1$). The fact that a *reduction in demand* is met by steps designed to *increase* price underscores the perversity of this arrangement.

Buffer stocks set a minimum and a maximum price for the commodity to be maintained respectively by purchases or by sales from central stocks of the commodity in question. In this case, the objective is to maintain the price within a predetermined range.

Operation of a buffer stock is illustrated in Figure 14-4. On both panels, (a) and (b), P_E is perceived as the long-run equilibrium price (with

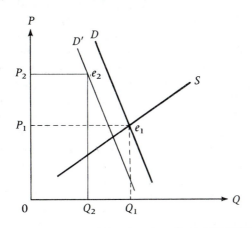

Figure 14-3
Effect of an Export Restrictions Scheme

Figure 14-4
Commodity Price Stabilization under a Buffer Stock ICA

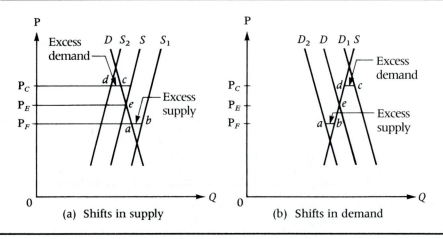

(a) Shifts in supply   (b) Shifts in demand

S and D representing the original supply and demand schedules). The buffer stock management decides to limit price fluctuations to a range $P_F - P_C$ where P_F is the floor price and P_C is the ceiling price. Should supply rise to S_1 in Panel (a) (for example, because of a bumper crop), price P_F is maintained by the buffer stock buying quantity $\overline{ab}$—the excess supply at that price. Conversely, should supply decline to S_2 (for example, because of a drought), the buffer stock maintains the ceiling price P_C by selling out of stocks quantity $\overline{cd}$ of the commodity—the excess demand at that price. Likewise, upward and downward shifts in demand, with a stable supply schedule, can bring about selling and buying operations, respectively, by the buffer stock. On Panel (b), when demand rises from D to D_1, P_C is maintained by sale of quantity $\overline{cd}$ out of central stocks. When demand declines from D to D_2, P_F is maintained by purchase of quantity $\overline{ab}$. All this can be accomplished by the buffer stock management standing ready to buy whatever quantities are offered to it at price P_F, and sell whatever quantities are requested at price P_C.

Over time, the stabilization operations are expected to narrow the price fluctuations from the solid to the dashed line in Figure 14-5.

Multilateral contracts specify a maximum price at which producing countries are obliged to sell stipulated quantities to consuming countries and a minimum price at which consuming countries are obliged to purchase stipulated quantities from producing countries. The operations of the contract in each case depend on its provisions.

All three mechanisms interfere with the allocative functions of the market, preventing shifts of resources between industries and thereby causing inefficiencies.

Figure 14-5
Price Fluctuations with and without a Buffer Stock

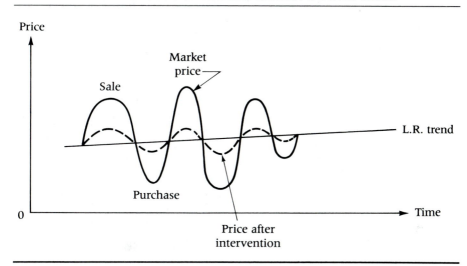

Several ICAs are, or have recently been, in operation. Most utilize buffer stocks or export quotas to stabilize prices. The International Wheat Agreement, negotiated in 1970, is in essence a consultative agreement, and calls for neither production or export controls nor for a central accumulation of stocks. The third (six year) International Coffee Agreement began in 1983. It contains standby provisions for export quotas and market sharing. In 1982, stagnant world coffee markets resulted in tension among the producing countries as each attempted to increase its market share. The sixth (five year) International Tin Agreement came into force in 1982. It utilizes buffer stocks and export controls to maintain prices between prescribed upper and lower limits. Long considered a "successful" ICA, this agreement collapsed in 1986 as a result of oversupply of the metal. While the demand for tin declined because of substitution by aluminum and plastic, supply rose as cash-starved producers from Malaysia to Bolivia mined ever greater quantities of the metal. Under these conditions it became impossible to maintain the price floor through purchases of tin by the buffer stock. The International Cocoa Agreement contains provisions for export quotas and buffer stocks, but its financial resources were exhausted in 1985. An ICA for natural rubber of the buffer stock variety entered into force in 1980, and its extension was under negotiations in 1986. Finally, ICAs on jute and tropical timber were reached in 1984 and 1985 respectively.

There is an inherent asymmetry in buffer stock agreements involving primary agricultural commodities such as coffee. Price support at the low level depends on the availability of financial resources, and those can be expanded if the participating countries agree to do so. But maintenance of the price ceiling depends on the availability of the commodity in stock. Once the stock is exhausted, nothing can prevent the price from rising above the ceiling, at least until the next harvest comes in, rendering the agreement "unoperational."

All past and present international commodity agreements suffer from attempts to fix and maintain a price different from the long-run equilibrium level. In most cases, it is difficult to determine what that price is. Even if it were possible to start at the "correct" level, that level changes over time in response to market forces. While these changes can go in all directions, the continuous pressure of the producing countries is only upward; in other words, they campaign for higher prices, which in turn lead to more production and larger surpluses (except in years of unusually high demand). Thus, agreements become a thinly disguised form of subsidy paid by the consuming nations (whose consumers pay the above-equilibrium prices) to the producing nations. And it is an inefficient method of subsidizing at that, for not only are consumers charged artificially high prices, but above-equilibrium prices stimulate excessive output. Moreover, the discrepancy between the equilibrium and the support prices usually leads to an accumulation of large stocks that are costly to store and maintain.

Besides the problem of financing and storing surpluses, many of the past and present agreements are threatened by noncompliance of small producers with the regulations, each small country thinking that its own action does not affect the world price, and by the incentive offered by high prices to the production of synthetic substitutes.

Because most agreements have not been particularly successful and are difficult to negotiate to begin with, attempts are being made to find other ways to combat the effects of violent price fluctuations on developing countries. A coordinated international effort is presently under way to diversify production of materials, and direct international financial support is available from the IMF to countries that experience a particularly severe decline in export earnings in any given year. Since it does not interfere with the workings of the market mechanism, such *compensatory financing* is a more efficient method of offsetting fluctuations in commodity prices or export earnings.

Not all international commodity agreements involve primary commodities, and not all are called forth by developing countries. The major exception is textiles. If any sector of the industrial countries should have contracted to make room for imports from developing countries, it is textiles. By reason of simple technology and relative labor intensity in the production process, this industry is the first candidate for introduction into a developing economy attempting to industrialize. Resources in the industrial nations can almost invariably be put to better use elsewhere. Yet well-known economic and political pressures prevail and keep the industry from contracting and imports from expanding. For a long time European countries restricted the importation of cotton textiles from the so-called low-wage countries in the Far East. Thus, Japanese, Taiwanese, and other Asian textiles were diverted to the American market, much to the dismay of the New England and North Carolina textile mills. No wonder American producers' clamor for protection, which was strongly supported by the United Textile Workers, grew louder and clearer all the time.

And their claim was *partly* backed by a valid argument. In addition to the general inefficiency perpetuated by the domestic price support of agricultural products in the United States, the program also subsidizes foreign textile mills by selling them raw cotton at reduced prices. In order to maintain the support price above the market level, the U.S. government is obliged to purchase all the domestic surpluses that are generated. As surpluses accumulate, there is pressure to dispose of them on foreign markets at a considerable discount. Thus, a foreign mill can purchase American cotton at a lower price than its New England competitor. And cheaper raw materials constitute a form of subsidy. The domestic industry in the United States wishes to counteract this subsidy by restricting imports of the final product.

But not all the industry's arguments are as logical. For the most part they follow the traditional lines that were proved invalid in a previous chapter, such as the relatively high wage rate they are obliged to pay compared with those paid by their foreign competitors. In general, their demand for import restrictions in the interest of "maintaining orderly markets" or "avoiding market disruptions" is nothing but a disguised request for a subsidy. But as often happens in public affairs, it is not the validity of the argument but the political and economic influence brought to bear by the debater that matters. As a result, the United States negotiated an agreement with Japan in the 1950s under which Japan agreed to impose "voluntary export quotas" on shipments of cotton textiles to the United States. Japan agreed to this "voluntary" control because the alternative was the imposition of mandatory import restrictions by the United States. The agreement did not help as much as expected. The newly freed share of the market was not captured by the domestic mills but was partly diverted to imports from other Far Eastern countries, such as Taiwan and Pakistan. The pressure for further restrictions continued unabated.

Because the European countries were interested in similar import limitations, the United States was able in the early 1960s to negotiate a long-term international commodity agreement to govern world trade in cotton textiles. Administered by the GATT, it now includes most producing and consuming nations and considerably limits the flow of international trade in cotton textiles. On January 1, 1974, a new four-year agreement went into force covering articles of cotton, wool, and synthetic fibers. It allowed importing countries to restrain textile imports when imports cause "market disruption," but required that such restrictions be used sparingly and be supervised by an international surveillance body set up under the GATT. This so-called Multifibre Arrangement among 51 countries, extended twice, regulates international trade in textiles. In addition, the United States and the EC have bilateral agreements with many supplying countries in which the latter undertake to further limit their textile exports to each of the two markets. In particular, strict limitations apply to the annual growth rate of imports. Late in 1985 Congress passed legislation imposing far stricter quotas on the import of textiles, shoes, and copper products. But it was vetoed by President Reagan.

Administrative, Technical, and Other Regulations

A myriad of government rules restrict the free flow of trade, although they may be ostensibly unrelated to protectionism. It is often difficult to determine whether these are bona fide technical regulations that happen to discriminate against imports or are regulations designed primarily to keep out imports.

For example, the French domestic tax on automobiles is graduated on the basis of a car's horsepower; as such, it raises the prices of American cars relative to domestic cars and can be regarded as discriminatory. An occasional Italian or British requirement that importers deposit at the government treasury for six months at no interest a sum equal to half the value of their imports is certainly a strong barrier to trade. And the European excise taxes on tropical products that are not produced at home serve merely to discourage imports. On the other hand, many Europeans regard the U.S. laws requiring automotive safety equipment as a protective device. And there is little doubt that the restrictions of minimum size on certain tomatoes sold in the United States discriminate against Mexican imports.

Other examples include complex customs procedures: a French ban on Scotch or bourbon advertisements, and a French requirement that all imported videotape recorders enter France through the tiny and inaccessible customs port of Poitiers, having a customs staff of only four; a limitation on the showing of foreign films on British television; and the Buy American Act, which requires the U.S. government to give American contractors a 12 percent edge in bidding for government contracts (50 percent for defense contracts). The complete list of such regulations is staggering. It ranges from preferences of national industries (such as railroads and airlines) for products of their own country, to laws designed to ensure that food is produced under hygienic conditions, to safety and other specifications of tractors and electrical equipment, and to the labeling requirements for various products.

Restrictions on *service* trade (banking, insurance, transportation, communication, etc.) have also multiplied in recent years. For example, American lawyers have encountered difficulties in establishing offices in Japan to represent their Japanese clients. Australia won't let foreign banks open branches or subsidiaries. Sweden bars local offices of foreign companies from processing payrolls abroad. France limits foreign equity in accounting firms. The EC restricts or excludes foreign vendors from its data communication network. Canada denies Canadian firms tax deductions for the cost of advertising on U.S. television stations near the border that is directed mainly at Canadian viewers. Argentina requires car importers to insure shipments with local insurance companies. Japanese airliners get cargo cleared more quickly in Tokyo than do foreign carriers. And, if a U.S. company wants to use American models for an advertisement in a West German magazine, it has to hire the models through a German agency—even if the ad is being photographed in Manhattan. Finally, some countries fail to provide protection for such intellectual property rights of foreign citizens as copyrights, trademarks, and patents.

A rather pervasive form of protection, practiced by many developing countries, is local content legislation. To sell cars, tractors and other capital goods in Brazil, Argentina, Mexico, or South Korea, a foreign manufacturer must set up domestic assembly operations, and guarantee that a minimum specified proportion of the value of the final product is locally made. A 1982 bill, introduced in the U.S. Congress, would apply the same principle to the U.S. auto market: Any manufacturer selling 200,000 or more cars in the U.S. would be required to use an average of 75 percent North American content (parts, labor, capital, etc.) in its cars. This would have had an adverse impact on the American consumer and national welfare would be similar to that of an import quota.[7] The bill failed to gain passage in the Congress.

Border Tax Adjustments

A major form of nontariff barriers that received prominent attention in recent years concerns rebates of domestic taxes to exporters. As a general rule, the GATT forbids export subsidies, including rebates of domestic taxes. The sole exception to this regulation is the rebate of indirect taxes to exporters. Indirect taxes are those levied on the product at some stage of its manufacture or sale, such as the excise or sales taxes in the United States and the value-added taxes in Europe. They are all borne eventually either by the final buyer or by the producer, depending on whether the price of the product goes up by the full amount of the tax or by less than that. In other words, the tax is levied directly on products, and only in an indirect manner is it shifted to individuals or productive resources. If and when the product is exported, the GATT's rule permits the government to rebate the tax to the exporter.

This permission does not apply to direct taxes—that is, taxes that are levied directly on people or on factors of production, such as the income tax or the corporate profits tax. The implicit rationale for this distinction is based on the poorly founded theory that indirect taxes are "shifted forward" and added in their entirety to the final price charged to the consumer,

---

[7] To the extent that a content protection scheme would force the establishment of plants in the U.S., it combines an element of tariff protection for the intermediate product with an element of subsidy for the final good. See G. Grossman, "The Theory of Domestic Content Protection and Content Preference," *Quarterly Journal of Economics*, November 1981, pp. 583–604. See also K. Krishna and M. Itoh, "Content Protection and Oligopolistic Interaction," mimeographed, NBER, 1985.

whereas direct taxes are paid at the source, either out of wages and salaries or out of profit, and do not affect the final price of the product. Consequently, only indirect taxes place exporters on an unfavorable competitive footing compared with their peers in other countries where such taxes may not exist or may not be as high; and only these taxes need to be rebated.

In discussing tariffs we noted that the incidence of a tax is a complex matter and cannot be determined merely from the way it is levied. In the case at hand there is no justification for the distinction made by the GATT. Direct taxes may be shifted to the consumer in precisely the same degree as indirect taxes are, depending on market conditions.

Be that as it may, the distinction has implications for trade between Europe and the United States. The United States relies mainly on direct taxes on income and profits to produce *federal* government revenue, and these are nonrebatable to exporters. This is not the case in most European countries. A major component of their public revenue comes from the value-added tax, which is a tax levied at each stage of the productive process on the value added at that stage. Because it is indirect, it is rebatable to exporters.

This provision of the GATT permits European countries to levy, in addition to the import duty, a border tax equal to the domestic value-added tax and at the same time rebate the domestic tax to exporters. These two measures together are known as border adjustments for internal taxes. With respect to the products affected, they are equivalent to a devaluation of the currency. In contrast, the United States levies a federal indirect tax (excise tax) on very few commodities and only those may qualify for border adjustment under the GATT's rule.

In GATT negotiations, the United States took the position that this rule is arbitrary and places European exporters at a competitive advantage, and that it should therefore be repealed or altered. Failing this, the administration considered rebating to American exporters the few indirect taxes levied by the federal government or even substituting a value-added tax for the corporate profits tax. But a country's tax system should be based on considerations of efficiency and equity, and not on the foreign competitive position of its industries. For this and other reasons, the value-added tax was not introduced in the United States. However, in 1971 Congress passed the Domestic International Sales Corporation (DISC) law, under which some 2000 export subsidiaries of U.S. companies enjoy deferment of the federal profits tax. The European countries viewed the DISCs as a violation of GATT rules, and the DISC provision was discontinued in 1984.

In fact, while the GATT's rule may be arbitrary and unjustified, it is not clear that it discriminates against American exporters or, if it does, what its impact is on transatlantic trade flows. It is possible that European producers are subject to the same direct taxes (and other social charges) as are their American counterparts and in addition must pay the rebatable indirect taxes. A thorough examination of the entire tax structure and its impact on trade is required to establish the claim of discrimination.

Cartels

Cartels are extensions of domestic monopolistic behavior into the international arena. When a group of business organizations of the same industry located in different countries, or a group of governments, agrees to limit competition and to regulate markets and restrict trade in some way, it is known as an *international cartel*. Unlike an ICA, a cartel agreement is limited to the suppliers, and does not include the consuming countries. For example, the International Air Transport Association is a 100-firm cartel incorporating all the major international airlines. Its rate-setting conferences meet annually to set fares and regulate other matters affecting commercial air traffic. Agreements require unanimous approval, each carrier having one vote regardless of size. Fares are then subject to the approval of the regulatory agency of each carrier's country, which in the case of U.S. carriers is the Civil Aeronautics Board. In a similar manner, freight rates along the major shipping routes are set by conferences that include all the major lines serving a particular route.

The Organization of Petroleum Exporting Countries (OPEC) is a cartel that in 1973–74 succeeded in quadrupling the price of crude oil (and doubling it again in 1979–80). The Arab members of that cartel also used an oil embargo as a political weapon. In the long run, the power of the cartel to raise prices may be restricted by increases in supplies from outside the cartel, such as in the continental United States, Alaska, and the North Sea; by the development of alternative sources of energy, such as coal, gas, atomic power, and solar energy; and by reduced consumption as a result of higher prices.[8]

Indeed during 1981–86 a global oil glut developed. Crude oil prices plummeted from $36 a barrel in the late 1970s to $15 a barrel by 1986, reducing the external surpluses of the major exporters. Countries like Nigeria and Mexico encountered balance-of-payments problems and were forced to impose import restrictions. The Soviet Union, which relies on oil and gold exports to finance imports from the West, faced major difficulties as the price of these two commodities dropped sharply.

Overt or illicit agreements often exist among major companies in the manufacturing and extractive industries. Their goals are many and varied, but in most cases they seek to fix prices, allocate world markets among the member firms to avoid competition, control technological research and development, and in other ways limit or alleviate competitive pressure. They may or may not tolerate smaller firms that are not members of the cartel and do not abide by its rules, depending on whether the latter's activities

---

[8] In the long run, a shortage of resources may develop. With that in mind, the *Law of the Sea* Conferences were organized in 1971 by the United Nations, in which the nations of the world are attempting to develop laws that will govern the distribution of the immense resources on and under the ocean floor. But after a decade of repeated attempts, an accord on the main issues still eludes the conferees. The United States opposes the agreement that was finally reached in 1982.

really disrupt the agreement or are merely a nuisance. When a major participant decides to opt out of the agreement, the entire operation of the cartel may be disrupted, much to the dismay of other members but to the joy of the consumers. Attempts by the U.S. Civil Aeronautics Board to introduce more competition in airline traffic have already reduced transatlantic fares by substantial amounts.

It is easy to see that cartel agreements are as harmful to the international economy as monopolies are to the domestic economy. They restrict output, misallocate resources, and extract higher prices from the public compared with conditions prevailing under competition. But international cartel action may even work counter to government policies. If the United States and Canada work out a free-trade arrangement in automobiles and parts, a private auto-marketing agreement can render it effectively void. By the same token, an agreement among the large French, British, German, and Italian automakers to allocate markets among themselves and fix prices can easily remove the salutary effects that the European Community hoped to achieve by eliminating official barriers to trade. The same applies to other major industries on the European continent. It does no good to eliminate tariffs and quotas if firms agree among themselves not to invade each other's territory or to avoid competition in other ways. For this reason, the European Community found it necessary to adopt rules of competition in industry.

It is one thing to realize the harmful effects of cartels and another to decide what to do about them. The United States has a relatively strong domestic antitrust tradition. In Europe, where that tradition is relatively weak, monopolistic practices are more acceptable. Lately there has been an increasing realization of their harmful effects, and some attempts are being made to curb them. The question is more complex internationally, where much production and trade is carried on by truly multinational companies that in an economic sense know no political boundaries. Should legislation be enacted to control these companies? Should governments seek to break up international cartels, or should their activities be permitted but placed under government control? These questions have to be answered before effective policy can be formulated.

Dumping

Another practice of private industry that may or may not become a subject of government action is dumping. Dumping occurs when a commodity is sold to foreign purchasers at a price lower than the price charged for the identical product on the domestic market. The word "identical" makes it difficult to establish the existence of dumping, because in making international price comparisons full allowance must be made for differences in specifications, including packaging and other superficial features. International standards exist for judging whether a commodity has been "dumped."

Government export subsidies are a form of dumping to be discussed in the last section. Our concern here is with dumping by private companies unrelated to government subsidies. It is customary to distinguish among three types of dumping: *Sporadic dumping* is disposal on foreign markets of an occasional surplus or overstock; it is tantamount to a domestic sale, and its effects are negligible. *Predatory dumping* occurs when a large home-based firm sells abroad at a reduced price in order to drive out competitors and gain control over the market, at which time it intends to reintroduce higher prices and use its newly acquired monopoly power to exploit that market. Potential rivals may then be discouraged from entering the field by the fear of a repeat performance on the part of the monopolist. This is the most harmful form of dumping.

Persistent dumping is a direct outgrowth of profit-maximizing behavior by monopolists. Consider a manufacturer who holds a monopoly position on the domestic market, where he is also protected from import competition by transport cost or government restrictions. In foreign markets, on the other hand, he faces the competition of producers from the host country as well as from third countries. Translated into economic terms, this situation implies that the demand elasticity is lower on the home market, where the consumer cannot turn to competing brands, than on foreign markets, where he can. The availability of close substitutes on foreign markets makes consumers highly responsive to price change in either direction. In other words, in terms of lost sales, the cost to the producer of charging a high price is lower at home than abroad. To maximize his overall net return, he would be led to charge a lower price abroad where he must meet competition than that charged at home where competitive pressure is lacking. Such dumping is harmful to the producers in the country receiving the dumped product, but this damage may be more than offset by the benefit to its consumers from the lower price.

□ A geometric representation of dumping is shown in Figure 14-6, comprising three panels: demand on the home and foreign markets, and a panel showing marginal cost and revenue. From the demand schedule on the home market we obtain the marginal revenue curve (MR_H). The demand on foreign markets yields the attendant marginal revenue (MR_F). Foreign demand is more elastic than home demand because of the availablility of competing brands, which are regarded as close substitutes. The two marginal revenue curves (MR_H and MR_F) are added *horizontally* at each price to obtain the total marginal revenue (MR_T) shown in the right-hand panel. The firm also has a marginal cost (MC) curve, and its intersection with MR_T determines the total quantity (Q_T) to be produced under profit-maximizing conditions.

□ How is Q_T divided between the two separate markets? Profit-maximizing behavior requires the division to be such that the marginal revenue in the two markets is equalized. Marginal revenue is the addition to total revenue derived from an increment of one unit of sales (or subtraction from a unit

Figure 14-6
A Monopolist Facing Separate Markets

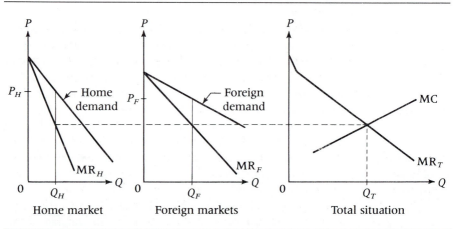

| Home market | Foreign markets | Total situation |

decrement). If MR_F is greater than MR_H, it would be profitable to shift sales from the home to the foreign market, since the addition to total revenue from the incremental foreign sales is larger than the loss of revenue from the reduced domestic sales. The opposite occurs if MR_H is greater than MR_F. Only equality of the two marginal revenues signals profit-maximizing equilibrium.[9]

☐ This position is shown in Figure 14-6. Quantities Q_H and Q_F are sold on the domestic and foreign markets, respectively; by construction they add up to the total quantity Q_T. Given the two quantities, the demand curves (not the marginal revenue) determine the prices prevailing on the two markets P_H and P_F, the domestic price being higher than its foreign counterpart. Indeed it can be shown mathematically that under profit-

[9] Following is a step-by-step procedure for drawing Figure 14-6:

(a) Draw two separate demand curves in each of the two markets—home market (left-hand panel) and foreign markets (center panel). Make the foreign demand curve flatter (more elastic) than the domestic demand schedule.

(b) From each demand schedule, obtain the marginal revenue curve. Graphically this can be done by extending the demand curve to the quantity axis, bisecting the resulting $\overline{0Q}$ distance, and connecting the midpoint with the beginning of the demand curve on the price axis.

(c) For each price, add horizontally the two marginal revenues in the two markets to obtain total marginal revenue, plotted as MR_T in the right-hand panel. Its intersection with the marginal cost curve (in the same panel) yields the total quantity produced.

(d) From the intersection of MC and MR_T draw a straight horizontal dashed line to meet the two marginal revenue curves. The points are those at which the marginal revenues in the two markets are equal. They determine the equilibrium division of the output between the two markets: Q_H and Q_F.

(e) Given these quantities, the price in each market is obtained by extending a vertical line from points Q_H and Q_F to the respective demand curves.

maximizing behavior the two prices would be inversely related to the two price elasticities.[10] ■

One condition necessary for all forms of dumping is separation of the domestic and foreign markets; otherwise, it is always possible for a foreign purchaser to resell the product on the home market and cut into the monopolist's profit. Thus, dumping is essentially price discrimination applied to the international arena. Indeed, it is easier to practice price discrimination internationally than nationally, because the domestic market cannot be fragmented into separate markets, while both transport costs and government restrictions often form an effective barrier between the domestic and foreign markets. On occasion the pressure of domestic monopolists for import quotas and other restrictions can be traced to their desire to effect such a separation and then practice price discrimination.

In actual practice it is difficult to distinguish the various types of dumping, and government policy, often formulated under pressure from import-competing industries, applies to all of them (although only the predatory variety is demonstrably harmful). The most common measure to counteract dumping in the importing country is the imposition of a *countervailing* import duty. Such a duty is allowed for in the American tariff legislation, but its imposition requires elaborate proceedings to prove that dumping does in fact exist.

Specifically, antidumping cases involve a two-step investigative procedure. First, the U.S. Commerce Department determines whether an imported product is being sold in the United States at prices below those prevailing in the exporting country ("sales at less than fair value"). In cases of positive findings, the International Trade Commission (ITC) institutes an investigation to determine whether the American industry "is being or is likely to be materially injured or is prevented from being established" by reason of such imports. In cases of affirmative determination, an antidumping duty is imposed. Such duties are assessed in addition to the normal tariff, and their size can vary with each shipment; it equals the amount by which the shipment is underpriced. In other words, exporters can avoid these duties by raising their export price, as Japanese TV exporters did in 1977. Antidumping duties are sanctioned by the GATT. In 1982–85 the ITC investigated over 400 dumping (otherwise known as "unfair trading practices") complaints, and granted relief in one fifth of all cases.

In 1978, the United States government inaugurated a novel system for administering the antidumping law in the case of steel products. In response to charges by U.S. steelmakers that foreign producers were dumping steel on the U.S. market, the administration introduced a *trigger price*

---

[10] An alternative definition of dumping is the sale of a commodity in a foreign market at a price below *production cost* (rather than home price). This can occur when the industry suffers excess capacity, so that the price charged both on the home and the foreign markets is below its full cost. Under this version, dumping can be inferred even when the home and foreign prices are the same. See W. Ethier, "Dumping," *Journal of Political Economy,* June 1982.

mechanism. For each steel product, it set a minimum import price equal to the price in the lowest-cost-producing country—in this case, Japan. Any shipment to the United States at a price below that level triggered the imposition of antidumping duties following a speeded-up investigation. This amounted to a government-sponsored floor or minimum prices for steel products.[11] The trigger price apparatus was supplemented by a "surge mechanism," which threatened restrictions whenever import quantities rose rapidly. The European Community has had similar import restrictions since January 1978. However, dissatisfaction of the U.S. steel companies with the operations of the two mechanisms led them to renew their complaints against foreign dumping, and to request stricter limitations on steel imports. As a result, the Administration negotiated VERs with all the steel exporting countries: Japan, Europe, and several LDCs. By the end of 1985 strict controls were in place, limiting U.S. imports of steel and steel products to 18–20 percent of the U.S. market, and allocating this share among supplying countries. The European Community has similar restrictions on its steel imports from Japan and the LDCs.

In the past most dumping complaints came from "traditional" industries such as shoes, textiles, and steel; today they come from the high-technology area as well. For example, in mid-1986, following the two-step investigation by the commerce department and the ITC, the U.S. imposed countervailing duties on Japanese computer chips (later removed).

Export Subsidies

In the previous sections we examined ways in which governments restrict imports or otherwise limit trade. But governments also use subsidies to stimulate exports. Export subsidies abound, GATT's rules to the contrary. They have often been a bone of contention between the U.S. and its trading partners.

In the field of agriculture both the U.S. and Europe employ domestic support prices, and then export some of their accumulated surpluses at low, subsidized prices. This is in violation of GATT's rules. At times a U.S.–EC rivalry appears, as when the U.S. attempted to recapture certain markets lost to subsidized EC grain exports. Under a 1985 plan, the U.S. would subsidize farm exports by offering the buying country a bonus in the form of grains from government-owned surpluses. And in mid-1986 Canada launched an investigation into allegations that U.S. corn exports were heavily subsidized—the first anti-dumping investigation *against* the U.S.

In the manufacturing sector, a popular way of subsidizing exports is by giving the foreign buyer a loan at below-market interest rates to finance the purchase. The subsidy measure is the difference between the market interest rate and the rate actually charged. Such loans, targeted for specific purchases, are important in the case of "big ticket" export items such as

---

[11] In line with the concept of effective protection, the introduction of a "minimum price" on a semiprocessed steel product that is used as a raw material for further fabrication amounts to a tax on the final product.

aircraft or machinery. They are made through a special agency of the government involved, which in the U.S. is the Export-Import Bank. A significant portion of European exports (such as the A300 airbus) are so financed, and American companies are reported to have lost business to such subsidized bids from foreign competitors. While the U.S. share in global subsidized credit has been modest, in 1985 the Reagan Administration decided to counter foreign subsidies through a special $300 million appropriation (dubbed a "war chest") to the Export-Import Bank.

To minimize such a "subsidy war," the OECD countries agreed on a minimum interest rate that may be charged on export credit.[12] The rates, adjusted periodically, vary according to the duration of the loan and the level of development of the loan-receiving country. Relatively poor countries are eligible for lower rates. In 1985 the minimum rates ranged from 9.85 to 12 percent.

But there is no limit to the ingenuity of nations in circumventing agreed-upon rules. In sales to LDCs, some industrial countries often mix development grants with export credits, thus enabling them to conceal very attractive credit terms under a guise of development assistance. In 1984, 15 industrial countries made 305 such "mixed credit" contracts valued at a total of $6.5 billion. A case in point occurred in April 1985 when a Japanese-led consortium won a Turkish contract to build a bridge over the Bosporus with a financial package that included more than $200 million in Japanese-government loans carrying a 5 percent interest rate. By calling the loans foreign aid rather than an export subsidy, Tokyo did not technically violate the OECD credit agreement.

While the many reasons for the subsidies vary, they usually have their roots in a mercantilist desire to promote exports and protect employment in specific industries. Subsidized credits have two effects. They direct resources to the export industries that are favored by the subsidized loans. And they transfer income from the exporting to the importing country. Since about two-thirds of these loans are made by the industrial countries to LDCs, the income transfers are from rich to poor countries. Appendix X presents a possible theoretical rationale for subsidizing the exports of oligopolistic industries.

Another form of export subsidy in the U.S. was the DISC tax-deferral provision. While it lasted, the provision yielded about $1 billion a year in tax benefits to qualifying companies, and thereby encourages exports.

Finally, the U.S. attempts to promote exports through the *Export Trading Company Act* of 1982. Under the terms of this legislation, an export trading company is defined as any group of companies and banks that joins forces with the specific objective of selling goods and services abroad. The act authorizes the commerce secretary to certify qualifying export trading companies for partial protection from U.S. antitrust statutes. This allows U.S. corporations to join forces to market their goods or services abroad even when antitrust laws bar them from similar joint ventures within the

---

[12] See OECD, *The Export Credit Financing Systems in OECD Member Countries*, Paris, 1982.

United States. It also allows bank holding companies to invest in export trading companies as much as 5 percent of their consolidated capital and surplus.

To qualify for certification, an export trading company has to show that its proposed business would not: substantially lessen competition; or restrain trade within the U.S.; unreasonably affect U.S. prices; substantially restrain exports of or unfairly compete against a U.S. competitor; or be likely to result in sales of the product to the U.S.

Review Questions

1. Evaluate the following statements:

    a. As instruments of protection go, a tariff is less harmful than a quota, and a quota is less harmful to the country than a VER.
    b. Protection is an expensive and inefficient way to create jobs.
    c. International commodity agreements constitute the best way of helping LDCs combat the effect of violent price fluctuations (of their exports) on their economies.
    d. The multifibre agreement represents an excellent way to organize international trade. We should apply it to steel and other industries.

2. Three of the U.S. industries demanding protection from foreign competition are: (a) footwear, (b) autos, (c) steel. Evaluate their demands and suggest what alternative policies might be followed in each case.

3. Suppose the U.S. steel industry is seeking protection from foreign imports. Compare and contrast (in terms of "equivalence" and related topics) the following measures of restricting steel imports: (a) tariff, (b) quota, (c) "Voluntary" Export Restraints. Use graphs as needed.

4. Explain how the tin buffer stock (ICA) functions. Why did it collapse in 1986?

5. Explain the terms:

    a. Border tax adjustments   d. OPEC
    b. Product upgrading   e. Export-credit subsidy
    c. International cartel   f. Export Trading Company Act (1982)

6. a. Define dumping and explain the three types of dumping.
    b. Show diagrammatically how persistent dumping may arise. Is this analysis equivalent to that of domestic price discrimination?
    c. What conditions are required for dumping to exist?
    d. Offer an alternative definition and explanation of dumping.
    e. What would an industry have to demonstrate in order to obtain protection from dumping? What form of protection is available? Give examples of industries that sought protection from dumping.

15 / U.S. Commercial Policy

A country's commercial policies are those that are designed to affect its trade relations with the rest of the world. Historically, the main commercial policy instrument employed by the United States has been the tariff, but in recent years greater reliance has been placed on nontariff barriers. Although in America's early years the tariff was used primarily for raising government revenue, it was later modified to serve the exclusive purpose of protecting domestic industry. Income and profit taxes became the major sources of revenue for the federal government. Because tariff rates have always been determined by Congress, they have reflected a host of political and economic pressures from diverse groups. The result was that the level of the American tariff in the first quarter of this century was high, reaching a peak in 1932 owing to the Smoot-Hawley Act of 1930. The tariff schedule was a long, complicated, and cumbersome document. However, in the mid-1930s the administration sought and obtained legislation for a gradual reduction in tariff rates subject to limits prescribed by Congress. And in the period following World War II this legislation enabled the United States to be the moving force behind a 40-year trend of international trade liberalization under the General Agreement on Tariffs and Trade (GATT). Following a discussion of the motivations behind U.S. foreign economic policies, this chapter will consider the major strands of that legislation.

Political Considerations in U.S. Commercial Policy

It is important to recognize that political and other considerations play a role in economic policies in general and in commercial policies in particular. Many countries regard foreign economic policies as a part of foreign policy and assign jurisdiction to their foreign minister in foreign trade matters.

Given the small share of foreign trade in the American economy and the emergence of the United States as the leading Western power, it may

not be surprising that political or military rather than economic considerations have often governed our commercial policy decisions in the post-war
period. This point can be abundantly illustrated by American attitudes toward
European affairs. Immediately after World War II, the United States supported the liberalization of intra-European trade and payments carried out
by the OEEC and the EPU, even though both arrangements discriminated
against American exports to western Europe. Although the then-acute dollar shortage provided an economic rationale for such policy, the real basis
for it was a desire to achieve political stability and military viability in Europe.

Similar thinking led the United States to back the establishment of the
European Community. The likelihood that the EC would unfavorably affect
American exports to its members, primarily in the sale of agricultural products, and the possible adverse effect of the newly created union on the
relative bargaining power of the United States in international economic
negotiations were evidently given little weight in the formulation of American policy. Instead, the overriding consideration was the presumed political
advantage to be drawn from a strong Europe in cold-war politics. It goes
without saying that the United States expected to remain the unchallenged
leader of a stronger Western alliance and hoped that the community would
be "outward looking" in its commercial policies.

The exclusive emphasis on political considerations changed somewhat
in the 1960s and was transformed into what might be called a political–
economic mix. In large measure, the change may be traced to the emergence of the EC as a strong bargaining unit in the GATT negotiations and
as a market whose policy can significantly affect U.S. exports. The fact that
the United States was facing an economic power of almost equal strength
across the bargaining table for the first time since World War II, coupled
with the impending adverse repercussions of EC discrimination on American exports, also contributed to the shift. The fear of trade diversion was
reinforced by serious concern about the U.S. balance-of-payments deficits.

In the 1980s, economic considerations gained further momentum with
the deep penetration of Japanese, European, and LDCs' exports of certain
highly visible products (steel, autos, TVs, footwear, and textiles) into the
American market. Their adverse impact on output, employment, and profits of selected U.S. industries deepened the protectionist sentiments in this
country. Indeed, some important industries demanded protection from
import competition, and it was often impossible for the Reagan administration to resist such demands. Protectionist sentiments in Europe were no
less intense.

The Reciprocal Trade Agreements Legislation

Since 1934 the cornerstone of American commercial policy has been the
Trade Agreements Act, and it has been continued through a dozen periodic
extensions. American participation in the GATT's tariff negotiations is
implicitly sanctioned by this legislation, as is the extent of duty reduction
permissible at any one round of bargaining. The provisions of the act as

well as their administration provide the most explicit clues to the motives behind U.S. commercial policies.

Two main lines of thought thread through the successive extensions of the reciprocal trade legislation, although their relative importance has varied from one extension to the next. On the one hand, the legislation has permitted continual, though limited, tariff reductions on U.S. imports. Since 1945, such reductions have been negotiated within the multilateral framework of the GATT, subject to the unconditional most-favored-nation principle. On the other hand, most extensions of the law have embodied a "no-injury" philosophy—trade liberalization was to be accomplished while "safeguarding" the interest of domestic industry. This philosophy found expression in the escape clause, peril point, and national security provisions of the act. The no-injury philosophy was also promoted diplomatically, by inducing exporting nations to "voluntarily" restrict the export of certain products to the United States.

To economists, the no-injury approach is clearly inconsistent with the general spirit of the reciprocal trade legislation. They regard tariff reduction first and foremost as a means to improve economic efficiency through increased international specialization. A larger volume of trade is expected to drive domestic resources away from relatively inefficient import-competing industries into industries that have competitive advantage. A similar process would take place abroad with the obvious result of increased efficiency all around. The safeguard provisions consititute a mechanism for preventing such shifts of resources. By protecting industries from import competition, they perpetuate allocative inefficiency and are therefore in direct conflict with what the act first set out to accomplish. We reduce tariffs and admit larger imports, but the instant such imports begin to have the beneficial effect of driving resources out of inefficient uses, we reverse course. This view of the main purpose of the tariff-reduction program is by no means universal. It is certainly not shared by many legislators and public officials. In these circles the program has been historically regarded as primarily a means of expanding American exports and strengthening the Western Alliance.

The Trade Agreements Act was first proposed by the Roosevelt Administration in 1934 as an antidepression measure designed to open up new export markets for American products. The offer of reciprocal tariff concessions was not an end in itself; it was meant to induce foreign countries to open their markets to American products. This view was superseded in the postwar period by a political objective. The program has come to be regarded as a means of strengthening the economies of friendly nations by opening the American market to some of their products, as symbolized by the slogan "Trade Not Aid." The dollar shortage after 1945 contributed considerably to this objective. Under these objectives, there exists no real inconsistency between extensive tariff reduction on the one hand and the prevention of injury to domestic interests on the other. If the U.S. goals are to open new export markets and cement the Western Alliance, why not attain them at the least cost in terms of displacement of domestic production?

The 1958 Extension and the "Safeguard" Provisions

This dual purpose of tariff reduction and the prevention of injury has been the major trend in reciprocal trade legislation since the Randall Report of 1954. The Randall Commission, set up by the Eisenhower Administration to study the goals of U.S. foreign economic policies, recommended the continuation of the Trade Agreements Program with appropriate safeguards to domestic industry. The subsequent extensions of the act during the 1950s—a three-year extension in 1955 and a four-year extension in 1958—contained liberal provisions for tariff reduction averaging 5 percent a year. In 1958, Congress authorized the President to offer tariff concessions of up to 20 percent, to be spread evenly over four years. It was under this authority that the so-called Dillon Round was negotiated in the GATT in 1961.

At the same time, however, Congress strengthened the protection to domestic interests against import competition. Three avenues of protection were open to domestic industries. Under the peril-point provision, the U.S. Tariff Commission[1] was required to determine *before* negotiations the level to which the tariff rate on each product could be lowered before causing serious injury to any domestic industry. The U.S. delegation is not authorized to offer concessions that would reduce rates below this level, although the peril point is hardly more than an educated guess.

Next, if, after a concession is granted, a domestic industry feels injured by import competition, it can apply for relief under the escape clause. A determination by the International Trade Commission of positive injury may lead to withdrawal of the concession if the president concurs with the Commission's recommendation. The escape clause is recognized in the GATT as a legitimate method of protecting domestic interests, and most trading nations find recourse to it when a domestic industry is threatened by "severe" import competition. Import restrictions can be reintroduced in such cases. But the country must then "compensate" its trading partners with liberalization of imports on some other products.

In each escape-clause investigation, the Tariff Commission must make three successive determinations. First, it must define the scope of the industry to be covered by the investigation. Because the impossibility of measuring cross elasticities precludes a precise definition of "industry," it is defined in the act as producers of "like or directly competitive products." The more broadly the industry is defined, the more difficult it is to prove injury, because injury to some segments of the industry may be more than offset by benefits to others (perhaps even from reciprocal expansion of exports), leaving the entire industry thriving. In contrast, a segmentation rule could lead to the use of the escape clause by an "industry" consisting of a few relatively inefficient producers.

Once the industry is defined, the Commission must determine whether or not serious injury has occurred. This can be interpreted either as an *absolute* decline in output or as a decline in the *share of the market* occupied

---

[1] In 1975 the name of this agency was changed to the International Trade Commission.

by the domestic industry. Under the second criterion, even an industry expanding in absolute terms can prove injury if imports have captured a larger share of a growing market. Finally, there remains the question of whether the decline must be traced to a "tariff concession," or just to general import competition, for an industry to qualify for relief. The language of the law and the philosophy of the commissioners make a difference in how difficult it is to prove injury. The escape clause is an alternative avenue of "relief" to that offered by the anti-dumping law.

The 1958 legislation strengthened the escape clause by expediting the investigative procedures of the Commission. It also increased considerably the president's authority to raise tariffs when escape-clause relief is granted. With respect to the Commission's determinations in escape-clause investigations, the legislation permitted a narrow definition of industry, thereby making it possible for a small segment of an industry to demonstrate injury, even when the industry as a whole experiences prosperity and growth. It also enabled domestic industries to base their claims for serious injury strictly on a decline in their share of the market, even if absolute levels of production and employment are on the increase.

A final avenue of relief is the national security clause, which permits withdrawal of concessions in cases where the affected domestic industry is essential to national security. For example, in 1986 the administration considered asking Japan to impose a VER on machine tool exports to the U.S. because such high-technology tools are used in manufacturing weapons.

It is abundantly clear that two main threads were woven through the reciprocal trade legislation. One was designed to liberalize imports into the United States, especially of industrial products, while the other was dedicated to "safeguarding" American industry from import competition.

It is reasonable to assume that in the early postwar period many concessions merely constituted reductions in "excess protection."[2] But toward the end of the 1950s the no-injury provisions were becoming increasingly incompatible with the main objective of the legislation, even for those who viewed the program strictly as a tool of foreign policy. The concessions granted by the United States during the previous generation had more than halved the level of the tariff, a reduction that practically eliminated all the "excess protection" in the tariff structure. It was no longer possible to grant many concessions without inflicting injury on domestic industries by simply curtailing the amount of "water" in the tariff. From then on, any significant amount of further trade liberalization, regardless of its objective, was likely to be injurious to domestic interests. To deal with this problem, economists have long advocated special provisions for adjustment assistance.

Trade-Adjustment Assistance

Given an adequate growth rate, the resources displaced by increased imports can shift to industries in which the United States enjoys comparative advan-

---

[2] "Excess protection" is one of several terms used to describe protection over and above what is necessary to keep out all imports; "water in the tariff" is another.

tage. But this process takes time. In the short run, a number of workers, firms, and communities might be hurt. And, in a society that assumes responsibility for the economic well-being of its members, such an impact of public policy cannot be overlooked.

Legislators and public officials interested in continuing the program began to recognize the need for finding an acceptable substitute for tariff relief under the escape clause. If most Americans stood to benefit from the increased efficiency resulting from trade liberalization, a way had to be found to compensate those who would incur the short-run losses caused by displaced domestic production. Thus, support gathered behind a program for trade-adjustment assistance.

Instead of protecting import-competing industries by the escape clause and thus perpetuating inefficiency, why not promote their transfer to lines of production in which they can compete effectively? The government could facilitate such movements of resources by means of a program designed to aid those who are injured by import competition. Under this program, whenever Tariff Commission investigations revealed that an industry had been injured by import competition generated by a previous tariff concession, its recommendation would not have to be limited to tariff relief. Instead, it could recommend direct assistance. To employers, the program would offer low-interest loans, aid in market research, and other assistance in moving to new lines of production. To workers, it would provide opportunities for retraining and offer to defray transportation costs to new locations. To communities injured by import competition, it would offer all assistance necessary to diversify the industrial base and adjust to the new circumstances.

The 1962 Trade Expansion Act

A trade-adjustment program was legislated for the first time by the Trade Expansion Act of 1962. Indeed, this was one of several drastic departures from the earlier reciprocal trade legislation. Under this program, workers made unemployed because of tariff concessions could obtain 65 percent of their weekly wage for 52 weeks plus an additional 26 weeks of pay if they were enrolled in a training program. Eligible firms could obtain technical and managerial assistance to help find new market outlets or develop new products, long-term, low-interest loans, and some minor tax relief.

Other liberal features of the 1962 act included a vast increase in the president's tariff-cutting authority. Under the act, the president was permitted to cut duties by up to 50 percent of their July 1962 level and to remove altogether duties that did not exceed 5 percent on that date. Also subject to removal were duties on agricultural commodities from the temperate and tropical zones. Tariff negotiations were to be conducted *on broad categories rather than on a product-by-product basis.*

It was under the authority of this legislation that the United States participated in the Kennedy Round of the GATT negotiations. What finally emerged from the five years of laborious bargaining (to be described in Chapter 16) was an average reduction of 35 percent on industrial tariff rates. These reductions took effect gradually over the 1967-72 period.

The Trade Reform Act of 1974

In 1974, Congress passed the Trade Reform Act, giving the administration new authority to reduce tariffs and thereby paving the way to the Tokyo Round (1975–79)[3] of the GATT negotiations (see Chapter 16). The act gave the president authority to reduce tariffs by 60 percent of their post-Kennedy-Round level, and to eliminate tariffs of 5 percent or less as a part of trade agreements with other countries. Duty reductions would be implemented in equal annual stages over several years. In addition, the president was granted authority to negotiate away nontariff barriers, but any such agreement may be disapproved by Congress within 90 days of its submission. Precise peril-point determination by the International Trade Commission (ITC)[4] in advance of negotiations is no longer required.

Escape-clause relief continues to be available to domestic industries. And the criteria for determining injury have been "liberalized" by making it unnecessary to link the injury to the tariff concessions (injury from import competition is now sufficient), and by requiring imports to be a substantial cause of the injury rather than a cause responsible for at least 51 percent of the injury ("major cause," defined as one that is greater than all other causes combined). Also, the industry may now be narrowly defined for the purpose of determining injury. The Commission must make its determination within 6 months after a petition has been filed.

Within 60 days of an affirmative determination by the International Trade Commission, the president must decide whether to provide import relief or direct the Secretary of Labor to expedite consideration of workers' petitions for adjustment assistance, or both. Should he decide against any action, he must report to Congress the considerations leading to his negative decision. Import relief can take the form of an increase in duty; imposition of a tariff on a duty-free item; suspension of the special treatment under provisions 806.3 or 807.0[5] of the tariff schedule; negotiation of orderly marketing arrangements with foreign countries (that is, VERs); quantitative restrictions (which, however, must allow imports of no less than the quantity imported in a recent representative period); or any combination of the above. In the case where import restrictions are imposed, the pres-

---

[3] Only the inaugural session was actually held in Tokyo. The actual negotiations took place in Geneva.

[4] This is the new name given to the Tariff Commission by the 1974 act.

[5] These provisions in the U.S. tariff code allow the reimportation to the United States of semifinished products manufactured abroad out of parts exported from the United States, with duty charged only on that part of the value of the imported product that has been added abroad. As a result, a variety of processing plants have been set up by American corporations in such countries as Mexico and Taiwan; thus, suspension of these provisions could harm certain developing countries.

ident is authorized to negotiate compensatory concessions with foreign countries. Any import relief is regarded as temporary and must be terminated not later than 5 years after it is granted, with a possible extension of 2 years. This phasing-out provision would presumably force the industry to adjust to increased imports. In 1985 the ITC voted relief in 32 out of 55 cases considered, and the President granted remedies in 18 of these cases.

An alternative avenue of relief is available to groups of *workers* hurt by import competition—they may apply to the Secretary of Labor for adjustment assistance. In making his determination, the Secretary need not find a causal link between increased imports and a previous tariff concession. Increased imports must be shown to have "contributed importantly" to the separation of a significant number or proportion of workers from employment (rather than be a "major cause"). Qualifying workers are then eligible for (a) supplementary unemployment compensation of up to 52 weeks, with maximum weekly benefits of 70 percent of the average statewide weekly wage; (b) retraining services; (c) job search allowance of 80 percent of cost and up to $500; and (d) relocation allowance subject to similar limitations as under (c). Adjustment assistance to eligible *firms* may take the form of loans not to exceed $1 million each, and loan guarantees of up to $3 million each. Finally, adjustment assistance is also available to "trade-impacted communities."

Until the mid-1970s the Trade Adjustment Assistance (TAA) program was hardly utilized. But the eased eligibility criteria in the 1974 act, coupled with the increased responsibility of the Labor Department in administering the program, has changed that. In the second half of the 1970s decade, one-half million workers received TAA funds. But only a small proportion of these workers participated in retraining, relocation, and related programs. Most of the money was spent on income maintenance as a supplement to the unemployment benefits. Instead of being retrained for new jobs, many laid-off workers in industries such as autos, apparel, and steel merely waited to be recalled to their old jobs while receiving generous TAA benefits. This use of the funds constitutes a disincentive to retraining and relocation. It is certainly inconsistent with the intent of the TAA legislation, if it does not abuse it altogether. This is one reason why the TAA program was sharply curtailed in the Reagan budget cuts of the 1980s. From a 1980 peak of $1.6 billion disbursed to 532,000 affected workers, the program shrunk by 1984 to $52 million, benefitting 16,000 workers.

The antidumping regulations were changed by the 1974 act to conform to the GATT's rules, which require, in addition to a finding of price discrimination, a determination of injury to domestic producers before countervailing duties can be imposed. On the other hand, the act gives the president authority to impose any type of import restrictions against countries employing unfair import restrictions on American products or those paying export subsidies, including subsidies of foreign supplies to third markets that displace American exports. Also, if a foreign country impairs its concession to the United States without compensation, the president is authorized to increase duties by not more than 50 percent above the statutory (1934) rate, or 20 percentage points above the July 1, 1975, rate, whichever is higher. Finally, articles that infringe a U.S. patent would be excluded from entry into the United States.

Next, in the event of persistent balance-of-payments deficits or a significant depreciation of the dollar, the president is authorized to impose a surcharge of up to 15 percentage points, or quantitative restrictions for a period not exceeding 150 days. In the case of large and persistent balance-of-payments surpluses or dollar appreciation, he is authorized to reduce duties by a maximum of 5 percentage points, or reduce or suspend other import restrictions for a period not to exceed 150 days.

The act also authorizes the president to extend most-favored-nation treatment to imports from countries not currently enjoying such treatment (mainly Communist countries) as a part of bilateral agreements. Such agreements would be restricted to a maximum period of 3 years (renewable once).

Finally, the act offers a Generalized System of Preferences (GSP) to the developing countries. It grants duty-free entry to the exports of manufactures, semi-manufactures, and selected other products from developing countries and territories. While the president may withdraw such treatment for any article or exporting country (for example, in connection with an injury finding by the International Trade Commission), he may not establish an intermediate preferential duty between zero and the most-favored-nation rate. The purpose of this program, which is similar to one introduced by other industrial nations, is to help promote the exports and economic development of developing countries (see Chapter 17).

Trade and Tariff Act of 1984

This legislation, signed into law on October 30, 1984, first, authorizes the president to negotiate reduction or elimination of barriers to: trade in services; trade in high-technology products and protection of intellectual property rights; and direct foreign investments. Secondly, the Act extends the U.S. GSP for 8½ years, through July 1993, but with explicit provisions for "graduation," namely removal of GSP benefits on products in which beneficiary countries have achieved a sufficient degree of competitiveness. Thirdly, authority is provided to negotiate a free-trade area with Israel.

It is under the provisions of this legislation that the U.S. administration is calling for a new round of trade negotiations in 1986-87.

The Political Economy of Protectionism

In their 1985 summit communique the heads of state of the seven largest industrial countries[6] stated: "Protection does not solve problems, it only creates problems." Why then is protectionism so widespread? As in other areas of national concern, commercial policies represent neither a majority vote nor the reasoned opinions of a single decision maker. They are a

---

[6]The U.S., U.K., Germany, France, Japan, Canada and Italy.

product of pressure groups vying for the attention of legislators and policymakers.

One reason that protection from foreign competition is so common is the strong lobbying incentive for groups that gain from protection, and the lack of such incentive for groups that stand to lose from protection. Any specific trade restriction inflicts damage on the community as a whole, and confers benefits on a few small groups. But although the total loss to society exceeds the benefits to the gaining groups (and thus there is a net loss), the losses from protection are diffused, whereas the gains are concentrated. A restriction on the entry of a foreign product, such as textiles, reduces the quantity supplied and hence raises the product's price. The main loser from such action is the consumer, who must pay the higher price. Thus the loss is diffused over 240 million consumers, each paying a slightly higher price. Similarly the U.S. sugar quota raises sugar prices (as well as the prices of goods made with sugar) by a few cents per pound, barely noticeable to the average buyer. Furthermore, in many cases consumers are not even aware of the relation between the price hike and protection. Consequently, they have little incentive to oppose the protective measure.

But the gains from protection are not diffused. Producers and workers in the protected industry, partly freed from the pressure of foreign competition, are able to charge a higher price for their product (such as domestic textiles). The benefits are heavily concentrated in the domestic manufacturers and labor unions of the particular industry. And the gains realized by each individual are sizable and visible. Hence the gainers, as a group, have an intense interest in the outcome. They are willing to engage in intense lobbying efforts and to expend large sums of money to assure a legislative outcome favorable to them.

This distribution of losses and benefits, and hence the interest of various political constituencies, explains why the pressure for protectionism is so great. There is a fundamental imbalance in the process of making trade policy; the advocates of protectionism start with a built-in advantage.

In recent years economists developed models designed to study the *structure* of protection; namely to explain why some industries are accorded high and others low protection.[7] Several partly conflicting hypotheses have

---

[7] For a sample of this literature see: Baldwin, R. E., "The Political Economy of Protectionism," Conference on Import Competition and Adjustment, NBER, Boston 1980; Brock, W. A. and Magee, S. P., "The Economics of Special Interest Politics: The Case of the Tariff," *American Economic Review* Papers and Proceedings 1978, 246–50; Caves, R. E., "Economic Models of Political Choice: Canada's Tariff Structure," *Canadian Journal of Economics*, 1976, 278–300; Findlay, R. and S. Wellisz, "Endogenous Tariffs, The Political Economy of Trade Restrictions and Welfare," in: J. N. Bhagwati, ed., *Import Competition and Response*, University of Chicago Press, Chicago 1982, 223–43; Finger, J. M., Hall, K. H., and D. P. Nelson, "The Political Economy of Administered Protection," *American Economic Review*, 1982, 452–66; Helleiner, G. K., "The Political Economy of Canada's Tariff Structure: An Alternative Model," *Canadian Journal of Economics* 1977, 318–26; Marvel, H. and Ray, E. J., "The Kennedy Round: Evidence on the Regulation of International Trade in the U.S.," *American Economic Review*, March 1983, 190–97; Pincus, J., "Pressure Groups and the Pattern of Tariffs," *Journal of Political Economy*, August 1975, 752–78.

emerged. The first one suggests that industries that are economically powerful and that find it easy to organize for a variety of purposes (e.g., few firms in the industry), are able to secure high-level protection relative to industries that are not well organized. Conversely if the product is used as an intermediate input by other industries (not by the final consumer), the ability and willingness of the using industries to exercise "countervailing power" may diminish the level of protection accorded to the product.

A second approach emphasizes the voting strength of those employed by the industry. It suggests that labor-intensive and geographically decentralized industries are able to secure higher protection than industries employing relatively few workers and much capital. A related hypothesis maintains that the aim of government in negotiating tariff cuts is to minimize labor adjustment costs. Hence protection is high in those industries where a large number of workers is likely to be injured by tariff cuts. A third approach claims that the objective of government is to ensure that low-income workers are not hurt by reduction in the level of protection.

Another view holds that protection is relatively high in those industries in which the country has a comparative cost disadvantage. Yet another view centers on international bargaining and suggests that in its trade policy a government attempts to influence the policies of other governments.[8] Hence protection is high on products exported by countries (such as LDCs) that are unwilling to liberalize their own imports. Finally, there exists a view that governments attempt to maintain the *status quo,* so that the protective structure mirrors the situation that existed at some historical period before the advent of large-scale trade liberalization.

Empirical tests undertaken thus far show that industries receiving the greatest protection are those characterized by a large number of workers, a high labor-output ratio, a small number of firms, and an historically high level of protection. Their workers tend to be unskilled and low paid. Because the empirical results are consistent with several of the hypotheses, the tests to date fail to discriminate between the conflicting theories.

Review Questions

1. What determinations must be made by the International Trade Commission in escape-clause investigations, and what bearing do they have on the ease of proving injury?

2. What were the main provisions of the: a. Trade Expansion Act, b. Trade Reform Act, c. Trade and Tariff Act?

3. If protection is inferior to free trade, why do we live in a protection-ridden world? What factors determine the structure of protection?

---

[8]Another strand of the political economy literature examines the threats and counter threats (with varying degrees of credibility) that countries employ in international bargaining to elicit certain policies from their trading partners. This was alluded to in the VER section of Chapter 16.

16 International and Regional Trade Organizations among Developed Countries

*T*he last forty years have witnessed a gradual liberalization of international trade in industrial products. The United States, through trade-agreements legislation, has become a driving force behind this process by inducing other countries to offer reciprocal tariff concessions, liberalizing quotas, and removing other restrictions. But the institutional framework for multilateral negotiations has been provided by several international organizations that also have established and policed rules of conduct in trade matters, and provided a strong impetus to the liberalization process. Internationally, they include the General Agreement on Tariffs and Trade (GATT) and the United Nations Conference on Trade and Development (UNCTAD); regionally, they consist of several customs unions and free-trade areas. The regional organizations of industrial nations are the European Communities[1] (EC), or Common Market, and the European Free Trade Area Association (EFTA).

These institutions are concerned primarily with trade matters, in contrast to the IMF and the European Monetary System (EMS), which are, respectively, international and regional organizations dealing with monetary exchange. It is important to recognize, however, that trade and payment restrictions are partly interchangeable in terms of their *effect* on trade flows if not in their intent. A tariff restricts imports by raising their prices, while exchange control lowers imports by limiting the amount of foreign

---

[1] Originally called the European Economic Community (EEC), its official name has been changed to the European Communities (EC), since it encompasses the European Economic Community, the European Coal and Steel Community, and Euratom. When discussing its earlier days we refer to it as the EEC, while in current affairs it is called the EC.

Apart from the regional organizations in Europe, the United States has a free-trade area with Israel, and special trading arrangements with the Caribbean basin. There is also discussion of freeing trade between the U.S. and Canada, and a Canadian Commission Report recommended in 1985 the establishment of a free-trade area between the two countries.

currencies available to finance them. A quota system can discriminate among various commodities and sources of supply by the manner in which the import licenses are issued. But the same end can be accomplished by means of exchange control, multiple exchange rates, and bilateral clearing agreements. Consequently, it is of little value to remove one type of restriction and leave the other intact. Policymakers generally recognize that a simultaneous attack on both fronts is necessary. Thus, members of the GATT must belong also to the IMF and must abide by its international currency rules. Similarly, the EEC did not come into existence until the European Payments Union succeeded in abolishing most payment restrictions on the Continent.

To place matters in proper perspective, Table 16-1 summarizes the two types of restrictions and the organizations set up to deal with them. The distinction is made on the basis of the intent of the policy involved, and even then it is often blurred, as in the case of import quotas. (Institutions set up to foster economic development are not included in our discussion.)

The "payments" side of the scheme was dealt with in Part 1. This chapter is concerned with the institutions serving mainly the developed countries that are listed in the "trade" column, although not necessarily in the order in which they are listed. Because proper organization of the material requires certain departures from chronological order, we begin with the European trade groups and continue with GATT. Discussion of the UNCTAD and regional schemes among the developing countries is reserved for Chapter 17.

Table 16-1
Trade and Payment Restrictions and the Organizations that Deal with Them

	Trade restrictions	Payment restrictions
Policy measures	Tariffs, quotas, nontariff barriers, others	Exchange control, multiple exchange rates, bilateral clearing agreements
International organizations	General Agreement on Tariffs and Trade (GATT)	International Monetary Fund (IMF)
	U.N. Conference on Trade and Development (UNCTAD)	
Regional organizations	European Communities (EC)	European Payments Union (EPU)
	European Free Trade Area Association (EFTA)	The European Monetary System (EMS)
	Customs unions and free trade areas in other parts of the world	The Sterling Area
		The French franc area

The European Communities[2]

Perhaps the most significant development in international trade matters after World War II was the establishment in 1958 of the European Economic Community (EEC), sometimes referred to as the European Common Market. Founded by the Treaty of Rome (signed in March 1957), it originally included six countries: West Germany, France, Italy, Belgium, the Netherlands, and Luxembourg. On July 1, 1977, the United Kingdom, Denmark, and Ireland acceded to the Community; Greece joined in 1981; while Spain and Portugal acceded on January 1, 1986, thereby raising the membership to twelve countries.

The founders of the EEC were motivated by the desire for political integration and considered economic union only a vehicle, albeit an important one, to attain that goal. But as of this writing very little has been accomplished on the political front, and the notes of discord emanating from European capitals are at times stronger than the sounds of cooperation. What meaningful progress there has been has taken place in the economic sphere.

Forerunners

Several organizations whose purpose was to promote economic cooperation in Europe preceded the EEC and in a sense can be considered its forerunners. First, the Organization of European Economic Cooperation (OEEC), encompassing practically all the countries of Western Europe, was established after World War II to coordinate reconstruction plans and channel American aid (under the Marshall Plan) to individual European countries.[3] Headquartered in Paris, this organization was also instrumental in bringing about liberalization of intra-European trade by gradually lifting import quotas. The European Payments Union, which led to the elimination of payment restrictions, was an offshoot of the OEEC. Today, with the United States, Canada, Japan, and Australia added to its membership roster, the organization is called the Organization for Economic Cooperation and Development (OECD) and is essentially a coordinative and consultative agency of the industrial nations.

A more direct forerunner of the EEC, and one that eventually merged with it, is the European Coal and Steel Community, established in 1951. Encompassing the original six EEC countries, it abolished trade restrictions and set up a common market for coal and steel products. It promulgated certain trade rules (such as rules of competition), and set up an administrative and judicial machinery to enforce them. In addition, an organization called Euratom provided for cooperation among the same countries in the

---

[2]See footnote 1.

[3]The American counterpart organization was the Economic Cooperation Administration. After several metamorphoses, it is now the Agency for International Development (AID) and is engaged in economic aid to developing countries.

development of atomic energy for peaceful uses. Finally, mention may be made of the three-nation customs union made up of the Benelux countries,[4] which became part of the EEC, and of various early attempts to integrate the four Scandinavian countries.

This is not to say that the groundwork for the EEC was so well laid that no stumbling blocks needed to be overcome. The obstacles were certainly formidable, but the earlier institutions demonstrated the strong desire for cooperation that existed in Europe. They also provided experience in solving problems and in some sense brought the countries to the brink of an economic union. Perhaps the final push toward integration was given by the realities of international politics, which dictated the need for bigness in international affairs if a country was not to become a "second-rate power" compared with Russia and the United States.[5] To many Europeans, this meant regional integration.

Trade Restrictions

The European Communities are first of all a customs union; the member countries abolished all tariffs and other trade restrictions among themselves and set up a common and uniform tariff against outsiders.[6] Thus, West German producers have free access to the French market (and vice versa), whereas Japanese and American producers must pay the common external tariff and in this sense are discriminated against. In the case of most industrial products, the common external tariff is the unweighted average of the tariff rates that existed in the constituent countries before integration. An incidental result of this averaging process is that EC tariff rates tend to concentrate around their overall average, with little dispersion. The EC has agreements for a free-trade area in manufactures with the EFTA countries so that free trade in manufactures prevails throughout Western Europe. However, the EC also imposes a variety of non-tariff barriers (such as VERs) on selective imports from Japan and other East Asian countries.

Agricultural Policy

Free trade was established for all products, industrial and agricultural alike. But because all the member countries support their agricultural sectors, they needed to develop common farm policies and impose tight and rather unusual import restrictions on many farm products. Not only are the governments directly involved in supporting agriculture, but the farm interests

---

[4] Belgium, Luxembourg, and the Netherlands.

[5] Following are some comparisons between the EC and the U.S.:

	EC	USA
Area (square miles)	639,833	3,615,122
Population (millions)	272	232
Civilian labor force (millions)	117	112
1984 GNP ($ billions)	2,200	3,628

[6] However many non-tariff barriers still obstruct trade among members of the EC.

in each country are both deeply entrenched and politically powerful. For this reason, agriculture contained the seeds of the widest diversity of views and the greatest intensity of conflict among the member countries.

Consider the case of grains. Before integration, the EEC countries operated independent price-support programs and these now had to be merged into one. But their interests with respect to the level of support diverged considerably. The West German farmers, being high-cost producers, campaigned for very high support levels that would keep them in business. The interest of West Germany as a whole would have been served far better by overhauling, rationalizing, and contracting the entire farm economy, transferring the freed resources to the industrial sector. But the farm unions exerted powerful political pressure at home, obliging the government to defend their interests. And so the West German official delegation insisted on very high support prices.

The French, on the other hand, pressured for lower support prices: low enough to permit them to undersell their West German competitors, but not down to a level that would permit imports from North America, Australia, or Argentina to undercut them. In other words, they wished to reserve for their own grains the great bulk of the EEC market. The United States wanted as low a support price as possible, both to stimulate consumption and to lower production inside the EEC, thereby leaving more room for imports. But America was not a party to the negotiations, and as to exerting influence, its moral position was undermined by its own agricultural support and protectionism. As in all cases of diversity, some compromise on the support price was reached after lengthy and laborious bargaining. The level at which prices are supported determines the cost of the Common Agricultural Policy (CAP) to the Community. The CAP occupies two thirds of the EC budget.[7] The system of agricultural protectionism is a by-product of the internal support system.

Several official terms should be defined for an understanding of the EC import-control program. The *target price* for grains is the support price that the Communities aim to maintain in the major consuming areas within the EC (the main population centers). It is determined every year following intensive bargaining between the producing and consuming interests within the EC. Small variations around that target are permitted and they determine the *intervention prices,* the minimum price at which the Communities buy grains to maintain the floor and the maximum price at which grains are sold out of official stocks to maintain the ceiling. For example, a target price of $4 per bushel and variations of 5 percent around it would produce intervention prices of $3.80 and $4.20. From the minimum price we subtract the cost of shipping grain overland (say, 5 cents) from the port of entry

---

[7]The annual EC budget is about $25 billion. Its revenue comes from the customs duties collected on manufactured goods imported into the EC, the levy collected on food imported into the EC and, by far the most important, a share of the domestic value-added tax (VAT) collected by EC member states.

to the main consuming area, to obtain the *threshold price* ($3.75 per bushel). This is the minimum import price that the Communities can tolerate if they are to maintain the minimum intervention price in the main population centers and avoid subsidizing foreign farmers.

In order to protect and preserve the threshold price, the European Communities employ a unique device known as the *variable levy*. It is an import tax amounting to the difference between the c.i.f. import price and the threshold price, and it varies with any changes in these two prices. In other words, changes in the internal target price (which indirectly determines the threshold price) or in the world price of grain (which determined c.i.f. import price) would bring about changes in the variable levy.

This levy is more vicious than a fixed tariff as a protective device. Under it, foreign exporters cannot maintain their sales volume by absorbing part of the duty. This would only increase the size of the variable levy. But that is precisely what the customs union wanted. By varying the target price, the Communities can regulate the volume of imported grains or the share of domestic consumption satisfied out of imports. As a general rule, a target price for each product is established once a year.

A variable levy is also imposed on imported fruits and vegetables. The equivalent of the target price in this case is the reference price, supposedly based on production costs in the most efficient producing region within the Communities. But this criterion may not be particularly meaningful because such a producing region may be inefficient by world standards. Also, as a practical matter, the reference price is often determined by intense bargaining between the producing and consuming countries inside the Communities. The variable levy on these imports is the difference between the reference price and the c.i.f. import price exclusive of import duty and domestic turnover taxes.

Although the EC may impose countervailing duties to prevent the importation of subsidized farm products, it may subsidize its own farm exports and dump accumulated surpluses in foreign countries. For example, high support prices for meat, cheese, milk, and butter encourage production and discourage consumption of these products. The resulting surpluses—referred to as "milk lakes" in the case of milk—are often exported at a subsidized price, much to the dismay of American farmers who lose foreign markets as a result. The U.S. government often counters this practice with a subsidy to American farm exports or by other means.[8]

In years of high international prices for food products, such as in 1972, the market price rises above the EC target levels, and no Communities support is necessary to maintain the price. In that case no variable levy is

---

[8]The 1985 "pasta war" is an example of U.S.-EC farm tensions. In response to preferential treatment given by the EC to Mediterranean (over American) citrus, the U.S. government imposed a prohibitive duty on European pasta. The EC then retaliated by increasing tariffs on imported U.S. lemons and walnuts. Other cases of mutual retaliation were in evidence in 1986. Often these are settled through the dispute-settling mechanism of the GATT.

imposed. In fact, in 1972–73, EC interest switched from protection and disposal of surpluses to an attempt to guarantee adequate supply.

In sum, the common agricultural policy consists of free trade within the Communities support prices for many products, and highly restrictive import schemes to "validate" the internal prices.[9] In the final analysis, the support price adopted by the Communities determines the level of internal consumption and production and therefore the volume of imports. The interest of foreign exporters such as the United States is served by the lowest support price possible; it is in direct conflict with the interest of producers inside the European Communities. However, EC policy also contains inducement to farmers to abandon agriculture in favor of jobs in the non-farm sectors, thereby shrinking the farm economy in the long run.

Other Rules

The EC agreement goes beyond trade matters, and thus the Communities are more than a customs union. First they ensure free mobility of capital and greater mobility of labor. Workers are free to seek employment any-where in the Communities, and the number of workers who migrate within the Communities runs into the millions. Second, and this is partly an out-come of the customs union, the treaty provides for coordination of fiscal and monetary policies. If the member nations give up some measure of independence in commercial policies, such coordination is necessary to min-imize balance-of-payments problems. Harmonization of tax and expendi-ture programs was deemed desirable to place producers in the 12 countries on an equally competitive footing. Thus, all EC members adopted the value-added tax as a major source of revenue, and the next big push is likely to be for a monetary union. But despite the EMS, this goal continues to elude the Community (see Chapter 10).

Another feature of the European Communities is that a sizable special fund was set up with the contributions of member countries to help accel-erate development in the more backward areas of the EC. This aspect of the organization is known as "regional policy." In addition, a whole array of rules was promulgated to assure competitive behavior in enterprises within the Communities and to prevent the development of cartels. The EC is becoming increasingly assertive in the areas of industrial policy and invest-ments regulations. Finally, a common transportation and energy policy was

---

[9]The CAP is a source of friction between the U.K. and the continental members of the EC. Before joining the EC, the U.K. operated a "deficiency payments" scheme in agriculture: Free trade existed in farm products, with world market prices prevailing inside the U.K., while British farmers were supported by a direct income subsidy. As a result food prices were low and farm imports were high by continental standards.

Upon accession to the EC, the U.K. abandoned the deficiency payments approach in favor of price support. Food prices rose sharply. But because of its traditionally high level of imports, the U.K. is saddled with a disproportionately large share of the CAP burden; for it pays huge sums in variable levy. For that it receives a refund from the Community, the size of which is a matter of annual dispute.

adopted, and the member nations cooperate closely (through Euratom) in the development and use of atomic energy.

Political Institutions

A set of political institutions, including a court of justice and a European parliament, were established to deal with EC matters and to move the EC members closer to political integration.

In the administrative branch of government, there are the Council of Ministers and the European Communities Commission. The council represents the 12 constituent governments, while the commission is the supranational decision-making body that presides over the vast bureaucracy at the Brussels headquarters. Regulations and directives issued by the Commission are legally binding, but major policies must be approved by the Council of Ministers.

The European Free Trade Area Association

Special significance attaches to the EC's relationship with the rest of Europe. At the time of the signing of the Treaty of Rome in 1957, an open invitation was issued to Western European countries to join the prospective organization, but for various reasons none except the Six was ready to sign. In particular, Great Britain did not wish to join for three main reasons. The British were generally dubious about the viability of any far-reaching agreement involving both Germany and France. They also did not wish to replace their form of agricultural support with that used on the Continent. Finally, joining the EEC would subject Great Britain to the common external tariff, making it impossible to maintain the imperial tariff preference system within the Commonwealth. Other countries did not join for reasons of international politics (neutrality in East-West relations).

As the EEC moved down the integration road, the British began to view with dismay the prospect of remaining outside. Consequently, they initiated negotiations for membership in the late 1950s. But as successive negotiations failed, the British initiated the formation of a smaller trading group, the European Free Trade Area Association (EFTA). Originally consisting of Great Britain, Austria, Switzerland, Portugal, Sweden, Norway, and Denmark (with Finland as an associate member) and headquartered in Geneva, EFTA is in essence a free-trade area for industrial goods, with some special provisions for trade in farm products.

A free-trade area differs from a customs union in that it does not have a common external tariff, and that difference presents a difficult problem of administration. Because the duty levied on imports from nonmember countries is not the same in all member countries, and because trade is free within the area, there is nothing to prevent a nonmember's exports from entering the high-duty member nation through a low-duty member. Thus, within the free-trade area, the lowest rate on each commodity becomes the effective rate for the entire area. This phenomenon is known as "trade deflection." In order to avoid it, the free-trade area must retain border checkpoints between its members (unnecessary in the case of a customs union) to investigate the origin of every commodity as it crosses the national boundary. Only if produced within the free-trade area is it accorded a duty-free status.

Even this approach can be circumvented. The outside producer can set up a final finishing plant for the product in the member country that has the lowest tariff, with value added accounting for not more than 10 percent of the final product, and ship from there to the entire free-trade area.[10] Thus, the integrating nations must decide what portion of the value of each product must be produced within the region in order for it to be accorded duty-free status. In the case of EFTA, the figure is 50 percent, and the rules (known as *rules of origin*) are enforced through the use of certificates of origin presented at border checkpoints.

The EFTA is a much looser organization than the European Communities. It does not have many of the Communities' institutional features; it has no common economic policies, and unlike the EC, it does not bargain as one unit in the GATT negotiations.

As the EC expanded and absorbed some member of EFTA, the EFTA was reduced in size and today it consists of: Austria, Finland, Ireland, Norway, Sweden, and Switzerland. It is retained as a formal organization. These countries contracted with the enlarged EC for free-trade arrangements in manufactured products as well as in a few nonmanufactures.

Special Trading Arrangements of the EC with Developing Countries

Two main factors were responsible for the contracting of special arrangements between the original six-member EEC and groups of developing countries: The preferences previously granted by France and Belgium to their respective colonies in Africa were to be "inherited" by the EEC; and the sheer impact of the integration on certain Mediterranean countries, about half of whose foreign trade is with EEC members, prompted them to negotiate for exemptions from, or reduction of, the EEC's external tariff.

Before enlargement of the Communities, the EEC had special "Association" agreements with the eighteen former French and Belgian colonies in Africa and with three East African countries. These were superseded in 1975 by a five-year association convention, signed in Lomé, Togo, between the enlarged EC and 57 Associated States (AS). The AS, now numbering 66, include the former associated countries, and the British commonwealth

---

[10] Here is an example from another region. Because there are no restrictions on U.S. imports from the Caribbean countries (under the so-called Caribbean initiative), Asian apparel firms have set up final assembly plants in these islands with the idea of exporting to the U.S.

countries in Africa, the Caribbean, and the Pacific.[11] This five-year treaty was renewed in 1980 and 1985.

Under the Convention, the Associated States receive economic assistance from the EC exceeding $5 billion over a period of five years. They are also granted technical assistance in a variety of forms.

The AS are also granted free access to EC markets for manufactured exports, as well as for agricultural products not subject to the Common Agricultural Policy (CAP) of the Communities. In addition, they have preferential access for their agricultural products subject to the CAP. EC rules of origin, which govern the preferential or free access to EC markets, were liberalized by considering the 66 countries as a single exporting unit. This means that successive working and processing operations can be carried out in a number of different countries and still qualify for duty-free entry to the EC.

Additionally, the Convention includes provisions for the stabilization of AS export earnings, known as STABEX.[12] It assures monetary transfers to AS exporters of primary products when their effective earnings from one-year exports to the EC fall below the average earnings of the previous four years. Also, a scheme called "Sysmin," provides aid for the rehabilitation of mining operations. Special arrangements were made to ensure a stable market for beef, rice, sugar, rum and bananas—items of extraordinary importance for several AS countries.

In addition to Africa, the Communities have contracted either association treaties or preferential trading agreements with most countries in the Mediterranean Basin. Trade agreements have also been concluded with Argentina, Uruguay, and Brazil, but these are of a nonpreferential nature.

The General Agreement on Tariffs and Trade

Following World War II, the trading nations convened in Havana and agreed to form an International Trade Organization (ITO) based on the charter negotiated there. But because the U.S. Senate failed to ratify ITO, it never came into being. As a substitute, the countries decided to set up an informal association, known as the General Agreement on Tariffs and Trade (GATT), to serve as a framework for multilateral tariff negotiations. Because Congress had already ratified the Trade Agreements Legislation, and the new organization could be regarded as merely an instrument to carry out that legislation, the administration did not consider it necessary to seek special ratification.

[11] The major developing members of the British Commonwealth—India, Bangladesh, Pakistan, Ceylon, Malaysia, and Singapore–were not offered Associate status by the EC. They benefit from the Generalized Scheme of Preferences (GSP), which favors all developing countries. The GSP will be discussed in Chapter 17; the preferences granted under it are more limited in nature than those embodied in the association treaties.

[12] For a description of the Lomé III agreement (including STABEX), see *Finance and Development*, September 1985, pp. 31–34,

Having adopted all the provisions of the defunct ITO, the GATT now sets and regulates the code of international trade conduct, which contains three fundamental principles: the principle of nondiscrimination embodied in the most-favored-nation clause (to be discussed next); a general prohibition of nontariff means of protection (such as quotas and export subsidies),[13] except for dealing with balance-of-payments difficulties; and the concept of consultation aimed at avoiding damage to the trade interests of the contracting parties. Special clauses deal with the position and needs of the developing countries. The GATT provides an institutional framework for multilateral negotiations on tariff reduction among the member nations. GATT's membership of ninety nations encompasses all the industrial countries, several East European countries, and fifty developing countries,[14] who are responsible in total for 80 percent of world trade. Member nations conducted seven major conferences and several minor ones to negotiate tariff concessions, the last one being the Tokyo Round (1975–79).

The Most-Favored-Nation Principle

All members of the GATT are expected to abide by a principle of nondiscrimination in levying tariffs known as the most-favored-nation (MFN) principle. This principle, however, can be interpreted in one of two ways. Under the conditional interpretation, if country A grants country B a tariff concession, it must also grant it to C (and all other countries), *provided* that C makes A an equivalent concession. The unconditional most-favored-nation interpretation requires A to apply any concession granted B to all other countries without expecting any equivalent concession from them.

On the face of it, the conditional MFN appears more equitable. If A and B negotiate mutual tariff concessions, why should these be applied indiscriminately to all other countries that have not conceded anything in return (they become "free riders")? But in practice the conditional MFN principle poses difficult problems. How does one define an "equivalent concession"? If Belgium and West Germany exchange tariff concessions on cars and bicycles, what should Belgium expect from Great Britain in return for a similar concession on cars? A British concession on bicycles may not

---

[13] As an interesting aside, it may be noted that subsidies sometimes help rather than hinder economic welfare. In a world with neither agricultural support programs nor other governmental interventions, the United States would be a major exporter of grains. If, under present conditions, the United States removed its export subsidies but retained its price support, it would cease to be an exporter of grains—clearly a move away from the optimal situation. This proposition has general application. In any *piecemeal* removal of the existing maze of governmental interventions, we should be careful that the move is toward rather than away from the best allocation of world resources. A *partial* movement toward the optimal use of resources is not necessarily an improvement over the existing situation. Each case must be judged on its own merit. This rule applies to a customs union (see Chapter 13), which constitutes a partial movement toward the optimal situation of universal free trade but may result in a reduction in world welfare.

[14] China applied for membership in July 1986.

be worth much to Belgians because the British themselves may manufacture bicycles much more efficiently. Thus, they will be forced to agree on something else that is in some sense "equivalent." The same would apply to all other members of the GATT not part to the original agreement. Translate this to ninety countries negotiating on thousands of products, and the outcome may be total confusion.

Carrying our example further, let us suppose that only countries that come up with equivalent concessions get the Belgian tariff reduction on cars. Belgium would thus be applying differential tariff rates on the same product, depending on its source. By the same token, the countries offering equivalent concessions would charge reduced rates on the products offered only if they originate in Belgium. A multiplicity of rates would prevail there also. And such multiplicity results in unhealthy discrimination between supplying countries and compounds the difficulty of administering the tariff.

It is because of these and other problems that the unconditional MFN principle was adopted by the GATT. But since countries do not like to grant what they consider "free concessions," they engaged in two practices to skirt the problem. First, each country might offer a tariff concession on a given product only to its major supplier, from whom it received a reciprocal concession; thus, only minor suppliers became "exempt" from the mutual practice. If there was more than one major supplier, the concession was negotiated with all of them. Second, countries have adopted a practice of redefining products for tariff purposes. In other words, a product can be broken into several narrow subcategories, the concession applied only to one of them. If supplying countries specialized according to certain features of the product (producing bicycles with a certain wheel size, for example), the concession could be granted only to one supplier and denied to others. But the tariff schedule itself became longer and more complicated. In the Kennedy and Tokyo rounds, negotiations were conducted on broad commodity categories (subject to the MFN) rather than on a product basis. Consequently, the "free rider" problem did not arise in the form described here.

There are several exceptions to the most-favored-nation rule under the GATT. First is a customs union, which involves free trade among members and a common and uniform tariff against outsiders: Nonmember countries must pay the common tariff, while member nations pay nothing when crossing into each other's markets, making for discrimination in favor of the members. The EEC was established under this exception. The only proviso attached is that most intra-area trade be liberalized and that the post-union common tariff not be more restrictive than the pre-union average tariff of the constituent countries.

The second exception is a free-trade area that calls for free trade among members but permits each to levy its own tariff against outsiders. Here the degree of discrimination against nonmember states depends on the tariff levels of the constituent nations, because no common external tariff is introduced. The EFTA, covering all trade in industrial products, was set up under this exception. A third exception allows for preferential treatment for trade between a country and its colonies or dominions.

In all cases of deviation from the most-favored-nation clause, the countries involved must seek a GATT waiver to the rule, and a waiver can also be granted under special circumstances not covered by the exception above. Outright violations of the principle do occur, however. Thus, the United States-Canada automobile agreement that liberalized trade in automobiles and their parts between the two nations discriminates against third countries and is in violation of the GATT. In recent years the frequent adoption of VERs and other discriminatory practices led to frequent violations of the MFN principle. Indeed many of the new protective devices are not subject to GATT's rules and procedures.

Developing countries are treated differently in two respects. First, they receive preferences in the markets of the industrial countries—a modification of the MFN rule. Second, the rule of reciprocity in the GATT negotiations does not apply to them. They obtain all concessions exchanged among the developed countries without themselves having to reciprocate.

The Tokyo Round

The major function of the GATT is to facilitate periodic multilateral negotiations for tariff reduction, subject to the unconditional most-favored-nation principle. As often as not, the scope of the negotiations is determined by the U.S. trade agreements legislation that prescribed (for the administration) the degree of latitude in tariff reduction, since the United States is the only major participant that requires prior enabling legislation. Thus the 1961 round, dubbed the Dillon Round, was made possible by the 1958 extension of the Trade Agreements Act. The Kennedy Round (1962–67) was negotiated under the authority of the 1962 Trade Expansion Act. And the Tokyo Round was negotiated under the authority of the 1974 Trade Reform Act.

Following five years of negotiations under the Tokyo Round, a final agreement was reached in April, 1979. It contained several provisions to liberalize non-tariff barriers, as well as substantial tariff reductions to be staged over an eight-year period beginning 1980. The agreement was approved by the U.S. Congress in July, 1979. In broad outline, five major areas of agreement emerged.[15]

International Trade Framework   Several changes were introduced into the GATT agreement. Notwithstanding the MFN clause, the differential and more favorable treatment accorded the developing countries (LDCs) as a matter of practice since the early 1960s, has now been codified. This

---

[15]See Kreinin and Officer, "Trade Liberalization Under the Tokyo Rounds—A Review of Their Effects on Trade Flows, Employment and Welfare," *Weltwirtschaftliches Archiv,* 1979, No. 3.

includes the Generalized System of Preferences (GSP), more favorable treatment under agreements concerning non-tariff barriers negotiated in GATT, regional trade arrangements among LDCs, non-reciprocity by LDCs in GATT tariff reductions, and special provisions favoring the least developed among the developing countries. LDCs were also granted permission to apply trade measures considered necessary to meet essential development needs. For all countries, an accord was reached on a mechanism for multilateral surveillance and for settlement of disputes. Consultations are now required when a country is forced to impose import restrictions for balance-of-payments purposes, or when it wishes to apply export restrictions that may deny other countries access to essential supplies.

Non-Tariff Barriers   Agreement was reached on five types of barriers. First, a revised set of customs valuation rules was introduced, under which the valuation is to be based primarily on the invoice price; but when that is not possible reliance on transaction value of identical or similar goods is permitted. Second, preferences given domestic suppliers in government procurement contracts on products (not services), when the contract is worth more than SDR 150,000 (about $165,000), will be reduced or eliminated. Third, the agreement calls for simplification and streamlining of import licensing procedures. Fourth, a special code was introduced, ensuring that domestic government subsidies do not harm the export interest of other countries (for example, in third markets), and that countervailing duties are imposed only in cases where imports cause injury to a domestic industry. And last, a special code of behavior was agreed upon, requiring that technical barriers to trade, imposed for reasons of health, safety, consumer, or environmental protection, should not create unnecessary obstacles to international trade. Disputes arising under the various new codes are settled by special multilateral committees to be established for this purpose.

Agriculture   Special arrangements were made for trade in bovine meat and in dairy products, while trade concessions were granted (separately), and had already been implemented, on the export of tropical food from LDCs.

Sectoral Agreement   The industrial countries eliminated all duties on civilian aircraft and parts.[16]

General Tariff Reductions   With respect to this all-important issue, the negotiators agreed to reduce tariffs on manufactured products, estimated to be $110 billion in 1976 trade value. The most important cuts have been concentrated in nonelectrical machinery, wood products, chemicals, and transport equipment, while less than average reductions were made in the

---

[16] Also, at the end of 1985, the U.S., Japan and Canada agreed to eliminate tariffs on computer parts.

textiles and leather sectors. Tariff concessions on agricultural products affect $12 billion of 1976 trade value (out of a total of $48 billion). The average depth of the tariff cut undertaken by the industrial countries has been estimated at 33–38 percent, while tariff rates on commodities of export interest to the LDCs were lowered by 26–37 percent. The cuts were staged over an 8-year period culminating on January 1, 1987.

Early in the Tokyo Round, the negotiating parties agreed to aim at a weighted-average tariff cut of between 30 and 40 percent. But that did not mean an equal (say, 35 percent) across-the-board reduction on all products. On the contrary, the negotiators were intent on not only lowering the level of tariff rates, but on "harmonizing" them—that is, reducing high tariff rates by a greater proportion than the lower ones. An example of a formula that would have such an effect is to reduce each tariff rate in a proportion equal to its own level (for instance, a 50 percent tariff would be cut by half to 25 percent; a 20 percent tariff would be cut by one-fifth to 16 percent, and so on).

Indeed, many months were spent on searching for an agreement on a tariff-reduction formula which would: (a) harmonize tariff rates, (b) achieve an agreed upon "average depth of cut," that is, a weighted-average reduction in all tariffs, and (c) insure that the tariff cuts be within the limits sanctioned by the U.S. legislation. In the end, the negotiators converged on a variant of a Swiss proposal: a tariff-reduction formula expressed as $Z = 16T/(16 + T)$ where T is the pre-Tokyo Round tariff rate, and Z the post-Tokyo Round tariff rate, both expressed in percentage terms. To see the strong harmonizing effect of this formula, consider the following examples:

T (percent)	Z (percent)
10	6.2
20	8.9
50	12.1
100	13.8
∞	16.0

Only initial tariff rates below 20 percent can be reduced according to the formula and still remain within the 60 percent reduction limit of the U.S. authority. Consequently, the formula was necessarily subject to the U.S. legislative constraint. Additional constraints were introduced by the "exceptions lists" tabled by the participants.

Strains on the International Trading System

Growing trade tensions in the 1980s have increased the case load of consultation within the GATT. The main pressure points as of 1986 are addressed in this section.

Both U.S. and the EC are weary of their massive trade deficits with Japan and of the deep Japanese penetration of their markets in certain highly visible products such as autos and steel as well as some high-technology products. Japan's low rate of industrial imports and its heavy agricultural protectionism have been a source of continuous agitation despite relaxation of certain import restrictions by Japan in the mid-1980s. Demands for "reciprocity legislation" echo in the halls of Congress, legislation that would permit limits on imports from countries denying the same access to American goods and services as the U.S. gives theirs. This action could shatter the MFN rule of GATT. Tensions between the U.S. and Japan continue despite the 1985 appreciation of the yen. And in 1986 these tensions spread to South Korea as the U.S. pressured Korea to liberalize its imports of goods and services. Trade disputes between the U.S. and the EC, especially in the field of agriculture, were exacerbated in 1986, partly as a result of the accession of Spain and Portugal to the community. The two countries imposed restrictions on the import of several farm products from the U.S., to which the U.S. threatened to retaliate. A process of mutual retaliation between the U.S. and the EC could have erupted had the issue not been resolved.

In the special case of steel, worldwide overcapacity and competition from the LDCs, Japan, and the EC have contributed to the massive unemployment in the U.S. steel industry. As a result the U.S. negotiated VERs with the main supplying countries, limiting imports to 18.6 percent of domestic consumption. The EC has similar arrangements with its main steel suppliers. Thus the global trading in steel appears to be managed in a manner akin to the multi-fibre agreement in textiles.

Government subsidization of export credit has become a major area of contention. The OECD countries reached an agreement on a lower limit below which subsidized export credit may not be offered, but various countries were accused of piercing this floor, partly in the guise of offering development assistance. Boeing and General Electric, for example, complained of contracts lost to foreign competitors by reason of subsidized credit.

Competition in high technology items is becoming very intense (even leading to industrial espionage) and is causing friction among the main trading nations. The industry is burdened by an assortment of requirements relating to maximum equity holding by foreigners, minimum local procurements of components, export performance, and shared technology. Protectionism in the area of *service* trade is also becoming an increasingly important source of tension.

U.S. demands that the West European nations limit their credits to eastern bloc countries, and otherwise control their high technology sales to the communist world, are a source of considerable discord. Of particular importance was the (1982) U.S. opposition to the construction of a Soviet-European pipeline to supply Siberian natural gas to Western Europe. The U.S. government denied the use of crucial American technology for the project and imposed a similar ban on European licensees and subsidiaries of American corporations, triggering a major dispute with the EC.

In a new departure into the trade aspects of foreign investments, the U.S. filed a complaint against Canadian practices under which foreign firms must meet minimum local content requirements, and export a minimum proportion of their output. These Canadian rules have since been partly relaxed. A new dispute between the U.S. and Canada erupted in mid-1986, when the U.S. levied a 35 percent (escape clause) tariff on a type of Canadian shingle, and threatened to take anti-dumping action against Canadian lumber. Canada retaliated by imposing a tariff on a range of imports from the U.S.

These are some examples of the general proliferation of non-tariff barriers and trade disputes. Analysis by GATT suggests that over 40 percent of all international transactions are conducted under some form of non-tariff restraint. Many of these impediments trigger complaints and petitions to GATT, and they pose a serious challenge to the ability of that organization to resolve trade disputes.

Apart from the specific issues outlined here, the mid-1980s witnessed intensification of protectionist sentiments in the U.S. Congress, triggered partly by large trade deficits. Indeed in mid-1986 both houses of Congress were considering protective trade legislation, including a provision that would require the president to restrict imports from any country that has large bilateral trade surpluses with the U.S. At the same time, the rise in protectionism in Europe was caused mainly by the large-scale unemployment there. To counter any movement in the direction of restriction of trade, and to foster greater trade liberalization, the U.S. administration has called for a new round of GATT negotiations to begin in 1987. Such negotiations would deal with liberalization of trade in services[17] and in high-technology products, as well as in reducing restrictions on direct foreign investments. Also under review would be improvements in the dispute-settling mechanism of the GATT.[18]

Thus far, we have focused the discussion on trade relations among the developed Western countries. Before turning to the special trade problems of developing countries, it appears useful to consider briefly East–West trade.

---

[17]The following are generally regarded as the principal services sectors involved in international trade:

- banking and financial services; insurance;
- freight by air, sea, or road, and port handling;
- passenger transportation and tourism;
- construction and engineering, architecture, repairs, and maintenance;
- films, sound recordings, communications, data processing, and printing;
- professional services (e.g., health, legal, accounting, and educational);
- other services (e.g., franchising, leasing).

[18]See M. Aho and J. Aronson, *Trade Talks: America Better Listen*, N.Y., Council on Foreign Relations, 1985; H. Stalson, *U.S. Service Exports and Foreign Barriers: An Agenda for Negotiations*, Washington, D.C., National Planning Association, 1985; and S. Anjara, "A New Round of Global Trade Negotiations," *Finance and Development*, June 1986.

Some Issues in East–West Trade[19]

When it comes to the size and composition of East–West trade, political considerations loom at least as important as economic ones. Judged strictly by population and national income, the potential for trade between the developed market-economy countries and the socialist states is vast. The OECD countries occupy one-quarter of the area of the globe, have one-fifth of the world's population, are responsible for over one-half of the world's industrial production, and have nearly two-thirds of the world's national income. The socialist countries[20] also occupy a quarter of the globe's area but have one-third of its population, and are responsible for over one-third of the world's industrial output and one-fourth of its national income. Yet East–West trade represents a mere 3 percent of world foreign trade turnover and a like proportion of the Western countries' foreign trade (although it represents a quarter of the socialist states' foreign trade). Western Europe accounts for most of this trade, while for the United States it is a minuscule share of total trade. However, trade between the U.S. and China has expanded in recent years.[21]

Most of the trade consists of exchange of manufacturing exports from the "West" for the exports of materials from the "East." As such, the commodity composition is similar to that of the trade between the industrialized market-economy countries and the developing countries.

Political, institutional, and economic forces originating in both East and West are responsible for the small size of these trade flows and present obstacles to their future growth. Market-oriented economies are generally geared to the satisfaction of consumer wants and permit market-determined prices to govern resource allocation. (Even publicly owned enterprises in market economies must function within the market atmosphere.) Government economic policies influence the decisions of private units indirectly through the market mechanism, and international trade is an extension of the domestic pricing system to the international arena. By contrast, in centrally planned economies, the economic plan determines resource allocation with minimal regard to market considerations. Often the plan emphasizes the development of heavy industries, with little regard to economic efficiency or comparative cost considerations. Price fixing is largely centralized in the planning commission, and price adjustments are often made to regulate income distribution rather than production. Domestic prices are effectively insulated from external influences.

---

[19] For an excellent treatment of this subject see Franklyn Holzman: *International Trade Under Communism—Politics and Economics*, New York, Basic Books, 1976; and "International Trade Practices of Centrally Planned Economies" *Columbia Journal of World Business*, Winter 1983.

[20] Including the U.S.S.R., Eastern Europe, China, Mongolia, North Korea, and Vietnam. However, China has introduced markets to some sectors of its economy.

[21] For more information, see U.S. International Trade Commission, *Reports on Trade Between the U.S. and Nonmarket Economy Countries*, Washington, D.C.

Foreign trade in centrally planned economies is determined in advance as part of the general economic plan. First to be determined are the kind and quantity of imports needed to meet the requirements of the plan (for example, to avoid production bottlenecks). Exports are then planned accordingly, as needed to pay for the desired imports. International trade is carried out within the framework of bilateral agreements. The socialist states do not have convertible currencies. Rather, exchange controls are strictly administered, and exchange rates do not relate domestic to foreign prices. The official exchange rate grossly overvalues most socialist countries' currencies. Because domestic prices are insulated from foreign prices and foreign trade is completely monopolized by state trading companies, tariffs lose their conventional significance. The state has direct means of protecting local industry and raising public revenue. The necessary imports are paid for at world prices and are sold domestically at domestic prices, while exports are purchased domestically at the internal prices and are sold abroad at whatever they can fetch on foreign markets. The state, rather than the relation between domestic and foreign prices, determines what will be traded and in what quantities.

Having decided on the commodity composition and volume of its trade, each socialist state first tries to meet its trading requirements within the socialist bloc. The U.S.S.R., Mongolia, Cuba, and the countries of Eastern Europe are organized in the Council for Mutual Economic Assistance (CMEA or COMECON). Trade among them is governed by bilateral agreements, and their accounts must be balanced bilaterally. But because internal price formation varies from one bloc country to another, their bilateral trade is governed by Western market prices. The CMEA established the International Bank for Economic Cooperation, which grants limited credit to finance intrabloc trade. For political reasons, and also because planners prefer to trade with each other rather than with thousands of individual businesses, intrabloc exchange is preferred by CMEA nations to trade with the West.

East–West trade is governed by bilateral trading agreements, and a significant portion of it is in the form of barter trade. The actual conduct of trade is lodged (in the East) in the hands of state foreign trade corporations that are each responsible for a number of products. It is with them that a private Western company must negotiate. Thus, as often as not, a Western exporter has no direct contact with the final user of his product, be it a store or a factory; nor is a Western importer usually permitted direct contact with the producer of his goods. Although there are now exceptions to this procedure in some East European countries, in many cases it presents an obvious technical complication to the conduct of trade.[22]

---

[22] Such separation is not unique to the foreign trade sector. It is reported that Soviet science serves industry badly because research institutes where inventions are made are controlled separately from the factories that are supposed to benefit from the research (*Wall Street Journal*, September 3, 1982).

While the limitations to trade emanating from the communist bloc are partly political, partly inherent in the nature of its economic system, and partly the result of the planners' aversion to foreign trade, the restrictions imposed by the West are all essentially political in nature. In 1950, the members of the OECD established the Coordinating Committee on Export Controls (COCOM), which restricted exports of strategic importance to the Eastern countries and also imposed certain restrictions on the credit terms granted to those countries. While the OECD's export restrictions have been liberalized over the years, the United States continued to apply its own much stricter controls over trade with the East, and consequently the scope of this trade has been much narrower than that of Western Europe. Only in 1972 did the president liberalize the U.S. control list to conform with the COCOM list of the OECD. While the embargo on China was lifted at that time, and trade and investment relations with that country have since been vastly expanded, the embargo on North Korea, Vietnam, and Cuba is still in force. Also in effect are special U.S. restrictions on granting credit to finance exports to the communist countries. On the import side, most communist countries do not receive most-favored-nation treatment in the U.S. Consequently, their exports to the United States are subject to the high U.S. statutory tariffs established in 1930,[23] which may be several times as high as the most-favored-nation rates.

Eastern bloc countries are quite interested in obtaining Western technology,[24] long-term Western credit to finance their imports, and most-favored-nation treatment for their exports. With respect to the latter request, a technical question arises concerning the sort of reciprocal concession they can offer. Tariff reduction has no meaning in a centrally planned economy, because the volume and source of their imports are determined by the planning commission and are unrelated to market prices. Thus, countries such as Poland, Romania, and Hungary (upon joining GATT) commonly reciprocate the MFN treatment by agreeing to increase imports by a certain percentage. China applied for GATT membership in mid-1986.

Of great importance in recent years have been contracts with Western firms to set up complete plants in the U.S.S.R. or in Eastern Europe. Because the communist countries do not permit equity ownership of such plants (ownership is held by the Eastern European government),[25] these contracts cannot be viewed as direct foreign investments in the normal sense of the word. Rather, they have come to be called *coproduction agreements*. While many types of arrangements are covered by this term, such an agreement generally involves a long-term contract under which a Western company

---

[23] Note, however, that these tariffs do not apply to much of the present U.S. imports from the U.S.S.R., because the duty is zero on raw materials.

[24] The technology can be embodied in the imported equipment, or it can be contracted for separately under licensing arrangements or sale of processes and know-how.

[25] In a radical departure from this rule, Romania and Hungary now allow some Western enterprises to own up to 49 percent equity in such ventures.

agrees to provide capital, technology, and sometimes managerial services for a project in an Eastern country. Ordinarily the contract calls for repayment and a return on investment mainly in the form of products derived from the project, and partly in foreign currency. Such agreements have been made by Western European and Japanese firms in Eastern Europe and in the U.S.S.R. Thus far, American participation has occurred largely through the European subsidiaries of American companies. An example is the case of the Siberian gas pipeline discussed in the previous section.

Review Questions

1. a. Explain the terms:

   • Trade creation of a customs union
   • Trade diversion of a customs union

   (Consult Chapter 13 as well).

   b. How would you go about estimating the trade creation and trade diversion of the *European Community? (What is the EC?)*
   c. Explain the meaning and functioning of the *variable levy* of the EC.
   d. What special arrangements does the EC have with developing countries?

2. a. What is the difference between a customs union and a free trade area? Give examples of each.
   b. How do the EC and EFTA differ from the GATT?
   c. How consistent are a CU and FTA with the MFN principle?

3. a. Outline the agreement reached in the Tokyo Round of trade negotiations.
   b. Why is there a need for another "round" in 1987? What would it deal with?

4. In what ways is East–West trade different from West–West trade? Why is East–West trade so limited in magnitude?

5. a. Is the trend toward trade liberalization proceeding smoothly, or are new protective devices (such as VERs) replacing the tariff as tariff rates decline?
   b. What are some of the strains in the international trading system?

17

Selected Trade Problems of Developing Countries

We now turn to the interests of the developing countries in international trade. It should be emphasized at the outset that foreign trade is not the central issue of the development problem. Exposure to foreign trade does spur economic development in a variety of ways, but the main impetus must come from within. Economic development requires the generation of a saving–investment process of sizable magnitude within an economic, social, and political environment conducive to growth. Because of the open nature of their economies, however, foreign trade is much more important to developing countries than it is to most developed nations. A general discussion of development is beyond the scope of this book; we shall be concerned merely with selected aspects of trade between the developed and developing countries.

Alternative Trade Approaches to Development

Two alternative trade approaches to economic development can be distinguished: import substitution and export-promotion strategies. Under the policy of import substitution, a country imposes high tariffs and non-tariff barriers to imports, and behind this shelter it expands domestic production to replace imports. Usually the country starts by producing nondurable consumer goods, which require labor-intensive and unsophisticated techniques. Once this easy stage is completed, further import substitution becomes increasingly difficult. Usually, the next step is to turn to the final processing of assembly-type commodities, generating a shift in the composition of imports away from these final products and toward intermediate and capital goods. To this end, the protective structure is escalated by the degree of processing, with final goods more highly protected than intermediate ones. The effective protection on final goods can at times reach 1000 percent.

This protection policy can have several results. First, the protective structure has produced many instances in which the foreign exchange costs of the intermediate imported goods are greater than the foreign exchange value of the final products in which they are embodied. (This is known as "negative value added.")[1] Likewise, waste that arises when LDCs attempt to "deepen" their production of manufactured products was discussed on page 308. Second, by restricting the demand for imports, the exchange value of the currency is artificially valued upward making it more difficult to export primary or manufactured products. Thus, the policy discriminates in favor of import-competing industries and against export industries. Production for domestic consumption is encouraged while production for exports is discouraged. Indeed, most LDCs pursue policies that are biased against their farm sectors, thereby lowering agricultural output, depressing rural income, and reducing exports.[2] But a unit of foreign exchange saved by import substitution costs more in terms of domestic resources than a unit of foreign exchange earned by exports.

Third, because the domestic market is usually too small to support an optimal-size plant, excess capacity tends to develop. While costs per unit in textile and shoe production decline only 10 percent when plant output doubles, in industries such as steel, pulp and paper, and chemicals, optimal-size plants can operate at almost half the per-unit cost of plants of the size that can be sustained by the internal markets of most developing countries. Thus, the widening of the internal market is one main benefit that accrues from regional integration among the developing countries. However, such steps are usually insufficient and must be supplemented by orienting exports toward the developed world. In sum, the fact that specialization and economies of scale cannot be fully exploited raises costs and prices well above the world market level.

Fourth, because the system of protection and other policies subsidize the importation of capital goods (at times coupled with artificially high wage rates brought about by union pressure), there is a strong incentive to use capital-intensive techniques regardless of the country's factor endowments. This is one reason why the rapid growth in industrial production in many developing countries is often not accompanied by a rapid growth in industrial employment. Finally, foreign capital that flows into the protected industries often does not generate export earnings but instead aggravates the debt-servicing problem.

---

[1] In Nigeria, for example, it has been shown that in the "important case of printing an imported cloth, the cost of the imported raw materials alone exceeds the value of the imports being replaced." (P. Killy, *Industrialization in an Open Economy; Nigeria 1945–1966*, Cambridge University Press, 1969, p. 126.) This is possible because the final product is sold in the heavily protected domestic market.

[2] These policies were discussed and criticized by the World Bank in its *1986 World Development Report*. See also *IMF Survey*, July 14, 1986.

Because of these problems, several developing countries—for example, Taiwan, South Korea, Singapore, and Brazil—have opted for an export-oriented strategy. This involves a change in the system of incentives in favor of exports, minimizing or eliminating the discrimination against them. Countries may even introduce a variety of fiscal incentives to increase exporters' earnings (such as export subsidies) or to reduce exporters' costs (such as reducing or removing duties on imported inputs or reducing the exporters' income taxes). Some countries (such as Mexico and Taiwan) established duty-free processing zones[3] into which inputs are imported duty free and from which final goods are exported after processing. Indeed, it is this measure coupled with the offshore provision[4] in the American tariff law that explains the existence in Mexico of hundreds of American plants, half of them just south of the California border. Similar extensive operations have been set up in Taiwan. In other cases, tariff rates have been reduced and harmonized, or the currency has been devalued (frequent minidevaluations in the case of Brazil). The major effect has been to expand the export of labor-intensive manufactured products and to avoid the establishment of insulated, highly inefficient domestic industries. Indeed, over the past decade there has been a sharp increase in manufactures exported from LDCs; however, most of it is accounted for by only ten countries and a significant portion of it is generated by multinational corporations. Although import substitution up to a certain point can be beneficial, the development experience of countries following export-promotion strategy has tended to be more favorable, in terms of growth rate and expansion of employment,[5] than that of countries developing strictly via import substitution.

Continued export-oriented growth requires adequate access to the markets of the developed countries. It is mainly in their demands for freer access to these markets that the developing countries have confronted the developed ones and have thrust their trade problems into the international arena. The focus of this confrontation has been centered in the United Nations Conference on Trade and Development (UNCTAD).

---

[3] Duty-free zones are not limited to LDCs. Most countries (including the United States) have such zones, usually located around port areas, where imports are checked before paying the duty and entering the country officially. The United States also has international banking zones where foreign deposits are accepted and foreign loans are made. These transactions are exempt from state income taxes and from certain Federal Reserve regulations.

[4] When a product made abroad out of U.S. components is reimported into the United States for further fabrication, only the value added abroad is subject to duty. Similar provisions exist in the tariff laws of Western European countries. They have proven highly beneficial in promoting LDCs' exports.

[5] See D. Nayyar, "Transnational Corporations and Manufactured Exports from Poor Countries," *Economic Journal*, March 1978; Anne Krueger: "Alternative Trade Strategies and Employment in LDCs," *American Economic Review*, May 1978, pp. 270–74; "Trade Policies in Developing Countries," in R. Jones and P. Kenen (eds.) *Handbook of International Economics*, Vol. I, North-Holland, 1984; and "Import Substitution Versus Export Promotion," *Finance & Development*, June 1985; and B. Balassa, *Change and Challenge in the World Economy*, N.Y., St. Martin's Press, 1985. For a different view see P. Streeten, "A Cool Look at Outward-Looking Strategies for Development," *The World Economy*, September 1982.

The United Nations Conference on Trade and Development (UNCTAD)

Most members of the United Nations are developing countries, yet international economic relations have been largely dominated by the score or so of industrial member nations. On several important grounds the developing countries feel that these relations serve exclusively the interest of the developed nations. In 1964, to provide a platform for their demands, the developing countries initiated an international conference known as the United Nations Conference of Trade and Development (UNCTAD). A permanent secretariat of the organization, under United Nations auspices, is headquartered in Geneva. A Trade and Development Board of fifty-five members meets twice a year, while plenary sessions of the entire membership (165 countries) are convened once in four years. In the mid-1970s, the discussions between developed and developing countries came to be dubbed the "North–South dialogue" or, alternatively, the demands for a "New International Economic Order." The current centerpiece of the dialogue is a proposed price stabilization scheme for primary commodities.

Demands Concerning Primary Products

Many of the complaints of the developing nations result from their dependence on the exportation of raw materials and agricultural products, commonly referred to under the heading "primary products." Over three-fourths of their nonpetroleum export earnings are made up of such commodities. Furthermore, in thirty of these countries, over 80 percent of the export earnings are derived from only three leading commodities; for another thirty-two countries, the figure lies between 60 and 80 percent. As a consequence, the price movements of primary commodities are of prime concern to them.

A long-standing complaint of these nations is that their commodity terms of trade, the ratio of the export price index to the import price index, has been declining or deteriorating over the long run. In other words, they can buy fewer imports for a given quantity of their exports. The theories behind the alleged decline in their export prices relative to import prices are many and varied. Much of their trade is an exchange of primary products for manufactured goods. It has been variably claimed that:

1. As world income grows, the demand for manufactured goods expands faster than the demand for primary products, so that the relative price of the latter declines.
2. Because primary products are marketed competitively, their prices are flexible, and any improvement in productivity is partly passed on to the foreign consumers in the form of reduced prices. On the other hand, monopolistic practices in manufacturing make prices rigid in a downward direction, so that the benefits of productivity increases are reaped

in the form of high earnings in the producing countries and not in the form of lower prices.

3. The development of synthetic substitutes lowers the demand for many primary materials and thereby depresses their prices.[6]

These and other theoretical arguments were marshaled to support the claim of a "secular deterioration in the terms of trade" of the developing countries. But these arguments can be countered by equally convincing propositions on the other side. And, more importantly, the vast number of empirical studies undertaken since the claim was first advanced in the 1950s are far from conclusive. (The claim was first advanced as an empirical proposition, and the theoretical rationale for it appeared only later.) The evidence on the problem is at best mixed and fails to substantiate the deterioration thesis.

Moreover, even a deterioration in the commodity terms of trade is not in itself an indication of decline in economic welfare. It all depends on the cause of the deterioration. To see this, imagine that Brazil achieves a 15 percent productivity improvement in coffee production, thereby increasing the world supply of coffee. If, as a result, world coffee prices decline by 5 percent, Brazil's commodity terms of trade also deteriorate and to the same extent. But the economic lot of Brazilian productive resources still improves by 10 percent. In other words, although Brazil now gets 5 percent fewer imports per unit of exports, it obtains 10 percent more imports per unit of productive services expended on export production.[7]

This alternative concept, the volume of imports obtainable per unit of input employed in the export industries, is known as the "single factoral terms of trade." It is measured by multiplying the commodity terms of trade by the productivity index in the export industries. In the present example, it is a better indicator of the effect of trade on economic welfare than are the commodity terms of trade. On the other hand, if the price of Brazilian coffee declined because of a shift in world taste from coffee to tea, then the commodity terms of trade would be an adequate indicator.

Be that as it may, demands to remedy the alleged "secular deterioration" by such methods as *indexing* the prices of primary commodities to those of manufactured goods[8] disappeared from the scene in the late 1970s. In part, this was due to strong resistance from the industrial countries, who regarded the proposal as highly inflationary. But equally important, the

---

[6] Conversely, environmental cleanup requirements in the industrial countries may prove beneficial to LDC exports, for they raise the prices of competitive products produced in the developed countries. Thus, a rise in price of synthetic rubber, attendant upon environmental regulations, would make natural rubber from Southeast Asia more competitive.

[7] On the other hand, "immiserizing growth" occurs when technological advance in the export industry increases output and consequently depresses prices by more than the rise in productivity, so as to result in a net loss to society. See J. Bhagwati, "Immiserizing Growth," *Review of Economic Studies,* June 1958.

[8] Under such an arrangement, prices of primary commodities would move up and down with the prices of manufactured goods, and in the same proportion.

proposal was divisive among the developing countries themselves. First, many primary products are produced in developed countries, so they would reap part of the "benefits." Second, the distribution of the benefits from indexing among the developing countries depends on which primary commodities are indexed. With so many conflicting interests represented, a negotiated solution seemed impossible. Finally, indexation involves great technical difficulties, such as storing accumulated surpluses and financing the program.

Additional claims advanced by the developing nations in the area of primary products have to do with agricultural protectionism in the industrial world. Direct quantitative barriers of all sorts are imposed on temperate-zone products (and on sugar), while tropical products are subject to excise taxes in Europe. Both the prices and volume of exports are artificially depressed by such measures. This lowers foreign exchange earnings of the developing countries and seriously handicaps their development efforts, which depend on imported equipment. A partial liberalization of trade in tropical products was achieved in the Tokyo Round of the GATT.

Currently, the most common complaint of the developing countries concerns violent short-run *fluctuations* in the prices of their exports, which in turn generate wide swings in export earnings and in domestic economic activity. Again, economic growth is said to be the casualty. Schematically, the two links in the argument are as follows:

<table>
<tr><td>Price fluctuations</td><td>⟶</td><td>Fluctuations in
Foreign Currency
Earnings</td><td>⟶</td><td>Retardation of Real
Growth and of
Investments</td></tr>
</table>

Because supply of and demand for primary products are price inelastic, large price fluctuations can be expected on *a priori* grounds and are verified in empirical studies.

However, the link from price fluctuations to variations in foreign currency earnings depends on whether the price changes are caused by shifts in the demand or the supply curve. Perhaps because the supply of agricultural commodities is dominated by weather conditions, supply shifts cause most of their price fluctuations (see Chapter 14, Figure 14–4, panel a). Here price and quantity move in opposite directions, so that foreign exchange earnings (price × quantity) need not fluctuate excessively. In the case of raw materials, most price fluctuations are caused by shifts in demand (Figure 14–4, panel b), perhaps because demand is dominated by economic conditions in the industrial countries. In this case, price and quantity move in the same direction, and sizable fluctuations in foreign currency earnings may be expected.

With respect to the second link, a host of cross-sectional empirical studies failed to establish a negative correlation between a degree of price or foreign currency fluctuations on the one hand, and growth rate in real

GNP or in investments on the other. At best, the empirical evidence is mixed. Although fluctuations may make planning more difficult,[9] they do not appear harmful to the development enterprise itself. However, policymakers in the developing countries are often more concerned with their ability to *plan* than with the growth performance in the private sector. And economic planning is handicapped by violent fluctuations in foreign exchange earnings.

To cope with this alleged problem UNCTAD developed a proposal for an "Integrated Commodity Program." It envisages international commodity agreements of the buffer stock variety for each of ten to eighteen primary commodities. The individual ICAs would be linked to a "common fund" of $6 billion, made up of contributions by producing and consuming countries (Scheme 17–A).

A buffer stock for each commodity would be operated independently, containing price fluctuations within predetermined lower and upper limits by buying and selling out of stock. Should the need for additional funds arise, they could be borrowed from the "common fund." An alleged advantage to operating many agreements jointly lies in the area of externalities. If the price of copper declines to its lower support level (necessitating copper purchases) at the time when the price of bauxite rises to its upper support level (calling for the sale of bauxite), then the proceeds from the sale of bauxite can be used to purchase copper (Scheme 17–B). That feature would reduce the capital necessary to operate the Common Fund. However, empirical evidence indicates that the prices of most primary commodities *fluctuate in unison* rather than in an offsetting fashion. For this and other reasons UNCTAD is said to grossly underestimate the amount necessary to operate the Common Fund. Furthermore, in cases of high and competing demands from the individual ICAs, how is the Common Fund to allocate

[9]For the role of planning in development, see Helen Hughes, "Private Enterprise and Development—Comparative Country Experience," *Finance and Development,* March 1982, pp. 22–25.

Scheme 17–A: The Common Fund Concept

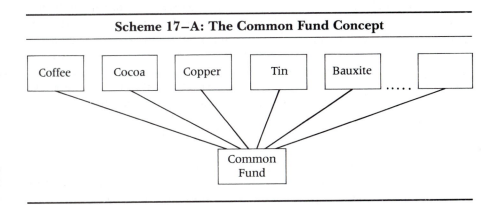

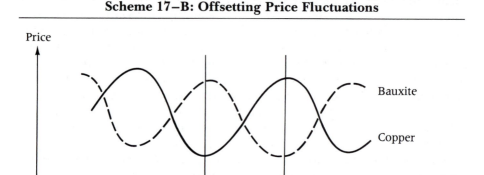

Scheme 17–B: Offsetting Price Fluctuations

its limited resources between their competing requirements? Finally, all the shortcomings of ICAs, outlined in Chapter 15, apply to this proposal as well.

Although the Integrated Commodity Program is the centerpiece of the so-called "New Order," the initial reaction of the major industrial countries was negative. They suggested that their past experiences with commodity agreements were far from encouraging, and certainly not positive enough to warrant such a far-reaching enterprise. Second, the necessary financial commitment, when realistically appraised, could not be justified. Such large sums, if used to *diversify* the economies of the developing countries, would be likely to yield greater dividends in terms of the stabilization of export earnings.

What emerged after lengthy negotiations is a proposal for a Common Fund of modest proportions: $470 million to finance the buffer stock operations for 18 commodities, and $350 million for market research and export promotion. But as of mid-1986 even this limited program has not been approved by enough countries to be implemented.

However, there exists a direct method of stabilizing foreign currency earnings: the compensatory finance facility of the IMF. It enables a member to borrow (at low interest) when its export earnings and financial reserves are low and to make repayments when they are high. The drawings, for up to 3–5 years, can occur when a country's export earnings over a 12-month period fall considerably short of the five-year average. This facility along with STABEX of the EC represent a more direct way of stabilizing foreign currency earnings than the roundabout means of price stabilization.

Manufactured Products

As for manufactured goods, the main complaint of the developing nations is that the tariff structure of the developed countries discriminates against them. First, rates are high on the labor-intensive simple-technology products in which they are interested. And, while multilateral concessions granted in GATT negotiations are extended to them without reciprocity, these concessions usually apply to commodities that are too sophisticated for them to manufacture. Indeed, when tariff rates on goods produced in the industrial world were lowered considerably, labor-intensive goods, such as textiles, were placed under direct quantitative restrictions. In part, this is due to the passive position that LDCs take in GATT negotiations. They generally offer no concessions of their own, preferring simply to receive the concessions that are exchanged among the industrial countries. These are granted to the LDCs under the MFN rule. But as a consequence, the negotiations between the United States, Europe, and Japan center on commodities that are of export interest only to the industrial countries. Indeed, it is in the interest of the developing countries to participate actively in GATT negotiations. Offering concessions would rationalize their import regimes,[10] and at the same time enable them to demand meaningful concessions from the industrial nations.

In the second place, the tariff structure of the industrial countries discourages industrialization elsewhere. In many cases, rates are low or nonexistent on raw materials and rise gradually with the degree of processing or fabrication to which the product has been subjected. This means that effective rates of protection on the finished products are much higher than the nominal rates (often more than double), which further accentuates the tariff escalation and reinforces the incentives of the nonindustrial countries to export goods in their raw form. A study of the post-Kennedy Round tariff rates on 123 processed materials showed a median nominal tariff rate in the United States of 8.6 percent and a median effective rate of 18 percent. The comparable figures for the EC were 12.2 and 33.1 percent, and for Japan they were 16.5 and 45.5 percent, respectively.[11] Certainly, the tariff structure that LDCs face discourages local processing of the products they export.

To offset and reverse this structure, the developing countries demanded tariff preferences for their manufactured exports in the markets of the industrial countries; they wished to be charged lower rates in the markets of each developed country than other industrial countries were charged for competitive products.

Analytically, preferences are analogous to customs unions, because they give rise to two static effects on trade flows:

1. *The trade-creation effect:* Tariffs are reduced on imports from the bene-

---

[10] See "Trade Policy Issues and Developments," IMF Occasional Paper no. 38, 1985. A 1986 UNCTAD study estimates that complete elimination of the post Tokyo-Round trade restrictions (on an MFN basis) would increase LDCs' exports by nearly 12 percent, or $30 billion. See UNCTAD Bulletin, February 1986.

[11] A.J. Yeats, "Effective Tariff Protection in the United States, the European Economic Community, and Japan," *Quarterly Review of Economics and Business*, Summer 1974, p. 45.

ficiary countries, which then displace some inefficient domestic production in the donor country.
2. *The trade-diversion effect:* The tariff discrimination embodied in the preferences results in imports from third countries being displaced by those from the beneficiary countries in the markets of the donor countries.

A recent study[12] suggests that the structure of effective tariff protection of manufacturing industries in the developed countries is *positively* correlated with the comparative advantage of the developing countries. Therefore, an across-the-board, duty-free access (without exceptions or limitations) granted to the developing countries' exports could provide them with an incentive to expand industries in which they have a comparative advantage. Conversely, effective protection in the developed countries was shown to be negatively correlated with their comparative advantage. Consequently, a truly generalized, limitation-free preference scheme would improve allocative efficiency in the developed countries as well. Insofar as the output displaced is that of labor-intensive, technologically unsophisticated industries, the resources in the developed countries would be forced to move to industries in which they possess a comparative advantage. But internal political pressures in the donor countries invariably work to limit this effect. As will be seen in what follows, most preferential schemes include restrictions designed to limit the trade-creation effect. The preferences granted by the EC, for example, are most generous on products in which the developing countries have the least comparative advantage.

Since the trade-diversion effect requires that a preferential margin be maintained, once preferences exist, the developing countries hold a vested interest in opposing general tariff reduction among the developed countries under the GATT.

When preferences were considered in the councils of nations during the 1960s, a host of substantive and administrative problems were raised. Yet sustained pressure from the developing nations, coupled with East–West politics and the vying for influence in the uncommitted world, kept the issue not only alive but in the forefront of international deliberations. These efforts came to fruition in the 1970s, when many industrial nations implemented preferential schemes in favor of the developing countries.

The Generalized System of Preferences (GSP)[13]

During 1971–72, Japan and the Western European countries introduced preferences in favor of the developing countries under UNCTAD sponsorship; the United States and Canada did so on January 1, 1976. Although it was originally envisaged that all industrial countries would adopt the same

---

[12]Z. Iqubal, "The Generalized System of Preferences and the Comparative Advantage of Less Developed Countries in Manufactures," (mimeographed), *International Monetary Fund*, April 1974.

[13]For a comprehensive study of the GSP, see Tracy Murray, *Trade Preferences for Developing Countries*, London, The Macmillan Press, 1977.

scheme in favor of all developing countries (hence the title "Generalized System"), it turned out that the schemes vary greatly in product coverage, list of beneficiary countries, and measures to safeguard domestic output and employment in the donor countries. Because of their importance as major markets, we describe in some detail the EC and the United States schemes.

The European Communities GSP

Under the EC scheme, manufacturing imports from developing countries enter the European Communities duty free, while similar goods originating in other developed countries are subject to the most-favored-nation rate, thereby giving a margin of preference to the developing countries equal to the Common External Tariff of the Communities.

In the case of nonagricultural products, the EC system is essentially a duty-free quota. The amount of each product accorded duty-free entry is subject to a ceiling. Once the ceiling has been reached in any year, further imports from developing countries are charged the full MFN rate of duty, but they revert to duty-free status at the start of the following year. In the case of the "sensitive products" (see below), entry is further restricted by subdividing the ceiling among the EC countries and assigning each member its own quota, so that the quotas effectively become country rather than EC tariff quotas. Because the distribution of the quota among EC members does not match the distribution of EC manufacturing imports from the beneficiary countries, the country quota further restricts the value of the preferences. For the purpose of reimposing the MFN tariff once the quota is exhausted, the EC scheme distinguishes between two types of commodities: sensitive and nonsensitive. "Sensitive" goods are those whose market it is feared will be disrupted by imports from beneficiaries. They constitute over one-half of EC manufacturing imports from the beneficiary countries, and restoration of duty is automatic. For the remaining, "nonsensitive" products, the restoration of the tariff must be ordered by the EC Commission. However, some of the products in the latter category are labeled "semi-sensitive" and are subject to surveillance. Another restrictive provision is that the preferential imports of each product from any one developing country are not allowed to exceed one-half the total ceiling for that product. For sensitive products, this "maximum amount limitation" is often limited to 20 to 30 percent of the total. In the case of textiles, duty-free entry is accorded only to the seven beneficiary countries subject to the GATT multi-fibre agreement (LTA), and to other beneficiaries who undertook, vis-à-vis the EC, bilateral commitments similar to those given in the LTA. In the agricultural field, the EC grants a preferential tariff reduction of 40 percent of the common external tariff on products subject to tariffs, or a similar reduction in the fixed amount of protection for products subject to variable levies.

The quota restrictions severely limit the usefulness of the Generalized System of Preferences (GSP) in promoting exports of the developing countries. A further restriction is imposed by the "rules of origin" governing the GSP. To qualify for duty-free entry, a product must be wholly produced in the preference-receiving country; if imported materials have been used, they must have been subject to "substantial transformation," the general criterion for such a transformation being that they must be categorized under a different four-digit BTN heading. However, there are many exceptions to the general rule governing substantial transformation, and a lengthy document explains the industrial transformation that various products must undergo to qualify for duty-free entry. Many developing countries find these specifications difficult to understand, much less to meet. In addition, given the way the program is administered, much of the government tariff revenue given up by the scheme would be absorbed by the European importers rather than transferred to the developing countries' exporters, for in many cases the importers simply offer reduced prices for imports covered by the scheme. Thus, even the so-called revenue transfer is limited.

Small as they were, the benefits conferred by the GSP were further diluted by the enlargement of the European customs union from six to twelve countries. There are two reasons why this happened. First, the original, relatively liberal, British and Danish schemes were abandoned in 1974 in favor of the more restrictive EC generalized system of preferences. Second, there was the establishment of a free-trade area in Europe. The trade-diversion effect of preferences has value only inasmuch as there are sources of supply over which the developing countries are preferred. Since mid-1977 the developing countries are no longer given preference over any Western European country. The only nonpreferred suppliers to Europe are the United States and Japan—with whom the developing nations compete in only a limited range of products—and the socialist states—who export largely the same products as the developing countries, but who price their exports in such a way as to absorb the preferential margin and remain competitive. Although these statements are subject to several qualifications, the conclusion is inescapable that the EC's contribution to expanding the export market of the developing nations is rather limited. The special preferences granted by the EC to the Associated States are more liberal.

The U.S. GSP

Although the U.S. GSP is more liberal than that of the EC, it contains limitations of its own. Under the Trade Reform Act of 1974, the United States grants duty-free entry to the exports of manufactures, semimanufactures, and selected other products from developing countries and territories. The ten-year program began in 1976, and was extended in 1985 for another 8½ years. There are, however, several important restrictions. First, many commodities of particular export interest to the developing countries are excluded, either because they are goods already subject to import-relief measures in the United States, such as textiles and steel, or because they are politically sensitive items, such as footwear, glass products, and watches. The act prohibits the president from designating as eligible for general preferences any article subject to import-relief measures, and requires withdrawal of preferential treatment from any article that becomes subject to import-relief or national security actions. Indeed, in cases where the International Trade Commission determines that injury exists, the president may terminate preferences rather than change the MFN rate charged to nonbeneficiary countries.

Second, preferential treatment does not apply to imports of an article from a particular developing country if that country supplies 50 percent of the total value of U.S. imports or more than $60 million[14] worth of the article. The $60 million exclusion rule would tend to become more restrictive over time owing to inflationary trends. Furthermore, the restriction makes no distinction between intramarginal and extramarginal exports. Unlike the quota system of the EC, the MFN tariff will apply to all imports of any item excluded by the rule. This constitutes a strong negative incentive for any developing country to export a commodity to the United States even $1 beyond the limit, as that would subject it to MFN duty on all the $60 million plus the $1.

Under a third exclusion, the preferential treatment is not accorded: to any country that discriminates against the United States by granting preferences to other developed countries, to members of OPEC, to countries participating in other cartel-like arrangements by withholding supplies of vital commodities, or to countries failing to cooperate in control of international drug traffic. Countries that do not enjoy MFN treatment (for example, the socialist states) are not eligible for the generalized system of preferences, nor are countries that have expropriated American property.

Finally, the rules of origin require that to qualify for preferences, at least 35 percent of the value of the product must be made in the beneficiary LDC, or 50 percent of its total value must be made in two or more LDCs. Partly because of these limitations, the U.S. GSP has limited effect on promoting the LDCs' exports to the United States. A new feature, known as *graduation*, was introduced when the GSP was extended in 1985. Under it preferential treatment is eliminated or phased out on those products from a particular country that would be competitive without duty-free status. On the other hand, some new benefits were extended to the *least* developed nations. Under the "graduation" provision, $839 million in imports from several LDCs stopped qualifying for duty-free entry as of mid-1986.[15]

Effect of the Tokyo Round on the GSP

Once the Tokyo Round Tariff Concessions are put into effect in 1987, there would be erosion in the margin of preferences accorded the developing

---

[14] This limit is subject to an expansion factor. The two ceilings are collectively referred to as the "competitive-need limitation." Under this provision, imports valued at $12 billion from Mexico, Taiwan, and Korea were removed from the GSP list in 1984.

[15] Duty-free imports under the GSP amounted to $13.3 billion in 1985. Two-thirds came from the top five LDC exporters: Taiwan, South Korea, Brazil, Mexico, and Hong-Kong.

countries under the GSP. But against that loss, the developing countries would be accorded, on a nonreciprocal basis, the benefit of the resulting tariff reductions under the GATT. And these benefits would be free of (a) the restrictions on beneficiaries and on commodity coverage, (b) quantitative limitation, (c) possible removal under domestic safeguard provisions, and (d) the 8½-year time limitation on the GSP program. Careful calculations have shown that these benefits may outweigh the losses occasioned by the erosion in the margin of preferences.[16] Moreover, it is entirely in the interest of the developing countries to plunge into the GATT negotiations as active participants—offering and receiving tariff concessions—rather than to remain passive recipients of nonreciprocal concessions. LDCs do not, as a general rule, need preferences to compete in the markets for which they have a comparative advantage.

Regional Integration among Developing Nations

There is an intense desire on the part of many nonindustrial nations to form regional economic groups among themselves. Customs unions and free-trade areas have been established with varying degrees of success in Central America, South America (the Latin American Free-Trade area), and East and West Africa. The main objective in most cases is to enlarge the domestic market.

Many countries adopt an "import substitution" development strategy. Instead of investing in and expanding their export sector, thereby pursuing development along lines dictated by comparative advantage, they impose restrictions on industrial products and set up their own import-substitution industries. This may or may not be justified, depending on the potential viability and competitive standing of these industries once they reach a certain size and become going concerns. They are certainly justified whenever infant-industry conditions prevail. Other arguments advanced on behalf of such a "balanced growth" strategy are the interdependence of industries in terms of technology and demand, and the unreliability of foreign markets as outlets for surplus products of concentrated production.

But in many cases the developing countries have proceeded on this development course far beyond any conceivable gain and at great cost to their economies in terms of allocative efficiency. Their import-control systems, consisting of tariffs, quotas, exchange controls, and multiple exchange rates, have become correspondingly complicated. Very often the prestige popularly attached to heavy industry is the major force spurring the government to move in this direction. In the end, however, development may be handicapped more than it is helped.

One factor that has an important bearing on the success or failure of such a strategy is the size of the market. The larger the market, the better

---

[16]See R. Baldwin and T. Murray, "MFN Tariff Reductions and LDC Benefits Under the GSP," *Economic Journal*, March 1977, pp. 30–46.

is the prospect that a new industry can someday reach an efficient size and become viable. Consequently, the small size of the domestic market strongly militates against import substitution. Since it is difficult to gain access to the vast markets of the industrial countries—because of competition from established enterprises and the tariff structure—the developing countries often choose to expand their own markets through regional integration.

In analytical terms, there are important differences between European integration and customs unions among developing countries. While in the first case, economic researchers have been mainly concerned with the effect on world welfare, the impact of, say, a West African Common Market on international trade flows is rather insignificant. The main concern in the latter case is with the effect of integration on the integrating countries themselves, and in that respect, trade creation as well as trade diversion *may* be beneficial. In Europe, trade diversion is considered harmful because it implies misallocation of fully employed resources from more efficient to less efficient pursuits. But in developing countries, the domestic labor drawn into trade-diverting activities may have been formerly unemployed or underemployed, so that its opportunity cost is at or near zero. There is another sense in which trade diversion in a customs union among developing countries may be welcome as "the lesser of two evils"—if the alternative to a trade-diverting, import-substituting customs union is a policy of import substitution pursued individually by the members of the union, each with a small national market. A study of the Central American Common Market[17] found the major benefits from integration to be: the savings of scarce foreign exchange (that is, foreign exchange has a scarcity value in excess of its market value) as members trade more with each other and import less from the rest of the world; the utilization of low opportunity-cost labor; and the exploitation of economies of scale.

An important issue that often crops up with this otherwise desirable approach is the distribution of the gains from integration. Because the integrating area consists of countries at different stages of development, new industries and other economic activity generated by the enlarged markets gravitate toward the most highly developed centers, much to the chagrin of those who represent the more backward regions. In East Africa, the developed center may be the Nairobi area. This tendency is often referred to as "polarization" of economic activity. The areas that were most advanced to begin with may come to dominate the entire customs union, while the less-advanced areas do not share in the gain from integration. To cope with this problem, several customs unions have adopted a scheme of allocating new industries among the nations that make up the union, in the hope of ensuring "equitable" distribution of the gain.

[17]See W.R. Cline and E. Delgado (eds.), *Economic Integration in Central America* (Washington, D.C., The Brookings Institution, 1978). For a critical examination of policies designed to promote "south–south" trade, see: Oli Havrylyshyn and Martin Wolf, "Promoting Trade Among Developing Countries: An Assessment," *Finance and Development*, March 1982.

Another common dilemma is the lack of adequate transportation facilities to make the enlarged market economically meaningful. It does little good to establish free-trade areas in South America if member countries find it cheaper to ship to North America and Europe than across the Andes. The natural trade orientation of many such members is toward the industrial nations, intracontinental trade constituting only 10 percent of total trade. Without adequate overland transportation facilities, they cannot hope to change that. A final question involves the exchange restrictions with which the developing governments are faced and that are often left intact when trade restrictions are removed. Meaningful integration cannot take place until exchange transactions are freed.

Other Issues

Issues relating to the international currency system were discussed at the end of Chapter 10. Aside from the LINK vehicle for obtaining development assistance, LDCs seek a considerable enlargement of financial and technical assistance,[18] offered either bilaterally or, preferably, through multilateral channels. Official financial aid has become increasingly important in the 1980s because commercial banks, concerned about the world economic scene, are reluctant to make loans to LDCs. In addition, LDCs want an untying of the bilateral aid component, thereby increasing its value in real terms. Finally, LDCs demand some long-term arrangement that would alleviate the burden of servicing their massive external debt, amounting to hundreds of billions of dollars. For example, Mexico's external debt of $90 billion has a crippling effect on its economy. International bankers are also concerned with the size of these debts from the viewpoint of bank solvency and the viability of the international banking system.

Review Questions

1. Compare and contrast an export-promotion and an import-substitution strategy of development.

2. a. Using 4 partial equilibrium diagrams explain clearly how an international *buffer stock* functions. (Consult Chapter 14 as well.)
   b. What problems arise in the operations of buffer stock agreements?
   c. How do buffer stocks fit in the current UNCTAD proposals for an integrated commodity program? Explain fully.

3. a. How did the Enlargement of the European Community affect the value of the European GSP for developing countries?
   b. How would the Tokyo Round affect the value of the GSP for the LDCs?

---

[18] Within UNCTAD, the developing countries also press for more efficient means of obtaining new technology and for technical aid in developing their tourist facilities and services.

c. Do the terms "trade diversion" and "creation" have a meaning in the analysis of preferences (such as the GSP)? If so, what?

4. Does the traditional analysis of customs unions apply without reservations to economic integration among LDCs?

5. Describe the main features of the GSP granted by the EC and the U.S.

18

International Mobility of Productive Factors

Introduction

*T*hus far in Part 2, we have dealt only with the merchandise-trade component of the balance of payments. Absent from the preceding chapters is an analysis of the capital account. That account was incorporated in Part 1, where the analysis centered on the implications of capital flows for balance-of-payments policies. Because a country's external position comprises both the current and the capital accounts, both have to be considered in discussing international financial relations.

By contrast, Part 2 has centered largely on the relation of international transactions to the domestic economy. It deals with the internal factors that motivate trade and the impact of trade (or, conversely, interferences with trade) on a country's well-being. Nothing has been said in this context about capital or labor movements. Far from being an accident, this omission is rooted in a long-standing assumption of classical economic theory: In attempting to demonstrate the gains from international trade and explain the commodity composition of trade, it is assumed that factors of production (labor, natural resources, and capital) are free to move only within each country; they cannot move between countries. To some extent, this assumption lingers on in many a theoretical discourse.

Observing the world around us, we notice a large-scale international mobility of capital. Although much of it is of the portfolio variety, direct investments in foreign countries by multinational enterprises have come to play a dominant role on the world scene. Also, despite social, cultural, and legal obstacles to mobility, people do move across national boundaries, sometimes in great numbers. Finally, while natural resources are obviously attached to their natural locations, extracted materials as well as manufactured machinery (both of which are included in merchandise trade) are probably more akin to productive factors (in their economic uses) than to final commodities. This, however, is a matter of interpretation.

Productive factors usually move from areas of low remuneration to areas of high remuneration, lowering their supply in the first region and raising it in the latter. The workings of the market then raise the earnings of the migrating factor in the land of departure and lower it in the land of arrival, thus tending to equalize factor rewards the world over. Under the Heckscher–Ohlin theory of international trade, this is what commodity trade is supposed to accomplish. Indeed, under the conditions of that model, commodity trade and factor mobility are substitutes for each other. If factors moved freely to a point where their remunerations were equalized across countries, there would be no international price differentials between commodities and therefore no room for international trade. Only lately have economists begun to develop models that incorporate both commodity and factor mobility,[1] and also begun to integrate the theory of optimum tariff with the theory of optimum tax on capital flows.[2]

The present chapter takes a step in this direction. Relaxing the assumption of immobile capital, it inquires into the costs and benefits of direct foreign investments. It is estimated that foreign subsidiaries of American corporations owned $233 billion of direct investments by the end of 1984, while foreign investment holdings in the United States were $160 billion. Of the total foreign assets owned by American companies, a large share is in petroleum and the extractive industries, but the majority is invested in manufacturing, a large part of it located in Western Europe. Foreign investments in manufacturing facilities in the United States are rising rapidly. Direct investments today are definitely a two-way flow. And at least thirteen American states have offices in Europe and/or Japan attempting to attract foreign investments to their locations.

At the risk of some repetition, we shall consider the impact of these investments on the balance of payments as well as on the economic welfare of the United States. The effect on the welfare of the host countries has been widely discussed in the development literature and will be only

---

[1] The following is an example of how the traditional results can change under such conditions: Suppose country A is more efficient than country B in the production of two products. But the degree of its advantage is identical in the two products, so that the price ratio is the same in both countries. Under the Heckscher–Ohlin model, and in the absence of factor mobility, there would be no trade (see Chapters 11 and 12). But with capital mobile, it would flow from B to A to exploit the more efficient environment, thereby raising the capital-labor ratio in A above that of B. Country A would then begin exporting the capital-intensive product and importing the labor-intensive one.

[2] A tariff imposed by a large country (with monopoly power) may affect not only its terms of trade, but also its terms of borrowing. Suppose the EC imports capital-intensive goods from the United States, and imposes a tariff on such imports. The terms of trade of the EC would improve and those of the United States, deteriorate. But in addition, U.S. (capital-intensive) exports would decline, reducing the price of capital in the United States. Consequently, the EC's terms of borrowing from the United States would also improve. Similarly, an EC tax on capital imports would improve its terms of trade as well as its terms of borrowing. The optimum tariff on imports would be higher under these conditions than when its indirect effect on capital flows were ignored.

summarized here. The final section of this chapter discusses briefly the economic implications of labor migration.

Motives for Direct Investments Abroad[3]

Both economic analysis and empirical studies trace the underlying motive for investing abroad to profit expectations. American enterprises invest in foreign countries when the prospects of profit from such investments exceed profits anticipated from the alternative uses of the funds. From the viewpoint of the national economy, the "alternative uses" consist of investments in the United States either by the same company or by others that can attain control over real resources by obtaining access to those funds. Thus, when investment funds flow to foreign countries, it may be assumed that, given the investment climate at home and abroad, expected profits (allowing for risk) from an incremental investment in foreign countries exceeded the profits expected from such activity in the United States. Factors affecting the relative "investments climate" include the general level of economic activity, existing and anticipated tax and tariff policies, and general institutional arrangements.[4] Certainly the high growth rate in the United States during 1981–85 attracted foreign investments to these shores. Thus between the end of 1983 and 1984 foreign investments in the U.S. rose by 16 percent, while U.S. investments abroad climbed only 3 percent.

But while such a statement lends itself to analysis with the economists' tool kit, it is too superficial for the understanding of business behavior under diverse circumstances. Indeed, when questioned directly about their motives, business organizations may not even mention increased profits. Rather, they tend to emphasize other factors, which in turn have direct or indirect bearing on net earnings.

The factors that contribute to the increased net earnings from foreign investments are so numerous and diverse as to defy an exhaustive survey. At the risk of some oversimplification, we shall lump them into two broad categories. The first category comprises cost or supply considerations that lower the costs of production and distribution, while the second includes market or demand considerations that influence profits by raising total revenue. Because profit is the difference between revenue and cost, what-

---

[3] In recent years, economists have attempted to develop theories that would explain the economic behavior of multinational enterprises. The hypotheses tested have ranged from portfolio diversification (Chapter 6), to sales maximization, to the product cycle theory (Chapter 12), to a desire to maintain a stake in rapidly growing markets, to other factors. However, a cohesive theory of the multinational corporation has not yet emerged. See R. Vernon and L. Wells, *Economic Environment of International Business*, N.Y., Prentice Hall, 1981; and R. Caves, *Multinational Enterprise and Economic Analysis*, Cambridge, Cambridge University Press, 1982.

[4] Another way of viewing the motivation for direct foreign investments is to focus on international profit differentials *within* an industry. Thus if expected profit in U.K. auto manufacturing exceeds that in U.S. auto production while the reverse is true for chemicals, then there would be a flow of direct investments from the U.S. to the U.K. in the auto industry and from the U.K. to the U.S. in the chemical industry.

ever factors raise revenue or lower cost also increase profit. Needless to say, the dichotomy is not clear-cut, and some factors can be classified under either heading.

Cost Considerations

The desire to increase profits by reducing costs certainly plays an important role in foreign investment decisions. It is useful to distinguish between two types of cost-reducing investments. The first arises from the need to obtain raw materials from abroad. Such materials may be either unavailable at home or obtainable only at extremely high costs. But they are essential to the production and sale of final products at home or abroad. Profit opportunities would remain unexploited without them.

Indeed, the vast American foreign investments in the extractive industries are motivated by the fact that the capital must go where the resources are. The product of such investments is a factor of production *complementary* to the labor and capital employed within the United States. Any diminution in the availability of this resource would directly harm the productivity and remunerations of the other two. This complementary factor includes primary materials, certain agricultural commodities (tropical products), and some semiprocessed goods brought back to the United States for further processing, with the final product marketed either here or abroad. Inclusion of the last item is dictated by the transportation costs of the primary products. When they are prohibitive or very high, the first stage of processing may have to take place at or near the extraction site, with the product brought home in a semiprocessed form. Investments in foreign transportation and communication links, which make possible or cheapen exports from the home country to otherwise isolated regions, can be regarded in the same light. Many of the American investments in developing countries are so motivated.

The second type of cost-reducing investment involves costs other than materials—primarily labor. Although to the company management it makes little difference where costs are cut, the national interest is likely to be affected differently. In the case of extractive industries, the resource whose cost is reduced is complementary to U.S. factors of production; it raises the productivity of American labor as well as capital and often leads to increased production within the United States. In some cases, such as oil, the resource is essential to the productive process in this country. On the other hand, when foreign investments are designed to lower labor costs, the savings occur in the employment of factors that are competitive with American resources. While such foreign investments raise the productivity of American capital, they tend to lower the productivity of American labor compared with similar investments in the United States.

Perhaps the most potent motive in the second category is the desire to take advantage of lower labor costs in foreign countries. The fact that wage rates in the United States are higher than in many other countries is not in itself an indication of higher labor costs. It is simply a reflection of the higher productivity of American labor. But when the wage differentials are not fully offset by productivity differentials, the result is lower labor cost in foreign countries. Industries in which the labor component is high relative to the capital component (the relatively "labor-intensive" industries) would be the first candidates for such cost differentials. But an unfavorable labor-cost differential may appear at times even in capital-intensive industries, when wage rates abroad lag considerably behind increases in productivity. The remarkable wage stability in Europe during the second half of the 1950s certainly contributed to that phenomenon, thereby stimulating American investments abroad. But in the late 1970s, U.S. labor costs were lower than their counterparts in certain European countries, motivating European companies to establish or purchase production facilities in the United States. Labor-cost differentials can be exploited by producing abroad and selling the final product in the host country, in third countries, or even back in the investing countries. Thus, many of the television sets imported into the United States, which compete with American-made sets, come from foreign operations of U.S. companies.

Another type of saving that can be secured by manufacturing abroad is in transportation costs. When the final product is perishable or has a high weight-to-value ratio, proximity to the main markets becomes very important. It may then be advantageous to replace exports by foreign production.

Government policies often play a direct role in inducing foreign investments. The outflow of capital may be motivated by a desire to take advantage of special tax treatment. More often, tariff policies both here and abroad bring about substantial relocation of plants. Successive reductions of duties by the United States can induce companies to produce abroad for sale in the United States. As American manufacturers lose their protective tariffs, they may not be able to compete against lower-cost imports, primarily of labor-intensive products. Consequently, they may set up production facilities in low-cost areas from which to supply the American market. Likewise, the establishment of the EC and the EFTA in Europe provided very strong incentives for American companies to invest there. Such investments enable producers to circumvent the discriminatory tariff wall they must face when exporting from the United States. And each facility in Europe can supply several national markets. Thus, the plant can be large enough to realize economies of scale and the benefits of specialization. Asian firms may invest in the Caribbean islands in order to gain duty-free access to the U.S. market. By the same token, there is little doubt that the high Canadian tariff constitutes a powerful inducement for American corporations to invest in Canada. Without it, the Canadian market could easily be supplied out of stateside locations.[5] Capital movement has become a substitute for the obstructed commodity movement.

[5] Canadian welfare may either rise or fall from such a policy. The tariff induces a U.S. corporation to set up a subsidiary in Canada. While the subsidiary may yield good profits, the corporation's worldwide profits would presumably fall; otherwise, it would have set up the

Tariff reduction in foreign countries has the opposite effect of making U.S. exports more competitive abroad, thus lessening the need to produce in foreign countries. In this case, export trade from the United States replaces the potential outward movement of capital. Finally, the depreciation of the dollar in the 1970s made U.S. investments abroad more expensive and foreign investments in the United States cheaper.[6] Correspondingly, there occurred a rather substantial increase in the inflow of European and Japanese direct investments into the United States. For American firms the dollar depreciation has tipped the balance between investing abroad and exporting from the United States in favor of exporting. For foreign firms the balance has been tipped in the opposite direction. But this reason disappeared in the 1980s, with the sharp appreciation of the U.S. dollar in 1981–85.

When a large company goes abroad, it sometimes becomes necessary for the enterprises that supply it at home, including banks that provide financial services, to set up overseas branches in order to provide orderly supplies to its foreign subsidiaries.

Marketing Considerations

On an abstract level, there exists a historical pattern according to which firms are induced to set up foreign branches as they become familiar with foreign markets through exports. The general widening of business horizons attendant upon the expansion of international trade leads businesses to increase their foreign investments. But sheer familiarity is merely an enabling condition. The desire to cater to specific market needs appears to

---

subsidiary even without the tariff. Because the corporation's marginal cost of supplying the Canadian market goes up, it would charge higher prices for its products. Hence, the burden of the tariff is split between the corporation and the Canadian consumer. Set against this consumer cost of protection are gains to Canada in the form of higher profit taxes and increased marginal product of labor. The latter gain could be large if prior to the foreign investments Canadian labor were paid more than its marginal social product, due to the existence of underemployment. To these benefits we may add the gain of external economies.

[6] However, the change in the relative price of investments in the United States and abroad is not a satisfactory explanation of the surge in foreign investments in the United States or of the possible decline in the rate of growth of U.S. investments overseas. This change is offset by the fact that a given return on U.S. investments abroad is now translated into more dollars, whereas a given dollar return on foreign investments in the United States is translated into smaller amounts of foreign currencies.

Other possible explanations for these phenomena are: (1) Currency overvaluation shrinks the domestic and foreign markets of the firm, resulting in excess capacity. It is also an incentive to move redundant capital abroad. (2) If the firm seeks to maximize sales (subject to a minimum profit constraint) rather than profits, overvaluation would lead it to move abroad. Devaluation reverses these trends. But the most potent explanation is that exchange rates are *perceived to be in disequilibrium*. In the 1960s and again in the 1980s, the dollar was generally regarded as overvalued relative to the European currencies. Consequently it was "cheap" for American investors to set up manufacturing facilities in Europe. And the return on these investments, expressed in European currencies, was expected to rise in terms of dollars when the overvaluation was corrected and the dollar depreciated. A reverse phenomenon occurred in the late 1970s.

be the real motivation. Initially, dissatisfaction with distribution techniques abroad may stimulate the establishment of a selling organization, including warehousing and service facilities, to market exports from the United States. As a second stage, the company is drawn to set up production or assembly and conversion plants so as to be close to its customers, provide better services, gear its product lines to local demands in specific markets, and, perhaps, satisfy the nationalistic feelings of its customers (or of the local government), thus increasing their acceptance of the product. However, as regards the last factor, we should hasten to add that nationalistic feelings also work in the opposite direction. As French, Canadian, and Mexican reactions indicate, there is a fairly widespread aversion to American control of foreign-based manufacturing facilities. Such feelings may not apply to minority share holdings, but most American companies strongly prefer majority interest. On balance, however, market and demand considerations constitute a potent factor in stimulating foreign investments. In addition, antitrust legislation in the United States, which often prevents firms from expanding through the acquisition of their competitors, may induce them to purchase such firms overseas.

Foreign Investments and Economic Welfare (Real Income)

World Welfare

It has long been an established proposition of economic theory that free movement of resources is beneficial to the world economy as a whole. When capital is attracted from one country to another by a higher rate of return, it flows from areas where it is relatively abundant and cheap to countries in which it is relatively scarce and expensive, until returns to it are equalized the world over. This flow is bound to be beneficial, because it raises total real output. The contribution of the marginal unit of capital to real output is less in the donor nation than in the host nation; in other words, capital is a relatively more important productive factor where it is scarce than where it is abundant. Thus, the addition to output it brings about in the receiving country exceeds the diminution to output in the giving (or investing) country, causing a net increase in their combined real output.

Host Country

As a general rule, the host country benefits considerably from foreign investments. Not only does its real product rise because of the contribution of new capital, but direct foreign investments usually bring with them managerial and technological know-how as well as access to inventions and innovations and to well-developed capital markets. If the level of training of the labor force rises as a result, the foreign capital is said to generate external economies to the benefit of other firms operating in the same industry. Foreign investments help the host country's balance of payments, both through the inflow of capital and export of products produced in the new plants. And finally, as income in the host country rises, so do savings, and the entire economy is consequently placed on a new and higher growth path. In the case of developing countries, an important element in export and growth can be the processing of assembly and component manufactures by vertically integrated multinational companies, who use these components in their operations in other countries.

Against this background, one might puzzle over the strong resentment that American investments generate in various host countries. Such nations as Mexico and Canada have enacted laws that, in one way or another, restrict foreign control or takeover of domestic enterprises. Likewise, India insists that (with some exceptions) multinational corporations operating in that country "dilute" their foreign ownership to under 50 percent by selling part ownership to Indian residents. And IBM's insistence on 100 percent corporate ownership led to its "withdrawal" from India in 1977 and from Nigeria in 1978. To some extent these phenomena may be explained by nationalistic or emotional feelings.

Foreign investments *performance standards* are common in host countries. They include a requirement that local subsidiaries of foreign companies export a minimum proportion of their output; and/or that they use in their production a minimum proportion of domestic materials and labor (local content requirements). These standards apply only to foreign investors and not to indigenous firms.[7] In 1983 a GATT panel found the Canadian local content standard (but not its minimum export requirements) in violation of GATTs rules. Canadian regulations of foreign investments were relaxed somewhat in 1985.

Some charges against foreign investors may rest on economic rather than emotional foundations, and these should be sorted out. The charge that foreign-owned enterprises exploit labor in the host country and take away natural resources at less than market value is in most cases exaggerated. Exploitation can occur only when monopoly power prevails. When exploration rights for a country's natural resources are sought by many firms, exploitation is unlikely. The host country benefits in terms of taxes, royalties, wages and salaries paid locally, and imported technology. However, when the investing company has monopoly power, "exploitation" is clearly possible and can undermine the terms of trade of the host country.[8] On the other hand, the producing countries can also organize a cartel and "exploit" the consuming countries, as was done by the OPEC nations. More serious is the complaint that foreign affiliates of American companies are governed by U.S. policies and laws that conflict with the policies of the host country. For example, a 1982 U.S. directive to European subsidiaries of

---

[7] For an analysis of the economic effects of such requirements see C. Davidson, S. Matusz and M. Kreinin, "Analysis of Performance Standards for Direct Foreign Investments," *Canadian Journal of Economics*, November 1985.

[8] For a more complete analysis see P. Streeten, "The Multinational Enterprise and the Theory of Development Policy," *World Development*, October 1973.

U.S. companies to withhold American technology from the construction of the Siberian–Western Europe gas pipeline caused an uproar in Europe.

A third allegation is that the major policy decisions of international companies and their research and development activities are centralized in the home office, leaving only routine work and less technical activities for the employees of foreign subsidiaries. However, in most cases, a profit-maximizing company is likely to use local talent to the extent that it is available, especially when the firm is subject to considerable pressure to do so. The charge that American companies are insensitive to local business practices in labor relations and other areas may be correct, but it is often the local practices that contribute to inefficiency and slow down economic growth. Finally, certain countries object to being "dominated" by foreign firms and especially dislike having their high-technology industries controlled by foreign capital. The charge of political domination is probably exaggerated, and in any case it does not fall within the purview of the economist. But the concentration of American capital in the technology- and science-intensive industries is to be expected, because the United States possesses a comparative advantage in these areas. However, far from being injurious, the imported technology is highly beneficial to the host country. In sum, although there are possible losses, on balance the capital-receiving country reaps a considerable gain in most cases.

Source (Investing) Country

Such a gain is not the likely outcome for the source country (for example, the United States). In order to isolate the effect of foreign investments on American real income from its impact on other economic magnitudes, we assume that the economy is operating at full employment and that it is continuously maintained at or about that level by fiscal and monetary means. Also, the balance of payments is assumed to be in equilibrium and to adjust rapidly and smoothly to transfers of capital via a freely fluctuating exchange rate. The question posed under these circumstances is how to distribute the aggregate savings generated by a fully employed economy between domestic and foreign investments so as to maximize real national product (or income). Put differently, will real national product be maximized if the distribution is left strictly to market decisions exercised by a multitude of profit-maximizing enterprises—if the location of each investment project depends on expected after-tax earnings here and abroad?

The answer is that, particularly in the manufacturing sector, foreign investments are likely to proceed considerably beyond what is warranted by the national interest, for several reasons. First, there are several types of risk that the firm may not fully consider before going abroad. The risk of unfavorable public regulations, such as regulations of profits, repudiation of loans, or even confiscation, affect the individual firm whether its investments are at home or abroad. But the national economy suffers only if the investments are abroad.

Second, there is a revenue loss to the U.S. government. In order to avoid double taxation (on grounds of equity), foreign investors are permitted to credit income taxes paid abroad against their domestic tax liability. Only the difference between the host country tax rate and that prevailing in the United States accrues to the U.S. government. In deciding where to invest, the private firm compares expected after-tax profit here and abroad; it is a matter of indifference to it which government receives the tax. But with corporate taxes ranging up to 46 percent of earnings, this is of great concern to the national government. A foreign investment yields tax revenue mainly to the host government, while the same investment in the United States yields profits that are taxed by the U.S. government. Under present institutional arrangements, foreign investments benefit the national interest only if after-tax profits abroad exceed net earnings before taxes in the United States. To some extent this fiscal loss is offset by the need for public expenditures to service home investments, a need that is absent in the case of foreign investments.

To recapitulate, for the private investor, the relevant comparison is between net-of-tax returns abroad and net-of-tax returns at home. In terms of world efficiency of resource use, the comparison should be made between gross returns abroad and gross returns at home. But in terms of national interest, the relevant comparison is between returns on investment made abroad after foreign tax and returns on investment made at home before tax. The national interest is served only if the former exceeds the latter.

Third, investments affect the productivity and remunerations of capital as well as labor and land. An addition to the capital stock, whether here or abroad, has the following effects: (1) Total real output rises as an increasing volume of capital is combined with a relatively stable amount of other resources, mainly labor and land; (2) the productivity of the incremental unit of capital, and therefore the rate of return to existing capital, tends to decline as the capital stock rises in proportion to other factors; and (3) the productivity of labor and land, and their rate of remuneration, tends to increase as each unit of these resources is combined with an increasing volume of capital in the productive process. The private firm is concerned only with the rate of return on capital when deciding where to locate its investment. The national view, on the other hand, cannot overlook the implications to other factors of production. In the case of foreign investments, it is the productivity of foreign labor and land that would rise. If the investments are undertaken at home, these benefits accrue to domestic resources. The point is abundantly illustrated by the American corporations that set up processing plants in Mexico just south of the border with the clear intention of bringing the finished product back to market in the United States. The incentive for doing this is the lower wage cost in Mexico. In the process, Mexican labor gains, and American labor loses as it is deprived of the use of the capital that crosses the border.

Combining the last two criteria, the national interest is served when returns on investments made abroad after foreign taxes exceed the returns on home investments before taxes by more than the loss in productivity of domestic labor.

Furthermore, the expansion of production attendant upon the new investments usually carries with it indirect benefits. These include improvement in the quality of labor, better production methods and techniques, and superior forms of organization. In the case of foreign investments, these benefits would be lost to the domestic economy. Indeed, because foreign investments require American technical and managerial talent, the movement of such personnel abroad deprives the U.S. economy of their services. (The U.S. is assumed to be the source country.)

This loss to the domestic economy may be more than offset in many instances by one important factor: The productivity of domestic capital and other resources depends in some measure on the capital endowment of the rest of the world. This phenomenon is most evident in the case of foreign investments in the extractive industries. The provision of primary materials from foreign sources (when domestic sources are not available) increases the productivity of domestic factors of production, because such materials are complementary to American capital and labor. In this case, there is a gain rather than a loss to domestic factors. Because a large share of U.S. investments in developing countries tends to concentrate in the extractive industries, the foreign policy objective of promoting investments in these areas (either as a substitute for or an addition to foreign aid) happens to coincide with the domestic economic interest.

On the other hand, half of the U.S. investments in Western Europe is concentrated in manufacturing industries. Here the argument outlined in the previous paragraph holds only to a limited extent. It is therefore suggested that foreign investments, motivated by private profit considerations, would exceed the amount justified by the national interest when that interest is defined as the maximization of real domestic income.

This is a fairly short-run analysis. In the long run, American investments abroad would increase income and output in the receiving countries, inducing increased imports from the United States. American output and employment would thereby be favorably affected. These benefits have not been included in the considerations above.

Finally, and most emphatically, the above argument constitutes a strictly one-sided view of America's stake in international investments. The other side is the rapidly increasing foreign investment in American manufacturing industries. In this case, the indirect benefits accrue to the United States, while the investment process proceeds beyond what is warranted from the foreign national point of view. Today, foreign investments are a two-way stream. The analysis does demonstrate that the assorted complaints emanating from various host countries that foreign investments are in some sense harmful to them are largely unfounded. Far from being damaging, these investments have made a tremendous contribution. The international diffusion of technological innovations and managerial know-how that takes place through the vehicle of the multinational enterprise sufficiently illustrates its contribution to the international economy. The interest of world welfare is best served by unobstructed flow of investment capital.

☐ **Taxing the Multinational Corporation**   Within the United States, an immediate policy problem is the tax treatment of direct foreign investments. It is alleged that the federal tax laws discriminate against investments in the United States and in favor of foreign investments and therefore constitute an inducement to invest abroad.

☐ Major federal tax concessions granted U.S. investments abroad are the foreign tax credit; tax deferral; and various tax preferences given to Western Hemisphere trade corporations, investments in the developing countries, and investment in the U.S. possessions. The first two concessions constitute the bulk of the loss in U.S. government revenues; we first consider the foreign tax credit.

☐ Foreign-incorporated subsidiaries and branches of American corporations are entitled to credit against their U.S. income tax the full amount of taxes they pay to foreign governments (at all levels of government). Thus, if the subsidiary earned $1000 and is operating in a country where profits are taxed at the rate of 30 percent, it would pay the host government $300 in taxes. Since the U.S. profit tax is 46 percent, its total tax liability to the American government is $460, from which the corporation is entitled to subtract the full amount of the foreign tax. Its tax obligation to the U.S. government becomes $460 − $300 = $160. If the foreign tax rate were 46 percent, the U.S. tax obligation of the above corporation (on its foreign profit) would be zero. But the credit cannot exceed the U.S. tax of 46 percent, so a corporation operating in a foreign country where the tax exceeds 46 percent has a total foreign and U.S. tax in excess of 46 percent[9] even though it pays no U.S. taxes.

☐ The rationale for this tax credit derives from the (public finance) principle of "horizontal equity," which requires equal tax treatment of persons with equal incomes. Applied to the case of foreign investments, the aim is to ensure the same total rate of taxation on domestic and foreign investments; it can be construed as horizontal equity on the international level. An alternative way of interpreting horizontal equity is to apply it on the national level. This would call for treating foreign-paid taxes in the same manner as domestically paid state and local taxes. The latter taxes are treated by the federal government as a cost of doing business. Thus, in our example, the $300 tax paid to the foreign government would be subtracted as a

---

[9] However, U.S. corporations operating in more than one foreign country can choose to calculate this credit either on a country-by-country basis or on the overall basis of lumping together taxes paid to all foreign governments. The latter option is advantageous if one foreign country levies a tax in excess of the 46 percent U.S. tax rate and another less than that.

business deduction from the $1000 profit, yielding taxable income of $700. The 46 percent U.S. federal tax would then be levied on the $700, resulting in a U.S. tax bill of $322. The total U.S. and foreign tax paid by the company on its overseas profits would then be $300 + $322 = $622, instead of the current $460. This in essence is what the Hartke–Burke bill proposed;[10] but it was never enacted into law.

☐ The tax deferral provision permits the profits of foreign incorporated subsidiaries of U.S. corporations to enjoy a deferment of U.S. tax until the profit is remitted to the parent corporation.[11] At best, this implies an interest-free loan from the U.S. government to the corporation for the duration of the deferral. But because much of the earnings retained abroad are reinvested in fixed assets, this virtually amounts to a permanent exemption from U.S. tax. Deferral clearly introduces a non-neutral incentive to invest abroad and is difficult to defend on the grounds of either equity or efficiency. No such deferral is available on domestic investments and the Hartke–Burke bill proposes the elimination of the deferral provision on foreign investments.[12]

☐ **The *Unitary Tax Issue***   A frequent complaint of several European countries relates to the *unitary tax* method used by 12 states (including California) to tax multinational companies. Under this system, a state levies its corporate income tax on multinational corporations on the basis of their worldwide earnings rather than on earnings from the business conducted within the state's boundaries. For example, if 10 percent of a company's sales, payroll and property are in California, 10 percent of all its global earnings are subject to the state's corporation tax. Thus a foreign company may be losing money on its U.S. operations and still be taxed on its worldwide profits. Additionally, because the state unitary method has no provision for credits for foreign taxes paid, the world-wide unitary method leads to international double taxation.

☐ As foreign countries (particularly Britain) threatened retaliation in 1985, the Reagan administration prepared to back legislation limiting the states' ability to use this method of taxation.   ∎

---

[10] It has been estimated that a change in the treatment of foreign profits from tax credit to tax deduction would produce an additional revenue to the U.S. government of $1.4 billion. See the *NBER Digest*, July 1982, p.3.

[11] In contrast to the tax credit rule, tax deferral applies also to dividend income on portfolio investments.

[12] The other types of tax concessions can be justified at least in part by the need to foster economic development: Western Hemisphere trade corporations are provided a 14 percentage point reduction in their U.S. tax liability. Corporations operating in developing countries were permitted to retain a variety of tax preferences, which were eliminated for other corporations in the 1962 Revenue Act. Finally, certain investments in U.S. possessions are treated as foreign corporations for the purpose of the U.S. income tax.

Effect on the U.S. Balance of Payments

We now drop the assumption of automatic balance-of-payments adjustment to capital outflow and ask what impact foreign investments have on the external accounts of the United States. On the face of it, the balance of payments is affected adversely by the amount of the capital outflow. But this oversimplified statement overlooks the relationship between the various balance-of-payments items and ignores the fact that capital outflow generates "favorable" movements of both goods and funds.

When an enterprise is established abroad, it immediately generates substantial exports in the form of capital equipment and materials required for plant operations. In subsequent years, the export of spare parts, materials, and additional equipment tends to continue, further mitigating the initial impact on the balance of payments.

Next, there is the return inflow of earnings into the United States. In any given year, this inflow represents earnings on investments made in past years. Put differently, an investment made at one time will generate earnings in subsequent years. And repatriated earnings constitute a major positive item in the U.S. balance of payments. It has been estimated that on the average, the payback period on the original capital outflow is five to ten years.

Third, we come to the least tangible aspect of foreign investments— the sales of the products of American subsidiaries, most of which are marketed in the host country, with the rest shipped to the United States or to third-country destinations. There are great variations in this mix among different industries and countries, but since we do not know what the situation would be in the absence of foreign investments it is rather difficult to evaluate their effects.

Most successful foreign ventures are expanded over the years through the investment of retained earnings and locally borrowed funds. Their book value rises correspondingly. These assets are obviously not available to the American monetary authorities for coping with the balance-of-payments deficit. But they do strengthen the long-run position of the United States and as such inspire confidence in the dollar as a transaction and reserve currency, thereby increasing the willingness of foreigners to hold and accumulate dollar assets.

Finally and most emphatically, foreign investment is a two-way street, and the 1970s witnessed a rapid growth of European and Japanese investments in the United States.

International Trade Theory and the Multinational Corporation

The emergence of the multinational corporation (MNC) as a major force on the world economic scene—with MNCs accounting for over one-fifth of all production—raises the fundamental question of whether the traditional theory of international trade still provides an adequate explanation of the economic world. Unfortunately, analytical work on this topic is still in its infancy, and the present exposition is of necessity rudimentary. It attempts to determine which strains of the theory are now the most relevant, and to what extent we need to modify important propositions made earlier in this book.

The Phenomenon of Transfer Pricing

International trade theory assumes that commodities are traded on world markets between independent firms, at market-determined (sometimes referred to as "arm's length") prices. But today, between one-fourth and one-third of world trade in manufactures is conducted *within* firms. MNCs tend to be vertically integrated companies, each producing the intermediate products (for example, components) necessary for its production processes as well as an array of final goods. Various components are manufactured by affiliates or subsidiaries of the corporation located in different countries, while the final assembly plants may be located in still other countries. As components and materials move through the production processes, they are transferred from one subsidiary to another, and therefore become part of international trade. Consequently, a large and growing proportion of international trade is actually intra-firm exchange. And the items entering such trade will be valued according to considerations other than those determining competitive market prices.

In this exchange the corporation is interested in maximizing its overall after-tax profit, rather than the profit of individual subsidiaries. The prices charged by one subsidiary on sales to another (located in a different country), known as *transfer prices*, may differ significantly from world prices. In particular, they are designed to minimize overall corporate income taxes and tariff payments. If tax rates differ between the countries in which the corporation's subsidiaries are located, the corporation will shift profits from the high to the low tax country. Thus, if the country into which components are imported has higher tax rates than the components-exporting country, the corporation will artificially *raise* the price of the components; it will underprice them when the opposite is the case. In this fashion it tries to maximize the profit of the subsidiaries in the low-tax country and minimize the profit of the subsidiaries in the high-tax country. A country raising its profit tax rates may find itself losing rather than gaining tax revenue as MNCs adjust to the new rates.

Second, the multinational corporation attempts to minimize its tariff payments to the country that imports components and intermediate goods. This requires underpricing of the exported components and involves shifting profits from the supplying to the importing country subsidiary. If profit tax rates are higher in the former than in the latter, the benefit to the corporation from the lower duty reinforces the gain from reduced profit taxes. In the reverse case, the two effects operate in opposite directions. In all cases, the pricing policies of the MNC on intra-firm (but international) trade would be affected by both tariff and tax considerations, and not merely by market forces of supply and demand.

Some implications of this phenomenon may now be considered. If a government imposes a tariff on some intermediate products to protect domestic producers, then the protective effect may be negated by an MNC exporting such products from other countries (to its assembly plant in the said country) at reduced prices. The government can counteract this by fixing component prices for duty purposes at a level close to market prices, by imposing antidumping duties, by converting *ad valorem* into specific tariffs, or by replacing tariffs with import quotas. But if the aim is to raise revenue, the tariff-imposing country may actually gain from the understatement of import values induced by an *ad valorem* tariff. Its loss in customs revenue could be more than offset by a gain in profits taxes. On the other hand, a government wishing to counteract the evasion of profits taxes by MNCs overstating import values can impose or raise tariffs on the imported components. This would encourage the corporation to underprice the components. The OECD is attempting to develop a code under which MNCs would adopt the same pricing policies as those followed by unrelated enterprises.

Finally, the computed effective rates of protection can be grossly distorted by transfer pricing. In particular, components can be so overpriced by the corporation that they appear to cost more than the value of the final product when the latter is valued at world market prices. This would give rise to an apparent case of "negative value added." Even in the absence of such an extreme result, the (erroneous) impression conveyed would be that of high protection for production of the final product in which the imported inputs are used (because the portion of the imported input in the value of the final product would appear artificially high).

The Commodity Composition of Trade

To what extent are the traditional theories (which rest on the assumption of immobile productive factors) still adequate in explaining the pattern of international trade? We can think of the MNC as a huge enclave cutting across national boundaries. It is an independent economic entity that buys and sells factors and goods, makes and receives transfers, and creates various external effects. Its linkages to a country in which it is operating include the employment of local labor and locally raised capital, the purchase of local materials and the sale of final products on the local market, the payment of taxes, and the creation of various externalities.

The corporation employs some productive factors that are immobile between countries—unskilled and skilled labor (and perhaps land)—in conjunction with two factors that move freely within the corporate empire, capital and knowledge. The return to the two mobile factors would be equalized between countries. But the relative factor intensities of the two immobile factors are still relevant in explaining the pattern of trade: Skilled-labor-intensive products would be produced in countries relatively well endowed with skilled labor, and unskilled-labor-intensive products, in countries relatively well endowed with unskilled labor. This result underscores the importance of labor skills, as against the simple capital/labor ratio, in explaining the commodity composition of trade, and is consistent with empirical findings (see Chapter 12).

Second, the two mobile factors would be attracted to those countries that are generally more efficient because of their physical infrastructure, political stability, and similar conditions. Such countries would therefore tend to produce and export products intensive in capital and knowledge. Third, the existence of transport costs, tariffs, and other import restrictions would induce the corporation to locate close to its main markets and to produce for them. On the other hand, when increasing returns to scale are important, there would be a tendency to limit the number of locations in which any product is produced. The existence of transport costs, along with economies of scale, will confer on countries with large domestic markets a comparative advantage in economies-of-scale-intensive goods.

The skill level of countries can change over time, requiring the MNC to adjust its production configuration. Likewise, knowledge may not be perfectly or instantly mobile within the corporation; it may take time to spread. To that extent, a corporate adjustment may be required, yielding a model similar to the product cycle approach.

This rudimentary discussion demonstrates—however tentatively—that it is possible to use various strains of the traditional theory to explain location and trade in a world in which MNCs play an important role. Explanations are no longer as simple as the Heckscher–Ohlin model and must be adapted to the new circumstances. Labor skill, economies of scale, transport costs, and the product cycle have become important ingredients. As long as some factors are reasonably immobile and others mobile, rather familiar results may be obtained. This takes us one point further. The concern of traditional economic theory with the effect of trade and import restrictions on the welfare of a country remains valid despite the increased mobility of factors in the MNC world. This is so because certain factors—namely labor, human capital embodied in the labor force, and capital embodied in the country's infrastructure—are largely immobile. And it is precisely the welfare of the immobile population that governments often seek to maximize.

International Migration of Labor

People do not move around as freely as capital. Not only are there legal obstacles to migration, but families tend to be socially and culturally rooted in their country of birth, and such attachments are difficult to overcome. Even language is sometimes a formidable obstacle to migration. Yet there are instances of large-scale migration; in particular, the European Communities have provided for free mobility of labor among the member countries. Indeed, highly industrialized areas in Europe (such as West Germany) where labor shortages are common, employ migrant workers on a large scale. Movement of people around the British Commonwealth is another instance of such migration, as is the migration of Mexican labor to the United States. Such cases are rare enough that they do not negate the proposition that labor is a *relatively* immobile factor. Yet it is important to examine the welfare implications of labor movements when they do occur.

Under ordinary circumstances people migrate in response to economic incentives; they move from their own country to another where they can command higher remuneration. The consequences of such migration parallel those of capital movements. In most cases migration is beneficial to world welfare. The migrants' marginal productive contribution, which is reflected in the income they command, is generally higher in the new country than in the old. In other words, the loss in production to the country from which they depart falls short of the gain in production to the country in which they settle, resulting in a net gain to the world as a whole. However, if the primary incentive to migration is not financial, the outcome may be different.

Migration also affects the income of factors of production in the two countries. If the migrating population owns no capital, the workers remaining behind in the country of emigration benefit while those in the country of immigration lose from migration;[13] the opposite consequences apply to capital.

So far, we have treated labor as a homogeneous factor of production. But in reality it is not, of course. Workers possess varying degrees of skills and training. International migration of highly trained scientific, technical, academic, and medical personnel, notably from the Commonwealth to Great Britain and from the developing countries to Europe and North America, has reached such proportions that it has become a cause for political and intellectual concern in many quarters. It is feared that this "brain drain" deprives developing countries, especially, of badly needed talents, and some concerned observers have even suggested the imposition of restrictions on the movement of highly trained people, or subjecting them to special taxes to be collected by their country of origin.

As was pointed out earlier, when migration takes place in response to economic incentives, it raises the real income of the world as a whole. The developing countries very often simply cannot productively absorb people who are highly trained in certain subjects, because the absorptive capacity of an economy depends on its level of development and degree of industrialization. On the other hand, there may be a crying need for these people

---

[13] See Berry and Soligo "Welfare Aspects of International Migration," *Journal of Political Economy*, October 1969; and Thompson and Clark, "Factor Movements With Three Factors and Two Goods in the U.S. Economy," *Economic Letters*, 1983, pp. 53–60.

in the industrial world. Thus, the difference between their marginal products in the two countries is very large, with migration easily resulting in a net gain to the world. In some cases, however, the country of emigration may justifiably demand compensation against the losses it incurs (even when these fall short of the gains to the receiving country), especially if it has spent resources to train the migrating specialists.

There are only two cases in which the "brain drain" may cause a loss to the world as a whole: first, if diverse taxation (or wage control) systems in the two countries distort the relationship between remuneration and marginal productivity[14] so that educated people move to countries where their marginal productivity is lower than in their native country; second, and more important, when the activity of educated people contributes to the welfare or productivity of others in the country of residence, a contribution known as "externality," and that externality is greater in the country of origin. Such contributions as leadership capacity, originality, creativity, and inventive ability come to mind as examples of "externalities." But it is only when they are not rewarded through the market that externalities may reverse the gain to world welfare that comes from free migration. It is true that on occasion there may be a strong case for compensating the countries of emigration for their losses. But the world as a whole nearly always benefits from unobstructed migration of trained labor. Moreover, the case against restrictions on international migration goes far beyond economics. It rests upon the cherished principles of personal freedom.

Review Questions

1. List some of the factors that induce companies to invest abroad.

2. Does the economic interest of a U.S. company investing abroad in manufacturing subsidiaries coincide with the interest of the U.S. as a country? If not, in what ways do the interests diverge? Why does the U.S. labor movement object to foreign investments by U.S. companies?

3. How are foreign subsidiaries of U.S. companies taxed? What are "transfer prices" and how are they affected by differential taxation? What is the "unitary tax issue"?

4. Why might the *labor skill* theory of the commodity composition of trade be appropriate in a world where production and trade are handled by *multinational corporations*? (Explain italicized terms.)

5. Examine the effects of direct foreign investments on the welfare of: a. the source country, b. the host country, c. the world as a whole.

6. What are the effects of direct foreign investments on the balance of payments of the source country?

---

[14] Migration of a star athlete from Sweden may be a case in point.

Appendices

APPENDIX I

Forums for Trade and Monetary Talks

The principal organizations and groups of countries that deal with the world's trade and monetary problems are described below.

General Agreement on Tariffs and Trade (GATT)   A multilateral trade treaty among governments, made up of 92 contracting parties, the GATT provides a framework for trade negotiations and lays down ground rules for the conduct of international trade.

International Monetary Fund (IMF)   Established in December 1945, it is the international organization with primary responsibility for international monetary matters. Each of its 149 member countries is assigned a quota, the size of which depends on the country's national income, international reserves, annual imports, variability of exports, and the ratio of exports to national income. In turn, the quota determines the member's voting power, its financial contribution to the Fund, and its ability to draw on the Fund's resources. The Fund's highest authority is the board of governors (consisting of a governor and an alternate governor appointed by the members), which meets once a year, and, when necessary, votes by mail. The general operations of the Fund are the responsibility of 21 executive directors, of which 6 are appointed by France, West Germany, Saudi Arabia, Japan, the United Kingdom, and the United States, and 15 are elected by groups of members.

World Bank   An international financial institution that makes loans for development to LDCs out of subscription capital as well as from funds raised on the world's capital markets.

The European Community (EC)   Sometimes referred to as the Common Market, its 12 members are West Germany, France, Italy, Belgium, the Netherlands, Luxembourg, the United Kingdom, Denmark, Ireland, Greece, Spain, and Portugal. Headquartered in Brussels, Belgium, the EC is a customs union and contains other features of economic integration.

The European Free Trade Area Association (EFTA)   A looser organization than the EC, it is made up of Austria, Finland, Sweden, Norway, Iceland, and Switzerland.

Group of Ten   This organization consists of the 10 major industrial countries (the U.S., U.K., Japan, West Germany, France, Italy, Belgium, the Netherlands, Canada, and Sweden) that agreed in October, 1962 to stand ready to lend their currencies to the IMF under the General Agreement to Borrow. The Group of Ten financial ministers and central bank governors meet from time to time to discuss international monetary issues. The first 5 countries on the list, known as the *Group of Five,* meet twice a year to coordinate policy.

Bank for International Settlements (BIS)   The BIS was originally set up in 1930 to promote cooperation between European central banks and to provide additional facilities for international financial transactions. It organizes regular meetings in Basel attended by the central bank governors of the major industrial nations and by the representatives of international organizations.

Organization for Economic Cooperation and Development (OECD)   Established in 1961 as successor to the Organization for European Economic Cooperation, it consists of 24 developed countries: the Group of Ten plus Australia, New Zealand, Austria, Denmark, Finland, Greece, Iceland, Ireland, Luxembourg, Norway, Portugal, Spain, Switzerland, and Turkey. Yugoslavia is an associate member. The OECD is concerned with a wide variety of economic matters.

Group of 77   A group of developing countries within the United Nations Conference on Trade and Development (UNCTAD). Originally numbering 77, the Group now has 127 members. UNCTAD was established under a UN General Assembly resolution on December 30, 1964 to deal with matters of international trade and development.

Group of 24   This organization is made up of 8 countries each in Africa, Asia, and Latin America deputed by the Group of 77 to consider monetary matters.

APPENDIX II

The Relationship Between Demand for a Foreign Currency (Dollar) and Supply of Domestic Currency (Mark)

In the German foreign-exchange market the demand for dollars *implies* supply of marks. Given the demand for dollars (left panel of Figure II-1), one can derive the supply of marks. At 4 D.M. = \$1, zero dollars are demanded; equivalently, at 1 D.M. = \$¼, zero marks are supplied (point *a* on both panels).

At 3 D.M. = \$1, \$1 billion is demanded (left-hand panel); equivalently, at 1 D.M. = \$⅓ (right-hand panel), 3 × 1 = 3 billion marks are supplied (point *b* on both panels). At 2 D.M. = \$1, \$2 billion are demanded; equivalently, at 1 D.M. = \$½, 2 × 2 = 4 billion marks are supplied (point *c*). At 1 D.M. = \$1, \$3 billion are demanded; equivalently, at 1 D.M. = \$1, 3 billion marks are supplied (point *d*). The

Figure II-1
Demand for Dollars and Supply of Marks

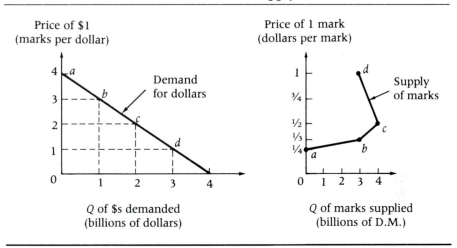

Price of $1
(marks per dollar)

Price of 1 mark
(dollars per mark)

Q of $s demanded
(billions of dollars)

Q of marks supplied
(billions of D.M.)

quantity of marks supplied at each mark price on the right-hand panel is equal to the area under the demand curve on the left-hand panel. The supply curve bends backward when the demand becomes inelastic.

Valuation of SDRs

The percentage weight of each of the five currencies included in the basket is converted into units of each currency, as shown in column 2 of the following table.

SDR Valuation on August 20, 1984				
Currency	Weight (in percent) (1)	Currency Amount (2)	Exchange Rate on Aug. 20, 1984 (3)	U.S. Dollar Equivalent (4)
U.S. dollar	42	0.5400	1.00000	0.540000
Deutsche mark	19	0.4600	2.87070	0.160240
French franc	13	0.7400	8.81150	0.083981
Japanese yen	13	34.0000	241.3800	0.140857
Pound sterling	13	0.0710	0.75775	0.093699
			Total	**1.018777**
		SDR value of US $1.00 =		**0.981569**
		U.S. dollar value of SDR =		**1.01878**

SOURCE: *IMF Survey.*

Each day the Fund converts these units of each currency into dollars at the prevailing exchange rate (columns 3 and 4). It then adds up the resulting 5 values of dollar equivalents to obtain the dollar value of 1 SDR for that day. The inverse of that figure is the SDR value of $1 U.S. Once the SDR value of a U.S. dollar is computed, the Fund calculates rates for the SDR against other currencies by using their market rates against the dollar.

APPENDIX III

Foreign-Trade Multiplier with Foreign Repercussions

It is possible to derive foreign-trade multiplier formulas that allow for foreign repercussions. Consider a two-country world in which country A and country B trade with each other. (In all notations, then, subscripts A and B denote country.) Any change in exports or imports of one country necessarily constitutes an equivalent change in imports or exports of the other. Each country's total income or production (Y) consists of consumption (C), investment (I), government purchases (G) of goods and services, and exports (X) (all of goods and services that are produced domestically). Changes in national income, brought about by any autonomous change in expenditures, consist of changes in these four expenditure components:

$$\Delta Y = \Delta C + \Delta I + \Delta G + \Delta X \tag{1}$$

For simplicity, assume that I and G are strictly autonomous. While a change in them generates changes in income, the reverse is not true; changes in Y do not induce changes in I or G. On the other hand, consumption and imports (that is, exports of the other country) have both autonomous and induced components. All autonomous changes in expenditures, from whatever source (investments, government expenditures, or the autonomous part of consumption) will be lumped under the term "exogenous shock" and labeled A. They are not affected by income changes.

By contrast, changes in income do induce changes in consumption, savings, and imports, the extent of which is determined respectively by the marginal propensities to consume (denoted by c), to save (s), and to import (m). In notation form:

$$\Delta S = \text{MPS} \times \Delta Y = s\Delta Y; \quad \Delta C = \text{MPC} \times \Delta Y = c\Delta Y; \quad \Delta M = \text{MPM} \times \Delta Y = m\Delta Y$$

where for each country $c + s + m = 1$. Remembering that the ΔX of each country equals the ΔM of its trading partner, we can now rewrite equation (1) for each of the two countries, incorporating the above assumptions:

$$\Delta Y_A = c_A \Delta Y_A + m_B \Delta Y_B + A_A \tag{2}$$

$$\Delta Y_B = c_B \Delta Y_B + m_A \Delta Y_{A} + A_B \tag{3}$$

That is, the change in income of each country is made up of the autonomous change in expenditures (A), an induced change in consumption, and a change in exports equaling the induced change in imports in the other country. It is the last item that forms the link between the two countries and reflects the foreign repercussions.

Given equations (2) and (3), our aim is to find an expression for ΔY resulting from an exogenous shock in terms of the marginal propensities and the autonomous change. From equation (3) we obtain:

$$\Delta Y_B - c_B \Delta Y_B = A_B + m_A \Delta Y_A; \; \Delta Y_B(1 - c_B) = A_B + m_A \Delta Y_A$$

$$\Delta Y_B = \frac{A_B + m_A \Delta Y_A}{1 - c_B} \tag{4}$$

Next, we substitute equation (4) into equation (2) to obtain:

$$\Delta Y_A = c_A \Delta Y_A + m_B \frac{A_B + m_A \Delta Y_A}{1 - c_B} + A_A \tag{5}$$

$$\Delta Y_A(1 - C_A) = A_A + m_B \frac{A_B + m_A \Delta Y_A}{1 - c_B}$$

Multiplying through by $(1 - c_B)$:

$$\Delta Y_A(1 - c_A)(1 - c_B) = A_A(1 - c_B) + m_B A_B + m_B m_A \Delta Y_A$$

Then,

$$\Delta Y_A[(1 - c_A)(1 - c_B) - m_B m_A] = A_A(1 - c_B) + m_B A_B$$

Remembering that $c + s + m = 1$, we obtain:

$$\Delta Y_A = \frac{A_A(1 - c_B) + m_B A_B}{(1 - c_A)(1 - c_B) - m_B m_A} = \frac{A_A(s_B + m_B) + m_B A_B}{(s_A + m_A)(s_B + m_B) - m_B m_A} \tag{6}$$

By similar procedures, we can solve the equations for the second country and obtain ΔY_B. Notice that $1 - c = m + s$ is the inverse of the simple multiplier. Given an increase in autonomous expenditures (A) in whatever form, in one or both countries, equation (6) tells us the resultant change in A's income.

Consider now the case in which the autonomous increase occurs in country A's exports to country B, arising from, say, a shift in B's taste for A's products. In other words, starting from an equilibrium position, A's exports to B (and B's imports from A) suddenly rise to a new annual level, higher than the old one by amount A. This produces a "shock" in A equal to A_A. But in country B, the autonomous increase in imports may or may not produce an equivalent negative shock.

At one extreme we may assume that all the new imports into B substitute for domestically produced goods. Thus the effect of the increase in imports is to reduce the autonomous component of domestic consumption (lower the consumption function) by the same amount. This is likely to approximate reality in a large diversified economy (such as the United States) that produces close substitutes for all its manufacturing imports. In terms of our notation, $A_A = -A_B$. Formula (6) then reduces to

$$\Delta Y_A = \frac{s_B A_A + m_B A_A - m_B A_A}{s_A s_B + s_A m_B + m_A s_B + m_A m_B - m_A m_B} \tag{7}$$

and the foreign-trade multiplier of A is

$$k = \frac{\Delta Y_A}{A_A} = \frac{s_B}{s_A s_B + s_A m_B + m_A s_B} = \frac{1}{s_A + m_A + m_B(s_A/s_B)} \tag{8}$$

(when both the numerator and the denominator are divided by S_B).

At the other extreme, assume that country B absorbs the entire increase in imports out of savings, so that there is no autonomous reduction in the consumption of domestic goods. In that case $A_B = 0$, and equation (6) becomes

$$\Delta Y_A = \frac{A_A(s_B + m_B)}{(s_A + m_A)(s_B + m_B) - m_B m_A} \tag{9}$$

The multiplier is

$$k = \frac{\Delta Y_A}{A_A} = \frac{s_B + m_B}{s_A s_B + s_A m_B + m_A s_B} = \frac{1 + (m_B/s_B)}{s_A + m_A + m_B(s_A/s_B)} \tag{10}$$

Between the two extremes fall any number of cases in which the impact of the increased imports in B is absorbed partly out of savings and partly out of consumption of domestic goods. Clearly the assumptions embodied in equation (8) constitute the most dampening effect that country B can have on the multiplier of country A through foreign repercussions.

APPENDIX IV

Stability of the Foreign-Exchange Market

Chapter 7 analyzed the "stability conditions" of the commodity markets on the assumption of infinite supply elasticities. Its first section developed the conditions under which devaluation of the home currency (pound sterling in our example) would improve (or revaluation would worsen) the balance of payments; that is, move the balance of payments in the desired *direction*. These elasticity conditions are directly related to the stability of the foreign-exchange market, and here we shall move from the "commodity space" to the "foreign-exchange space" to demonstrate the relationship.

The foreign-exchange market is said to be *stable* if changes in the exchange rate induce a movement in the balance of payments in the "right" or desired direction. Devaluation is expected to improve and revaluation to worsen the country's external payments position. In other words, stability requires that devaluation of the currency (pound sterling in our example) increase the difference *inpayments minus outpayments*, both expressed in terms of dollars. It was seen in Chapter 7 that, in terms of the foreign currency, outpayments necessarily decline while inpayments may move in either direction. But even when inpayments decline, stability may obtain if the decline is outpaced by a greater reduction in outpayments.

Figures 7-3 and 7-4 in Chapter 7, which demonstrated these relationships with respect to commodity trade, can be transformed into a chart that deals directly

Figure IV-1
Stable U.K. Foreign-Exchange Market, I

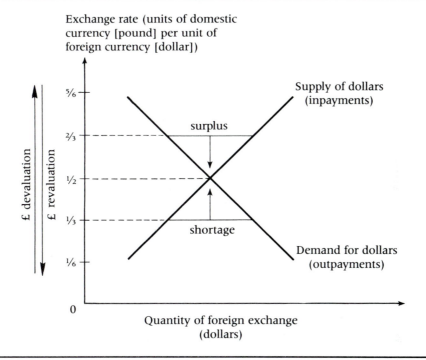

Exchange rate (units of domestic
currency [pound] per unit of
foreign currency [dollar])

£ devaluation

£ revaluation

⁵⁄₆

²⁄₃

½

⅓

⅙

0

Supply of dollars
(inpayments)

surplus

shortage

Demand for dollars
(outpayments)

Quantity of foreign exchange
(dollars)

in foreign currency flows. Consider Figure IV-1. The horizontal axis measures the quantity of foreign exchange demanded (outpayments) or supplied (inpayments). It is equivalent to the area under the $S_{U.S.}$ or $D_{U.S.}$ curves in the upper panel of Figures 7-3 and 7-4, respectively—that is, the quantity of merchandise traded times its dollar price. Movements along the vertical axis (the exchange rate) are equivalent to shifts in, say, the supply curves in the commodity space as the exchange rate changes. The exchange rate is defined in such a way that devaluation is portrayed as moving upward along the vertical axis; that is, as a greater number of domestic currency units per dollar.

Since devaluation always reduces outpayments, the demand-for-dollars curve is of necessity negatively sloped. It is derived from Figure 7-3 by relating changes in the exchange rate to changes in the area under $S_{U.S.}$ at points of equilibrium (quantity times dollar price). The inpayments line is derived from the upper panel of Figure 7-4 by relating the areas under the equilibrium points on $D_{U.S.}$ to changes in the exchange rate as reflected in shifts of $S_{U.K.}$. The inpayments line can slope in either direction, depending on the elasticity of $D_{U.S.}$ In Figure IV-1 it is positively sloped, showing a rise in the supply of dolars in case of devaluation and reflecting a relatively elastic $D_{U.S.}$. In other words, this case shows the outpayments line negatively sloped and the inpayments line positively sloped, so that the slope (or elasticity) of inpayments exceeds that of outpayments. In sum, Figure IV-1 shows the

Figure IV-2
Stable U.K. Foreign-Exchange Market, II

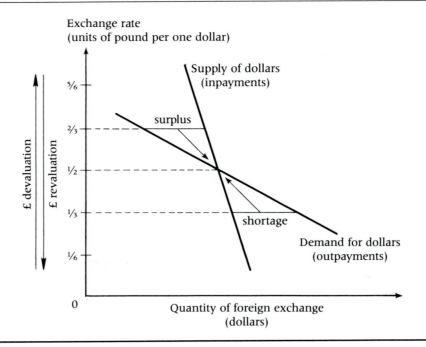

foreign-exchange market when devaluation lowers outpayments and raises inpayments and when revaluation does the reverse. On both counts devaluation improves and revaluation worsens the balance of payments, and the foreign-exchange market is clearly stable. In Figure IV-1 the dollar is undervalued and the pound is overvalued at $1 = £⅓, resulting in excess demand for dollars (a dollar shortage). A devaluation of the pound is indicated, which would push the exchange rate toward the equilibrium point of $1 = £½ (or £1 = $2). Conversely, at an exchange rate of $1 = £⅔, the dollar is overvalued and the pound is undervalued, resulting in an excess supply of dollars (a dollar surplus). A revaluation of the pound is indicated, which would push the exchange rate toward equilibrium. In both cases the movement is in the "right" direction, indicating a stable foreign-exchange market.

While the outpayments line must be negatively sloped, the inpayments line can slope either way, depending on the U.S. import-demand elasticity.

In Figure IV-2, the inpayment curve is negatively sloped, indicating relatively inelastic U.S. import demand, but it is steeper than the outpayment line (cuts it from above). Although both slopes are negative, the slope of the inpayment line is greater than that of the outpayment line. This is still a stable situation, for it represents the case where the adjustment in outpayments exceeds that in inpayments. As before, at $1 = £⅓ (or £1 = $3) the dollar is undervalued and the pound overvalued, creating excess demand (shortage) for dollars. Devaluation of the pound

Figure IV-3
Unstable U.K. Foreign-Exchange Market

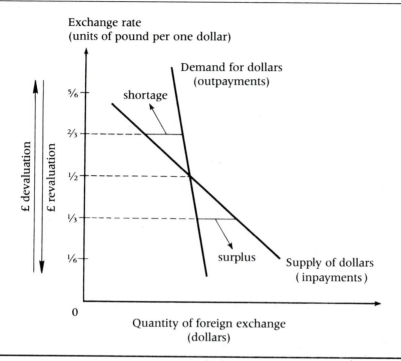

sterling reduces inpayments, but it lowers outpayments by a greater amount, so that the quantity *inpayments minus outpayments* increases, and the market moves toward equilibrium. Conversely, at $1 = £⅔, the dollar is overvalued (and the pound is undervalued), creating excess supply of dollars. Revaluation of the pound sterling pushes the market toward the equilibrium exchange rate of £1 = $2.

Finally, consider the case in which both lines are negatively sloped, but the outpayments line is steeper than the inpayments line (Figure IV-3). In other words, the slope of the inpayments line is less (has a higher negative number) than that of the outpayments line. Devaluation reduces both inpayments and outpayments, but the decline in inpayments is greater for any given devaluation, so that the difference *inpayments minus outpayments* declines rather than rises. This is the foreign-exchange equivalent of the case in which the sum of the demand elasticities is below 1 (in absolute value), with supply elasticities being infinite. In this case, when $1 = £⅓, there is excess supply (surplus) of dollars and revaluation is indicated, while at $1 = £⅔ there is excess demand for dollars (a dollar shortage), which calls for devaluation of the pound. In both cases the indicated action drives the market away from, rather than toward, equilibrium. This is an unstable foreign-exchange market, and it occurs when the inpayment line has a lower slope than the outpayment line.

Cases of multiple equilibria are also possible. Figure IV-4 shows an example of an unstable equilibrium and two stable equilibria on either side of it.

Figure IV-4
U.K. Foreign-Exchange Market—Multiple Equilibria

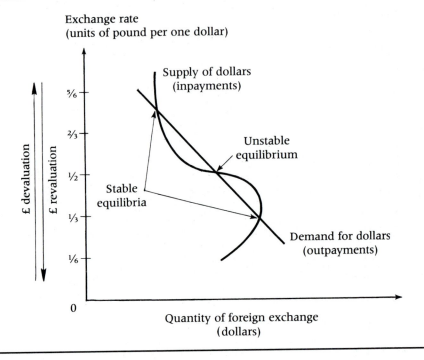

Exchange rate
(units of pound per one dollar)

Supply of dollars
(inpayments)

Unstable
equilibrium

Stable
equilibria

Demand for dollars
(outpayments)

£ devaluation

£ revaluation

$5/6$

$2/3$

$1/2$

$1/3$

$1/6$

0

Quantity of foreign exchange
(dollars)

APPENDIX V

Policies to Attain Internal and External Balance

Two convenient diagrams are often used to demonstrate the policy options open to a country attempting to attain internal and external balance. These are described below.

Expenditures-Changing and Expenditures-Switching Policies

In the first case, assume that international capital movements do not exist. External balance then implies balance on the goods and services account. With respect to domestic conditions, assume that unemployment or inflation are caused only by deficient or excessive demand, respectively. In such a case recession and inflation cannot coexist.

Figure V-1 shows real expenditures on the horizontal axis and a ratio of international to domestic prices (or costs) on the vertical axis. Because the vertical

Figure V-1
The Swan[1] Diagram of Internal and External Balance

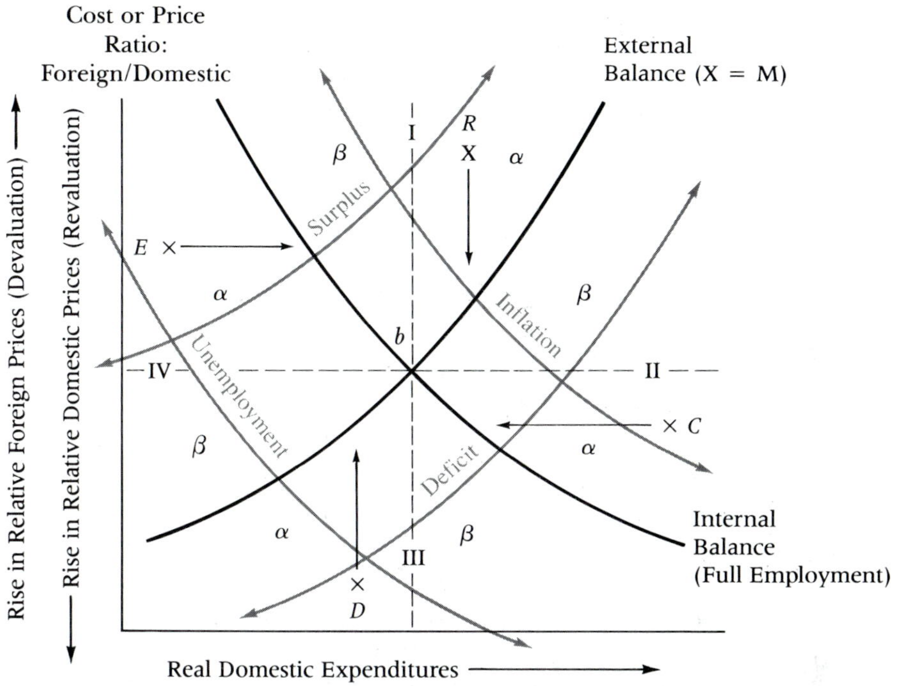

axis is in a form of a ratio of foreign over domestic prices, an increase in foreign prices (domestic prices remaining unchanged) implies moving upward along the axis, while an increase in domestic prices (foreign prices remaining unchanged) implies moving downward along the axis. Thus the vertical axis can be viewed as an index of the country's competitive position. An upward movement along it means increased competitiveness leading to higher exports and lower imports. Conversely, a downward movement means lower exports and greater imports.

The internal balance or full-employment line is the locus of all combinations of real expenditures and cost ratios that yield full employment without inflation. The higher the domestic prices relative to foreign prices (limiting exports and encouraging imports), the higher must real domestic expenditures be to maintain full employment. Hence the internal balance curve slopes downward from left to right. Above the line (and to its right) are combinations of real expenditures and cost ratios that yield inflation, while below it and to the left are combinations that yield unemployment.

---

[1] This diagram was originally presented in T. W. Swan, "Longer-Run Problems of the Balance of Payments," reprinted in R. Caves and H. Johnson, *Readings in International Economics*, Homewood, Illinois, Irwin, 1968, pp. 455–64.

In contrast, the external balance line slopes upward and to the right. It represents combinations of real expenditures and cost ratios that yield equality between exports and imports of goods and services. In this case the higher the domestic expenditures, the more competitive (that is, a higher foreign to domestic price ratio) must the country be to maintain external balance. Below the line (and to its right) are expenditures—price ratio combinations yielding deficits in the balance on goods and services, while above it (and to the left) are combinations yielding surpluses.

The two lines divide the space into the following four regions:

Region	Domestic Condition	External Condition
I	Inflation	Surplus
II	Inflation	Deficit
III	Unemployment	Deficit
IV	Unemployment	Surplus

Regions II and IV represent "consistent" situations calling, respectively, for fiscal and monetary policies that contract and expand real domestic expenditures. These are known as expenditures-changing policies. The effect of such measures is shown by straight horizontal lines, such as the lines starting at points *C* (contractionary domestic policies) and *E* (expansionary domestic policies). Regions I and III represent inconsistent situations calling for policies that would change relative prices and induce people to switch expenditures between foreign and domestic goods; these are expenditures-switching policies. In region I the main therapy is revaluation, which makes the country less competitive and also combats the inflation. Conversely, in region III the main action called for is currency devaluation, which improves the country's competitive position and expands income. The impact of these two policy measures is shown by straight vertical lines, such as those starting, respectively, from points *R* and *D*.

The objective of economic policy is to attain a combination of internal and external balance. Such a situation obtains only at pont *b*, the intersection of the two balance curves. Point *b* cannot be reached by employing only one policy measure, except in the rare cases where the straight policy lines happen to pass through it (that is, the dashed lines). In all other cases a *combination* of expenditures-changing and expenditures-switching policies is called for.

Consider the consistent region IV, which calls for expansionary domestic policies to combat the external surplus as well as the domestic unemployment. Only if the initial situation happens to be positioned exactly to the left of *b* will expansionary policies land the economy right on the mark. Starting from point *E*, for example, expansion up to the internal balance line would still leave the country with an external surplus. Getting to point *b* requires expansion beyond the internal balance line, accompanied by currency revaluation. Likewise, point *C* requires contractionary domestic policies accompanied by devaluation; point *D* calls for devaluation plus domestic expansion; and point *R* calls for revaluation and domestic contraction.

Indeed, it is possible to divide the space into four policy zones circumscribed by the straight-dashed lines and the internal and external balance lines as follows:

Zone	Desired Policy	
	Domestic	External
Iα and IIβ	Contraction	Revaluation
IIα and IIIβ	Contraction	Devaluation
IIIα and IVβ	Expansion	Devaluation
IVα and Iβ	Expansion	Revaluation

In no zone is one policy measure sufficient to attain external and internal balance, the sole exception being situations on the dashed lines.

Fiscal and Monetary Policies; Capital Movements Responsive to Interest Changes

The foregoing analysis made no distinction between fiscal and monetary policies in the domestic arena and also assumed away capital movements. It can now be extended and modified by assuming international capital transfers to be responsive to interest rate differentials, and by distinguishing between the effect of fiscal and monetary policies on the rate of interest. In effect this adds one policy instrument to the arsenal, since expenditure-changing policies are no longer viewed as one policy.

In the domestic economy, the *IS* curve represents the loci of equilibrium points in the commodities market while the *LM* curve shows the points of equilibria in the money market. Their intersection yields equilibrium real income (Y) and rate of interest (i). This is shown in Figure V-2.

Figure V-2
Domestic Equilibrium

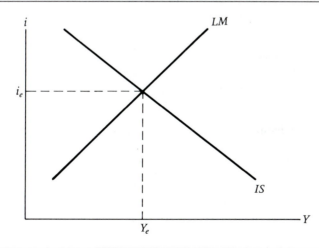

Figure V-3
External Balance

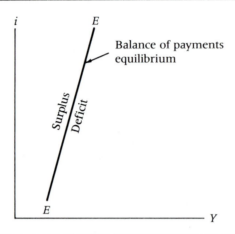

If international capital movements are assumed to be governed by the country's interest rate (relative to foreign rates), it is possible to identify combinations of real income and interest rates that would yield equilibrium in the balance of payments. The loci of such points is shown as the *EE* curve on Figure V-3. The higher the country's income, the greater the deficit on goods and services, and the higher must be its interest rate to attract sufficient foreign funds so as to produce external balance. The more sensitive capital is to interest differentials, the greater is the effect of higher interest rates in offsetting the impact of a given rise in income on the balance of payments, and the flatter the *EE* curve. At the extreme, if capital were completely mobile, the *EE* curve would be flat; the country's interest rate cannot deviate from world interest rates. By contrast, if capital were completely immobile the *EE* curve would be vertical. In view of the portfolio approach to capital movements, the *EE* curve is drawn fairly steeply in Figure V-3. Changes in the exchange rate (or other changes in relative prices) would affect the curve as follows: Depreciation of the country's currency (or improved competitive position via domestic price changes) shift the *EE* curve to the right, reducing the deficit area and increasing the surplus area. Appreciation (or making the country less competitive) moves the *EE* curve to the left. All this assumes that the Marshall-Lerner stability conditions are met.

Superimposing the *EE* curve upon the *IS* and *LM* curves provides the equilibrium loci in the commodities, money, and foreign-exchange markets.[2] If the three curves intersect at one point, as is the case in Figure V-4, we obtain the combination of real income and interest rate that yields domestic and external equilibrium, with the domestic equilibrium below full employment (equilibrium is to the left of $Y_{F.E.}$). External balance obtains, but internal balance is lacking.

---

[2]Such a diagram was originally presented in D. Wrightsman, "IS, LM and External Equilibrium," *American Economic Review,* March 1970, pp. 203–8.

Figure V-4
Underemployment Equilibrium

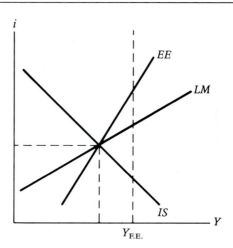

In Figure V-5 neither internal nor external balance obtains, but the situation is consistent. Domestic equilibrium obtains at point *A*, the intersection of the *IS* and *LM* curves. Because it is to the left of the *EE* line, point *A* implies an external surplus. And because it is to the left of the full-employment income ($Y_{F.E.}$), it implies unemployment. Internal and external balance can be attained at point *H* by a proper mix of fiscal and monetary policies, namely by shifting the *IS* and *LM* curves.

Figure V-5
Internal and External Imbalance—"Consistent" Situation

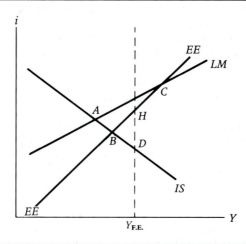

Figure V-6
Internal and External Imbalance—"Inconsistent" Situation

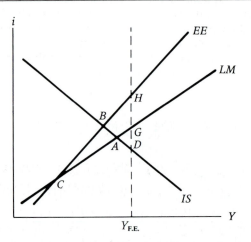

By contrast, Figure V-6 portrays an "inconsistent" situation. The equilibrium income and interest rate, at point A, yield both an external deficit (it is to the right of the EE curve) and internal unemployment (it is to the left of the full-employment income, $Y_{F.E.}$). Had point A been to the right of $Y_{F.E.}$, we would have had inflation and deficit—a consistent situation.

Starting from point A, external balance can be restored by monetary contraction, moving LM upward to intersect IS at point B;[3] or by fiscal contraction, moving IS downward to intersect LM at point C. Monetary contraction accomplishes the task with a smaller loss of real income than does fiscal contraction (C is farther than B from $Y_{F.E.}$). Monetary contraction *lowers* income and *raises* the rate of interest, and both changes contribute to the improvement in the balance of payments; fiscal contraction, on the other hand, lowers income and *lowers* the rate of interest, an interest change that is unfavorable to the balance of payments.

If full employment is the objective, then monetary expansion can reach it (by shifting LM downward and to the right) at point D, while fiscal expansion can reach it at point G (by shifting the IS curve upward and to the right). The cost in terms of external deficit is greater in the case of monetary expansion, which lowers the rate of interest, than in the case of fiscal expansion, which raises it.

Finally, *internal* and *external* balance can be achieved at point H by a proper mix of fiscal expansion and monetary contraction.

Thus far the discussion has assumed a fixed exchange rate. Exchange-rate adjustment is a powerful tool in attaining external and internal balance. Starting from the original situation shown in Figure V-6, devaluation of the currency would have the following effects: (1) The EE curve would shift downward and to the right

---

[3] Under the pure gold standard this would happen automatically, because the external deficit would shrink money supply, moving LM upward and to the right until it intersects the IS curve at point B. The same argument is made by the monetary approach (see Chapter 8).

as the country becomes more competitive and the area of deficit shrinks; (2) The *IS* curve would shift upward and to the right as output of the export- and import-competing industries expands; and (3) The *LM* function would shift upward and to the left as prices rise and real money supply declines. The likely net result is a convergence toward equilibrium at a higher rate of income and employment. But it would be purely accidental for external and internal balance to be reached by merely adjusting the exchange rate. For that, the devaluation should be accompanied by proper domestic measures.

APPENDIX VI

(A) A Proposal for Rules for Intervention in the Foreign-Exchange Markets

Professors Ethier and Bloomfield of the University of Pennsylvania, searching for the simplest possible intervention guidelines,[1] suggest that the most realistic and easily enforceable rule is one which embodies a minimum of regulation and which specifies only what intervention is *not* permissible. They came up with two rules:

1. No central bank shall sell its own currency at a price below its reference rate by more than a certain fixed percentage (possibly zero) or buy its own currency at a price exceeding its reference rate by more than the fixed percentage.
2. The structure of the reference rates shall be revised at periodic prespecified intervals through some defined international procedure.

Rule 1 is illustrated by the following diagram. A country would never have an obligation to intervene. Its only obligation is to *avoid* intervening in such a way as to appreciate the rate (by selling foreign exchange) when the rate is above *A* or depreciate it when it is below *B*. (Within the band $\overline{AB}$ any intervention is permissible.)

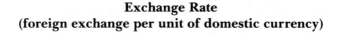

Exchange Rate
(foreign exchange per unit of domestic currency)

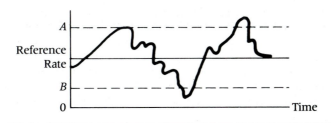

---

[1] W. Ethier and A. Bloomfield, "Managing The Managed Floats," *Essays in International Finance,* Princeton University, No. 112, October 1975.

Free floats, "leaning against the wind," or "moderating" seasonal or cyclical exchange fluctuations, would be compatible with rule 1 and no quantitative limitation would be imposed on these types of intervention. Intervention to change the composition of reserves can be undertaken only when it is consistent with rule 1. What would not be allowed is to accentuate departures of market rates from reference rates. Competitive exchange-rate behavior (such as competitive depreciation) is not consistent with the proposed rule. Reference rates may be defined in terms of SDRs. Rule 2 would permit periodic revision of these rates by international consensus, but some technical indicators, such as changes in reserve holdings or even a form of "purchasing power parity," would have to be devised to guide the decision-making process.

(B) Evaluating Official Intervention in the Foreign-Exchange Market

In a recent article, Professor Dean Taylor evaluates official foreign-exchange intervention in the 1970s using Friedman's profit criterion. He finds that monetary authorities have resisted exchange-rate movements, causing a misallocation of resources when a shift in the equilibrium exchange rate occurred.

The following are his main conclusions: "With the possible exception of France, not one of the central banks in this study has succeeded in its objective of stabilizing the exchange markets. Some have incurred substantial losses and have adversely affected exchange-rate movements. Generally the authorities follow a policy of 'leaning against the wind' by resisting exchange-rate changes. In some cases, this resistance has led to pegging the existing exchange rate when its equilibrium level changes. The authorities are able to hold out for a limited time but are eventually forced to allow the adjustment to take place, and lose substantial sums in the process."[2]

(C) On the Relative Effectiveness of Fiscal and Monetary Policy under Alternative Exchange-Rate Regimes

Consider a small country, with liquid capital highly mobile internationally, so that interest rates cannot diverge from world interest rates (in terms of Appendix V this means a flat EE curve):

(1) With a fixed exchange rate, fiscal policy is fully effective in changing income. The accompanying diagram shows the Hicksian *IS* and *LM* curves on the income-interest rate space. The initial equilibrium is at point *a*, yielding Y_1 and i_1, with i_1 equal to the world interest rate. Suppose the government expands fiscally, borrowing the needed funds on the money market, without any new money being created. In Figure VI-B, the *IS* curve shifts to IS_2 and the equilibrium to point *b*. But the rise in interest rates attracts foreign capital, raising the domestic money supply, with the inflow lasting until interest rate is back to its original level, i_1, equal to the world rate. In terms of the diagram, *LM* shifts to LM_2, and the final equilib-

---

[2]Dean Taylor, "Official Intervention in the Foreign Exchange Market, or, Bet against the Central Bank," *Journal of Political Economy*, April 1982, p. 357.

Figure VI-B
Fiscal Policy Under a Fixed Exchange Rate

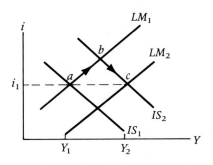

rium is at point *c*, yielding income Y_2. The rise in income is not hampered by an increase in the domestic interest rate.

By contrast, monetary policy is ineffective in changing income. Starting from equilibrium point *a*, an increase in money supply shifts the *LM* curve to LM_2. But equilibrium point *b* involves an interest rate below the world's level (i_1). Capital flows out, reducing the domestic money supply, until the original interest level is restored, with the *LM* curve reverting back to LM_1. Income remains at Y_1. (See Figure VI-C.)

(2) With a freely floating exchange rate, fiscal policy is ineffective. Starting from equilibrium point *a*, fiscal expansion shifts the *IS* curve to IS_2 and the equilibrium point to *b*. The rise in interest rate above world level would attract foreign capital. But in this case, it leads to appreciation of the currency. This lowers ($X - M$), leading to a multiple reduction in income. *IS* reverts to its original position, (IS_1), leaving income unchanged. (Figure VI-D.)

By contrast monetary policy is fully effective. Starting from equilibrium point *a*, the rise in money supply shifts LM_1 to LM_2 and the equilibrium point moves to *b*. The decline in interest rate below world level would generate an outflow of capital.

Figure VI-C
Monetary Policy Under a Fixed Exchange Rate

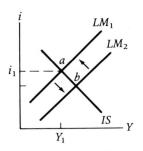

Figure VI-D
Fiscal Policy Under a Freely Floating Exchange Rate

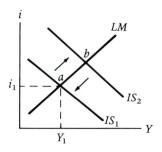

But in this case, the exchange rate depreciates. The resulting rise in $(X - M)$ leads to a multiple increase in income. The *IS* curve shifts to IS_2 until world interest rate is reached at equilibrium point *c*. Income rises from Y_1 to Y_2. (Figure VI-E.)

Figure VI-E
Monetary Policy Under a Freely Floating Exchange Rate

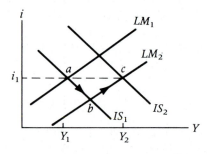

APPENDIX VII

The Factor Proportions Theory

Students thoroughly familiar with advanced price theory will recognize that the transformation curve of a country can be derived from its contract curve, which in turn is the locus of points of tangency between two sets of isoquants, each set pertaining to one of the country's two industries. The Edgeworth-Bowley box diagram is used to delineate the country's fixed amount of resources, made up of two productive factors (for example, labor and capital), and the contract curve is drawn inside the box. That curve is the locus of points of efficient allocation of the two productive factors between the two industries; from any point off the contract curve

Figure VII-1
The Edgeworth–Bowley Box Diagrams

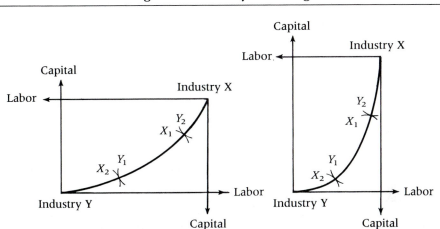

Country B   Country A

one can move to *certain points* on that curve and increase the output produced by the given quantity of the two factors. We can thus show the contract curves for countries A and B from which the respective transformation curves in Figure 11-10 can be derived.

The assumptions of the factor proportions model, outlined in chapter 12, are built into the two diagrams (Figure VII-1). Besides pure competition and perfect internal factor mobility, the model's assumptions are as follows:

(a) The isoquants of industry X are identical in both countries; so are the isoquants of industry Y.

(b) Industry Y is labor intensive relative to industry X and X is capital intensive relative to industry Y, and this relationship holds for both countries. Translated into a multicommodity world, this assumption means that the *ranking* of industries by the labor/capital ratio required for production (that is, the factor use ratio) would be the same in both countries even if the factor price ratio varied. This assumption is known as the nonreversibility of factor intensities.

(c) Both commodities are produced under diminishing returns but constant returns to scale. The latter assumption implies that any straight ray from each origin (say of industry Y) will intersect the isoquants of the industry depicted on the origin (for example, the Y isoquants) at points of equal slopes. The economic meaning of this is that all such points of intersection show equal ratios between the marginal physical productivities of the two factors in the given industry. In other words, under constant returns to scale, the marginal productivity of a factor in a given industry is independent of the scale of operations and depends only on its ratio to the other factor in use (that is, on the factor use ratio). And the factor use ratio is identical along a straight ray from the origin; it is equal to the constant slope of that ray.

(d) Country A is capital abundant relative to country B, while B is labor abundant relative to country A. This is indicated by the relative size of the two boxes.

Figure VII-2
Post-trade Production Equilibrium

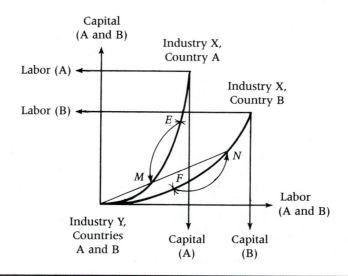

As a next step, place the box diagram of country A on top of the one of country B, in such a way that their origins for industry Y will coincide. This is shown in Figure VII-2, where the isoquants are deleted for the sake of clarity. The identical Y isoquants for both countries coincide exactly, while the identical X isoquants start at two different points of origin. Any ray from the (joint) origin of Y, such as $\overline{YMN}$, intersects the contract curves of the two countries at points M and N, where the Y isoquants common to the two countries have equal slopes. In other words, the ratio of the marginal products of the two factors in industry Y is the same in both countries. Since within each country, factor mobility ensures that the ratio of the marginal products of the two factors is the same in industries Y and X, that ratio must also be the same in industry X of the two countries. Geometrically this means that the straight line connecting M with the origin of industry X in country A is parallel to the straight line connecting N with the origin of industry X in country B (not drawn).

Equality of the marginal products ensures that the output mixes at point M for country A and at point N for country B would result in identical product prices (or price ratios) in the two countries. And this is the requirement for post-trade equilibrium. Depending on demand patterns (which are shown by indifference curves in Figure 11-10 but cannot be shown on a box diagram), the pretrade output mix was E in country A and F in country B. The opening of trade moved that mix to points M and N, respectively. The relatively capital-abundant country A moved to specialize more in the relatively capital-intensive product X; and the relatively labor-abundant country B moved to specialize more in the relatively labor-intensive product Y. Specialization is incomplete in both countries as is the case in Figure 11-10. Thus there is one-to-one correspondence between the output mix in the factor "space" and in the commodity "space." *As long as specialization is incomplete* (that is, each country produces some of both products), not only would commodity prices be equalized between the two countries at the post-trade production equilibrium points such as *M* and *N*, but factor prices would also be equalized.

But the number of such post-trade production equilibrium points is unlimited, as there are unlimited rays from the joint origin Y that would intersect the two contract curves. Which one would prevail depends on the relative international prices of the two products. If Y's price rises relative to X, the ray shifts counter-clockwise and more Y is produced in both countries, while if the price of X rises relative to Y, the ray shifts clockwise, and more X is produced in both countries. Thus the "relevant" ray must depend on conditions of demand as well as supply; it must be derived from Figure 11-10, where demand is also depicted, in a way that ensures the identity of the two trade triangles. Only then is the final equilibrium uniquely determined.

Not all points on the two contract curves are "pairable" in the sense of inter-secting a straight ray from origin Y, in much the same way that not all points along the two transformation curves are pairable in the sense of having equal slopes. Thus the price of Y relative to that of X can rise to a point where the *ray from the joint origin* Y *becomes the diagonal of country B's box diagram*. Here country B completely specializes in industry Y, and further increases in the relative price of Y can lead only country A to move upward along its contract curve to produce more Y and less X. Conversely, if the price of X relative to that of Y rises to a point where the *ray from the joint origin* Y *becomes tangent to country A's contract curve*, then country A is completely specialized in X and produces no Y. Further increases in the relative price of X would lead only country B to move downward along its contract curve toward greater specialization in X.

Thus the two rays whose descriptions are italicized in the previous paragraph delineate the limits to incomplete specialization. All rays falling within these limits indicate incomplete specialization and correspond to points of equal slopes of the two transformation functions in the commodity space (Figure 11-10). The size of *the range of incomplete specialization* depends on two factors:

(a) It varies directly with the similarity of relative factor endowments of the two countries. The more the factor endowment ratios differ the more the shapes of the two box diagrams differ (this can be readily seen by adding labor to country B, leaving all else unchanged) and the smaller the range of pairable points along a ray from joint origin Y.

(b) It varies inversely with the similarity of the production isoquants of X and Y. The more alike they are, the less the "belly" of the two contract curves and the smaller the range of "pairable" points along a ray from origin Y. The extreme case, which corresponds to the Ricardian model of constant opportunity costs, is the one of identical isoquants of the two commodities. The contract curve of each country becomes the diagonal of its box diagram, and there is no range of incomplete specialization. Once trade opens up, country A moves to specialize completely in product X, and country B in product Y.

The Mobile Factor in a Sector-Specific Model

In the sector-specific model described in Chapter 12, labor is the mobile factor; it is combined with capital in sector M, and with land in sector A. How is the fixed quantity of labor in a (fully employed) economy distributed between the two sectors?

Figure VII-3
Wage Rate Determination

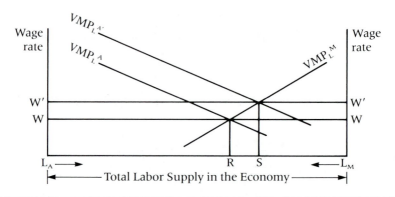

In Figure VII-3, the total labor supply is shown along the horizontal axis. Labor in sector A is measured rightward from origin L_A, while labor in sector M is measured leftward from origin L_M. Since labor is subject to diminishing returns in each sector, the value of the marginal product of labor in manufacturing[1] (VMP_L^M) schedule slopes negatively, measured leftward from origin L_M. Likewise the VMP_L^A is measured rightward from origin L_A. They intersect at height W, the equilibrium wage rate in the economy: $W = VMP_L^M = VMP_L^A$. The allocation of labor between the two sectors is at point R: $L_A R$ in agriculture, and $L_M R$ in manufacturing. When trade opens up, food prices rise, so that the VMP_L^A shifts upward to $VMP_L^{A'}$. The labor allocation point moves from R to S as more labor is employed in sector A and less in M. The wage rate rises (to W'), but not by as much as the increase in food prices. So the wage rate falls relative to the price of food but rises relative to the price of manufactures. Workers may gain or lose from free trade depending on whether they consume mostly manufactured goods or mostly food.[2]

APPENDIX VIII

Elasticity of Import Demand and the Domestic Demand and Supply Elasticities

The elasticity of import demand for a given product is positively (and uniquely) related to the domestic demand and supply elasticities, and negatively related to the share of imports in domestic consumption and production.

---

[1] The price of manufacturing times labor's marginal physical product.
[2] For further elaboration see R. Ruffin and R. Jones, "Protection and Real Wages: A Neoclassical Ambiguity," *Journal of Economic Theory*, April 1977.

Remembering that the volume of imports (Q_m) is the difference between the quantities demanded (Q_d) and supplied (Q_s) at home, we an derive the import-demand elasticity (Σ_D) from the definition of elasticity, as follows:

$$\Sigma_D = \frac{-P}{Q_m} \times \frac{\Delta Q_m}{\Delta P} = \frac{-P}{Q_m} \times \frac{\Delta(Q_d - Q_s)}{\Delta P}$$

$$= \frac{-P}{Q_m} \times \frac{\Delta Q_d}{\Delta P} + \frac{P}{Q_m} \times \frac{\Delta Q_s}{\Delta P}$$

Next, we multiply and divide the first term of the last expression by Q_d and the second term by Q_s:

$$\Sigma_D = \frac{\dfrac{-P}{Q_d} \times \dfrac{\Delta Q_d}{\Delta P} \times Q_d}{Q_m} + \frac{\dfrac{P}{Q_s} \times \dfrac{\Delta Q_s}{\Delta P} \times Q_s}{Q_m}$$

$$= \frac{\epsilon_d \times Q_d}{Q_m} + \frac{\epsilon_s \times Q_s}{Q_m}$$

where ϵ_d and ϵ_s represent domestic demand and supply elasticities, respectively. Thus,

$$\Sigma_D = \frac{Q_d}{Q_m} \times \epsilon_d + \frac{Q_s}{Q_m} \times \epsilon_s$$

Elasticity of Export Supply and the Domestic Demand and Supply Elasticities

The export-supply elasticity of a given product is positively related to the domestic demand and supply elasticities and negatively related to the share of exports in domestic production and consumption. Remembering that the volume of exports (Q_e) is the difference between the quantities supplied and demanded domestically (Q_s and Q_d), we can derive the export-supply elasticity (Σ_x) from the definition of elasticity, as follows:

$$\Sigma_x = \frac{P}{Q_e} \times \frac{\Delta Q_e}{\Delta P} = \frac{P}{Q_e} \times \frac{\Delta(Q_s - Q_d)}{\Delta P} = \frac{P}{Q_e} \times \frac{\Delta Q_s}{\Delta P} - \frac{P}{Q_e} \times \frac{\Delta Q_d}{\Delta P}$$

Next, we multiply and divide the first term by Q_s and the second term by Q_d:

$$\Sigma_x = \frac{\dfrac{P}{Q_s} \times \dfrac{\Delta Q_s}{\Delta P} \times Q_s}{Q_e} - \frac{\dfrac{P}{Q_d} \times \dfrac{\Delta Q_d}{\Delta P} \times Q_d}{Q_e} = \frac{\epsilon_s \times Q_s}{Q_e} + \frac{\epsilon_d \times Q_d}{Q_e}$$

where ϵ_s and ϵ_d represent domestic supply and demand elasticities, recalling that the demand elasticity is negative. Thus:

$$\Sigma_x = \frac{Q_s}{Q_e} \times \epsilon_s + \frac{Q_d}{Q_e} \times \epsilon_d$$

A Country's Share in World Export Markets and the Elasticity of Demand for Its Exports

The elasticity of demand for a country's exports of a given product is inversely related to its share in the world market.

If W is the world demand for imports of a given product and C is the quantity exported by competing sources (other countries), then $W - C$ is the quantity exported by the country in question. Let η_x be the elasticity of demand for the country's exports of the product; then

$$\eta_x = \frac{-P}{W - C} \times \frac{\Delta(W - C)}{\Delta P} = -\frac{P}{W - C}\left(\frac{\Delta W}{\Delta P}\right) - \frac{P}{W - C}\left(-\frac{\Delta C}{\Delta P}\right)$$

$$= \frac{-P(\Delta W/\Delta P)}{W - C} + \frac{P(\Delta C/\Delta P)}{W - C}$$

Multiply and divide the first term by W and the second term by C:

$$\eta_x = \frac{W(-P/W)(\Delta W/\Delta P)}{W - C} + \frac{C(P/C)(\Delta C/\Delta P)}{W - C} = \frac{W}{W - C}\eta_w + \frac{C}{W - C}e_c$$

where η_w is the world demand elasticity for the product and e_c is the supply elasticity from competing sources.

One important implication of this relation is that even if the demand for a certain product is relatively inelastic, the demand for a particular country's exports of the product can be highly elastic if it has only a small share in total world markets. Applying this to the domestic market we can see how the demand for wheat can be inelastic but the demand for a single farmer's wheat infinitely elastic, when he accounts for a very small share in the total supply.

Import-Demand and Export-Supply Elasticities and the Incidence of a Tariff

In Figure VIII-1 the pretariff international price is $\overline{OP}$ and the quantity traded is $\overline{OQ}$, as determined by the intersection of the import-demand and export-supply curves. A specific tariff of size t is then imposed, shifting export supply leftward to the broken line. Domestic price in the importing country rises by fraction s of the tariff, while its terms of trade improve by a fraction $(1 - s)$. The quantity traded declines by ΔQ. Our objective is to find an expression for s.

The elasticity of the import-demand curve at point E is

$$|\Sigma_D| = \frac{\Delta Q}{Q} \times \frac{P}{\Delta P} = \frac{\Delta Q}{\overline{OQ}} \times \frac{\overline{OP}}{st} \tag{1}$$

From that we obtain:

$$\frac{\Delta Q}{\overline{OQ}} = |\Sigma_d|\frac{st}{\overline{OP}} \tag{2}$$

The elasticity of the export-supply curve at point E is

$$\Sigma_s = \frac{\Delta Q}{\overline{OQ}} \times \frac{\overline{OP}}{\Delta P} = \frac{\Delta Q}{\overline{OQ}} \times \frac{\overline{OP}}{(1 - s)t} \tag{3}$$

Substituting (2) into (3) gives

$$\Sigma_s = |\Sigma_d| \frac{st}{\overline{OP}} \times \frac{\overline{OP}}{(1-s)t} = |\Sigma_D| \frac{s}{1-s}$$

(4)

Therefore,

$$\frac{s}{1-s} = \frac{\Sigma_s}{|\Sigma_D|}$$

and

$$\Sigma_S - s\Sigma_S = s \times |\Sigma_D|$$
$$s(|\Sigma_D| + \Sigma_S) = \Sigma_S$$
$$s = \frac{\Sigma_S}{|\Sigma_D| + \Sigma_S}$$

Dividing through by Σ_S, we obtain

$$s = \frac{1}{|\Sigma_D|/\Sigma_S + 1}$$
$$(1-s) = \frac{|\Sigma_D| + \Sigma_S - \Sigma_S}{|\Sigma_D| + \Sigma_S}$$
$$= \frac{|\Sigma_D|}{|\Sigma_D| + \Sigma_S}$$
$$= \frac{1}{1 + \Sigma_S/|\Sigma_D|}$$

Clearly it is the *relative* size of the import-demand and export-supply elasticities that determines the incidence of the tariff. In turn, these elasticities are related to the

---

Figure VIII-1
Incidence of a Tariff

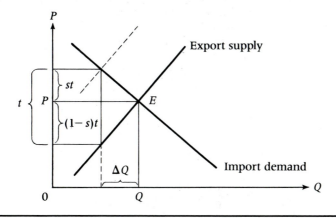

domestic supply and demand elasticities in the respective countries (as spelled out in the previous sections of this appendix).

The expressions above assume that the government does nothing with the tariff revenue. If, however, we assume that these funds are distributed to the population in the form of a general income subsidy, the expressions must be modified to take into account the added demand for imports arising from the added income (the marginal propensity to import). Also, this is a partial equilibrium formula, which refers only to a tax on a single product. A different, full-equilibrium formula would apply when analyzing the incidence of a tariff levied across the board on all products.

Similar formulas apply to the incidence of domestic indirect taxes, except that domestic rather than international elasticities are involved.

Economic Cost of the Tariff

In Chapter 13 the economic cost of the tariff was analyzed with the use of producers' and consumers' surpluses and changes in government revenue. But the analysis was restricted to a small country whose terms of trade remain unaffected, so that all the effects of the tariff are visible inside the importing country. This can be extended to the more general case of a two-country world, where the terms of trade are affected by the tariff.

Figure VIII-2 is similar to Figure 13-3. The free-trade price is P_E, while the tariff-ridden price in the importing country is P_t^M and that in the exporting country is P_t^X. The following changes occur in the importing country:

Consumers' surplus declines by the area $g + h + i + j$.

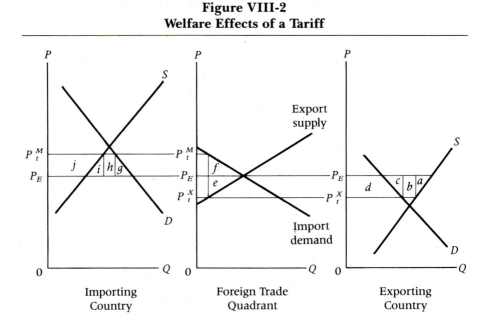

Figure VIII-2
Welfare Effects of a Tariff

Importing Country

Foreign Trade Quadrant

Exporting Country

Producers' surplus increases by area j.

Government revenue increases by area h.

The net deadweight loss equals the sum of the triangular areas $i + g$. The following changes take place in the exporting country:

Producers' surplus declines by area $a + b + c + d$.

Consumers' surplus increases by area d.

Government revenue accruing to the *importing* country increases by area b.

> (Area b is a transfer from the exporting to the importing country. It does not affect worldwide welfare because whereas it is a loss to the exporting country, it is an equal gain to the importing country.)

The net deadweight loss equals the areas of triangles $a + c$.

The net loss to the importing country is triangles i and g, while the net gain is rectangle b. Its *optimum tariff* is the tariff rate that would maximize the net gain, the area $[b - (g + i)]$. The exporting country sustains a net loss measured by the area $a + b + c$, of which b is a transfer to the importing country. To the world taken as a whole, the *net* deadweight *loss* from the tariff is triangles $a + c + i + g$. Geometrically, we have $i + g = f$, because their height is the same, and the base of f equals the combined bases of i and g, both being the difference between the free-trade imports and the tariff-ridden imports. By identical reasoning, areas $a + c = e$. Thus, in the foreign trade quadrant, the net welfare cost of the tariff to the world taken as a whole (that is, disregarding distributional effects) is area $e + f$. Without further marking of the diagram, it can be seen that if the tariff is removed in two successive steps of equal size, the first 50 percent reduction would improve world welfare by a far greater amount (trapezoid area) than the second and final reduction (remaining triangle).

Static Effects of a Customs Union[1]

In Figure VIII-3 assume that S_a and D_a are the internal supply and demand curves in country A for a given product. S_b and S_c are the export-supply curves of countries B and C to country A, with C being a more efficient producer than B. S_b^t and S_c^t are the same two supply curves subject to a 100 percent tariff imposed by country A. Curve S^t indicates total supply of the commodity in country A $(S_a + S_b^t + S_c^t)$. Price P_1 is established. Country A produces Q_a domestically and imports Q_b and Q_c from countries B and C, respectively.

When countries A and B form a customs union to the exclusion of C, the relevant supply curve in country B becomes S_b, while S_c^t remains in effect in country C.[2] Total supply in country A's market becomes S_{CU}, consisting of $S_a + S_b + S_c^t$. The price in country A drops to P_2; domestic supply declines to Q_{a1}; imports from country B rise to Q_{b1}; and imports from country C diminish to Q_{c1}. These changes can be quantified in terms of their effect on producers' surpluses in all three countries, and on consumers' surpluses and government tariff revenue of country A. The following observations relate to each panel of the diagram:

---

[1]Reprinted with permission from M. E. Kreinin, *Kyklos*, December 1973.

[2]This assumes that A's tariff against outsiders remains unchanged, which is characteristic of a free-trade area rather than of a customs union. But the diagram can be adjusted to account for any modification in that tariff rate.

Figure VIII-3
Welfare Effects of a Customs Union

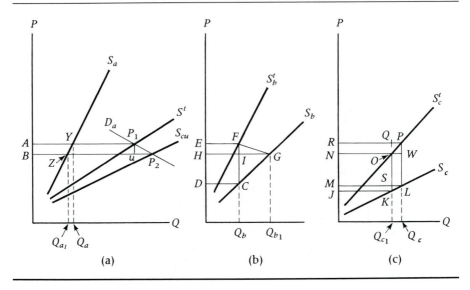

(a)   (b)   (c)

(a) Country A enjoys an increase of consumers' surpluses of BAP_1P_2 and suffers a reduction of producers' surpluses amounting to $BAYZ$. There is a *gain of* ZYP_1P_2.

(b) Country B enjoys a gain in producers' surplus of $HGCD$. Country A faces a loss in government tariff revenue of $CDEF$. Since area $DCHI$ is common to both, we obtain in part (b) *a loss of EHIF and a gain of ICG.*

(c) Tariff revenue of country A declines from $RPLM$ to $NOKJ$. Subtracting the area $NOSM$, common to both, we get a loss of $RNOP + POSL$ and a gain of $MJKS$. At the same time, producers' surpluses of country C decline by $MJKL$. Thus Figure VIII-3c yields the *following loss: RNOP + POSL − MJKS + MJKL = RNOP + POSL + LSK = RNOP + POKL.*

Area ZYP_1P_2 [the net gain in (a)] is equal by construction to areas $EFGH$ in (b) plus $RNOP$ in (c). Subtracting from this net gain in (a) the losses $EHIF$ in (b) and $RNOP$ in (c), we are left with a net gain of FIG in (b). Adding it to the earlier gain CIG, we obtain a *net gain of CFG* in part (b), to be weighed against the *net loss of POKL* in part (c). The net effect on world welfare depends on the relative size of the two areas.

APPENDIX IX

A Domestic Monopolist Under a Tariff and a Quota

In this section we shall formally demonstrate the proposition that when domestic production is carried on by a monopolist, a tariff would curtail his monopoly power by more than an "equivalent" quota—a quota that allows the same volume of imports

---

Figure IX-1
A Monopolist Under a Tariff and a Quota

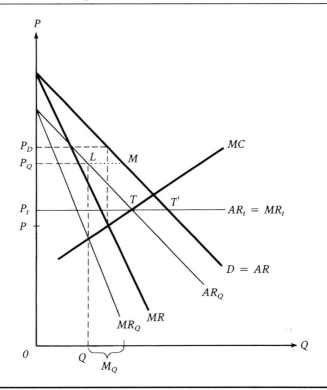

---

as under the tariff. In Figure IX-1, assume that domestic demand is represented by average revenue curve AR, yielding marginal revenue MR, and that the monopolist's marginal cost is represented by MC. In the absence of international trade, the quantity produced and sold domestically is shown by the intersection of MR and MC, with the resulting price $\overline{OP_D}$.

Assume now that the international price of the commodity is $\overline{OP}$. If the economy is opened up to international trade, with a tariff $\overline{PP_t}$ imposed on the commodity, then the domestic price cannot rise above $\overline{OP_t}$. In fact, the demand curve would then become kinked: $\overline{P_tTT'D}$. Along its flat portion it coincides with the marginal revenue, MR_t. Domestic output would then be $\overline{P_tT}$, where T is the intersection of the MC and the MR_t curves, while imports would equal $\overline{TT'}$, *all sold at price $\overline{OP_t}$.*

If the import volume under the tariff regime, $\overline{TT'}$ is converted into a quota, then we have a dominant supplier model, under which the monopolist need only accommodate himself to a fixed amount of imports. Graphically, the market demand curve remains unaffected, but the demand curve facing the monopolist is AR_Q, obtained by shifting the market AR leftward (horizontally) by the amount of the quota. The corresponding marginal revenue curve, MR_Q, is then generated. Domestic output is determined by the intersection of MC and MR_Q, yielding price $\overline{OP_Q}$. The quantity imported, LM (shown as M_Q on the horizontal axis) is the same as that under a tariff regime ($LM = TT'$), but the price charged, and therefore monopoly profit accruing to the importers, is higher.

APPENDIX X
Trade Policy Under Oligopoly

(A) *Rationale For Policy Intervention*

In a perfectly competitive environment, the only possible justifications for trade intervention by the government are the following:

1. Imposition of an optimum tariff on imported goods designed to improve the terms of trade, or of a tax on imported capital, designed to improve the terms of borrowing;
2. Infant industry protection but only if a direct subsidy is not feasible;
3. Possible offset to a domestic distortion, but only when domestic measures are not available.

These reasons have not been considered important enough to justify a drastic departure from the traditional stance favoring free trade.

   In recent years economists have redirected their attention to oligopolistic markets, where the number of firms producing a product and making independent decisions is very small. This has become known as a *strategic* environment. The main feature distinguishing it from a competitive environment is the *emergence and persistence of economic profits*. "Strategic trade policy" is a term coined to describe measures that can shift the equilibrium generated by oligopolistic interchange.[1]

   In oligopolistic markets nations compete for their share of global economic profits. A primary objective of strategic trade policy is to enable *our* firms or government to capture a bigger share of these profits than would be the case without the policy. *Our* share of global oligopoly profits can be increased by expanding the market share of U.S. firms. In the case of export industries, an export subsidy (or in its absence, a subsidy for R & D) would enable *our* oligopolistic firms to capture a larger share of the export markets. If the resulting increase in their economic profits exceeds the cost of the subsidy, the policy improves *our* national welfare, albeit at the expense of others. In the case of imported products produced by foreign oligopolists, the imposition of a tariff enables *our* oligopolists to expand their market share. The resulting increase in economic profits of *our* firms plus the rise in gov-

[1] Following are some references to this recently developed strand of the literature:
Baldwin, R. "Incentives and Rent Seeking: Trade Policy and Subsidization," (mimeographed), 1984. Brander, J., and Spencer, B. "Tariff Protection and Imperfect Competition," In *Monopolistic Competition in International Trade* (H. Kierzkowski, ed.). Oxford: Oxford University Press, 1982. Brander, J., and Spencer, B. "Export Subsidies and International Market Share Rivalry," (mimeographed), 1982. Dixit, A. and Grossman, G. "Targeted Export Promotion with Several Oligopolistic Industries," Princeton Discussion Paper, 1984. Grossman, G. and Richardson, D. "Strategic Trade Policy: A Survey of Issues and Early Analysis," Princeton *Special Papers in International Economics*, 1985.

ernment tariff revenue enhances national economic welfare. The nature of these policies will be explained with the help of simple diagrams.

In the simplest case assume that *we* import a product produced by a foreign monopolist. There are no domestic producers of that product, so that the foreign monopolist is in fact a global monopolist. He is assumed to produce at constant cost conditions, so that the marginal cost (*MC*) curve is horizontal.

Figure X-1 depicts the profit-maximizing position of the monopolist selling in *our* market, where *D* represents the demand in our market for the foreign-produced product, and *MR* is the resulting marginal revenue curve. The intersection of *MC* and *MR* determines the quantity *Q* that *we* import from the foreign monopolist. Price *P* is charged, and the excess of *P* over *MC* is economic profit per unit of output. Total economic profit extracted from our market by the foreign monopolist is the shaded area. A specific import tariff would raise the *MC* curve to *MC^t*, reduce the quantity imported from *Q* to *Q^t*, and increase the price to the consumers from *P* to *P^t*. Foreign monopoly profit declines to the rectangular area bounded by points *MC^t*, *P^t*, *a*, *b*. However, because of the decline in quantity, not all the change in foreign monopoly profit is appropriated by *our* government. Rather, that area is the rectangle bounded by points *MC*, *MC^t*, *c*, *b*. The loss in consumer surplus is represented by area *P*, *P^t*, *a*, *d*.

In the case described in Figure X-1, the policy intervention is beneficial because the foreign monopoly profit appropriated by the government exceeds the loss to domestic consumers. The optimal tariff is the level that maximizes the difference between the gain in government revenue and the loss to the domestic consumers. Since that varies with the shape of the demand curve, knowledge of the demand elasticity is needed to determine the level of tariff. Similar information on the shape

Figure X-1
Foreign monopolist selling in *our* market: A tariff reduces foreign monopoly profits.

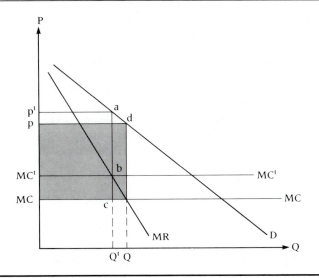

and level of the marginal cost curve (which is not necessarily horizontal) is also required.

In a reverse case, assume that *our* firm is the global monopolist with a constant MC curve, exporting to foreign countries (in which there are no local producers), and that the local and foreign markets are segregated. This is shown in Figure X-2, where D is foreign demand, MR is marginal revenue from foreign sales, and the intersection between MC and MR determines the profit-maximizing quantity of exports, Q. Price is set at P, and monopoly profit per unit is the difference between P and MC along the price axis. Total monopoly profits extracted from foreigners is the shaded area. A specific export subsidy (government subsidy of X dollars per unit of output) to the local monopoly firm lowers its marginal costs to MC^S, reduces the export price from P to P^S (namely, *our* terms of trade deteriorate) and raises quantity to Q^S. Economic profit appropriated from foreign markets increases to the rectangular area bounded by points MC^S, P^S, a, b. The subsidy cost to the government is the rectangular area bounded by MC, MC^S, a, b. Here it is smaller than the gain in monopoly profit. The difference between the gain in monopoly profit and the cost of the subsidy is the net gain to the country. Its size depends on the shape of the demand curve. Again, information on the cost structure and the demand elasticity is needed to determine the optimal size of the subsidy, namely, the subsidy that would maximize the excess of appropriated profits over the subsidy cost.

Since GATT's rules prohibit an export subsidy, its place can be taken by subsidy for research and development (R & D). Because it applies to all output rather than just to exports, the cost of that subsidy could be higher. But against the greater cost, there are two benefits: First, the price to the domestic consumers declines. And second, the R & D has external spillover effects, as well as the "learning by doing" effect.

Figure X-2
A domestic monopolist selling abroad: A subsidy increases domestic monopoly profits.

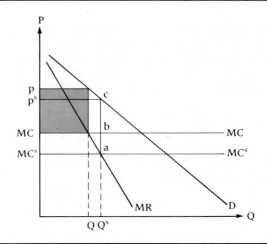

These simple examples can be generalized to include other situations. Suppose a domestic and a foreign firm (such as Boeing and the European Airbus Industrie) compete in a third market. If the government of one of the countries provides export or R & D subsidies to its domestic firm, this producer may be able to capture a larger share of the world market and increase its profits net of the subsidy. Thus, the country could gain in terms of income and employment. But such a policy risks retaliation by other countries.

Other extensions of the analysis include its applicability to oligopolistic markets, and to cases where firms enjoy increasing returns to scale or benefit from "learning by doing." In the latter cases protection of domestic markets and promotion of export markets can reduce per unit costs, thereby saving resources.

This analysis, which suggests that there is room for beneficial policy intervention in oligopolistic markets, is subject to serious limitations that considerably weaken the case for intervention.

(B) *Limitations of the Oligopoly Analysis*

1. Existence of Oligopoly Profits   The foregoing argument for policy intervention rests on the existence of global oligopoly profits to be appropriated. Yet in many industries such profits do not exist. At best the degree of monopoly power and hence the level of monopoly profit varies greatly between industries. At times a single industry has an oligopolistic subsector (mainframe computers) and competitive subsectors (microcomputers). Moreover, ease of entry (and hence persistence of monopoly profits) varies a great deal. Much of oligopoly profits is *transitory*, and exists only until technology is diffused, and/or entry of new firms occurs.

Any optimal strategic trade intervention would have to be limited to the concentrated industries. It would require the policy maker to differentiate between industries and trading partner. This means the demise of the MFN even in pretense. It also means that *discretion* would have to be substituted for *rules* in the conduct of trade policy. This opens the door to a great deal of unproductive rent-seeking activity, where groups and industries seek protection or subsidies through lobbying and bloc voting.

2. R & D   The second, related, rationale for policy intervention is the existence of positive externalities associated with R & D. Yet it is not clear that the capital markets do not account for spillover effects. Moreover, R & D intensity varies greatly among industries. There are also variations by the degree of "learning by doing," and by the level of external benefits or spillover derived. These variables are not even susceptible to measurement. Again, the complexity of the task rules out a rationally developed trade policy.

3. Factor Inputs in Fixed Supply   Suppose several oligopolistic industries use a common resource (such as scientists and or engineers) that is scarce and inelastic in supply. Any form of protection or subsidy to one such industry would enable it to draw the scarce resource from the nonsubsidized oligopolistic industries. The latter would have to contract. The profit-shifting gains from targeting any one industry are dissipated by the profit-shifting losses of other industries. For example, if a certain scientific skill is used in both the aircraft and computer industries, a subsidy to the first industry would cause the second one to contract. Profits captured by the aircraft industry could be matched by profits lost to the computer industry.

4. Need for Information   A sensible strategic policy requires rather exacting and elaborate information, regarding demand elasticities, economic profits, cost structure, costs and spillover effects of R & D, slope of the learning curve, degree and types of scale economies, potential number of competitors, and so forth. Knowledge of firms' behavior, and of their response to government policy and to announcements by competitors is also needed. This type of information is not available at the present state of the art.

5. Retaliation   Strategic policy attempts to improve *our* situation at the expense of others, by appropriating global profits. What is gained by one country is lost to another. As such, the policy invites retaliation. And a process of mutual retaliation can be harmful to all. This indicates the superiority of a cooperative approach to the distribution of profit, provided that a mechanism can be devised to enforce and verify agreements, so as to avoid circumventing it.

6. Redistribution   As shown in Figure X-1, domestic and foreign consumers may have to pay a higher price to enable *our* firms to capture foreign monopoly profits. Such redistribution may not be socially acceptable.

7. Multinational Corporations   A key requirement for the strategic trade policies is that *our* firms and projects be distinguishable from *theirs*. Yet many firms are transnationally owned, and many projects are joint ventures by firms with different nationalities. Trade policies that redistribute profits toward some favored project, or toward some favored firm, would fail to aid *us* significantly, unless our residents have disproportionate shares in the favored projects or firms.

Given these limitations, the suitability of strategic trade policy, in the form of tariffs and subsidies is highly questionable.

Bibliography

General References

Instructors wishing to supplement the text with relevant articles may wish to consult the following list of "readers" (paperbacks):

Adams, John (ed.). *The Contemporary International Economy: A Reader.* N.Y.: St. Martin's Press, 1985. Covers topics in international trade, finance, and development.

Balassa, Bela (ed.). *The Changing Patterns in Foreign Trade and Payments.* Third edition. New York: W. W. Norton, 1978. Covers selected policy issues.

Baldwin, R. E., and J. O. Richardson (eds.). *International Trade and Finance.* Second edition. Boston: Little, Brown, 1981. Readings covering both trade and finance; theory as well as policy.

Kapoor, A., and P. Drab (eds.). *The Multinational Enterprise in Transition.* Princeton: The Darwin Press, 1972.

Meier, Gerald M. *Problems of Trade Policy.* New York: Oxford University Press, 1973. Covers commercial policy.

Meier, Gerald. *Problems of World Monetary Order.* Second edition. New York: Oxford University Press, 1982. Covers topics in international finance.

Officer, L., and T. Willet (eds.). *The International Currency System.* Columbia, Missouri: Lucas Brothers, 1973.

For more advanced topics, see R. Jones and P. Kenen (eds.), *Handbook of International Economics,* North-Holland, 1984. Each chapter is devoted to a comprehensive survey of a topic in international trade or finance, and contains an extensive bibliography.

Survey Articles

Following is a list of articles and monographs, each surveying a portion of the field of international economics. They are usually accompanied by extensive bibliographies that are useful to students pursuing further work in a specific area.

International Finance

Dornbusch, R., *Open Economy Macroeconomics*, N. Y., Basic Books, 1980.

Goldstein, Morris, "Have Flexible Exchange Rates Handicapped Macroeconomic Policy?" Princeton Special Series in International Economics, No. 14, June 1980.

Grubel, Herbert G., "The Demand for International Reserves: A Critical Review of the Literature," *Journal of Economic Literature*, Dec. 1971, pp. 1148–66.

Hodjera, Z., "International Short Term Capital Movements: A Survey of Theory and Empirical Analysis," *IMF Staff Papers*, 1973.

Isard, Peter, *Exchange Rate Determination: A Survey of Popular Views and Recent Models*, Princeton Studies in International Finance, No. 42, 1978.

Ishyama, Y., "The Theory of Optimum Currency Areas: A Survey," *IMF Staff Papers*, June 1975.

Kenen, P., *Capital Mobility and Financial Integration: A Survey*, Princeton Studies in International Finance, No. 39, 1976.

Kreinin, M., and L. Officer, *The Monetary Approach to the Balance of Payments: A Survey*, Princeton Studies in International Finance, No. 43, 1978.

Krueger, Anne O., "Balance of Payments Theory," *Journal of Economic Literature*, Mar. 1969, pp. 1–26.

McKinnon, Ronald, "The Exchange Rate and Macroeconomic Policy: Changing Postwar Perceptions," *Journal of Economic Literature*, June 1981.

Officer, L., "The Purchasing Power Parity Theory—A Survey," *IMF Staff Papers*, March 1976, and *Purchasing Power Parity: Theory, Evidence, and Relevance*, Greenwich, CT.: JAI Press, 1982.

Tower, E., and D. Willett, *The Theory of Optimum Currency Areas and Exchange Rate Flexibility*, Princeton Special Papers in International Economics, No. 11, May 1976.

Williamson, J., "International Liquidity—A Survey," *Economic Journal*, September 1973.

International Trade

Baldwin, R., *Non Tariff Distortions of International Trade*, Washington: The Brookings Institution, 1970.

Bhagwati, Jagdish, "The Pure Theory of International Trade," *Economic Journal*, Mar. 1964.

Bhagwati, Jagdish (ed.), *The New International Economic Order*, Cambridge: MIT Press, 1977.

Black, J., "Arguments for Tariffs," *Oxford Economic Papers*, June 1959.

Corden, W. M., *The Theory of Protection*, New York: Oxford University Press, 1971.

Greenway, David (ed.), *Current Issues in International Trade*, London: Macmillan, 1985.

Krauss, Melvyn B., "Recent Developments in Customs Union Theory: An Interpretive Survey," *Journal of Economic Literature*, June 1972, pp. 413–36.

Kravis, Irving, "A Survey of International Comparisons of Productivity," *Economic Journal*, May 1976.

Kreinin, M. E., and L. H. Officer, "Tariff Reductions under the Tokyo Round: A Review of Their Effects on Trade Flows, Employment, and Welfare," *Weltwirtschaftliches Archiv*, 1979, No. 3.

Magee, S. P., "Factor Market Distortions, Production and Trade: A Survey," *Oxford Economic Papers*, March 1973.

Stern, Robert, "Tariffs and Other Measures of Trade Control: A Survey of Recent Developments," *Journal of Economic Literature*, September 1973, pp. 857–88.

Sources of Country and Regional Statistics

Following are the most widely used sources of data used in international economics.

United States

U.S. Department of Commerce, *Survey of Current Business* (monthly)
Federal Reserve Board, *Federal Reserve Board, Federal Reserve Bulletin* (monthly)
Council of Economic Advisors, *Economic Report of the President* (annually)
U.S. International Trade Commission, *Annual Reports on the Trade Agreements Program*, as well as numerous reports on specific topics or industries.
Office of the United States Trade Representative, *Annual Reports.*

Industrial Countries

U.S. Department of Commerce, *International Economic Indicators* (quarterly)
OECD, *Quarterly National Accounts Bulletin* (quarterly)
OECD, *Main Economic Indicators* (monthly and annually)

All Countries

IMF, *International Financial Statistics* (monthly)
World Bank, *World Development Report* (annually); *World Atlas* (annually)
GATT, *International Trade* (annually)
IMF, World Bank, and GATT, *Annual Reports*
United Nations, *Monthly Bulletin of Statistics*
United Nations Economic Commissions Reports about the Main Regions of the World
UNCTAD, *Handbook of International Trade and Development Statistics*

For authoritative analyses of current problems confronting individual countries (and their policies), as well as of timely issues in international trade and finance, see the semi-annual, *Economic Policy,* published by Cambridge University Press for the London-based Center for Economic Policy Research.

Index